Westmoreland County, Virginia
MARRIAGE RECORDS
1850–1880
Annotated

Wesley E. Pippenger

HERITAGE BOOKS
2018

HERITAGE BOOKS
AN IMPRINT OF HERITAGE BOOKS, INC.

Books, CDs, and more—Worldwide

For our listing of thousands of titles see our website
at
www.HeritageBooks.com

Published 2018 by
HERITAGE BOOKS, INC.
Publishing Division
5810 Ruatan Street
Berwyn Heights, Md. 20740

International Standard Book Number
Paperbound: 978-0-7884-5839-2

TABLE OF CONTENTS

INTRODUCTION

This work is a compilation of data found in 1,510 marriage records of Westmoreland County, Virginia, for the years 1850 through 1880. Records previous to 1851 were published by Stratton Nottingham in his *The Marriage License Bonds of Westmoreland County, Virginia, From 1786 to 1850*. However, this compiler found that many records for 1850 were not included in Nottingham's work, presumably because they were in the form of a marriage license and he only selected marriage bonds. Not all of these marriage records are found at the courthouse in Montross, as 27 are found only in church records and 19 in neighboring counties. Fifty-four licenses were issued for which there is no further information or minister return. The gentleman who was married the most (four times) is George Philander Chinn.

The data here are derived from multiple sources, including: marriage licenses or applications, minister returns of marriage, consents by guardian or parent, or entries in either of two bound marriage registers, and supplemented with family Bible records, cemetery records, military records, and other publications. The index, which is made up of over 12,000 entries, contains a heading for C.S.A. to list 212 Confederate soldiers identified. Please note that a considerable amount of information about cemetery burials can be found on the Internet at the website *Findagrave.com*, and may be consulted for accuracy and thoroughness.

Original records have been microfilmed by the Library of Virginia, and each of the items used are listed below along with the reel number of the film found at the Library. Not all recorded parts of a marriage are necessarily found together on microfilm. The parties are presumed to be residents of Westmoreland County at the time of the record unless otherwise stated. Also, the place of marriage is presumed to be Westmoreland County unless otherwise noted.

With respect to consents or other notes in the file at the courthouse in Montross, Virginia, the name of the bride or groom is not repeated herein unless the signature is different from the clerk's recording of the names. If either party did not sign their name completely, it is noted, i.e. Sally [her X mark] Smith. Some difficulty is found with surnames being spelled differently between multiple, or within the same, record. For instance, it is difficult to determine between Carey or Casey, Clark or Clarke, Morris or Morriss, Sanders or Saunders, Sanford or Sandford, Venie or Veney, etc. The spelling found on a person's tombstone may be used when found.

Data have been presented as found in the original records by considering all individual pieces found. Oddly, the date of marriage on the minister return and in either of the two marriage registers (state and local copy) differs frequently. In these cases, the date found on the minister return portion of the marriage license is used. Also, the compiler has inserted information from outside sources in brackets, i.e. "[ ]", or in nearly 1,100 footnotes. These additional sources include a range of published marriage records from Westmoreland and surrounding counties. Additional publications used are found in the Bibliography. Specific sources are listed at the end of each item.

Wesley E. Pippenger
Little Egypt
Tappahannock, Virginia

ABBREVIATIONS AND SOURCE CODES

Abbreviations

a.k.a.	Also known as	FB	Free Blacks
B	Black	Inf.	Infantry
a.	Born	LVA	Library of Virginia
bur.	Buried	M.G.	Minister of [the] Gospel
C.S.A.	Confederate States Army	(M)	Mulatto
C	Consent	q.v.	Latin for *quod vide*, meaning to see
Cav.	Cavalry		elsewhere
Co.	County	Reg.	Regiment
(C)	Colored	res.	residence of, or resided in
d.	Died	Rev.	Reverend
Dr.	Doctor		

Old style abbreviations are used for states, i.e. Va. for Virginia, or Mass. for Massachusetts.

Source Codes

CP   Cople Parish Register, 1861-1892 [LVA Misc. Reel 5874]

DC   Virginia Death Certificate, 1912-2014 online at *Ancestry.com.*

DR   Register of Deaths, 1854-1896. Note: There are no entries for 1853-1856, 1862-1863, 1878-1880 or 1890. [LVA Reel 75]

M15   Marriage Bonds Vol. 15, 1847-1854 [Minister Returns]. [LVA Reel 89]

M16   Marriage Bonds Vol. 16, 1855-1859 [Minister Returns]. [LVA Reel 89]

M16a   Marriage Bonds Vol. 16, 1855-1859 (continued) [Minister Returns]. [LVA Reel 90]

M17   Marriage Bonds Vol. 17, 1860-1865 [Certificates]. [LVA Reel 90]

M17a   Marriage Bonds Vol. 17, 1860-1865 (continued) [Certificates]. [LVA Reel 91]

M18   Marriage Licenses, 1866-1871. [LVA Reel 92]

M19   Marriage Licenses, 1872-1878. [LVA Reel 93]

NN   The *Northern Neck News* (Warsaw, Va.). Some entries are found for the period 1879-1886.

R   Register of Marriage Licenses Issued [With Marriage Certificates], 1850-1920. [LVA Reel 133]

R1   Register of Marriages, 1854-1908. [LVA Reel 74]

SC   *The Southern Churchman* newspaper (Alexandria, Va.)

SP   Records of St. Peter's Episcopal Church, 1847-1999 [LVA Reels 2072-2074]

VG   *The Virginia Genealogist*; volume and page

WP   Washington Parish Register, 1847-1991 [LVA Reel 2075]

The 1870 and 1880 Federal census records may have been used to determine race of non-white parties.

ACTS
of the
GENERAL ASSEMBLY
of the
STATE OF VIRGINIA

ACT REQUIRING VITAL STATISTICS

Chapter 25
An Act Concerning the Registration of Births, Marriages and Deaths,
Passed April 11, 1853

Three registers to be kept by clerk.

1. Be it enacted by the general assembly, that from and after the first day of January eighteen hundred and fifty-four, the clerk of every county and corporation court shall keep three books, to be called, respectively, the register of marriages, the register of births, and the register of deaths.

Duty of ministers.

What set forth in his record.

2. Henceforth it shall be the duty of every minister or other person celebrating a marriage, and of the clerk or keeper of the records of any religious society which solemnizes marriages by the consent of the parties in open congregation, at once to make a record of every marriage between white persons solemnized by or before him, and within two months after such marriage to return a certificate thereof, signed by him, to the clerk of the court of the county or corporation in which the same is solemnized. Such record and certificate shall set forth, as far as the same can be ascertained, the date and place of the marriage, the full names of both the parties, their ages and condition before the marriage (whether single or widowed), the places of their birth and residence, the names of their parents and the occupation of the husband.

Abstract by clerk.

3. The clerk to whom such certificate shall be returned, shall file and preserve the same in his office, and within twenty days after receiving the same, record a full abstract thereof in his register of marriages, setting out, in convenient tabular form, all the circumstances therein stated and the name of the person signing the certificate, and make an index of the names of both the parties married.

If marriage out of state.

4. If at the time of celebrating any marriage out of this state, either or both of the parties thereto be a resident or residents of this state, a certificate or statement thereof, verified by the affidavit of any person present at such celebration, may be returned to the clerk of the court of the county or corporation in which the husband resides, if he be such resident, and otherwise, of the county or corporation in which the wife resides, and an abstract thereof shall be recorded by him in the manner prescribed in the third section.

Penalty on minister for noncompliance.

5. If any minister who shall give bond in order to his being authorized to celebrate marriage in this state, shall fail to comply with the second section, the condition of such bond shall be deemed to be thereby broken, and he shall be subject to the penalty hereinafter prescribed for such failure.

6. Every such clerk of a court shall, on or before the first day of the next November term of his court, post at the front door of his courthouse a copy of the second section, with a statement of the penalties for violations thereof.

7. Every commissioner of the revenue shall make an annual registration of the births and deaths in his district. When he ascertains the personal property subject to taxation, he shall ascertain the births and deaths that have occurred in the year ending on the thirty-first day of December preceding, and such circumstances as he is hereinafter required to record. He shall ascertain the births and deaths in each family from the head of such family, if practicable.

8. He shall record in a book to be kept by him for that purpose, so far as can be ascertained, the date and place of every such birth; the full name of the child, (if it has a name;) the sex and color thereof; and if colored, whether free or slave; also whether the child was born alive or stillborn; the full name of the mother; and if the child be free and born in wedlock, the full name, occupation and residence of the father; if the child be a slave, the name of the owner; if there be more than one child born at one birth, the fact and number shall be stated; and any other circumstances of interest relating to any birth.

9. Every such commissioner shall in like manner record in a book to be kept by him for that purpose, the place and date of every death in his district during the year ending on the preceding thirty-first day of December; the full name, sex, age, condition (whether married or not,) and color of the deceased; and if colored, whether free or slave; also the occupation, if any, of the deceased, and his or her place of birth, the names of his or her parents, and (if the deceased was married) the name of the husband or wife; and if the deceased was a slave, the name of the owner; also the disease or cause of the death, so far as such facts can be ascertained.

10. The commissioner shall make and subscribe an affidavit, upon each of the books so to be kept by him, to the effect that he has pursued the directions in this act, according to the best of his skill; and he shall return his said books to the clerk of the court of his county or corporation on or before the first day of June.

11. Such clerk shall thereupon record a full abstract of the contents of the said book, containing a record of births, in his said register of births, setting forth, in convenient tabular form, all the circumstances hereinbefore required to be recorded, with references to the commissioners' books, and making an alphabetical index of the names of the free children born, and (when they have no names) of the names of the parents, and also of the names of the owners of the slaves born, placing in the index the dates of the births.

12. He shall in like manner record a full abstract of the contents of the said book, containing a record of deaths, in his said register of deaths, setting forth, in convenient tabular form, all the circumstances hereinbefore required to be recorded, with reference to the commissioners' book, and making an alphabetical index of the names of the deceased and the names of the owners of deceased slaves, and placing in the index the dates of the deaths.

13. Every such clerk of a court shall file and preserve in his office the books so deposited with him by the commissioners.

14. He shall transmit to the auditor of public accounts a copy of his register of marriages during the preceding year, on or before the first day of March in each year, and a copy of his

register of births and register of deaths during the preceding year, on or before the first day of August in each year.

Abstract of audi-
tor.
When report to
legislature.

15. Such copies shall be filed and preserved in the said auditor's office, and from them the auditor shall prepare an abstract annually of marriages, births and deaths in each county and corporation, and make a report upon said registrations once in every period of two years, to be laid before the general assembly.

Registers to be
prima facie evi-
dence.

16. The said books to be kept by the clerks, and copies, (or of any part thereof,) certified by the clerk lawfully having custody thereof, shall be prima facie evidence of the facts therein set forth in all cases.

Pay of clerk
for copies.

17. A clerk shall be entitled to ten cents for every copy of an entry in said books relating to a marriage, birth or death, to be paid by the party requiring the copy.

How commis-
sioner to obtain
his information.

18. If a commissioner in any case cannot obtain the requisite information concerning any birth or death from the head of the family, as before required, he shall obtain the same from such persons as are hereinafter required to give it; or if that cannot be done, from any other persons, always recording the name of the person giving the information.

Physicians and
surgeons.
Their duties.

19. Every physician and surgeon shall, in a book to be kept by him, make a record at once of the death of every person dying in this state, upon whom he has attended at the time of such death, setting out as far as practicable the circumstances herein required to be recorded by a commissioner respecting deaths. He shall give to a commissioner of the revenue, whenever called on by him for that purpose, annually, a copy of such record, so far as the same relates to deaths in such commissioner's district.

Coroners; their
duties.

Penalty for
failure.

20. Every coroner shall keep a like record of the deaths in relation to which he acts officially, and give a copy thereof to any commissioner of the revenue, whenever called on by him for that purpose, annually, so far as the same relates to deaths in such commissioner's district. For every neglect or failure to perform any duty required of him by this section, a coroner shall forfeit twenty dollars.

Entries by com-
missioner.

21. The commissioner shall make such entries or corrections in his record of deaths as may be supplied or warranted by the copies so to be furnished to him by physicians, surgeons and coroners, noting the source of the information.

If head of family
absent, what his
duty.
Penalty for re-
fusal to give in-
formation.

22. The head of any family, if he be not at his residence when the commissioner calls there to obtain the information required by this act to be obtained of him, shall give the same information to the proper commissioner of the revenue on or before the first day of June in the same year; and for a failure or neglect to do so, shall forfeit one dollar. If any head of a family, being lawfully requested to give any such information, shall refuse to give the same, he shall forfeit ten dollars.

Penalty of com-
missioner for
failure of duty.

23. If any commissioner of the revenue fail to obtain any information respecting a birth or death, which he is by this act authorized or required to obtain, and which he can produce, he shall for every such failure and for every failure to record the information acquired by him respecting a birth or death, according to this act, forfeit five dollars.

For failure to

24. If any commissioner of the revenue fail to perform the duties required of him by the tenth

section of this act, he shall forfeit fifty dollars.

*Penalty of clerk
for failure of
duty.*

25.   If any clerk of a court fail to perform the any duty required of him by the third section of this act, he shall forfeit ten dollars for every such offence; and if he fail to perform any duty required of him by the eleventh, twelfth, thirteenth or fourteenth section, he shall, for every such offence, forfeit fifty dollars.

26.   If any clerk of a court, commissioner of the revenue, physician, surgeon, coroner or minister celebrating a marriage, or clerk or keeper of the records of any religious society, shall, in any book, register or record, which such officer or person is by this act required to keep or make, or in any copy or certificate which by this act he is required to make or give, knowingly make any false, erroneous or fraudulent entry, record, registration or written statement, he shall for every such offence forfeit not less than one hundred nor more than five hundred dollars.

27.   If any person, upon whose information or statement any record or registration may lawfully be made under this act, shall knowingly give any false information, or make any false statement to be used for the purpose of making any such record or registration, he shall forfeit not less than fifty nor more than three hundred dollars for every such offence.

28.   The auditor of public accounts shall furnish the clerk of every county and corporation court and every commissioner of the revenue with all forms and instructions which he may deem necessary or proper for carrying this act into effect.

29.   This act shall take effect **the first day of July eighteen hundred and fifty three.**

MINISTERS FEATURED IN RECORDS

Bagby, George F., M.G. Served Nomini Baptist Church beginning c.1856, and Bruington Baptist Church in King and Queen County in 1858.

Bain, William F. (1831-1902). Methodist Episcopal Church South. Buried in Cedar Grove Cemetery of Fauquier County. Son of Rev. George A. and Frances M. Bain.

Balderson, William (1781-1854). No further information.

Battaile, Benjamin Robinson (d. 1883), physician. Married Elizabeth Brown Clark. Served Popes Creek Baptist Church.

Baynham, William Armistead (1813-1887). Minister of the Gospel. Baptist. Memorial tablet at Enon Baptist Church, Supply, Virginia. His first wife Virginia d. 1853.

Bayton, Thomas J. Record 1867.

Beale, Frank Brown (1852-1908). Buried Upper King and Queen Baptist Church. Son of Gen. Richard Lee Turberville Beale (1819-1893) and Lucy Maria Brown (d. 1894). Served Nomini Baptist, 1856-1857 and after 1875; Menokin Baptist, 1872. Married 1883 in King and Queen County to Susie M.H. Garnett. Namesake of Beale Memorial Baptist Church in Tappahannock, Va.

Beale, George William (1842-1921). Served Popes Creek Baptist Church from 1868. Buried Coan Church, Heathsville, Va. Son of Richard Lee Turberville Beale. Served in the 9th Va. Cav., C.S.A.

Billingsley, Joseph A. Records 1867-1874.

Bird, John. Baptist. Served in Essex County. Record 1854.

Bradley, Paul. Records 1880.

Brooke, Pendleton. In 1879, appointed nineteenth Rector of Cople Parish, resigned in 1885.

Butts, D.G.C. Served the Methodist Episcopal Church South. Records 1873-1880.

Chesley, John William (1825-1917). Started 1 FEB 1854 in Washington Parish, resigned 1 APR 1857. Served in Talbot and St. Mary's Cos., Md. Records 1854-1867.

Claybrook, Frederick William (1844-1914). Son of Richard A. Claybrook and Charlotte T. Brown. First served Oak Grove Baptist Church from 1875 to 1880, served Lebanon Baptist, then Farnham Bapist, 1880-1886. Twice married. Buried at Morattico Baptist Church, Kilmarnock, Va.

Covington, Y.S.D. Methodist Episcopal Church South. Record 1857.

Crocker, William Andrew (1827-1901). Buried Calvary United Methodist Church Cemetery. Son of James Crocker and Frances Hiles Woodley. Served the Methodist Episcopal Church South in Warsaw, Va. in 1874; Heathsville Circuit. Married to Frances Keaton Jennings (1827-1898).

Dashiell, Thomas Grayson (1830-1893). He was first married in July 1854 to Wilhelmina (d. 1862), daughter of Rev. Dr. Sparrow, and married secondly to Kate (d. 1888), daughter of Rev. William Sparrow. He was founder of St. Mark's Church in Richmond.

Davis, F.A. Records 1867-1870.

Davis, Joseph Hoomes (1809-1879). Methodist. Son of William Edwards Davis and wife Mary, bur. in the Beale Family Cemetery, located at *Hickory Hill*, off of Route 626 near Hague, Va.

Dobb, Penfield. Record 1852.

Fisher, Andrew. Served North Farnham Episcopal, 1859-1860. Served as Rector in Richmond County parishes until 1871. Married Margaret Poe.

Fones, Henry Harrison (1840-1922). M.G. Served in Co. G, 15th Va. Cav., C.S.A. Served Oak Grove Baptist Church from 1880 to 1882. Rappahannock Baptist up to 1887 and again 1888-1894; Farnham Baptist, 1887-1888, and other locations. Buried Rappahannock Baptist Church cemetery. Served in several military companies, and Chaplin in the 55th Va. Inf., C.S.A. Married to Susan Ann Pullen. Records 1866-1880.

Garlick, J.C. Record 1850.

Gaskins (a.k.a. Gaskings), William (C). Records 1876-1880.

Gibbs, E.A. Records 1872.

Godwin, John. Minister of the Gospel. Records 1853.

Graham, Jeremiah "Jerry" (C). Served as the first pastor of Galilee Baptist Church until his resignation in 1871.

Henley, Robert Y. Disciples of Christ and the Reformed Baptist Church. Record 1852.

Hunnicutt, James W. Record 1852.

Johnson, B.H. Record 1852.

Johnson, Thomas Tasker (C) (1821-1904). Founded Potomac Baptist Church and Zion Baptist Church. Married Bettie Lee Johnson.

King, Henry P.F. (d. 1899). Served the Methodist Protestant Church and the Methodist Episcopal Church.

Lamkin, J.J. Record 1858.

Latane, William Catesby (d. 1906). Protestant Episcopal Church. Rector of Washington Parish from 1875 to 1906.

Lewis, Robert L. (C) (d. 1896). Served Galilee Baptist Church and Clarksville Baptist Church.

Lloyd, John J. Record 1876.

Locke, Thomas Estep (1812-1897). Married Lucy Armistead Nelson on 21 DEC 1841 in Lunenburg Co. Started 3 NOV 1857 in Washington Parish, Rector of St. Peter's Church, resigned 1869. Buried in Ivy Hill Cemetery, Alexandria, Va.

McDaniel, John. Served in King George Co. Records 1844-1853.

McDonald, James (1806-1893). Methodist Episcopal Church.

McGuire, Edward Brown (1818-1881). Son of Rev. Edward Charles McGuire, Rector of St. George's Parish, Fredericksburg, and his wife Judith Carter Lewis. He commenced his ministry in 1842 in Meherrin Parish of Greenville Co., then St. Paul's in Hanover, St. David's in King William, Cople in Westmoreland, St. Anne's in Essex, and Hanover in King George Co.

McGuire, William (1828-1887). Son of Rev. Edward Charles McGuire. Served was first a minister of the Protestant Episcopal Church and served Washington Parish from 1 OCT 1847 to 1853; later served the Reformed Episcopal Church. Married Marietta Heber Alexander of King George Co. They had two daughters.

Montague, Howard William (1810-1876). Baptist, seved Bethel Baptist Church in Caroline County, Mt. Zion Baptist Church at Dunbrooke, and Ephesus Baptist Church at Dunnsville, Essex County.

Montague, Philip. Baptist. Well known in Essex and King and Queen Counties.

Nash, Bushrod W. Union Baptist denomination.

Nevitt, Thomas G. Record 1877.

Newton, John B., Dr., was registrar of Cople Parish and practiced medicine. He served St. John's Episcopal Church in Tappahannock before moving to Westmoreland County where he lived in the rectory of Cople Parish.

Northam, George Henry (1828-1896). Baptist. Served Nomini Baptist Church after the death of his father, and again after 1866. Son of George Northam (1793-1854) who was pastor of Nomini and Menokin Baptist until his death in 1854. The son was first married in 1850 to Elizabeth Mary Sanford Walker (1827-1856), then Catharine A. Saunders. Buried at Jerusalem Baptist Church, Emmerton, Va.

Payne, John (d. 1874). Served Washington Parish from 1871 to 1874. First buried at *Cavalla*,[1] first removed to St. Paul's Episcopal Church Cemetery, Alexandria, Va., then to the Episcopal Seminary at Alexandria, Va.

---

[1] Payne, p. 127, notes that *Cavalla* in Westmoreland Co. is named for Cavalla, Liberia, West Africa.

Porter, James F. [or S.] Record 1863.

Pullen, John (1804-1869). Minister of the Gospel. Served Rappahannock Baptist, 1842-1867, and Popes Creek Baptist from 1848 until his death. Buried Rappahannock Baptist Church.

Reamy, Robert Neale (1817-1894). Served Rappahannock Baptist in 1867, assisted at Welcome Baptist. Son of James I. Reamy. Buried Reamy Family Cemetery at Foneswood, Va. Married to Virginia Jane Owens (1822-1900).

Rich, Edmond (C). Records 1878-1880.

Rodefer, Charles P. (b. 1838). Married 1864 in Lynchburg, Va. to Anna Lee Johnson, daughter of William H. Johnson and Louisa Taylor. He was a chaplain in C.S.A.

Rosser, John C. Record 1879.

Rowe, John Gallatin (1827-1891). M.G. Son of George Rowe and Lucy Leitch. Founded Bowling Green Methodist Church in Bowling Green, Caroline County. Married Margaret Ann Purcell.

Roy, John, Rev. (C) (d. 1874 at age 60). First pastor of Shiloh Baptist Church in 1860's, and served at Grant's Hill Baptist Church until his death. Son of Boller and Maria Roy.

Russ, Charles, Jr. (C) (a.k.a. Rust), of Tucker Hill. Served Potomac Baptist Church and Zion Baptist Church. Buried behind the old church in *Gawn's Woods*.

Sanford, Robert James (1822-1889), M.D., served as captain in Co. 2, 111th Va. Mil. and Co. B, 40th Va. Inf., C.S.A. Buried at Carmel United Methodist Church. Married to Ellen Harvey Lawson Bailey.

Smith, John C. (C), of Hague, Va. Served Salem Baptist Church.

Taylor, Walter C. Records 1871-1874.

Thomas, Thomas G. (C). Founding pastor of Clarksville Baptist Church, c.1868. Served Mount Zion Baptist Church.

Tucker, Beverley Dandridge (1846-1930). Buried Zion Episcopal Church, Charles Town, W. Va. Episcopal Bishop, served St. John's Episcopal Church at Warsaw, 1873-1882. Married Anna Maria Washington (1851-1927).

Tuttle, Edmund B. Started 15 MAR 1853 in Washington Parish.

Walker, W.W. Methodist Protestant Church. Prisoner in 1864 at Point Lookout, Md.

Ward, William Norvell (1805-1881). Protestant Episcopal clergyman. Graduated in 1834 from the Theological Seminary in Alexandria, first served in Spotsylvania Co. Son of Seth Ward and Martha Norvell. Married in 1836 in Leesburg, Va. to Mary Smith Blincoe. Served North Farnham Episcopal from 1840-1853. Instrumental in organizing the 55th Virginia Infantry of the C.S.A. Buried in Hollywood Cemetery of Richmond.

Watts, Charles E. Record 1870.

Watts, Emanuel (C) (d. 1883). Served Little Zion Church, Oak Grove, Va., and Grant's Hill Baptist Church for a short while.

Weaver, James A. (1810-1885). Served Nomini Baptist Church. Buried at Nomini Baptist Church.

Wharton, Dabney Miller, D.D. (1804-1887). Son of John and Sally Wharton. In 1843, he was appointed seventeenth Rector of Cople Parish, and served St. James (1860-1887). Married first to Ann Ophelia Pearce (1807-1866). They were first buried in a Wharton Family Cemetery at *Lawfield*, but now found at St. James Church. Memorialized at St. James Episcopal Church in Warsaw.

Wheelwright, J.H. Served the M.E. Church. Record 1857.

White, John W., served the M.E. Church. Records 1876-1878.

Wiles, Alfred. Records 1851-1852.

Williams, E.L. Record 1851.

Young, Henry (C). Baptist. Records 1870.

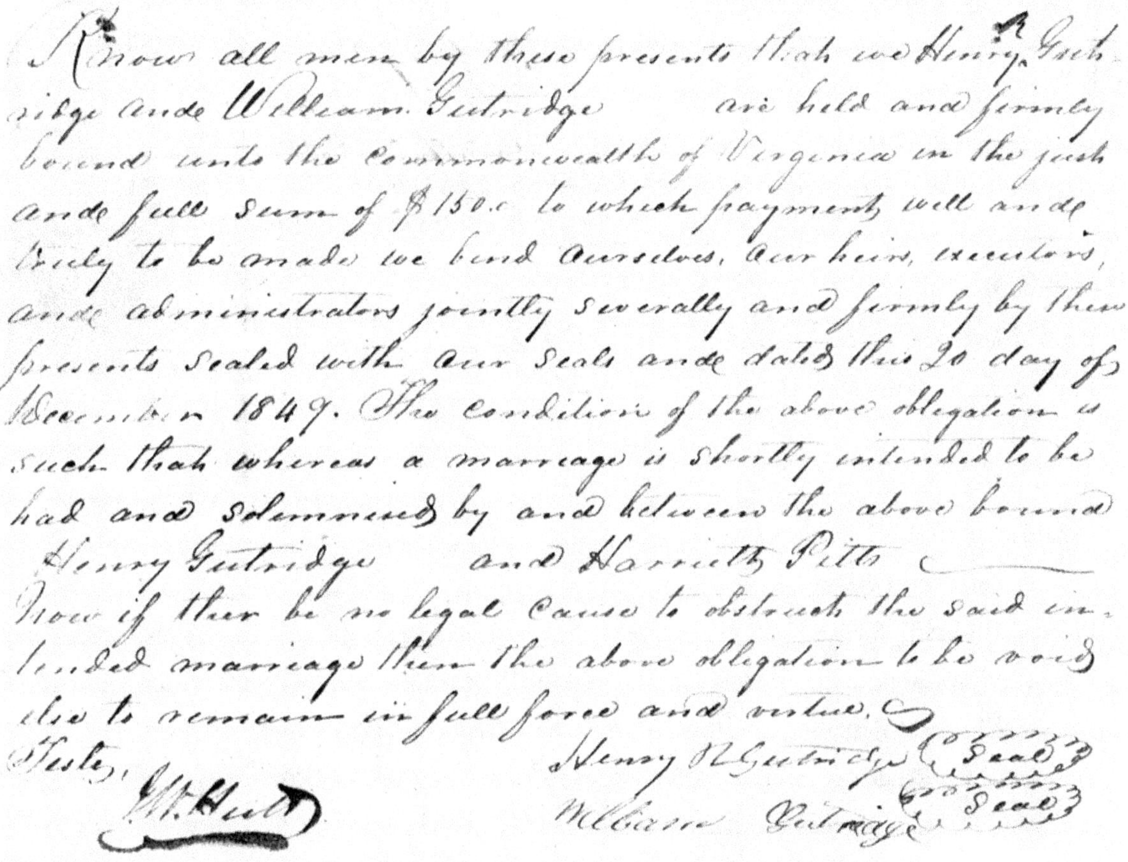

Know all men by these presents that we Henry Guth-ridge and William Gutridge are held and firmly bound unto the Commonwealth of Virginia in the just and full sum of $150.. to which payment, will and truly to be made we bind Ourselves, Our heirs, executors, and administrators jointly severally and firmly by these presents Sealed with Our Seals and dated this 20 day of December 1849. The condition of the above obligation is such that whereas a marriage is shortly intended to be had and solemnized by and between the above bound Henry Gutridge and Harriett Pitts Now if there be no legal cause to obstruct the said in-tended marriage then the above obligation to be void else to remain in full force and virtue.

Teste,   Henry R Gutridge (Seal)
W Hull   William Gutridge (Seal)

Figure 1 - Sample Bond used until about 1850

MARRIAGE LICENSE.

VIRGINIA, *Westmoreland County* to wit:

To any Person Licensed to Celebrate Marriages:

You are hereby authorized to join together in the Holy State of Matrimony, according to the rites and ceremonies of your Church, or religious denomination, and the laws of the Commonwealth of Virginia, *Arnold Lucas* and *Willie Ann McGuire*

Given under my hand, as Clerk of the *County* Court of *Westmoreland* this *21st* day of *August* 186*4*.

Warner Hunt CLERK.

CERTIFICATE TO OBTAIN A MARRIAGE LICENSE,
To be annexed to the License, required by Act passed 15th March, 1861.

Time of Marriage, *23d Augt 1866*

Place of Marriage, *Westmoreland County Va*

Full names of Parties Married, *Arnold Lucas Willie Ann McGuire*

Age of Husband, *23 years*

Age of Wife, *23 years*

Condition of Husband, (widowed or single,)

Condition of Wife, (widowed or single,)

Place of Husband's Birth, *Westmoreland County Va*

Place of Wife's Birth, *Westmoreland County Va*

Place of Husband's Residence, *Westmoreland County Va*

Place of Wife's Residence, *Westmoreland County Va*

Names of Husband's Parents, *Father unknown Polly Lucas*

Names of Wife's Parents, *Father unknown Maranda Templeman alias McGuire*

Occupation of Husband, *Farmer*

Given under my hand this *21st* day of *August* 186*6*

William M Hudson *Arnold Lucas* CLERK.

MINISTER'S RETURN OF MARRIAGE.

I CERTIFY, that on the *23* day of *August*, 186*6*, at *Westmoreland Co*, I united in marriage the above named and described parties, under authority of the annexed License.

G H Northam

☞ The Minister celebrating a Marriage is required, within TEN days thereafter, to return the License to the Office of the Clerk who issued the same, with an endorsement thereon of the FACT of such marriage, and of the TIME and PLACE of celebrating the same.

Figure 2 - Sample Marriage License 1, pre-printed form A

Marriage License

Virginia:

        Westmoreland County, To wit:

To any person licensed to celebrate marriages
You are hereby Authorized to join together in Holy
Matrimony according to the rites and ceremonies
of Your church or religious denomination and
the laws of the Commonwealth of Virginia:
Armistead Curre Belfield and Eliza Ann Dishman
    Given under my hand as Clerk of the county
Court of Westmoreland County This 13th day of
December 1869

                         Jno L Smith Clk

Certificate

Time of Marriage	14th December 1869
Place of Marriage	Fairview Westmoreland
Full Names of Parties	Armistead Curre Belfield and Eliza Ann Dishman
Age of Husband	30 Years
Age of Wife	24 Years
Condition of Husband	Single
Condition of Wife	Single
Place of Husbands Birth	Westmoreland County Va
Place of Wifes Birth	Westmoreland County Va
Place of Husbands Residence	Westmoreland County Va
Place of Wifes Residence	Westmoreland County Va
Names of Husbands Parents	Thomas M. & Fannie F Belfield
Names of Wifes Parents	Charles & Eliza F Dishman
Occupation	Farmer.

Given under my hand this 13 day of December
1869

                    A C Belfield

Figure 3 - Sample Marriage License 2, hand written format

Marriage License.

Virginia, *Westmoreland County* to-wit:

To any Person Licensed to Celebrate Marriages:

You are hereby authorized to join together in the Holy State of Matrimony, according to the rites and ceremonies of your Church, or religious denomination, and the laws of the Commonwealth of Virginia,

Robert Ethelwald Sanford

and *Bettie Asberry Collins*

Given under my hand, as Clerk of the County Court of *Westmoreland* this *8th* day of *November* 1888

J Warren Hutt Clerk.

CERTIFICATE TO OBTAIN A MARRIAGE LICENSE.

To be annexed to the License, required by Acts passed 15th March, 1861, and February 27th, 1866.

Time of Marriage, *8th of Nov 1888*	Place of Husband's Birth, *Westm'd Co V'a*
Place of Marriage, *Westm'd Co V'a*	Place of Wife's Birth, *Westm'd Co V'a*
Full Names of Parties Married, *Robert Ethelwald Sanford & Bettie Asberry Collins*	Place of Husband's Residence, *Westm'd Co V'a*
	Place of Wife's Residence, *Westm'd Co V'a*
Color, *White*	Names of Husband's Parents, *Richard & Fanny A Sanford*
Age of Husband, *21 years*	
Age of Wife, *22*	Names of Wife's Parents, *Geo W & Ann Eliza-beth Collins*
Condition of Husband, (widowed or single) *single*	
Condition of Wife, (widowed or single) *single*	Occupation of Husband, *Farmer*

Given under my hand this *8th* day of *November* 1888

J Warren Hutt Clerk.

MINISTER'S RETURN OF MARRIAGE.

I Certify, That on the *8th* day of *November* 1888, at *Antioch Westmoreland County* I united in Marriage the above-named and described parties, under authority of the annexed License.

J. B. Beale

☞ The Minister celebrating a marriage, is required, within TEN days thereafter, to return the license to the Office of the Clerk who issued the same, with an endorsement thereon of the FACT of such marriage, and of the TIME and PLACE of celebrating the same.

Figure 4 - Sample Marriage License 3, pre-printed form B

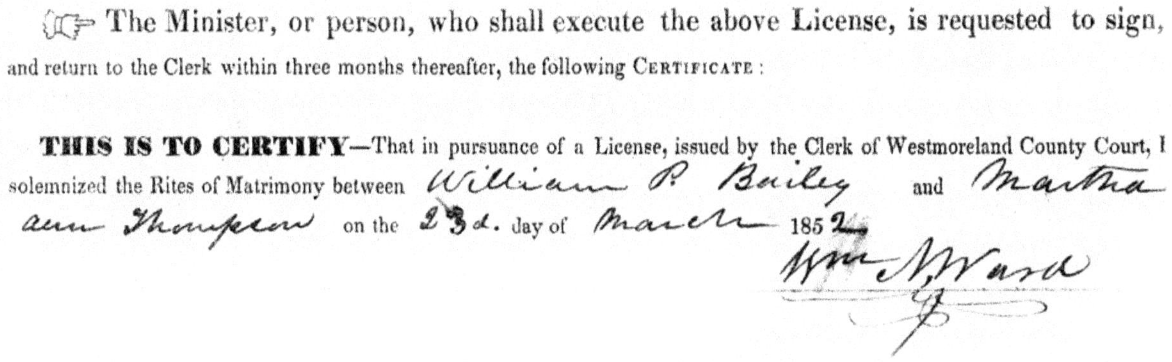

☞ The Minister, or person, who shall execute the above License, is requested to sign, and return to the Clerk within three months thereafter, the following CERTIFICATE:

THIS IS TO CERTIFY—That in pursuance of a License, issued by the Clerk of Westmoreland County Court, I solemnized the Rites of Matrimony between *William P Bailey* and *Martha ann Thompson* on the 23d. day of *March* 1852

Wm N Ward

Figure 5 - Sample Minister Return, single entry

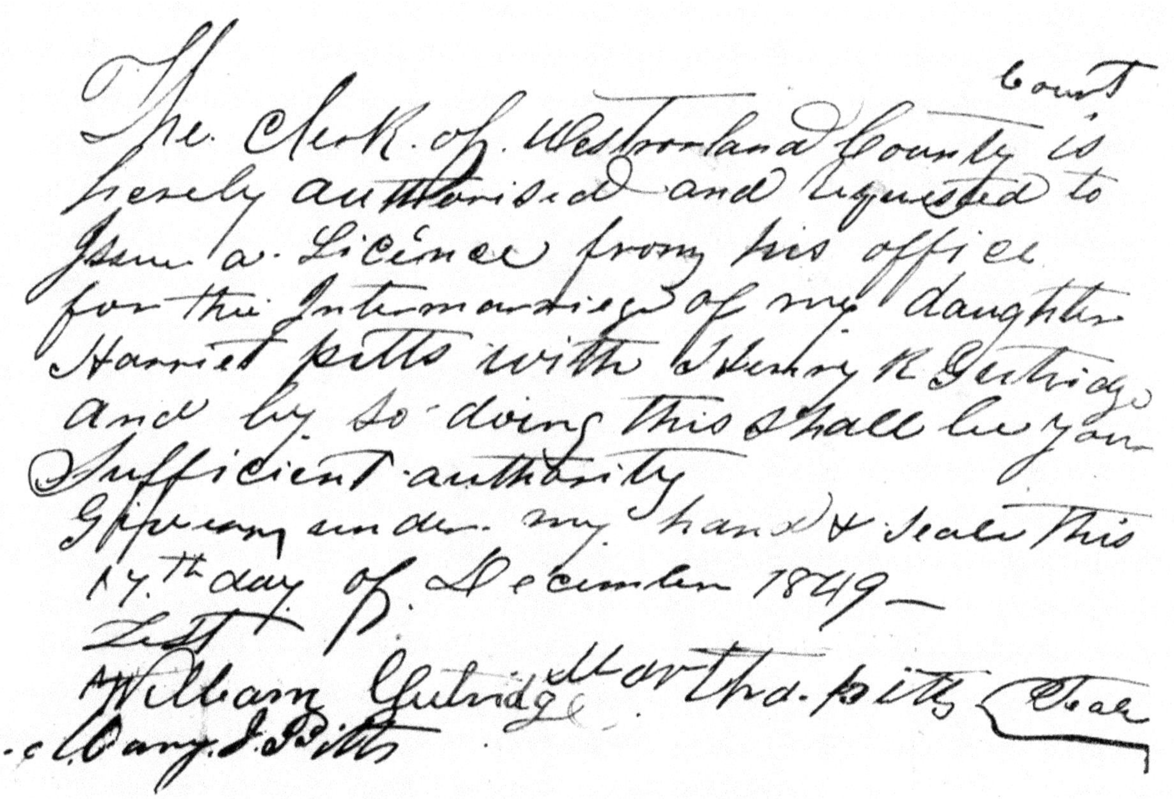

The Clerk of Westmoreland County Court is hereby authorised and requested to Issue a License from his office for the Intermarriage of my daughter Harriet pitts with Henry R Gentridge and by so doing this shall be your Sufficient authority Given under my hand & seal this 17th day of December 1849 —

William Gentridge Martha pitts (Seal)

Figure 6 - Sample Consent by Parent

A

Adams, James J. to Sarah R. King. License 7 OCT 1852. Married 7 OCT 1852 by Wm. N. Ward. [M15:52-24, R:23]

Adams, Joseph J. to Rachel A. Hayes. JOSEPH J. ADAMS, age 25, single, b. Brooklyn, N.Y., res. King George Co., son of J.J. and Mary Adams, to RACHEL A. HAYES, age 22, single, b. Perryville, Lycoming Co., Pa., daughter of Ambrose and Sarah C. Hayes. License 5 FEB 1876. Filed 12 FEB 1876. [M19 license not on film; R:118; R1:64-6 no return]

Alexander, Edward Porter (1835-1910), Lieut., later Brigadier General of C.S.A., son of Adam Leopold Alexander (1803-1882) and Sarah Hillhouse Gilbert (1805-1855),[1] first to Bettie Jacqueline Mason. Married 3 APR 1860 by Rev. Thomas E. Locke at *Cleveland*, the residence of William Roy Mason. [WP]

Alexander, Thornton (C) to Lucy Fowler. THORNTON ALEXANDER, farmer, age 24, single, b. Westmoreland Co., son of Beverly and Nancy Alexander, to LUCY FOWLER, age 21, single, b. Westmoreland Co., daughter of Oliver and Mary Fowler. License 19 FEB 1879. Married 20 FEB 1879 at Mrs. J. Tyler's by Thomas T. Johnson. [M20; R:128; R1:76-16]

Allaway, James to Emma Elizabeth Gregory (d. 1883 of bilious fever). JAMES ALLAWAY, farmer, age 22, single, b. Northumberland Co., son of James and Lucy Allaway, to EMMA ELIZABETH GREGORY, age 19, single, b. Westmoreland Co., daughter of James [A.] and Sarah Gregory. License 27 DEC 1875. Married 5 JAN 1876 by F.B. Beale. [DR:57-3 gives mother of Emma as Sarah Grayson; M19; R:116; R1:63-3]

Alzerodt, John C. to Virginia Butler. License 25 DEC 1852. Married 26 DEC 1852 by Penfield Dobb. [M15:52-29, R:25]

Anderson, Daniel (a slave belonging to L. Washington), to Eliza [blank] (a slave belonging to G.M. Carter). Married 11 NOV 1860 at St. Peter's Church by Rev. T.E. Locke. [WP]

Anderson, Philip to Grace "Gracy" Rowand (C). PHILIP ANDERSON, farmer, age 22, single, b. Cumberland Co., son of Philip and [Marinda] Anderson, to GRACY ROWAND, age 28, single, b. Westmoreland Co., daughter of Rhody and Emily Rowand. Signed Philip [his X mark] Anderson, wit. Joseph Jones. License 1 JAN 1867. Married 3 JAN 1867 at *Sandy Point*[2] by J.H. Davis. [M18; R:85; R1:26-10]

Anadale, Robert P. (1828-1873), served in Co. A, 15th Va. Cav., C.S.A., to Mary M. Tallent (1827-1911).[3] ROBERT ANNADALE [sic], farming, age 25, single, b. Westmoreland Co., son of Thomas

---

[1] Charles C. Alexander and Virginia W. Alexander, *Alexander Kin*, Vol. II (Greenville, S.C.: Southern Historical Press, Inc., 1990), p. 325, for discussion of the family of Dr. Adam Alexander of Liberty Co., Ga. and his son Adam Leopold Alexander.
[2] The *Sandy Point* home is described in the *Northern Neck News*, 28 APR 1893, p. 1.
[3] Robert P. Annadale and his wife Mary M. Tallent were buried in the Weaver-Annadale Cemetery, located off of Route 644.

Annadale [and Nancy Ann Carpenter], to MARY TALENT [sic], age 26, single, b. Westmoreland Co., daughter of William Tallent. License 26 DEC 1853. Married 29 DEC 1853 at Thomas Annadale's by Rev. John Pullen. [M15:54-16b; R:37; R1:1-12]

Anadale, Thomas (d. testate[1] 1874 of old age), to Rachel M. Carpenter. THOMAS ANNEDALE [sic], farmer, age about 50, widower, b. Westmoreland Co., son of Robert and Mary [Good] Annadale, to RACHEL M. CARPENTER, age about 21, single, b. Westmoreland Co., daughter of Mary Carpenter. License 6 APR 1854. Married 6 APR 1854 at Robert Mariner's by John Pullen. [DR:31-1; M15:54-16; R:43; R1:1-7]

Anthony, Dangerfield to Emma Jane Hinson. DANGERFIELD ANTHONY, farmer, age 26, single, b. Richmond Co., son of Thomas and Nancy [Jenkins] Anthony, to EMMA JANE HINSON, age 24, single, b. Westmoreland Co., daughter of William F. and Betsy Hinson. License 25 MAR 1880. Married 25 MAR 1880 by R.N. Reamy. [M20; R:133; R1:82-1]

Anthony, James Dangerfield to Mary Ann Barrett. JAMES DANGERFIELD ANTHONY, farmer, age 21, single, b. Richmond Co., son of Thomas and Nancy [Jenkins] Anthony, to MARY ANN BARRETT, age 15, single, b. Richmond Co., daughter of James and Mealy Barrett. Signed by James D. [his X mark] Anthony, wit. W.S. McKenney. License 2 FEB 1874. Married 2 FEB 1874 by B.R. Battaile. [M19; R:112; R1:57-7]

Anthony, John (d. by 1867), to Emily Franklin. JOHN ANTHONEY [sic], farmer, age 34, single, b. Westmoreland Co., son of John and Keturah [Thomas] Anthony,[2] to EMILY FRANKLIN, age 34, single, b. Westmoreland Co., daughter of Thomas and Harriet [Sutton] Franklin.[3] Consent 15 MAY 1860 by bride, wit. Thomas J. Linthicum. License 16 MAY 1860. Married 17 MAY 1860. [M17:60-23; R:74]

Anton, Benjamin (d. by 1866), to Alice Howsen. License 16 JUL 1850. Married 17 JUL 1850 by George Northam. [M15:50-18, R:1 not in *Nottingham*]

Anton, James Wesley (1856-1914), to Sallie Robertson Self (1857-1917).[4] JAMES WESLEY ANTON, mechanic, age 21, single, b. Westmoreland Co., son of Benjamin and Alice [Howsen] Anton, *q.v.*, to SALLIE R. SELF, age 21, single, b. Westmoreland Co., daughter of Joseph and Mary Self. License 3 SEP 1878. Married 5 SEP 1878 at *Afton*[5] by F.W. Claybrook. [M19; R:126; R1:74-13]

Anton [or Anthon], Robert to Elizabeth Gregory. License 26 NOV 1850. Married 27 NOV 1850 by George Northam. [M15:50-24, R:3 not in *Nottingham*]

Anton, Robert to Frances Morris. ROBERT ANTON, farmer, age 45, widowed, b. Westmoreland Co., son of Robert and Betsy Anton, to FRANCES MORRIS, age 45, single [sic], b. Westmoreland Co., daughter of William and Catharine McKennney. Consent 19 JUN 1866 by bride, wit. John

---

[1] Deeds & Wills No. 40, p. 81, will of Thomas Anadale, proved 28 SEP 1874, names wife Rachel.
[2] John Anthony and Kettura Thomas were married by bond 2 OCT 1821 in Westmoreland Co.
[3] Thomas Franklin was married to Harriet Sutton by bond 9 FEB 1814 in Westmoreland Co.
[4] James W. Anton and his wife Sarah R. Self were buried at Yeocomico Episcopal Church.
[5] *Afton* was built c.1840.

Howell. License 16 JUN 1866. Married 17 JUN 1866 by Elder James A. Weaver. [M18; R:83; R1:24-7]

Anton, Zachariah to Mary Jane Housen. ZACHARIAH ANTON, farmer, age 21, single, b. Westmoreland Co., son of Samuel and Elizabeth [Gregory] Anton,[1] to MARY JANE HOUSEN, age 19, single, b. Westmoreland Co., daughter of John W. and Felicia Housen. License 30 JAN 1860. Married 2 FEB 1860 by James A. Weaver. [M17:60-7; R:72; R1:17-1]

Armstrong, Henry S. (d. 1883 of pneumonia), to Mary Elizabeth Dishman (d. 1893 of pneumonia). HENRY S. ARMSTRONG, mariner, age 34, widowed, b. New Castle Co., Del., son of Andrew and Mary Armstrong, to MARY E. DISHMAN, age 19, single, b. Westmoreland Co., daughter of John T. [Triplett] Dishman [1796-1866] and Mary H. [Harlowe McDaniel] [1814-1880]. License 10 JUN 1857. Married 11 JUN 1857 at Leeds Town by W.A. Baynham. [DR:57-4, 94-1; M16a:57-19; R:61; R1:9-6]

Ashburn, Steptoe to Sarah "Sally" J. Ashburn. STEPTOE ASHBURN, sailor, age about 36, widower, b. Northumberland Co., son of Henry and Elizabeth Ashburn, to SALLY J. ASHBURN, age about 24, single, b. Lancaster Co., daughter of James and Sally Ashburn. License 14 JAN 1854. Married 19 JAN 1854 at Leedstown by John Bird, M.G. of the Baptist denomination, Essex Co. [M15:54-1; R:37; R1:1-1]

Ashton, Anthony (C) (d. 1877 of consumption), to Frances Newman. ANTHONEY ASHTON [sic], farmer, age 28, single, b. Westmoreland Co., son of Matilda Ashton, father unknown, to FRANCES NEWMAN, age 22, single, b. Westmoreland Co., daughter of Emanuel and Caroline [Lucas] Newman.[2] License 23 NOV 1864. Married 24 NOV 1864 at the residence of the bride's father by D.M. Wharton. [DR:39-1; M17a:64-13; R:80; R1:21-7]

Ashton, Austin to Anna Pierce. AUSTIN ASHTON, farmer, age 23, single, b. Westmoreland Co., son of Jane Ashton, father unknown, to ANNA PIERCE, age 22, single, b. Westmoreland Co., daughter of Thornton and Sally Pierce. Signed Austin [his X mark] Ashton, wit. C.C. Baker.[3] License 20 JAN 1868. Married 23 MAY 1868 at *Sherland* by J.H. Davis. [M18; R:89; R1:31-11]

Ashton, Blain to Sally Grimes. License 6 JUN 1855. [R:49]

Ashton, Daniel to Letty Taylor. License 17 DEC 1852. Married 17 DEC 1852 by George Northam, L.M.G. [M15:52-28, R:25]

Ashton, Daniel (C), second to Frances Ashton (d. 1872 of small pox). DANIEL ASHTON, farmer, age 34, widowed, b. Westmoreland Co., son of [Charles and] Matilda Ashton, to FRANCES ASHTON, age 24, single, b. Westmoreland Co., daughter of Blane and Susan Ashton. Signed Daniel Ashton, wit. John Goodridge. License 5 DEC 1860. Married 6 DEC 1860. [DR:20-1; M17:60-38; R:76]

---

[1] Samuel Anton was married to Susannah Gregory by bond 20 JUL 1824 in Westmoreland Co.
[2] Emanuel Newman was married to Caroline Lucas by bond 21 DEC 1836 in Westmoreland Co.
[3] Charles C. Baker (1820-1889), son of John and Sarah Baker, served in Co. E, 55th Va. Inf., C.S.A. He was buried at Andrew Chapel United Methodist Church.

Ashton, Daniel, third to Mary Elizabeth Johnson (d. 1882 of dropsy). DANIEL ASHTON, sailor, age 48, widowed, b. Westmoreland Co., son of Charles and Matilda Ashton, to MARY ELIZABETH JOHNSON, age 25, single, b. Westmoreland Co., daughter of Charles and Ann Johnson. Signed by Daniel [his X mark] Ashton, wit. W.S. McKenney. License 14 JAN 1874. Married 15 JAN 1874 at C. Johnson's by G.W. Beale, minister. [DR:52-5; M19; R:111; R1:56-16]

Ashton, Dock (C) to Lizzie Rich. DOCK ASHTON, farmer, age 22, single, b. Westmoreland Co., son of Kelsic and Mary Ashton, to LIZZIE RICH, age 23, single, b. Essex Co., daughter of William and Catharine Rich. License 5 MAR 1880. Married 10 MAR 1880 at Little Zion Church by Emanuel Watts. [M20; R:132; R1:81-13]

Ashton, Fleet William to Winny Ann Ashton. FLEET WILLIAM ASHTON, farmer, age 20, single, b. Westmoreland Co., son of Winny Ashton, father unknown, to WINNY ANN ASHTON, age 20, single, b. Westmoreland Co., daughter of Sally Ashton, father unknown. Wit. J.H. Sisson. License 1 JUN 1859. Married 2 JUN 1859. [M16a:59-16; R:70]

Ashton, Jacob to Felicia Ashton. JACOB ASHTON, farmer, age 44, single, b. Westmoreland Co., son of Blane and Crissy Ashton, to FELICIA ASHTON, age 26, single, b. Richmond Co., daughter of Matilda Ashton, father unknown. Signed Jacob [his X mark] Ashton, wit. W.E. Baker. License 25 JAN 1860. Married 26 JAN 1860. [M17:60-5; R:72]

Ashton, James (C) to Maria Champe Vessels (C). JAMES ASHTON, farmer, age 24, single, b. Westmoreland Co., son of Kelsic and Mary [Tate] Ashton,[1] to MARIA CHAMPE VESSELS, age 23, single, b. Essex Co., daughter of David and Eliza Vessels. Signed James [his X mark] Ashton. License 22 FEB 1876. Married 23 FEB 1876 at *Locust Farm* by Emanuel Watts, pastor Little Zion Church, Oak Grove, Va. [M19; R:118; R1:64-8]

Ashton, James to Alice Henry, black. JAMES ASHTON, farmer, age 25, widowed, b. Westmoreland Co., son of Kelsick and Mary [Tate] Ashton, to ALICE HENRY, age 20, single, b. Essex Co., daughter of Milly Gaskins. License 6 MAR 1880. Married 10 MAR 1880 at *Blenheim* by William C. Latane, Presbyter P.E. Church, wit. Henry Streets. [M20; R:132; R1:81-12; WP]

Ashton, Joseph to Hester Ann Newman. JOSEPH ASHTON, farmer, age 25, single, b. Westmoreland Co., son of George and Julia [Tate] Ashton,[2] to HESTER ANN NEWMAN, age 23, single, b. Westmoreland Co., daughter of Emanuel and Caroline [Lucas] Newman.[3] Signed Joseph [his X mark] Ashton. License 22 DEC 1869. Married 23 DEC 1869 by D.M. Wharton, Rector, Montross Parish. [M18; R:97; R1:40-33]

Ashton, McDaniel to Mary Elizabeth Williams. McDANIEL ASHTON, farmer, age 20, single, b. Westmoreland Co., son of Jesse and Amelia Ashton, to MARY ELIZABETH WILLIAMS, age 19, single, b. Westmoreland Co., daughter of Levi and Martha Williams. Signed M.D. [his X mark] Ashton]. License 25 NOV 1868. Married 1 DEC 1868 by D.M. Wharton. [M18; R:93; R1:36-1]

Ashton, Robert to Pheobe Ann Henry. License 16 JAN 1858. [R:63]

---

[1] Kelsick Ashton and Mary Tate were married by bond 10 DEC 1845 in Westmoreland Co.
[2] George Ashton and Julia Tate were married by bond 3 JAN 1844 in Westmoreland Co.
[3] Emanuel Newman and Caroline Lucas were married by bond 21 DEC 1836 in Westmoreland Co.

Ashton, Rodham (C) to Betsey Lawrence. License 11 FEB 1857. [R:59]

Ashton, Samuel to Maria Johnson. License 5 DEC 1855. [R:51]

Askins, Thomas Henry (1832-1901), served in Co. E, 40th Va. Inf., C.S.A., to Julia W. Gawen (b. 1832, d. 1892 of LaGrippe).[1] THOMAS H. ASKINS, mechanic, age 25, single, b. Westmoreland Co., res. *Centreville*,[2] son of Charles L. and Nancy Askins, to JULIA W. GAWEN, age 25, single, b. Westmoreland Co., res. *Wilmington*, daughter of William and Alice J. [Jefferson Garner] Gawen.[3] License 21 JUL 1857. Married 23 JUL 1857 at Yeocomico Church by T. Grayson Dashiell. [DR:90-48; M16a:57-23; NN; R:61; R1:9-14]

Atkins, Alvey Lee to Ella Myrtle Gutridge. ALVEY LEE ATKINS, farmer, age 49, widowed, b. and res. King William Co., son of Reuben and M.A. Atkins, to ELLA MYRTLE GUTRIDGE, age 20, single, b. Westmoreland Co., daughter of William A. and F.J. Gutridge. License 20 DEC 1879. Married 21 DEC 1879 at *Middle Brow* by F.W. Claybrook. [M20; R:131; R1:79-14]

Atwell (see Atwill)

Atwill, Benjamin Brown (1844-1918),[4] served Co. C, 9th Va. Cav., C.S.A., first to Elizabeth "Betsy" Ford Jones (d. 1878).[5] BENJAMIN BROWN ATWILL, farmer, age 23, single, b. Westmoreland Co., son of Samuel B. and Jane A. [Brown] Atwill,[6] to ELIZABETH FORD JONES, age 21, single, b. Westmoreland Co., daughter of [Dr.] Joseph and Mary F. [Chandler] Jones [d. 1890].[7] License 3 MAR 1868. Married 3 MAR 1868 by D.M. Wharton. [M18; R:90; R1:32-11]

Atwell, Samuel to Miss Ella Marshall. Married 31 AUG 1860 by Rev. T.E. Locke at *Shiloh*, King George Co. [WP]

Atwill, Stephen Bailey (1852-1905), to Mary Susan "Mollie" Bailey (1855-1940).[8] STEPHEN BAILEY ATWILL, merchant, age 25, single, b. Westmoreland Co., son of Samuel B. and [Judith A. Brown] Atwill, to MARY SUSAN BAILEY, age 22, single, b. Westmoreland Co., daughter of Robert S. [Sydnor] and Constance E. [Eugenia Hutt] Bailey, *q.v.* License 10 DEC 1877. Married 13 DEC 1877 at Carmel [Church] by J.H. Davis. [M19; R:123; R1:71-7]

Atwill, Thomas Frank (d. 1893 of dispepsia), to Elizabeth Ellen Johnson. THOMAS FRANK ATWELL [sic], farmer, age 22, single, son of James K. and Eliza [Jane Muse] Atwill, *q.v.*,[9] to ELIZABETH ELLEN JOHNSON, age 21, single, b. Westmoreland Co., daughter of William and Elizabeth Johnson. Consent 26 NOV 1860 by bride, wit. H.B. Belfield. License 26 NOV 1860. Married 27 NOV 1860 by H.P.F. King. [M17:60-36, 36a, 36b; R:76; R1:17-4]

---

[1] Thomas H. Askins and wife Julia Gawen were buried at Carmel United Methodist Church Cemetery, Kinsale, Va.
[2] Centreville was built c.1849 and was the home of the William Carey Family.
[3] William Gawen and Alice Jefferson Garner, daughter of Catherine Garner, were married by bond 14 DEC 1818 in Westmoreland Co.
[4] Benjamin Brown Atwill was buried at Yeocomico Episcopal Church, Tucker Hill, Va.
[5] Betsy Atwill was buried in The Glebe Cemetery, located in front of *Glebe Mansion*.
[6] Samuel B. Atwill and Jane A. Brown were married by bond 20 DEC 1842 in Westmoreland Co.
[7] Dr. Joseph Jones and Mary F. Chandler were married by bond 5 JUN 1845 in Westmoreland Co.
[8] Stephen Bailey Atwill and his wife Mary S. Bailey were buried in the Bailey Family Cemetery, located at *The Great House*, in Kinsale, Va. The Great House was re-built in 1827 by Maj. Robert Bailey and is said to have been copied from the floor plan of *Kirnan*.
[9] James K. Atwill and Eliza J. Muse were married by bond 11 FEB 1836 in Westmoreland Co. Eliza Jane was a daughter of Thomas S. Muse by his first wife Sally Higdon who were married by bond 25 JUL 1810 in King George Co.

Augustien [or Augustine], Charles Hoffman, to Florence Baynum Owens. CHARLES HOFFMAN AUGUSTIEN, schoolmaster, age 26, single, b. Burlington Co., N.J., son of Frederick A. Augustien [d. 1885 at his residence *Monrovia*] and Beula B. [Hullins] [d. 1889 of malarial fever], to FLORENCE BAYNUM OWENS, age 23, single, b. King George Co., daughter of Ed. W. [Edward Willis] [d. 1883[1]] and J.V. Owens. License 27 NOV 1875. Married 1 DEC 1875 at *Bleak Hall*, the residence of Mr. Owens by F.W. Claybrook. [DR:66-114[2], 80-57; M19; R:116; R1:62-8; WP]

Ayers, John W.F. to Lydia Anna Eliason. JOHN W.F. AYERS, planter, age 22, single, b. Harrisburg, Pa., son of James B. and Eliza M. Ayers, to LYAID ANNA ELIASON [sic], age 18, single, b. St. Georges, Del., daughter of Ebenezer and Sarah A. Eliason. License 12 JAN 1855. Married 14 JAN 1855 in Montross, Va. by H.P.F. King, minister of the M.E. Church South. [M16:55-4; R:47; R1:3-1]

B

Bailey, James Warren to Anna Ha[ce] Cridlin (d. 1872 of dysentery). JAMES WARREN BAILEY, farmer, age 32, [divorced], b. Augusta, Me., son of James H. and Martha Bailey, to ANNA H. CRIDLIN, age 20, single, b. Westmoreland Co., daughter of William and Nancy Cridlin. License 31 JUL 1869. Planned marriage 1 AUG 1869. [DR:22-2 gives father Burton Cridlin; R:95; R1:39-2 no return]

Bailey, James Warren to Ella Vernillia Carpenter. JAMES WARREN BAILEY, farmer, age 35, widower, b. Augusta, Me., son of J.H. [James] and Martha Bailey, to ELLA VERNILLIA CARPENTER, age 22, single, b. Westmoreland Co., daughter of Alexander and Mary [Jane Miller] Carpenter.[3] License 6 DEC 1872. Married 8 DEC 1872 at Gustavus Miller's by Robert N. Reamy. [M19; R:107; R1:51-16]

Bailey, Jeremiah (C) to Fannie Deane. JEREMIAH BAILEY, farmer, age 21, single, b. Westmoreland Co., son of James and Rebecca Bailey, to FANNIE DEANE, age 19, single, b. Westmoreland Co., daughter of James and Easter Deane. License 17 DEC 1878. Married 19 DEC 1878 at Zion Baptist Church by Rev. Charles [his X mark] Russ, wit. Thos. Brown, Jr. [M19; R:127; R1:76-1]

Bailey, John Lawson (1844-1898), served in Co. D, 8th Va. Inf., C.S.A., to Nannie Ballantyne Bailey (1853-1931).[4] JOHN LAWSON BAILEY, carpenter, age 32, single, b. Westmoreland Co., son of Stephen G. and Harriet A. Bailey, to NANNIE BALENTYNE BAILEY [sic], age 23, single, b. Westmoreland Co., daughter of William B. [Ball] and Ann E. [Elizabeth Murphy] Bailey. License 4 DEC 1876. Married 5 DEC 1876 at *Kinsale*, the home of William B. Bailey by J.H. Davis. [M19; NN; R:120; R1:67-5]

---

[1] WP shows that Edward Willis Owens died 25 JUL 1883, age 61, and was buried at *Locust Farm*.
[2] DR:66-114, entry for Frederick A. Augustine, b. York, Pa., d. 14 DEC 1885 of liver disease, age 63, son of George and Rosina Augustine, father of F.A. Augustine.
[3] Alexander Carpenter and Mary Jane Miller were married by bond 28 JAN 1850 in Westmoreland Co.
[4] John Lawson Bailey and his wife Nannie Ballantyne Bailey were buried in the Bailey Family Cemetery, located at *The Great House* in Kinsale, Va.

Bailey, John Portues (b. 1829, d. testate 1889[1]), builder of *Plain View*, to Georgianna Smith Hutt (1843-1920).[2] JOHN PORTUES BAILEY, farmer, age 39, single, b. Westmoreland Co., son of [Maj.] Robert Bailey and Ann P. [Portues Ball], to GEORGIANNA SMITH HUTT, age 2[5], single, b. Westmoreland Co., daughter of William and Elizabeth J. Hutt. License 23 DEC 1868. Married 31 DEC 1868 by W.F. Bain. [Bible; M18; R:94; R1:37-1]

Bailey, Robert Sydnor (1822-1868), second to Constance Eugenia Hutt (b. 1833, d. 1894 at *Bankton*).[3] License 13 NOV 1851. Married 14 NOV 1851 by A. Wiles. [M15:51-22; NN; R:11]

Bailey, Robert (C) to Lucretia Kelsic. ROBERT BAILEY, farmer, age 34, single, b. and res. Richmond Co., son of Ellen Bailey, father unknown, to LUCRETIA KELSIC, age 20, single, b. Richmond Co., daughter of Meredith and Lucy Kelsic. Signed by Robert [his X mark] Bailey, wit. W.S. McKenney. License 24 DEC 1873. Married 25 DEC 1873 by Thomas G. Thomas. [M19; R:110; R1:56-1]

Bailey, Thomas to Elizabeth Tate. License 26 JAN 1858. [R:63]

Bailey, William Ball (1824-1911), son of Maj. Robert Bailey (d. 1844) and Ann Portues Ball (d. 1855 in 64th year), first to Ann Elizabeth Murphy (1832-1932),[4] daughter of John Ballantine Murphy (1790-1867) and Million Brown Wishart (d. 1834). License 13 APR 1852. Married 15 APR 1852 by Edward B. McGuire. [Bible; M15:52-15; R:19]

Bailey, William P. to Martha Ann Thompson. License 22 MAR 1852. Bond 23 MAR 1852 by William N. Ward. [M15:52-12; R:17]

Balderson, Cornelius [or Carolinus] "Corry" L. (1851-1925), to Elvira Ella White (1857-1924).[5] CORIOLINUS BALDERSON [sic], farmer, age 23, single, b. Westmoreland Co., son of Uriah Balderson [b. 1814, d. testate 1887[6]] and Delila Balderson [1809-1890],[7] to ELIVIRA ELLA WHITE, age 18, single, b. Westmoreland Co., daughter of Granville White and Leanna [Orinthia Mothershead].[8] License 9 APR 1875. Married 11 APR 1875 by H.H. Fones. [M19; R:115; R1:61-3]

Balderson, Daniel to Mrs. Mary Finch White. DANIEL BALDERSON, mechanic, age about 38, single, b. upper part of Richmond Co., son of [Rev.] William Balderson [c.1781-1854] and Frances his wife, to MARY WHITE, age about 25, widow, b. Westmoreland Co., daughter of William Finch and [Harriet] Sorrel. License 26 JAN 1856. Married 29 JAN 1856 at Spencer Sorrel's by John Pullen, M.G. [M16:56-3; R:53; R1:5-3]

---

[1] Deeds & Wills No. 48, p. 412, will of John P. Bailey of *Plain View*, proved 23 SEP 1889.

[2] John Portues Bailey and wife Georgianna Smith Hutt were buried in the Bailey Family Cemetery, located at *The Great House* in Kinsale, Va.

[3] Robert Sydnor Bailey and his second wife Eugenia Hutt were buried in the Bailey Family Cemetery, located at *The Great House* in Kinsale, Va.

[4] William Ball Bailey and his wife Ann Elizabeth Murphy were buried in the Bailey Family Cemetery, located at *The Great House* in Kinsale, Va.

[5] Cornelius "Corro" L. Balderson and his wife Ella Elvira White were buried in the Balderson Family Cemetery, located off of Route 622 at *Panorama*, Montross, Va.

[6] Deeds & Wills No. 47, p. 324, will of Uriah Balderson, proved 24 OCT 1887, names wife Delila Balderson and son Corra L. Balderson.

[7] Uriah Balderson, son of Ebenezer Balderson and Ann Clark, and Delila Balderson were married by bond 15 FEB 1836 in Richmond Co. Uriah Balderson, son of Ebenezer Balderson and Elizabeth Hardwick, and wife Delila Balderson were buried in the Balderson-Ridgely Family Cemetery, located off of Route 622.

[8] Granville White and Leannah Mothershead, daughter of Sarah Mothershead, were married by bond 3 MAR 1838 in Westmoreland Co.

Balderson, Daniel Smith (1849-1936), to Emma Sophia White (1853-1932).[1] DANIEL SMITH BALDERSON, farmer, age 24, single, b. Westmoreland Co., son of Uriah Balderson [d. testate 1887] and Delila Balderson, *q.v.*, to EMMA SOPHIA WHITE, age 20, single, b. Westmoreland Co., daughter of Granville White and Leanna [Orinthia Mothershead], *q.v.* License 18 FEB 1874. Married 19 FEB 1874 by W.C. Taylor. [M19; R:112; R1:57-15]

Balderson, Edward (d. by 1864[2]), to Frances J. Fones, daughter of Samuel R. Fones and Nancy Wilson.[3] License 27 JAN 1853. Married [2]7 JAN 1853 by John Pullen. [M15:53-1, R:27]

Balderson, George Cornelius (b. 1852, d. 1932 of pneumonia), to Mary Elizabeth Jenkins (1858-1920).[4] GEORGE CORNELIUS BALDERSON, farmer, age 24, single, b. Richmond Co., son of Marl. [Marlborough B.] Balderson [1825-1915] and Susan D. [Oliffe] [d. by 1852],[5] to MARY ELIZABETH JENKINS, age 20, single, b. Richmond Co., daughter of James H. Jenkins and Mary A. [Sanders].[6] License 11 JAN 1877. Married 14 JAN 1877 at Mr. Jenkins' (the bride's father) by F.W. Claybrook. [DC; M19; R:121; R1:68-11]

Balderson, George Washington (b. 1844, d. 1926 of pneumonia), served in Co. G, 15th Va. Cav., C.S.A., to Mrs. Sarah Jane Hart Fones (1841-1891).[7] GEORGE WASHINGTON BALDERSON, farmer, age 21, [single], b. and res. Richmond Co., son of Theoderick N. [Noel] Balderson [1814-1890] and [Dorothea] L. [Lane Saunders] [1821-1903],[8] to SARAH JANE FONES, age 24, widow, b. Westmoreland Co., daughter of Fielding R. and Ann E. Hart. License 23 NOV 1865. Married 26 NOV 1865 at *Foneswood* by John Pullen. [DC; M17a:65-12; NN; R:81; R1:22-7]

Balderson, Philip Montague (1837-1909), served in Co. A, 15th Va. Cav., C.S.A., first to Lucy Jane Annadale (d. 1886 age 45).[9] PHILIP MONTAGUE BALDERSON, farmer, age 27, single, b. Richmond Co., son of Uriah [Balderson] [d. testate 1887[10]] and Delila Balderson, *q.v.*, to LUCY ANNIDALE [sic], age 21, single, b. Westmoreland Co., daughter of Thomas Annadale [and Nancy Ann Carpenter]. License 14 OCT 1864. Married 16 OCT 1864 at Mrs. White's by John Pullen. [DR68-42, 72-77[11]; M17a:64-10; R:80; R1:21-3]

Balderson, Warner Harrison (b. 1847, d. 1936 of nephritis), to Norsey Ann Oliff (1847-1913).[12] WARNER HARRISON BALDERSON, farmer, age 21, single, b. Richmond Co., son of William R. Balderson and Amelia [Ambrose],[13] to NORSEY ANN OLIFF, age 21, single, b. Richmond Co.,

---

[1] Daniel Smith Balderson and his wife Emma Sophia White were buried in the Balderson-Ridgely Family Cemetery, located off of Route 622.
[2] Frances married (2) on 12 JUL 1864 at Alexandria, Va. by Rev. Thomas Drumm, rector of Christ Church, to Charles Guy, fisherman, b. Stafford Co., son of Benjamin and Susan Guy. Charles Guy d. 28 OCT 1874 in his 53rd year and was buried in the Methodist Protestant Cemetery in Alexandria, Va.
[3] Samuel R. Fones and Nancy Wilson were married by bond 26 OCT 1815 in Westmoreland Co., with William Sanders, security.
[4] George C. Balderson and wife Mary E. Jenkins were buried at Popes Creek Baptist Church, Baynesville, Va.
[5] Marlborough B. Balderson, son of Rev. William R. Balderson, and Susannah D. Olliffe, daughter of William S. Olliffe, were married by bond 11 NOV 1846 in Richmond Co. Marlborough died 18 FEB 1915 of arterio sclerosis and was buried near Potomac Mills.
[6] James H. Jenkins and Mary Sanders had a marriage license 20 OCT 1851 in Richmond Co. Married 22 OCT 1851 by Rev. William Balderson.
[7] George W. Balderson and wife Sarah J. Fones were buried at Rappahannock Baptist Church, Newland, Richmond Co., Va.
[8] Theoderick N. Balderson and Dorothea Lane Saunders, daughter of Daniel Saunders and Mary Mothershead, were married 12 OCT 1838 in St. Mary's Co., Md.
[9] Philip Montague Balderson and his wife Lucy Jane Annadale were probably buried in the Balderson-Ridgely Family Cemetery, located off of Route 622.
[10] Deeds & Wills No. 47, p. 324, will of Uriah Balderson, proved 24 OCT 1887, names wife Delila Balderson and son Philip M. Balderson.
[11] DR:72-77, entry for Uriah Balderson, b. Richmond Co., d. 8 OCT 1887 of cancer, age 75, son of Ebenezer and Annie Balderson.
[12] Warner H. Balderson and wife Norsey A. Oliff were buried at Rappahannock Baptist Church, Newland, Va.
[13] William Balderson, Jr. and Amelia Ambrose were married by bond 5 FEB 1833 in Richmond Co.

daughter of Jesse Oliff and Bethuel [Jenkins].[1] Signed Warner H. [his X mark] Balderson, wits. Wm. Green, J.W. Hutt. License 7 JAN 1869. Married 18 JAN 1869 by Robert N. Reamy. [M18; R:94; R1:37-9]

Ball, George (C) to Juliet Figget[t]. License 25 APR 1857. [R:59]

Ball, John to Prescilla Weldon. JOHN BALL, farmer, age 25, single, b. Westmoreland Co., son of George and Elizabeth Ball, to PRESCILLA WELDON, age 21, single, b. Westmoreland Co., daughter of Sample Weldon [and Sally Gaskins], *q.v.* Signed John [his X mark] Ball, wits. J.W. Hutt and Wm. S. McKenney. License 12 FEB 1868. Married 14 FEB 1868 at *Hickory Hill* by J.H. Davis. [M18; R:90 has Priscilla Winkfield in error; R1:32-8]

Ball, Thomas (C) to Melvina Washington. THOMAS BALL, farmer, age 22, single, b. Westmoreland Co., son of Fanny Ball, father unknown, to MELVINA WASHINGTON, age 20, single, b. Westmoreland Co., daughter of Eliza Washington, father unknown. Signed Thomas [his X mark] Ball, wit. J.H. Sisson. License 24 NOV 1869. Married 25 NOV 1869 by John C. Smith. [M18; R:96; R1:39-16]

Ball, William Henry (C) to Matilda Burton. WILLIAM HENRY BALL, farmer, age 22, single, b. Westmoreland Co., son of William Ball and Feby [Burrell] [d. 1883], to MATILDA BURTON, age 22, single, b. Westmoreland Co., daughter of Thomas and Lucy Burton. License 18 SEP 1878. Married 19 SEP 1878 at the residence of the bride's parents by Edmond Rich. [DR:57-8[2]; M19; R:126; R1:74-16]

Banket, Robert (C) to Mary Streets. ROBERT BANKET, farmer, age 21, single, b. Westmoreland Co., son of Dunmore and Caroline Banket, to MARY STREETS, age 17, single, b. Westmoreland Co., daughter of Moses and Lucinda Streets. License 13 NOV 1876. Married 15 NOV 1876 at Little Zion Church by Emanuel Watts, pastor, Little Zion Church. [M19; R:119; R1:66-14]

Bankhead, John (C) to Alice Garland. JOHN BANKHEAD, waggoner, age 24, single, b. Westmoreland Co., son of John and Charlotte Bankhead, to ALICE GARLAND, age 20, single, b. Westmoreland Co., daughter of Peter and Peggy Garland. License 27 NOV 1877. Married 28 NOV 1877 at Little Zion Church by Emanuel Watts, pastor. [M19; R:123; R1:71-5]

Banks, Albert to Elizabeth Roy. ALBERT BANKS, farmer, age 22, single, b. Westmoreland Co., son of William and Caroline Banks, to ELIZABETH ROY, age 21, single, b. Westmoreland Co., daughter of John and Eliza Roy. Married 31 DEC 1867 at B.F. Smoot's Mill[3] by R.N. Reamy. [M18; R1:31-1]

Barber, Charles Crocker to Sallie Elizabeth Askins. CHARLES CROCKER BARBER, farmer, age 23, single, b. Westmoreland Co., son of Henry D. Barber and Felicia B. [Beale], *q.v.*, to SALLIE ELIZABETH ASKINS, age 21, single, b. Westmoreland Co., daughter of Thomas H. Askins and Julia [W. Gawen], *q.v.* License 25 FEB 1880. Married 26 FEB 1880 at Yeocomico Church by Pendleton Brooke, P.E. Ch. [CP; M20; R:132; R1:81-9]

---

[1] Jesse Oliff and Bethuel Jenkins were married by bond 13 MAY 1842 in Westmoreland Co.
[2] DR:57-8, entry for Phoebe Ball (C), d. 30 DEC 1883 of consumption, age 40, daughter of Spencer and Polly Burrell, wife of William Ball.
[3] Smoot's Grist Mill became Cook's Mill.

Barber, Ellison W., served in Co. C, 9th Va. Cav., C.S.A., to Mary E.F. Garner (d. 1872 of pneumonia). ELERSON W. BARBER, farmer, age 22, single, b. Westmoreland Co., [no parents given], to MARY E.F. GARNER, age 18, single, b. Westmoreland Co., daughter of James and Elizabeth Garner. License 26 SEP 1854. Married 28 SEP 1854 at the house of James Garner by H.P.F. King. [DR:20-5; M15:54-10; R:45; R1:2]

Barber, Henry D. to Felicia Beale. License 18 AUG 1852. Married 19 AUG 1852 by George Northam, L.M.G. [M15:52-20, R:21]

Barker, Beckwith (d. 1862), served in Co. C, 47th Va. Inf., C.S.A., to Lucy Ann Head. BECKWITH BARKER, sailor, age 24, single, b. Westmoreland Co., son of Joseph and Betsy Barker, to LUCY ANN HEAD, in her 17th year, single, b. Westmoreland Co., daughter of Uriah Head and [Mahala] Ann [Dameron].[1] License 8 MAR 1858. Married 11 MAR 1858 at residence of Mrs. Head by Thomas E. Locke, Rector of St. Peter's Church, Washington Parish. [M16a:58-10; R:63; R1:11-7; SP; WP]

Barker, William "Billie" Sedwick (1844-1927), served in Co. E, 55th Va. Inf., C.S.A., to Eolia Reed (1855-1931).[2] WILLIAM SEDWICK BARKER, farmer, age 31, widowed, b. Westmoreland Co., son of John Barker [d. testate 1884[3]] and Frances [DeAtley], to EOLIA REED, age 21, single, b. Westmoreland Co., daughter of William and Jane Reed. License 27 DEC 1875. Married 5 JAN 1876 at Capt. Baxter's by F.W. Claybrook. [M19; R:117; R1:63-4]

Barnes, Charles W. to Julia A. Smith. License 5 JAN 1853. Married 13 JAN 1853 by Wm. N. Ward. [M15:53-2, R:25]

Barnett, Thornton (C) to Alice Turner. THORNTON BARNETT, farming, age 70, single, b. King George Co., son of Benjamin and Sarah Barnett, to ALICE TURNER, age 70, single, b. Westmoreland Co., parents unknown. Signed Thornton [his X mark] Barnett, wit. J.W. Hutt. License 16 FEB 1874. Married 21 FEB 1874 at Mattox, Va. by Emanuel Watts, pastor. [M19; R:112; R1:57-13]

Barrack, Richard Henry to Martha Jane Edmonds (d. 1882). RICHARD HENRY BARRACK, waterman, age 18, single, b. Westmoreland Co., son of George G. and Maria Barrack, to MARTHA JANE EDMONDS, age 17, single, b. Westmoreland Co., daughter of William [F.] and Alice Edmonds. Consent 10 AUG 1860 by father William [his X mark] Edmonds, wits. Lewis T. Miller, Austin C. Edmonds. Consent 10 AUG 1860 by father George G. Barrack, wits. Lewis T. Miller, Wm. [his X mark] Edmonds. License 11 AUG 1860. Married 14 AUG 1860 [at the residence of Mr. Edmonds] by Thomas E. Locke, Rector of Washington Parish. [M17:60-28, 28a, 28b, 28c; R:74; R1:17-15; SC; WP]

Bartlett, Elijah, member of 1864 Home Guard, C.S.A., to Lavinia Bartlett. ELIJA BARTLETT, farmer, age 25, single, b. Westmoreland Co., son of Samuel Bartlett and Mahala [Carter],[4] to LAVINIA BARTLETT, age 21, single, b. Westmoreland Co., unknown parents. Signed Elija [his X

---

[1] Uriah Head and Mahala Ann Dameron were married by bond 22 JUL 1830 in Westmoreland Co.
[2] William S. Barker and his wife Eolie Reed were buried at Popes Creek Baptist Church, Baynesville, Va.
[3] Deeds & Wills No. 44, p. 358, will of John Barker, proved 25 FEB 1884, names wife Frances Barker and son William.
[4] Samuel Bartlett and Mahala Carter, daughter of Daniel Carter, were married by bond 26 SEP 1832 in Richmond Co.

mark] Bartlett, wit. Wm. S. McKenney. License 5 MAR 1874. Married 8 MAR 1874 at R.N. Reamy's by Robert N. Reamy. [M19; R:112; R1:58-3]

Bartlett, James to Elizabeth Ann Mothershead. JAMES BARTLETT, workman, age 23, b. Richmond Co., son of John Bartlett and Elizabeth Mothershead,[1] to ELIZABETH ANN MOTHERSHEAD, age 21, b. Westmoreland Co., daughter of William M. Mothershead and Elizabeth Bartlett. License 7 MAR 1857. Married 8 MAR 1857 at the residence of Elizabeth Mothershead by John G. Rowe, M.G. [M16a:57-10; R:59; R1:8-13]

Bartlett, Richard to Mrs. Sarah Frances Jenkins Franklin, widow of James Edward Franklin, *q.v.* RICHARD BARTLETT, laborer, age 24, single, b. Richmond Co., son of Samuel Bartlett and Mahala [Carter], *q.v.*, to SARAH FRANCES FRANKLIN, age 28, widow, b. Westmoreland Co., daughter of Henry Jenkins. License 23 MAY 1874. Married 24 MAY 1874 by B.R. Battaile. [M19; R:113; R1:58-10]

Bartlett, Robert H. to Virginia Kennedy. ROBERT H. BARTLETT, farmer, age 26, single, b. Westmoreland Co., son of Joseph and Sarah Bartlett, to VIRGINIA KENNADAY [sic], age 23, single, b. Westmoreland Co., daughter of Thomas and Sarah Jane Kennaday. License 15 OCT 1856. Married 16 OCT 1856 at the residence of Thos. Kennaday by H.P.F. King, minister of the M.E. Church South. [M16a:56-28; R:57; R1:7-5]

Bartlett, William (d. by 1870), to Elmira Green (d. 1873 near Oak Grove), daughter of George and Sarah Green. License 22 MAY 1851. Married 22 MAY 1851 by John Pullen. [DR:28-2; M15:51-13; R:9]

Bartlett, William Henry, first to Mary Jane Bryant (d. by 1878). WILLIAM H. BARTLETT, sailor, age 25, single, b. Richmond Co., son of Henry and [Curlista][2] Bartlett, to MARY J. BRYANT, age 19, single, b. Westmoreland Co., daughter of Jonathan and Sarah "Sally" Bryant. Signed William H. [his X mark] Bartlett. License 5 JAN 1859. Married 6 JAN 1859 by H.P.F. King, M.G. [M16a:59-2 and 2a; R:66; R1:14-1]

Bartlett, William Henry, second to Mrs. Jane Sanford McGuinness. WILLIAM HENRY BARTLETT, farmer, age 35, widowed, b. Westmoreland Co., son of Henry and Curlista Bartlett, to JANE McGUINNESS, age 35, widow, b. Westmoreland Co., daughter of Richard and Dorinda Sanford. License 4 JUN 1878. Married 5 JUN 1878 by H.H. Fones. [M19; R:126; R1:74-3]

Barton, Howard T. (1823-1893), Dr., C.S.A., to Mrs. Fairinda F. Washington Payne (d. 1866),[3] widow of James H. Payne. HOWARD T. BARTON, physician, will be 34 years old in a few days, single, b. Fredericksburg, Va., res. Berryville, Clarke Co., son of Thomas B. [Bowerbank] Barton [1792-1871] and S.C.S. [Susan C. Stone] [1796-1875],[4] to FAIRINDA F. PAYNE, age 35, widow, b. Jefferson Co., res. Westmoreland Co., daughter of Perrin and Fairinda Washington. License 20 NOV 1857. Married 23 NOV 1857 at *The Point* by T. Grayson Dashiell, minister of the Episcopal Church. [M16a:57-38; R:62; R1:10-11; SP; WP]

---

[1] John Bartlett and Elizabeth Mothershead, daughter of John Mothershead, were married by bond 13 JAN 1819 in Richmond Co.
[2] Another copy at 59-2 gives mother of the bride as Farresty Bartlet.
[3] Howard T. Barton and his wife Fairinda were buried in Stonewall Jackson Memorial Cemetery, Lexington, Rockbridge Co., Va.
[4] Thomas B. Barton and his wife Susan, daughter of William S. Stone (d. 1820) were buried in Fredericksburg Cemetery.

Baxter, William Henry to Harriett Frances Pitts. WILLIAM HENRY BAXTER, farmer, age 19, single, b. Westmoreland Co., son of Joseph Baxter and Ann Maria [Deatley],[1] to HARRIETT FRANCES PITTS, age 16, single, b. Westmoreland Co., daughter of Larkin Pitts [d. testate 1868[2]] and Martha "Patsey" [Ingram].[3] License 11 DEC 1867. Married 12 DEC 1867 at Larkin Pitts' residence by Thomas E. Locke, Rector of St. Peter's Church, Washington Parish. [DR:15-48; M18; R:88; R1:30-5; WP gives bride as Henrietta]

Baylor, George to Mrs. Mary Annie Payton Washington. GEORGE BAYLOR, laborer, age 23, single, b. Essex Co., son of James and Lucinda Baylor, to MARY ANNIE WASHINGTON, age 21, widow, b. Westmoreland Co., daughter of Ned and Rose Payton. License 14 JAN 1878. Married 17 JAN 1878 by R.N. Reamy. [M19; R:124; R1:72-6]

Baylor, James to Sarah Johnson. JAMES BAYLOR, farmer, age 23, single, b. Essex Co., son of Hilliard and Sally Baylor, to SARAH JOHNSON, age 21, single, b. Westmoreland Co., daughter of Edward and Mary Johnson. License 19 DEC 1870. Planned marriage 20 DEC 1870. [R:100; R1:44-13 no return]

Baylor, Samuel to Gabriella Fortune, colored persons, divorced.[4] SAMUEL BAYLOR, farmer, age 23, single, b. Essex Co., son of James Baylor and Cynthia [Gardner], to GABRIELLA FORTUNE, age 17, single, b. Essex Co., daughter of Humphry and Louisa Fortune. License 2 APR 1879. Married 3 APR 1879 at Grant's Hill Church by William C. Latane, Presbyter P.E. Church. [M20; R:128; R1:77-6; WP]

Baylor, Stephen to Elizabeth Tibbs. STEPHEN BAYLOR, farmer, age 21, single, b. Essex Co., son of Edmond and Charity Baylor, to ELIZABETH TIBBS, age 18, single, b. Westmoreland Co., daughter of Daniel and Caroline Tibbs. License 11 JAN 1879. Married 11 JAN 1879 by R.N. Reamy. [M20; R:128; R1:76-11]

Beacham, John G. to Mrs. Letty A. Rice English (d. 1895 of LaGrippe). JOHN G. BEAUCHAMP [sic], sailor, age 43, widower, b. Northumberland Co., res. Washington, D.C., son of James G. Beauchamp and Jane [Lamkin],[5] to LETTY A. ENGLISH, age 38, widow, b. Westmoreland Co., daughter of Thomas and Ann Rice. License 1 JUN 1858. Married 2 JUN 1858 at John M. [Middleton] Branson's by H.P.F. King, minister of the M.E. Church. [DR:101-40; M16a:58-17; R:64; R1:12-2 has Beauchamp]

Beacham, Joseph William (1850-1920), to Lydia Ann Self (1845-1925).[6] JOSEPH WILLIAM BEACHAM, farmer, age [2]7, single, b. Westmoreland Co., son of Nathaniel Beacham and Martha [Spurling],[7] to LYDIA ANN SELF, age 35, single, b. Westmoreland Co., daughter of Peter [Lamkin] Self and Susan [Rebecca Garner].[8] License 7 JAN 1879. Married 9 JAN 1879 at the residence of Mrs. Peter Self by R.J. Sanford. [M20; R:128; R1:76-10]

---

[1] Joseph Baxter and Ann Maria Deatley, daughter of Matthew Deatley, were married by bond 29 JUL 1844 in Westmoreland Co.
[2] Deeds & Wills No. 37, p. 519, will of Larkin Pitts, proved 23 MAR 1868.
[3] Larkin Pitts and Patsey Ingram were married by bond 19 APR 1830 in Essex Co.
[4] In Essex Co. we find that Samuel Baylor was married 27 DEC 1883 to Bettie Sale. His status there is divorced, and notes "from the bonds of matrimony by decree of the Westmoreland Circuit Court, October 16th 1883, for the adultery of wife."
[5] James G. Beacham and Jane Lamkin were married by bond 13 JAN 1807 in Northumberland Co.
[6] Joseph W. Beacham and wife Lydia A. Self were buried at Ebenezer United Methodist Church, Oldhams, Va. Ebenezer was built at Oldhams Crossroads in 1838.
[7] Nathaniel Beacham and Martha Spurling were married by bond 30 DEC 1839 in Westmoreland Co.
[8] Peter S. Self and Susan R. Garner were married by bond 31 MAR 1838 in Westmoreland Co.

Beacham, Nathaniel to Mrs. Susan Rebecca Garner Self, widow of Peter Lamkin Self, *q.v.* NATHANIEL BEACHAM, farmer, age 54, widowed, b. Northumberland Co., son of Thomas Beacham, to SUSAN R. SELF, age 44, widow, b. Westmoreland Co., daughter of C.W. Garner. Signed Nathaniel [his X mark] Beacham, wit. C.C. Baker. License 19 FEB 1867. Married 19 FEB 1867 by R.J. Sanford. [M18; R:86; R1:27-8]

Beacham, Robert J. (d. by 1869), to Mary Catharine Delano. License 7 SEP 1852. Married 9 SEP 1852 by William N. Ward. [M15:52-22, R:23]

Beacham, Robert to Susan R. Self (1853-1936).[1] ROBERT BEACHAM, farmer, age 23, single, b. Westmoreland Co., son of Robert [J.] Beacham and Mary [Catharine Delano], *q.v.*, to SUSAN R. SELF, age 25, single, b. Westmoreland Co., daughter of Peter [Lamkin] Self and Susan [Rebecca Garner]. License 21 JAN 1878. Married 24 JAN 1878 at Mrs. Susan Beacham's by R.J. Sanford. [M19; R:124; R1:72-13]

Beale, Daniel C. to Martha Ann M. Dement. DANIEL C. BEALE, farmer, age 24, single, b. Westmoreland Co., son of William [S.] Beale and Frances [G. Garner],[2] to MARTHA A. DEMENT, age 24, single, b. Westmoreland Co., daughter of George Dement and Elizabeth [Harrison].[3] License 23 MAR 1855. Married 28 MAR 1855 by H.P.F. King. [M16:55-10; R:49; R1:3-4]

Beauchamp (see Beacham)

Beckwith, John W., Jr. (1831-1890), elected second Bishop of Georgia in 1867, to Ella B. Brockenbrough (1837-1887).[4] JOHN BECKWITH, JR., clergyman of the church, age 26, single, b. Raleigh, N.C., res. Maryland, son of John and Margaret C. Beckwith of *Chatham*,[5] to ELLA BROCKENBROUGH, age 19, single, b. King William Co., daughter of John F. [Fauntleroy] Brockenbrough [1812-1865[6]] and Frances A. [Ann Carter].[7] License 28 JUL 1857. Married 29 SEP 1857 at *Chatham* by T. Grayson Dashiell, clergyman. [M16a:57-31; R:61; R1:10-8]

Beddoe, Newton G. to Martha Olliffe. NEWTON G. BEDDOE, farmer, age 30, widower, b. Richmond Co., son of John Beddoe and Ann Balderson,[8] to MARTHA OLLIFFE, age 26, single, b. Richmond Co., daughter of Lofty Oliffe and Susan Jones.[9] License 25 JUL 1855. Married 26 JUL 1855 by B.W. Nash, regular ordained minister of the Union Baptist denomination. [M16:55-15; R:49; R1:4-3]

Beddoe, William Henry (b. 1831, d. 1891),[10] served in Co. E, 55th Va. Inf., C.S.A., to Elizabeth J. Eskridge. WILLIAM H. BEDDOE, farming, age about 25, single, b. upper dist. of Richmond Co., son of [William] Beddoe and Mary his wife, to ELIZABETH J. ESKRIDGE, age about 23, single, b.

---

[1] Susan Self Beacham was buried at Ebenezer United Methodist Church, Oldhams, Va.
[2] William S. Beale and Frances G. Garner were married by bond 29 DEC 1823 in Westmoreland Co.
[3] George Dement and Elizabeth Harrison were married by bond 31 JAN 1827 in Westmoreland Co.
[4] John W. Beckwith and his wife Ella were buried in Bonaventure Cemetery of Savannah, Ga.
[5] CF1859-13, *John Barber & ux v. John W. Beckwith & ux &c.*
[6] Deeds & Wills No. 41, p. 172, plat and division of the estate of John F. Brockenbrough, dec.
[7] John Fauntleroy Brockenbrough and Frances Ann Carter were married by bond 2 MAY 1833 in Richmond Co. William Stebbins Hubard, *Descendants of William Brockenbrough (1650-1700)*, p. 41, at #106, states that her name was Frances Ball Carter.
[8] John Beddoo and Nancey Balderson were married by bond 20 SEP 1800 in Westmoreland Co., with Jacob Miller, security.
[9] Lofty Oliffe and Susannah Jones were married by bond 23 AUG 1819 in Westmoreland Co., with William Balderson, security.
[10] William H. Beddoo was buried at Providence United Methodist Church, Lerty, Va.

Westmoreland Co., daughter of Burrell S. [Simms] Eskridge [1806-1886] and Elizabeth [Kilmon].[1] License 23 APR 1856. Married 24 APR 1856 at Joseph He[n]nage's by John Pullen, M.G. [DR:88-17; M16:56-12; R:55; R1:6-1]

Belfield, Armistead Curre (c.1837-1922),[2] served Co. C, 47th Va. Inf., C.S.A., to Eliza Ann Dishman. ARMISTEAD CURRE BELFIELD, farmer, age 30, single, b. Westmoreland Co., son of Thomas M. [Meriwether] Belfield [1796-1873], of *Greenwood*, and Fannie F. [Sanford] [d. testate 1883],[3] to ELIZA ANN DISHMAN, age 24, single, b. Westmoreland Co., daughter of Charles [Triplett] Dishman [1806-1866] and Eliza T. [Smith] [1812-1854].[4] License 13 DEC 1869. Married 14 DEC 1869 by D.M. Wharton, Rector of Montross Parish. [M18; R:96; R1:40-22]

Belfield, Henry Bathurst (b. 1833, d. 1917[5] of cancer of the mouth), undertaker, first to Mary A. Johnson (d. 1896 of chronic diarrhea). HENRY B. BELFIELD, wheelwright, age 27, single, b. Westmoreland Co., son of Thomas M. [Meriwether] Belfield and Frances F. [Fairfax Sanford] [d. testate 1883], *q.v.*, to MARY A. JOHNSON, age 24, single, b. Westmoreland Co., daughter of William Johnson and Elizabeth [A. Mothershead].[6] License 2 MAR 1857. Married 3 MAR 1857 at the residence of William Johnson by H.P.F. King, minister of the M.E. Church. [DR:105-3; M16a:57-9; R:59; R1:8-11]

Belfield, Leroy Daingerfield (d. 1885 of bronchitis), served in Co. C, 47th Va. Inf., C.S.A., to Mary Elizabeth Ogden Spilman. LEROY DAINGERFIELD BELFIELD, farmer, age 26, single, b. Westmoreland Co., son of Thomas M. [Meriwether] and Frances F. [Sanford] Belfield, *q.v.*, to MARY ELIZABETH OGDEN SPILMAN, age 17, single, b. North Carolina, daughter of William and Mary Spilman. License 25 NOV 1868. Married 6 DEC 1868 by Robert N. Reamy. [DR:65-73; M18; R:93; R1:36-2]

Belfield, Mottram Sydnor, Corp. (b. c.1829), served in Co. A, 15th Va. Cav., C.S.A., to Anne Lamkin (d. 1889 of dysentery).[7] SYDNOR BELFIELD, farming, age about 27, single, b. Westmoreland Co., son of Thomas M. [Meriwether] Belfield [1796-1873][8] and Frances [F. Sanford] [d. testate 1883] his wife, *q.v.*, to ANNE LAMKIN, age about 22, single, b. Westmoreland Co., daughter of Mathew Lamkin and Mary [E.] his wife. License 20 OCT 1856. Married 26 OCT 1856 at Mr. Lamkins' by John Pullen, M.G. [DR:79-13; M16a:57-35; R:57; R1:8-6]

Bendler, Hiram H. to Sarah F. Hudson. HIRAM H. BENDLER, blacksmith, age 22, single, b. Camden Co., N.J., son of Jacob S. and Mary Bendler, to SARAH F. HUDSON, age 17, single, b. Westmoreland Co., daughter of Robert H. Hudson and Elizabeth [Self].[9] License 16 JUL 1871. Married 19 JUL 1871 at Robert H. Hudson's by R.J. Sanford. [M18; R:102; R1:47-1]

---

[1] Burrel S. Eskridge and Elizabeth Kilmon were married by bond 14 MAY 1829 in Westmoreland Co. Burrell Simms Eskridge and his wife Elizabeth Kilmon were buried in the Eskridge Family Cemetery, located off of Route 214 near the entrance to *Stratford Hall*.
[2] A.C. Belfield was buried at Grant United Methodist Church.
[3] Thomas M. Bellfield and Frances F. Sandford, daughter of Sebbella Sandford, were married by bond 21 NOV 1821 in Westmoreland Co. Deeds & Wills No. 44, p. 136, will of Fannie F. Belfield, proved 25 JUN 1883.
[4] Charles Dishman and Eliza T. Smith, daughter of William Windsor Smith and Elizabeth Monroe, were married by bond 6 SEP 1830 in Westmoreland Co.
[5] DC: Henry Bathurst Belfield was buried at Andrew Chapel United Methodist Church.
[6] William Johnson and Elizabeth A. Mothershead were married by bond 12 DEC 1822 in Westmoreland Co.
[7] Mottram Sydnor Belfield and his wife Ann Lampkin are thought to be buried in the Belfield Family Cemetery, located off Route 3 near Montross, Va.
[8] Thomas M. Belfield, private, captain in Shackleford's Co., 41st Va. Mil., War of 1812, was buried in the Belfield Family Cemetery, near Montross, Va.
[9] Robert H. Hudson and Elizabeth Self, daughter of Moses Self, were married by bond 15 JUN 1848 in Richmond Co.

Bennett, John R. to Almira Spilman [also Spillman]. License 28 DEC 1852. Married 29 DEC 1852 by Jas. W. Hunnicutt. [M15:52-30, R:25]

Berry, Robert to Mrs. Mary Jane Bankhead Henderson (d. 1877), colored people. ROBERT BERRY, farmer, age 23, single, b. Westmoreland Co., son of James and Patsey Berry, to MARY JANE HENDERSON, age 21, widow, b. Westmoreland Co., daughter of Dunmon and Caroline Bankhead. Signed Robert [his X mark] Berry, wits. J.W. Hutt and R.F. Parker. License 24 DEC 1867. Married 29 DEC 1867 at the Methodist Church, Oak Grove, Va., by Thomas E. Locke, Rector of St. Peter's Church. [DR:39-3; M18; R:88; R1:30-13; WP]

Berry, William to Anna Maria Watts (1842-1917), colored people. WILLIAM BERRY, farmer, age 22, single, b. Westmoreland Co., son of James and Patsy Berry, to MARIA WATTS, age 23, single, b. Westmoreland Co., daughter of Robert Watts and Lucy [Mericks]. Signed Wm. [his X mark] Berry, wit. C.C. Baker. License 24 DEC 1867. Married 29 DEC 1867 at the Methodist Church, Oak Grove, Va., by T.E. Locke. [DC; M18; R:88; R1:30-14; WP]

Berryman, Edmond (C), first to Winny Ann Reed. EDMOND BERRYMAN, farmer, age 36, single, b. Westmoreland Co., son of Isaac and Lydia Berryman, to WINNY ANN REED, age 23, single, b. Westmoreland Co., daughter of John and Lucy Reed. License 10 FEB 1866. Planned marriage 17 FEB 1866. [R:82; R1:23-10 no return]

Berryman, Edmond (C), second to Isabella Nelson. EDMOND BERRYMAN, farmer, age 40, widowed, b. Westmoreland Co., son of Isaac and [Lydia] Berryman, to ISABELLA NELSON, age 21, single, b. Westmoreland Co., daughter of John and Sally Nelson. Signed Edmund [his X mark] Berryman, wit. C.C. Baker. License 30 DEC 1867. Married 3 JAN 1868 at their residence by R.J. Sanford. [M18; R:89; R1:31-8]

Berryman, William Alexander (C) (d. 1882 of cancer), to Charlotte Conway. WILLIAM ALEXANDER BERRYMAN, farmer, age 65, single, b. Westmoreland Co., son of [William and Phyllis Berryman], to CHARLOTTE CONWAY, age 37, single, b. Westmoreland Co., daughter of Spencer and Dilly Conway. License 25 DEC 1874. Married 26 DEC 1874 by Emanuel Watts, pastor Little Zion Church. [M19; R:114; R1:59-15]

Beverly, Peter (C) to Mrs. Ellen Smith Willis. PETER BEVERLY, farmer, age 30, widowed, b. Hanover Co., son of Peter and Violet Beverly, to ELLEN WILLIS, age 25, widow, b. Essex Co., daughter of Daniel and Judy Smith. License 2 JUL 1877. Married 4 JUL 1877 at *Gran[t's] Hill* by R.N. Reamy. [M19; R:122; R1:70-5]

Bird, Hiram to Sarah Fortune. HIRAM BIRD, blacksmith, age 23, single, b. Essex Co., son of Henry and Susan Bird, to SARAH FORTUNE, age 22, single, b. Essex Co., daughter of Robert and Mary Fortune. Signed Hiram [his X mark] Bird, wits. J.F. Bispham, J.W. Hutt. License 30 DEC 1867. Married 31 DEC 1867 at *Blumsberry* by R.N. Reamy. [M18; R:89; R1:31-7]

Bird, John (C) to Henrietta Holmes. JOHN BIRD, farmer, age 21, single, b. Westmoreland Co., son of Henry and Harriet Bird, to HENRIETTA HOLMES, age 19, single, b. Essex Co., daughter of Eady Holmes, father unknown. License 22 DEC 1879. Married 24 DEC 1879 at Little Zion Church by Emanuel Watts, pastor, Little Zion Church. [M20; R:131; R1:80-2]

Bird, Mortimer (C) to Judy Ann Fortune. MORTIMER BIRD, farmer, age 25, single, b. Caroline Co., son of Vestilia Bird, father unknown, to JUDY ANN FORTUNE, age 23, single, b. Essex Co., daughter of Robert Fortune and Mary [Bird].[1] License 12 JAN 1877. Married 16 JAN 1877 at Little Zion Church by E. Watts. [M19; R:121; R1:68-12]

Bispham, Robert Armstrong to Maggie Hamilton Scates. ROBERT ARMSTRONG BISPHAM, farmer, age 23, single, b. Westmoreland Co., son of John F. Bispham [d. 1872 of heart disease] and Catharine M. [Templeman] [d. 1870 of pneumonia], to MAGGIE HAMILTON SCATES, age 21, single, b. Richmond Co., daughter of Ransdell and Julia A. Scates (now Julia A. Spence). License 29 OCT 1872. Married 29 OCT 1872 at Montross, Va. by G.H. Northam. [DR:19-1[2], 21-15[3]; M19; R:106; R1:51-7]

Blackwell, Adam to Maria Sevear. ADAM BLACKWELL, farmer, age 46, widowed, b. Caroline Co., son of [Seth] and Rachel Blackwell, to MARIA SEVEAR, age 46, widow, b. Westmoreland Co., parents unknown. License 23 DEC 1870. Planned marriage 24 DEC 1870. [R:100; R1:45-1 no return]

Bluit, Richard (C) to Nancy Campbell. RICHARD BLUIT, farmer, age 23, widower, b. King George Co., son of Davis and Milly Bluit, to NANCY CAMPBELL, age 27, single, b. Caroline Co., daughter of George and Rachel Campbell. Signed Richard [his X mark] Bluit, wit. J.W. Hutt. License 29 DEC 1875. Married 30 DEC 1875 at Little Zion Church, Oak Grove, Va., by Emanuel Watts, pastor. [M19; R:117; R1:63-8]

Bolding, Charles T. to Louisa Ingram. CHARLES T. BOLDING, farming, age 23, single, b. Fredericksburg, Va., son of Elijah and Mary Bolding, to LOUISA INGRAM, age 20, single, b. Essex Co., daughter of Godfrey Ingram and Mary J. [Coghill].[4] Signed Charles T. [his X mark] Bolding, wit. W.S. McKenney. License 15 AUG 1871. Married 15 AUG 1871 at Henry Reamy's by Robert N. Reamy. [M18; R:102; R1:47-6]

Boothe, Samuel J. to Cornelia F. Reynolds. SAMUEL J. BOOTH [sic], waterman, age 30, single, b. Westmoreland Co., son of Samuel J. Booth and Mary W. [Wright],[5] to CORNELIA F. REYNOLDS, age 19, single, b. Westmoreland Co., daughter of Joseph Reynolds and Martha B. [McKenney].[6] License 7 JAN 1857. Married 14 JAN 1857 at the residence of the wife's father by W.W. Walker, minister of the Methodist Protestant Church. [M16a:57-5; R:57; R1:8-12]

Bowen, Albert S. (1847-1922),[7] served in Co. C, 47th Va. Inf., and Co. D, 40th Va. Inf., C.S.A., to Mary Frances Bowen. ALBERT BOWEN, farmer, age 21, single, b. Westmoreland Co., son of Thomas Bowen and Nancy [Burr],[8] to MARY FRANCES BOWEN, age 21, single, b. Richmond Co., daughter of William and Rebecca Bowen. License 8 JAN 1867. Married 14 JAN 1867 at the residence of the husband's father by D.M. Wharton. [M18; R:85; R1:26-14]

---

[1] Robert Fortune and Mary Bird, daughter of John Bird, were married by bond 3 JUN 1840 in Essex Co.
[2] DR:19-1, entry for Catharine Bispham, housekeeper, d. in 1870 of pneumonia, age 54, daughter of Sam. and Cath: Templeman, born and died in Montross Township, wife of John F. Bispham.
[3] DR:21-15, entry for Jno. F. Bispham, farmer, widower, d. 28 SEP 1872 of heart disease, age 53, son of Wm. and Mary Bispham.
[4] Godfrey Ingram and Mary Coghill, daughter of John Coghill, were married in AUG 1850 in Essex Co. by Rev. William A. Baynham.
[5] Samuel J. Boothe and Mary W. Wright were married by bond 27 JUN 1817 in Westmoreland Co.
[6] Joseph Reynolds and Martha McKenney, daughter of Reubin McKenney, were married by bond 16 DEC 1834 in Westmoreland Co.
[7] Albert Bowen is memorialized at Nomini Baptist Church, Montross, Va.
[8] Thomas Bowen and Ann Burr were married by bond 8 FEB 1837 in Westmoreland Co.

Bowen, Arthur to Harriet Nickins, colored persons. ARTHUR BOWEN, farmer, age 22, single, b. Essex Co., son of Billy and Letty Bowen, to HARRIET NICKINS, age 21, single, b. Essex Co., daughter of Thomas and Lucy Nickins. Signed Arthur [his X mark] Bowen, wits. J.W. Hutt, J.W. Harvey. License 16 JUL 1869. Married 17 JUL 1869 in St. Peter's Church, Oak Grove, Va., by Thomas E. Locke, Rector. [M18; R:95; R1:38-15; WP]

Bowen, Lewis Smith (d. 1882 of dropsy of heart), served in Co. D, 40th Va. Inf., C.S.A., to Maria Elizabeth Drake. LEWIS SMITH BOWEN, carpenter, age 25, single, b. Richmond Co., son of William S. and Ann ["Nancy"] Bowen, to MARIA ELIZABETH DRAKE, age 22, single, b. Westmoreland Co., daughter of John Drake and Mary [Ann Green].[1] License 23 DEC 1867. Married 26 DEC 1867 at B.F. Smoot's Mill by R.N. Reamy. [DR:56-1; M18; R:88; R1:30-12]

Bowen, Robert to Nancy Baylor. ROBERT BOWEN, farmer, age 22, single, b. Essex Co., son of Ruben and Maria Bowens [sic], to NANCY BAYLOR, age 21, single, b. Essex Co., daughter of Hilliard and Sarah Baylor. License 17 DEC 1870. Planned marriage 17 DEC 1870. [R:100; R1:44-12 no return]

Bowen, Zedekiah to Elender Scott. License 3 FEB 1852. Married 5 FEB 1852 by George Northam, L.M.G. [M15:52-6, R:15]

Bowler [or Boulware[2]], Carolinus to Margaret Worrell. CAROLINUS BOWLER, farmer, age 35, single, b. Westmoreland Co., son of Oliver and Molly Pursley [sic], to MARGARET WORRELL, age 25, single, b. Westmoreland Co., daughter of [Antin] and Jane Worrell. License 19 SEP 1878. Married 20 SEP 1878 at the residence of Bowler by Wm. C. Latane, Presbyter P.E. Church. [M19; R:126; R1:75-1; WP]

Bowler, Leroy to Lucy Jane Kay. LEROY BOWLLER [sic], farmer, age 22, single, b. Spotsylvania Co., son of Fielding and Alice J. Bowler, to LUCY JANE KAY, age 22, single, b. Westmoreland Co., daughter of Emma Kay, father unknown. License 18 JUL 1878. Married 21 JUL 1878 at Mrs. Obe Bowler's by Wm. C. Latane, Presbyter, P.E. Church, wit. Charles Worrell. [M19; R:126; R1:74-5; WP]

Bowler, Obedia (d. 1876), to Sarah "Sally" Pursley. OBEDIA BOLER [sic], farmer, age 37, single, b. King George Co., son of Malinda Boler, to SALLY PURSLEY, age 22, single, b. Westmoreland Co., daughter of Ataway and Ellen Pursley. License 5 JUN 1867. [DR:38-5[3]; R:86; R1:28-6 no return]

Bowling, Wallace to Frances Ellen Doleman (d. 1887 of bloody flux). WALLACE BOWLING, soldier, age 28, single, b. St. Mary's Co., Md., son of Charles and Ann S. Bowling, to FRANCES ELLEN DOLEMAN, age 22, single, b. Westmoreland Co., daughter of Jacob V. and Leanner Doleman. Married 18 FEB 1864. Married 18 FEB 1864 at Mrs. Doleman's by John Pullen. [DR:72-70; M17:64-1; R:80; R1:20-9]

---

[1] John Drake and Mary Ann Green were married by bond 6 DEC 1838 in Westmoreland Co.
[2] Deeds & Wills No. 42, p. 137, bill of sale by Carolinas Bolware.
[3] DR:38-5, entry for Obidiah Bowler, white, d. 18 SEP 1865 of bronchitis, age 45, illegitimate son of Sarah J. Bowler, husband of Sarah Bowler.

Boyes, Thomas to Ann M. Chatham. THOMAS BOYES, seaman, age 50, single, b. New York, res. Washington, D.C., son of Ely and Margaret Boyes, to ANN M. CHATHAM, age 35, single, res. Westmoreland Co., names of parents incomplete. Certificate signed by Thos. E. Marshall, Provost Marshall, Capt. 2nd N.H. Vols. Married 20 SEP 1865 at the bride's residence by H.P.F. King. [M17a:65-8]

Bradley, Arthur (C) to Lizzie Jones (C). ARTHUR BRADLEY, farmer, age 34, single, b. Westmoreland Co., son of Smith and Sarah Bradley, to LIZZIE JONES, age 21, single, b. Westmoreland Co., daughter of Lavina Jones, father unknown. License 14 DEC 1878. Married 15 DEC 1878 at Little Zion Church by Emanuel Watts, pastor. [M19, R:127; R1:75-16]

Bradley, Thomas (C) (d. 1884 of measles), to Susannah Stewart. THOMAS BRADLEY, farmer, age 21, single, b. Westmoreland Co., son of Smith [d. 1876 of congestive chill] and Sarah Bradley, to SUSANNAH STEWART, age 21, single, b. Westmoreland Co., daughter of John and Mary Stewart. License 30 DEC 1880. Married 31 DEC 1880 at *Church Point* by Wm. C. Latane, Presbyter P.E. Church. [DR:38-4[1], 63-152 race is white; M20; R:134; R1:84-16; WP]

Bradley, William (C) (d. 1881 of kidney disease), to Mrs. Sarah Streets Pierce, widow of Thomas H. Pierce, *q.v.* WILLIAM BRADLEY, farmer, age 52, widower, b. Westmoreland Co., son of [John] Jack and Harriet Bradley, to SARAH PIERCE, age 26, widow, b. Westmoreland Co., daughter of Theodoric Stacy [sic]. License 6 JUN 1877. Married 9 JUN 1877 at Little Zion Church by Emanuel Watts, pastor. [DR:51-6; M19; R:122; R1:70-1]

Bradshaw, Thomas Aaron to Elizabeth Tyler Franklin. THOMAS AARON BRADSHAW, sailor, age 22, single, b. Somerset Co., Md., son of Solomon H. and Mary M. Bradshaw, to ELIZABETH TYLER FRANKLIN, age 22, single, b. Westmoreland Co., daughter of James Franklin. License 5 JUN 1872. Married 6 JUN 1872 at James Franklin's by R.J. Sanford. [M19; R:105; R1:50-12]

Branch, Thomas (1802-1888), to Ann Adams Wheelwright (1827-1908).[2] THOMAS BRANCH, commission merchant, age 54, widower, b. Chesterfield Co., res. Petersburg, Va., son of Thomas Branch and Mary [Patterson], to ANN ADAMS WHEELWRIGHT, age 29, single, b. Westmoreland Co., daughter of Joseph and Louisa D. Wheelwright. License 21 APR 1857. Married 22 APR 1857 at *Exeter*, Westmoreland Co. by J.H. Wheelwright, minister of the M.E. Church. [M16a:57-13; R:59; R1:9-2]

Brann, James Presley, first to Louisa James Franklin. JAMES PRESLEY BRANN, farmer, age 22, single, b. Westmoreland Co., son of William and Fanny Brann, to LOUISA JAMES FRANKLIN, age 20, single, b. Westmoreland Co., daughter of James M. and Mary Franklin. Signed Jas. P. [his X mark] Brann, wit. J.W. Hutt. License 14 DEC 1872. Married 19 DEC 1872 by R.J. Sanford. [M19; R:107; R1:52-4]

Brann, James Presley, second to Mary Elizabeth Swayne. JAMES PRESTLY BRANN [sic], farmer, age 30, widowed, b. Westmoreland Co., son of William [d. 1881 of consumption] and Fanny Brann, to MARY ELIZABETH SWAYNE, age 22, single, b. Northumberland Co., daughter of William and

---

[1] DR:38-4, entry for Smith Bradley, d. 17 SEP 1876 of congestive chill, age 50, son of Arthur and Harriet Bradley.
[2] Thomas Branch and his second wife Ann Adams Wheelwright were buried in Blandford Cemetery, Petersburg, Va.

Millie Swayne. License 28 APR 1880. Married 29 APR 1880 at Hague, Va., by Pendleton Brooke, P.E. Ch. [DR:48-4; M20; R:133; R1:82-8]

Branson, Benjamin Harding (1840-1911), served Co. K. 40th Va. Inf. and 9th Va. Cav., C.S.A., to Elizabeth Ann Courtney (1848-1921).[1] BENJAMIN HENRY BRANSON [sic], farmer, age 28, single, b. Westmoreland Co., son of John M. [Middleton] Branson and Ann R. [Rice] [d. testate 1875[2]],[3] to ELIZABETH ANN COURTNEY, age 20, single, b. Westmoreland Co., daughter of James R. Courtney and Mary R. [Sutton].[4] License 9 MAR 1869. Married 9 MAR 1869 at the residence of James R. Courtney by J.H. Davis. [M18; R:95; R1:38-2]

Branson, John William (b. 1836, d. 1892 of paralysis), served Co. C, 9th Va. Cav., C.S.A., to Ann Marian Hardwick (1839-1910).[5] JOHN WILLIAM BRANSON, farmer, age 22, single, b. Westmoreland Co., son of John M. [Middleton] Branson and Ann R. [Rice], *q.v.*, to ANN MARIAN HARDWICK, age 19, single, b. Westmoreland Co., daughter of Hiram and Eliza [R.] Hardwick [d. testate 1882[6]]. License 14 DEC 1858. Married 15 DEC 1858 by J.J. Lamkin. [DR:90-50; M16a:58-37 and 37a; NN; R:66; R1:13-4; R1:14-2]

Branson, Solomon Redman (d. 1872 of suicide), to Elizabeth Alice Garland (d. 1888). SOLOMON R. BRANSON, farmer, age 22, single, b. Westmoreland Co., [son of John M. [Middleton] Branson [d. testate 1866[7]] and Ann [R. Rice], *q.v.*], to ELIZABETH A. GARLAND, age 19, single, b. Richmond Co., parents not given. Minister return by H.P.F. King. License 9 FEB 1854. Married 5 FEB 1854 at the residence of Miss Elizabeth McClanahan. [DR:20-3; M15:54-17; NN; R:39; R1:1-2]

Branson, William T. (b. 1811, d. 1883 of asthma), to Sarah Elizabeth Norwood (1831-1917).[8] WILLIAM T. BRANSON, farmer, age 59, single, b. Westmoreland Co., son of Vincent T. and Elizabeth Branson, to SARAH ELIZABETH NORWOOD, age 36, single, b. Westmoreland Co., daughter of John and Hannah[9] Norwood. License 21 FEB 1871. Married 21 FEB 1871 by Walter C. Taylor. [DR:57-11; M18; R:101; R1:46-3]

Braxton, John Staige, Capt. (1829-1879),[10] farmer and merchant, served in the 30th Va. Inf., C.S.A., to Olivia J. Wright. License 8 JUL 1851. [R:9 no return]

Brent, Elias Carter, served in Co. D, 9th Va. Cav., C.S.A., to Eliza Fitzhugh Payne. ELIAS CARTER BRENT, farmer, age 23, single, b. Northumberland Co., son of William H. and Catharine M. Brent, to ELIZA FITZHUGH PAYNE, age 17, single, b. King George Co., daughter of George Payne, mother unknown. License 5 JAN 1859. Married 6 JAN 1859 in King George Co. [M16a:59-3; R:66]

[1] Benjamin H. Branson and his wife Elizabeth Ann Courtney were buried at Carmel United Methodist Church, Kinsale, Va.
[2] Deeds & Wills No. 40, p. 193, will of Ann R. Branson, proved 26 JUL 1875, names son Benjamin H. Branson.
[3] John M. Branson and Ann R. Rice were married by bond 17 MAR 1828 in Westmoreland Co.
[4] James R. Courtney and Mary R. Sutton were married by bond 6 JAN 1848 in Westmoreland Co.
[5] John W. Branson and his wife Anne M. were buried at Carmel United Methodist Church, Kinsale, Va.
[6] Deeds & Wills, Bk. 42, p. 352, will of Eliza R. Hardwick, proved 28 AUG 1882, mentions daughter Annie M. Branson.
[7] Deeds & Wills, Bk. 37, p. 250, will of John Middleton Branson, proved 26 NOV 1866, names son Solomon Redman Branson.
[8] William T. Branson and his wife Sarah Elizabeth Norwood were buried in the Norwood Family Cemetery, located off of Route 3 between Montross, Va. and Templeman's Crossroads.
[9] Mallory, p. 106, in data for the Norwood Family Cemetery, gives Sarah Elizabeth Norwood as the daughter of John Norwood and Sarah Porter. John Norwood and Sally Porter, daughter of Edward Porter, were married by bond 3 NOV 1813 in Westmoreland Co.
[10] John S. Braxton was buried in Fredericksburg Cemetery.

Brent, Horace (C) to Nancy Thompson. HORACE BRENT, farmer, age 22, single, b. Westmoreland Co., son of David [d. 1886 of dropsy] and Fanny Brent, to NANCY THOMPSON, age 22, single, b. Westmoreland Co., daughter of George and Easter Thompson. Signed Horace [his X mark] Brant, wit. J.W. Hutt. License 11 FEB 1870. Married 13 FEB 1870 by John C. Smith. [DR:68-9[1]; M18; R:98; R1:42-3]

Brent, Horace (C) to Elizabeth Lucas. HORACE BRENT, farmer, age 30, divorced, b. Westmoreland Co., son of David and Fanny Brent, to ELIZABETH LUCAS, age 25, single, b. Westmoreland Co., daughter of Arrena Lucas. License 25 SEP 1878. Married 26 SEP 1878 at L. Toleman's by John W. White, M.G. [M19; R:126; R1:75-3]

Briant (see Bryant)

Britton, Peter (C) to Melissa Jane Burton. PETER BRITTON, farmer, age 23, single, b. Westmoreland Co., son of Mary Britton, to MELISSA JANE BURTON, age 20, single, b. Westmoreland Co., daughter of Thomas and Lucy Burton. License 11 SEP 1878. Married 12 SEP 1878 by Edmond Rich. [M19; R:126; R1:74-15]

Brohawn, John to Olivia A. Lyell. JOHN BROHAWN, merchant, age 23, single, b. Dorchester Co., Md., father unknown, mother Sarah Slakum, to OLIVIA A. LYELL, age 17, single, b. Richmond Co., daughter of Robert and Mary Lyell. License 13 SEP 1855. Married 13 SEP 1855 by H.P.F. King, minister of the M.E. Church. [M16:55-18; R:49; R1:4-2]

Brooks, Albert to Elizabeth Roy. License 26 DEC 1867. [R:89]

Brooks, Horace Alexander, Dr. (1841-1907), served Co. C, 9th Va. Cav., C.S.A., to Hallie Fenton Brown (b. 1842, d. 1866 of fever).[2] HORACE ALEXANDER BROOKS, physician, age 24, single, b. and res. Baltimore, Md., son of Nathaniel C. and Mary E. Brooks, to HALLIE FENTON BROWN, age 22, single, b. Westmoreland Co., daughter of George F. Brown and Martha Fenton [Taliaferro].[3] License 2[7] NOV 1865. Married 28 NOV 1865 at *Peckatone*,[4] by Rev. Brooks. [CR; DR:11-1; R:81; R1:22-9 no return]

Brooks, James S. (1856-1904),[5] to Mary Streets. JAMES BROOKS, farmer, age 22, single, b. Westmoreland Co., son of Thomas and Anna Brooks, to MARY STREETS, age 22, single, b. Westmoreland Co., daughter of Beverly and Sallie Streets. License 14 JAN 1878. Married 16 JAN 1878 at *Blenheim* by Wm. C. Latane, M.G. [DC; M19; R:124; R1:72-7; WP]

Brooks, Solomon (C) to Susan Lane. SOLOMON BROOKS, farmer, age 22, single, b. Westmoreland Co., son of Solomon and Julia Brooks, to SUSAN LANE, age 21, single, b. Westmoreland Co., daughter of Richard and Lotty Lane. Signed Solomon [his X mark] Brooks, wit. J.H. Sisson. License 16 FEB 1870. Married 24 FEB 1870 by John C. Smith. [M18; R:98; R1:42-5]

---

[1] DR:68-9, entry for David Brent (C), d. 1 OCT 1886 of dropsy, son of William and Nancy Brent, father of Horace Brent.
[2] Dr. Horace Alexander Brooks and his wife Hallie Fenton Brown were buried at Yeocomico Episcopal Church, Tucker Hill, Va.
[3] George F. Brown and Martha F. Taliaferro were married by bond 28 NOV 1838 in Westmoreland Co.
[4] Soon after 1865, *Peckatone* was purchased by Samuel Hardwick, and the Murphy Family moved to *Spring Grove*. *Peckatone* burned in 1886.
[5] James S. Brooks was buried at Grant Hill Baptist Church, Leedstown, Va.

Brooks, Stephen, first to China Sarah Sale (d. by 1880). STEPHEN BROOKS, farmer, age 22, single, b. Westmoreland Co., son of Stephen and Eliza Brooks, to CHINA SARAH SALE, age 21, single, b. Westmoreland Co., daughter of Richard and Eliza Sale. License 7 JUN 1867. Married 8 JUN 1867 at *Auburn*[1] by J.H. Davis. [M18; R:87; R1:28-7]

Brooks, Stephen, second to Mrs. Mary Homes. STEPHEN BROOKS, farmer, age 34, widowed, b. Westmoreland Co., son of Stephen and Eliza Brooks, to MARY HOMES, age 36, widow, b. Westmoreland Co., daughter of Fannie Henry. License 25 JUN 1880. Married 26 JUN 1880 by Pendleton Brooke, P.E. Ch. [M20; R:132; R1:83-4]

Brown, Benjamin Franklin, Dr., of *Boscobel* (d. 1889 of bilious dysentery),[2] son of Richard T. Brown and Lucy [Spark],[3] to Elizabeth M. Taliaferro. License 27 DEC 1852. Married 30 DEC 1852 by Wm. McGuire, Rector Cople Parish. [CP; DR:81-112; M15:52-31; R:25]

Brown, Charles Edwin, first to Mary Dianna Hall (d. 1873 of consumption). CHARLES EDWIN BROWN, age 22, single, b. Westmoreland Co., son of W.W. [William W.] Brown and E.A. [Eleanor Ann Costin], *q.v.*, to MARY DIANNA HALL, age 21, single, b. Westmoreland Co., daughter of William B. Hall and Mary B. [Omohundro].[4] License 15 JAN 1873. Married 18 JAN 1873 at *Plain View* by G.H. Northam. [DR:27-26; M19; R:108; R1:53-2]

Brown, Charles Edwin, second to Sybbella Walker Muse. CHARLES EDWIN BROWN, farmer, age 25, widowed, b. Westmoreland Co., son of William W. Brown [d. 1872 of consumption] and [Eleanor] Ann [Costin],[5] to SYBBELLA WALKER MUSE, age 2[8], single, b. Westmoreland Co., daughter of James [H.] Muse and Elizabeth [B. Walker]. License 30 NOV 1875. Married 30 NOV 1875 at Montross, Va. by W.A. Crocker. [DR:21-1; M19; R:116; R1:62-9]

Brown, Christopher Parkinson, served in Co. C, 40th Va. Inf., C.S.A., to Ann Gregory. License 19 NOV 1853. Married 20 NOV 1853 by George Northam, L.M.G. [M15:53-20, R:35]

Brown, George Fulton, of *Poplar Hill* (b. 1848 at *Lee Hall*, d. 1909 of typhoid fever at *Wilton*), to Mary Estelle Phineas Arnest (1852-1924).[6] GEORGE FULTON BROWN, farmer, age 28, single, b. Westmoreland Co., son of [Col.] Thomas Brown [d. 1880 at *Buena Vista*] and Sarah S. [Cox],[7] to MARY ESTILL ARNEST, age 24, single, b. Franklin Co., Mo., daughter of Joseph Nicholas Arnest. License 14 NOV 1876. Married 21 NOV 1876 at Yeocomico Church by John J. Lloyd. [CP; D&W 41, p. 3; M19; R:120; R1:66-15]

Brown, Hanibald (C) to Virginia Isabella Burton. HANIBALD BROWN, farmer, age 24, single, b. Richmond Co., son of George and Lucinda Brown, to VIRGINIA ISSABELLA BURTON [sic], age 16, single, b. Westmoreland Co., daughter of Thomas and Lucy Burton. License 11 DEC 1878. Married 1 DEC 1878 by Edmond Rich. [M19, R:127; R1:75-14]

---

[1] *Auburn* was built c.1830 by the Campbell Family.
[2] Dr. Brown was buried at Yeocomico Episcopal Church, Kinsale, Va.
[3] Richard T. Brown and Lucy Spark were married by bond 27 MAR 1806 in Westmoreland Co., with Alexander Parker, security.
[4] William B. Hall and Mary B. Omohundro were married by bond 10 OCT 1843 in Westmoreland Co., with E.B. Omohundro, security.
[5] William W. Brown and Eleanor A. Coston were married by bond 9 APR 1849 in Westmoreland Co.
[6] George F. Brown and his wife Mary E. were buried at Yeocomico Episcopal Church, Kinsale, Va.
[7] Thomas Brown and Sarah S. Cox were married by bond 3 JUL 1843 in Westmoreland Co., with James S. Lyell, security. They were buried in the graveyard at *Lee Hall*.

Brown, Henry to Mary Washington, colored persons. HENRY BROWN, coachman, age 28, single, b. Anne Arundel Co., Md., son of Charles and Elizabeth Brown, to MARY WASHINGTON, age 18, single, b. Westmoreland Co., parents unknown. Signed Henry [his X mark] Brown, wit. J.W. Hutt. Married 26 SEP 1868 by Thomas E. Locke, Rector, Washington Parish. [M18; R1:35-3; WP]

Brown, John Noah (d. by 1866), to Virginia Ann Douglass. JOHN NOAH BROWN, farmer, age 22, single, b. Westmoreland Co., son of John and Sarah Brown, to VIRGINIA ANN DOUGLASS, age 17, single, b. Westmoreland Co., daughter of Lemuel Douglass and Sarah [Palmer].[1] License 4 APR 1860. Married 5 APR 1860 by H.P.F. King, M.G. [M17:60-20 and 20a; R:74; R1:17-9]

Brown, Merideth M. (d. 1895 of white rising), to Maria J. Jenkins. MERIDETH M. BROWN, farming, going on age 25, single, b. Westmoreland Co., son of Christofer C. Brown and Fanny [Frances Marmaduke] his wife,[2] to MARIAH J. JENKINS [sic], going on age 27, single, b. Westmoreland Co., daughter of Richard W. Jenkins and Jane his wife. License 10 NOV 1855. Married 4 NOV 1855 at Popes Creek Church by John Pullen, M.G. [DR:101-12; M16:55-20, R:49; R1:4-4]

Brown, Philip [Bush] to Alice Marie Collinsworth (d. 1888). PHILIP BROWN, farmer, age 23,[3] single, b. Westmoreland Co., son of John and Susan Brown, to ALICE M. COLLINSWORTH, age 23, single, b. Westmoreland Co., daughter of [John W.] and Martha C. Collinsworth. License 4 MAY 1859. Married 4 MAY 1859 at Sandy Valley Church by H.P.F. King, M.G. [DR:75-2; M16a:59-12 and 12a; R:68; R1:16-5]

Brown, Robert Smith to Virginia Margaretta Butler. ROBERT SMITH BROWN, waterman, age 27, single, b. Westmoreland Co., son of George H. Brown and Mary E. [S. Lyell],[4] to VIRGINIA MARGARETTA BUTLER, age 27, single, b. Westmoreland Co., daughter of F.T.A. Butler and Frances R. [Brown].[5] License 20 OCT 1873. Married 20 OCT 1873 at the residence of the bride's father by D.G.C. Butts, minister of the M.E. Church South. [M19; R:109; R1:54-11]

Brown, Thomas, Jr., of *Locust Farm*, to Charlotte "Lottie" Elizabeth Claybrook. THOMAS BROWN, merchant, age 29, single, b. Westmoreland Co., son of Thomas Brown and Sarah S. [Cox][6] [d. 1874], to CHARLOTTE ELIZABETH CLAYBROOK, age 29, single, b. Northumberland Co., daughter of Richard A. and Charlotte T. Claybrook. Signed Thomas Brown, Jr. License 3 DEC 1875. Married 7 DEC 1875 at Yeocomico Church by F.W. Claybrook. [CP; DR:30-33[7]; M19; R:116; R1:62-11; SC]

Brown, William to Sarah Ann Foxwell. License 31 DEC 1851. Married 6 JAN 1852 by John Pullen. [M15:52-1, R:13]

Brown, William to Martha Jane Sutton. WILLIAM BROWN, farmer, age 33,[8] widower, b. Westmoreland Co., son of William and Patsy Brown, to MARTHA JANE SUTTON, age 23, single,

---

[1] Lemuel Douglass and Sarah Palmer were married by bond 30 DEC 1841 in Westmoreland Co., with Joseph H. Moone, security.
[2] Christopher Brown and Frances Marmaduke were married by bond 22 SEP 1825 in Westmoreland Co., with George Coates, security.
[3] Another copy at 59-12a gives age of groom 20, age of bride 25.
[4] George H. Browne and Mary E.S. Lyell were married by bond 14 DEC 1841 in Westmoreland Co., with O.E.P. Hazard, security.
[5] Francis T.A. Butler and Rebecca F. Brown were married by bond 26 MAY 1845 in Westmoreland Co., with Thomas T. Beale, security.
[6] Thomas Brown and Sarah S. Cox were married by bond 3 JUL 1843 in Westmoreland Co., with James S. Lyell, security.
[7] DR:30-33, entry for Sarah Brown, d. 28 NOV 1874 of pneumonia, age 51, daughter of Presley and Ricarda Cox, wife of Thomas Brown.
[8] Another copy at 59-13a gives age of groom 37, age of bride 22, and birthplace of groom as Richmond Co.

b. Westmoreland Co., daughter of William Sutton and Catharine "Kitty" [Nash].[1] Signed Wm. [his X mark] Brown, wit. J.H. Sisson. License 10 MAY 1859. Married 12 MAY 1859 at the residence of John Sutton by H.P.F. King, M.G. [M16a:59-13 and 13a; R:68; R1:16-6]

Bryan, William Butler to Mary J. Augustine. WILLIAM BUTLER BRYAN, farming, age 22, single, b. King George Co., son of James Bryan and Catharine [Allensworth],[2] to MARY J. AUGUSTINE, age 20, single, b. New Jersey, daughter of Frederick [A.] and Beula [B.] Augustine [Augustien]. License 22 JAN 1872. Married 28 JAN 1872 at the residence of Frederick A. Augustine by Howard W. Montague, M.G. [M19; R:104; R1:49-10]

Bryant, George (C) to Ellen Newman. GEORGE BRYANT, farmer, age 35, single, b. Westmoreland Co., son of Louisa Bryant, father unknown, to ELLEN NEWMAN, age 31, single, b. Westmoreland Co., daughter of George and Mary Newman. License 29 NOV 1876. Married 30 NOV 1876 at her home by Jerry Graham. [M19; R:120; R1:67-3]

Bryant, George (C) (d. 1917 of heart trouble), to Mrs. Eliza Hungerford Taylor. GEORGE BRYANT, farmer, age 28, single, b. Westmoreland Co., son of James and Rebecca Bryant [d. 1889], to ELIZA TAYLOR, age 30, widow, b. Westmoreland Co., daughter of Taliaferro and Maria Hungerford. License 21 FEB 1877. Married 23 FEB 1877 at her home by Jerry Graham. [DC; DR:79-11; M19; R:121; R1:69-2]

Bryant, George (C) to Ella Virginia Hutcherson. GEORGE BRYANT, farmer, age 30, widowed, b. Westmoreland Co., son of James and Rebecca Bryant, to ELLER VIRGINIA HUTCHERSON [sic], age 26, single, b. Westmoreland Co., daughter of Matilda Hutcherson, father unknown. License 6 OCT 1880. Married 7 OCT 1880 at *Grape Hill* by Rev. Robert Lewis, pastor of Galilee Church. [M20; R:134; R1:83-13]

Bryant, George Henry to Sarah Yardly. GEORGH [sic] HENRY BRYANT, farmer, age 54, widowed, b. Westmoreland Co., son of Reuben Bryant and Sarah [Mothershead],[3] to SARAH YARDLY, age 39, single, b. Westmoreland Co., daughter of William and Elizabeth Yardly. Married 10 OCT 1866 at G.H. Bryant's by John Pullen. [M18; R:84; R1:25-1]

Bryant, James Henry to Roberta Jane Gutridge. JAMES H. BRYANT, farmer, age 24,[4] single, b. Westmoreland Co., son of Mary Ann Bryant, father unknown, to ROBERTA J. GUTRIDGE, age 19, single, b. Westmoreland Co., daughter of Albert M. Gutridge and Mary [Ann Nash].[5] Signed James H. [his X mark] Bryant, wit. J.H. Sisson. License 15 SEP 1859. Married 16 SEP 1859 by B.W. Nash, minister of the Baptist Church. [M16a:59-23 and 23a; R:70; R1:15-3]

Bryant, John to Mary Caroline Jenkins. JOHN BRYANT, waterman, age 22, single, b. Westmoreland Co., son of Reuben and Elizabeth Bryant, to MARY CAROLINE JENKINS, age 18, single, b. Somerset Co., Md., daughter of Littleton and Sarah Jane Jenkins. Signed John [his X mark] Bryant. License 2 JAN 1867. Married 3 JAN 1867 at *Ragged Point* by J.H. Davis. [M18; R:85; R1:26-11]

---

[1] William Sutton and Kitty Nash were married by bond 6 JAN 1835 in Westmoreland Co., with William T. Brown and William H. Sanford, securities.
[2] James Bryan and Catharine Allensworth were married in JAN 1842 in King George Co.
[3] Reuben Briant and Sally Mothershead were married by bond 11 MAR 1816 in Westmoreland Co., with Nathaniel Mothershead, security.
[4] Another copy at 59-23a gives age of groom as 23 and bride as 18.
[5] Albert M. Gutridge, son of Elizabeth Gutridge, and Mary Ann Nash were married by bond 1 FEB 1838 in Westmoreland Co.

Bryant, John R. to Martha C. Gutridge.   JOHN R. BRYANT, farmer, age 24, single, b. Westmoreland Co., son of James and Nancy Bryant, to MARTHA GUTRIDGE, age 19, single, b. Westmoreland Co., daughter of Albert [M.] Gutridge and Mary [Ann Nash], *q.v.* License 17 FEB 1858. Married 28 FEB 1858 at Chilton's X Roads by H.P.F. King, minister of the M.E. Church. [M16a:58-7; R:63; R1:11-4 incorrectly has Mary C. Gutridge]

Bryant, Jonathan, Jr. (1843-1915),[1] served in Co. E, 55th Va. Inf. and Co. A, 15th Va. Cav., C.S.A., first to Charlotte Killman (d. 1872 of dropsy). JOHNATHAN BRYANT [sic], farmer, age 24, single, b. Westmoreland Co., son of Jonathan Bryant and S.A. [Sarah Ann "Sallie" Buckler][2] [b. Md., d. 1881], to CHARLOTTE KILLMAN, age 21, single, b. Westmoreland Co., daughter of Martin M. Killman and Ann [Weaver].[3] License 30 NOV 1868. Married 3 DEC 1868 by D.M. Wharton. [DR:21-4, 50-5; M18; R:93; R1:36-3; SC]

Bryant, Jonathan, Jr. (1843-1915), second to Sophia Frances Oliff (d. 1881). JONATHAN BRYANT, farmer, age 29, widowed, b. Westmoreland Co., son of Jonathan Bryant and Sarah A. [Ann Buckler], *q.v.*, to SOPHIA FRANCES OLIVE [sic], age 24, single, b. Richmond Co., daughter of [William and] Sophia [Frances Carter] Oliff.[4] Signed Johnothon Bryant [sic]. License 24 MAY 1875. Married 27 MAY 1875 at Montross, Va. by H.H. Fones. [DR:50-4; M19; R:115; R1:61-5]

Bryant, Richard (C) to Easter M. Lee.   RICHARD BRYANT, farmer, age 24, single, b. Westmoreland Co., son of Louisa Bryant, father unknown, to EASTER M. LEE, age 19, single, b. Westmoreland Co., daughter of Robert and Edey Lee. Signed Richard [his X mark] Bryant, wit. Wm. Green. License 25 JAN 1869. Married 25 JAN 1869 by Jerry Graham. [M18; R:94; R1:37-12]

Bryant, Richard Henry Washington, served in Co. A, 15th Va. Cav., C.S.A., to Mrs. Elizabeth Ann Reed (b. 1825, d. 1891), widow of James Sutton (d. testate 1866). RICHARD HENRY WASHINGTON BRYANT, farmer, age 36, single, b. Westmoreland Co., son of John B. Bryant and Elizabeth A. [Eskridge],[5] to ELIZABETH ANN SUTTON, age 42, widow, b. Westmoreland Co., daughter of John Reed [1795-1869] and Kitty [Mariah Kelly][6] [d. 1849].[7] License 9 NOV 1871. Married 9 NOV 1871 at Chilton's X Roads by Walter C. Taylor. [DR:88-2; M18; R:103; R1:48-3]

Bryant, Vernon (1833-1903),[8] served in Co. A, 15th Va. Cav., C.S.A., to Mrs. Mary E. Hinson Bryant. VERNON BRYANT, carpenter, age 37, single, b. Westmoreland Co., son of John B. Bryant and Elizabeth [A. Eskridge], *q.v.*, to MARY E. BRYANT, age 35, widow, b. Richmond Co., daughter of Austin Hinson [and Mahaley Hueson].[9] License 21 JAN 1871. Married 23 JAN 1871 by G.W. Beale. [M18; NN; R:101; R1:45-11]

Bryant, William W. to Elizabeth Sutton (d. 1861). WILLIAM W. BRYANT, farmer, age 28, single, b. Westmoreland Co., son of Reuben and Mary Bryant, to ELIZABETH SUTTON, age 23, single, b. Westmoreland Co., son of Samuel Sutton and Elizabeth [Crask], *q.v.*[10] License 25 FEB 1857.

---

[1] Jonathan Bryant was buried in the Bryant Family Cemetery, located near the intersection of Routes 609 and 1601.

[2] Jonathan Briant and Sally Buckler were married by bond 13 FEB 1834 in Westmoreland Co., with Martin Killmon, security.

[3] Martin Killmon and Ann Weaver were married by bond 10 FEB 1845 in Westmoreland Co., with Burrell S. Eskridge, security.

[4] William Oliff, Jr. and Sophia Carter were married by bond 23 DEC 1835 in Richmond Co., with John S. Carter, security.

[5] John B. Bryant and Elizabeth Eskridge were married by bond 29 DEC 1831 in Westmoreland Co., with Richard Omohundro, security.

[6] John Reed and Kitty M. Kelly were married by bond 28 NOV 1822 in Westmoreland Co., with Richard Reed, security.

[7] John Reed and his wife Kitty Mariah Kelly were buried in the Reed-Sanford Family Cemetery, located off of Route 643 near Route 622.

[8] Vernon Bryant was buried at Popes Creek Baptist Church, Baynesville, Va.

[9] Austin Hinson and Mahaley Hueson were married by bond 17 MAR 1829 in Westmoreland Co., with James Guttridge, security.

[10] Samuel Sutton and Elizabeth Crask were married by bond 24 DEC 1817 in Westmoreland Co., with Joseph Sutton, security.

Married 26 FEB 1857 at the residence of Mr. Bryant by H.P.F. King, minister of the M.E. Church. [Bible; M16a:57-8; R:59; R1:8-10]

Bryant, William White to Emily Carpenter. WILLIAM WHITE BRYANT, farmer, age 40, widowed, b. Westmoreland Co., son of Reuben Bryant and Sarah [Mothershead], *q.v.*, to EMILY CARPENTER, age 22, single, b. Westmoreland Co., daughter of Joseph and Polly Carpenter. License 23 MAY 1863. Married 28 MAY 1863 at the residence of Mrs. Elizabeth Poor by Robert N. Reamy. [M17:63-5; R:79; R1:20-2]

Buckner, William (C) to Fannie Nugul. WILLIAM BUCKNER, farmer, age 60, single, b. Caroline Co., son of Edmund and Lucy Buckner, to FANNIE NUGUL, age 31, single, b. Westmoreland Co., daughter of Davy and Maria Nugul. Signed William [his X mark] Bucker, wit. J.W. Hutt. License 22 MAY 1869. Married 24 OCT 1869 by John C. Smith. [M18; R:95; R1:38-9]

Bulger, Robert (d. 1881 of pneumonia), son of Thomas and Mary Bulger, to Elizabeth A. Bartlett. License 20 DEC 1853. Married 23 DEC 1853 by John Pullen. [DR:50-7; M15:53-22, R:35]

Bulger, William S. to Frances E. Hammock. WILLIAM S. BULGER, farmer, age 45, widower, b. Richmond Co., son of John Bulger and Susanna [Smith],[1] to FRANCES E. HAMMOCK, age 16, single, b. Richmond Co., father unknown, mother Charlotte Hammock.[2] License 2 JAN 1855. Married 2 JAN 1855 at the residence of Mrs. Delano by H.P.F. King, Minister of the M.E. Church South. [M16:55-1; R:47; R1:2]

Bunday, Eli to Mrs. Betsy Richards Fortune (d. by 1874), widow of Richard Fortune,[3] colored people. ELI BUNDAY, house carpenter, age 42, widowed, b. Westmoreland Co., son of William and Eliza Bunday, to BETSY FORTUNE, age 39, widow, b. Essex Co., daughter of Peter and Sucky Richards. License 26 DEC 1866. Married 27 DEC 1866 at Peter Richards' residence by Thomas E. Locke. [M18; R:85; R1:26-8; WP]

Bunday, Eli to Lucy Ann Jenkins (d. 1882 of consumption). ELI BUNDAY, carpenter, age 49, widowed, b. Westmoreland Co., son of William and Eliza Bunday, to LUCY ANN JENKINS, age 17, single, b. Spotsylvania Co., daughter of Horace and Elizabeth ["Betty"] Jenkins. License 16 FEB 1874. [DR:56-6; R:112; R1:57-12 no return]

Bunday, Henry (C) to Harriet Jackson. HENRY BUNDAY, farmer, age 23, single, b. Essex Co., son of Reuben and Betsy Bunday, to HARRIET JACKSON, age 21, single, b. Westmoreland Co., daughter of Ed. and Judy Jackson. Signed Henry [his X mark] Bunday, wit. Wm. S. McKenney. License 28 JAN 1876. Married 29 JAN 1876 at Little Zion Church by Emanuel Watts, pastor, Little Zion Church. [M19; R:117; R1:64-4]

Bundy, Henry Howard (C) to Mrs. Mary Harris, widow of Solomon Harris. HENRY HOWARD BUNDY, laborer, age 22, single, b. Caroline Co., son of Louisa Fortune, to MARY HARRIS, age 24, widow, b. Essex Co., daughter of [Eliza] Hoomes. Signed Henry H. [his X mark] Bundy, wit. W.S. McKenney. License 8 JAN 1873. Married 9 JAN 1873 by John Roy. [M19; R:108; R1:52-15]

---

[1] John Bulger, Jr. and Susanna Smith were married by bond 7 DEC 1807 in Richmond Co., with William Smith, security.
[2] Charles Hammack and Charlotte P. Deatley were married by bond 16 AUG 1830 in Richmond Co., with Thomas Hale, security.
[3] Richard Fortune and Elizabeth Richards, daughter of Peter Richards, were married by bond 30 APR 1850 in Essex Co., with Henry Richards, security.

Bundy, Levi to Emily Hungerford, free colored persons. Married 28 MAY 1854 at St. Peter's Church by Rev. J.W. Chesley. [SP; WP]

Bundy, Thomas (C) to Fenton Garnett. THOMAS BUNDY, laborer, age 19, single, b. Westmoreland Co., son of Diana Bundy, father unknown, to FENTON GARNETT, age 18, single, b. Westmoreland Co., daughter of Malinda Garnett, father unknown. License 25 SEP 1871. Married 25 SEP 1871 by Emanuel Watts, Pastor of Little Zion Church. [M18; R:103; R1:47-11]

Burgess, Henry to Virginia Purcell. HENRY BURGESS, miller, age 36, widowed, b. Essex Co., res. King George Co., son of William and Harriet Burgess, to VIRGINIA PURCELL, age 20, single, b. Westmoreland Co., daughter of George and Emily Purcell. Signed Henry [his X mark] Burgess, wit. Wm. S. McKenney. License 4 NOV 1874. Married 8 NOV 1874 by Jos. A. Billingsley. [M19; R:113; R1:59-4]

Burl, Austin to Mary Thompson. AUSTIN BURL, farmer, age 21, single, b. Westmoreland Co., son of Thomas and Judy F. Burl, to MARY THOMPSON, age 18, single, b. Westmoreland Co., daughter of Francis Thompson. Signed Austin [his X mark] Burle, wit. W.S. McKenney. License 8 JAN 1874. Married 8 JAN 1874 at S. Johnson's by G.W. Beale, minister. [M19; R:111; R1:56-8]

Burnet, Oldham to Margaret Barnes. OLDHAM BURNET, farmer, age 40, widowed, b. Westmoreland Co., son of Charles and Hannah Burnet, to MARGARET BARNES, age 37, widow, b. St. Mary's Co., Md., daughter of Joshua and Betsey Barnes. Signed Oldham [his X mark] Burnet, wit. Wm. S. McKenney. License 29 APR 1876. Married 4 [MAY] 1876 at my house by Thomas T. Johnson. [M19; R:118; R1:64-15]

Burnett, Fleet (C) to Mary Elizabeth Weldon. FLEAT BURNETT [sic], sailor, age 24, single, b. Westmoreland Co., son of Austin and Louisa Burnett, to MARY ELIZABETH WELDON, age 18, single, b. Westmoreland Co., daughter of Priscilla Ball alias Weldon, father unknown. License 2 JUN 1877. Married 7 JUN 1877 at Potomac Church by Thomas T. Johnson. [M19; R:122; R1:69-14]

Burrell (also see Burwell)

Burrell, Fleet to Julie Ashton (d. 1874 of pneumonia), daughter of Jennie Ashton. License 22 JAN 1867. [DR:30-2; R:85]

Burrell, Fleet William (d. 1885 of consumption), to Amanda Virginia Thompson. FLEET WILLIAM BURRELL, farmer, age 28, widowed, b. Northumberland Co., son of Mary Burrell, father unknown, to AMANDA VIRGINIA THOMPSON, age 20, single, b. Westmoreland Co., daughter of John and Judy Thompson. License 25 AUG 1875. Married 26 AUG 1875 at John Thompson's by F.B. Beale. [DR:64-6; M19; R:115; R1:61-12]

Burrel, George (C) to Martha Ann Pinn. GEORGE BURREL, farmer, age 22, single, b. Westmoreland Co., son of Nancy Burrel, father unknown, to MARTHA ANN PINN, age 21, single, b. Westmoreland Co., daughter of Peter and Elsie Pinn. License 13 OCT 1880. Married 14 OCT 1880 at Galilee Church by Rev. Robert Lewis, pastor of Galilee Church. [M20; R:134; R1:83-14]

Burress, Richard S. to Jane Oliffe. License 2 FEB 1852. Married 3 FEB 1852 by John Pullen. [M15:52-3, R:15]

Burton, George W. to Mary J. Boothe. License 8 FEB 1853. Married 9 FEB 1853 by John Godwin. [M15:53-5; R:27]

Burton, Jesse to Mrs. Ann Gainey Spence. JESSE BURTON, farmer, age 68, widower, b. Westmoreland Co., son of Daniel and Dianah Burton, to ANN SPENCE, age 40, widow, b. Richmond Co., daughter of William and Harriet Gainey. License 10 FEB 1869. Planned marriage 18 FEB 1869. [R:94; R1:37-15 no return]

Burwell (also see Burrell)

Burwell [or Burrill], Joshua to Henrietta Hill (C). JOSHUA BURWELL, farmer, age 21, single, b. Westmoreland Co., son of [Daniel] and Sarah Burwell, to HANEY HILL, age 21, single, b. Westmoreland Co., daughter of Ned and Amelia Hill. License 22 FEB 1866. Married 25 FEB 1866 at the Rector of the Episcopal Church by Chas. P. Rodefer, minister. [CP; M18; R:82; R1:23-12]

Bushrod, Henry (C) to Nancy Gordon (d. 1888 of heart disease). HENRY BUSHROD, farmer, age 26, single, b. Westmoreland Co., son of Wesley [d. 1874 of pneumonia] and Easter Bushrod, to NANCY GORDON, age 24, single, b. Richmond Co., daughter of Samuel and Peggy [or Milly] Gordon. Signed Henry [his X mark] Bushrod, wit. C.C. Baker. License 10 JUN 1867. Married 22 JUN 1867 at the Rectory, Washington Parish by Thomas E. Locke. [DR:32-1, 73-125, 77-122; M18; R:87; R1:28-8]

Bushrod, Robert (C) to Lucy Nickens. ROBERT BUSHROD, farmer, age 23, single, b. Westmoreland Co., son of West [Wesley] and Easter Bushrod, to LUCY NICKENS, age 21, single, b. Westmoreland Co., daughter of James and Tina Nickens. Signed Robert [his X mark] Bushrod, wit. Wm. S. McKenney. License 23 NOV 1875. Married 24 NOV 1875 at Little Zion Church by Emanuel Watts, pastor of Little Zion Church. [M19; R:116; R1:62-7]

Butler, Beckwith to Ricardia Lee McGuire. BECKWITH BUTLER, sailor, age 24, single, b. Westmoreland Co., son of Beckwith Butler and Elizabeth [Smoot][1] [d. 1871 of consumption], to RICARDIA LEE McGUIRE, age 22, single, b. Westmoreland Co., daughter of Henry and Ricardia McGuire. Signed Beckwith [his X mark] Butler, wit. J.W. Hutt. License 28 AUG 1868. Married 30 AUG 1868 by H.P.F. King. [DR:19-2; M18; R:92; R1:35-4]

Butler, Edward to Mrs. Mary Douglass Weaver. EDWARD BUTLER, farmer, age 30, single, b. Westmoreland Co., son of Beckwith Butler and Elizabeth [Smoot], to MARY WEAVER, age 25, widow, b. Westmoreland Co., daughter of Lemuel Douglass and Sally [Palmer].[2] License 3 DEC 1878. Married 3 DEC 1878 at William Palmer's by J.H. Davis. [M20; R:127; R1:75-8]

Butler, Henry (C) to Mrs. Polly Whiting Haggot. HENRY BUTLER, farmer, age 40, widowed, b. Prince George's Co., Md., son of Thomas and Hannah Butler, to POLLY HAGGOT, age 29, widow,

---

[1] Beckwith Butler and Elizabeth Smoot were married by bond 29 JUN 1829 in Westmoreland Co., with Samuel Davis, security.
[2] Lemuel Douglass and Sarah Palmer were married by bond 30 DEC 1841 in Westmoreland Co., with Joseph H. Moone, security.

b. Westmoreland Co., daughter of Ellic and Terry Whiting. Signed Henry [his X mark] Butler, wit. J.H. Sisson. License 20 OCT 1869. Married 21 OCT 1869 by John C. Smith. [M18; R:95; R1:39-7]

Butler, John Stuart to Sarah Elizabeth King. JOHN STUART BUTLER, farmer, age 27, single, b. Westmoreland Co., son of William B. Butler and Mary [P. Harrison],[1] to SARAH ELIZABETH KING, age 27, single, b. Westmoreland Co., daughter of Hiram S. King and Hannah H. [Harrison].[2] License 1 MAY 1868. Married 31 MAY 1868 by H.P.F. King. [M18; R:91; R1:33-7]

Butler, John W. to Nancy R. McKenney. JOHN W. BUTLER, carpenter, age 25, single, b. Westmoreland Co., son of William A. Butler and Susan P. [Tiffey],[3] to NANCY R. McKENNEY, age 18, single, b. Westmoreland Co., daughter of Presley and Nancy R. McKenney. Signed John W. Butler, wit. Jno. [R.] Bennett. Consent 7 MAY 1860 by bride's parents, wit. Jno. R. Bennett. License 7 MAY 1860. Married 9 MAY 1860. [M17:60-22; R:74]

Butler, Oscar to Emeline Davis (d. 1877 in childbirth). OSCAR BUTLER, farmer, age 29, single, b. Westmoreland Co., son of Beckwith Butler and Elizabeth [Smoot], *q.v.*, to EMELINE DAVIS, age 22, single, b. Westmoreland Co., daughter of Joseph and Ann Davis License 28 DEC 1875. Married 30 DEC 1875 at *Willis Grove* by F.B. Beale. [ER:39-14 has Eveline Butler; M19; R:117; R1:63-7]

Butler, Samuel Newyear to Mrs. Susan Hannah Sanford Stephens, widow of John Stephens, *q.v.* SAMUEL NEWYEAR BUTLER, farmer, age 24, single, b. Westmoreland Co., son of William [d. 1874] and Mary Butler, to SUSAN HANNAH STEPHENS, age 18, widow, b. Westmoreland Co., daughter of William [S.] and Mary B. Sanford. Signed Saml. N. [his X mark] Butler, wit. C.C. Baker. License 17 DEC 1868. Married 25 DEC 1868 by R.J. Sanford. [DR:30-1[4]; M18; R:93; R1:36-13]

Butler, William Henry[5] to Mary Ann Dozier (d. 1889 aged 53).[6] WILLIAM BUTLER, shoemaker, age 32, single, b. Westmoreland Co., son of Beckwith Butler and Elizabeth [Smoot], to ANN DOZIER, age 32, single, b. Richmond Co., daughter of Martin Dozier and [Elizabeth] Betsy [Butler].[7] License 13 JAN 1870. Married 13 JAN 1870 by D.M. Wharton, Rector of Montross Parish. [DR:81-115; M18; R:97; R1:41-8]

C

Cameron, John to Charlotte Davis. JOHN CAMERON, farmer, age 22, single, b. Westmoreland Co., son of Arshabal [Archibald] and Massey Cameron, to CHARLOTTE DAVIS, age 21, single, b. Westmoreland Co., daughter of Lewis and Mary Davis. License 6 JAN 1873. [R:107; R1:52-14 no return]

Cammel, Thomas (C) to Cynthia Ann Jones. THOMAS CAMMEL, laborer, age 23, single, b. Westmoreland Co., son of Lewis and Edie Cammel, to CYNTHIA ANN JONES, age 22, single, b.

---

[1] William B. Butler and Mary P. Harrison were married by bond 14 JAN 1834 in Westmoreland Co., with James M. English, security.
[2] Hiram S. King, son of Sally R. King, and Hannah Harrison were married by bond 1 JUL 1822 in Richmond Co., with William Brickey, Sr., security.
[3] William A. Butler and Susan Tiffey were married by bond 14 DEC 1829 in Westmoreland Co., with John Bayne, security.
[4] DR:30-1, entry for William B. Butler, farmer, d. 12 MAY 1874 of dropsy, age 73, son of James Butler.
[5] A William H. Butler (1844-1921) with wife Annie were buried in St. Peter's Cemetery, Oak Grove, Va. He served in Co. C, 15th Va. Cav., C.S.A.
[6] Mary A. Butler was buried in the Butler Family Cemetery, located off of Route 3 near Flat Iron Corner.
[7] Martin Dozier and Elizabeth Butler were married by bond 9 FEB 1827 in Westmoreland Co., with William Sutton, security.

Westmoreland Co., daughter of Letty Jones. License 12 MAY 1876. Married 12 MAY 1876 at Sandy Point by Thomas T. Johnson. [M19; R:118; R1:65-2]

Campbell, Isaac, first to Emily Hungerford. ISAAC CAMPBELL, sailor, age 25, single, b. Westmoreland Co., son of B.W. and Kitty Campbell, to EMILY HUNGERFORD, age 22, single, b. Westmoreland Co., daughter of Thomas and Sophia Hungerford. License 24 DEC 1866. Married 25 DEC 1866 by J.H. Davis. [R:85; R1:26-5]

Campbell, Isaac (C), second to Lucy Ann Johnson. ISAAC CAMPBELL, sailor, age 35, widowed, b. Westmoreland Co., son of William and Kitty Campbell, to LUCY ANN JOHNSON, age 23, single, b. Westmoreland Co., daughter of Richard and Jenny Johnson. License 13 DEC 1876. Married 22 DEC 1876 near Tucker Hill by William Gaskins. [M19; R:120; R1:67-6]

Campbell, John (C) (d. 1896 by drowning), to Frances Barnard. JOHN CAMPBELL, sailor, age 2[9], single, b. Northumberland Co., son of Sampson and Charlotte Campbell, to FRANCES BARNARD, age 17, single, b. St. Mary's Co., Md., daughter of Margaret Barnard, father unknown. License 8 JUN 1876. Married 8 JUN 1876 at *Talty Hall* by Thomas T. Johnson. [DR:107-44; M19; R:119; R1:65-10]

Campbell, Joseph (C) to Georgeanna Taylor. JOSEPH CAMPBELL, farmer, age 22, single, b. Westmoreland Co., son of Joseph and Maria [Campbell], to GEORGEANNA TAYLOR, age 24, single, b. Westmoreland Co., daughter of Jessie and Pollie Taylor. License 15 APR 1879. Married 17 APR 1879 at *Harrisville* by Chas. [his X mark] Rust. [M20; R:128; R1:77-8]

Campbell, Richard (C) to Lizzie Redman. RICHARD CAMPBELL, laborer, age 23, single, b. Westmoreland Co., son of William and Catharine Campbell, to LIZZIE REDMAN, age 23, single, b. Westmoreland Co., daughter of Leer Redman, father unknown. Signed Richard [his X mark] Campbell, wit. J.W. Hutt. License 13 MAY 1869. Married 15 MAY 1869 by John C. Smith. [M18; R:95; R1:38-6]

Campbell, Solomon (C) (d. 1932 of chronic nephritis),[1] to Rosa Ashton. SOLOMON CAMPBELL, farmer, age 23, single, b. Westmoreland Co., son of Joseph Campbell and Bettie [Johnson], to ROSA ASHTON, age 19, single, b. Westmoreland Co., daughter of Stewart and Roxanna Ashton. License 20 AUG 1878. Married 22 AUG 1878 at the bride's residence by Rev. William Gaskings. [DC; M19; R:126; R1:74-9]

Campbell, William (C) (d. 1936 of cerebral hemorrhage),[2] to Maria Berryman. WILLIAM CAMPBELL, farmer, age 22, single, b. Essex Co., son of [Ethan] and Ellen Campbell, to MARIA BERRYMAN, age 21, single, b. Westmoreland Co., daughter of Warren and Maria Berryman. License 6 NOV 1880. Married 6 NOV 1880 at Little Zion Church by Emanuel Watts, pastor, Little Zion Church. [M20; R:134; R1:84-1]

Carey, George (C) to Mrs. Mary Ashton. GEORGE CAREY, farmer, age 60, widowed, b. Westmoreland Co., parents unknown, to MARY ASHTON, age 30, widow, b. Westmoreland Co.,

---

[1] DC: Solomon Campbell was buried at Zion Church, and that his wife was Rose Askins.
[2] DC: William Campbell was buried in a family cemetery.

daughter of Ann Ashton. License 15 SEP 1877. Married 20 SEP 1877 at Potomac Church by Thomas T. Johnson. [M19; R:123; R1:70-10]

Carey, John to Eliza Wright. JOHN CAREY, farmer, age 45, single, b. Westmoreland Co., son of Cornelius and Betsy [Elizabeth Jones] Cary [sic],[1] to ELIZA WRIGHT, age 30, single, b. Westmoreland Co., daughter of Solomon and Emily Wright. License 26 NOV 1877. Married 6 DEC 1877 at *The Glebe* by F.B. Beale. [M19; R:123; R1:71-3]

Carey, Richard (C) to Lucy Thompson (C). License 13 DEC 1854. [R:45]

Carey, Thomas to Fanny Richardson. License 28 OCT 1857. [R:62]

Carey, Thomas to Amanda Harrison. THOMAS CARY, farmer, age 22, single, b. Westmoreland Co., son of Stafford Carey and Judy [Gaskins],[2] to AMANDA HARRISON, age 22, single, b. Westmoreland Co., daughter of Polly Harrison, father unknown. Signed Thos. [his X mark] Carey, wit. C.C. Baker. License 18 DEC 1866. Married 20 DEC 1866 at the residence of the minister by J.H. Davis. [M18; R:84; R1:26-1]

Carey, Thomas (b. 1856, d. 1924 of chronic endocarditis),[3] to Sallie Weldon. THOMAS CAREY, farmer, age 21, single, b. Westmoreland Co., son of Richard Carey and Lucinda [Thompson], to SALLIE WELDON, age 21, single, b. Westmoreland Co., daughter of Harry and Jane Weldon. License 10 JAN 1877. Married 11 JAN 1877 by F.B. Beale. [M19; R:121; R1:68-10]

Carey, William to Eliza A. Smith, free people of color. License 10 MAR 1852. Married 11 MAR 1852 by E.B. [Edward Brown] McGuire. [M15:52-9; R:17]

Carroll, Solomon Redman to Mary Jane Windows. SOLOMON R. CAROL [sic], farmer, age 21,* single, b. Westmoreland Co., son of John and Eliza [Carroll], to MARY J. WINDOWS, age 24,* single, b. Dorchester, Md.,* res. Baltimore, Md., daughter of Henry and Eliza Windows. License 7 OCT 1858. Married 7 OCT 1858 at *Traveller's Rest* by George F. Bagby, M.G. [M16a:58-22[4]; R:64; R1:12-7]

Carter, Arthur (1839-1930),[5] to Affire Hinson. ARTHUR CARTER, farmer, age 24, single, b. and res. Richmond Co., son of John S. and Nancy Carter, to AFFIRE HINSON, age 25, single, b. Westmoreland Co., daughter of Vincent and [Frances] Hinson.[6] Signed Arthur [his X mark] Carter, wit. Wm. E. Baker. License 10 MAR 1870. Married 10 MAR 1870 by Robert N. Reamy. [DC; M18; R:98; R1:42-11]

Carter, Daniel Brooks (d. 1901), to Sydna A. Carpenter. DANIEL BROOKS CARTER, farmer, age 36, widowed, b. and res. Richmond Co., son of Daniel Carter and Sarah [Hinson],[7] to SYDNA A. CARPENTER, age 19, single, b. Westmoreland Co., daughter of Joseph Carpenter and Shady

---

[1] Cornelius Cary and Elizabeth Jones were married by bond 11 NOV 1829 in Westmoreland Co., with Edmund Tate, security.
[2] Stafford Carey and Judy Gaskins were married by bond 29 NOV 1842 in Westmoreland Co., with Thomas Carey, security.
[3] DC: Thomas Carey was buried in a private cemetery.
[4] Another copy at 58-22a gives middle names for bride and groom, * ages 22 and 22, birthplace of wife as Somerset Co., Md., and place of marriage as Machodoc Church. Machodoc Meeting House was built as a Baptist church in 1856 at Machodoc Crossroads.
[5] DC: Arthur Carter was buried at Ephesus Christian Church, Flat Iron, Va.
[6] Vincent Hinson and Fanny Roe were married by bond 11 FEB 1829 in Westmoreland Co., with Rodney Moxley, security.
[7] Daniel Hinson and Sally Hinson were married by bond 30 OCT 1822 in Westmoreland Co., with Daniel Carter, security.

[Hinson].[1] License 7 JAN 1876. Married 9 JAN 1876 at Mrs. S. Carpenter's by R.N. Reamy. [M19; NN; R:117; R1:63-12]

Carter, Edward Landon (d. 1871 at *Woodland*, Loudoun Co.), to Mary Ridgley Arnest. EDWARD LANDON CARTER, farmer, age 42 last birthday, single, b. *Sudley*, Fairfax Co., son of Landon Carter [d. testate 1858 in Loudoun Co.[2]] and Courtney Norton, to MARY RIDGLEY ARNEST, age 31 last birthday, single, b. *Nomony Hall* [sic], daughter of John Arnest and Juliet Sterett. License 2 SEP 1856. Married 3 SEP 1856 at *Nomini Hall*[3] by T. Grayson Dashiell, clergyman. [M16a:56-25; R:57; R1:6-9]

Carter, Henry (C) to Charlotte Johnson. HENRY CARTER, farmer, age 55, widowed, b. Westmoreland Co., son of George and Harriet Carter, to CHARLOTTE JOHNSON, age 30, single, b. King George Co., daughter of Edward and Maria Johnson. Signed Henry [his X mark] Carter, wit. J.W. Hutt. License 7 JUL 1872. Married 12 JUL 1872 at Leeds Town by John Roy. [M19; R:106; R1:50-1r]

Carter, Henry to Ginny Taylor. HENRY CARTER, wood chopper, age 28, single, b. Westmoreland Co., son of Harry and Jane Carter, to GINNY TAYLOR, age 29, single, b. Westmoreland Co., daughter of Jack and Sophia Taylor. Signed Henry [his X mark] Carter, wits. Hy. Harford, J.W. Hutt. License 29 JUL 1868. Married 30 JUL 1868 at *Hickory Hill* by J.H. Davis. [M18; R:92; R1:34-13]

Carter, Jefferson to Sarah Jackson. JEFFERSON CARTER, blacksmith, age 70, single, b. Westmoreland Co., son of Gaff and Milly Carter, to SARAH JACKSON, age 40, single, b. Westmoreland Co., daughter of Alex and Sarah Jackson. Signed Jefferson [his X mark] Carter, wit. J.W. Hutt. License 6 MAY 1868. Married 7 MAY 1868 at *Hickory Hill* by J.H. Davis. [M18; R:91; R1:33-9]

Carter, John (C) to Maria Smith. JOHN CARTER, laborer, age 37, widowed, b. Lunenburg Co., son of David and Chloe Carter, to MARIA SMITH, age 30, single, b. Essex Co., daughter of Daniel and Judy Smith. Signed John [his X mark] Carter, wit. Wm. S. McKenney. License 3 JAN 1876. Married 6 JAN 1876 at Little Zion Church by Emanuel Watts, pastor of Little Zion Church. [M19; R:117; R1:63-10]

Carter, Moses to Gracy Nickens, colored persons. MOSES CARTER, farmer, age 23, single, b. Essex Co., son of Aaron and Jane Carter, to GRACY NICKENS, age 21, single, b. Essex Co., daughter of Davey and Elizabeth Nickens. Signed Moses [his X mark] Carter, wit. J.H. Sisson. License 22 OCT 1869. Married 23 OCT 1869 at Dr. Wirt's farm by Thomas E. Locke, Rector of Washington Parish. [M18; R:96; R1:39-9; WP]

Carter, Nathaniel Edward to Rosa Graham (d. 1888 of dropsy). NATHANIEL EDWARD CARTER, farmer, age 24, single, b. Prince William Co., son of Nathaniel and Frances Carter, to ROSA GRAHAM, age 19, single, b. Westmoreland Co., daughter of Jerry and Harriet Graham. License 27 DEC 1872. Married 1 JAN 1873 at *Millwood*. [DR:75-15; M19 no minister signature; R:107; R1:52-11]

---

[1] Joseph Carpenter and Shady Hinson were married by bond 7 MAR 1849 in Westmoreland Co., with Frederick Poor, security.
[2] Loudoun Co. Wills, Bk. 2M, p. 292, will of Landon Carter, of *Wood Land*.
[3] *Nomini Hall* burned to the ground in October 1850 while occupied by the John Arnest Family. It had been built by Robert "King" Carter for his son Robert, and was inherited by his son Robert Carter.

Carter, Rawleigh William Downman, served in Co. D, 9th Va. Ca., C.S.A., to Jane Champ Payne. RAWLEIGH WILLIAM DOWNMAN CARTER, farmer, age 41, widower, b. Northumberland Co., son of R.D. [Raleigh Downman] Carter [1796-1863] and Judith [Gaskins],[1] to JANE CHAMP PAYNE, age 30, single, b. Richmond Co., daughter of George and Jane C. Payne. License 14 DEC 1874. Married 15 DEC 1874 at Oak Grove, Va. by E.B. McGuire. [M19; R:113; R1:59-11; WP]

Carter, Robert to Emily Cary. ROBERT CARTER, farmer, age 45, widower, b. Westmoreland Co., son of Emanuel and Polly Smith, to EMILY CARY, age 27, single, b. Westmoreland Co., daughter of Thomas and Rachal Cary [sic]. Signed Robert [his X mark] Carter, wit. W.S. McKenney. License 8 FEB 1871. Married 9 FEB 1871 by G.W. Beale, minister. [M18; R:101; R1:45-15]

Carter, Thomas A. to Martha Hinson. License 28 DEC 1857. [R:63]

Carter, Vincent to Ellen Belfield (1857-1922).[2] VINCENT CARTER, farmer, age 21, single, b. Richmond Co., son of Joseph Carter and Mary [Lewis], to ELLEN BELFIELD, age 19, single, b. Westmoreland Co., parents unknown. License 27 AUG 1878. Married 29 AUG 1878 at the residence of Miss Jones by D.M. Wharton. [DC; M19; R:126; R1:74-10]

Carter, Walter (d. by 1877), to Elizabeth Bankhead, colored people. WALTER CARTER, farmer, age 22, single, b. Westmoreland Co., son of William and Rosetta Carter, to ELIZABETH BANKHEAD, age 20, single, b. Westmoreland Co., daughter of John and Charlotte Bankhead. Signed Walter [his X mark] Carter, wit. C.C. Baker. License 21 DEC 1869. Married 26 DEC 1869 at Henderson Smith's residence by Thomas E. Locke, Rector, Washington Parish. [M18; R:97; R1:40-29; WP]

Carter, William (C) to Caroline Berryman. WILLIAM CARTER, farmer, age 25, single, b. King George Co., son of Henry and Martha Carter, to CAROLINE BERRYMAN, age 21, single, b. Westmoreland Co., daughter of Warren and Maria Berryman. License 20 DEC 1879. Married 23 DEC 1879 at Little Zion Church by Emanuel Watts, pastor, Little Zion Church. [M20; R:131; R1:79-16]

Carter, William (C) to Peggy Smith. WILLIAM CARTER, farmer, age 24, single, b. Westmoreland Co., res. King George Co., son of Lewis and Matilda Carter, to PEGGY SMITH, age 18, single, b. Westmoreland Co., daughter of George and Sallie Smith. License 15 JAN 1878. Married 17 JAN 1878 in Washington Township by Emanuel Watts, pastor, Little Zion Church. [M19; R:124; R1:72-10]

Carter, William H., Sr. to Mrs. Sallie W. Gooding, widow of John Gooding.[3] WILLIAM H. CARTER, builder, age 49, widower, b. Lancaster Co., Va., son of Joseph and Frances E. Carter, to SALLIE W. GOODING, age 39, widow, b. Baltimore Co., Md., name of parents blank. License 15 DEC 1856. Married 15 DEC 1856 in Montross, Va. by George Northam, M.G. [M16a:56-34; R:57; R1:8-1]

---

[1] Rawleigh D. Carter, widower, and Judith Gaskins, were married by bond 13 APR 1829 in Westmoreland Co., with John D. Leland, security.
[2] DC: Ellen Carter was buried near Zacata, Va.
[3] CF1859-08, *Arthur Brown v. Admr. of John Gooding &c.*

Carver, William V. to Lavinia H. Van Ness. WILLIAM V. CARVER, seaman, age 25, single, b. Vinalhaven, Me., son of John and Rhoda Carver, to LAVINIA H. VAN NESS, age 20, single, b. *Chatham*, daughter of Benjamin and Delia Van Ness. License 21 FEB 1855. Married 27 FEB 1855 at *Chatham*, the residence of Benjamin Van Ness by J.W. Chesley, minister of the Prot. Epis. Church. [M16:55-8, R:49; R1:3-5; SP; WP]

Cary, Vanness to Felicia Corbin (C) (d. 1892 of asthma). VANNESS CARY, farmer, age 24, single, b. Westmoreland Co., son of Stafford Cary and Judy [Gaskins], *q.v.*, to FELICIA CORBIN, age 26, single, b. Westmoreland Co., daughter of Nancy Corbin, father unknown. License 3 DEC 1879. Married 4 DEC 1879 at Potomac Church by Thomas T. Johnson. [DR:92-55; M20; R:130; R1:79-4]

Catrup, Samuel Porter (1836-1896), to Catherine Ann Bailey (1845-1933).[1] SAMUEL PORTER CATRUP, printer, age 24, single, b. Talbot Co., Md., res. Baltimore, Md., son of Samuel H. [1809-1872] and Sarah Jane Catrup [1811-1882], to CATHRINE ANN BAILEY[sic], age 24, single, b. Westmoreland Co., daughter of Stephen G. and Harriet A. Bailey. License 6 DEC 1869. Married 7 DEC 1869 at *Kinlocque* by R.J. Sanford. [M18; R:96; R1:40-20]

Chamberlain, John Lee (d. 1874 of heart disease), to Elizabeth Ann Davis (d. testate 1886[2]). JOHN LEE CHAMBERLAIN, merchant, age 69, widower, b. Richmond Co., son of John Chamberlain and Rachel [Alderson],[3] to ELIZABETH ANN DAVIS, age 41, single, b. Westmoreland Co., daughter of Samuel Davis. License 29 SEP 1870. Married 29 SEP 1870 by H.H. Fones. [DR:31-14; M18; R:99; R1:44-1]

Chambers, Leonard to Eliza Taylor. LEONARD CHAMBERS, brick mason, age 24, single, b. Westmoreland Co., son of Thomas Chambers and Patsey [Astin],[4] to ELIZA TAYLOR, age 22, single, b. Westmoreland Co., daughter of Charles and Rose Taylor. Signed Leonard [his X mark] Chambers, wits. J.W. Hutt, Ben. Walker. License 12 FEB 1861. Married 14 FEB 1861. [M17:61-4; R:77]

Chandler, Frank (C) to Judy McHeart. FRANK CHANDLER, farmer, age 23, single, b. Westmoreland Co., son of Maria Rust, father unknown, to JUDY McHEART, age 21, single, b. Westmoreland Co., daughter of Spencer and Mary McHeart. License 18 FEB 1880. Married 19 FEB 1880 at *Auburn* by Charles Rust. [M20; R:132; R1:81-7]

Chandler, John Henry (1843-1909), served Co. K, 40th Va. Inf., C.S.A., to Georgie Anna Blackistone (1846-1910).[5] JOHN HENRY CHANDLER, farmer, age 35, single, b. Westmoreland Co., son of H. [Harriet] [d. 1865 of typhoid pneumonia] and L.P. [Lewis] Chandler, to GEORGIE ANNA BLACKISTONE, age 32, single, b. St. Mary's Co., Md., daughter of G.W. and J. Blackistone. License 26 NOV 1878. Married 26 NOV 1878 at the residence of the bride's father by D.M. Wharton. [DR10-61; M19; R:127; R1:75-7]

Churchwell, George to Fenton Pierce. License 12 JAN 1859. [R:68]

---

[1] Samuel P. Catrup and his wife Catherine were buried in Mount Olivet Cemetery, Baltimore, Md.

[2] Deeds & Wills No. 46, p. 171, will of Elizabeth Chamberlain, proved 26 APR 1886, names half-brothers Joseph E., Charles W. and Lewis Davis, brothers John and Richard Davis.

[3] John Chamberlain and Rachel Alderson, daughter of Mary Alderson, were married by bond 16 DEC 1791 in Richmond Co.

[4] Thomas Chambers and Patsy Astin were married by bond 6 JAN 1827 in Westmoreland Co., with Rodham Astin, security.

[5] J.H. Chandler and his wife Georgia Blackistone were buried at St. James Episcopal Church, Montross, Va.

Clark, Addison Judson to Frances Elizabeth Dishman. ADISSON JUDSON CLARK [sic], farmer, age 22, single, b. King George Co., son of Overton [J.] Clark and Nancy [Hudson],[1] to FRANCES ELIZABETH DISHMAN, age 19, single, b. Westmoreland Co., daughter of James [Andrew] Dishman [1798-1873] and [his second wife] Ann [V. Kent] [1804-1859].[2] License 17 SEP 1860. Married 18 SEP 1860. [M17:60-31; R:74]

Clarke, Alfred Rudolph to Annie Withers. ALFRED RUDOLPH CLARKE, carpenter, age 28, single, b. England, son of John [R.] and C.R. Clarke, to ANNIE WITHERS, age 17, single, b. Westmoreland Co., daughter of Mary F. Withers, father unknown. License 15 JAN 1878. Married 16 JAN 1878 at *Sherland* by F.B. Beale. [M19; R:124; R1:72-9]

Clark, Hempsel to Mary Elizabeth Wright (1831-1917).[3] HEMPSEL CLARK, farmer, age 69, widowed, b. and res. Richmond Co., son of Ransdell and Nancy Clark, to MARY ELIZABETH WRIGHT, age 46, single, b. Westmoreland Co., daughter of M.M. [Mottrom Middleton] Wright [1800-1858] and Malinda A. [Ann Lamkin] [1809-1868].[4] License 2 JUN 1879. Married 3 JUN 1879 by W.A. Crocker. [M20; NN; R:129; R1:77-13]

Clark, Richard Jackson (1856-1908), to Julia Ann Bryant (1858-1890).[5] RICHARD JACKSON CLARK, waterman, age 21, single, b. Westmoreland Co., son of Richard Clark [d. 1871 by suicide] and Harriet [P. Burkley], to JULIA ANN BRYANT, age 19, single, b. Westmoreland Co., daughter of John R. and Clementha Bryant. License 17 NOV 1877. Married 29 NOV 1877 by H.H. Fones. [DR:24-6; M19; R:123; R1:71-4]

Clarke, Robert Lewis to Sarah Elizabeth Moxley. ROBERT LEWIS CLARKE, farmer, age 26, single, b. Westmoreland Co., son of Richard and Harriet Ann Clarke, to SARAH ELIZABETH MOXLEY, age 26, single, b. Westmoreland Co., daughter of Richard Moxley and [Ann] Rebecca [Stone]. License 6 DEC 1873. Married 10 DEC 1873 at *The Cottage* by Walter C. Taylor. [M19; R:110; R1:55-3]

Clark, Thomas Washington to Mary McGuire. THOMAS WASHINGTON CLARK, farmer, age 60, widowed, b. Westmoreland Co., son of James Clark and Penelope [Sanford],[6] to MARY McGUIRE, age 50, single, b. Westmoreland Co., daughter of Travis McGuire and Rebecca [Sutton].[7] License 25 JAN 1865. Married 5 FEB 1865 at the residence of the bride by H.P.F. King. [M17a:65-3; R:81; R1:21-16]

Clark, Thomas William (1855-1942), first to Theodosia Ernest Smith (1859-1936).[8] THOMAS WILLIAM CLARK, farmer, age 22, single, b. Richmond Co., res. Northumberland Co., son of H.J. [Hiram James] Clark and A.B. [Ann Lewis], to THEODOSIA SMITH, age 19, single, b.

---

[1] Overton J. Clarke and Nancy J. Hudson were married 9 SEP 1828 in King George Co. by Lovell Marders.
[2] James Dishman and Ann V. Kent were married by bond 31 OCT 1836 in Westmoreland Co., with Thomas Sandy, security.
[3] Mary E. Wright Clark was buried in a Wright Family Cemetery at *Cabin Point*.
[4] Mottrom M. Wright and Malinda Lamkin [daughter of Lewis Lamkin and Griffentello Claughton] were married by bond 6 APR 1830 in Richmond Co., with Charles L. Bell as security. Mottram M. Wright and his wife Malinda A. Lamkin were buried in a Wright Family Cemetery, located off of Route 203 near Oldhams, Va.
[5] Richard J. Clark and his wife Julia Ann Bryant were buried in the Chisford-Stratford Area Community Cemetery, located off of Route 609 on property owned by the Hinson Family.
[6] James Clark and Penelope Sanford, daughter of Reuben Sanford, were married by bond 28 MAY 1796 in Westmoreland Co., with John Grinnan, security.
[7] Travis McGuire and Beckey Sutton were married by bond 3 FEB 1809 in Westmoreland Co., with Joseph Sutton, security.
[8] Thomas W. Clarke and his wife Theodosia were buried at Smithland Baptist Church, Coan, Va.

Westmoreland Co., daughter of James [& B.]A. Smith. License 3 [APR] 1878. Married 10 APR 1878 at James R. Smith's by R.N. Reamy. [M19; R:125; R1:73-11]

Clark, Watt Alfred (C) to Elizabeth Thompson. WATT ALFRED CLARKE, laborer, age 26, single, b. Westmoreland Co., son of Henry and Rebecca Clarke [d. 1886], to ELIZABETH THOMPSON, age 18, single, b. Westmoreland Co., daughter of John and Ricardia Thompson. Signed Watt Alfred Clark. License 25 FEB 1874. Married 26 FEB 1874 at Henry Clark's by Jerry Graham. [DR:68-50; M19; R:112; R1:57-16]

Clark, William to Virginia Jasper. WILLIAM CLARK, farming, age 23, single, b. Westmoreland Co., son of James and Elizabeth Clark, to VIRGINIA JASPER, age 27, single, b. Westmoreland Co., daughter of Samuel and Leucinda Jasper. License 6 MAY 1854. Married 7 MAY 1854 at Popes Creek Church by John Pullen. [M15:54-3; R:43; R1:1-13]

Claughton, Jasper to Ellen Smith. JASPER CLAUGHTON, farmer, age 20, single, b. Northumberland Co., son of Jasper and Fanny Claughton, to ELLEN SMITH, age 22, single, b. Westmoreland Co., daughter of James and Martha Young. License 5 MAR 1866. Married 5 MAR 1866 at Wm. Cary's by J.H. Davis. [M18; R:83; R1:23-13]

Claybrook, Edwin Coke [or Cole], of *Glenburney* (b. 1842, d. 1893 of epilepsy), served Co. C, 9th Va. Cav., C.S.A., to Judith White Newton (b. 1843 at *Linden*, d. 1895 of kidney trouble).[1] EDWIN COKE CLAYBROOK, lawyer, age 24, single, b. Northumberland Co., son of Richard A. Claybrook [d. 1873 of heart disease] and Charlotte T. [Brown] [d. 1884 of paralysis], to JUDITH WHITE NEWTON, age 23, single, b. Westmoreland Co., daughter of Willoughby Newton [1802-1874] and Mary [Stevenson Brockenbrough] [b. 1810, d. testate 1888[2]], *q.v.* License 14 JAN 1867. Married 15 JAN 1867 at the residence of the bride's father [*Linden*] by Andrew Fisher. [CP; DR:26-15[3], 60-10[4], 94-26, 101-20; M18; NN; R:85; SC]

Clayton, Adderson (C) to Hannah Johnson. ADDERSON CLAYTON, farmer, age 33, single, b. Westmoreland Co., son of Betsy Clayton, to HANNAH JOHNSON, age 26, single, b. Westmoreland Co., daughter of Henry and Mary Johnson. License 14 MAY 1876. Married 18 MAY 1876 at my house by Thomas T. Johnson. [M19; R:118; R1:65-1]

Clevinger, John to Emily Jane McGuire. JOHN CLEVINGER, farmer, age 34, single, b. Bedford Co., Pa., son of Peter and Mary Clevinger, to EMILY JANE McGUIRE, age 31, widow, b. Westmoreland Co., daughter of Sarey McGuire, father unknown. License 4 DEC 1877. Married 4 DEC 1877[5] by G.H. Northam. [M20' R:123; R1:71-6]

---

[1] Edwin Coke Claybrook and his wife Judith were buried at Yeocomico Episcopal Church, Kinsale, Va.

[2] Deeds & Wills No. 47, p. 428, will of Mary S. Newton of *Linden*, proved 23 APR 1888, names daughter Judith White Claybrook. The *Linden* house was gutted by fire in November 1879. For description see *Northern Neck News*, 15 DEC 1893, p. 1.

[3] DR:26-15, entry for Richard A. Claybrook, attorney at law, b. Middlesex Co., d. 4 DEC 1873, of [supposed] heart disease, age 59, son of Richard and Elizabeth Claybrook, husband of Charlotte T. Claybrook.

[4] DR:60-10, entry for Charlotte Claybrook, d. 15 AUG 1884 of paralysis, age 70, daughter of Richard and Lucy Brown, widow, mother-in-law of Thomas Brown.

[5] There are several conflicting points here: (1) the Register of Licenses notes that the license was issued 4 DEC 1877, and (2) this date is confirmed by the license itself, while (3) the date of marriage on the Minister's Return of Marriage is 4 DEC 1878, and (4) the license is filmed with 1879 records.

Coakley, William B. (1846-1912),[1] served in Co. I, 9th Va. Cav., C.S.A., to Lillian Jane Hutt (1857-1942). WILLIAM COAKLEY, farmer, age 33, single, b. and res. King George Co., son of William B. Coakley and Caroline [Marshall],[2] to LILLIE JANE HUTT [sic], age 21, single, b. Westmoreland Co., daughter of [Edwin] Hutt and Susan J. [Brown], *q.v.* License 24 DEC 1879. Married 25 DEC 1879 at the residence of the bride's father by D.M. Wharton. [M20; R:131; R1:80-5; SC]

Coats, Carter Samuel (d. 1875 of pneumonia), served in Co. G, 15th Va. Cav., C.S.A., to Maria Hinson. CARTER SAMUEL COATS, farmer, age 28, single, b. Richmond Co., son of Samuel and Nancy Coats, to MARIA HINSON, age 20, single, b. Westmoreland Co., daughter of Vincent Hinson and Fanny [Roe].[3] License 1 APR 1859. Married 3 APR 1859 by John Pullen. [M16a:59-10, 10a and 10b; R:68; R1:14-11]

Coats, Cornelius to Margaret Weldon (C). CORNELIUS COATS, farmer, age 22, single, b. and res. Richmond Co., son of Sandy and Lucinda Coats, to MARGARET WELDON, age 25, single, b. Richmond Co., daughter of Sample Weldon and Sally [Gaskins] (C).[4] License 29 DEC 1874. Married 31 DEC 1874 at Sample Weldon's by Jerry Graham. [M19; R:114; R1:60-8]

Coats, George Beriah, first to Maria A. Reamy. GEORGE B. COATS, farming, age 25, single, b. in upper part of Richmond Co., son of James Coats, Sen. and Elizabeth his wife, to MARIA A. REAMEY [sic], age 15, single, b. in upper part of Richmond Co., daughter of John Reamy and Jane his wife. License 25 JUL 1855. Married 29 JUL 1855 at Leucy Peed's in upper part of Westmoreland Co. by John Pullen. [M16:55-16; R:49; R1:3-10]

Coats, George Beriah, second to Frances Elizabeth Barker. GEORGE BERIAH COATS, farmer, age 35, widowed, b. Richmond Co., son of James and Elizabeth Coats, to FRANCES ELIZABETH BARKER, age 22, single, b. Westmoreland Co., daughter of John [d. testate 1884] and [Frances] Barker, *q.v.* License 14 FEB 1865. Married 16 FEB 1865 at John Barker's by John Pullen. [M17a:65-5; R:81; R1:22-2]

Coats, John W., served in Co. K, 9th Va. Cav., C.S.A., to Elizabeth A. Sanders. JOHN W. COATES [sic], farming, age about 21, single, b. upper dist. of Richmond Co., res. near Carter's Wharf, son of James Coats and Elizabeth his wife, to ELIZABETH A. SANDERS, age about 19, single, b. Westmoreland Co., daughter of John Sanders and Mary his wife. License 4 JAN 1858. Married 6 JAN 1858 at John Sanders' by John Pullen, M.G. [M16a:58-4; R:63; R1:11-14]

Coats, Richard Spicer to Mrs. Lucy Ann Bartlett Gutridge. RICHARD SPICER COATS, farmer, age 57, widowed, b. Westmoreland Co., son of William and Franky Coats, to LUCY ANN GUTRIDGE, age 36, widow, b. Richmond Co., daughter of Samuel Bartlett and Mahal[a] [Carter].[5] License 8 SEP 1864. Married 8 SEP 1864 at the residence of George Gutridge by Robert N. Reamy. [M17a:64-9; R:80; R1:21-2]

---

[1] William B. Coakley and his wife Lillian were buried at St. Paul's Episcopal Church, Nomini Grove, Va.
[2] William B. Coakley and Caroline Marshall were married 19 DEC 1844 in King George Co. by Rev. Philip Montague.
[3] Vincent Hinson and Fanny Roe were married by bond 11 FEB 1829 in Westmoreland Co., with Thomas P.W. Neale, security.
[4] Sample Weldon and Sally Gaskins, free persons of colour, were married by bond 2 JUN 1828 in Richmond Co., with George Henry, security.
[5] Samuel Bartlett and Mahala Carter, daughter of Daniel Carter, were married by bond 26 SEP 1832 in Richmond Co., with John S. Carter, security.

Coats, Robert Alexander (1858-1924), to Rebecca Damaious Smith (1860-1934).[1] ROBERT ALEXANDER COATS, farmer, age 22, single, b. Richmond Co., son of John A. Coats and E. [Elizabeth "Betty" Sanders], to REBECCA DAMAIOUS SMITH, age 19, single, b. Westmoreland Co., daughter of J.R. and A. Smith. License 20 DEC 1880. Married 22 DEC 1880 by R.N. Reamy. [M20; R:134; R1:84-10]

Coats, William Salathiel (b. 1829, d. 1888 of Bright's disease), served Co. A, 15th Va. Cav., C.S.A., son of James B. Coats and Elizabeth Carpenter,[2] to Emily Gutridge (1834-1913),[3] daughter of James Gutridge and Susan Hinson. License 10 MAR 1852. Married 11 MAR 1852 by John Pullen. [M15:52-10; R:17]

Coghill, Winter [or Winton] to Sarah Jane Barrack. License 1 APR 1852. Married 4 APR 1852 by John Pullen. [M15:52-14; R:19]

Cole, John (1820-1893), to Alice Elizabeth "Ailsy" Douglass (1834-1879).[4] License 10 NOV 1851. Married 13 NOV 1851 by Wm. N. Ward, M.G. in the Prot. Epis. Ch. [M15:51-21; R:11]

Cole, Leroy (C) to Virginia Smith. LEROY COLE, farmer, age 22, single, b. Westmoreland Co., son of Samuel and Lucy Cole, to VIRGINIA SMITH, age 20, single, b. Westmoreland Co., daughter of Emanuel Smith and Juli[et] [Ashton].[5] Signed Leroy [his X mark] Cole, wit. J.H. Sisson. License 20 JAN 1870. Married 20 JAN 1870 by John C. Smith. [M18; R:98; R1:41-12]

Collins, George W.,[6] plasterer, to Elizabeth Ann Reed. License 25 NOV 1850. Married 12 DEC 1850 by George Northam. [M15:50-26; R:3 not in *Nottingham*]

Collins, John Henry to Ann McGuire. JOHN HENRY COLLINS, brick mason, age 55, widowed, b. Essex Co., son of John and Elizabeth Collins,[7] to ANN McGUIRE, age 38, single, b. Westmoreland Co., daughter of William and Sarah McGuire. License 24 DEC 1864. Married 29 DEC 1864 at the residence of Capt. Henry Weaver by H.P.F. King. [M17a:64-17; R:81; R1:21-11]

Combs, Stansberry (1823-1909),[8] to Susan Winkfield (d. 1882). STANSBERRY COMBS, farmer, age 45, single, b. King George Co., son of Edmond and Nancy Combs, to SUSAN WINKFIELD, age 30, single, b. King George Co., daughter of Polly Winkfield. License 21 JAN 1874. Married 22 JAN 1874 at Wm. Worrell's by John Payne. [DR:56-8; M19; R:111; R1:57-2; WP]

Compton, Samuel Gilbert, Dr. (1831-1892),[9] surgeon, served in 18th Bat. Va. Heavy Art., C.S.A., first to Eugenia Brockenbrough (1839-1862).[10] SAMUEL GILBERT COMPTON, planter, age 27,

---

[1] Robert A. Coates and his wife Rebecca D. were buried in the Smith Family Cemetery, located off of Route 203 near Oldhams, Va., then the graves were removed to Beulah Baptist Church.
[2] James Coats and Elizabeth Carpenter were married c.1812 by bond in Westmoreland Co.
[3] William S. Coates and his wife Emily were buried at St. Peter's Cemetery, Oak Grove, Va.
[4] John Cole and his wife Alice were buried at Carmel United Methodist Church, Kinsale, Va.
[5] Emanuel Smith and Juliet Ashton were married by bond 7 JAN 1830 in Westmoreland Co., with James G. Donoho, security.
[6] George W. Collins served in Co. A, 15th Va. Cav., C.S.A., as a musician through 1862, and chief bugler. Deserter by 1865 and suspected to be in Westmoreland Co., resided at Templemans, age 72 in 1902. Deeds & Wills Bk. 74, p. 274, will of George W. Collins, dated 18 AUG 1904, proved 6 JUN 1912.
[7] John Collins (d. 1815) was married to Mrs. Elizabeth Bray, widow of Charles Bray (d. 1803) by bond 6 FEB 1806 in Essex Co., with Jesse Boughan, security.
[8] Stansbury Combs was buried in the Combs Burying Ground, Rollins Fork, King George Co., Va.
[9] Dr. Compton was buried in the Compton Family Cemetery, Rapides Parish, La.
[10] Eugenia Compton was buried with her parents in Oak Hill Cemetery, Georgetown, D.C.

single, b. and res. Parish of Rapides, La., son of John Compton [1779-1855] and Amelia B. [Baillio] [1799-1859], to EUGENIA BROCKENBROUGH, age 21, single, b. King William Co., daughter of John F. [Fauntleroy] Brockenbrough [1812-1865] and Frances A. [Ann Carter] [1816-1866], *q.v.* License 28 JUN 1859. Married 28 JUN 1859 at *Chatham*. [M16a:59-17; R:70]

Cook, Baly to Mary J. Rose. BALY COOK, farming, age about 23, single, b. Westmoreland Co., son of Stewart Cook and Eliza [Hinson],[1] to MARY J. ROSE, age about 24, single, b. King George Co., daughter of Henry Rose and Mahaly [Jones].[2] License 2 DEC 1858. Married 4 JAN 1858 at Samson Nash's by John Pullen, M.G. [M16a:58-1 and 58-1a; R:66; R1:13-7]

Cook, Charles L. to Catharine Washington. CHARLES L. COOK, farmer, age 25, single, b. Westmoreland Co., son of Samuel Cook and Mariah Dickens,[3] to CATHARINE WASHINGTON, age 21, single, b. Westmoreland Co., daughter of Samuel Washington and Mariah Cook. License 4 JUL 1857. Married 5 JUL 1857 by Bushrod W. Nash, of the Union Baptist denomination. [M16a:57-21; R:61; R1:9-8]

Cook, George to Julia Washington (d. 1871 in child birth). GEORGE COOK, farmer, age 22, single, b. Westmoreland Co., son of Austin Cook and [Elizabeth] Ann [Mothershead],[4] to JULIA WASHINGTON. age 24, single, b. Westmoreland Co., daughter of Samuel and Maria* Washington. Signed George [his X mark] Cook, wit. J.H. Sisson. License 26 FEB 1870. Married 27 FEB 1870 by Robert N. Reamy. [DR:19-4 *gives mother as Elizabeth Washington; M18; R:98; R1:42-8]

Cook, George to Lucy Cook. GEORGE COOK, laborer, age 22, widowed, b. Westmoreland Co., son of Austin Cook and [Elizabeth] Ann [Mothershead], *q.v.*, to LUCY COOK, age 22, single, b. Westmoreland Co., daughter of Stewart Cook and Eliza Hinson, *q.v.* Signed George [his X mark] Cook, wit. W.S. McKenney. License 22 MAR 1871. Married 26 MAR 1871 by Robert N. Reamy. [M18; R:102; R1:46-11]

Cook, James to Charlotte Green. JAMES COOK, farmer, age about 21, single, b. upper dist. of Westmoreland Co., son of Stewart Cook and Eliza [Hinson] his wife, *q.v.*, to CHARLOTTE GREEN, age about 20, single, b. Westmoreland Co., daughter of White Green and Susan his wife.[5] License 27 DEC 1855. Married 27 DEC 1855 at William Weaver's by John Pullen, M.G. [M16:55-28; R:51; R1:4-9]

Cook, John Lewis to Charlotte Oliff (d. 1874). JOHN LEWIS COOK, farmer, age 26, single, b. Westmoreland Co., son of James S. and Eliza Cook, to CHARLOTTE OLIFF, age 17, single, b. Washington, D.C., daughter of Rodham P. [Porter] and [Lucinda] Oliff. License 9 JAN 1867. Married 10 JAN 1867 at the residence of Rhodam P. Oliff by R.N. Reamy. [DR:32-3; M18; R:85; R1:26-16]

Cooke, Samuel to Mrs. Julia Ann Jennings. SAMUEL COOKE, farmer, age 49, widower, b. Westmoreland Co., son of James and Sally Cooke, to JULIA ANN JENNINGS, age 38, widow, b.

---

[1] Steward Cooke and Eliza Hinson were married by bond 25 APR 1833 in Westmoreland Co., with Meredith Lucas, security.
[2] Henry Rose and Maholy Jones [sic] were married 6 APR 1831 in King George Co.
[3] Samuel Cook and Maria Dekins, daughter of James Dekins [sic], were married by bond 2 NOV 1830 in Westmoreland Co., with Meredith Lucas, security.
[4] Austin Cooke and Elizabeth Ann Mothershead were married by bond 2 SEP 1833 in Westmoreland Co., with William L. Mothershead, security.
[5] Whiting Green and Susannah Ryls were married by bond in MAY 1816 in Westmoreland Co., with Silas Short, security.

Richmond Co., daughter of John [Reddon] and Nancy. License 8 JUL 1854. Married 9 JUL 1854 at Samuel Cooke's by John Pullen, M.G. [M15:54-6; R:43; R1:2]

Cook, William Henry to Eliza Ann Cook. WILLIAM HENRY COOK, farmer, age 27, single, b. Westmoreland Co., son of John and Ann Cook, to ELIZA ANN COOK, age 25, single, b. Westmoreland Co., daughter of William S. and Eliza Cook. License 9 SEP 1867. Married 12 SEP 1867 at the residence of Henry Edmons [sic] by R.N. Reamy. [M18; R:87; R1:29-6]

Cookman, Ezekiel Judson (1842-1926), served in Co. E, 37th Va. Reg. and Co. C, 40th Va. Inf., C.S.A., to Fannie Chinn Cralle (1835-1885).[1] EZEKIEL JUDSON COOKMAN, mechanic, age 25, single, b. and res. Northumberland Co., son of Jeremiah Cookman and Elizabeth [Jane Headley],[2] to FANNIE CHINN CRALLE, age 24, single, b. Northumberland Co., daughter of [Darius] Griffin Cralle [1801-1848] and Mariah G. [Gatewood Gordon] [1805-1873]. License 30 APR 1868. Married 30 APR 1868 by R.N. Reamy. [DR:71-6; M18; R:91; R1:33-6]

Corbin, Joseph (C) to Elizabeth Reed. JOSEPH CORBIN, farmer, age 24, single, b. Westmoreland Co., son of Fleet and Nancy Corbin, to ELIZABETH REED, age 21, single, b. Westmoreland Co., daughter of Clarissa Reed, father unknown. Consent 15 FEB 1861 by bride Elizabeth [her X mark] Reid, wit. Robert [his X mark] Newman. License 12 FEB 1861. Married 17 FEB 1861. [M17:61-5; R:77]

Corbin, Simeon to Maria Jenkins. SIMEON CORBIN, laborer, age 22, single, b. Westmoreland Co., son of [Fleet] and Nancy Corbin, to MARIA JENKINS, age 22, single, b. Westmoreland Co., daughter of Ann Thompson. Signed Simeon [his X mark] Corbin, wit. J.H. Sisson. Consent 10 MAY 1860 by mother of bride Ann [her X mark] Thomson, also signed Maria [her X mark] Jenkins, wit. George Cairey. License 17 MAY 1860. Married 20 MAY 1860. [M17:60-24 and 24a; R:74 incorrectly has Ann Jenkins]

Costenbader, Robert Oscar (1858-1918),[3] to Lucy Ella Hall. ROBERT OSCAR COSTENBADER, laborer, age 20, single, b. Westmoreland Co., son of William H. [Henry] Costenbader [1836-1903][4] and Ira Ann [Daughtry] [d. 1867], to LUCY ELLA HALL, age 18, single, b. Westmoreland Co., daughter of William H. Hall and Lucinda [E. Gutridge], *q.v.* License 19 DEC 1878. Married 24 DEC 1878 at Potomac Mills by F.W. Claybrook. [M19; R:127; R1:76-2; WP]

Costenbader, William Henry (1836-1903), served in Co. E, 55th Va. Inf., C.S.A., second[5] to Emuella "Ella" Jane Pitts (1850-1898).[6] WILLIAM HENRY COSTENBADER, millwright, age 34, widowed, b. Pennsylvania, son of Henry and Caroline Costenbader, to EMUELLA JANE PITTS, age 18, single, b. Essex Co., daughter of Larkin Pitts [d. 1868] and Martha [Ingram], *q.v.* License 11 DEC 1867. Married 12 DEC 1867 at the residence of Larkin Pitts by Thomas E. Locke, Rector of St. Peter's Church, Washington Parish. [DR:15-48; M18; R:88; R1:30-5; WP]

---

[1] Ezekiel J. Cookman and his first wife Fannie were buried at Gibeon Baptist Church, Village, Va.
[2] Jeremiah Cookman and Elizabeth J. Headley were married by bond 13 JAN 1834 in Northumberland Co., with Benjamin Dawson, security.
[3] Robert O. Costenbader was buried at Popes Creek Baptist Church, Baynesville, Va.
[4] William H. Costenbader, who served in Co. E, 55th Va. Inf., C.S.A., was buried at St. Peter's Cemetery, Oak Grove, Va.
[5] DR:14-50, entry for I.A. Costenbader, wife of W.H. Costenbader, d. 4 JUL 1867 in childbirth, age 33.
[6] Deeds & Wills No. 46, pp. 144, 149. William H. Costenbader made a homestead claim in 1886. He was buried at Oak Grove Cemetery, Oak Grove, Va. William and his wife Ella were buried in St. Peter's Cemetery, Oak Grove, Va. NN:22 OCT 1897 [sic], p. 2, announces the death of Mrs. E.J. Costenbader.

Courtney, Addison to Catharine Yeatman. ADDISON[1] COURTNEY, farmer, age 21, single, b. Richmond Co., son of Leonard Courtney and Mary [Alderson],[2] to CATHARINE YEATMAN, age 23, single, b. Westmoreland Co., daughter of Mollie [Patty] Yeatman [sic], father's name unknown. License 1 DEC 1858. Married 2 DEC 1858 by James A. Weaver. [M16a:58-33; R:66; R1:15-2]

Courtney, Bushrod English (1835-1900),[3] served Co. K, 40th Va. Inf. and Co. C, and 9th Va. Cav., C.S.A., to Georgianna Unruh. BUSHROD E. COURTNEY, farmer and merchant, 23, single, b. Westmoreland Co., son of William J. Courtney [d. 1869 of dropsy] and Elizabeth B. [Lamkin],[4] to GEORGIANNA UNRUH, age 18, single, b. Alexandria, Va., res. Kinsale, Va., daughter of Charles Benner and Susan Unruh. License 30 NOV 1858. Married 1 DEC 1858 in Yeocomico Church by T. Grayson Dashiell, clergyman. [DR:17-7[5]; M16a:58-31 and 31a; R:66; R1:13-1; SC]

Courtney, David Crenshaw, served in Co. C, 9th Va. Cav., C.S.A., to Flora Ann Lewis. DAVID CRENSHAW COURTNEY, farmer, age 49, widowed, b. Westmoreland Co., son of William J. Crenshaw and Nancy [Crenshaw],[6] to FLORA ANN LEWIS, age 45, single, b. Westmoreland Co., daughter of George W. and Polly Lewis. License 11 AUG 1873. Married 13 AUG 1873 by R.J. Sanford. [M19; R:109; R1:54-7]

Courtney, Henry to Malinda Burrell. HENRY COURTNEY, farmer, age 24, single, b. Richmond Co., son of Henry and Maria Courtney, to MALINDA BURRELL, age 21, single, b. Richmond Co., daughter of Thomas and Julia Burrell. Signed Henry [his X mark] Courtney, wit. J.W. Hutt. License 28 DEC 1875. Married 30 DEC 1875 by F.B. Beale. [M19; R:117; R1:63-6]

Courtney, James Andrew (1853-1909),[7] first to Harriet Sophronia Wilson (d. 1893 of cholera). JAMES ANDREW COURTNEY, farmer, age 25, single, b. Richmond Co., son of William and Mary Ann Courtney, to HARRIET SOPHRONIA WILSON, age 25, single, b. Westmoreland Co., daughter of Robert Wilson and Fanny [Bennett].[8] License 10 JAN 1877. Married 11 JAN 1877 by G.H. Northam. [DR:94-27; M19; R:121; R1:68-9]

Courtney, James C. (d. 1871 of dropsy), farmer, to Mary Murphy. License 20 OCT 1853. Married 25 OCT 1853 by William N. Ward. [DR:23-1; M15:53-18; R:33]

Courtney, Jeremiah to Mrs. Cynthia Ann Pope Courtney, widow of Zachariah Courtney, *q.v.* JEREMIAH COURTNEY, carpenter and farmer, age 57, widowed, b. Westmoreland Co., son of Benjamin Courtney and Mary [Smith],[9] to CYNTHIA ANN COURTNEY, age 29, widow, b. Westmoreland Co., daughter of John Pope and Susan [McCluskey].[10] License 19 NOV 1864. Married 24 NOV 1864 at Mrs. Susan Pope's by William F. Bain. [M17a:64-14; R:80; R1:21-6]

---

[1] Another copy at 58-33a gives groom's name as Anderson Courtney, and varies with names of parents.
[2] Leonard Courtney and Mary Alderson were married by bond 4 NOV 1812 in Richmond Co., with Thomas S. Davis, security.
[3] B.E. Courtney was buried at Yeocomico Episcopal Church, Tucker Hill, Va.
[4] William J. Courtney and Elizabeth B. Lamkin [widow of Benedict Lamkin] were married by bond 3 JUL 1834 in Westmoreland Co., with John English, security. Note: Elizabeth B. English was married by bond 19 MAY 1825 to Benedict Lamkin.
[5] DR:17-7, entry for Wm. J. Courtney, d. 7 SEP 1869 of dropsy, age 83, farmer, notes his parents as Benjamin and Nancy Courtney.
[6] William Courtney and Nancy Crenshaw were married by bond 22 MAR 1813 in Westmoreland Co., wit. John Crenshaw.
[7] James A. Courtney and his second wife Virginia Emeline Atkins were buried at Gibeon Baptist Church, Village, Va.
[8] Robert Wilson and Frances Bennett were married by bond 10 JAN 1850 in Westmoreland Co., with James Johnson, security.
[9] Benjamin Courtney and Mary Smith were married by bond 27 AUG 1801 inn Westmoreland Co., wit. Jeremiah Jeffries.
[10] John Pope and Susan McCluskey were married by bond 11 JUN 1834 in Westmoreland Co., with James K. Johnson, security.

Courtney, John Richard to Lucy Ann Brann. JOHN RICHARD COURTNEY, farmer, age 40, widower, b. Westmoreland Co., son of Malachi Courtney [d. 1869 of heart disease] and Mary [Brown],[1] to LUCY ANN BRANN, age 30, single, b. Westmoreland Co., daughter of William Brann and Fanny [Frances Y. McKenney].[2] Signed by John R. [his X mark] Courtney, wit. Wm. S. McKenney. License 28 OCT 1872. Married 31 OCT 1872 by R.J. Sanford. [DR:17-8; M19; R:106; R1:51-6]

Courtney, John Robert (1854-1924),[3] farmer, served in Co. A, 55th Va. Vol. Inf., C.S.A., first to Margaret E. Brown (d. 1866 of palpitation of heart), daughter of James and Betsey Brown. License 10 NOV 1851. Married 12 NOV 1851 by George Northam, L.M.G. [DR:11-8; M15:51-20; R:11]

Courtney, Thomas to Mary Newman. THOMAS COURTNEY, farmer, age 32, single, b. Richmond Co., son of Leonard Courtney and Mary [Alderson], *q.v.*, to MARY NEWMAN, age 30, single, b. Westmoreland Co., daughter of Jane [Newman], father unknown. Signed Thomas [his X mark] Courtney, wit. John Goodridge. Consent by bride. License 1 OCT 1860. Married 2 OCT 1860. [M17:60-32 and 32a; R:74]

Courtney, Zachariah (d. by 1864), to Cynthia Ann Pope. ZACHARIAH COURTNEY, farmer, age 48, single, b. Westmoreland Co., son of Benjamin Courtney and Mary [Smith], *q.v.*, to SCYNTHIA ANN POPE [sic], age 21, single, b. Westmoreland Co., daughter of John Pope and Susan [McCluskey], *q.v.* License 19 OCT 1854. Married 19 OCT 1854 at the residence of John Dunnahaw by H.P.F King, M.G. [M15:54-12; R:45; R1:2]

Cox, Abraham F., Dr. (d. 1902 in Alexandria, Va.),[4] physician, served in Co. C, 9th Va. Cav., C.S.A., to Virginia C. Cox. ABRAHAM F. COX, teacher, age 24, single, b. Fredericksburg, Va., son of Peter and Jane Cox, to VIRGINIA C. COX, age 30, single, b. Westmoreland Co., daughter of James Cox and Hannah [Jackson].[5] License 13 DEC 1856. Married 15 DEC 1856 at the residence of John L. Bailey. [M16a:56-33; R:57; R1:7-7]

Crabb, Cyrus Edwin to Mrs. Josepha J. Crabb Edwards (1828-1874),[6] widow of William Edwards, *q.v.* CYRUS E. CRABB, boot maker, age 28, single, b. Westmoreland Co., son of William P. Crabb and Eliza [Ann Yeatman][7] [d. 1871 of consumption], to JOSEPHA J. EDWARDS, age 28, widow, b. Westmoreland Co., daughter of William and Sally Crabb [sic]. License 25 AUG 1856. Married 27 AUG 1856 at her residence by H.P.F. King, minister of the M.E. Church. [DR:24-18 gives daughter of Henry and A. Yeatman; M16a:56-24; R:55; R1:6-8]

Crabb, George Henry (1846-1924),[8] served in the 43rd Va. Cav., C.S.A., to Mary Lillian Courtney (1854-1915).[9] GEORGE HENRY CRABB, farmer, age 28, single, b. Westmoreland Co., son of Benedict P. Crabb and Eliza Ann [Smith] [d. 1883], to MARY LILLIAN COURTNEY, age 22, single,

---

[1] Malachi Courtney and Mary Brown were married by bond 15 AUG 1826 in Westmoreland Co., with William Courtney, security.
[2] William Courtney and Frances Y. McKenney were married by bond 26 FEB 1839 in Westmoreland Co., with Joseph McKenney, security.
[3] John R. Courtney was buried at Exol Church, Contra, King & Queen Co., Va.
[4] Dr. Abraham F. Cox was buried in St. Paul's Episcopal Church Cemetery, in Alexandria, Va. I erroneously typed and indexed him as Abraham F. Fox in my *Tombstone Inscriptions of Alexandria, Virginia, Volume 5*, p. 348.
[5] James Cox and Hannah Jackson were married by bond 12 JUN 1804 in Westmoreland Co., with John Watt, security.
[6] Josepha J. Crabb was buried at Nomini Baptist Church, Montross, Va.
[7] William P. Crabb and Eliza Ann Yeatman, daughter of Ann H. Yeatman, were married by bond 7 NOV 1827 in Westmoreland Co., with G.G. Mothershead, security.
[8] Buried with marker George Henry Crabbe, at Lebanon United Methodist Church, Templeman, Va.
[9] Mary Lillian Courtney Crabb was buried at Lebanon United Methodist Church, Templeman, Va.

b. Westmoreland Co., daughter of James R. Courtney and Mary [R. Sutton].[1] License 23 MAY 1876. Married 24 MAY 1876 at the residence of Mr. James Courtney by John [W.] White. [DR:57-24[2]; M19; R:118; R1:65-7]

Crabb, William M.M. (d. 1881), to Elizabeth S. Sturman. License 27 OCT 1852. Married 7 NOV 1852 by Ro. Y. Henley. [M15:52-26; NN; R:23]

Cralle, Fielding (C) to Gracy Tibbs. FIELDING CRALLE, farmer, age 22, single, b. Westmoreland Co., son of Lewis and Sarah Cralle, to GRACY TIBBS, age 23, single, b. Westmoreland Co., daughter of Robert and Maria Tibbs. License 8 JAN 1877. Married 11 JAN 1877 at Washington Crawley's house by Thomas T. Johnson. [M19; R:121; R1:68-7]

Cramp (also see Crump)

Cramp, Michael, of Washington, D.C., to Mary Ann Ashton. MICHAEL CRAMP, fisherman, age 35, single, b. Kensington, Pa., son of John and Fanny Cramp, to MARY ANN ASHTON, age 20, single, b. King George Co., daughter of Alexander and Louisa Ashton. License 20 DEC 1855. Married 24 DEC 1855 at *Spring Grove* [the residence of Alexander Ashton] by J.W. Chesley, minister of the Prot. Epis. Church. [M16:55-27; R:51; R1:4-11; SP; WP]

Crawley [or Cralle], Kenner to Letitia Armstrong. KENNER CRAWLEY, sailor, age 23, single, b. Westmoreland Co., son of Lewis and Sarah Crawley, to LETITIA ARMSTRONG, age 18, single, b. Westmoreland Co., daughter of Scipio and Julia Armstrong. Signed Kenner [his X mark] Crawley, wit. W.S. McKenney. License 15 JUL 1873. Married 17 JUL 1873 at Julia Armstrong's by R.J. Sanford. [M19; R:109; R1:54-5]

Crocker, Joseph Henry to Emma Clara Bailey. JOSEPH HENRY CROCKER, farmer, age 22, single, b. Kennebec Co., Me., son of L. and M.E. Crocker, to EMMA CLARA BAILEY, age 21, single, b. Westmoreland Co., daughter of James W. [Warren] Bailey and Ella V. [Vernillia Carpenter], *q.v.* License 28 JUN 1880. Married 28 JUN 1880 by R.N. Reamy. [M20; R:134; R1:83-5]

Crocket, David to Linda Parlor. DAVID CROCKET, laborer, age 27, single, b. Westmoreland Co., son of William and Ellen Crocket, to LINDA PARLOR, age 20, single, Richmond Co., daughter of Thomas and Livina Parlor. Signed David [his X mark] Crocket, wit. W.S. McKenney. License 26 DEC 1872. Married 26 DEC 1872 at *Crook House* by D.M. Wharton. [M19; R:107; R1:52-10 has Davy Crocket]

Crowell, Luther Peck to Eveline Rosetta Harvey. LUTHER PECK CROWELL, teacher, age 24, single, b. Chautaugua Co., N.Y., son of Solomon Crowell and Anna Peck, to EVELINE ROSETTA HARVEY, age 36, single, b. Westmoreland Co., daughter of John Harvey and Lucy Jett. License 20 SEP 1856. Married 21 SEP 1856 at Mrs. Mary J. Stewart's by John G. Rowe, M.G. [M16a:56-27; R:57; R1:7-1]

[1] James R. Courtney and Mary R. Sutton were married by 6 JAN 1848 in Westmoreland Co., with R.W. Yeatman, security.
[2] DR:57-24, entry for Eliza A. Crabbe, d. 20 SEP 1883 in Montross, Va. of old age, age 69, widow, daughter of Henry and Sallie Smith, mother of George H. Crabbe.

Croxton, James Carter (1844-1915), served in Co. A, 15th Va. Inf., C.S.A., to Emily Demaris Lamkin (1836-1911).[1] JAMES CARTER CROXTON, farmer, age 21, single, b. Westmoreland Co., son of Carter Croxton [1802-1858][2] and Mary Ann [Clarkson] [1814-1887],[3] to EMILY DEMARIS LAMKIN, age 17, single, b. Westmoreland Co., daughter of Lewis A.L. Lamkin and Margaret J. [Jacques].[4] License 25 SEP 1865. Planned marriage 27 SEP 1865. [R:81; R1:22-4 no return]

Crump (also see Cramp)

Crump, Samuel (C) to Mrs. Mary Taylor McHart. SAMUEL CRUMP, farmer, age 40, widower, b. Norfolk, Va., son of Thomas and Sally Crump, to MARY McHART, age 35, widow, b. Westmoreland Co., daughter of Nelson and Polly Taylor. License 18 JUL 1871. Married 20 JUL 1871 by John C. Smith. [M18; R:102; R1:47-2]

Crutchfield, Allen to Mrs. Charlotte Johnson Criss. ALLEN CRUTCHFIELD, farmer, age 20, single, b. Spotsylvania Co., son of Alfred and Charlotte Crutchfield, to CHARLOTT CRISS [sic], age 25, widow, b. Westmoreland Co., daughter of John and Maria Johnson. Signed Allen [his X mark] Crutchfield. License 24 NOV 1869. Married 25 NOV 1869 by G.W. Beale. [M18; R:96; R1:39-14]

Crutchfield, Lewis (C) to Jane Newman. LEWIS CRUTCHFIELD, farmer, age 21, single, b. Spotsylvania Co., son of Alfred and Charlotte Crutchfield, to JANE NEWMAN, age 22, single, b. King George Co., daughter of Martha Newman. Signed Lewis [his X mark] Crutchfield, wit. J.W. Hutt. License 2 MAR 1870. Married 3 MAR 1870 by J.H. Davis. [M18; R:98; R1:42-9]

Curley, Bowling (d. 1884 of lung disease), to Mrs. Susan A. Miller Young. BOLDING CURLEY [sic], farmer, age 47, widowed, b. King George Co., son of John ["Jack"] and Hetty Curley, to SUSAN A. YOUNG, age 25, widow, b. Westmoreland Co., daughter of Richard Miller. License 25 SEP 1862. Married 26 SEP 1862 at Chilton's Crossroads by H.P.F. King. [DR:62-128; M17:62-13; R:78; R1:19-5]

Curley, James (C) to Fenton Ashton. JAMES CURLEY, farmer, age 25, single, b. Amelia Co., daughter of Ashley and Louisa Curley, to FENTON ASHTON, age 19, single, b. Westmoreland Co., daughter of Kelsick Ashton and Mary [Tate].[5] License 18 SEP 1877. Married 18 SEP 1877 at Little Zion Church by Emanuel Watts, pastor, Little Zion Church. [M19; R:123; R1:70-12]

Curry, James (C) to Mary Elizabeth Dean. JAMES CURRY, laborer, age 21, single, b. Richmond Co., son of Lucas and Dinah Curry, to MARY ELIZABETH DEAN, age 19, single, b. Westmoreland Co., daughter of Winny Ann Dean, father unknown. License 20 JAN 1880. Married 22 JAN 1880 at *Plainfield* by Thomas T. Johnson. [M20; R:131; R1:80-14]

Curry, Thomas (C) to Adline Williams. THOMAS CURRY, farmer, age 30, single, b. Richmond Co., son of James and Sally Curry, to ADLIAN WILLIAMS, age 25, single, b. Alabama, daughter of

---

[1] James C. Croxton and wife Emily D., and his parents, were buried in the Croxton Family Cemetery, located on *Clear Spring Farm*, off of Route 612 near Lyells, Va. Also, see Deeds & Wills No. 4, p. 316, will of Elizabeth C. Wilson who requests burial in a walnut coffin at *Clear Spring*, and names brothers R.A. Croxton and William H. Croxton.
[2] Also see Deeds & Wills 45, p. 177 for division of property to brothers James C. Croxton and Richard Albert Croxton.
[3] Carter Croxton, Jr. and Mary Ann Clarkson were married by bond 22 DEC 1830 in Essex Co., with George Wright, security.
[4] Lewis A. Lamkin and Margarett S. Jaques were married by bond 15 APR 1839 in Northumberland Co., with M.B. Cralle, security.
[5] Kelsick Ashton and Mary Tate were married by bond 10 DEC 1845 in Westmoreland Co., with Ludwell Ashton, security.

Littleton and Tempsy Williams. Signed Thos. [his X mark] Curry, wit. J.W. Hutt. License 30 NOV 1869. Married 2 DEC 1869 by John C. Smith. [M18; R:96; R1:40-19]

D

Dade, Richard H. to Nancy Dickins. License 7 APR 1853. Married 26 APR 1853 by John McDaniel. [M15:53-13, R:29]

Daiger, Charles Edward (b. 1852, d. 1931 of chronic nephritis), to Mary Jane Allen (1858-1929).[1] CHARLES EDWARD DAIGER, mechanic, age 27, single, b. Baltimore City, Md., son of Joseph and Sabina Daiger, to MARY JANE ALLEN, age 21, single, b. Westmoreland Co., daughter of W.H. and Frances J. Allen. License 4 JUN 1879. Married 5 JUN 1879 at Carmel Church by W.W. Walker. [DC; M20; R:129; R1:77-14]

Dameron, Charles L. (b. 1847, d. 1926 of pneumonia), to Calvina Garner (1855-1936).[2] CHARLES L. DAMERON, farmer, age 24, single, b. Richmond Co., son of John [C.] Dameron and Lucy [Jane Hall],[3] to CARROLL GARNER [sic], age 17, single, b. Westmoreland Co., daughter of Vincent M. [Milton] Garner and Margaret [L. Dement].[4] Signed Charles L. [his X mark] Dameron. License 12 JAN 1872. Married 21 JAN 1872 at Ge[n]. Beale's by G.W. Beale, M.G. [DC; M19; R:104; R1:49-8]

Dameron, Dandridge Champin (d. b 1876), to Sarah Frances Douglas. DANDRIDGE CHAMPIN DAMERON, farmer, age 24, single, b. Westmoreland Co., son of Robert and Lucy Dameron, to SARAH FRANCIS DOUGLAS, age 19, single, b. Westmoreland Co., daughter of Lemuel Douglas and Sarah [Palmer] [sic].[5] Signed Dandridge C. [his X mark] Dameron, wit. Wm. S. McKenney. License 5 JAN 1875. Married 7 JAN 1875 at *Willis Grove* by Frank B. Beale. [M19; R:114; R1:60-10]

Dameron, John (b. 1851, d. 1921 of mycarditis), and Mrs. Sarah Frances Douglas Dameron, widow of Dandridge Champin Dameron, *q.v.* JOHN DAMERON, farmer, age 25, single, b. Richmond Co., son of John [C.] Dameron and Lucy [Jane Hall], *q.v.*, and SARAH DAMERON, age 23, widow, b. Westmoreland Co., daughter of Lemuel Douglas and Sarah [Palmer], *q.v.* License 18 DEC 1876. Married 26 DEC 1876 at *Sherland* by F.B. Beale. [DC; M19; R:120; R1:67-8]

Dameron, Lucius Edward to Ella E. Bramble (1853-1928).[6] LUCIUS EDWARD DAMERON, farmer, age 22, single, b. Richmond Co., son of John [C.] Dameron and Lucy [Jane Hall], *q.v.*, to ELLA E. BRAMBEL [sic], age 21, single, b. Northumberland Co., daughter of Thomas [H.] [Bramble] and Sallie [Snow].[7] License 26 DEC 1874. Married 29 DEC 1874 at Mr. Carey's by Frank B. Beale. [M19; R:114; R1:60-4]

Dameron, Luke to Frances A. Johnson. License 24 MAR 1852. Married 25 MAR 1852 by Wm. N. Ward. [M15:52-13; R:19]

---

[1] Charles E. Daiger and his wife Mary Jane were buried at Carmel United Methodist Church, Kinsale, Va.
[2] Charles L. Dameron and his wife Calvina were buried at Carmel United Methodist Church, Kinsale, Va.
[3] John C. Dameron, Jr. and Lucy Jane Hall were married 12 JAN 1842 in Richmond Co. by Rev. William N. Ward.
[4] Vincent M. Garner and Margaret L. Dement were married by bond 13 MAY 1848 in Westmoreland Co., with Peter L. Self, security.
[5] Lemuel Douglass and Sarah Palmer were married by bond 30 DEC 1841 in Westmoreland Co., with Joseph H. Moone, security.
[6] Lucius and Ella Dameron were buried at Carmel United Methodist Church, Kinsale, Va.
[7] Thomas H. Bramble and Sally Snow were married by bond 10 JUN 1839 in Northumberland Co., with James A. Holt, security.

Dameron, Luke to Mrs. Eliza Jane Gaskins Johnson, widow of John Johnson, *q.v.* LUKE DAMERON, farmer, age 45, widowed, b. Westmoreland Co., son of John and Susan Dameron, to ELIZA JOHNSON, age 25, widow, b. Westmoreland Co., daughter of Patrick Gaskins and Sally [Sarah Gaskins].[1] License 20 AUG 1867. Married 21 AUG 1867 at Ebenezer Church by F.A. Davis. [M18; R:87; R1:29-5]

Dameron, Robert to Catharine Ann Gregory. ROBERT DAMERON, farmer, age 22, single, b. Westmoreland Co., son of Robert and Lucy Dameron, to CATHARINE ANN GREGORY, age 23, widow, b. Westmoreland Co., parents unknown. License 29 JAN 1867. Planned marriage 31 JAN 1867. [R:86; R1:27-6 no return]

Dameron, Robert H. (d. 1871 of congestive chill), to Sarah "Sally" Housen (d. 1871 in child bed). ROBERT H. DAMERON, farmer, age 46, widowed, b. Northumberland Co., son of John and Susan Dameron, to SALLY HOWSEN [sic], age 20, single, b. Westmoreland Co., daughter of Stewart [and Sallie] Housen. License 27 JAN 1862. Married 29 JAN 1862 at Fleet Anton's house by W.W. Walker. [DR:19-11, 23-8; M17:62-7; R:78; R1:18-13]

Dameron, Robert Henry to Rebecca Garner. ROBERT HENRY DAMERON, farmer, age 21, single, b. Richmond Co., son of John [C.] Dameron and Lucy [Jane Hall], *q.v.*, to REBECCA GARNER, age 20, single, b. Westmoreland Co., daughter of Vincent M. [Milton] Garner and Margaret [L. Dement], *q.v.* Robert Henry [his X mark] Dameron, wit. W.S. McKenney. License 12 JAN 1872. Married 17 JAN 1872 at Ge[n]. Beale's by G.W. Beale, minister. [M19; R:104]

Darnaby, George Edward to Sarah Frances Reed (C) (d. 1927 of nephritis). GEORGE EDWARD DARNABY, shoemaker and farmer, age 22, single, b. Westmoreland Co., son of Mary Blue alias Darnaby, father unknown, to SARAH FRANCES REED, age 18, single, b. Westmoreland Co., daughter of James Reed and Rose [Taylor]. License 17 MAR 1877. Married 18 MAR 1877 at *Atwillton* by Thomas G. Nevitt. [DC; M19; R:122 has George Edwin Darnaby; R1:69-9]

Davis, Charles Willis to Lucy Fenton Mothershead. CHARLES WILLIS DAVIS, farmer, age 25, single, b. Westmoreland Co., son of Samuel Davis and Ann [Quisenbury],[2] to LUCY FENTON MOTHERSHEAD, age 20, single, b. Westmoreland Co., daughter of Charles C. Mothershead [d. testate 1882] and Elizabeth [H.] [Dozier].[3] License 6 JAN 1869. Married 7 JAN 1869 by G.H. Northam. [M18; R:94; R1:37-8]

Davis, George William (1856-1923), to Mary Jane Stephens (b. 1851, d. 1898 at Cole's Point).[4] GEORGE WILLIAM DAVIS, farmer, age 21, single, b. Alexandria, Va., son of Henderson and Jane Davis, to MARY JANE STEVENS [sic], age 16, single, b. Westmoreland Co., daughter of Jerry and Ann Stephens [sic]. Signed George W. [his X mark] Davis, wit. J.H. Sisson. License 20 OCT 1870. Married 21 OCT 1870 at the residence of Jerry Stephens by R.J. Sanford. [M18; NN; R:100; R1:44-3]

---

[1] Patrick Gaskins and Sarah Gaskins were married by bond 14 JAN 1842 in Westmoreland Co., with William Bailey, security.
[2] Samuel Davis and Ann Quisenbury were married by bond 18 MAR 1835 in Westmoreland Co., with Nicholas Quisenbury, security.
[3] Charles C. Mothershead and Elizabeth Dozier were married by bond 21 DEC 1831 in Westmoreland Co., with William Johnson, security.
[4] George W. Davis and his wife Mary Jane were buried at St. Paul's Catholic Church, Hague, Va.

Davis, John to Eliza J. Ferguson. JOHN DAVIS, farmer, age 24, single, b. Richmond Co., son of John Davis and Sarah his wife, to ELIZA J. FERGUSON, age 24, single, b. Richmond Co., daughter of James T. Ferguson and Eliza his wife. License 2 JAN 1855. Married 4 JAN 1855 at Ebenezer [United] Methodist Church by Wm. N. Ward, M.G. [M16:55-3; R:47; R1:10-3]

Davis, John to Hannah Sanford. JOHN DAVIS, farmer, age 20, single, b. Richmond Co., son of William and Sally Davis, to HANNAH SANFORD, age 19, single, b. Westmoreland Co., daughter of Lawrence [M.] Sanford and Mary Jane [Beale].[1] Signed John [his X mark] Davis, wit. Wm. S. McKenney. License 6 NOV 1875. Married 7 NOV 1875 at the residence of Lawrence Sanford by R.J. Sanford. [M19; R:116; R1:62-3]

Davis, John H. to Nancy Killman. License 2 JUL 1853. [R:31 no return]

Davis, John Henry to Harriet J. Killman. JOHN HENRY DAVIS, tailor, age 37, widowed, b. Westmoreland Co., son of Henry and Sarah Davis, to HARRIET J. KILLMAN, age 22, single, b. Westmoreland Co., daughter of Martin Killman and Fanny [Briant].[2] License 30 DEC 1861. Married 1 JAN 1862 at the residence of Martin Killman by H.P.F. King. [M17:62-1; R:77; R1:18-8]

Davis, John Thomas to Mrs. Eliza Jane Wroe Short. JOHN THOMAS DAVIS, farmer, age 21, single, b. Fairfax Co., son of Henson and Jane Davis, to ELIZA JANE SHORT, age 22, widow, b. Westmoreland Co., daughter of John Wroe. License 2 OCT 1868. Married 4 OCT 1868 by R.J. Sanford. [M18; R:92; R1:35-6]

Davis, John W. to Sarah Ann Annadale. JOHN W. DAVIS, farmer, age 27, single, b. Westmoreland Co., son of Samuel Davis and Ann [Quisenbury], *q.v.*, to SARAH ANN ANNADALE, age 26, single, b. Westmoreland Co., daughter of Thomas and Nancy Annadale. License 24 MAY 1855. Married 27 MAY 1855 by H.P.F. King. [M16:55-12; R:49; R1:3-8]

Davis, John William (d. by 1869), to Frances Ann Beddo. JOHN WILLIAM DAVIS, farmer, age 38, widowed, b. Westmoreland Co., son of Samuel and Nancy Davis, to FRANCES BEDDO, age 19, single, b. Westmoreland Co., daughter of Hezekiah and Ann Beddo. License 28 DEC 1863. Married 30 DEC 1863 at John W. Davis's by John Pullen. [M17:63-10; R:80; R1:20-8]

Davis, Joseph William Luttrell, second[3] to Elender Jane Scott (d. 1886 of consumption). JOSEPH WILLIAM LUTTRELL DAVIS, shoemaker, age 58, widower, b. Westmoreland Co., son of Samuel and Frances Davis, to ELENDER JANE SCOTT, age 34, single, b. Westmoreland Co., daughter of George and Anne Scott. License 14 JUN 1876. Married 15 JUN 1876 at Mr. Howell's by J.H. Davis. [DR:68-17, 71-19 for 1887; M19; R:119; R1:65-11]

Davis, Lewis Weston (d. 1923), to Catharine Ann Mothershead. LEWIS WESTON DAVIS, farmer, age 24, single, b. Westmoreland Co., son of Samuel Davis and Ann [Quisenbury], *q.v.*, to CATHARINE ANN MOTHERSHEAD, age 26, single, b. Westmoreland Co., daughter of Charles C. Mothershead and Betsey E. [Elizabeth Dozier], *q.v.* Signed Lewis W. [his X mark] Davis, wit. W.S.

---

[1] Lawrence M. Sanford and Mary J. Beale, daughter of William L. Beale, were married by bond 14 MAR 1843 in Westmoreland Co., with Willis Garner, security.
[2] Martin Killmon, Jr. and Fanny Briant, daughter of Frances Briant, were married by bond 11 MAY 1825 in Westmoreland Co., with James Briant, security.
[3] DR:19-10, entry for Ann E. Davis, d. 7 DEC 1871 of pneumonia, age 45, daughter of James and Hanna Sanford, wife of Joseph W.L. Davis.

McKenney. License 3 OCT 1872. Married 3 OCT 1872 at Providence Church by Walter C. Taylor. [M19; R:106; R1:51-2]

Davis, Richard H. to Mrs. Ann Beddoe. RITCHARD H. DAVIS [sic], farming, age about 24, single, b. Westmoreland Co., son of Samuel Davis and Ann his wife, to ANN BEDOWE [sic], age about 33, widow, father not known, mother Elizabeth. License 12 APR 1856. Married 18 APR 1856 at Felishia Nash's by John Pullen, M.G. [M16:56-10; R:55; R1:5-9]

Davis, Samuel Grayson (d. 1888), to Mary Elizabeth "Bettie" Sanford. SAMUEL GRAYSON DAVIS, farmer, age 21, single, b. Westmoreland Co., son of Joseph W.L. Davis and Ann E. [Sanford],[1] to MARY ELIZABETH SANFORD, age 18, single, Northumberland Co., daughter of William and Mary B. Sanford. License 21 FEB 1877. Married 22 FEB 1877 at the residence of John S. Butler by R.J. Sanford. [DR:75-20; M19; R:121; R1:69-3]

Davis, Simon (C) to Mrs. Easter Maluns. SIMON DAVIS, farmer, age 47, single, b. Westmoreland Co., son of Peter and Hannah Davis, to EASTER MALUNS, age 40, widow, b. Northumberland Co., parents unknown. Signed Simon [his X mark] Davis, wit. C.C. Baker. License 8 FEB 1871. Married 9 FEB 1871 by Jerry Graham. [M18; R:101; R1:45-16]

Davis, William (C) to Julia Coventon. WILLIAM DAVIS, farmer, age 45, single, b. Essex Co., son of William Davis and Martha [Bunday],[2] to JULIA COVENTON, age 26, b. Essex Co., daughter of Matilda Coventon [Covington], father unknown. License 28 SEP 1878. Married 29 SEP 1878 at Little Zion Church by Emanuel Watts, pastor. [M19; R:126; R1:75-4]

Davis, William H. to Ann Maria Bispham. WILLIAM H. DAVIS, farmer, age 25, single, b. Richmond Co., son of William and Pegga Davis, to ANN MARIA BISPHAM, age 23, single, b. Richmond Co., daughter of William Bispham and Mary [Asbury].[3] License 24 MAR 1856. Married 27 MAR 1856 at the residence of J.B. Reed by H.P.F. King, minister of the M.E. Church. [M16:56-9; R:53; R1:5-10]

Davis, William J. to Mary Jane Harrison. License 25 JUN 1855. [R:49]

Day, Edwin to Lucy Rice. EDWIN DAY, farmer, age 29, single, b. Westmoreland Co., son of Washington and Easter Day, to LUCY RICE, age 21, single, b. Westmoreland Co., daughter of John Rice. License 10 JAN 1877. Married 11 JAN 1877 by H.H. Fones. [M19; R:121; R1:68-8]

Day, Washington, Sr. (C) to Ellen Homes. WASHINGTON DAY, SR., gardener, age 65, widower, b. Westmoreland Co., son of William and Patty Day, to ELLEN HOMES, age 36, single, b. Westmoreland Co., daughter of Brooks Homes. Signed Washington [his X mark] Day, Sr., wit. W.S. McKenney. License 5 FEB 1874. Married 5 FEB 1874 by John Roy. [M19; R:112; R1:57-9]

Dean, James (C) to Alice Miles. JAMES DEANE [sic], farmer, age 23, single, b. Westmoreland Co., son of James and Easter Dean [sic], to ALICE MILES, age 21, single, b. St. Mary's Co., Md., daughter of Oldham and Margarett Burnett. License 13 AUG 1879. Married 14 AUG 1879 at Zion Church by Charles [his X mark] Rust. [M20; R:129; R1:78-8]

---

[1] Joseph W.L. Davis and Ann E. Sanford were married by bond 20 JAN 1846 in Westmoreland Co., with William Wroe, security.
[2] William Davis and Martha Bunday were married by bond 20 DEC 1830 in Essex Co., wit. James R. Micou.
[3] William Bispham and Mrs. Mary Asbury (widow) were married by bond 19 JUL 1820 in Richmond Co., with Joseph Belfield, security.

Dean, John (C) to Amanda Scott. JOHN DEAN, farmer, age 21, single, b. Westmoreland Co., son of James and Easter Dean, to AMANDA SCOTT, age 22, single, b. Westmoreland Co., daughter of Nathaniel and Rebecca Scott. Signed John [his X mark] Dean. License 16 FEB 1870. Married 17 FEB 1870 by John C. Smith. [M18; R:98; R1:42-4]

Dean, Peter (C) to Eliza Newman. PETER DEAN, farmer, age 25, single, b. Westmoreland Co., son of James and Nancy Dean, to ELIZA NEWMAN, age 30, single, b. Westmoreland Co., daughter of Judy Newman, father unknown. License 11 MAY 1878. Married 16 MAY 1878 at my residence by Rev. William Gaskings. [M19; R:125; R1:73-14]

Deatley, Matthew Walter to Mary Virginia Reed. MATHEW W. DEATLEY [sic], waterman, age 19, single, b. *Laurel Grove*, Westmoreland Co., son of Matthew Deatley and Maria [Mitchell],[1] to MARY VIRGINIA REED, age 20, single, b. near Oak Grove, Westmoreland Co., daughter of James and Amelia F. Reed. License 18 FEB 1857. Married 19 FEB 1857 at *Locust Farm* [the residence of Mrs. Reed] by J.W. Chesley, minister of the Prot. Epis. Church. [M16a:57-6; R:59; R1:8-8; SP]

Deatley, William, served in Co. C, 47th Va. Inf., C.S.A., to Mrs. Susan Dishman White, widow of William White (d. 1856).[2] WILLIAM DEATLEY,[3] farmer, age 30, single, b. Westmoreland Co., son of Meredith and Susan Deatley, to Mrs. SUSAN WHITE, age 38, widow, b. Westmoreland Co., daughter of Jane Dishman. License 25 JAN 1858. Married 28 JAN 1858 at the bride's residence by Thomas E. Locke, Rector of St. Peter's Church, Washington Parish. [M16a:58-5; R:63; R1:11-6; SP; WP]

Deatley, William Berkley (1846-1921), to Mary Medora Jones (1844-1921).[4] Married 6 NOV 1868 at *Peach Hill*, King George Co., by Rev. Thomas E. Locke. [WP]

Delano, Augustine Rice (1851-1912), to Sarah Rebecca English (1854-1943).[5] AUGUSTINE RICE DELANO, farmer, age 22, single, b. Westmoreland Co., son of Augustus [d. testate[6] 1867 of kidney disease] and Mary Delano, to SARAH REBECCA ENGLISH, age 19, single, b. Westmoreland Co., daughter of Samuel W. English and Sarah [Ann Delano].[7] License 8 OCT 1873. Married 9 OCT 1873 at Samuel W. English's by R.J. Sanford. [DR:13-10; M19; R:109; R1:54-9]

Delano, Augustus to Mary Elizabeth Spurlin. AUGUSTUS DELANO, carpenter, age 32, single, b. Westmoreland Co., son of George and Nancy Delano, to MARY ELIZABETH SPURLIN, age 32, single, b. Westmoreland Co., parents unknown. License 28 MAR 1859. Married 31 MAR 1859 by T. Grayson Dashiell, clergyman. [M16a:59-9 and 33; R:68; R1:14-6]

Dickins, John to Sarah F. Tate. JOHN DICKINS, farmer, age 37, widower, b. Westmoreland Co., son of James and Susan Dickins, to SARAH F. TATE, age 22, single, b. Westmoreland Co., daughter of Marshall [d. 1881] and Elizabeth Tate. Signed John [his X mark] Dickins, wit. C.C. Baker. License 30 NOV 1874. Married 4 DEC 1874 by Howard W. Montague, M.G. of Christ. [M19; R:113; R1:59-8; WP]

---

[1] Mathew Deatly and Maria Mitchell were married by bond 29 DEC 1820 in Westmoreland Co., with William Deatly, security.
[2] William White and Susan Dishman were married by bond 14 MAR 1836 in Westmoreland Co., with Samuel Dishman, security.
[3] The surname is sometimes found as DeAtley.
[4] William B. Deatley and his wife Mary M. were buried in the Deatley Family Cemetery, Oak Grove, Va.
[5] Augustus "Gus" Delano and wife Sarah Rebecca were buried at Ebenezer United Methodist Church, Oldhams, Va.
[6] Deeds & Wills No. 37, p. 481, will of Augustus Delano, proved 27 JAN 1868, names son Augustus Rice Delano.
[7] Samuel W. English and Sarah Ann Delano were married by bond 23 DEC 1844 in Westmoreland Co., with Benedict Walker, security.

Dickins, John to Rosabell Combs. JOHN DICKINS, farmer, age 46, widower, b. Westmoreland Co., son of James and Susan Dickins, to ROSABELL COMBS, age 22, single, b. King George Co., daughter of Hannah Combs. Signed John [his X mark] Dickins, wit. J.W. Hutt. License 17 JUN 1872. Married 8 JUL 1872 at *Cavalla* by John Payne. [M19; R:106; R1:50-13; WP]

Dickson, James to Felicia Harrison. JAMES DICKSON, farmer, age 22, single, b. Westmoreland Co., son of Solomon and Emily Dickson, to FELICIA HARRISON, age 22, single, b. Westmoreland Co., daughter of Samuel and Letty Harrison. License 25 SEP 1866. Married 27 SEP 1866 at Machodoc [Church] by G.H. Northam. [M18; R:84; R1:25-2]

Diggs, John to Eliza Ann Burgess. JOHN DIGGS, farmer, age 22, single, b. Westmoreland Co., son of John and Sally Diggs, to ELIZA ANN BURGESS, age 21, single, b. Westmoreland Co., daughter of James and Mary Burgess. License 21 MAR 1877. Married 22 MAR 1877 at *Mount Pleasant*[1] by F.B. Beale. [M19; R:122 incorrectly has Mary Burgess; R1:69-10]

Dishman, Robert L. to Lucinda H. Sisson. ROBERT L. DISHMAN, farmer, age 22, single, b. King George Co., son of William [J.] and Elizabeth Dishman, to LUCINDA H. SISSON, age 22, single, b. Westmoreland Co., daughter of William R. Sisson and Ann E. [Harvey].[2] License 14 FEB 1855. Married 14 FEB 1855 at Montross, Va. by H.P.F. King, minister of the M.E. Church. [M16:55-7, R:49; R1:2]

Dixson [or Dixon], Cephas Noah to Susan Virginia Newman (d. 1885 of pneumonia). CEPHAS NOAH DIXSON, farmer, age 21, single, b. Westmoreland Co., son of Solomon and Emily Dixon, to SUSAN VIRGINIA NEWMAN, age 21, single, b. Westmoreland Co., daughter of William H. and Malinda Newman. License 12 DEC 1870. Married 15 DEC 1870 by G.H. Northam. [DR:64-14; M18; R:100; R1:44-9]

Dixon, George W. to Redelia Evans. GEORGE W. DIXSON [sic], waterman, age 28, single, b. Northumberland Co., son of James [d. 1893] and Julia Dixson, to REDELIA EVANS, age 17, single, b. Dorchester Co., Md., daughter of John and Sarah Evans. License 25 FEB 1878. Married 5 MAR 1878 by F.B. Beale. [DR:94-29; M19; R:125; R1:73-5]

Dixon, Robert (C) to Lucy Ann Wright. ROBERT DIXSON [sic], farmer, age 20, single, b. Westmoreland Co., son of Solomon and Emily Dixson, to LUCY ANN WRIGHT, age 19, single, b. Westmoreland Co., daughter of Solomon and Emily Wright [sic]. License 17 JUN 1880. Married 17 JUN 1880 at *The Glebe* by F.B. Beale. [M20; R:133; R1:83-3]

Dixon, Solomon (C) to Barbary Ann Thompson. SOLOMON DIXON, farmer, age 50, widowed, b. Westmoreland Co., son of William and Frances Dixon, to BARBARY ANN THOMPSON, age 20, single, b. Westmoreland Co., daughter of Lucy [Cary], father unknown. Signed Solomon [his X mark] Dixon, wits. J.W. Hutt, G.W. Goldsby. License 2 DEC 1868. Married 10 DEC 1868 by G.H. Northam. [M18; R:93; R1:36-4]

Dixon, Solomon to Sallie Magumby. SOLOMON DIXON, farmer, age 30, single, b. Westmoreland Co., son of Solomon and Emily Dixon, to SALLIE MAGUMBY, age 23, single, b. Westmoreland Co.,

---

[1] See Deeds & Wills No. 41, p. 283 for sale of *Mount Pleasant* from Willoughby Newton, Jr., a bankrupt.
[2] William R. Sisson and Ann E. Harvey were married by bond 24 MAY 1825 in Westmoreland Co., with Joseph F. Harvey, security.

daughter of Edwin and Adeline Magumby. License 1 JUN 1878. Married 6 JUN 1878 at *Hickory Hill* by J.H. Davis. [M19; R:125; R1:74-2]

Dixon, Travis (C) to Mrs. Nancy Taliaferro Washington (C). TRAVIS DIXON, laborer, age 60, widowed, b. King George Co., son of William and Winny Dixon, to NANCY WASHINGTON, age 39, widow, b. Westmoreland Co., daughter of William and Sarah Taliaferro. License 2 DEC 1876. Married 2 DEC 1876 at Little Zion Church by E. Watts, Little Zion Church. [M19; R:120; R1:67-4]

Dobyns, Thomas Mitchell (1825-1873),[1] served in Co. D, 37th Reg. Va. Mil. and Home Guards, C.S.A., of *Indian Banks*, Richmond Co., second to Anna Demaris Wright (1834-1909).[2] THOMAS MITCHELL DOBYNS, farmer, age 49, widowed, b. Lancaster Co., res. Northumberland Co., son of Washington Dobyns [b. 1777], mother unknown [Priscilla Glascock],[3] to ANNA DEMARIS WRIGHT, age 31, single, b. Westmoreland Co., daughter of Mottrom M. Wright and Malinda A. [Ann Lamkin].[4] License 14 DEC 1868. Married 15 DEC 1868 by J.H. Davis. [M18; R:93; R1:36-10]

Dodd, George (b. 1843 at *Edge Hill*, d. 1923 of myocarditis in King George Co.),[5] mason, son of John Dodd, to Martha Inscoe. Married 17 JAN 1872 at *Cavalla* by Rev. John Payne. [DC; WP]

Dodd, Landon to Elizabeth Williams. License 28 MAY 1855. [R:49]

Doleman, William Henry (1842-1911), served in Co. E, 55th Va. Inf., C.S.A., first to Lucinda "Lucy" Frances Hinson (1843-1878).[6] WILLIAM HENRY DOLEMAN, sailor, age 19, single, b. Westmoreland Co., son of Austin Doleman and Elizabeth [A. Marmaduke], to LUCINDA FRANCES HINSON, age 18, single, b. Richmond Co., daughter of William F. Hinson, mother unknown [Mary Ann Neale]. License 6 JAN 1862. Married 7 JAN 1862 at the residence of Elizabeth Tallent by H.P.F. King. [M17:62-3; R:78; R1:18-9]

Doleman, William Henry (1842-1911), *q.v.*, second to Mary Susan Hinson (1861-1935). WILLIAM HENRY DOLEMAN, farmer, age 37, widower, b. Westmoreland Co., son of Austin Doleman and Elizabeth [A. Marmaduke], to MARY SUSAN HINSON, age 18, single, b. Westmoreland Co., daughter of R. [Rodham Neale] Hinson and Martha [F. Eliffe], *q.v.* License 22 MAY 1879. Married 1 JUN 1879 by Elder James A. Weaver. [M20; R:129; R1:77-12]

Donahue, George Northam to Bettie Hopkins Thrift. GEORGE NORTHAM DONNAHUE [sic], merchant, age 24, b. Richmond Co., son of William H. and Margaret [N.] Donahue, to BETTIE HOPKINS THRIFT, age 19, single, b. Westmoreland Co., daughter of Joseph B. and Mary A. Thrift. License 31 MAR 1875. Married 1 APR 1875 at the residence of Joseph Thrift by R.J. Sanford. [M19; R:115; R1:61-2]

---

[1] Thomas M. Dobyns and his first wife Margaret Sarah Beauchamp/Beacham, daughter of Joseph and Sarah Beacham of Northumberland Co., were buried in the Beauchamp Family Cemetery in Cherry Point, now graves found at Melrose United Methodist Church, Lewisetta, Va.
[2] Anna D. Thrift, widow of Thomas Mitchell Dobyns, and widow of Jeremiah C. Thrift, was buried in a Wright Family Cemetery, located off of Route 203 near Oldhams, Va.
[3] Washington Dobyns and Priscilla Glascock were married by bond 18 NOV 1812 in Richmond Co., with Henry M. Dobyns, security.
[4] Mottrom M. Wright and Malinda Lamkin were married by bond 6 APR 1830 in Richmond Co., with Charles L. Bell, security.
[5] DC: George Dodd was buried at *Edge Hill*.
[6] William H. Doleman and both his wives Lucy and Susan were buried at Providence United Methodist Church, Chiltons, Va.

Donahue, Richard Sedwick to Ella Virginia Rowe (d. 1888 of spinal meningitis).[1] RICHARD SEDWICK DONAHUE, age 27, single, b. Westmoreland Co., son of William H. [d. 1883 of paralysis of the brain] and Margaret [N.] Donahue, to ELLA VIRGINIA ROWE, age 22, single, b. Westmoreland Co., daughter of William and Dorothy Rowe. License 11 NOV 1875. Married 14 NOV 1875 by R.J. Sanford. [DR:57-22, 75-17; M19; R:116; R1:62-4]

Douglas, Edward Filmore (b. 1851, d. 1935 of influenzal pneumonia),[2] to Susan Virginia English. EDWARD FILMORE DOUGLASS [sic], farmer, age 25, single, b. Westmoreland Co., son of Lemuel Douglas and Sarah [Palmer[3]], *q.v.*, to SUSAN VIRGINIA ENGLISH, age 24, single, b. Westmoreland Co., daughter of Samuel [W.] English and Sarah A. [Ann Delano], *q.v.* License 1 JAN 1877. Married 2 JAN 1877 by R.J. Sanford. [DC; M19; R:121; R1:68-4]

Douglass, Rodeham to Mary Morris (d. 1869 of bilious fever). License 8 MAR 1853. Married 16 MAR 1853 by George Northam, L.M.G. [DR:17-10[4]; M15:53-9; R:27]

Douglass, Solomon Rody (1852-1900), to Mary Bettie Hall (1865-1971).[5] SOLOMON RODY DOUGLASS, farmer, age 23, single, b. Westmoreland Co., son of Rody [Rodeham] and Mary [Morris] Douglass, *q.v.*, to MARY BETTIE HALL, age 18, single, b. Richmond Co., daughter of Samuel and Olivia Hall. License 14 JUL 1880. Married 15 JUL 1880 by R.N. Reamy. [M20; R:134; R1:83-8]

Dowling, Cornelius (C) to Edith Watts. CORNELIUS DOWLING, farmer, age 24, single, b. King George Co., son of Seymour and Virginia Dowling, to EDITH WATTS, age 20, single, b. Westmoreland Co., daughter of Emanuel and Hannah Watts. Signed Cornelius [his X mark] Dowling, wit. J.W. Hutt. License 19 DEC 1874. Married 24 DEC 1874 by Emanuel Watts, pastor Little Zion Church. [M19; R:113; R1:59-14]

Dozier, John Thomas to Mary Lee Weaver (b. 1860).[6] JOHN THOMAS DOZIER, farmer, age 24, single, b. Westmoreland Co., son of Richard Dozier and Ann [Rebecca Carroll[7]], to MARY LEE WEAVER, age 19, single, b. Westmoreland Co., daughter of John [Henry] Weaver [d. testate 1890[8]] and [Emily] Maria [Bragg].[9] License 14 JAN 1880. Married 15 JAN 1880 by F.B. Beale. [M20; R:131; R1:80-12]

Dozier, William Churchwell (d. 1867 of drowning), to Lucinda Peed. WILLIAM CHURCHWELL DOZIER, shoemaker, age 31, single, b. Westmoreland Co., son of Martin Dozier and Elizabeth [Butler],[10] to LUCINDA PEED, age 19, single, b. Westmoreland Co., daughter of William and

---

[1] Ella Rowe Donahue is probably buried in the Sandy Valley Cemetery, located off of Route 202.
[2] Edward F. Douglas was buried at Ebenezer United Methodist Church, Oldhams, Va.
[3] DC for Edward F. Douglas gives his mother as Sarah Brinnan.
[4] DR:17-10, entry for Mary Douglass, d. 15 OCT 1869 of bilious fever, housekeeping, daughter of Wm. and Fanny Morriss.
[5] Solomon R. Douglas and wife Mary B. were buried at Currioman Baptist Church, Chiltons, Va. Her tombstone notes she was also the wife of F.L. Entwisle and E.M. Farr.
[6] John T. Dozier and his wife Mary Lee Weaver were buried in the Weaver-Sanford Family Cemetery, located off of Route 645, between Zacata, Va. and Hinnom, Va.
[7] Richard Dozier and Ann Rebecca Carroll were married by bond 19 DEC 1848 in Westmoreland Co., with Benjamin Short, security. CF1854-15, *George Carroll v. Solomon Carroll &c.* Records & Inventories Bk. 20, p. 377, John Carroll died intestate in 1848. His daughter Ann has intermarried with Richard Dozier. DR:7-17 shows death for Rebecca Dozier on 1 SEP 1861 at age 80.
[8] Deeds & Wills No. 49, p. 49, will of John Weaver, proved 24 FEB 1890, names daughter Mary Lee Dozier.
[9] John Weaver, son of Henry Weaver, and Emily M. Bragg, were married by bond 23 NOV 1849 in Westmoreland Co., with Robert M. Bragg, security.
[10] Martin Dozier and Elizabeth Butler were married by bond 9 FEB 1827 in Westmoreland Co., with William Sutton, security.

Lucinda Peed. License 26 DEC 1859. Married 27 DEC 1859 by John Pullen. [DR:13-16; M16a:59-31 and 31b; R:72; R1:17-7]

Dozier, William Richard, served in Co. C, 9th Va. Cav., C.S.A., to Susan Fox Harvey. WILLIAM RICHARD DOZIER, farmer and deputy sheriff, age 35, widower, b. Westmoreland Co., son of Vincent Dozier and Susan [Smith],[1] to SUSAN FOX HARVEY, age 27, single, b. Westmoreland Co., daughter of Joseph F. and Frances Ann Harvey. License 11 JUL 1854. Married 12 JUL 1854 at *Brodfield* by W.W. Walker, Methodist Protestant minister. [M15:54-7; R:43; R1:1-15]

Drake, Benjamin to Eveline Jasper.[2] License 22 OCT 1850. Married 24 OCT 1850 by John Pullen. [M15:50-23; R:3 not in *Nottingham*]

Drake, Benjamin to Mrs. Mary McGuire Clarke. BENJAMIN DRAKE, farmer, age 62, widowed, b. Westmoreland Co., son of Henry and Betsy Drake, to MARY CLARKE, age 58, widow, b. Westmoreland Co., daughter of Travis McGuire and Rebecca [Sutton], *q.v.* Signed Benjamin [his X mark] Drake, wit. Wm. Stewart McKenney. License 19 MAR 1873. Married 20 MAR 1873 at the residence of Benj. Drake by D.G.C. Butts. [M19; R:108; R1:53-14]

Drake, Thomas (d. 1869), to Mary Elizabeth Lefever (d. 1873 of measles at Baynesville, Va.). THOMAS DRAKE, farmer, age 21, single, b. Westmoreland Co., son of John Drake and Mary [Ann Green],[3] to MARY ELIZABETH LAFEVRE [sic], age 23, single, b. Westmoreland Co., daughter of Nathaniel Lefevre and Martha [Pursley].[4] License 2 JAN 1866. Married 4 JAN 1866 at Nathaniel Lefevre's by John Pullen. [DR:28-8; M18; R:82; R1:22-15; WP]

Dunlap, John I. to Jane Tate. License 16 AUG 1850. Married 21 AUG 1850 by John Pullen. [M15:50-21; R:1 not in *Nottingham*]

Dyer, John to Elizabeth N. Hazzard. License 10 JUL 1851. Married 17 JUL 1851 by George Northam, L.M.G. [M15:51-14; R:9]

E

Edmonds, Austin Christopher to Jane M. Thompson. AUSTIN CHRISTOPHER EDMONDS, blacksmith, age 24, single, b. Westmoreland Co., son of William Edmonds and Alice [Short],[5] to JANE M. THOMPSON, age 31, single, b. King George Co., parents unknown. Consent 23 JUN 1860 by bride. License 23 JUN 1860. Married 26 JUN 1860 by H.P.F. King. [M17:60-27, 27a, 27b; R:74; R1:17-10]

Edmonds, Henry Lewis to Elizabeth Moss. HENRY LEWIS EDMONDS, farmer, age 29, single, b. Westmoreland Co., son of James Edmonds [d. 1866 of consumption] and Alice [Cook],[6] to ELIZABETH MOSS, age 21, single, b. Richmond Co., daughter of Thomas Moss and Polly

---

[1] Vincent Dozier and Susan Smith were married by bond c.1811 in Westmoreland Co., with James Dozier, security.
[2] DR:15:17, entry for Everlina Drake, d. 1 DEC 1867, age 44, unknown cause, daughter of Lucie and Saml. Jackson [sic], wife of Ben Drake.
[3] John Drake and Mary Ann Green were married by bond 6 DEC 1838 in Westmoreland Co., with George Green, security.
[4] Nathaniel Lefever and Martha Pursley were married by bond 20 OCT 1838 in Westmoreland Co., with William Peed, security.
[5] William Edmonds and Alcy Short were married by bond 29 OCT 1832 in Westmoreland Co., with Uriah E. Head, security.
[6] James Edmonds and Alice Cook were married by bond 21 NOV 1822 in Westmoreland Co., with John Massey, security.

[Massey].[1] Signed H.L. [his X mark] Edmonds, wit. J.W. Hutt. License 28 MAY 1867. Married 29 MAY 1867 at Henry L. Edmonds' by Henry H. Fones. [DR:11-11; M18; R:86; R1:28-3]

Edmonds, Richard A. to Sarah A. Jones. RICHARD A. EDMONDS, farmer, age 25, single, b. Westmoreland Co., son of James Julian and Alice Maria Edmonds, to SARAH A. JONES, age 23, single, b. Westmoreland Co., daughter of Robert Jones and Lucy Ann Carter. Signed Richard A. [his X mark] Edmonds, wit. W.S. McKenney. License 8 MAR 1871. Married 9 MAR 1871 by B.R. Battaile. [M18; R:102; R1:46-9]

Edwards, Charles Richard (d. 1886 of pneumonia), to Mrs. Virginia Ann Douglass Brown, widow of John Noah Brown, *q.v.* CHARLES RICHARD EDWARDS, house joiner, age 33, single, b. Westmoreland Co., son of Richard Edwards and Ann [Maria McKenney],[2] to VIRGINIA ANN BROWN, age 23, widow, b. Westmoreland Co., daughter of Lemuel Douglass and Sally [Sarah Palmer], *q.v.* License 25 APR 1866. Married 26 APR 1866 by G.H. Northam. [DR:69-57; M18; NN; R:83; R1:23-15]

Edwards, Richard Batten (b. 1842, d. 1921),[3] served in Co. A, 15th Va. Cav., C.S.A., to Willie Ann Eliza Washington Reed (d. 1876 of bilious or typhoid fever). RICHARD BATTEN EDWARDS, farmer, age 25, single, b. Westmoreland Co., son of Richard Edwards and Ann [Maria McKenney], *q.v.*, to WILLIE ANN ELIZA WASHINGTON REED, age 17, single, b. Westmoreland Co., daughter of Joseph B. and Elizabeth Reed. License 18 JUN 1867. Married 20 JUN 1867 by G.H. Northam. [DC; DR:35-19 for 1876, and DR:39-26 for 1877; M18; R:87; R1:28-10]

Edwards, Robert Armstrong, served in Co. K, 9th Va. Cav., C.S.A., to Ida Atwill. ROBERT ARMSTRONG EDWARDS, farmer, age 21, single, b. Westmoreland Co., son of William and Christian Edwards, to IDA ATWILL, age 22, single, b. Caroline Co., daughter of Daniel and E. Atwill. License 2 NOV 1880. Married 4 NOV 1880 at Lebanon M.E. Church by Paul Bradley. [M20; R:134; R1:83-16]

Edwards, Simon Dorsey, served in Co. A, 15th Va. Cav., C.S.A., first to Lucy Asberry Reed (d. 1871 in childbirth). SIMON DORSEY EDWARDS, farmer, age 24, single, b. Westmoreland Co., son of Richard R. Edwards and Ann [Maria McKenney], to LUCY ASBERRY REED, age 17, single, b. Westmoreland Co., daughter of Joseph B. and Elizabeth Reed. Consent 1[0] DEC 1860 by father Joseph B. Reed, wit. George W. Collins. License 11 DEC 1860. Married 12 DEC 1860 by H.P.F. King. [DR:24-2; M17:60-39, 39a, 39b; R:76; R1:17-12]

Edwards, Simon Dorsey, second to Mary Paulina George (d. 1893). SIMON DORSEY EDWARDS, farmer, age 36, widowed, b. Westmoreland Co., son of Richard [R.] Edwards and Ann [Maria McKenney], *q.v.*, to MARY PAULINA GEORGE, age 20, single, b. Westmoreland Co., daughter of P.C. [Philander Chinn] George and Ann [E. Atwill], *q.v.* License 20 MAY 1874. Married 21 MAY 1874 at the home of Thomas Edwards by W.A. Crocker. [M19; NN; R:113; R1:58-9]

---

[1] Thomas Moss and Mary Massey were married by bond 7 APR 1828 in Westmoreland Co., with Matthew Jenkins, security.
[2] Richard Edwards and Ann Maria McKenney, daughter of Gerard McKenney, were married by bond 22 JAN 1829 in Westmoreland Co., with Gerard McKinney, security.
[3] DC: Richard B. Edwards was buried at Beulah Church.

Edwards, Thomas (d. testate 1879[1]), to Virginia McKenney. THOMAS EDWARDS, farmer, age 65, widowed, b. Westmoreland Co., son of William and Frances Edwards, to VIRGINIA McKENNEY, age 44, single, b. Westmoreland Co., daughter of Armstrong McKenney and Jane [Steward].[2] Married 2 DEC 1858 by H.P.F. King, minister of the M.E. Church. [M16a:58-34 and 34a; R1:13-5]

Edwards, Thomas William (d. 1887 of consumption), to Christian Armstrong McKenney. THOMAS WILLIAM EDWARDS, shoemaker, age 34, widowed, b. Westmoreland Co., son of Thomas Edwards and Elizabeth [S. Templeman],[3] and CHRISTIAN A. McKENNEY, age 29, single, b. Westmoreland Co., daughter of Armstrong McKenney and Jane [Steward], *q.v.* License 3 NOV 1858. Married 4 NOV 1858 at Templeman's X Roads by H.P.F. King, minister of the M.E. Church. [DR:72-84; M16a:58-26 and 26a; R:64; R1:12-9]

Edwards, Thomas William (d. 1887 of consumption), to Mrs. Mary Ann Hunter Jenkins (d. 1886 of consumption), widow of John S. Jenkins, *q.v.* THOMAS WILLIAM EDWARDS, mechanic, age 54, widowed, b. Westmoreland Co., son of Thomas Edwards and Elizabeth [S. Templeman], *q.v.*, to MARY ANN JENKINS, age 50, widow, b. Westmoreland Co., daughter of John and Sarah ["Sallie"] Hunter. License 20 FEB 1878. Married 21 FEB 1878 at the bride's residence by John W. White, M.G. [DR:69-54, 72-84; M19; R:125; R1:73-4]

Edwards, Thomas William Brown (d. 1887 of congestion of the bowel), served in Co. C, 9th Va. Cav., C.S.A., to Amanda G. Atwill. THOMAS W.B. EDWARDS, farmer, age 23, single, b. Westmoreland Co., son of William Edwards and Sarah ["Sallie"] [N. Taylor],[4] to AMANDA G. ATWILL, age 24, single, b. Westmoreland Co., daughter of Samuel B. and Mary Atwill. License 26 DEC 1855. Married 27 DEC 1855 by H.P.F. King, minister of the M.E. Church. [DR:72-85; M16:55-29, R:51; R1:4-12]

Edwards, William (d. by 1856), to Josepha J. Crabb. License 9 OCT 1850. Married 13 OCT 1850 by J.C. Garlick. [M15:50-22; R:3 not in *Nottingham*]

Edwards, William McKendrie (b. 1845, d. 1917 of paralysis),[5] served in the 43rd Va. Cav., C.S.A. (Mosby's Rangers), to Mary Anna Jenkins.[6] WILLIAM McKENDRIE EDWARDS, farmer, age 27, widowed, b. Westmoreland Co., son of Richard L. Edwards and Ann Maria [McKenney] [d. 1886],[7] to MARY ANN JENKINS, age 25, widow, b. Westmoreland Co., daughter of John S. Jenkins and Harriet [H. Hunter].[8] License 13 JAN 1874. Married 14 JAN 1874 at Templeman's X Roads by Walter C. Taylor. [DC; DR:69-5[9]; M19; R:111; R1:56-14]

Edwards, Wiscum Montgomery to Sallie Brown Sutton. WISCUM MONTGOMERY EDWARDS, engineer, age 28, single, b. Caroline Co., son of John and Frances Edwards, to SALLIE BROWN

---

[1] Deeds & Wills No. 4, p. 422, will of Thomas Edwards, proved 22 SEP 1878, mentions wife but not named.
[2] Armstrong McKenney and Jane Steward were married by bond 12 AUG 1813 in Westmoreland Co., with Nathaniel Clopton, security.
[3] Thomas Edwards and Elizabeth S. Templeman were married by bond 17 OCT 1817 in Westmoreland Co., with Samuel Templeman, Jr., security.
[4] William Edwards and Sarah N. Taylor were married by bond 26 JUN 1826 in Westmoreland Co., with Robert Bailey, security.
[5] William M. Edwards was buried in the Edwards Family Cemetery, located off of Route 621 near Nomini Grove, Va. His death certificate gives place of burial as West Farm.
[6] Deeds & Wills No. 44, p. 338.
[7] Richard Edwards and Ann Maria McKinney, daughter of Gerard McKinney, were married by bond 22 JAN 1829 in Westmoreland Co.
[8] John S. Jenkins and Harriett H. Hunter were married by bond 4 JUN 1845 in Westmoreland Co., with M.M. Marmaduke, Jr., security.
[9] DR:69-5, entry for Anna M. Edwards, d. 13 FEB 1886 of dropsy, age 83, daughter of James and Frances McKenney, mother of W.M. Edwards.

SUTTON, age 21, single, b. Westmoreland Co., daughter of John Sutton and Mary [Y. McKenney], *q.v.* License 10 APR 1880. Married 13 APR 1880 by F.B. Beale. [M20; R:133; R1:82-5]

Eliff (also see Oliff)

Eliff, George Washington to Mary Elizabeth Mothershead. GEORGE WASHINGTON ELIFFE [sic], carpenter, age 22, single, b. Westmoreland Co., son of Henry Eliff and Fanny [Frances Stone], *q.v.*, to MARY ELIZABETH MOTHERSHEAD, age 26, single, b. Westmoreland Co., daughter of Charles C. Mothershead and Elizabeth [Dozier], *q.v.* License 6 MAR 1860. Married 6 MAR 1860 by George F. Bagby. [M17:60-14 and 46; R:72; R1:17-3]

Eliff, Henry to Mrs. Ann N. "Nancy" McNeil Messick, widow of Joseph Messick.[1] HENRY ELIFF, farmer, age 52, widower, b. Richmond Co., son of George and Frances Eliff, to ANN M. MESIC [sic], age 37, widow, b. Westmoreland Co., daughter of John R. and Lucinda McNeel [or McNeil]. License 22 DEC 1856. Married 25 DEC 1856 at his residence by H.P.F. King, minister of the M.E. Church South. [M16a:56-36; R:57; R1:8-4]

Eliff, James Henry to Frances Pope Edwards. JAMES H. ELIFF, house carpenter, age 25, single, b. Westmoreland Co., son of Henry Eliff and Frances [Stone],[2] to FRANCES P. EDWARDS, age 38, single, b. Westmoreland Co., daughter of Thomas Edwards and Elizabeth [S. Templeman], *q.v.* License 23 JUN 1858. Married 23 JUN 1858 at the residence of Thomas Edwards by H.P.F. King, minister of the M.E. Church. [M16a:58-20[3]; R:64; R1:12-6]

Eliff, Joseph Stone, served in Co. A of 15th Va. Cav., C.S.A., to Mary Catherine Thompson. JOSEPH STONE ELIFF, farmer, age 40, single, b. Westmoreland Co., son of Henry Eliff and Frances [Stone], *q.v.*, to MARY CATHRON THOMPSON [sic], age 20, single, b. King George Co., daughter of William D. Thompson and Ellen [Moxley].[4] License 12 OCT 1870. Married 13 OCT 1870 at *Chatham* by G.W. Beale, minister Baptist Church. [M18; R:100; R1:44-2]

Elmore, John William (d. by 1873), to Rebecca Jane Barnett. JOHN WILLIAM ELMORE, farmer, age 22, single, b. Westmoreland Co., son of Edmund [T.K.] Elmore and Mary [Barnett],[5] to REBECCA JANE BARNETT, age 19, single, b. Westmoreland Co., daughter of Levi Barnett [d. 1864 of bilious fever at *Water View*] and Martha [Pope].[6] License 2 OCT 1867. Married 3 OCT 1867 by G.H. Northam. [DR:8-14[7]; M18; R:87; R1:29-11]

England, William Clarence (1845-1926), served in Co. E, 47th Va. Inf., C.S.A., to Emma Catharine Sutton (1855-1916).[8] WILLIAM [CLARENCE] ENGLAND, merchant, age 30, single, b. Orange Co., son of John F. England [d. 1884 age 70] and Emily [W. Loving],[9] to EMMER CATHARINE SUTTON [sic], age 20, single, b. Westmoreland Co., daughter of James Sutton and Elizabeth [Reed], *q.v.*

---

[1] Joseph Messack and Nancy McNeil were married by bond 4 JUN 1841 in Westmoreland Co., with James S. Dozier, security.

[2] Henry Eliff and Frances Stone, daughter of Alice Stone, were married by bond 28 FEB 1824 in Westmoreland Co., with William Bulger, security.

[3] Another copy at 58-20a gives middle names for both bride and groom.

[4] William D. Thompson and Ellen Moxley were married 14 FEB 1850 in King George Co. by Rev. John McDaniel.

[5] Edmund T.K. Elmore and Mary Barnett were married by bond 16 AUG 1841 in Westmoreland Co., with John B. Carroll, security.

[6] Levi Barnett and Martha Pope, daughter of John Pope, were married by bond 7 OCT 1839 in Westmoreland Co., with Richard Pritchett, security.

[7] Entry in Death Register for Levi Barnett gives parents as William and Eliza Barnett.

[8] William C. England and his wife Emma were buried at Currioman Baptist Church, Chiltons, Va.

[9] John F. England and Emily Loving were married 27 DEC 1841 in Caroline Co., wit. Edwin B. Loving.

License 16 MAY 1876. Married 17 MAY 1876 at *Bushfield* by John W. White. [Bible; M19; R:118; R1:65-4]

Engle, Edward McCrady to Frances Scott Wirt. EDWARD McCRADY ENGLE, attorney at law, age 39, single, b. Charleston, S.C., res. Jacksonville, Fla., son of John and Susan L. Engle, to FRANCES SCOTT WIRT, age 26, single, b. Westmoreland Co., daughter of William and Elizabeth Wirt. License 30 MAY 1874. Married 1 JUL 1874 at *Wirtland* by Jno. Payne. [M19; R:113; R1:58-11; WP]

English, Benjamin Smith (1819-1893),[1] second to Kate Stewart (d. 1882 of consumption). BENJAMIN SMITH ENGLISH, farmer, age 58, widowed, b. Westmoreland Co., son of James and Jane English, to KATE STEWART, age 28, single, b. Westmoreland Co., daughter of John T. and Sarah E. Stewart. License 22 DEC 1879. Married 23 DEC 1879 at the residence of the bride's mother by W.A. Crocker. [DR:52-31; M20; R:131; R1:80-1]

English, George Washington (1847-1926), to Mary Frances 'Mollie" Lewis (1856-1924).[2] GEORGE WASHINGTON ENGLISH, farmer, age 25, single, b. Westmoreland Co., son of Samuel [Walter] English and Sarah [Ann Delano], to MARY FRANCES LEWIS, age 18, single, b. Westmoreland Co., daughter of John W. Lewis and Ellen [E. King], *q.v.* License 11 FEB 1874. Married 12 FEB 1874 at the bride's father's by W.A. Crocker. [M19; R:112; R1:57-10]

English, James McKendrie (1843-1917),[3] served in Co. C, 9th Va. Cav., C.S.A., to Martha Dorathea Beale (d. 1869 of pneumonia). JAMES McKENDRIE ENGLISH, carpenter, age 25, single, b. Westmoreland Co., son of Benjamin S. [Smith] English and Mary F. [Frances Smith],[4] to MARTHA DORATHEA BEALE, age 24, single, b. Westmoreland Co., daughter of Sydnor Beale and Sarah A. [M. Parks].[5] License 14 DEC 1868. Married 16 DEC 1868 at the residence of Capt. Beauchamp by H.P.F. King. [DR:17-11; M18; R:93; R1:36-11]

English, John William (d. 1884 of consumption), to Susan Williams Robinson (1854-1934).[6] JOHN WILLIAM ENGLISH, farmer, age 20, single, b. Westmoreland Co., son of Benjamin Smith English and Mary [Frances] Smith, *q.v.*, to SUSAN WILLIAM ROBINSON [sic], age 18, single, b. Westmoreland Co., daughter of William [B.] Robinson and Ann M. [Wright].[7] License 9 MAY 1872. Married 9 MAY 1872 at the residence of George Jeffries by R.J. Sanford. [DR:60-20; M19; R:105; R1:50-5]

English, Joseph William (1840-1909), served in Co. F or 3, 86th Va. Inf., C.S.A., to Lucy Jane Reynolds (1845-1901).[8] JOSEPH WILLIAM ENGLISH, farmer, age 29, single, b. Westmoreland Co., son of John English and Letty [A. Rice],[9] to LUCY JANE REYNOLDS, age 23, single, b. Westmoreland Co., daughter of Henry and Lucetta Reynolds. License 10 JUL 1868. Married 12 JUL 1868 by W.W. Walker. [M18; R:92; R1:34-10]

---

[1] B.S. English and his first wife Mary F. Smith were buried in the English Family Cemetery, located off of Route 603 near Acorn, Va.
[2] George W. English and his wife Mary F. were buried at Ebenezer United Methodist Church, Oldhams, Va.
[3] James M. English was buried at Ebenezer United Methodist Church, Oldhams, Va.
[4] Benjamin S. English and Mary F. Smith were married by bond 18 JAN 1841 in Westmoreland Co., with Moses Chilley, security.
[5] Sydnor Beale and Sarah A.M. Parks, daughter of Arthur Parks, were married by bond 22 JAN 1838 in Westmoreland Co., with Henry Beale, Jr., security.
[6] DC: Susan W. English was buried at Carmel United Methodist Church, Kinsale, Va.
[7] William B. Robinson and Ann M. Wright were married by bond 29 FEB 1836 in Westmoreland Co., with William R. McKenney, security.
[8] Joseph W. English and his wife Lucy J. were buried at Ebenezer United Methodist Church, Oldhams, Va.
[9] John English and Letty A. Rice were married by bond 16 DEC 1833 in Westmoreland Co., with William T. Branson, security.

Epps, Silas (C) to Willie Ann Johnson. SILAS EPPS, farmer, age 22, single, b. Essex Co., son of Bartlett [d. 1874 of pneumonia] and Philis Epps, to WILLIE ANN JOHNSON, age 21, single, b. Westmoreland Co., daughter of Dennis and Sally Johnson. License 5 JAN 1878. [DR:32-6; R:124 license not on film; R1:72-2 no return]

Eskridge, Benjamin (C) to Virginia Ashton. BENJAMIN ESKRIDGE, farmer, age 22, single, b. Westmoreland Co., son of Frederick and Letty Eskridge, to VIRGINIA ASHTON, age 22, single, b. Westmoreland Co., daughter of Stewart and Roxana Ashton. Signed Benjamin [his X mark] Eskridge, wit. W.S. McKenney. License 30 MAR 1872. Married 31 MAR 1872 at Gen. Beale's by G.W. Beale, minister. [M19; R:105; R1:50-3]

Eskridge, George (C) to Alice Ann Nelson. GEORGE ESKRIDGE, farmer, age 33, single, b. Westmoreland Co., son of Henry Eskridge and China [Lacy] (C) [d. 1882], to ALICE ANN NELSON, age 20, single, b. Westmoreland Co., daughter of Joseph and Eliza Nelson. Signed George [his X mark] Eskridge, wit. C.C. Baker. License 27 DEC 1867. Married 1 JAN 1868 by Jerry Graham. [DR:52-32[1]; M18; R:89; R1:31-4]

Eskridge, Joseph (C) to Elizabeth "Betsey" Carey (d. 1891 of consumption). JOSEPH ESKRIDGE, farmer, age 37, single, b. Westmoreland Co., son of [Catharine] Eskridge, to BETSEY CAREY, age 37, single, b. Westmoreland Co., daughter of William [Carey]. License 8 JAN 1867. Married 10 JAN 1867. [DR:87-4; R:85; R1:26-15 no return]

Eskridge, Vernon (1839-1903), served Co. A, 15th Va. Cav., C.S.A., to Sarah Elizabeth Bryant (b. 1844, d. 1896 of consumption).[2] VERNON ESKRIDGE, farmer, age 30, single, b. Westmoreland Co., son of B.S. [Burrell] Eskridge [d. testate 1886[3]] and Elizabeth [Kilmon],[4] to SARAH ELIZABETH BRYANT, age 25, single, b. Westmoreland Co., age James Y. and [H]anny Bryant. License 15 DEC 1870. Married 15 DEC 1870 near *Stratford* by H.H. Fones. [DR:105-9[5]; M18 face of license not on film; R:100; R1:44-11]

Evans, Abraham to Alice Ann Franklin (d. 1885 of consumption). ABRAHAM EVANS, captain of vessel, age 27, single, b. Somerset Co., Md., son of Mitchell and Margarett Evans, to ALICE ANN FRANKLIN, age 22, single, b. Westmoreland Co., daughter of James M. [d. testate 1878[6]] and Mary Franklin. License 18 MAY 1869. Married 20 MAY 1869 at the home of James Franklin by J.H. Davis. [DR:64-15; M18; R:95; R1:38-8]

Evans, Christopher D.J. (1819-1900), served Co. A, 15th Va. Cav. and Co. C, 9th Va. Cav. as gunsmith and blacksmith, C.S.A., first to Clementina M. Jenkins. License 13 JAN 1852. Married 13 JAN 1852 by George Northam, L.M.G. [M15:52-2; R:15]

Evans, Christopher D.J. (1819-1900), second to Frances A. Balderson (1839-1904).[7] CHRISTOPHER D.J. EVANS, blacksmith, age 33, b. Sussex Co., Del., widower, son of C.D.J. and

---

[1] DR:52-32, for China Eskridge, b. King Greorge Co., d. 15 JUN 1882 of old age, age 80, daughter of Ben and Charlotte Lacy, wife of Henry Eskridge.

[2] Vernon Eskridge and his wife Sarah E. were buried at Grant United Methodist Church, Lerty, Va.

[3] Deeds & Wills No. 46, p. 236, will of Burrell S. Eskridge, proved 26 JUL 1886, names son Vernon Eskridge.

[4] Burrel S. Esksridge and Elizabeth Kilmon were married by bond 14 MAY 1829 in Westmoreland Co., with Tarpley Bryant, security.

[5] DR:105-9 gives her parents as John and Mary Jamison.

[6] Deeds & Wills No. 41, p. 237, will of James M. Franklin, proved 18 JAN 1878, names daughter Alice Evans.

[7] Christopher D.J. Evans and his wife Frances A. were buried at St. James Episcopal Church, Montross, Va.

Priscilla Evans, to FRANCES BALDERSON, age 19, single, b. Richmond Co., daughter of Uriah Balderson [d. testate 1887[1]] and Delila [Balderson], *q.v.* License 7 DEC 1858. Married 9 DEC 1858 at the house of the lady's parents by H.P.F. King, M.G. [M16a:58-36 and 36a; R:66; R1:12-14]

Evans, James to Emma Chatam. JAMES EVANS, waterman, age 21, single, b. Dorchester Co., Md., son of John H. and Sarah Evans, to EMMA CHATAM, age 22, single, b. Westmoreland Co., daughter of Patrick and Annie M. Chatam. License 16 FEB 1880. Married 1[8] FEB 1880 by F.B. Beale. [M20; R:132; R1:81-6]

Everett, Charles Washington to Mary Catharine Pope. CHARLES WASHINGTON EVERETT, farmer, age 22, single, b. Richmond Co., son of Charles and Elizabeth Everett, to MARY CATHARINE POPE, age 15, single, b. Westmoreland Co., daughter of John Pope and Susan [McCluskey].[2] License 12 MAY 1859. Married 12 MAY 1859 at Yeocomico Church by T. Grayson Dashiell, clergyman of Prot. Episcopal Church. [M16a:59-14 and 14a; R:68; R1:14-12]

F

Fairfax, Ferdinando, Dr. (1801/3-1873), second to Mary Jane Jett (b. 1833, d. 1864 in Tipton Co., Tenn.). FERDINANDO FAIRFAX, physician and surgeon, age 48, widower, b. *Shannon Hill*, Jefferson Co., Va., son of Ferdinando Fairfax [b. 1769, d. 1820 at *Mount Eagle*, near Alexandria, Fairfax Co.] and Eliza Blair [Cary] [1770-1822],[3] to MARY JANE JETT, age 24, single, b. *Lock Harbor*, daughter of James Jett [1779-1857] and Ethelwalda [Sanford]. License 27 NOV 1855. Married 28 NOV 1855 at *Lock Harbour* by T. Grayson Dashiell. [M16:55-23, R:51; R1:5-2; SC]

Fairfax, William Henry, Dr. (1834-1907),[4] served in Co. K, 40th Va. Inf., and as surgeon in the 15th Va. Cav., C.S.A., to Eleanor Griffith (b. 1843, d. by 1880). WILLIAM HENRY FAIRFAX, physician, age 32, single, b. King George Co., res. Tipton Co., Tenn., son of [Dr.] Ferdinando Fairfax and [his first wife] Mary [Ann Jett], to ELEANOR GRIFFITH, age 23, single, b. Westmoreland Co., daughter of Edward C. Griffith and Mary E. [Cox].[5] License 25 FEB 1867. Married 26 FEB 1867 at *Locust Farm* by Andrew Fisher. [CP; M18; R:86; R1:27-9; SC]

Faris, Daniel T. to Jane Sanford. License 26 FEB 1851. Married 27 FEB 1851 by John Pullen. [M15:51-10; R:7]

Faucett, Henry to Sarah Newman. HENRY FAUCETT, farming, age 21, single, b. and res. Richmond Co., son of John and Susan Faucett, to SARAH NEWMAN, age 21, single, b. Westmoreland Co., daughter of Edmund Newman and Caroline [Lucas].[6] Signed Henry Faucett, wit. C.C. Baker. License 16 OCT 1860. Married 18 OCT 1860. [M17:60-35; R:76]

Fauntleroy, George (C), first to Eliza Ball (d. 1877). GEORGE FAUNTLEROY, farmer, age 32, single [sic], b. Westmoreland Co., son of Sampson[7] and Lavina Fauntleroy, to ELIZA BALL, age

---

[1] Deeds & Wills No. 47, p. 324, will of Uriah Balderson, proved 24 OCT 1887, names wife Delila Balderson and daughter Frances Evans.
[2] John Pope and Susan McCluskey were married by bond 11 JUN 1834 in Westmoreland Co., with James K. Johnson, security.
[3] Ferdinando Fairfax was married 18 FEB 1769 to his cousin Eliza Blair Cary, third daughter of Wilson Miles Cary, of *Ceeley's*, near Hampton, Va.
[4] William Henry Fairfax was buried at Yeocomico Episcopal Church, Tucker Hill, Va.
[5] Edward C. Griffith and Mary E. Cox were married by bond 6 NOV 1838 in Westmoreland Co., with Joseph Jones, security.
[6] Edmund Newman and Caroline Lucas were married by bond 21 DEC 1836 in Westmoreland Co., with Richard Ashton, security.
[7] DR:15-19, entry for Sampson Fauntleroy, d. 12 JUN 1868 of consumption, age 64.

18, single, b. Westmoreland Co., daughter of John R. and Hannah Ball. Signed by George [his X mark] Fauntleroy, wit. W.S. McKenney. License 7 JAN 1874. Married 8 JAN 1874 at Zion Church by Thomas T. Johnson. [DR:39-27; M19; R:111; R1:56-7]

Fauntleroy, George (C), second to Fanny Jones. GEORGE FAUNTLEROY, farmer, age 27, widowed, b. Westmoreland Co., son of Sam[p]son and Lavina Fauntleroy, to FANNY JONES, age 21, single, b. Westmoreland Co., daughter of John and Nicey Jones. License 17 MAR 1880. Married 18 MAR 1880 at *Springfield* by Charles Rust. [M20; R:132; R1:81-15]

Fauntleroy, Griffin (C) (d. 1881 of pneumonia), to Henrietta Johnson. GRIFFIN FAUNTLEROY, farmer, age 21, single, b. Westmoreland Co., son of Joseph and Levicy Fauntleroy, to HENRIETTA JOHNSON, age 17, single, b. Westmoreland Co., daughter of Washington and Olivia Johnson. License 20 AUG 1879. Married 21 AUG 1879 at *Laurel Hill* by Charles [his X mark] Rust. [DR:48-18; M20; R:129; R1:78-9]

Fauntleroy, Joseph (C) to Margaret Smith. JOSEPH FAUNTLEROY, farmer, age 21, single, b. Westmoreland Co., son of Joseph and [Lorica] Fauntleroy, to MARGARET SMITH, age 18, single, b. Westmoreland Co., daughter of John and Milly Smith. License 10 OCT 1877. Married 11 OCT 1877 at Rugged Point by Charles Rust. [M19; R:123; R1:70-13]

Fauntleroy, Robert (C) to Sarah Thompson. ROBERT FAUNTLEROY, farmer, age 28, single, b. Westmoreland Co., son of Thomas and Harriet Fauntleroy, to SARAH THOMPSON, age 17, single, b. Westmoreland Co., daughter of Austin and Sarah Thompson. Signed Robert [his X mark] Fauntleroy, wit. J.W. Hutt. License 30 DEC 1868. Married 31 DEC 1868 by R.J. Sanford. [M18; R:94; R1:37-4]

Fauntleroy, Simon (C) (d. 1899), to Georgianna Jackson. SIMON FAUNTLEROY, farmer, age 24, single, b. Westmoreland Co., son of Emanuel and Heny Fauntleroy, to GEORGIANNA JACKSON, age 20, single, b. Westmoreland Co., daughter of Armistead and Ellen Jackson. Signed Simon [his X mark] Fauntleroy, wit. J.W. Hutt. License 30 DEC 1868. Married 30 DEC 1868 by Jerry Graham, parson. [M18; NN; R:94; R1:37-3]

Fendla, William S. (d. 1863 of typhoid fever in camp), farmer, served in Co. H, 40th Va. Inf., C.S.A., to Elizabeth Edwards. License 30 DEC 1851. Married 31 DEC 1851 by A. Wiles. [M15:51-26; R:13]

Fessenden, John Milton, Col. to Mrs. Sarah Ann Murphy Richards, widow of William Richards, *q.v.* JOHN MILTON FESSENDEN, civil engineer, age 60, widowed, b. Warren, R.I., res. Boston, Mass., son of John and Abby M. Fessenden, to SARAH ANN RICHARDS, age 40, widow, b. Westmoreland Co., daughter of Robert Murphy and Eliza B. [Newton].[1] License 25 JUN 1868. Married 25 JUN 1868 at *Spring Grove* (the residence of the bride's mother) by D.M. Wharton, Rector, Montross Parish. [CP; M18; R:91; R1:34-7; SC]

Fisher, Adolphus to Elizabeth Trigger. Married 22 DEC 1864 at the Washington Parish rectory by Rev. T.E. Locke. [WP]

---

[1] Robert Murphy and Eliza B. Newton were married by bond 18 MAY 1818 in Westmoreland Co., with William L. Rogers, security.

Fisher, Charles Henry (C) to Jane Waughs. CHARLES HENRY FISHER, sailor, age 28, single, b. Westmoreland Co., son of Isaac [d. 1887] and Susan Fisher, to JANE WAUGHS, age 21, single, b. Westmoreland Co., daughter of Lewis and Sarah Waughs. Signed Charles [his X mark] Henry Fisher, wit. Wm. S. McKenney. License 26 AUG 1874. Married 21 AUG 1874 at Little Zion Church by Thomas T. Johnson. [DR:71-21; M19; R:113; R1:58-14]

Fisher, Emanuel (C) to Agness Weldon. EMANUEL FISHER, waterman, age 23, single, b. Westmoreland Co., son of Isaac and Susan Fisher, to AGNESS WELDON, age 21, single, b. Westmoreland Co., daughter of Thomas and Laura Weldon. License 26 DEC 1876. Married 28 DEC 1876 at *Cabin Ford*[1] by F.B. Beale. [M19; R:121; R1:68-2]

Fisher, Lee (C) (d. 1930 of valvular heart disease), first to Maria Catharine Rust. LEE FISHER, farmer, age 22, single, b. Westmoreland Co., son of Isaac and Susan Fisher, to MARIA CATHARINE RUST, age 19, single, b. Westmoreland Co., daughter of Charles and Charlotte Rust. License 2 JAN 1878. Married 2 JAN 1878 at Dr. [Bround's] by Thomas T. Johnson. [DC; M19; R:124; R1:72-1]

Fitzhugh, Henry Battaile (1839-1909),[2] of *Sherwood Forest*, served in Co. B, 9th Va. Reg., C.S.A., first to Mary Bankhead Lewis, bapt. 25 APR 1848. HENRY B. FITZHUGH, age 27, single, b. Stafford Co., son of Henry Fitzhugh [d. 1883], and [Jane] Elizabeth [Downman] [1817-1881], to MARY B. LEWIS, daughter of John B. and Elizabeth Lewis. Married 3 FEB 1867 at *Shellfield*, Westmoreland Co., by Rev. Henry Wall. [License not found; SC; SP; WP]

Fones, Lewis to Bessada Jones. License 22 DEC 1851. Married 23 DEC 1851 by John Pullen. [M15:51-25; R:13]

Fones, Lewis to Mrs. Eliza Ann Reamy Gutridge, widow of Richard Corbin Gutridge. LEWIS FONES, farmer, age 49, widowed, b. Richmond Co., parents unknown, to ELIZA ANN GUTRIDGE, age 50, widow, b. Richmond Co., daughter of Joshua Reamy, mother unknown. Signed Lewis [his X mark] Fones, wit. J.W. Hutt. License 1 FEB 1870. Married 3 FEB 1870 by Robert N. Reamy. [M18; R:98; R1:42-2]

Fones, Robert Amos (b. c.1835, d. 1876 of dispepsia), appointed first postmaster of Foneswood, Va. in 1871, to Julia Ann Dishman (1939-1906).[3] ROBERT AMOS FONES, teacher, age 21, single, b. Westmoreland Co., son of James B. Fones and Mary Ann [Gutridge],[4] to JULIA ANN DISHMAN, age 16, single, b. Westmoreland Co., daughter of John T. [Triplett] Dishman [d. 1866 of consumption] and Mary H. [Harlowe McDaniel]. License 14 NOV 1855. Married 15 NOV 1855 at Leeds Town, Va. by John Pullen, M.G. [DR:11-10, 38-6; M16:55-21; R:51; R1:4-5]

Fortune, Archy to Laura Amanda Vessels, colored people. Married 2 APR 1867 at *Roxbury* by Thomas E. Locke. [WP]

Fortune, Philip (C) to Susan Fortune. PHILIP FORTUNE, farmer, age 28, single, b. Essex Co., son of M. Fortune, to SUSAN FORTUNE, age 20, single, b. Essex Co., daughter of [Robert] Fortune

---

[1] *Cabin Ford* was built c.1835 by Richard Lee Turberville Beale.
[2] Henry B. Lewis was buried in Hollywood Cemetery, Richmond, Va.
[3] Robert A. Fones and his wife Julia A. were buried at Ephesus Christian Church, Flat Iron, Va.
[4] James B. Fones and Mary Ann Gutridge were married by bond 19 DEC 1833 in Westmoreland Co., with Richard C. Gutridge, security.

and Mary [Bird].[1] License 15 JUN 1880. Married 17 JUN 1880 by R.N. Reamy. [M20; R:133; R1:83-2]

Fortune, Philip (C) to Mary Susan Richards. PHILIP FORTUNE, farmer, age 30, single, b. Essex Co., son of [Robert] Fortune and Mary [Bird] [d. 1874], to MARY SUSAN RICHARDS, age 28, single, b. Essex Co., daughter of [Peter] and Sucky Richards. License 18 JAN 1873. [DR:32-8; R:108; R1:53-4 no return]

Fortune, William (C) to Vernilia Bird. WILLIAM FORTUNE, mechanic, age 49, widowed, b. Essex Co., son of Thomas Fortune and Judy [Key],[2] to VERNILIA BYRD [sic], age 20, single, b. Caroline Co., daughter of Tazwell and Selena [Bird]. License 17 DEC 1877. Married 18 DEC 1877 at Little Zion Church by Emanuel Watts, pastor, Little Zion Church. [M19; R:123; R1:71-12]

Fortune, William (C) to Maria Fortune (d. 1876 of congestive chill). WILLIAM FORTUNE, carpenter, age 46, divorced with liberty to marry, b. Essex Co., son of Thomas Fortune and Judy [Key], *q.v.*, to MARIA FORTUNE, age 32, single, b. Essex Co., daughter of [William and] Harriett Fortune. Signed William [his X mark] Fortune, wit. W.S. McKenney. License 12 JAN 1874. Married 13 JAN 1874 at Oak Grove, Va. by Emanuel Watts, minister of Little Zion Church. [M19; R:111; R1:56-10]

Foxell, John Lewis (1846-1905), to Mary Jane Sorrell (1853-1890).[3] JOHN FOXELL, waterman, age 27, single, b. Westmoreland Co., son of [William Foxell and] Adeline Jasper, to MARY JANE SORRELL, age 19, single, b. Westmoreland Co., daughter of John W. [Wesley] Sorrell and Sarah "Sally" [Sanford].[4] Signed John [his X mark] Foxell, wit. W.S. McKenney. License 24 DEC 1873. Married 24 DEC 1873 by Walter C. Taylor. [M19; R:110; R1:55-15]

France, Joseph (d. 1905 of asthma),[5] to Charlotte Hall. JOSEPH FRANCE, farmer, age 33, widower, b. and res. Richmond Co., son of John France and Elizabeth [Hall],[6] to CHARLOTTE HALL, age 19, single, b. Westmoreland Co., daughter of Richard and Eliza Ann Hall. License 6 FEB 1866. Married 6 FEB 1866 at Richard Hall's by Henry H. Fones. [M18; R:82 has John France; R1:23-9]

Francis, Noah to Susan R. Bailey. License 4 FEB 1859. [R:68]

Frank, Cornelius Alexander (1847-1931), to Mrs. Indiana Jane Armstrong Reamy (1851-1928), widow of William Kelley Reamy, *q.v.*[7] CORNELIUS ALEXANDER FRANK, farmer, age 28, single, b. King George Co., son of Joshua [1823-1865] and Alice [1823-1900] France [sic],[8] to INDIANA JANE REAMEY [sic], age 25, widow, birthplace unknown, daughter of Henry [S.] Armstrong, mother unknown [Jane]. License 8 NOV 1877. Married 18 NOV 1877 by H.H. Fones. [M19; R:123; R1:70-16]

---

[1] Robert Fortune and Mary Bird, daughter of John Bird, were married by bond 3 JUN 1840 in Essex Co., with Peter Bird, security.
[2] Thomas Fortune (d. 1880), son of Humphrey Fortune (d. 1820), and Judith Key (d. 1860), daughter of Killis Key, were married by bond 23 DEC 1813 in Essex Co., with Elisha Johnson, security.
[3] John L. Foxell and his wife Mary J. were buried at Currioman Baptist Church, Chiltons, Va.
[4] John Wesley Sorrell and Sarah Sanford were married by bond 23 DEC 1847 in Westmoreland Co., with George H. Bryan, security.
[5] Joseph France was buried in the France Family Cemetery, Newland, Va.
[6] John France, widower, and Elizabeth Hall, were married by bond 16 MAY 1829 in Richmond Co., with John Saunders, security.
[7] Cornelius A. Frank and his wife Mary Indiana were buried in St. Peter's Cemetery, Oak Grove, Va.
[8] Joshua Frank and Ailsy Wilkerson were married 7 JAN 1843 in King George Co. by Rev. Philip Montague.

Franklin, James Edward (d. by 1874), to Sarah Frances Jenkins. JAMES EDWARD FRANKLIN, farmer, age 22, single, b. Westmoreland Co., son of Zachariah Franklin and Lucy [Hinson],[1] to SARAH FRANCES JENKINS, age 20, single, b. Richmond Co., daughter of Enoch and Selina Jenkins. Signed Jas. E. [his X mark] Franklin. License 10 MAR 1868. Married 12 MAR 1868 at Mr. Pursley's residence by Thomas E. Locke, Rector, Washington Parish. [M18; R:90; R1:32-12; WP]

Franklin, John Belfield, second[2] to Susan F. Self. JOHN BELFIELD FRANKLIN, farmer, age 37, widowed, b. Charles Co., Md., son of James M. [d. testate 1878] and Mary W. Franklin, to SUSAN F. SELF, age 25, single, b. Westmoreland Co., daughter of Wat and Lucy Self.[3] License 28 AUG 1877. Married 30 AUG 1877 at *Shannon* by G.W. Beale. [M19; R:122; R1:70-8]

Franklin, Joseph William to Virginia Tate. JOSEPH WILLIAM FRANKLIN, farmer, age 23, single, b. Westmoreland Co., son of John and Lucy Franklin, to VIRGINIA TATE, age 21, single, b. Westmoreland Co., daughter of Jordon and Mary Tate. Signed Joseph W. [his X mark] Franklin, wit. Wm. S. McKenney. License 19 APR 1876. Married 20 APR 1876 at Mary Tate's by Robt. N. Reamy. [M19; R:118; R1:64-14]

Franklin, Samuel R. to Jane Ann Lewis. SAMUEL R. FRANKLIN, farmer, age 22, single, b. and res. Richmond Co., son of Samuel [R.] Franklin and Susan S. [Sisson],[4] to JANE ANN LEWIS, age 19, single, b. Westmoreland Co., daughter of John W. and Ellen [P.] Lewis. License 28 MAR 1870. Married 30 MAR 1870 by James A. Weaver. [M18; R:98; R1:42-13]

Frazer, Austin to Maria Howard (d. 1884 of consumption). AUSTIN FRAZER, farmer, age 34, widowed, b. King George Co., son of Edmond and Sallie Frazer, to MARIA HOWARD, age 21, single, b. Westmoreland Co., daughter of Benjamin and Loucinda Howard. License 11 DEC 1879. Married 14 DEC 1879 by H.H. Fones. [M20; R:130; R1:79-10]

Fultine, William (C) to Eliza Smith. WILLIAM FULTINE, farmer, age 21, single, b. Westmoreland Co., son of William and Betsey Fultine, to ELIZA SMITH, age 18, single, b. Westmoreland Co., daughter of Jerry and Susan Smith. William [his X mark] Fultin [sic]. License 27 DEC 1871. Married 29 DEC 1871 at Zion Church by Thomas T. Johnson. [M18; R:104; R1:49-2]

Funsten, Oliver Ridgeway, Jr.(1845-1894), served in Co. D, 6th Va. Cav. and others, C.S.A., to Lucy Pratt Lewis (1844-1909).[5] OLIVER RIDGEWAY FUNSTEN, JR., farmer, age 25, single, b. and res. Clarke Co., son of O.R. [Sr.] [1817-1871] Funsten and Mary C. [Catherine Meade] [1816-1847], to LUCY PRATT LEWIS, age 22, single, b. Westmoreland Co., daughter of George W. [d. testate 1879[6]] and Jane B. Lewis. License 9 JUN 1868. Married 10 JUN 1868 at *Claymont*, the residence of the bride's father [G.W. Lewis] by Thomas E. Locke, Rector, Washington Parish. [M18; R:91; R1:34-5; SC; WP]

---

[1] Zachariah Franklin and Lucy Hinson were married by bond 2 FEB 1825 in Westmoreland Co., with William Tallent, security.
[2] DR:35-20, entry for Sarah E. Franklin, b. Somerset Co., Md., d. 3 DEC 1876 of consumption, age 29, daughter of David and Caroline Messick, wife of John B. Franklin.
[3] Walter D. Self and Lucy S. Brann were married by bond 15 APR 1845 in Westmoreland Co., with Robert M. Self, security.
[4] Samuel R. Franklin and Susan S. Sisson were married by bond 24 FEB 1841 in Richmond Co., with James Johnson, security.
[5] O.R. Funsten, Jr. and his wife Lucy Pratt Lewis were buried in Thornrose Cemetery, Staunton, Va.
[6] Deeds & Wills No. 41, p. 378, will of George W. Lewis, proved 26 MAY 1879, names daughter Lucy Pratt Funsten.

Furlong, John (d. testate 1894[1]), to Mrs. Mary Jane Sandy Sanford (b. 1829, d. 1887 of heart disease),[2] widow of Col. William H. Sanford (1791-1875), *q.v.* JOHN FURLONG, bookkeeper, age 68, widowed, b. Baltimore City, Md., res. Alexandria City, Va., son of William and Sarah Furlong, to MARY JANE SANFORD, age 51, widow, b. Richmond Co., daughter of John Sandy and Fannie [Robinson Sanford]. License 27 DEC 1879. Married 27 DEC 1879 at *Springfield* by F.B. Beale. [DR:76-78; M20; R:131; NN; R1:80-6]

G

Gaines, Moses (C) to Catherine Watts. MOSES GAINES, farmer, age 22, single, b. Westmoreland Co., son of Travis and Martha Gaines, to CATHERINE WATTS, age 19, single, b. Westmoreland Co., daughter of Emanuel and Hannah Watts. Signed Moses [his X mark] Gaines. License 11 JAN 1872. Married 13 JAN 1872 by Emanuel Watts, Pastor, Little Zion Church, Oak Grove, Va. [M19; R:104; R1:49-5]

Gainey, Zachariah to Susan Smith. ZACHARIAH GAINEY, farmer, age 18, single, b. Westmoreland Co., son of William Gainey and Fanny Ball, to SUSAN SMITH, age 22, single, b. Westmoreland Co., daughter of Carter Travis, mother not known. Signed Zachariah [his X mark] Gainey, wit. J.H. Sisson. License 18 OCT 1869. Married 19 OCT 1869. [M18; R:95; R1:39-6]

Gaiters, Edmund (C) to Eliza Ann Thompson. EDMUND GAITERS, farmer, age 28, single, b. Richmond Co., son of Osburn and Celia Gaiters, to ELIZA ANN THOMPSON, age 23, single, b. Westmoreland Co., daughter of Manda Montague, father unknown. License 14 MAR 1877. Married 15 MAR 1877 at Joseph Thomson's by Jerry Graham. [M19; R:121; R1:69-7]

Gardner, David S. to Emily Frances Laycock. DAVID S. GARNER [sic], blacksmith, age 32, single, b. Connecticut, son of James and Reitta Gardner, to EMILY FRANCES LAYCOCK, age 20, single, b. Westmoreland Co., daughter of John [P.] Laycock and Elizabeth [Brown].[3] License 10 MAR 1858. Married 10 MAR 1858 at Ebenezer Church by W.W. Walker, M.G. [M16a:58-9; R:63; R1:11-10]

Garland, James Parker (C) to Mary Samuel. JAMES PARKER GARLAND, blacksmith, age 23, single, b. Lunenburg Co., son of Peter and Peggy Garland,[4] to MARY SAMUEL, age 16, single, b. Essex Co., daughter of Leanna Samuel. License 18 DEC 1876. Married 19 DEC 1876 at Little Zion Church by Emanuel Watts, pastor, Little Zion Church. [M19; R:120; R1:67-9]

Garland, Simon (C) to Fanny Quarles. SIMON GARLAND, blacksmith, age 32, single, b. Lunenburg Co., son of Robin and Fanny Garland, to FANNY QUARLES, age 20, single, b. Westmoreland Co., daughter of Joshua and Caroline Quarles (C) [d. 1895]. Signed Simon [his X mark] Garland. License 3 JUN 1875. Married 5 JUN 1875 at Troy [Creek] by Emanuel Watts, pastor of Little Zion Church. [DR:104-46; M19; R:115; R1:61-7]

Garner, Thornton to Martha Barker. THORNTON GARNER, farming, age 22, single, b. King George Co., son of Thornton Garner and Hanna his wife, to MARTHA BARKER, daughter of Daniel

---

[1] Deeds & Wills No. 52, p. 350, will of John Furlong, of Montross, Va., proved 25 JUN 1894.
[2] John Furlong and his wife Mary Jane were buried at Andrew Chapel United Methodist Church, Montross, Va.
[3] John P. Laycock and Elizabeth Brown were married by bond 29 MAY 1834 in Westmoreland Co., with Nelson R. Dozier, security.
[4] Norris, p. 578, Peter and Peggy Garland helped establish Little Zion Baptist Church. Their son Simon was the first black mailman in Westmoreland Co.

Barker and Leucinda [Smith] his wife. License 23 OCT 1854. Married 24 OCT 1854 at Henry Hall's by John Pullen, M.G. [M15:54-13; R:45; R1:2]

Garnett, Henry (C) to Fanny Robinson. HENRY GARNETT, farmer, age 2[6], single, b. Essex Co., son of Emma Smith, to FANNY ROBINSON, age 21, single, b. Essex Co., daughter of Judy Robinson. License 29 DEC 1874. Married 29 DEC 1874 by John Roy. [M19; R:114; R1:60-7]

Garnett, Robert (C) to Martha Ann Taliaferro. ROBERT GARNETT, farmer, age 21, single, b. Caroline Co., son of Albert and Malinda Garnett, to MARTHA ANN TALIAFERRO, age18, single, b. Caroline Co., daughter of Turner and Sally Taliaferro. Signed Robert [his X mark] Garnett, wit. W.S. McKenney. License 24 DEC 1872. Married 26 DEC 1872 at Little Zion Church, Oak Grove, Va. by Emanuel Watts, pastor. [M19; R:107; R1:52-8]

Gaskins, Alfred to Mary Jane Travis (C) (d. 1885). ALFRED GASKINS, farmer, age 21, single, b. Westmoreland Co., son of Hiram and Juliet Gaskins, to MARY JANE TRAVIS, age 21, single, b. Westmoreland Co., daughter of Sally Travis, father unknown. Signed Alfred [his X mark] Gaskins, wit. Wm. S. McKenney. License 27 DEC 1871. Married 28 DEC 1871 at Hague, Va. by Thomas T. Johnson. [DR:64-26; M19; R:104; R1:49-3]

Gaskins, Andrew (C) (d. 1883 of congestive chill), to Hannah E. Johnson. ANDREW GASKINS, laborer, age 23, single, b. Northumberland Co., son of Albert and Rosetta Gaskins (C) [d. 1888], to HANNAH E. JOHNSON, age 23, single, b. Westmoreland Co., daughter of Olmstead and Sarah Johnson. Signed Andrew [his X mark] Gaskins, wit. W.S. McKenney. License 16 DEC 1873. Married 18 DEC 1873 at *Olivista* by Thomas T. Johnson. [DR:57-37, 75-24; M19; R:110; R1:55-7]

Gaskins, Bartlett (C) (d. 1885), to Ann Thompson (d. 1872). BARTLETT GASKINS, farmer, age 60, widowed, b. Westmoreland Co., son of Thomas and Sally Gaskins, to ANNIE THOMPSON, age 50, single, b. Westmoreland Co., daughter of Maria [Hacket] Thompson, father unknown. Signed Bartlett [his X mark] Gaskins, wits. J.E. Sturman, J.W. Hutt. License 22 APR 1867. Married 25 APR 1867 at the residence of J.H. Davis by J.H. Davis. [DR:20-16, 64-20; M18; R:86; R1:28-1]

Gaskins, Bartlett (C) to Mrs. Mary Thomson. BARTLETT GASKINS, farmer, age 70, widowed, b. Westmoreland Co., son of Thomas and Sally Gaskins, to MARY THOMSON, age 50, widow, b. Westmoreland Co., parents unknown. Signed Bartlett [his X mark] Gaskins. License 19 NOV 1873. Married 20 NOV 1873 at *Hickory Hill* by J.H. Davis. [M19; R:109; R1:54-14]

Gaskins, Edmond to Harriet Pratt, colored persons. EDMOND GASKINS, farmer, age 55, widower, b. Westmoreland Co., son of Davy and Judy Gaskins, to HARRIET PRATT, age 21, single, b. Westmoreland Co., daughter of Owen and Ann Pratt. Signed Edmond [his X mark] Gaskins, wit. J.W. Hutt. License 8 DEC 1868. Married 24 DEC 1868 by Thomas E. Locke, Rector, Washington Parish. [M18; R:93; R1:36-7; WP]

Gaskins, Edward (a.k.a. Edmond) (C) to Mrs. Milly Jackson. EDWARD GASKINS, farmer, age 60, widowed, b. Westmoreland Co., son of David and Judy Gaskins, to MILLY JACKSON, age 35, widow, b. Essex Co., parents unknown. License 17 DEC 1877. Married 19 DEC 1877 at Little Zion Church by Emanuel Watts, pastor, Little Zion Church. [M19; R:123 has Edmond Gaskins; R1:71-11]

Gaskins, Moses Henry (C) (b. c.1857, d. 1936 of valvular heart disease), to Mary Ann Smith. MOSES HENRY GASKINS, farmer, age 23, single, b. Westmoreland Co., son of Peter and Caroline Gaskins, to MARY ANN SMITH, age 21, single, b. Westmoreland Co., daughter of Julia Ann Smith, father unknown. License 12 MAY 1880. Married 13 MAY 1880 at *Cherry Grove* by Chas. [his X mark] Rust. [DC; M20; R:133; R1:82-11]

Gaskins, Peter, free colored, to Caroline Henry. Married by T. Grayson Dashiell. [M16:55-24a (no bride given) date 15 DEC 1855; M16:56-1 date 22 JAN 1856; R:53]

Gaskins, Richard Henry (C) to Mrs. Emily Cralle Gauf. RICHARD HENRY GASKINS, farmer, age 30, widowed, b. Westmoreland Co., son of George and Ellen Gaskins, to EMILY GAUF, age 30, widow, b. Westmoreland Co., daughter of Lewis and Sally Crallee [sic]. Signed Richard H. [his X mark] Gaskins, wit. J.W. Hutt. License 18 OCT 1872. Married 19 OCT 1872 at Potomac Baptist Church by Thomas T. Johnson. [M19; R:106; R1:51-5]

Gaskins, Samuel (C) to Sarah Harrison. SAMUEL GASKINS, farmer, age 24, single, b. Westmoreland Co., son of Peter and Caroline Gaskins, to SARAH HARRISON, age 21, single, b. Westmoreland Co., daughter of Polly Harrison, father unknown. License 15 DEC 1880. Married 16 DEC 1880 at *Cherry Grove* by Charles Rust. [M20; R:134; R1:84-7]

Gaskins, William A. (C) (d. 1888), to Lorinda Harrison. WILLIAM GASKINS, farmer, age 26, single, b. Westmoreland Co., son of Bartlet[t] Gaskins and Mary [Ann Peck],[1] to LORINDA HARRISON, age 23, single, b. Westmoreland Co., daughter of Samuel Harrison and Letty [Henry].[2] Signed William [his X mark] Gaskins, wit. Wm. E. Baker. Consent 27 APR 1860 by Samuel Harrison for his daughter Lorinda to marry, wit. S.R. Branson. License 1 MAY 1860. Married 3 MAY 1860. [DR:75-23; M17:60-21 and 21a; R:74]

Gawen, James Braxton (d. 1872 of consumption), served in Co. K, 40th Va. Inf., C.S.A., to Sarah "Sallie" Elizabeth Dunnahaw. JAMES BRAXTON GOWEN [sic], farmer, age 28, single, b. Westmoreland Co., son of William Gawen [d. 1844] and Alice J. [Jefferson Garner], to SALLIE ELIZABETH DUNNAHAW, age 22, single, b. Westmoreland Co., daughter of Richard H. and Sallie E. Dunnahaw. License 11 DEC 1866. Married 15 DEC 1866 by G.H. Northam. [DR:20-15; M18; R:84; R1:25-15]

Gawen, Joseph A. to Jane L. Brown (d. 1869 of heart disease). JOSEPH A. GAWEN, merchant, age 35, single, b. Westmoreland Co., son of William Gawen [d. 1844] and Alice [Jefferson Garner], to JANE L. BROWN, age 17, single, b. Westmoreland Co., daughter of John and Susan Brown. License 26 FEB 1860. Married 29 FEB 1860 by George F. Bagby. [DR:17-13; M17:60-12; R:72; R1:17-2]

Gawen, Robert Hall (1842-1911),[3] served Co. K, 40th Va. Inf., C.S.A., first to Anna Dunnahaw [Donahue] (d. 1871 in child birth). ROBERT HALL GAWEN, farmer, age 27, single, b. Westmoreland Co., son of William Gawen [d. 1844] and Alice J. [Jefferson Garner],[4] to ANNA

---

[1] Barlett Gaskins and Mary Ann Peck were married by bond 21 OCT 1829 in Westmoreland Co., with Samuel Harrison, security.
[2] Samuel Harrison and Letty Henry were married by bond 19 MAY 1829 in Westmoreland Co., with Henry Johnson, security.
[3] Robert Hall Gawen was buried at Yeocomico Episcopal Church, Tucker Hill, Va.
[4] CF1859-10, *Alice Gawen v. Admr. of William Gawen.*

DUNNAHAM, age 19, single, b. Alabama, daughter of Richard and Anna Dunnahaw. Married 5 MAY 1870 by G.H. Northam. [DR:23-11; M18; R:99; R1:43-3]

Gawen, Robert Hall (1842-1911), second to Mrs. Sarah Elizabeth Dunnahaw [a.k.a. Donahue] Gawen (1844-1910), widow of James Braxton Gawen, *q.v.* ROBERT HALL GAWEN, farmer, age 30, widowed, b. Westmoreland Co., son of William Gawen [d. 1844] and Alice [Jefferson Garner], to SARAH ELIZABETH GAWEN, age 28, widow, b. Westmoreland Co., daughter of Richard [H.] and Sally [E.] Dunnahaw. License 21 NOV 1872. Married 21 NOV 1872 at St. James Church in Montross, Va. by D.M. Wharton. [M19; R:107; R1:51-13]

Gowen, Thomas Arthur (d. 1872 in Northumberland Co.), to Mrs. Mary Young McKenney Sutton, widow of John Sutton, *q.v.* THOMAS ARTHUR GOWEN, farmer, age 70, widowed, b. Westmoreland Co., son of John and Mary Gowen, to MARY YOUNG SUTTON, age 44, widow, b. Westmoreland Co., daughter of James McKenney and Sallie [Sutton].[1] License 5 DEC 1866. Married 10 DEC 1866 by G.H. Northam. [DR:20-17; M18; R:84; R1:25-14]

Gawen, William Presley (d. 1889 of consumption), to Elizabeth Ann Murphy. WILLIAM PRESLEY GAWEN, merchant, age 25, single, b. Westmoreland Co., son of William Gawen [d. 1844] and Alice J. [Jefferson Garner][2] [d. 1882 of pneumonia], to ELIZABETH ANN MURPHY, age 24, single, b. Westmoreland Co., daughter of James B. Murphy and Susan [B. Lowe].[3] License 22 SEP 1859. Married 23 SEP 1859 by T. Grayson Dashiell. [DR:52-40, 81-146; M16a:59-24 and 24a; R:70; R1:15-1]

Gemeny, Edgar Jero. to Caroline Virginia Courtney. EDGAR J. GEMENY, carpenter, age 28, single, b. Alexandria, Va., son of John and Matilda Gemeny [d. 1877], to CAROLINE VIRGINIA COURTNEY, age 19, single, b. Westmoreland Co., daughter of William J. Courtney and Elizabeth B. [Lamkin].[4] License 27 DEC 1867. Married 1 JAN 1868 at Carmel [Church] by J.H. Davis. [DR:39-34; M18; R:89; R1:31-5]

George, Philander Chinn, first to Ann E. Atwill. License 21 JUN 1852. Married 22 JUN 1852 by H.H. Gary. [M15:52-19, R:21]

George, Philander Chinn (1830-1899),[5] served in Co. C, 9th Va. Inf. as ambulance driver, C.S.A., second to Sarah "Sallie" Harriet Brown. PHILANDER CHINN GEORGE, farmer, age 33, widowed, b. Lancaster Co., son of Spencer George and Pauline [Lawson][6] [d. 1883], to SALLIE HARRIET BROWN, age 23, single, b. Westmoreland Co., daughter of William W. and Jane Brown. License 20 MAY 1863. Married 21 MAY 1863 at Col. W.W. Brown's by William F. Bain. [DR:57-39[7]; M17:63-4; NN; R:79; R1:20-1]

George, Philander Chinn (1830-1899), third to Sarah Frances Edwards. PHILANDER CHINN GEORGE, farmer, age 38, widowed, b. Lancaster Co., son of Spencer George and Pauline

---

[1] James McKenney and Sally Sutton were married by bond 16 DEC 1806 in Westmoreland Co., with Daniel Morris, security.
[2] William Gawen and Alice Jefferson Garner, daughter of Catherine Garner, were married by bond 14 DEC 1818 in Westmoreland Co., with Augustus L. Gallagheare, security.
[3] James B. Murphy and Susan B. Lowe, were married by bond 2 SEP 1839 in Westmoreland Co., with James Lowe, security.
[4] William J. Courtney and Elizabeth B. Lamkin were married by bond 3 JUL 1834 in Westmoreland Co., with John English, security.
[5] Philander C. George was buried at Lebanon United Methodist Church.
[6] Spencer George and Pauline Lawson, daughter of H.C. Lawson, were married by bond 13 NOV 1826 in Lancaster Co.
[7] DR:57-39, entry for Paulina Greorge, widow, b. Lancaster Co., d. 22 DEC 1883 of old age, age 75, daughter of Henry C. and Mary Lawson, mother of Philander C. George.

[Lawson], *q.v.*, to SARAH FRANCES EDWARDS, age 33, single, b. Westmoreland Co., daughter of William and Sarah E. Edwards. Married 2 APR 1868 at the residence of T.W.B. Edwards by H.P.F. King. [M18; R1:32-14]

George, Philander Chinn (1830-1899), fourth to Henrietta Lyell Atwill. PHILANDER CHINN GEORGE, farmer, age 44, widowed, b. Lancaster Co., son of Spencer George and Pauline [Lawson], *q.v.*, to HENRIETTA LYELL ATWILL, age 25, single, b. Westmoreland Co., daughter of Daniel Atwill. License 30 OCT 1876. Married 2 NOV 1876 at Lebanon Church by John W. White. [M19; R:119; R1:66-10]

Gibson, Thomas (C) to Mary Chatman. THOMAS GIBSON, farmer, age 53, widowed, b. Westmoreland Co., son of Simon and Silvey Gibson, to MARY CHATMAN, age 31, single, b. Westmoreland Co., parents unknown.[1] Signed Thomas [his X mark] Gibson, wit. C.C. Baker. License 3 SEP 1868. Married 26 SEP 1868 by Jerry Graham, parson. [M18; R:92; R1:35-5]

Gilbert, William Ewell to Julia Augusta English. WILLIAM EWELL GILBERT, farmer, age 20, single, b. and res. Northumberland Co., son of William and Mary Gilbert, to JULIA AUGUSTA ENGLISH, age 23, single, b. Westmoreland Co., daughter of Samuel W. English and Sarah A. [Ann Delano].[2] License 7 FEB 1868. Married 11 FEB 1868 at Mrs. Delano's by R.J. Sanford. [M18; R:90; R1:32-5]

Gilchrist, Jesse to Mary Jane Nickens, colored persons. JESSE GILCHRIST, farmer, age 26, single, b. Westmoreland Co., son of Daniel and Patsey Gilchrist, to MARY JANE NICKENS, age 23, single, b. Essex Co., daughter of Davey and Elizabeth Nickens. License 22 OCT 1869. Married 23 OCT 1869 at Dr. Wirt's farm by Thomas E. Locke, Rector of Washington Parish. [M18; R:96; R1:39-8; WP]

Gill, Benjamin Snow to Virginia Frances Delano. BENJAMIN SNOW GILL, farmer, age 23, single, b. New Castle Co., Del., son of Benjamin R. and Mary R. Gill, to VIRGINIA FRANCES DELANO, age 22, single, b. Westmoreland Co., daughter of George and Nancy Delano. License 9 MAY 1864. Married 10 MAY 1864 at the home of Augustus Delano by W.W. Walker, V.D.M. [M17:64-3; R:80; R1:20-11]

Gillis, Newton to Susan Coventon [Covington]. NEWTON GILLIS, farmer, age 21, single, b. Richmond Co., son of Syrus and Judy Gillis, to SUSAN COVENTON, age 18, single, b. Essex Co., son of Emily Coventon, father unknown. License 14 JUN 1879. Married 14 JUN 1879 by R.N. Reamy. [M20; R:129; R1:78-2]

Goldsby, George Washington (d. 1889 of carbunkle), to Lucy Muse. GEORGE WASHINGTON GOLDSBY, hotel keeper, age 51, widowed, b. Fredericksburg, Va., son of David and Matilda Goldsby [d. 1873], to LUCY MUSE, age 34, single, b. Westmoreland Co., daughter of James H. Muse and Elizabeth [B. Walker].[3] License 22 DEC 1869. Married 23 DEC 1869 by D.M. Wharton, Rector of Montross Parish. [DR:26-20, 79-24; M18; R:97; R1:40-31]

---

[1] The names Daniel and Hannah have been crossed through onlicense.
[2] Samuel W. English and Sarah Ann Delano were married by bond 23 DEC 1844 in Westmoreland Co., with Benedict Walker, security.
[3] James A. Muse and Elizabeth B. Walker were married by bond 27 JAN 1834 in Westmoreland Co., with James H. Payne, security.

Good, James H. (C) to Elmira Waughn. JAMES H. GOOD, house carpenter, age 34, widowed, b. Essex Co., son of Phil Good and Sally [Johnston],[1] to ELMIRA WAUGHN, age 24, single, b. Westmoreland Co., daughter of James and Ann Waughn. Signed James H. [his X mark] Good, wit. John Goodridge. License 22 DEC 1859. Married 22 DEC 1859. [M16a:59-29; R:70]

Good, James to Martha Pierce. License 3 JUN 1852. Married 3 JUN 1852 by E.B. McGuire. [M15:52-18; R:19]

Good, James (C) to Martha Jane Roan. JAMES GOOD, carpenter, age 39, widowed, b. Essex Co., son of Philip Good and Sally [Johnston], *q.v.*, to MARTHA JANE ROAN, age 23, single, b. Westmoreland Co., daughter of John and Lucy Roan. Signed James [his X mark] Good, wits. W.T. Bispham, J.W. Hutt. License 30 MAY 1866. Married 31 MAY 1866 by J.H. Davis. [M18; R:83; R1:24-4]

Good, James (C) to Virginia Thompson. JAMES GOOD, miller, age 51, widowed, b. Essex Co., son of Phil Good and Sallie [Johnston], *q.v.*, to VIRGINIA THOMPSON, age 24, widow, b. Westmoreland Co., daughter of William and Ann Thompson. License 7 MAY 1879. Married 8 MAY 1879 at Potomac Church by F.B. Beale. [M20; R:129; R1:77-10]

Gordon, Benjamin (C) to Winnieann Travis. BENJAMIN GORDON, farmer, age 43, single, b. Westmoreland Co., son of Edwin and Susan Gordon, to WINNIEANN TRAVIS, age 26, single, b. Westmoreland Co., daughter of Carter and Sally Travis. License 2 JUN 1870. Married 2 JUN 1870 by Thomas T. Johnson, minister. [M18; R:99; R1:43-8]

Gordon, Hyson Freeling (b. 1845, d. 1916 in Baltimore, Md.), to Josephine Nora Winstead (b. 1856, d. 1946 of heart disease).[2] HYSON FREELING GORDON, farmer, age 30, single, b. Richmond Co., son of John and Fannie Gordon, to JOSEPHINE NORA WINSTEAD, age 16, single, b. Richmond Co., daughter of John [H.] Winstead and Dianah [H. Lewis].[3] Signed H.F. Gordon. License 29 DEC 1873. Married 30 DEC 1873 by R.J. Sanford. [DC; M19; R:111; R1:56-2]

Gordon, Jeremiah (C) to Emily Ann Wilson. JEREMIAH GORDON, farmer, age 35, single, b. Northumberland Co., son of Joseph and Nelly Gordon, to EMILY ANN WILSON, age 24, single, b. Westmoreland Co., daughter of Richard E. and Elizabeth Wilson. Signed Jeremiah [his X mark] Gordon, wit. Wm. S. McKenney. License 1 JUN 1875. Married 4 JUN 1876 at [Hone] Pt. by Thomas T. Johnson. [M19; R:115; R1:61-6]

Gordon, Robert Henry (C) (1848-1919), to Maria Stewart.[4] ROBERT HENRY GORDON, farmer, age 29, single, b. Westmoreland Co., son of Osburn and Lucy Gordon, to MARIA STEWART, age 18, single, b. Westmoreland Co., daughter of Richard and Harriet Stewart. License 30 JAN 1877. Married 1 FEB 1877 at Richard Stewart's house by Thomas T. Johnson. [M19; R:121; R1:68-15]

---

[1] Philip Goode and Sally Johnston [or Johnson] were married by bond 24 DEC 1816 in Essex Co., with Elijah Johnston, security.
[2] Freeling Hyson Gordon and his wife Josephine N. were buried at Gibeon Baptist Church, Village, Va.
[3] John H. Winstead, son of Samuel Winstead, and Diannah M. Lewis, daughter of Sarah Lewis, were married 22 OCT 1852 by Rev. William F. Barrack in Richmond Co.
[4] Robert H. Gordon and his wife Maria were buried at Potomac Baptist Church, Hague, Va.

Gouldman, Thomas,[1] served in Co. A, 15th Va. Cav., C.S.A., to Susan Ann Gutridge (1842-1915).[2] THOMAS GOULDMAN, farmer, age 24, single, b. Westmoreland Co., son of John Gouldman and Martha [Parker], to SUSAN ANN GUTRIDGE, age 23, single, b. Westmoreland Co., daughter of James Gutridge [d. 1868] and Susan [Hinson].[3] License 22 JAN 1868. Married 23 JAN 1868 at James Gutridge's by R.N. Reamy. [DC; DR:15-22; M18; R:89; R1:31-12]

Gowen (see Gawen)

Graham, Ewell (C) to Ella (or Levinor[4]) Lewis. EWELL GRAHAM, farmer, age 23, single, b. Westmoreland Co., son of Charles and Patty Graham, to ELLA LEWIS, age 19, single, b. Westmoreland Co., daughter of Levinor Lewis, father unknown. Signed Ewell [his X mark] Graham, wit. Wm. Green. License 25 JAN 1869. Married 30 JAN 1869 by Jerry Graham. [M18; R:94; R1:37-11]

Graham, James Spiers to Mrs. Sarah Adelaide Collins Smith. JAMES SPIERS GRAHAM, farmer, age 39, widowed, b. Glasgow, Scotland, son of John and Jane Spiers, to SARAH ADELAIDE SMITH, age 32, widow, b. Northampton, Mass., daughter of David and Mary Ann Collins. License 27 MAR 1880. Married 27 MAR 1880 by Paul Bradley. [M20; R:133; R1:82-2]

Graham, Jeremiah "Jerry," Rev. (C), second[5] to Mrs. Mary Newman. JERRIE GRAHAM [sic], minister of the gospel, age 62, widowed, b. Westmoreland Co., son of James and Philis Graham, to MARY NEWMAN, age 52, widow, b. Westmoreland Co., parents unknown. Signed J. [his X mark] Graham, wit. J.W. Hutt. License 19 DEC 1874. Married 24 DEC 1874 at the house of Mary Newman by Thomas G. Thomas. [M19; R:113; R1:59-13]

Grant, Milton (C) to Mrs. Mary Downing Richardson. MILTON GRANT, farmer, age 23, single, b. Westmoreland Co., son of Solomon and Eliza Grant, to MARY RICHARDSON, age 36, widow, b. Westmoreland Co., daughter of John and Fanny Downing. Signed by Milton [his X mark] Grant, wit. W.S. McKenney. License 4 FEB 1874. Married 5 FEB 1874 at [Wm.] C. Taylor's by Jerry Graham. [M19; R:112; R1:57-8]

Gravatt, Andrew to Mary Jane Gouldman. ANDREW GRAVATT, farmer, age 38, widowed, b. and res. Caroline Co., son of J.C. [John Cherbury] and A. [Amanda Broaddus] Gravatt,[6] to MARY JANE GOULDMAN, age 28, single, b. Westmoreland Co., daughter of Thomas and Pheby Gouldman. License 23 NOV 1868. Married 6 DEC 1868 Howard W. Montague, M.G. of the L.J. Christ of the Baptist faith. [M18; R:93 incorrectly has James Gravatt; R1:35-16 has James Gravatt]

Gray, Robert to Fannie Franklin. ROBERT GRAY, carpenter, age 46, widowed, b. Fairfax Co., res. Washington, D.C., son of Robinson and Ruth Gray, to FANNIE FRANKLIN, age 23, single, b. Westmoreland Co., daughter of James M. and Mary Franklin. License 22 MAY 1867. Married 22 MAY 1867 at the residence of J.M. Franklin by J.H. Davis. [M18; R:86; R1:28-2]

---

[1] Perhaps John Thomas Gouldman, who was buried in the Gutridge Family Cemetery, located on Route 642 near Foneswood, Va.
[2] Susan Ann Gutridge Gouldman was buried in the Gutridge Family Cemetery, located on Route 642 near Foneswood, Va.
[3] James Gutridge and Susan Hinson were married by bond 11 JAN 1820 in Westmoreland Co., with George H. Sisson, security.
[4] On the License, the name Levinor has been crossed through and replaced with Ella; however, Levinor remains on the Certificate.
[5] DR:30-9, entry for Harriet Graham, d. 20 SEP 1874 of paralysis, wife of Jeremiah Graham.
[6] John Cherbury Gravatt (1798-1875) and his wife Amanda Broaddus (1807-1889) were buried in Greenlawn Cemetery of Bowling Green, Va. They were married in 1825 in Caroline Co.

Grayson, John (C) to Louisa Watts. JOHN GRAYSON, farmer, age 33, single, b. King George Co., son of John and Adeline Grayson, to LOUISA WATTS, age 21, single, b. Westmoreland Co., daughter of Robin and Lucy Watts. Signed John [his X mark] Grayson, wit. Wm. S. McKenney. License 23 DEC 1874. Married 30 DEC 1874 by Emanuel Watts, pastor Little Zion Church. [M19; R:114; R1:60-1]

Green, George to Mary Ellen Williams. GEORGE GREEN, sailor or waterman, age 23, single, b. Charles Co., Md., b. Westmoreland Co., son of William and [Rue] Green, to MARY ELLEN WILLIAMS, age 18, single, b. Westmoreland Co., daughter of Robert and Maria Williams. License 26 AUG 1875. Planned marriage 27 AUG 1875. [M19 no return; R:115; R1:61-13]

Green, Moses W., first to Amanda E. Franklin. MOSES W. GREEN, mechanic, age 28, single, b. Orange Co., son of George W. Green and Sally [Sarah F.] his wife, to AMANDA E. FRANKLIN, age [3]1, single, b. Westmoreland Co., daughter of Zachariah Frankling [sic] and Leucy [Hinson][1] his wife. License 16 FEB 1858. Married 18 FEB 1858 at Mrs. Franklin's in Mattox, Va. by John Pullen, M.G. [M16a:58-6; R:63; R1:11-13]

Green, Moses W., second to Jane C. Cristie Pursley. MOSES W. GREEN, farmer, age 31, widowed, b. Orange Co., son of George W. and Sarah F. Green, to JANE C. CRISTIE PURSLEY, age 20, single, b. Westmoreland Co., daughter of William Pursley and Margaret Ann [Wilkins].[2] License 2 JUN 1861. Married 2 JUN 1861 at Popes Creek Church by John Pullen. [M17:61-11; R:77; R1:18-4]

Greenlaw, Shakespear Byron (1842-1918), of *Oak Grove*, to Charlotte Ann Carter (1847-1885).[3] SHAKESPEAR BYRON GREENLAW, farmer, age 24, single, b. King George Co., son of William Greenlaw [1802-1854] and Sarah [Ann Underwood],[4] to CHARLOTTE ANN CARTER, age 22, single, b. Westmoreland Co., daughter of George M. Carter and Mary [T. Rice].[5] License 2 AUG 1869. Married 4 AUG 1869 at the residence of the bride's father by Thomas E. Locke, Rector, Washington Parish. [M18; R:95; R1:39-3; SC; WP]

Gregory, James to Frances Bowen. JAMES GREGORY, farmer, age 23, single, b. Westmoreland Co., son of John Gregory and Frances [Howsen],[6] to FRANCES BOWEN, age 19, single, b. Westmoreland Co., daughter of Hanah Bowen [sic]. Married 18 MAY 1858 by James A. Weaver, minister of the Union Baptist Church. [M16a:58-14; R1:12-5]

Gregory, John Brooks to Mary "Polly" Ann Ennis (d. 1885 of dropsy). JOHN BROOKS GREGORY, farmer, age 22, single, b. Westmoreland Co., son of John Gregory and Fanny [Howsen], *q.v.*, to POLLY ANN ENNIS, age 20, single, b. Westmoreland Co., daughter of [Billy and] Jane E. Ennis,[7] father unknown. Signed John B. Gregory, wit. Chas. C. Baker. Consent 11 MAR 1861 by mother Jain Elizabeth [her X mark] Ennis, signed by bride Polly Ann [her X mark] Ennis, wit. John Howell. License 12 MAR 1861. Married 14 MAR 1861. [DR:64-22; M17:61-6 and 6a; R:77]

---

[1] Zachariah Franklin and Lucy Hinson were married by bond 2 FEB 1825 in Westmoreland Co., with William Tallent, security.
[2] William Pursley and Ann Margaret Wilkins were married by license 1 APR 1830 in Westmoreland Co., with James Peed, security.
[3] Shakespear B. Greenlaw and his wife Charlotte were buried at St. Peter's Cemetery, Oak Grove, Va.
[4] William Greenlaw and his wife Sarah Ann Underwood were buried in the Greenlaw Family Cemetery, *Ellerslie*, King George Co.
[5] George M. Carter and Mary T. Rice were married by bond 12 DEC 1834 in Westmoreland Co., with Thomas L. Muse, security.
[6] John Gregory and Fanny Howson were married by bond 8 NOV 1830 in Westmoreland Co., with Robert Anton, security.
[7] William Ennis and Jane McKenney were married by bond 14 APR 1845 in Westmoreland Co., with Fleet B. Anton, security.

Gregory, Levi to Mary Ann Shackleford. LEVI GREGORY, miller, age 35, single, b. Westmoreland Co., son of Thomas Gregory and Elizabeth [King],[1] to MARY ANN SHACKLEFORD, age 18, single, b. Westmoreland Co., daughter of John Shackleford and Martha [Newman].[2] License 30 JUN 1864. Married 30 JUN 1864 at the residence of the bride's father by H.P.F. King. [M17:64-4; R:80; R1:20-12]

Gregory, Matthew D. to Sarah Ann Howell. License 21 NOV 1853. Married 21 NOV 1853 by George Northam, L.M.G. [M15:53-21; R:35]

Gregory, Samuel Templeman to Catharine Ann Merinder. SAMUEL TEMPLEMAN GREGORY, farmer, age 36, single, b. Westmoreland Co., son of James Gregory and Isabella [Templeman],[3] to CATHARINE ANN MERINDER, age 19, single, b. Westmoreland Co., daughter of John and Mary Merinder. Consent 15 SEP 1860 by bride Catharine Ann [her X mark] Merinder, wit. John Howell. License 17 SEP 1860. Married 16[4] SEP 1860 by H.P.F. King. [M17:60-30 and 30b; R:74; R1:16-13]

Gresham, Samuel Preston to Mary Stuart Harvey. SAMUEL PRESTON GRESHAM, merchant, age 23, single, b. and res. Lancaster Co., son of Samuel Gresham and Sarah C. [Chilton],[5] to MARY STUART HARVEY, age 19, single, b. Alexandria, Va., daughter of George C. and Mary S. Harvey. License 25 DEC 1858. Married 29 DEC 1858 by H.P.F. King, M.G. [M16a:58-41 and 41a; R:66; R1:13-3]

Griffith, Edward Colville to Julia Rebecca Hungerford (1826-1903), daughter of John Washington and Eleanor Anne Hungerford.[6] License 28 MAR 1853. Married 6 APR 1853 by Wm. McGuire, Rector of Montross and Cople Parishes. [M15:53-11; R:29]

Griffith, Frederick, Dr. (b. 1841, d. 1877 of consumption),[7] served Co. C, 9th Va. Cav., C.S.A., to Fannie Brockenbrough Tyler. FREDERICK GRIFFITH, physician, age 22, single, b. Westmoreland Co., son of Edward C. Griffith and [Mary] Elizabeth [Cox],[8] to FANNIE BROCKENBROUGH TYLER, age 18, single, b. Essex Co., daughter of Wat H. [Henry] Tyler and Jane L. [Louisa Blake].[9] License 5 FEB 1863. Planned marriage 10 FEB 1863. [CP; R:79; R1:19-13 no return]

Griggs, Hudson Porter, served in Co. A, 15th Va. Cav., C.S.A., to Martha Ann McGuire. HUDSON P. GRIGGS, farmer, age 29, single, b. Westmoreland Co., son of Henry Griggs and Lucy [Dozier],[10] to MARTHA A. McGUIRE, age 22,[11] single, b. Westmoreland Co., daughter of William McGuire and Lucy [Thomas].[12] License 8 NOV 1858. Married 10 NOV 1858 by H.P.F. King, minister of the M.E. Church. [M16a:58-29 and 29a; R:66; R1:12-11]

---

[1] Thomas Gregory and Elizabeth King were married by bond 29 MAY 1823 in Westmoreland Co., with John Gregory, security.

[2] John Shackleford and Martha Newman were married by bond 20 JAN 1842 in Westmoreland Co., with Fleet Gregory, security.

[3] James Gregory and Isabella Templeman were married by bond 5 MAR 1812 in Westmoreland Co., with Gerrard McKenney, security.

[4] Minister return by H.P.F. King gives date of marriage as 17 SEP 1860, while it is 16 SEP 1860 on certificate.

[5] Samuel Gresham and Mrs. Sarah C. Chilton, widow of Fauntleroy Chilton, and sister of Richard Mitchell, were married by bond 16 MAY 1831 in Lancaster Co.

[6] Julia Rebecca Griffith was buried in the Hungerford-Griffith Family Cemetery, located at Leedstown, Va.

[7] Dr. Frederick Griffith was buried at Yeocomico Episcopal Church, Tucker Hill, Va.

[8] Edward C. Griffith and Mary E. Cox were married by bond 6 NOV 1836 in Westmoreland Co., with Joseph Jones, security.

[9] Dr. Wat Henry Tyler and Jane Louisa Blake, daughter of Benjamin and Elizabeth Blake, were married 26 DEC 1843 in St. John's Episcopal Church, Tappahannock, Va.

[10] Henry Griggs and Lucy Dozier were married by bond 25 SEP 1820 in Westmoreland Co., with James Dozier, security.

[11] Another copy at 58-29a gives age of the bride as 21.

[12] William McGuire and Lucy Thomas were married by bond 7 FEB 1827 in Westmoreland Co., with Henry Pritchet, security.

Griggs, Robert to Elizabeth Roane. License 24 MAR 1858. [R:63]

Griggs, William (C) to Mary McCoy (d. 1876 of heart disease). WILLIAM GRIGGS, farmer, age 30, widower, b. Westmoreland Co., son of Nancy Griggs, to MARY McKOY [sic], age 23, single, b. Westmoreland Co., daughter of Rodham and Agness [Douglass] McCoy, *q.v.* Signed Wm. [his X mark] McCoy, wit. J.W. Hutt. License 11 JAN 1870. Married 13 JAN 1870 at the residence of Rhodam McCoy [sic] by J.H. Davis. [DR:37-8; M18; R:97; R1:41-7]

Griggs, William (C) (d. 1893 of rheumatism), to Elizabeth Thompson. WILLIAM GRIGGS, farmer, age 31, widowed, b. Westmoreland Co., son of Nancy Griggs, father unknown, to ELIZABETH THOMPSON, age 28, single, b. Westmoreland Co., daughter of John and Judy Thompson. License 7 NOV 1877. Married 8 NOV 1877 by Thomas T. Johnson. [DR:96-49; M19; R:123; R1:70-15]

Grissett, Cyrus to Mrs. Virginia "Jennie" Dempcy. CYRUS GRISSETT, farmer, age 49, widower, b. Westmoreland Co., son of Thomas Grissett and Mary [Murry], *q.v.*, to VIRGINIA DEMPCY, age 31, widow, b. Westmoreland Co., daughter of John and Elizabeth [Cook] [Massey].[1] Signed Cyrus [his X mark] Grissitt, wit. J.W. Hutt. License 4 SEP 1869. Married 5 SEP 1869 at Popes Creek Church by Robert N. Reamy. [M18; R:95; R1:39-5]

Grissett, Milton, first to Martha Jane Beverton (d. by 1876). MILTON GRISETT, sailor, age 27, single, b. Westmoreland Co., son of Thomas Grissett and Mary [Murry],[2] to MARTHA JANE BEVERTON, age 17, single, b. Westmoreland Co., daughter of Francis Beverton and Ellen [Yardley].[3] Married 17 JUN 1858 at the rectory of St. Peter's Church by Thomas E. Locke, Rector of St. Peter's Church, Washington Parish. [M16a:58-19[4]; R1:12-3; SP]

Grissett, Milton (d. 1904),[5] served in Co. A, 15th Va. Cav., C.S.A., *q.v.*, second to Cornelia Reamy. MILTON GRISSETT, farmer, age 44, widowed, b. Westmoreland Co., son of Thomas Grissett and Mary [Murry], *q.v.*, to CORNELIA REAMEY [sic], age 15, single, b. Richmond Co., daughter of Robert [G.] Reamy and Maria [L. Carter].[6] License 15 MAY 1876. Married 15 MAY 1876 by H.H. Fones. [M19; R:118; R1:65-3]

Grissett, William to Dorathea Stevens (a.k.a. Stephens). License 23 AUG 1852. Married 26 AUG 1852 at Mrs. Sampson's by Wm. McGuire, Rector Washington Parish. [M15:52-21; R:21; SP; WP]

Gutridge, George C. to Susan A. Pitts. License 7 MAR 1856. [R:53]

Gutridge, George C., served in Co. C, 9th Va. Cav., C.S.A., to Martha Lucas. GEORGE GUTRIDGE, farmer, age 25, single, b. Westmoreland Co., son of George and [Daisy] Gutridge, to MARTHA LUCAS, age 26, single, b. Westmoreland Co., daughter of William N. Lucas and Nancy [Washington].[7] Signed George [his X mark] Gutridge, wit. J.W. Hutt. License 5 JUN 1867. Married 6 JUN 1867 at St. Peter's Church, Oak Grove, Va. by Thomas E. Locke. [M18; R:86; R1:28-5; WP]

---

[1] John Massey and Elizabeth Kook were married by bond 30 NOV 1826 in Westmoreland Co., with William B. Fleet, security.
[2] Thomas Grissett and Mary Murphy were married by bond 12 JAN 1825 in Westmoreland Co., with John Mozingo, security.
[3] Francis Bevelton and Ellen Yardley were married by bond 18 DEC 1834 in Westmoreland Co., with Walker Winkfield, security.
[4] Another copy at 58-19a notes that the place of proposed marriage is Popes Creek Church, and that the age of the bride is 16 years.
[5] Milton Gressitt is buried at Popes Creek Baptist Church, Baynesville, Va.
[6] Robert G. Reamy and Maria L. Carter were married 27 DEC 1849 in Richmond Co. by Rev. John Pullen.
[7] William N. Lucas and Nancy Washington were married by bond 23 DEC 1839 in Westmoreland Co., with William R. Sisson, security.

Gutridge, George Corbin to Mary Jane Pitts. GEORGE CORBIN GUTRIDGE, farmer, age 32, single, b. Westmoreland Co., son of Richard C. [Corbin] Gutridge and Eliza A. [Ann Reamy],[1] to MARY JANE PITTS, age 34, single, b. Westmoreland Co., daughter of William Pitts [d. 1843[2]] and Martha Pitts.[3] License 3 AUG 1864. Married 4 AUG 1864 at Mrs. Richard Gutridge's by John Pullen. [M17a:64-7; R:80; R1:20-15]

Gutridge, George Washington, served in Co. E, 15th Va. Cav., C.S.A., to Louisa Jane Barker (d. 1882 of dropsy). GEORGE WASHINGTON GUTRIDGE, farmer, age 26, single, b. Westmoreland Co., son of Albert M. Gutridge and Mary A. [Ann Nash],[4] to LOUISA JANE BARKER, age 19, single, b. Westmoreland Co., daughter of Alexander ["Sandy"] Barker and Amelia [Ann Moore].[5] Signed Geo. W. [his X mark] Gutridge, wit. J.W. Hutt. License 21 DEC 1869. Married 23 DEC 1869 at Albert Gutridge's by Thomas E. Locke. [DR:56-14; M18; R:97; R1:40-27; WP]

Gutridge, Griffin T. [or F] (d. 1870 of congestive chill at Mattox Creek, age 60), to Elizabeth Jenkins. License 11 APR 1853. Married 14 APR 1853 by John Pullen. [DR:18-14; M15:53-12; R:29]

Gutridge, Henry Randall (d. 1848, murdered 1882), to Pauline Gutridge (1856-1947).[6] HENRY RANDALL GUTTRIDGE, farmer, age 22, single, b. Westmoreland Co., son of Richard C. [Corbin] Guttridge [d. by 1870] and Eliza Ann [Reamy], *q.v.*, to PAULINA GUTTRIDGE, age 18, single, b. Westmoreland Co., daughter of Henry R. [Randall] Guttridge and Harriett [V. Pitts].[7] License 13 JAN 1871. [DR:51-14; NN; R:101; R1:45-10 no return]

Gutridge, James Christopher to Elizabeth Frances Brown. JAMES CHRISTOPHER GUTRIDGE, farmer, age 23, single, b. Richmond Co., son of Newton and Harriet H. Gutridge, to ELIZABETH FRANCES BROWN, age 30, single, b. Richmond Co., daughter of William A. and Bettie H. Brown. Signed J. [his X mark] C. Gutridge, wit. J.W. Hutt. License 2 JAN 1874. Married 4 JAN 1874 by Walter C. Taylor. [M19; R:111; R1:56-6]

Gutridge, John James to Catharine Luzella Gutridge (d. 1874 in childbirth). JOHN JAMES GUTRIDGE, laborer, age 27, single, b. Westmoreland Co., son of A.M. [Albert] Gutridge and Mary Ann [Mason][8] [d. 1882 of consumption], to CATHARINE LUZELLA GUTRIDGE, age 18, single, b. Westmoreland Co., daughter of G.T. [Griffith] and Elizabeth Ann Gutridge. Signed John [his X mark] J. Gutridge, wit. W.S. McKenney. License 6 MAY 1873. Married 12 MAY 1873 at *Cavalla* by John Payne. [DR:32-9, 56-15; M19; R:109; R1:54-3; WP]

Gutridge, Ransdell S., served in Co. C, 47th Va. Inf., C.S.A., to Elizabeth Ann Anthoney. RANSDELL S. GUTRIDGE, farmer, age 21, single, b. Westmoreland Co., son of Richard C.

---

[1] Richard C. Gutridge and Eliza Reamy, daughter of Joshua Reamy, were married by bond 15 OCT 1832 in Westmoreland Co., with John Morris, Sr., security.
[2] CF1851-04, *Martha Pitts &c. v. Admr. of William Pitts.*
[3] William Pitts and Martha Pitts were married by bond 14 DEC 1821 in Essex Co., with John Coghill, security.
[4] Albert M. Gutridge, son of Elizabeth Gutridge, and Mary Ann Nash, were married by bond 1 FEB 1838 in Westmoreland Co., with Samuel Roe, security.
[5] Sandy A. Barker and Amelia Ann Moor, daughter of Mary Moor, were married by bond 12 JAN 1837 in Westmoreland Co., with Townsend Barker, security.
[6] The surname is also found as Guttridge. Henry R. Gutridge was buried in the Gutridge Family Cemetery, located on Route 642 about ½ mile from its intersection with Route 624.
[7] Henry Gutridge and Harriett Pitts, daughter of Martha Pitts, were married by bond 20 DEC 1849 in Richmond Co., with William Gutridge, security.
[8] DR:56-15, for Mary A. Gutridge, d. 25 APR 1882 of consumption, age 65, daughter of James and Polly Mason, mother of John J. Gutridge.

[Corbin] Gutridge and Eliza Ann [Reamy], *q.v.*, to ELIZABETH ANN ANTHONEY, age 21, single, b. Richmond Co., daughter of Thomas and Ann Anthoney. License 29 MAR 1861. Married 30 MAR 1861 by Robert N. Reamy. [M17:61-7 and 7b; R:77; R1:17-16]

Gutridge, Richard H. to Eliza Ann Cradeling. License 3 APR 1851. Married 7 APR 1851 by William Balderson. [M15:51-11; R:9]

Guttridge, William A. (d. testate 1882[1]), to Frances Jane Atkins. License 2 DEC 1854. [R:45]

H

Hackett, John (C) to Mrs. Maria Peirce Tiffey (d. 1886 of pneumonia). JOHN HACKETT, farmer, age 41, widowed, b. Westmoreland Co., son of John and Maria Hackett, to MARIA TIFFEY, age 41, widow, b. Westmoreland Co., daughter of Thornton and Elizabeth Peirce. Signed John [his X mark] Hackett, wit. J.H. Sisson. License 30 AUG 1869. Married 2 SEP 1869 by John C. Smith. [DR:68-29; M18; R:95; R1:39-4]

Haislip, Joseph to Julia Jane Mothershead. JOSEPH HAISLIP, age 42, widower, b. Charles Co., Md., son of Joseph and Margaret Haislip, to JULIA JANE MOTHERSHEAD, age 33, single, b. Westmoreland Co., daughter of G.G. [George] Mothershead and Hannah [C. Baber], *q.v.* License 25 DEC 1854. Married 1 JAN 1855 at the residence of Mrs. Hannah [Sydnor] by H.P.F. King of the M.E. Church. [M15:54-15; R:47; R1:2]

Haislip, Joseph B., served in Co. C, 9th Va. Cav., C.S.A., to Mrs. Hannah C. Mothershead Sydnor, widow of Richard B. Sydnor, Jr. (1822-1850).[2] JOSEPH B. HAISLIP, house painter, age 22, single, b. Charles Co., Md., son of Joseph and Sarah Haislip, to HANNAH C. SYDNOR, age 29, widow, b. Westmoreland Co., daughter of G.G. [George] Mothershead and Hannah [C. Baber].[3] License 22 DEC 1857. Married 23 DEC 1857 at the residence of Mrs. Julia J. Haislip by H.P.F. King, minister of the M.E. Church. [M16a:57-39; R:62; R1:10-12]

Hale, Oswald to Betsy Epps. OSWALD HALE, farmer, age 21, single, b. Essex Co., son of Judy Hale, father unknown, to BETSY EPPS, age 25, single, b. Essex Co., daughter of Easter Epps, father unknown. License 21 NOV 1866. Married 23 NOV 1866 at John Dishman's by John Pullen. [M18; R:84; R1:25-12]

Hall, Abraham (C) to Betsey Berryman. ABRAHAM HALL, farmer, age 45, single, b. Westmoreland Co., son of Abraham [d. 1887] and Fanny Hall, to BETSEY BERRYMAN, age 36, single, b. Westmoreland Co., daughter of Lavinia Johnson, father unknown. Signed Abraham [his X mark] Hall and bride. License 18 MAY 1876. Married 18 MAY 1876 at my house by Thomas T. Johnson. [DR:71-27; M19; R:118; R1:65-5]

Hall, Alfred Benjamin to Mrs. Frances Ann Beddo Davis, widow of John William Davis, *q.v.* ALFRED BENJAMIN HALL, farmer, age 23, single, b. Westmoreland Co., son of Williamson Hall

---

[1] Deeds & Wills No. 42, p. 365, will of William A. Guttridge, proved 25 SEP 1882, names wife Frances Jane Guttridge.
[2] Richard B. Sydnor, Jr., son of Richard B. Sydnor (1795-1851) and Elizabeth Wright, and Hannah C. Mothershead were married by bond 19 APR 1847 in Westmoreland Co., with James C. Harvey, security.
[3] George C. Mothershead and Hannah C. Baber were married by bond 15 JAN 1816 in Westmoreland Co., with William G. Sturman, security.

and Rachel [Sanford],[1] to FRANCES ANN DAVIS, age 23, widow, b. Westmoreland Co., daughter of Hezekiah and Ann Beddo. License 26 JAN 1869. Married 28 JAN 1869 at Mrs. R. Davis' by H.H. Fones. [M18; R:94; R1:37-13]

Hall, Andrew to Bettie Norman, colored persons. ANDREW HALL, farmer, age 25, single, b. Somerset Co., Md., son of Simon and Ann Hall, to BETTIE NORMAN, age 22, single, b. Westmoreland Co., daughter of Madison and Maria Norman. License 13 NOV 1880. Married 13 NOV 1880 by Wm. C. Latane, Presbyter P.E. Church. [M20; R:134; R1:84-2; WP]

Hall, Frederick Layson (d. 1887 of pneumonia), to Alcinda V. Brewer. FREDERICK LAYSON HALL, farmer, age 22, single, b. Westmoreland Co., son of Henry Hall and Elizabeth [Silba],[2] to ALCINDA V. BREWER, age 18, single, b. Westmoreland Co., daughter of Eliza Brewer. Signed Fredk. L. [his X mark] Hall, wit. Wm. S. McKenney. License 28 DEC 1874. Married 31 DEC 1874 at *Flamstead Hill* by B.R. Battaile. [DR:73-145; M19; R:114; R1:60-6]

Hall, George A. to Sarah E. Brewer (d. 1873 of congestion near Longwood). GEORGE A. HALL, farmer, age 27, single, b. Westmoreland Co., son of Henry Hall and Elizabeth [Silba], *q.v.*, to SARAH E. BREWER, age 19, single, b. Westmoreland Co., daughter of Eliza ~~Hall~~ Brewer. License 23 OCT 1871. Married 24 OCT 1871 at William Peed's by Robert N. Reamy. [DR:28-17; M18; R:103; R1:48-1]

Hall, James Claughton (b. 1845, d. 1918 of paralysis),[3] served in Co. C, 9th Va. Cav., C.S.A., to Mary Sibbella Walker. JAMES CLAUGHTON HALL, farmer, age 24, single, b. Westmoreland Co., son of William B. Hall [d. 1869 of pneumonia] and Mary B. [Bates Omohundro][4] [d. 1888 age 70],[5] to MARY SIBELLA WALKER, age 22, single, b. Westmoreland Co., daughter of William G. Walker and Elizabeth [Sanford].[6] License 29 APR 1869. Married 28 APR 1868 at *Woodbine* by G.H. Northam. [DC; DR:15:28, 76-80; M18; R:95; R1:38-3]

Hall, Peter Martin to Mary Elizabeth Claughton. PETER MARTIN HALL, farmer, age 39, single, b. and res. Northumberland Co., son of Peter Hall and Mary [T. Haynie],[7] to MARY ELIZABETH CLAUGHTON, age 32, single, b. Westmoreland Co., daughter of Peter C. Claughton and Hannah [R. Lamkin].[8] License 24 DEC 1861. Married 2[5] DEC 1861 at minister's residence by W.W. Walker. [M17:61-13; R:77; R1:18-6]

Hall, Richard to Emily Bryant. RICHARD HALL, laborer, age 25, widowed, res. Richmond Co., son of Kit and Matilda Hall, to EMILY BRYANT, age 22, single, b. Westmoreland Co., daughter of Louisa Bryant, father unknown. License 20 DEC 1876. Planned marriage 22 DEC 1876. [M19 no return; R:120; R1:67-14]

---

[1] William Williamson Hall and Rachel Sanford were married by bond 14 DEC 1844 in Westmoreland Co., with Edwin G. Reed, security.
[2] Henry Hall and Elizabeth Silba were married by bond 13 JAN 1837 in Westmoreland Co., with John Spillman, security.
[3] James C. Hall was buried at Menokin Baptist Church.
[4] William B. Hall and Mary B. Omohundro were married by bond 10 OCT 1843 in Westmoreland Co., with E.B. Omohundro, security.
[5] William B. Hall and his first and second wives were buried in the Omohundro Family Cemetery at *Fruit View*, located near Nomini Grove, Va. He married his first wife, Mary Ann Omohundro, b. 1807, on 12 OCT 1825.
[6] William G. Walker and Elizabeth Sanford were married by bond 17 APR 1884 in Westmoreland Co., with Joseph S. Lyell, security.
[7] Peter Hall and Mary T. Haynie were married by bond 20 DEC 1815 in Northumberland Co., with Willis W. Hudnall, security.
[8] Peter C. Claughton and Hannah R. Lamkin were married by bond 26 NOV 1824 in Westmoreland Co., with James C. Wright, security.

Hall, Richard Madison (d. by 1871), to Mary Ann Healy. RICHARD MADISON HALL, farmer, age 33, widowed, b. Westmoreland Co., son of William B. Hall and Mary A. [Ann Omohundro],[1] to MARY ANN HEALY, age 20, b. Northumberland Co., daughter of Nathan and Mary A. Healy. License 6 FEB 1860. Married 9 FEB 1860 by G.H. Northam. [M17:60-9; R:72; R1:16-12]

Hall, Robert Marcus (a.k.a. Marshall) (1836-1916), first to Mary Ann Jennings (d. 1865 of dropsy). ROBERT M. HALL, farmer, age 26, single, b. Richmond Co., son of Richard Hall and Eliza [A. Yeatman], to MARY ANN JENNINGS, age 26, single, b. Richmond Co., daughter of Smith and [Elizabeth] Betsy Jennings. License 22 APR 1861. Married 23 APR 1861 at Robert M. Hall's by John Pullen. [DR:9-41; M17:61-9; R:77; R1:18-2]

Hall, Robert Marcus (a.k.a. Marshall) (1835-1916), served in Co. A, 15th Va. Cav., C.S.A., second to Sarah Ann Jennings. ROBERT MARCUS HALL [sic], miller, age 31, widowed, b. Richmond Co., son of Richard Hall and Eliza [A. Yeatman][2] [d. 1876], to SARAH ANN JENNINGS, age 25, single, b. Richmond Co., daughter of Smith and Elizabeth Jennings. License 18 DEC 1867. Married 19 DEC 1867 by H.H. Fones. [DR:37-11; M18; R:88; R1:30-7]

Hall, Sheldon M., first to Columbia H. Northam. License 26 OCT 1853. Married 28 OCT 1853 by John Pullen. [M15:53-22; R:33]

Hall, Sheldon M. (d. 1867 of consumption), served in Co. C, 9th Va. Cav., C.S.A., second to Julia A. Drake. SHELDON M. HALL, farmer, age 26, widowed, b. Westmoreland Co., res. *Forest View*, names of parents obliterated [son of William Hall], to JULIA A. DRAKE, age 16, single, b. Westmoreland Co., daughter of R. and Julia Drake. License 7 APR 1857. Married 8 APR 1857 near Morning Grove by G.H. Northam, minister of the Baptist persuasion. [DR:13-26; M16a:57-12; R:59; R1:9-4]

Hall, William H. (d. 1880 of consumption), served in Co. B, 40th Va. Inf., C.S.A., to Lucinda E. Gutridge. License 27 DEC 1851. Married 30 DEC 1851 by John Pullen. [M15:51-27; NN; R:13]

Hall, William Spicer to Alice Logan Pound. WILLIAM SPICER HALL, farmer, age 27, single, b. Westmoreland Co., son of Henry Hall and Elizabeth [Silba], *q.v.*, to ALICE LOGAN POUND, age 17, single, b. Westmoreland Co., daughter of William H. and Martha Pound. License 5 OCT 1867. Married 6 OCT 1867 in St. Peter's Church by Thomas E. Locke, Rector of St. Peter's Church. [M18; R:88; R1:29-12; WP]

Hall, William Wallis to Sarah Agnes Newton. WILLIAM WALLIS HALL, farmer, age 23, single, b. and res. Richmond Co., son of Robert and Sibby Hall, to SARAH AGNES NEWTON, age 26, single, b. Westmoreland Co., daughter of Isaac Newton and Hannah [Mathaney].[3] License 23 FEB 1870. Married 23 FEB 1870 by H.H. Fones. [M18; R:98; R1:42-6]

Hammonds, Berry to Ellen Jones. License 27 JUL 1852. [R:21 no return]

---

[1] William B. Hall and Mary Ann Omohundro, daughter of Richard Omohundro, were married by bond 10 OCT 1825 in Westmoreland Co., with George G. Mothershead, security. The couple are buried at *Fruit View*.
[2] Richard Hall and Eliza A. Yeatman were married by bond 29 DEC 1830 in Richmond Co., with William Burgess, security.
[3] Isaac Newton and Hannah Mathaney were married by bond 4 MAY 1826 in Westmoreland Co., with George Mathaney, security.

Hammonds, John to Martha Tate. JOHN HAMMONDS, sailor, age 24, single, b. Westmoreland Co., son of James Edmonds [sic] and Susan his wife, to MARTHA TATE, age 16, single, b. Westmoreland Co., daughter of Henry Tate and Synta [Johnson][1] his wife. License 4 FEB 1854. Married 5 FEB 1854 at Susan Hammons' by John Pullen. [M15:54-16, R:39; R1:1-8]

Hammonds, John to Margaret Winkfield. JOHN HAMMONDS, waterman, age 27, widowed, b. Westmoreland Co., son of James Edwards and Susan Hammonds, to MARGARET WINKFIELD, age 20, single, b. Westmoreland Co., daughter of Henry Winkfield and Precilla [Lucas].[2] Signed John [his X mark] Hammonds, wit. J.H. Sisson. License 18 FEB 1860. Married 21 FEB 1860 by H.P.F. King. [M17:60-11 and 11a; R:72; R1:16-4]

Hardwick, Albin Lindsey (a.k.a. Albion L.) (1831-1907), served as lieutenant in Co. 2, 111th Va. Mil., C.S.A., to Eveline Hunter Branson (1842-1898).[3] ALBIN L. HARDWICK [sic], merchant, age 27, single, b. Westmoreland Co., son of Hiram Hardwick and Elizabeth R. [Barnes] [b. Northumberland Co., d. 1882 of cancer], to EVERLINE H. BRANSON, age 17, single, b. Westmoreland Co., daughter of John M. Branson and Ann R. [Rice].[4] License 10 JAN 1859. Married 12 JAN 1859 by H.P.F. King. [DR:52-42; M16a:59-4 and 4a; R:66]

Hardwick, Benjamin William (1848-1918),[5] to Roberta Frances Rock (d. 1885 of dropsy). BENJAMIN WILLIAM HARDWICK, farmer, age 27, single, b. Westmoreland Co., son of Hiram Hardwick and Eliza [Elizabeth R. Barnes], *q.v.*, to ROBERTA FRANCIS ROCK [sic], age 24, single, b. Richmond Co., daughter of James Rock and Sarah [Ann Hardwick].[6] License 23 MAR 1878. Married 27 MAR 1878 at Carmel Church by J.H. Davis. [DR:64-29 has mother Susan Rock; M19; NN; R:125; R1:73-10]

Hardwick, Henry Clay (1845-1920),[7] served in Co. C, 9th Va. Cav., C.S.A., to Elizabeth "Bettie" Rock (c.1850-1920). HENRY CLAY HARDWICK, harness maker, age 33, single, b. Westmoreland Co., son of Hiram [H.] Hardwick and Eliza [Elizabeth R. Barnes], *q.v.*, to BETTIE ROCK, age 21, single, b. Richmond Co., daughter of James Rock and Sarah [Ann Hardwick], *q.v.* License 29 JAN 1880. Married 5 FEB 1880 at *Peckatone* by R.J. Sanford. [M20; R:132; R1:81-1]

Hardwick, Samuel Redman (b. c.1819, d. 1876 of pneumonia),[8] to Susan Frances Bailey. SAMUEL REDMAN HARDWICK, farmer, age 46, widowed, b. Richmond Co., son of John Hardwick and Elizabeth [Morgan], to SUSAN FRANCES BAILEY, age 28, single, b. Westmoreland Co., daughter of [Stephen] and Harriet Bailey. License 1 APR 1863. Married 7 APR 1863 at Dr. Robert Sanford's by William F. Bain. [CP; DR:35-30; M17:63-3; R:79; R1:19-16]

Harford, Henry (c.1822-1874), served in Co. C, 47th Va. Inf., C.S.A., to Marian Bradford Sisson (b. 1839, d. 1870 of congestive chill).[9] HENRY HARFORD, merchant, age 33, single, b. Richmond Co., son of Henry and Susan Harford, to MARIAN B. SISSON, age 18, single, b. Westmoreland

---

[1] Henry Tate and Sintha Johnson were married by bond 10 JAN 1831 in Westmoreland Co., with Campbell Tate, security.
[2] Henry Winkfield and Sillar Lucas were married by bond 4 JAN 1826 in Westmoreland Co., with Meredith Lucas, security.
[3] Albion L. Hardwick and his wife Eveline H. were buried at Carmel United Methodist Church, Kinsale, Va.
[4] John M. Branson and Ann R. Rice were married by bond 17 MAR 1828 in Westmoreland Co., with Newyear C. Branson, security.
[5] Benjamin W. Hardwick was buried at Carmel United Methodist Church, Kinsale, Va.
[6] James Rock, of Northumberland Co., and Sarah Ann Hardwick, were married by bond 5 JAN 1837 in Richmond Co., with John Hardwick, Jr., security. VG:24, p. 63. Married 12 JAN 1837 in Richmond Co. by Rev. William Forester.
[7] Henry C. Hardwick and his wife Bettie were buried at Carmel United Methodist Church, Kinsale, Va.
[8] Samuel R. Hardwick was buried with his wife Rebecca Marmaduke (d. 1876) in the Hardwick Family Cemetery, located at *River View*.
[9] Henry Harford and his wife Marion B. were buried at Andrew Chapel United Methodist Church, Montross, Va.

Co., daughter of William [R.] Sisson and Ann [E. Harvey].[1] License 19 FEB 1856. Married 19 FEB 1856 at Montross, Va. by J.W. Chesley, minister of the Prot. Epis. Church. [DR:19-12; M16:56-5; R:53; R1:5-4]

Harford, Henry (d. 1874 of dropsy),[2] served in Co. C, 47th Va. Inf., C.S.A., to Mary "Mollie" Lyell. HENRY HARFORD, merchant, aga 49, widowed, b. Richmond Co., son of Henry Harford and Susan [English],[3] to MARY LYELL, age 32, single, b. Westmoreland Co., daughter of Joseph L. Lyell and Susan R. [Dishman].[4] License 13 NOV 1872. Married 13 NOV 1872 at St. James Church in Montross, Va. by D.M Wharton. [DR:31-12; M19; R:106; R1:51-10; SC]

Harrington, Columbus Levin to Sallie Frances Crabb. COLUMBUS LEVIN HARRINGTON, merchant, age 26, single, b. Dorchester Co., Md., son of John and Elizabeth Harrington, to SALLIE FRANCES CRABB, age 21, single, b. Westmoreland Co., daughter of William P. Crabb and Eliza A. [Ann Yeatman].[5] Signed Columbus [his S mark] Harrington. License 12 SEP 1859. Married 14 SEP 1859. [M16a:59-22; R:70; R1:15-5]

Harris, Charles Edward to Eliza Jane Sanford. CHARLES EDWARD HARRIS, merchant, age 26, single, b. Richmond Co., son of James M. Harris and Amanda J. [Quay],[6] to ELIZA JANE SANFORD, age 23, single, b. Westmoreland Co., daughter of Richard Sanford and Frances A. [Ann Sydnor], *q.v.* License 17 MAY 1879. Married 18 MAY 1879 at Oldhams X Roads by W.A. Crocker. [M20; NN; R:129; R1:77-11]

Harris, David W. to Frances F. Webb. License 13 AUG 1853. Married 13 AUG 1853 by Wm. N. Ward. [M15:53-18; R:33]

Harris, Elija to Jennie Brooks. ELIJA HARRIS, farmer, age 22, single, b. Westmoreland Co., son of Silas and Betsy Harris, to JENNIE BROOKS, age 23, single, b. Westmoreland Co., daughter of Bartlette and Mary Brooks. License 5 JUL 1879. Married 5 JUL 1879 by R.N. Reamy. [M20; R:129; R1:78-5]

Harriss, Francis John to Marietta Addlade McGinniss. FRANCIS JOHN HARRISS, farmer, age 27, single, b. Wilmington, Del., res. Richmond Co., son of John A. and Althsa Harriss, to MARIETTA ADDLADE McGINNISS, age 21, single, b. Kent Co., Md., daughter of William C. and Margaret McGinniss. License 25 APR 1870. Married 4 MAY 1870 at the residence of Wm. C. McGinniss by F.A. Davis. [M18; R:99; R1:43-2]

Harris, Joseph W. to Mary A. McKenney. JOSEPH W. HARRIS, farmer, age 22, single, b. Westmoreland Co., son of Charles W. and Mary Ann Harris, to MARY A. McKENNEY, age 21, single, b. Westmoreland Co., daughter of Samuel McKenney and Priscilla [R. Sutton].[7] License 11 DEC 1871. Married 14 DEC 1871 by G.H. Northam. [M19; R:103; R1:48-7]

---

[1] William R. Sisson and Ann E. Harvey were married by bond 24 MAY 1825 in Westmoreland Co., with Joseph F. Harvey, security.
[2] Henry Harford was buried at Andrew Chapel United Methodist Church, Montross, Va.
[3] Henry Harford, Sr., and Susan English, were married by bond 3 JUN 1822 in Richmond Co., with William A. Packett, security.
[4] Joseph L. Lyell and Susan R. Dishman were married by bond 25 MAR 1830 in Westmoreland Co., with Joseph F. Harvey, security.
[5] William P. Crabb and Eliza Ann Yeatman, daughter of Ann H. Yeatman, were married by bond 7 NOV 1827, with G.G. Mothershead, security.
[6] James M. Harris and Amanda J. Quay, daughter of Sarah Ann Harris, were married 27 NOV 1851 in Richmond Co. by Rev. Alfred Wiles.
[7] Samuel McKenney and Priscilla R. Sutton were married by bond 5 JAN 1847 in Westmoreland Co., with James Crask, security.

Harris, Solomon (d. by 1873), to Mary Lawrence. SOLOMON HARRIS, farmer, age 25, single, b. Essex Co., son of Elias and Susan Harris, to MARY LAWRENCE, age 23, single, b. Essex Co., daughter of Eliza Homes, father unknown. License 20 DEC 1867. Signed Solomon [his X mark] Harris, wit. C.C. Baker. Married 21 DEC 1867 at Smoot's Mill by R.N. Reamy. [M18; R:88; R1:30-9]

Harris, Walter (C) to Lavina Jenkins. WALTER HARRIS, farmer, age 27, single, b. Westmoreland Co., son of [Mason] and Hannah Harris, to LAVINA JENKINS, age 25, single, b. Westmoreland Co., daughter of Daniel and Fannie Campbell. License 1 JAN 1867. Married 3 JAN 1867 at *Bay View* by J.H. Davis. [M18; R:85; R1:26-9]

Harrison, Henry (C) to Sarah Rebecca Gaskins. HENRY HARRISON, farmer, age 22, single, b. Westmoreland Co., son of Sam Harrison [d. 1887] and [Letty] [Henry],[1] to SARAH REBECCA GASKINS, age 21, single, b. Westmoreland Co., daughter of Bartlett Gaskins and Mary [Ann Peck], *q.v.* License 20 DEC 1865. Married 21 DEC 1865 at the house of Bartlett Gaskins. [DR:71-25; M18; R:82]

Harrison, James to Allice Reed. JAMES HARRISON, farmer, age 24, single, b. Westmoreland Co., son of Ann Harrison, father unknown, to ALLICE REED, age 21, single, b. Westmoreland Co., daughter of Elizabeth Reed, father unknown. License 23 JAN 1877. Married 25 JAN 1877 at *King Kopsico* by F.B. Beale. [M19; R:121; R1:68-13]

Harrison, James William to Hester Ann Reynolds. JAMES WILLIAM HARRISON, carpenter, age 25, single, b. Westmoreland Co., son of William H. and Ann T. Harrison, to HESTER ANN REYNOLDS, age 21, single, b. Westmoreland Co., son of Joseph Reynolds and Martha [McKenney].[2] Consent by bride and Joseph [his X mark] Reynolds, wit. Samuel H. Self. License 26 NOV 1860. Married 18 DEC 1860 by Elder James A. Weaver. [M17:60-40, 40a and 40b; R:76; R1:17-14]

Harrison, Samuel to Betsey Chambers. SAMUEL HARRISON, farmer, age 26, single, b. Westmoreland Co., son of Littleton and Julia Ann Ashton, to BETSEY CHAMBERS, age 22, single, b. Westmoreland Co., daughter of Thomas and Patsey Chambers. License 2 DEC 1863. Married 3 DEC 1863 at Patsy Chambers' by D.M. Wharton. [M17:63-9; R:80; R1:20-7]

Harrison, Samuel to Harriet Ball. SAMUEL HARRISON, mechanic, age 70, widowed, b. Westmoreland Co., son of Henry and Judy Harrison, to HARRIET BALL, age 25, single, b. Westmoreland Co., daughter of George and Betty Ball. License 27 MAY 1876. Married 27 MAY 1876 at *Cabin Ford* by F.B. Beale. [M19; R:119; R1:65-8]

Harrison, Samuel S. to Elizabeth A. Wroe. SAMUEL S. HARRISON, farmer, age 47, widower, b. Westmoreland Co., son of John S. Harrison and Julia [Leecock],[3] to ELIZABETH A. WROE, age 31, single, b. Westmoreland Co., daughter of Samuel C. Wroe and Eliza [Olive].[4] Consent 28 MAY

---

[1] Samuel Harrison and Letty Henry were married by bond 19 MAY 1829 in Westmoreland Co., with Henry Johnson, security.
[2] Joseph Reynolds and Martha McKenney, daughter of Reuben McKenney, were married by bond 16 DEC 1834 in Westmoreland Co., with William R. McKenney, security.
[3] John Harrison, son of Samuel Harrison, and Julia Leecock, were married by bond 29 MAR 1813 in Westmoreland Co., wit. Jeremiah Leecock.
[4] VG:24, p. 25, Samuel C. Wroe and Elizer Allive were married 9 APR 1929 in Westmoreland Co. by Rev. Jeremiah Jeffries.

1860 by bride, Elizabeth [her X mark] A. Wroe, wit. Robt. Beale. License 28 MAY 1860. Married 3 JUN 1860. [M17:60-25 and 25a; R:74]

Harrison, Thomas H. (C) to Amanda Furlong Carter. THOMAS H. HARRISON, farmer, age 25, single, b. Westmoreland Co., son of Beverly and Ann Harrison, to AMANDA F. CARTER, age 17, single, b. Westmoreland Co., daughter of Thornton and Maria Carter. License 23 JAN 1878. Married 24 JAN 1878 at Easter Montague's by Thomas T. Johnson. [M19; R:125; R1:72-15]

Harrison, William to Rachael Thompson. License 30 JAN 1851. Married 30 JAN 1851 by George Northam, L.M.G. [M15:51-6; R:7]

Hart, William Fielding to Bernice F. Smoot. WILLIAM FIELDING HART, farmer, age 25, single, b. Westmoreland Co., res. Richmond Co., son of Fielding Hart and Ann [E. Pittman],[1] to BERNICE F. SMOOT, age 18, single, b. Caroline Co., daughter of Benjamin F. Smoot and Lucy A. [Mothershead], *q.v.* License 30 MAY 1870. Married 2 JUN 1870 by H.H. Fones. [M18; R:99; R1:43-5]

Harvey, George Carmichael, Jr. (1841-1906), served in Co. K, 40th Va. Inf., C.S.A., to Lizzie Northen. GEORGE CARMICHAEL HARVEY, merchant, age 28, single, b. Alexandria, Va., son of George C. [Carmichael, Sr.] Harvey and Mary S. [Susan Cox],[2] to LIZZIE NORTHEN, age 19, single, b. Westmoreland Co., daughter of John H. and Margaret Northen. License 26 OCT 1871. Married 26 OCT 1871 at Mrs. Margaret Northen's by W.F. Bain. [M18; R:103; R1:48-2]

Harvey, John M. to Lavinia Harvey. JOHN M. HARVEY, farmer, age 3[5], single, b. Westmoreland Co., son of Octavus A. Harvey and Susan M. [Maria Muse],[3] to LAVINIA HARVEY, age 29, single, b. Westmoreland Co., daughter of Joseph F. and Frances A. Harvey. License 2 JUN 1857. Married 2 JUN 1857 by Y.S.D. Covington, minister of the M.E. Church South. [M16a:57-16; R:61; R1:9-11]

Harvey, John Washington (1846-1920),[4] served in Co. C, 9th Va. Cav., C.S.A., first to Mary Ann Goodridge (d. 1871). JOHN WASHINGTON HARVEY, merchant, age 21, single, b. Westmoreland Co., son of Joseph F. Harvey and Ann [W. Hungerford],[5] to MARY ANN GOODRIDGE, age 18, single, b. Missouri,* daughter of John Goodridge and Mary J. [Greer] [d. 1885 of liver disease]. License 18 DEC 1867. Married 18 DEC 1867 at the residence of the bride's father by D.M. Wharton, Rector of Montross Parish. [DR:23-8, * gives her place of birth as King George Co., 65-86[6]; M18; R:88; R1:30-8]

Harvey, John Washington (1846-1920), second to Kate Gatewood Chandler (1844-1909).[7] JOHN WASHINGTON HARVEY, merchant, age 28, widower, b. Westmoreland Co., son of Joseph F. [Fox] Harvey and Ann W. [Hungerford] [d. 1851], *q.v.,* to KATE GATEWOOD CHANDLER, age 29,

---

[1] Fielding Hart and Ann E. Pittman were married by bond 8 AUG 1836 in Caroline Co.

[2] George Carmichael Harvey, Sr. (1810-1854) and his wife Mary Susan Cox (1814-1899) were buried in the Harvey Family Cemetery, located at *Melrose Farm* near Acorn, Va. A marker with his name is found at Yeocomico Episcopal Church, Tucker Hill, Va.

[3] Octavius Harvey and Susanna Maria Muse, daughter of Charles Muse and his cousin wife Lucy Muse, were married by bond 23 DEC 1816 in Westmoreland Co., with Joseph Fox, security.

[4] John W. Harvey was buried at St. James Episcopal Church.

[5] Joseph F. Harvey and Ann W. Hungerford were married by bond 18 OCT 1843 in Westmoreland Co., with William Hutt, security.

[6] DR:65-86, entry for Mary J. Goodridge, b. Caroline Co., d. 18 FEB 1885 of liver disease, age 59y11m7d, daughter of James and Mildred Greer, wife of John Goodridge.

[7] John W. Harvey and his wife Kate were buried at St. James Episcopal Cemetery, Montross, Va.

single, b. Westmoreland Co., daughter of Hanibal Chandler and Lucy P. [Bowcock] [d. testate 1889[1]].[2] License 15 DEC 1874. Married 15 DEC 1874 by D.M. Wharton, Rector of Montross Parish. [M19; R:113; R1:59-12]

Harvey, Patrick Robb (b. 1849, d. 1884 of pneumonia), to Constance Eugenia McKenney (1852-1945).[3] PATRICK ROBB HARVEY, merchant, age 23, single, b. Westmoreland Co., son of Joseph F. [Fox] Harvey and Ann [W. Hungerford], *q.v.*, to CONSTANCE EUGENIA McKENNEY, age 21, single, b. Westmoreland Co., son of William P. McKenney and Mary Y. [Young Hutt].[4] License 12 NOV 1873. Married 12 NOV 1873 at the residence of the bride's mother in Montross, Va. by D.M. Wharton. [DR61-84; M19; R:109; R1:54-13; SC]

Harvey, R.L. to Lucie J. Edwards. R.L. HARVEY, occupation nothing, age 21, single, b. Northumberland Co., son of L.G. [Lewis] Harvey and M. [Martha Lee],[5] to LUCIE J. EDWARDS, age 19, single, b. Westmoreland Co., daughter of William and S.E. Edwards. License 28 JUL 1857. Married 5 AUG 1857 at West Farm the residence of T.W.B. Edwards by John G. Rowe, M.G. [M16a:57-25; R:61; R1:10-4]

Harwood, John Baylor (d. 1864 killed in action at Ashland, Va.), served in Co. K, 9th Va. Cav., C.S.A., to Richard Anna Omohundro (1841-1871), of *Fruit View*. JOHN BAYLOR HARWOOD, schoolmaster, age 22, single, b. Essex Co., son of Richard H. and Mary Harwood, to RICHARD ANNA OMOHUNDRO, age 17, single, b. Westmoreland Co., daughter of Richard [Fleming] Omohundro and Mary [B. Claughton]. License 13 DEC 1858. Married 15 DEC 1858 by George H. Northam. [M16a:58-38; R:66; R1:15-10]

Hatton, John Chaney to Anna William Jett. JOHN CHANEY HATTON, carpenter, age 31, single, b. Somerset Co., Md., res. Northumberland Co., son of Francis A. and Mary W. Hatton, to ANNA WILLIAM JETT, age 21, single, b. Northumberland Co., daughter of William Jett. License 2 DEC 1871. Married 3 DEC 1871 at Ebenezer Church by W.W. Walker. [M18; R:103; R1:48-6]

Hayden, Marcellus (b. 1845, d. 1916 of general debility), to Alyda Bell Boyer. MARCELLUS HAYDEN, waterman, age 27, single, b. Lancaster Co., son of Hiram Hayden and Alice [Ashbourne],[6] to ALYDA BELL BOYER, age 19, single, b. New York City, daughter of Thomas and Caroline Boyer. License 13 OCT 1876. Married 18 OCT 1876 by F.B. Beale. [DC; M19; R:119; R1:66-7]

Head, Stephen (d. 1918 of paralysis),[7] to Caroline Rollins [or Rawlings]. STEPHEN HEAD, farmer, age 26, single, b. Westmoreland Co., son of Uriah Head and Mary [Short],[8] to CAROLINE ROLLINS, age 23, single, b. King George Co., daughter of Austin Rollins and Elizabeth [Inscoe].[9] Signed Stephen [his X mark] Head, wit. C.C. Baker. License 23 APR 1868. Married 24 APR 1868

---

[1] Deeds & Wills No. 48, p. 389, will of Lucy P. Chandler, proved 26 AUG 1889, names daughter Kate.

[2] Hanibal Chandler and Lucy P. Bowcock, daughter of Henry Bowcock, were married by bond 20 MAY 1842 in Westmoreland Co., with Thomas Jett Redmon, security.

[3] Patrick R. Harvey and his wife Constance were buried at Andrew Chapel United Methodist Church, Montross, Va.

[4] William P. McKenney and Mary Young Hutt were married by bond 13 DEC 1849 in Westmoreland Co., with Charles C. Baker, security.

[5] Lewis G. Harvey, widower, and Martha Lee, were married by bond 7 JAN 1833 in Northumberland Co., with George G. Lee, security.

[6] Hiram Hayden and Alice Ashbourne, daughter of Griffin Ashbourne, were married by bond 12 JAN 1843 in Lancaster Co.

[7] DC: Stephen Head was buried at Oak Grove, Va.

[8] Uriah Head and Mahala Ann Dameron were married by bond 22 JUL 1830 in Westmoreland Co., with William Butler, security.

[9] Austin Rollins and Elizabeth Inscoe were married 17 SEP 1839 in King George Co.

at the Rectory by Thomas E. Locke, Rector of Washington Parish. [DC; M18; R:90; R1:33-1; WP gives bride as Rawlings]

Henderson, John (C) to Rebecca Hacket. JOHN HENDERSON, farmer, age 40, widowed, b. Westmoreland Co., son of Henry and Martha "Mollie" Henderson, to REBECCA HACKET, age 21, single, b. Richmond Co., daughter of Jesse and Jane Hacket. Signed John [his X mark] Henderson, wit. Wm. S. McKenney. License 15 JAN 1876. Married 16 JAN 1876 by R.J. Sanford. [M19; R:117; R1:63-16]

Henderson, Robert (C) to Rose Anne Taylor (d. 1877 in child birth). ROBERT HENDERSON, farmer, age 22, single, b. Westmoreland Co., son of Mary Henderson, to ROSE ANN TAYLOR, age 21, single, b. Westmoreland Co., daughter of Rose Taylor, father unknown. Signed Ro. [his X mark] Henderson, wit. J.W. Hutt. License 17 DEC 1867. Married 19 DEC 1867 at James Reed's by D.M. Wharton. [DR:39-41; M18; R:88; R1:30-6]

Hennage, William (1834-1898), served as private in Co. 5, 111th Va. Mil., C.S.A., to Arebella Cornelia Balderson (1844-1916).[1] WILLIAM HENNAGE, farmer, age 26, single, b. Westmoreland Co., son of William Hennage and Ann [N. Hazard],[2] to AREBELL CORNELIA BALDERSON [sic], age 15, single, b. Westmoreland Co., daughter of Uriah Balderson [d. testate 1887[3]] and Delila Balderson, *q.v.* License 18 DEC 1860. Married 20 DEC 1860 by H.P.F. King. [M17:60-42 and 42a; R:76; R1:17-13]

Henry, Alexander (C) to Winny A. Smith. License 26 JAN 1859. [R:68]

Henry, Frederick to Hannah Johnson. License 4 DEC 1855. [R:51]

Henry, George (C) to Mary Corbin. GEORGE HENRY, farmer, age 48, widowed, b. Westmoreland Co., son of Daniel and Sally Henry, to MARY CORBIN, age 30, single, b. Westmoreland Co., daughter of Fleet and Nancy Corbin. Signed George [his X mark] Henry, wit. Wm. S. McKenney. License 28 FEB 1872. Married 29 FEB 1872 at Zion Church by Rev. Thomas T. Johnson. [M19; R:105; R1:49-14]

Henry, John (d. by 1865), to Mary Richardson. License 24 SEP 1857. [R:62]

Henry, Prince (C) to Anna Smith. PRINCE HENRY, farmer, age 29, single, b. Westmoreland Co., son of Nancy Henry, to ANNA SMITH, age 23, single, b. Westmoreland Co., daughter of William and Charlotte Smith. License 18 JAN 1870. Married 20 JAN 1870 by G.W. Beale, minister. [M18; R:97; R1:41-11]

Henry, William to Kitty Newman. WILLIAM HENRY, farmer, age 21, single, b. Richmond Co., son of Eve Henry, father unknown, to KITTY NEWMAN, age 22, single, b. Westmoreland Co., daughter of Frederick and Jenny Newman. Signed Wm. [his X mark] Henry, wit. Wm. E. Baker. License 6 FEB 1860. Married 7 FEB 1860. [M17:60-8; R:72]

---

[1] William Hennage and his wife Arrybella Cornelia Balderson were buried in the Hennage Family Cemetery, located off of Route 622 near Montross, Va.
[2] William Henage and Ann N. Hazard were married by bond 20 MAR 1821 in Westmoreland Co., with Josiah Hazard, security.
[3] Deeds & Wills No. 47, p. 324, will of Uriah Balderson, proved 24 OCT 1887, names wife Delila Balderson and daughter Cornelia Henage.

Heren, Thomas A. to Martha T. Branson. THOMAS A. HEREN, sailor, age 26, single, b. Gloucester Co., son of Thomas and Harriet A. Heren, to MARTHA T. BRANSON, age 22, single, b. Westmoreland Co., daughter of John M. Branson and Ann [R. Rice], *q.v.* License 30 JUN 1856. Married 1 JUL 1856 at the residence of J.M. Branson by H.P.F. King, minister of the M.E. Church. [M16a:56-18; R:55; R1:6-6]

Hess, Jacob to Mrs. Martha R. Weaver Davis. JACOB HESS, farmer, age 24, single, b. Germany, son of Goodlow and Zershenny Hess, to MARTHA R. DAVIS, age 30, widow, b. Westmoreland Co., daughter of Presley Weaver and Mary [Alverson].[1] License 17 MAY 1858. Married 23 MAY 1858 at my residence by H.P.F. King, minister of the M.E. Church. [M16a:58-16; R:64; R1:11-15]

Hickman, Henry (C) to Ursly Holmes. HENRY HICKMAN, laborer, age 21, single, b. Westmoreland Co., son of Nat. and Ann Hickman, to URSLY HOLMES, age 21, single, b. Essex Co., daughter of Willis and Ellen Holmes. Signed Henry [his X mark] Hickman, wit. W.S. McKenney. License 17 DEC 1875. Married 18 DEC 1875 at Little Zion Church by Emanuel Watts, pastor of Little Zion Church. [M19; R:116; R1:62-13]

Hill, Samuel C. (C) to Lucy Ann Burton. SAMUEL C. HILL, farmer, age 24, single, b. Westmoreland Co., son of Edward and Julia Hill, to LUCY ANN BURTON, age 23, single, b. Westmoreland Co., daughter of Frederick and Purcilla Burton. License 15 JAN 1878. Married 17 JAN 1878 at Mr. John [T.] Rice's [d. 1887], *Laurel Spring*[2] by Chas. [his X mark] Russ, wit. Joseph N. Arnest. [M19; R:124; R1:72-8]

Hinson, George Andrew (b. 1853, d. 1935 of a hip fracture), to Alphia Etta Saunders (1856-1944).[3] GEORGE ANDREW HINSON, farmer, age 25, single, b. Richmond Co., son of Andrew [J.] Hinson and Maria [Ann Oliff],[4] to ALPHIA ETTA SAUNDERS, age 23, single, b. Washington, D.C., daughter of [William] Henry Saunders and M.A. [Maria A. Jones]. License 3 DEC 1879. Married 4 DEC 1879 by H.H. Fones. [DC; M20; R:130; R1:79-5]

Hinson, George W. to Jane E. Poe. GEORGE W. HINSON, house carpenter, age 24, widower, b. Richmond Co., son of Austin Hinson and Mahalah [Hueson], *q.v.*, to JANE E. POE, age 22, single, b. Westmoreland Co., daughter of Frederic[k] and Letty Poe. License 2 APR 1857. Married 2 APR 1857 at the residence of Mrs. Poe by H.P.F. King, minister of the M.E. Church. [M16a:57-11; R:59; R1:9-3]

Hinson, James to Mrs. Maria Jane Carter Reamy. JAMES HINSON, farmer, age 38, single, b. Westmoreland Co., son of Vincent Hinson and Frances [Roe],[5] to MARIA JANE REAMY, age 43, widow, b. Richmond Co., daughter of Daniel and Sarah Carter. License 12 NOV 1870. Married 13 NOV 1870 by B.R. Battaile. [M18; R:100; R1:44-5]

Hinson, James Henry, served in Co. D, 40th Va. Inf., C.S.A., to Mary Jane Bowen. JAMES HENRY HINSON, farmer, age 27, single, b. Westmoreland Co., son of Thomas Hinson and Ann [Riley],[6] to MARY JANE BOWEN, age 28, single, b. Westmoreland Co., daughter of Thomas and Nancy

---

[1] Presley Weaver and Mary Alverson were married by bond 21 JAN 1824 in Westmoreland Co., with Joshua Reamy, security.
[2] *Laurel Spring*, the home of Thomas Rice, was enlarged in 1844. John T. Rice who died in 1887 was buried there.
[3] George A. Hinson and his wife Alphia were buried at Chiltons, Va.
[4] Andrew J. Hinson and Mariah Ann Oliff were married 22 JAN 1851 in Richmond Co. by Rev. William Balderson.
[5] Vincent Hinson and Fanny Roe were married by bond 11 FEB 1829 in Westmoreland Co., with Thomas P.W. Neale, security.
[6] Thomas Hinson and Ann Riley were married by bond 22 SEP 1841 in Westmoreland Co., with Rodney Moxley, security.

Bowen. Signed James H. [his X mark] Hinson, wit. W.S. McKenney. License 27 JAN 1873. Married 30 JAN 1873 by H.H. Fones. [M19; R:108; R1:53-5]

Hinson, John to Elizabeth Ann Peed. License 12 DEC 1853. Married 14 DEC 1853 by John Pullen. [M15:53-22; R:35]

Hinson, John C. to Ann Oliver. JOHN C. HINSON, farmer, age 32, single, b. Westmoreland Co., son of Fenner Hinson and Becky [Rebeckah Carpenter],[1] to ANN OLIVER, age 20, single, b. Westmoreland Co., daughter of Austin and Phoebe Oliver. Wit. C.C. Baker. License 24 JAN 1859. Married 25 JAN 1859 by John Pullen. [M16a:59-5 and 5a; R:68; R1:14-8]

Hinson, Julius J. to Ann Nash. JULIUS J. HINSON, farmer, age 21, single, b. Westmoreland Co., daughter of John and Ann Hinson, to ANN NASH, age 19, single, b. Westmoreland Co., daughter of Lewis and Mary Ann Nash. License 24 JAN 1870. Married 27 JAN 1870 by G.H. Northam. [M18; R:98; R1:41-13]

Hinson, Rodham "Rhody" Neale (d. 1898), first to Martha F. Eliff (d. 1868 of dropsy). RODHAM NEALE HINSON, farming, age 27, single, b. Westmoreland Co., son of William [F.] Hinson [and Mary Ann Neale], to MARTHA F. ELIFFE [sic], age 17, single, b. Westmoreland Co., daughter of Henry Eliff. License 26 DEC 1854. Married 27 DEC 1854 at Henry Eliffe's by John Pullen. [DR:15-31; M15:54-16a; NN; R:37; R1:1-10]

Hinson, Rodham Neale, second to Mrs. Mary Olverson. RODHAM HINSON, farmer, age 45, widowed, b. Westmoreland Co., son of William F. Hinson and [Mary] Ann [Neale],[2] to MARY OLVERSON, age 40, widow, b. Westmoreland Co., parents unknown. Signed R.N. Hinson. License 10 OCT 1871. Married 12 OCT 1871 at *Kenmore*[3] by G.W. Beale, M.G. [M18; R:103; R1:47-14]

Hinson, Thomas Polk, served in Co. A, 15th Va. Cav., C.S.A., to Frances Ann Butler. THOMAS POLK HINSON, farmer, age 2[5], single, b. Richmond Co., son of Reuben Hinson and Polly [Mary M. Hinson],[4] to FRANCES ANN BUTLER, age 25, single, b. Westmoreland Co., daughter of Christopher and Lucy Butler. License 19 MAR 1867. Married 24 MAR 1867 at Henry Travers' by Henry H. Fones. [M18; R:86; R1:27-13]

Hinson, William F. to Mary Ann Hinson. WILLIAM F. HINSON, farming, age about 51, widower, b. Richmond Co., son of John Hinson and Mary his wife, to MARY ANN HINSON, age about 26, single, b. Westmoreland Co., daughter of Fenner Hinson and Rebecka[h] [Carpenter] his wife. License 7 JUL 1856. Married 13 JUL 1856 at Fenner Hinson's by John Pullen, M.G. [M16a:56-20; R:55; R1:6-11]

Hinson, William Sandy to Olivia A.V. Ambrose. WILLIAM SANDY HINSON, farmer, age 23, single, b. and res. Richmond Co., son of [J.] K. and Susan Hinson, to OLIVIA A.V. AMBROSE, age 22, single, b. Westmoreland Co., daughter of Sally Ambrose, father unknown. Signed William S. [his

---

[1] Fenner Hinson and Rebeckah Carpenter were married by bond 21 JUL 1824 in Westmoreland Co., with Beriman Ramey, security.
[2] William F. Hinson and Mary Ann Neale, daughter of Lucinda Miller, were married by bond 23 JAN 1826 in Westmoreland Co., with Thomas Neale, security.
[3] *Kenmore* was built c.1867 by John Newton Murphy on property originally part of nearby *Spring Grove*.
[4] Reubin and Mary M. Hinson, daughter of William Hinson, were married by bond 25 SEP 1833 in Westmoreland Co., with Oliver E.P. Hazard, security.

X mark] Hinson, wit. J.W. Hutt. License 1 JAN 1870. Married 2 JAN 1870 to Robert N. Reamy. [M18; R:97; R1:41-6]

Hinson, Zachariah Taylor to Mary Catharine Tate. ZACHARIAH TAYLOR HINSON, farmer, age 24, single, b. Richmond Co., son of Presley Hinson and Ann [Hinson],[1] to MARY CATHARINE TATE, age 24, single, b. Westmoreland Co., daughter of William Tate and Betsy [Elizabeth Hinson].[2] License 10 FEB 1875. Married 11 FEB 1875 in Richmond Co. by Robert N. Reamy. [M19; R:114; R1:60-16]

Hipkins, Parker (a servant belonging to G.M. Carter), to Amy [blank] (a servant belonging to T.E. Locke). Married [ ] JUL 1860 by Rev. Thomas E. Locke at Washington Parish rectory. [WP]

Hoban, Peyton (C) (1835-1900),[3] a deacon of Little Zion Baptist Church, to Mrs. Elizabeth "Betty" Bankhead Carter, widow of Walter Carter, *q.v.* PEYTON HOBAND [sic], farmer, age 40, widowed, b. Westmoreland Co., son of Harry and Mary Hoban[d], to BETTY CARTER, age 28, widow, b. Westmoreland Co., daughter of John and Charlotte Bankhead. License 23 MAY 1877. Married 24 MAY 1877 at Little Zion Church by Emanuel Watts, pastor. [M19; R:122; R1:69-13]

Hodges, James Washington (C) to Mary Fauntleroy. JAMES WASHINGTON HODGES, farmer, age 23, single, b. Montgomery Co., Md., son of Washington and Louisa Hodges, to MARY FAUNTLEROY, age 30, widow, b. Westmoreland Co., daughter of Sampson and Lavinia Fauntleroy. License 21 OCT 1879. Married 23 OCT 1879 at my residence by Rev. William Gaskings. [M20; R:130; R1:78-14]

Hodgkin, John Benoni, Dr., first to Sarah Elizabeth Rust (1848-1877).[4] JOHN BENONI HODGKIN, dentist, age 32, single, b. Alexandria Co., res. Alexandria, Va., son of Robert Hodgkin and Elizabeth [Fraser],[5] to LIZZIE RUST, age 22, single, b. Delaware, daughter of John [C.] Rust [1815-1886] and Elizabeth [Ellen Rose] [1822-1912]. License 14 JUN 1870. Married 15 JUN 1870 in Oak Grove Church by Thomas E. Locke, Rector of Christ Church, Albemarle Co. [M18; R:99; R1:43-9; SC; WP]

Hogan, Colbert Hank (1844-1881), to Hannah Calvin Victoria Purcell (1850-1895).[6] COLBERT HANK HOGAN, farmer, age 24, b. Westmoreland Co., son of Richard J. Hogan and Mary [King],[7] to HANNAH CALVIN VICTORIA PURSELL [sic], age 18, b. Richmond Co., daughter of Hiram M. [Morgan] Purcell [1816-1877] and Hannah L. [Lane Middleton] [1819-1904].[8] License 27 JAN 1868. Married 29 JAN 1868 at the residence of Hiram Pursel by Elder James A. Weaver. [M18; R:89; R1:31-14]

---

[1] Presley Hinson and Ann Hinson were married by bond 16 JAN 1849 in Richmond Co., with Meredith Hinson, security.
[2] William Tate and Elizabeth Hinson, daughter of Ann Hinson, were married by bond 20 DEC 1847 in Westmoreland Co., with Samuel C.F. Butler, security.
[3] Peyton Hoban, Sr. was buried at Little Zion Baptist Church, Oak Grove, Va.
[4] Sarah Elizabeth Rust Hodgkin, and her parents, were buried in the Rust Family Cemetery at *Waverly.*
[5] War of 1812 Pension File for Robert Hodgkin shows that he was married first 10 SEP 1817 in Alexandria, Va. to Clara Taylor [d. 18 FEB 1831], and married second 28 JUN 1831 to Elizabeth Fraser. Robert was born 26 MAR 1796 and died 27 MAR 1876 in Alexandria, and his wife Elizabeth died 26 DEC 1883 in Alexandria. Occupation wheelwright. Robert and Clara were buried in Trinity United Methodist Church Cemetery in Alexandria, Va.
[6] Colbert H. Hogan and his wife Hannah were buried in the Hugh Middleton Family Cemetery, Oldhams, Va.
[7] Richard J. Hogan and Mary King were married by bond 10 MAY 1832 in Westmoreland Co., with John L. Middleton, security.
[8] Hiram M. Pursell and Hannah L. Middleton, daughter of Jeremiah Middleton, were married by bond 26 JAN 1841 in Westmoreland Co., with Samuel W. English, security. They were buried in the Purcell Family Cemetery, Oldhams, Va.

Hogan, Eric Taylor to Georgianna A. Self.[1] ERIC TAYLOR HOGAN, farmer, age 25, single, b. Westmoreland Co., son of R.J. [Richard] Hogan and Mary J. [King], *q.v.*, to GEORGIANNA SELF, age 20, single, b. Westmoreland Co., daughter of George L. Self and Mary [B. Davis].[2] Signed Eric T. [his X mark] Hogan, wit. Wm. S. McKenney. License 20 JUN 1874. Married 21 JUN 1874 at Richard Hogin's by R.J. Sanford. [M19; R:113; R1:58-12]

Hogan, Harry (C) to Mrs. Sally West Tinsley, widow of Littleton Tinsley, *q.v.* HARRY HOGAN, farmer, age 22, single, b. Westmoreland Co., son of Payton and Winny Hogan, to SALLY TINSLEY, age 23, widow, b. Westmoreland Co., daughter of Edmond and Sally West. License 8 SEP 1879. Married 8 SEP 1879 at Little Zion Church by Emanuel Watts, pastor. [M20; R:130; R1:78-12]

Hogan, Richard Christopher (1839-1905),[3] served Co. A, 15th Va. Inf., C.S.A., to Eunice Bailey. RICHARD CHRISTOPHER HOGAN, farmer, age 21, single, b. Westmoreland Co., son of Richard [J.] Hogan [d. 1892] and Mary [King], *q.v.*, to EUNICE BAILEY, age 21, single, b. Maine, parents unknown. Consent 16 MAR 1860 by bride, wit. Saml. C. Jackson. License 16 MAR 1860. Married 17 MAR 1860. [DR91-53; M17:60-17, 17a, 17b; R:72]

Holliday, James Robinson, served in Co. C, 9th Va. Cav., C.S.A., to Mrs. Rebecca Jane Barnett Elmore, widow of John William Elmore, *q.v.* JAMES ROBINSON HOLLIDAY, school teacher, age 33, single, b. Westmoreland Co., son of William Holliday [d. by 1859] and Susan R. [Robinson],[4] to REBECCA JANE ELMORE, age 24, widow, b. Westmoreland Co., son of Levi Barnett and Martha [Pope], *q.v.*[5] License 8 FEB 1873. Married 11 FEB 1873 at Martha Barnett's by G.W. Beale, minister. [M19; R:108; R1:53-8]

Holmes, Jacob to Ann Elizabeth Doleman. JACOB HOLMES, sailor, age 32, single, b. and res. Baltimore City, Md., son of Jacob and Mary Holmes, to ANN ELIZABETH DOLEMAN, age 26, single, b. Westmoreland Co., daughter of Jacob V. and Leanna Doleman. License 7 JUN 1875. Married 8 JUN 1875 by H.H. Fones. [M19; R:115; R1:61-8]

Homes, Robert to Sarah Baylor. ROBERT HOMES, laborer, age 23, single, b. King George Co., son of Seymore and Betsy Homes, to SARAH BAYTON, age 21, single, b. Essex Co., daughter of Edmon[d] and Charity Baylor. License 8 MAR 1878. Married 9 MAR 1878 by R.N. Reamy. [M19; R:125; R1:73-7]

Homes, Thomas to Margaret M. Smith. License 14 MAY 1853. Married 18 MAY 1853 by Wm. McGuire, Rector of Cople and Montross Parishes. [M15:53-15; R:31]

Horner, Henry Jabez (1854-1909), to Susan Alice Butler (1841-1889).[6] HENRY HORNER, farmer, age 24, single, b. Derbyshire, England, son of Jabez Horner and Eliza [Ford],[7] to SUSAN ALICE

---

[1] E.T. Hogan and wife Georgianna were buried at Gibeon Baptist Church, Village, Va.

[2] George Self and Mary B. Davis were married 1 MAR 1853 in Richmond Co. by Rev. George H. Northam.

[3] Richard C. Hogan was buried at Ebenezer United Methodist Church.

[4] William Holliday and Susan R. Robinson were married by bond 11 DEC 1837 in Westmoreland Co., with Steptoe T. Rice, security.

[5] Levi Barnett and Martha Pope, daughter of John B. Pope, were married by bond 7 OCT 1839 in Westmoreland Co., with Richard Pritchett, security.

[6] Henry J. Horner and his wife Susan Alice Butler were buried in the Horner Family Cemetery, located on *Chesterfield Farm*, off of Route 640.

[7] Jabez Horner (a.k.a. Henry Jabez Horner) (1820-1890) and his wife Eliza Ford (1817-1905) were buried in the Horner Family Cemetery, located on *Chesterfield Farm*, off of Route 640. Mallory, p. 66, notes that he and his wife came to the U.S. in 1854 with the organ for St. Peter's Episcopal Church, Oak Grove, Va. WP notes the burial for Mrs. Jabez Horner in 1905.

BUTLER, age 24, single, b. Westmoreland Co., daughter of William A. Butler and Susan P. [Tiffey], *q.v.* License 12 MAR 1867. Married 14 MAR 1867 at Mrs. Sisson's residence by Thomas E. Locke. [M18; R:86; WP]

Howard, Robert C. (C) to Charlotte Smith.[1] ROBERT HOWARD, farmer, age 23, single, b. and res. King George Co., son of Henry and Hester Howard, to CHARLOTTE SMITH, age 19, single, b. Westmoreland Co., daughter of Maria Smith. License 13 FEB 1878. Married 14 FEB 1878 in Washington Township by Emanuel Watts, pastor, Little Zion Church. [M20; R:125; R1:73-3]

Howarth, Thomas A. to Amanda J. Dishman (d. 1867). THOMAS A. HOWARTH, seafaring, age 19, single, b. Essex Co., son of John H. and Martha A. Howarth, to AMANDA J. DISHMAN, age 19, single, b. Westmoreland Co., daughter of John [Triplett] Dishman and Mary H. [Harlowe McDaniel].[2] License 7 FEB 1855. Married 8 FEB 1855 at Leeds Town, Va. by W.A. Baynham, M.G. [DR:13-25; M16:55-6; R:47; R1:3-7]

Howlet, James to Julia Ann Nickens, colored people. JAMES HOWLET, laborer, age 22, single, b. Caroline Co., son of Henry and Betsey Howlet, to JULIA ANN NICKENS, age 21, single, b. Essex Co., daughter of David and Betsy Nickens. Signed James [his X mark] Howlet, wit. J.W. Hutt. License 16 JUL 1869. Married 17 JUL 1869 in St. Peter's Church by Thomas E. Locke, Rector. [M18; R:95; R1:39-1; WP]

Hubbard, John (C) to Mrs. Mary Thompson Hacket. JOHN HUBBARD, farmer, age 49, widowed, b. Westmoreland Co., son of Jennie Hubbard, father unknown, to MARY HACKCET, age 36, widow, b. Westmoreland Co., daughter of Gerard and Ellen Thompson. License 15 NOV 1880. Married 17 NOV 1880 at Henry Johnson's house by Thomas T. Johnson. [M20; R:134; R1:84-3]

Hubbert, Erye (C) to Elizabeth Walker. ERYE HUBBERT, farmer, age 22, single, b. Westmoreland Co., son of Samuel and Winnie Hubbert, to ELIZABETH WALKER, age 21, single, b. Westmoreland Co., daughter of Ditta Walker, father unknown. License 10 DEC 1879. Married 11 DEC 1879 at my residence by Rev. William Gaskings. [M20; R:130; R1:79-9]

Hudson, Carlos B. to Victoria E. Courtney (d. 1857 in childbirth age 20).[3] CARLOUS B. HUDSON [sic], farmer, age 45, widower, b. Northumberland Co., father unknown, mother Polly Hudson, to VICTORIA E. COURTNEY, age 17, single, b. Westmoreland Co., daughter of William J. [Jeffries] Courtney and Elizabeth [B. English Lamkin], *q.v.* License 26 FEB 1855. Married 6 MAR 1855 at the residence of W.J. Courtney by H.P.F. King, minister of the M.E. Church South. [DR:1-31; M16:55-9, R:49; R1:3-3]

Hudson, Clement Wilson, Capt. to Mary Elizabeth Spilman. CLEMENT WILSON HUDSON, mariner, age 37, widower, b. Delaware, res. Seaford, Del., son of Benjamin and Margaret Hudson, to MARY ELIZABETH SPILMAN, age 25, single, b. Westmoreland Co., daughter of John Spilman and Thursday [Hoult].[4] License 29 MAY 1868. Married 2 JUN 1868 at the residence of Robt. Spilman, Leedstown, by Thomas E. Locke. [M18; R:91; R1:34-1; SC; WP]

---

[1] Robert C. and Charlotte Howard were buried at Spy Hill Cemetery, King George Co.
[2] John Dishman and Mary McDaniel, daughter of Mary Simms, were married by bond 18 JAN 1830 in Westmoreland Co., with John Hunter, security.
[3] Victoria E. Courtney Hudson was buried in the Courtney Family Cemetery, located on *Royal Oak Farm* near Kinsale, Va.
[4] John Spilman and Thirza Hoult were married by bond 3 MAY 1815 in Westmoreland Co., with Abraham White, security.

Hudson, Joseph Davis (1842-1918), first to Susan Delano. JOSEPH DAVIS HUDSON, shoemaker, age 23, single, b. Westmoreland Co., son of William R. [Reed] Hudson and Catharine [Davis],[1] to SUSAN DELANO, age 18, single, b. Westmoreland Co., daughter of George and Nancy Delano. License 22 JAN 1866. Married 23 JAN 1866 at the house of Augustus Delano by W.W. Walker. [M18; R:82; R1:23-4]

Hudson, Joseph Davis (1842-1918),[2] second to Lucy Anne Stephens. JOSEPH HUDSON, farmer, age 30, widowed, b. Westmoreland Co., son of William R. [Reed] Hudson and Catharine [Davis], *q.v.*, to LUCY ANNE STEPHENS, age 15, single, b. Westmoreland Co., daughter of Jeremiah and Ann Stephens. License 15 MAY 1872. Married 16 MAY 1872 at the residence of Richard R. King by R.J. Sanford. [M19; R:105; R1:50-8]

Hudson, Robert Henry (1826-1901), served in Co. E, 55th Va. Inf., C.S.A., to Mrs. Mary Catharine Delano Beacham (1836-1904),[3] widow of Robert J. Beacham, *q.v.* ROBERT HENRY HUDSON, carpenter, age 43, widower (divorced), b. Westmoreland Co., son of Corbin S. Hudson and Elizabeth W. [Wroe],[4] to MARY CATHARINE BEACHAM, age 32, widow, b. Westmoreland Co., daughter of George of Nancy Delano. License 28 MAY 1869. Married 3 JUN 1869 by W.W. Walker. [M18; R:95; R1:38-10]

Hudson, William Henry to Elizabeth Lewis. WILLIAM HENRY HUDSON, farmer, age 22, single, b. Westmoreland Co., son of William R. and Mary Hudson, to ELIZABETH LEWIS, age 19, single, b. Northumberland Co., daughter of Frances Lewis, father unknown. License 7 MAY 1861. Married 8 MAY 1861 at *Pleasant View* by O.M.T. Samuels. [M17:61-10; R:77; R1:18-3]

Hughes, Thomas to Bettie P. Tiffey, in 1869 at Montross, Va. by Rev. D.M. Wharton. [SC]

Hungerford, Elza (C) to Louisa Taylor (d. 1888 of cancer). ELZA HUNGERFORD, farmer, age 35, single, b. King George Co., daughter of Willie and Betsey Hungerford, to LOUISA TAYLOR, age 30, single, b. King George Co., daughter of [Joseph and Mary] Maria Taylor. Signed Elza [his X mark] Hungerford, wit. J.W. Hutt. License 26 DEC 1870. Married 29 DEC 1870 by Jerry Graham. [DR:76-83; M18; R:100; R1:45-2]

Hungerford, Philip C. to Amelia Jane Spence (d. 1880). PHILIP C. HUNGERFORD, merchant, age 26, single, b. Montross, Va., son of [Maj.] Henry Hungerford [b. 1788, d. 1866 of cramp][5] and [his first wife] Amelia [Spence],[6] to AMELIA J. SPENCE, age 20, single, b. Richmond Co., daughter of John and Elizabeth Spence. License 15 OCT 1855. Married 16 AUG 1855 in St. James Church, Montross, Va. by J.W. Chesley, minister of the Prot. Epis. Church. [DR:12-51; M16:55-19; NN; R:49; R1:4-6; SC]

Hunter, Alick (C) to Fanny Williams. ALICK HUNTER, farmer, age 23, single, b. Essex Co., son of Peter and Lucy Hunter, to FANNY WILLIAMS, age 22, single, b. Westmoreland Co., daughter

---

[1] William R. Hudson and Catharine Davis, daughter of Caty Alderson, were married by bond 18 DEC 1828 in Richmond Co., with George Delano, security.
[2] Joseph D. Hudson was buried near Acorn, Va.
[3] Robert H. Hudson and his wife Mary were buried at Ebenezer United Methodist Church, Oldhams, Va.
[4] Corbin Hudson and Elizabeth Wroe were married by bond 1 JUN 1825 in Westmoreland Co., with Mathew R. King, security.
[5] Maj. Henry Hungerford (1788-1866), a veteran of the War of 1812, son of Lt. Thomas Hungerford and Ann Washington, and his wife Amelia Spence (d. 1831 age 37), were was buried in the Hungerford-Griffith Family Cemetery, located at Leedstown, Va.
[6] Henry Hungerford and Amelia Spence were married by bond 12 MAR 1818 in Westmoreland Co., with Thomas Spence, Sr., security.

of Jane Williams. Signed Alick [his X mark] Hunter, wit. W.S. McKenney. License 24 DEC 1872. Married 25 DEC 1872 at Little Zion Church, Oak Grove, Va. by Emanuel Watts, pastor. [M19; R:107; R1:52-7]

Hunter, Simon Peter (C) to Dolly Peterson. SIMON PETER HUNTER, farmer, age 29, single, b. Essex Co., son of Peter and Lucy Hunter, to DOLLY PETERSON, age 22, single, b. Essex Co., daughter of Philip and Amy Peterson. Signed Simon Peter [his X mark] Hunter, wit. Wm. S. McKenney. License 13 AUG 1874. Married 15 AUG 1874 by John Roy. [M19; R:113; R1:58-13]

Hurtt, Henry Nickols to Lou Kate Beale. HENRY NICKOLS HURTT, merchant, age 26, single, b. and res. Baltimore, Md., son of Henry N. and Rebecca B. Hurtt, to LOU KATE BEALE, age 21, single, b. Westmoreland Co., daughter of Henry and Susan R. Beale. License 15 APR 1867. Married 17 APR 1867 by F.A. Davis. [M18; R:86; R1:27-16]

Hutt, Charles Warren (1842-1906),[1] served in Co. K, 40th Va. Inf., C.S.A., prisoner of war at Point Lookout, Md., to Bettie Lee Brown. CHARLES WARREN HUTT, merchant, age 23, single, b. Westmoreland Co., son of Edwin Hutt and Nancy N. [McClanahan],[2] to BETTIE LEE BROWN, age 22, single, b. Westmoreland Co., daughter of William W. and Jane [Frances] Brown. License 10 JAN 1866. Married 14 JAN 1866 at the residence of W.W. Brown by H.P.F. King. [M18; R:82; R1:23-1]

Hutt, Edwin (b. 1819, d. 1889 of consumption),[3] served in Co. 4, 111th Va. Mil., C.S.A., to Susan J. Brown. EDWIN HUTT, merchant, age 35, widower, b. Westmoreland Co., son of Garrard [Jarrett] and Ellener Hutt, to SUSAN J. BROWN, age 22, single, b. Westmoreland Co., daughter of William W. and Jane Frances Brown. Married 25 NOV 1856 at the residence of W.W. Brown by H.P.F. King, minister of the M.E. Church South. [DR:79-25; M16a:56-31; R1:7-9]

Hutt, Joseph Warren (1839-1907), served in the 111th Va. Mil., C.S.A., to Elizabeth Elbert "Lizzie" Costin (b. 1837, d. 1894 of paralysis).[4] JOSEPH WARREN HUTT, clerk of county court, age 23, single, b. Westmoreland Co., to ELIZABETH ELBERT [COSTIN], age 16, single, b. Westmoreland Co. [daughter of John E. and Elizabeth Costin]. Minister return by H.P.F. King. License 8 MAR 1854. Married 8 MAR 1854 at the residence of Col. W. Brown. [DR:98-8; M15:54-17a; NN; R:43; R1:1-5]

Hutt, William Ogle (1847-1909),[5] served in Co. C, 9th Va. Cav., C.S.A., to Lulie Virginia Omohundro (1859-1941). WILLIAM OGLE HUTT, farmer, age 31, single, b. Westmoreland Co., son of Edwin Hutt and Nancy N. [McClanahan], *q.v.*, to LULIE VIRGINIA OMOHUNDRO, age 19, single, b. Westmoreland Co., daughter of John M. [Meredith] Omohundro [1827-c.1890] and Elizabeth [Porter]. License 31 DEC 1878. Married 1 JAN 1879 at the residence of John M. Omohundro by D.G.C. Butts. [M20; R:127; R1:76-7]

Hynson (see Hinson)

---

[1] C. Warren Hutt was buried at St. Paul's Episcopal Church.
[2] Edwin Hutt, son of Gerard Hutt, and Nancy N. McClanahan, daughter of John McClanahan, were married by bond 29 NOV 1837 in Westmoreland Co., with O.E.P. Hazard, security.
[3] Edwin Hutt was buried at St. Paul's Episcopal Church.
[4] Joseph W. Hutt and his wife Lizzie were buried at Andrew Chapel United Methodist Church, Montross, Va.
[5] William O. Hutt was buried at St. Paul's Episcopal Church.

I

Ingram, Augustus Robert to Virginia Alice Coghill. AUGUSTUS ROBERT INGRAM, farmer, age 25, single, b. Essex Co., son of Godfrey Ingram and Mary [Coghill], *q.v.*, to VIRGINIA ALICE COGHILL, age 16, single, b. Essex Co., daughter of John Coghill and Virginia [Parker].[1] License 31 MAY 1880. Married 1 JUN 1880 by R.N. Reamy. [M20; R:133; R1:82-15]

Ingram, William to Margaret J. Ashburn. License 1 AUG 1853. [R:33 no return]

Inscoe, George W. to Milly Trigger. Married 1 FEB 1861 at the Washington Parish rectory by Rev. T.E. Locke. [WP]

Inscoe, John Dye (b. 1826, d. 1902 in D.C.),[2] served Co. E, 15th Va. Cav., C.S.A., to Christianna Coakley. JOHN DYE INSCOE, farmer, age 48, single, b. King George Co., son of Thomas [d. 1864] and Frances Inscoe, to CHRISTIANNA COAKLEY, age 35, single, b. King George Co., daughter of John and Sarah Coakley. License 12 JAN 1874. Married 15 JAN 1874 at the residence of John Inscoe by John Payne. [DR:8-7; M19; R:111; R1:56-11; WP]

Inscoe, John Washington (1848-1923),[3] to Elizabeth "Bessie" Morgan. JOHN WASHINGTON INSCOE, farmer, age 20, single, b. Westmoreland Co., son of Frances Inscoe, to ELIZABETH MORGAN, age 21, single, b. King George Co., daughter of Meredith Morgan and D[ulaney Jane Inscoe].[4] Signed John W. [his X mark] Inscoe, wit. J.W. Hutt. License 23 DEC 1867. Married 24 DEC 1867 at the rectory by Thomas E. Locke, Rector of St. Peter's Church. [M18; R:88; R1:30-11; WP]

J

Jackson, Alexander to Eve Fisher. ALEXANDER JACKSON, waterman, age 24, single, b. Westmoreland Co., son of Samuel and Sarah Jackson, to EVE FISHER, age 27, single, b. Westmoreland Co., daughter of Isaac and Susan Fisher. License 22 NOV 1876. Married 23 NOV 1876 at *Traveller's Rest* by F.B. Beale. [M19; R:120; R1:66-16]

Jackson, John (C) to Margaret Scott. JOHN JACKSON, farmer, age 23, single, b. Westmoreland Co., son of Samuel and Sarah Jackson, to MARGARET SCOTT, age 26, single, b. Westmoreland Co., daughter of Thornton and Jennie Scott. License 25 NOV 1878. Married 28 NOV 1878 at *Boscoville* by Chas. [his X mark] Russ, wit. Joseph N. Arnest. [M19; R:126; R1:75-6]

Jackson, John J. (d. 1894 age 83), to Mary Jane Head (d. 1892 age 63).[5] JOHN JACKSON, farmer and shoemaker, age about 40, single, b. Caroline Co., son of Robert Jackson and Sarah his wife, to MARY JANE HEADE [sic], age 17, single, b. Westmoreland Co., daughter of Uriah [E.] Head and Mary [Mahala Ann Dameron].[6] License 9 FEB 1854. Married 13 FEB 1854 at the residence of the minister, John Pullen. [M15:54-16a; R:39; R1:1-9]

---

[1] John Coghill, Jr. and Virginia Parker were married on 6 OCT 1853 in Essex Co.
[2] John D. Inscoe is buried with wife Anna W. in St. Peter's Cemetery, Oak Grove, Va.
[3] John W. Inscoe was buried at Grace Church.
[4] Meredith Morgan and Dulaney Jane Inscoe were married 20 FEB 1844 in King George Co. by Rev. John McDaniel.
[5] John J. Jackson and his wife Mary Jane Head were buried in the Jackson Family Cemetery, located off of Route 638 near Oak Grove, Va.
[6] Uriah Head and Mahala Ann Dameron were married by bond 22 JUL 1830 in Westmoreland Co., with William Butler, security. Mary Ann (a.k.a. Mahala) Dameron Head Yeatman was buried in the Jackson Family Cemetery, located off of Route 638 near Oak Grove, Va. It is thought that her husband Uriah E. Head was buried here as well.

Jackson, Samuel Richard, of *Green Hill* (1828-1909), to Lucy Frances Rice (1836-1877).[1] SAMUEL RICHARD JACKSON, farmer and merchant, age 29, single, b. Westmoreland Co., son of Richard Jackson and Sophia J. [Scates],[2] to LUCY FRANCES RICE, age 21, single, b. Westmoreland Co., daughter of John T. Rice and Mary C. [Robinson].[3] License 29 OCT 1857. Married 4 NOV 1857 at *Laurel Spring* by H.P.F. King, minister of the M.E. Church. [M16a:57-36; R:62; R1:10-9]

Jackson, William (C) (1851-1921), to Eliza Jane Booten. WILLIAM JACKSON, sailor, age 23, single, b. Westmoreland Co., son of Samuel and Sarah Jackson, to ELIZA JANE BOOTEN, age 21, single, b. Westmoreland Co., daughter of Charles and Priscilla Booten. Signed William [his X mark] Jackson, wit. W.S. McKenney. License 17 DEC 1873. Married 18 DEC 1873 at Harrisville, Va. by G.W. Beale, minister. [DC; M19; R:110; R1:55-9]

Jackson, William (C) to Margaret Hover. WILLIAM JACKSON, sailor, age 21, single, b. Westmoreland Co., son of Henry and Fanny Jackson, to MARGARET HOVER, age 22, single, b. Westmoreland Co., daughter of Patin [sic] and Winny Hover. License 15 DEC 1880. Married 16 DEC 1880 at Little Zion Church by Emanuel Watts, pastor, Little Zion Church. [M20; R:134; R1:84-8]

Jenkins, Harry (C) (d. 1894 of heart failure), to Marietta Taliaferro. HARRY JENKINS, farmer, age 25, single, b. Spotsylvania Co., son of Horace [d. 1894] and [Elizabeth] Betsy Jenkins [d. 1886], to MARIETTA TALLIAFERRO [sic], age 18, single, b. Westmoreland Co., daughter of Turner and Sally Taliaferro. License 27 FEB 1878. Married 28 FEB 1878 at Little Zion Church by Emanuel Watts, pastor. [DR:70-114, 100-48 and 49; M19; R:125; R1:73-6]

Jenkins, James to Emily Reamy. JAMES JENKINS, farmer, age 25, single, b. Westmoreland Co., son of Margaret Jenkins, father unknown, to EMILY REAMY, age 25, single, b. Richmond Co., daughter of Robert N. Reamy and Jane [Owens]. License 27 SEP 1866. Married 28 SEP 1866 at the residence of the minister by D.M. Wharton. [M18; R:84; R1:25-3]

Jenkins, James Payne (1840-1905), served in Co. C, 9th Va. Cav., C.S.A., to Katherine Caroline Crabbe (1841-1911).[4] JAMES PAYNE JENKINS, carpenter, age 27, single, b. Westmoreland Co., son of James P. Jenkins and Nancy [Ann Moxley],[5] to CATHERINE CAROLINE CRABB [sic], age 25, single, b. Westmoreland Co., daughter of William P. Crabb and Eliza [Ann Yeatman], *q.v.* License 21 OCT 1868. Married 22 OCT 1868 by G.H. Northam. [M18; R:92; R1:35-8; R1:37-7]

Jenkins, James Payne (1840-1905),[6] served in Co. C, 9th Va. Cav., C.S.A., to Augusta Green. JAMES PAYNE JENKINS, farmer, age 28, widower, b. Westmoreland Co., son of Margaret Jenkins [sic], father unknown, to AUGUSTA GREEN, age 19, single, b. Westmoreland Co., daughter of George and Cardellia Green. Signed James P. [his X mark] Jenkins, wit. Wm. Green. License 6 JAN 1869. Married 7 JAN 1869 at the rectory by Thomas E. Locke, Rector, Washington Parish. [M18; R:94; WP]

---

[1] S.R. Jackson and wife Lucy F. Robinson were buried in the Jackson Family Cemetery, located at *Green Hill*, off of Route 202 near Mount Holly, Va.

[2] Richard Jackson and Sophia Scates, daughter of James Scates, were married by bond 13 MAR 1821 in Westmoreland Co., with M.C. Harvey, security.

[3] John T. Rice and Mary C. Robinson were married by bond 29 AUG 1831 in Westmoreland Co., with William M. Dameron, security.

[4] James P. Jenkins and his wife Katherine Crabbe were buried at St. James Episcopal Cemetery, Montross, Va.

[5] James P. Jenkins and Ann Moxley were married by bond 27 OCT 1831 in Westmoreland Co., with Jacob V. Doleman, security.

[6] James P. Jenkins was buried at St. James Episcopal Church.

Jenkins, Jesse (C) to Mary Jane Johnson. JESSIE JENKINS, farmer, age 23, single, b. Westmoreland Co., son of Eliza Jenkins, father unknown, to MARY JANE JOHNSON, age 18, single, b. Westmoreland Co., daughter of John and Frances Johnson. License 20 OCT 1864. Married 23 OCT 1864 at John Johnson's by H.P.F. King. [M17a:64-11; R:80; R1:21-4]

Jenkins, John Lewis (d. 1900), to Mary Jane Eliff.[1] JOHN L. JENKINS, house carpenter, age 22, single, b. Westmoreland Co., son of James Jenkins and Nancy [Ann Omohundro] , to MARY JANE ELIFF, age 15, single, b. Westmoreland Co., daughter of Henry Eliff and Frances [Stone].[2] License 1 JAN 1858. Married 5 JAN 1858 at Andrew Chapel by H.P.F. King, minister of the M.E. Church. [M16a:58-2; R:63; R1:11-3]

Jenkins, John S. (1824-1856),[3] to Mary A. Hunter, daughter of John and Sarah Hunter, *q.v.* License 18 JAN 1853. [R:25 no return]

Jenkins, Littleton Francis to Harriet Ann Stephens. LITTLETON FRANCIS JENKINS, farmer, age 28, single, b. Westmoreland Co., son of Littleton and Jane Jenkins, to HARRIET ANN STEPHENS, age 17, single, b. Westmoreland Co., daughter of Jeremiah and Alice Stephens. License 23 APR 1878. Married 26 APR 1878 by F.W. Claybrook. [M19; R:125; R1:73-13]

Jenkins, Richard to Emma Sophronia Cole. RICHARD JENKINS, farmer, age 24, single, b. Wicomico Co., Md., son of Littleton and Sarah J. [Jane] Jenkins [d. 1876], to EMMA SOPHRONIA COLE, age 22, single, b. Westmoreland Co., daughter of George W. and Margaret Cole. Signed Richard [his X mark] Jenkins, wit. J.W. Hutt. License 1 JUN 1870. Married 2 JUN 1870 at the bride's mother's by Charles E. Watts. [DR:35-32; M18; R:99; R1:43-7]

Jenkins, Richard W. to Jane Mothershead. RICHARD W. JENKINS, farmer, age 54, single, b. Westmoreland Co., son of Smith Jenkins and Jemima [Washington],[4] to JANE MOTHERSHEAD, age 54, single, b. Westmoreland Co., daughter of John Mothershead and [Celia Massey].[5] License 17 OCT 1857. Married 18 OCT 1857 at his residence by H.P.F. King, minister of the M.E. Church. [M16a:57-33; R:62; R1:10-7]

Jenkins, William Bartlett to Charlotte B. Davis. WILLIAM BARTLETT JENKINS, farmer, age 33, widowed, b. Richmond Co., son of James and Frances Jenkins, to CHARLOTTE B. DAVIS, age 19, single, b. Richmond Co., daughter of Thomas L. and Ann Davis. Wit. J.W. Hutt. License 8 APR 1859. Married 12 APR 1859 by T. Grayson Dashiell, clergyman. [M16a:59-11 and 33; R:68; R1:14-7]

Jett, Edward Starke to Latitia Ann Franklin. EDWARD STARKE JETT, carpenter, age 26, single, b. Westmoreland Co., son of James H. Jett and Jane [White],[6] to LATITIA ANN FRANKLIN, age 19, single, b. King George Co., daughter of Betty Franklin. License 2 NOV 1872. Married 3 NOV 1872 at *Spring Garden* by Howard W. Montague, M.G. of Christ. [M19; R:106; R1:51-8]

---

[1] John Lewis Jenkins and his wife Mary Jane Eliff were possibly buried in the Jenkins Family Cemetery, located off of Route 645 near Zacata, Va.
[2] Henry Eliff and Frances Stone, daughter of Alice Stone, were married by bond 28 FEB 1824 in Westmoreland Co., with William Bulger, security.
[3] John S. Jenkins was buried in the Edwards Family Cemetery, located off of Route 621 near Nomini Grove, Va.
[4] Smith Jenkins and Jemima Washington were married by agreement 6 DEC 1792 in Westmoreland Co.
[5] John Mothershead and Celia Massey were married by bond 19 AUG 1801 in Westmoreland Co., with Thomas Massey, security.
[6] James H. Jett and Jane White were married by bond 23 MAR 1831 in Westmoreland Co., with William White, security.

Jett, James H. (d. 1867 of consumption), to Mrs. Amelia F. Thomas Reede. JAMES H. JETT, mechanic, age 46, widower, b. Mattox, Va., son of Taliaferro and Amelia Jett, to AMELIA F. REEDE, age 42, widow, b. King George Co., daughter of Massy Thomas and Margaret his wife. License 5 SEP 1857. Married 8 SEP 1857 at Mrs. Reed's in Mattox, Va. by John Pullen, M.G. [DR:13-30; M16a:57-29; R:61; R1:11-12]

Johnson, Aaron Arthur (C) to Mary Ann Williams (C). AARON ARTHUR JOHNSON, farmer, age 25, single, b. Westmoreland Co., son of Thomas T. and Betty Johnson, to MARY ANN WILLIAMS, age 22, single, b. Westmoreland Co., daughter of Abram and Jane Williams. License 30 DEC 1874. Married 31 DEC 1874 at Harris' near Sandy Point by Thomas T. Johnson. [M19; R:114; R1:60-9]

Johnson, Adam (C) to Bettie Frances Patrick. ADAM JOHNSON, farmer, age 21, single, b. Hanover Co., son of Adam and Charlotte Johnson, to BETTIE FRANCES PARTRICK [sic], age 21, single, b. Essex Co., daughter of Henry and Mary Patrick. Signed Adam [his X mark] Johnson, wit. W.S. McKenney. License 12 SEP 1873. Married 14 SEP 1872 by Emanuel Watts, pastor of Little Zion Church. [M19; R:109; R1:54-8]

Johnson, Albert to Virginia Smith. ALBERT JOHNSON, farmer, age 22, single, b. Westmoreland Co., son of Margaret Johnson, father unknown, to VIRGINIA SMITH, age 20, single, b. Westmoreland Co., daughter of John and Milly Smith. License 2 JUN 1877. Married 7 JUN 1877 at Rugged Point by Chas. [his X mark] Rust, wit. Joseph N. Arnest. [M19; R:122; R1:69-15]

Johnson, Ananias to Rose Wright, colored persons. ANANIAS JOHNSON, farmer, age 23, single, b. Westmoreland Co., son of R. and M.A. Johnson, to ROSE WRIGHT, age 28, single, b. Westmoreland Co., daughter of J.H. and Millie Wright. License 24 DEC 1879. Married 25 DEC 1879 at *Blenheim* by Wm. C. Latane, Presbyter P.E. Church. [M20; R:131; R1:80-4; WP]

Johnson, Andrew to Coodie Harrison. ANDREW JOHNSON, sailor, age 23, single, b. Westmoreland Co., daughter of George and Caty Johnson, to COODIE HARRISON, age 18, single, b. Westmoreland Co., daughter of Fanny Harrison, father unknown. Signed Andrew Johnson, wit. Chas. C. Baker. License 24 JAN 1860. Married 26 JAN 1860. [M17:60-4; R:72]

Johnson, Benjamin to Alice Jane Virginia Nelson (C) (d. 1885 of heart disease). BENJAMIN JOHNSON, farmer, age 22, single, b. Essex Co., son of Robert and Letty Johnson, to ALICE JANE VIRGINIA NELSON, age 21, single, b. Westmoreland Co., daughter of James and Maria Nelson. License 6 JAN 1871. [DR:66-134; R:100; R1:45-6 no return]

Johnson, Charles to Jenny Hinson. CHARLES JOHNSON, farmer, age 21, single, b. Westmoreland Co., son of Alice Johnson, father unknown, to JENNY HINSON, age 23, single, b. Westmoreland Co., parents unknown. Signed Charles [his X mark] Johnson, wit. C.C. Baker. License 28 JAN 1868. Married 30 JAN 1868 at *Hickory Hill* by J.H. Davis. [M18; R:89; R1:32-1]

Johnson, Charles (C) to Hannah Stewart. CHARLES JOHNSON, farmer, age 21, single, b. Westmoreland Co., son of James and Fanny Johnson, to HANNAH STEWART, age 20, single, b. Westmoreland Co., daughter of Samuel and Peggy Stewart. Signed Charles [his X mark] Johnson, wit. J.W. Hutt. License 21 DEC 1874. Married 23 DEC 1874 by Emanuel Watts, pastor of Little Zion Church. [M19; R:114; R1:59-14]

Johnson, Charles (C) to Charlotte Ann Young. CHARLES JOHNSON, age 23, widowed, b. Westmoreland Co., son of James and Fanny Johnson, to CHARLOTTE ANN YOUNG, age 17, single, b. Westmoreland Co., daughter of Johnson and Edy Young. License 18 DEC 1876. Married 20 DEC 1876 at Little Zion Church by Emanuel Watts, pastor, Little Zion Church. [M19; R:120; R1:67-10]

Johnson, Charles Henry to Susan Dickens. License 7 DEC 1857. [R:62]

Johnson, Cornelius (C) (d. 1882 of dropsy), to Bettie Campbell. CORNELIUS JOHNSON, farmer, age 40, single, b. Westmoreland Co., son of Griffin and [Mahala] Hany Johnson, to BETTIE CAMPBELL, age 31, single, b. Westmoreland Co., daughter of Solomon and Lucy Robinson. Signed Cornelius [his X mark] Johnson, wit. J.W. Hutt. License 21 DEC 1869. Married 23 DEC 1869 at Sandy Point by J.H. Davis. [DR:52-50; M18; R:96; R1:40-26]

Johnson, Daniel to Annie Epps. DANIEL JOHNSON, farmer, age 25, single, b. Essex Co., son of Jacob and Matilda Johnson, to ANNIE EPPS, age 21, single, b. Essex Co., daughter of Bartlett and Phillis Epps. License 29 DEC 1877. Married 29 DEC 1877 by R.N. Reamy. [M19; R:124; R1:71-16]

Johnson, Dennis to Betsy Hall. License 7 APR 1856. [R:55]

Johnson, Dennis to Susan West (C). DENNIS JOHNSON, farmer, age 19, single, b. Westmoreland Co., son of Margaret Johnson, father unknown, to SUSAN WEST, age 19, single, b. Westmoreland Co., daughter of Solomon and Kitty West. License 10 SEP 1880. Married 11 SEP 1880 at *Blenheim* by Wm. C. Latane, Presbyter P.E. Church. [M20; R:134; R1:83-12; WP]

Johnson, Elza to Emma Kay. ELZA JOHNSON, farmer, age 45, single, b. Westmoreland Co., son of William and Nancy Johnson, to EMMA KAY, age 25, single, b. Westmoreland Co., daughter of Taylor and Elizabeth Kay. Signed Elza [his X mark] Johnson, wit. W.S. McKenney. License 21 JAN 1874. Married 22 JAN 1874 at Wm. Worrell's by John Payne. [M19; R:111; R1:57-3; WP has Susan Kay]

Johnson, Frederick to Charlotte Tate. FREDERICK JOHNSON, farmer, age 30, widowed, b. and res. Richmond Co., son of William and Mary Johnson, to CHARLOTTE TATE, age 22, single, b. Westmoreland Co., daughter of Ewell and Gracy Tate. License 6 JUN 1863. Married 25 JUL 1863 by H.P.F. King. [M17:63-7; R:80; R1:20-5]

Johnson, Frederick to Mrs. Martha Pratt Haines. FREDERICK JOHNSON, farmer, age 21, single, b. Westmoreland Co., son of Charles and Ann Johnson, to MARTHA HAINES, age 29, widow, b. Westmoreland Co., daughter of Peter and Lucy Pratt. License 24 JUL 1879. Married 24 JUL 1879 at Mr. Rice's by F.W. Claybrook. [M20; R:129; R1:78-7]

Johnson, Frederick B. to Elisey Johnson. License 23 DEC 1851. Married 27 DEC 1851 by John McDaniel. [M15:51-28, R:13]

Johnson, George (C) to Lucinda Richardson. GEORGE JOHNSON, farmer, age 21, single, b. Westmoreland Co., son of William Settles and Sucky Johnson, to LUCINDA RICHARDSON, age 21, single, b. Westmoreland Co., daughter of Benjamin Richardson. Signed George [his X mark]

Johnson, wit. J.H. Sisson. License 23 APR 1870. Married 24 APR 1870 by Jerry Graham. [M18; R:99; R1:43-1]

Johnson, George, Jr. (d. 1874 of pneumonia), to Frances Young. GEORGE JOHNSON, farmer, age 23, single, b. Westmoreland Co., son of George and Catharine Johnson, to FRANCES YOUNG, age 18, single, b. Westmoreland Co., daughter of James and Betsy Young. Signed George [his X mark] Johnson, wit. J.W. Hutt. License 24 AUG 1871. Married 24 AUG 1871 by John C. Smith. [DR:30-14; M18; R:102; R1:47-7]

Johnson, Henderson to Eliza Johnson. HENDERSON JOHNSON, farmer, age 25, single, b. Northumberland Co., son of Sampson and Mollie Johnson, to ELIZA JOHNSON, age 22, single, b. Westmoreland Co., daughter of Benjamin and Maria Johnson. Signed Henderson [his X mark] Johnson, wits. J.W. Hutt, F.S. Sisson. License 26 MAR 1868. Married 26 MAR 1868 at *Hickory Hill* by J.H. Davis. [M18; R:90; R1:32-13]

Johnson, Henry Washington (C) to Winney Ann Braxton. HENRY WASHINGTON JOHNSON, farmer, age 20, single, b. Westmoreland Co., son of Samuel and Tempe Johnson, to WINNEY ANN BRAXTON, age 18, single, b. Westmoreland Co., daughter of Daniel and Ellen Braxton. Signed Henry W. [his X mark] Johnson, wit. W.S. McKenney. License 19 NOV 1874. Married 19 NOV 1874 on Mrs. Harris' land by Thomas T. Johnson. [M19; R:113; R1:59-5]

Johnson, Hiram Hazard (c.1840-1910),[1] served in Co. C, 47th Va. Inf., C.S.A., to Martha Ann Brown. HIRAM JOHNSON, farmer, age 24, single, b. Westmoreland Co., son of Robert Hazard [Johnson[2]] and Sally Jenkins, to MARTHA ANN JOHNSON, age 24, single, b. Westmoreland Co., daughter of Christopher and Fanny Brown. License 8 JUL 1863. Married 9 JUL 1863 at the residence of the bride by H.P.F. King. [M17:63-8; R:80; R1:20-6]

Johnson, Ignacius to Fanny Dixson (d. 1891 of consumption). IGNACIUS JOHNSON, farmer, age 29, single, b. Westmoreland Co., son of Charles and Leoana Johnson, to FANNY DIXSON, age 23, single, b. Westmoreland Co., daughter of Solomon and Emily Dixson. Signed Ignacious [his X mark] Johnson, wit. J.H. Sisson. License 23 NOV 1869. Married 25 NOV 1869 by J.H. Davis. [DR:87-32; M18; R:96; R1:39-13]

Johnson, James to Suckey Jett, slaves belonging to Dr. F.D. Wheelwright. Married 14 SEP 1861 at the Washington Parish rectory by Rev. T.E. Locke. [WP]

Johnson, James to Ann Carter. JAMES JOHNSON, farmer, age 20, single, b. Westmoreland Co., son of John and Sarah Johnson, to ANN CARTER, age 21, single, b. Westmoreland Co., unknown parents. Signed James [his X mark] Johnson, wit. J.F. Bispham. License 26 JAN 1867. Married 31 JAN 1867 at *Long Wood* by R.N. Reamy. [M18; R:86]

Johnson, James Edmond to Henrietta Garner. JAMES EDMOND JOHNSON, farmer, age 32, single, b. Westmoreland Co., son of Charles N. and Ann Johnson, to HENRIETTA GARNER, age 23, single, b. Westmoreland Co., daughter of Isaac and Juli[et] Garner. License 13 MAR 1878. Married 13 MAR 1878 by F.B. Beale. [M19; R:125; R1:73-9]

---

[1] Hiram H. Johnson was buried in an unmarked grave at Providence United Methodist Church.
[2] Mallory, p. 188, explains that Hiram took Johnson as a surname after his mother married Benjamin Johnson.

Johnson, James S. to Sallie A. Hunter. JAMES S. JOHNSON, wheelwright, age 32, single, b. Stafford Co., son of William Johnson and Elizabeth [A. Mothershead][1] [d. 1882 of dropsy], to SALLIE A. HUNTER, age 25, single, b. Westmoreland Co., daughter of John [d. by 1860][2] and Sallie T. Hunter. License 12 JAN 1857. Married 13 JAN 1857 at the residence of Mrs. Sallie T. Hunter by H.P.F. King, minister of the M.E. Church South. [DR:55:12[3]; M16a:57-4; R:59; R1:8-3]

Johnson, James W. to Augusta Barker, daughter of John [d. testate 1884] and Frances Barker, *q.v.* License 22 MAR 1853. Married 24 MAR 1853 by John Pullen. [M15:53-10; R:29]

Johnson, James William to Elizabeth Lucas.[4] JAMES WILLIAM JOHNSON, laborer, age 20, single, b. Westmoreland Co., son of James and Susan Johnson, to ELIZABETH LUCAS, age 20, single, b. Westmoreland Co., daughter of Briddy and Jane Lucas. License 23 DEC 1862. Planned marriage 23 DEC 1862. [R:79; R1:19-10 no return]

Johnson, Jerry (C) to Ann Smith. JERRY JOHNSON, farmer, age 50, single, b. Westmoreland Co., son of Jerry and Nelly Johnson, to ANN SMITH, age 23, single, b. Westmoreland Co., daughter of John and Susan Smith. License 19 JUL 1876. Married 20 JUL 1876 at my house by Thomas T. Johnson. [M19; R:119; R1:65-13]

Johnson, John (C) (d. by 1867), to Eliza Jane Gaskins. JOHN JOHNSON, farmer, age 25, single, b. Westmoreland Co., son of Charles and Leanna Johnson, to ELIZA JANE GASKINS, age 21, single, b. Westmoreland Co., daughter of Patric[k] Gaskins and Sally [Sarah Gaskins].[5] License 23 SEP 1862. Married 25 SEP 1862. [R:78; R1:19-4 no return]

Johnson, John to Mrs. Patty Dangerfield Johnson. JOHN JOHNSON, farmer, age 36, single, b. Westmoreland Co., son of John and Lavina Johnson, to PATTY JOHNSON, age 25, widow, b. Westmoreland Co., daughter of Leroy and Maria Dangerfield. Signed John [his X mark] Johnson, wit. J.H. Sisson. License 14 JAN 1870. Married 18 JAN 1870 by G. Wm. Beale, minister. [M18; R:97; R1:41-9]

Johnson, John (C) to Mary Frances Davis. JOHN JOHNSON, laborer, age 26, single, b. Westmoreland Co., son of John and Hannah Johnson, to MARY FRANCIS DAVIS [sic], age 18, single, b. Essex Co., daughter of William and Mary Davis. Signed John [his X mark] Johnson, wit. W.S. McKenney. License 15 AUG 1871. Married 17 AUG 1871 by John Roy, pastor of church at Grant's Hill. [M19; R:102; R1:47-5]

Johnson, John to Mary Thompson. JOHN JOHNSON, farmer, age 25, single, b. Westmoreland Co., son of Samuel and Tempe Johnson, to MARY THOMPSON, age 21, single, b. Westmoreland Co., daughter of Roberta Straughan, father unknown. License 30 JAN 1877. Married 1 FEB 1877 at Cabin Point by Frank B. Beale. [M19; R:121; R1:68-16]

---

[1] William Johnson and Elizabeth A. Mothershead were married by bond 12 DEC 1822 in Westmoreland Co., with Daniel Mothershead, security.
[2] CF1860-07, *Guardian of Thomas S. Jenkins &c. v. Mary A. Jenkins &c.*
[3] DR:52-12, entry for Elizabeth Johnson, d. 25 NOV 1882 of dropsy, age 76, daughter of Daniel and Catharine Mothershead, mother of James S. Johnson.
[4] The couple is probably buried in the Johnson Family Cemetery, located near the intersection of Routes 3 and 204.
[5] Patrick Gaskins and Sarah Gaskins were married by bond 14 JAN 1842 in Westmoreland Co., with William Bailey, security.

Johnson, John to Judy Thompson. JOHN JOHNSON, farmer, age 21, single, b. Westmoreland Co., son of Washington and Olivia Johnson, to JUDY THOMPSON, age 26, single, b. Westmoreland Co., daughter of Polly Thompson, father unknown. License 5 MAY 1879. Married 8 MAY 1879 at Col. Thos. Brown's by F.W. Claybrook. [M20; R:128; R1:77-9]

Johnson, John Jefferson (C) to Virginia Thompson. JOHN JEFFERSON JOHNSON, farmer, age 22, single, b. Westmoreland Co., son of Edward and Mary Johnson, to VIRGINIA THOMPSON, age 22, single, b. Westmoreland Co., daughter of James and Julia Ann Thompson. Signed by J.J. [his X mark] Johnson, wit. J.W. Hutt. License 13 DEC 1873. Married 18 DEC 1873 by John Roy. [M19; R:110; R1:55-5]

Johnson, John Richard, second[1] to Georgeanna Thompson. JOHN RICHARD JOHNSON, farmer, age 27, widowed, b. Westmoreland Co., son of Samuel and Tempy Johnson, to GEORGEANNA THOMPSON, age 21, single, b. Westmoreland Co., daughter of Roberta Straughan, father unknown. License 28 JAN 1879. Married 30 JAN 1879 at *Bushfield* by F.B. Beale. [M20; R:128; R1:76-14]

Johnson, Joseph to Arena Kelly (d. 1888 of liver complaint). JOSEPH JOHNSON, no occupation, age 24, single, b. Westmoreland Co., son of Charles and Leanna Johnson, to ARENA KELLY, age 24, single, b. Westmoreland Co., daughter of Vincent Kelly and Atway [Astin].[2]* License 3 DEC 1855. Married 6 DEC 1855 at residence of Charles Johnson by T. Grayson Dashiell. [DR:75-37[3]; M16:55-24; R:51]

Johnson, Joseph (C) to Julia Maiden. JOSEPH JOHNSTON [sic], farmer, age 34, widowed, b. Westmoreland Co., son of Lewis and Hannah Johnson, to JULIA MAIDEN, age 34, single, b. Westmoreland Co., daughter of Daniel Maiden. License 16 JUN 1877. Married 17 JUN 1877 at Little Zion Church by Emanuel Watts, pastor, Little Zion Church. [M19; R:122; R1:70-2]

Johnson, Josephas (C) to Georgeanna Thompson. JOSEPHAS JOHNSON, farmer, age 44, widowed, b. Westmoreland Co., son of Reuben Johnson and Fanny [Johnson],[4] to GEORGEANNA THOMPSON, age 18, single, b. Richmond Co., daughter of Dunkin and Malinda Thompson. License 10 JUN 1880. Married 10 JUN 1880 at the residence of the bride by Edmond Rich. [M20; R:133; R1:83-1]

Johnson, Lewis to Louisa Tate (C) (d. 1867). LEWIS JOHNSON, farmer, age 30, single, b. Westmoreland Co., son of Thomas and Hannah Johnson, to LOUISA TATE, age 30, single, b. Westmoreland Co., daughter of Hopeful Tate [d. 1871] and Maria [Tate].[5] License 19 MAR 1862. Married 22 MAR 1862 by G.H. Northam. [DR:13-31, 24-1; M17:62-10; R:78; R1:19-1]

Johnson, Lewis to India Newman. LEWIS JOHNSON, farmer, age 36, widower, b. Westmoreland Co., son of Thomas and Hannah Johnson, to INDIA NEWMAN, age 21, single, b. Westmoreland

---

[1] DR:39-48, entry for Mary Johnson, d. 10 OCT 1877 in childbirth, age 21, daughter of Roberta Straughan, wife of John Johnson.
[2] Vincent Kelly and Attoway Astin, daughter of Winneyford Astin, were married by bond 19 JAN 1831 in Westmoreland Co., with Emanuel Smith, security.
[3] DR:75-37, entry for Irena Johnson (C), d. 10 OCT 1888 of liver complaint, age 57, * daughter of Marcus and Judy Kelly, wife of Joseph Johnson.
[4] Reuben Johnson and Fanny Johnson were married by bond 21 JAN 1829 in Westmoreland Co., with Samuel Johnson, security.
[5] Hopeful Tate and Maria Tate were married by bond 23 JAN 1832 in Westmoreland Co., with Samuel Tate, security.

Co., daughter of Emanuel Newman and Caroline [Lucas].[1] Signed Lewis [his X mark] Johnson, wit. J.H. Sisson. License 29 DEC 1869. Married 30 DEC 1869 by H.H. Fones. [M18; R:97; R1:41-5]

Johnson, Moses Arthur (C) to Georgeanna Smith. MOSES ARTHUR JOHNSON, farmer, age 26, widowed, b. Westmoreland Co., son of Susan Johnson, to GEORGEANNA SMITH, age 22, single, b. Westmoreland Co., daughter of Emanuel Smith and Juliet [Ashton].[2] Signed by Moses [his X mark] Johnson, wit. Wm. S. McKenney. License 21 DEC 1875. Married 23 DEC 1875 at Fort Hill by Thomas T. Johnson. [M19; R:116; R1:62-15]

Johnson, Muscoe to Mary Louisa Patrick, colored persons. MUSCOE JOHNSON, farmer, age 21, single, b. Essex Co., son of Richard and Mary Johnson, to MARY LOUISA PATRICK, age 21, single, b. Essex Co., daughter of Henry and Mary Patrick. License 27 DEC 1878. Married 28 DEC 1878 at *Claymont* by Wm. C. Latane, Presbyter P.E. Church. [M20; R:127; R1:76-4; WP]

Johnson, Peter (C) to Martha Gaskins. PETER JOHNSON, farmer, age 21, single, b. Westmoreland Co., son of Margaret Johnson, father unknown, to MARTHA GASKINS, age 23, single, b. Westmoreland Co., daughter of Thomas and Mary Gaskins. License 2 JUN 1880. Married 3 JUN 1880 at the bride's residence by Charles [his X mark] Rust. [M20; R:133; R1:82-16]

Johnson, Philip Demerritt, served in Co. D, 9th Va. Cav., C.S.A., to Mary Ann Yeatman. PHILIP DEMERRITT JOHNSON, farmer, age 22, single, b. Westmoreland Co., son of William and Elizabeth Johnson, to MARY ANN YEATMAN, age 19, single, b. Westmoreland Co., daughter of Thomas J. Yeatman and Susan [P. Hunter].[3] License 26 SEP 1867. Married 26 SEP 1867 by G.H. Northam. [M18; R:87; R1:29-9]

Johnson, Philip to Lavina Lee. PHILLIP JOHNSON [sic], waterman, age 25, single, b. Westmoreland Co., son of Betsy Johnson, to LAVINA LEE, age 24, single, b. Westmoreland Co., daughter of Humphrey and Lucy Lee. Signed Phillip [his X mark] Johnson, wit. Wm. S. McKenney. License 9 APR 1874. Married 9 APR 1874 by H.H. Fones. [M19; R:112; R1:58-5]

Johnson, Primus to Frances Smith, free people of color. PRIMUS JOHNSON, age 21, to FRANCES SMITH, age 20. License 20 DEC 1853. Married 30 DEC 1853 by Wm. N. Ward, Minister in the P.E. Church. [M15:53-24; R:37]

Johnson, Richard to Emily Beale. RICHARD JOHNSON, farmer, age 39, widower, b. Westmoreland Co., son of Griffin and Haney Johnson, to EMILY BEALE, age 22, single, b. Westmoreland Co., daughter of George and Sophia Beale. Signed Richard [his X mark] Johnson, wit. H. Chandler. License 30 NOV 1869. Married 2 DEC 1869 by John C. Smith. [M18; R:96; R1:40-18]

Johnson, Richard (C) to Letitia Walker. RICHARD JOHNSON, farmer, age 60, widowed, b. Westmoreland Co., son of Jessie and Fanny Johnson, to LETITIA WALKER, age 25, single, b. Westmoreland Co., daughter of Sookey Walker, father unknown. Signed Richard [his X mark] Johnson, wit. Wm. S. McKenney. License 2 OCT 1871. Married 7 OCT 1871 by Emanuel Watts, Pastor of Little Zion Church. [M18; R:103; R1:47-13]

---

[1] Emanuel Newman and Caroline Lucas were married by bond 21 DEC 1836 in Westmoreland Co., with Richard Ashton, security.
[2] Emanuel Smith and Juliet Ashton were married by bond 7 JAN 1830 in Westmoreland Co., with James G. Donoho, security.
[3] Thomas J. Yeatman and Susan P. Hunter were married by bond 11 DEC 1839 in Westmoreland Co., with Bennett P. Crabb, security.

Johnson, Robert Noah to Willie Tate, black. ROBERT NOAH JOHNSON, farmer, age 28, single, b. Westmoreland Co., son of William and Hannah Johnson, to WILLIE TATE, age 21, single, b. Westmoreland Co., daughter of William and Fannie Tate. License 29 JAN 1880. Married 29 JAN 1880 at my residence by D.M. Wharton. [M20; R:132; R1:81-2]

Johnson, Samuel to Frances Thompson (d. 1881 of consumption). SAMUEL JOHNSON, farmer, age 60, widowed, b. Westmoreland Co., son of Nat. and Phoebe [Johnson], to FRANCES THOMPSON, age 45, single, b. Westmoreland Co., parents unknown [Gerard and Polly Thompson]. License 21 JUL 1876. Married 21 JUL 1876 at *Avries* by Frank B. Beale. [DR:48-29; M19; R:119; R1:65-14]

Johnson, Samuel to Sallie Parker. SAMUEL JOHNSON, laborer, age 21, single, b. Essex Co., son of Becky Johnson, father unknown, to SALLIE PARKER, age 22, single, b. Westmoreland Co., daughter of Richard Parker, mother unknown. License 25 AUG 1879. Married 26 AUG 1879 by B.R. Battaile. [M20; R:129; R1:78-10]

Johnson, Thomas to Carty Smith. THOMAS JOHNSON, farmer, age 21, single, b. Westmoreland Co., son of Whitfield and Sarah Ann Johnson, to CARTY SMITH, age 23, single, b. Westmoreland Co., daughter of William and Jennie Smith. License 10 DEC 1878. Married 12 DEC 1878 at *Bushfield* by F.B. Beale. [M20; R:127; R1:75-13]

Johnson, Thomas Sydnor to Susanna Lucas (d. 1887 of pneumonia). THOMAS SYDNOR JOHNSON, farmer, age 28, single, b. Westmoreland Co., son of Charles Johnson and Ann Lewis, to SUSIANNA LUCAS [sic], daughter of Anderson [or Andrew] and Julia Ann Lucas. Signed Thomas S. [his X mark] Johnson, wit. W.S. McKenney. License 11 FEB 1873. Married 13 FEB 1873 at Anderson Lucas' by G.W. Beale, M.G. [DR:72-99; M19; R:108; R1:53-9]

Johnson, Whitfield to Sarah Harrison. License 1 MAR 1854. [R:41]

Johnson, William (C) to Lucy Miller. WILLIAM JOHNSON, farmer, age 25, single, b. Hanover Co., son of Adam and Charlotte Johnson, to LUCY MILLER, age 21, single, b. Essex Co., daughter of Arthur and Mary Miller. Signed William [his X mark] Johnson, wit. W.S. McKenney. License 30 MAY 1872. Married 2 JUN 1872 at Little Zion Church at Oak Grove by Emanuel Watts, pastor. [M19; R:105; R1:50-10]

Johnson, William to Phillis Ann White. WILLIAM JOHNSON, farmer, age 21, single, b. Westmoreland Co., son of Charlotte Johnson, to PHILLIS ANN WHITE, age 30, single, b. Henrico Co., parents unknown. Signed Wm. [his X mark] Johnson. License 5 JAN 1875. Married 7 JAN 1875 at *Auburn* by Frank B. Beale. [M19; R:114; R1:60-11]

Johnson, William (C) to Mary Susan Newman (C). WILLIAM JOHNSON, farmer, age 20, single, b. Richmond Co., son of Frederick and Martha Johnson, to MARY SUSAN NEWMAN, age 21, single, b. Westmoreland Co., son of Francis and Laurinda Newman. License 28 NOV 1876. Married 30 NOV 1876 at Little Zion Church by Emanuel Watts, pastor, Little Zion Church. [M19; R:120; R1:67-2]

Johnson, William to Sarah Lee. WILLIAM JOHNSON, farmer, age 22, single, b. Westmoreland Co., son of Fanny Johnson, father unknown, to SARAH LEE, age 21, single, b. Westmoreland Co., daughter of Henry and Rebecca Lee. License 19 DEC 1877. Married 20 DEC 1877 at *Little Blackground* by F.B. Beale. [M19; R:124; R1:71-14]

Johnson, William Hamilton (1857-1909), to Susan Virginia Howard (1858-1923),[1] colored persons. WILLIAM HAM.* JOHNSON, laborer [in saw mill], age 22, single, b. Caroline Co., son of Nelson and Susan Johnson, to SUSAN VIRGINIA HOWARD, age 21, single, b. Westmoreland Co., daughter of Benjamin and Lucinda Howard. License 17 FEB 1879. Married 19 FEB 1879 at *Popes Creek Farm* by Wm. C. Latane, Presbyter P.E. Church. [M20; R:128; R1:76-15; WP]

Johnson, William Littleton to Mrs. Henrietta [Hill] Burrel. WILLIAM LITTLETON JOHNSON, farmer, age 23, single, b. Richmond Co., son of Letty Johnson, father unknown, to HENRIETTA BURREL, age 30, widow, b. Westmoreland Co., daughter of Edwin and Judy [Hill]. License 29 AUG 1876. Married 31 AUG 1876 by William Gaskins. [M19; R:119; R1:66-2]

Jones, Beverly to Mrs. Jane Lane. BEVERLY JONES, farmer, age 25, single, b. Westmoreland Co., son of Lucy Jones, father unknown, to JANE LANE, age 27, widow, b. Westmoreland Co., parents unknown. Signed Beverly [his X mark] Jones, wit. W.S. McKenney. License 11 MAY 1876. Married 13 MAY 1876 at Salem Church by F.B. Beale. [M19; R:118; R1:64-16]

Jones, Charles to Sally Gaskins (C). CHARLES JONES, farmer, age 70, single, b. Westmoreland Co., son of Moor[e] and Judy Moncure, to SALLY GASKINS, age 45, widow, b. Westmoreland Co., daughter of Thomas and Sally Gaskins. License 5 FEB 1866. Married 8 FEB 1866 at the rectory of Cople Parish by Chas. P. Rodefer, minister. [CP; M18; R:82; R1:23-7]

Jones, George Washington (1841-1922), served in Co. E, 55th Va. Inf., C.S.A., to Elizabeth Frances Sanford (1844-1901).[2] GEORGE W. JONES, sailor, age 21, single, b. Richmond Co., son of Rebecca Jones, father unknown, to ELIZABETH F. SANFORD, age 19, single, b. Westmoreland Co., daughter of William J. [James] Sanford and [Frances] Fanny [Holbrook].[3] License 17 DEC 1862. Married 17 DEC 1862 at the residence of Mary Kelly by H.P.F. King. [M17:62-16; R:79; R1:19-8]

Jones, Hiram M. to Sallie H. Douglass. License 25 JAN 1853. [R:27 no return]

Jones, Lewis to Harriet Homes. LEWIS JONES, laborer, age 21, single, b. Essex Co., son of Barnaby Hedgman and Susan Jones, to HARRIET HOMES, age 27, single, b. Essex Co., daughter of Davy and Farissey Homes. Signed Lewis [his X mark] Jones, wits. J.E. Sturman, J.W. Hutt. License 15 OCT 1867. Married 19 OCT 1867 at B.F. Smoot's mill by R.N. Reamy. [M18; R:88; R1:29-13]

Jones, Nelson to Jane Peirce [a.k.a. Pierce]. NELSON JONES, farmer, age 21, single, b. Westmoreland Co., son of Moses Thompson and Lucy Jones, to JANE PEIRCE, age 20, single, b. Westmoreland Co., daughter of William Peirce and Hannah [McCoy].[4] Signed Nelson [his X mark] Jones. License 25 FEB 1870. Married 27 FEB 1870 by John C. Smith. [M18; R:98; R1:42-7]

---

[1] William H. Johnson and his wife Susan were buried at Grant Hill Baptist Church, Leedstown, Va. * His name also appears as William Hamlin Johnson.
[2] George W. Jones and his wife Elizabeth were buried at Providence United Methodist Church, Chiltons, Va.
[3] William J. Sanford and Fanny Holbrook were married by bond 12 AUG 1830 in Westmoreland Co., with Thomas M. Belfield, security.
[4] William Peirce and Hannah Macoy were married by bond 9 JUL 1828 in Westmoreland Co., with Joseph Thompson, security.

Jones, Patrick to Emiline Wright. PATRICK JONES, farmer, age 27, single, b. Westmoreland Co., son of Patrick [d. 1885] and Nancy Jones, to EMELINE WRIGHT, age 18, single, b. Westmoreland Co., daughter of Solomon and Emily Wright. Signed Patrick [his X mark] Jones, wit. J.W. Hutt. License 4 JAN 1871. Married 5 JAN 1871 by G.W. Beale. [DR:64-41; M18; R:100; R1:45-5]

Jones, Patrick, second[1] to Mrs. Nancy Dean. PATRICK JONES, farmer, age 63, widower, b. Westmoreland Co., parents unknown, to NANCY DEAN, age 35, widow, b. Westmoreland Co., daughter of Maria Henry. Signed Patrick [his X mark] Jones. License 8 JAN 1874. Married 12 JAN 1874 at Potomac Church by G.W. Beale, minister. [M19; R:111; R1:56-9]

Jones, Robert to Eliza Jane Thompson. ROBERT JONES, farmer, age 25, single, b. Westmoreland Co., son of ~~William and Ann~~ Judy Lee, to ELIZA JANE THOMPSON, age 20, single, b. Westmoreland Co., daughter of William and Ann Thompson. Signed Robert [his X mark] Jones, wit. W.S. McKenney. License 11 MAR 1873. Married 20 MAR 1873 at Carlos Hudson's by G.W. Beale, minister. [M19; R:108; R1:53-13]

Jones, Solomon to Sarah Ann Tate. SOLOMON JONES, farmer, age 24, single, b. Westmoreland Co., son of Lucy Jones, father unknown, to SARAH ANN TATE, age 22, single, b. Westmoreland Co., daughter of Jordon Tate and Betsy [Thompson].[2] License 2 JUL 1870. Married 3 JUL 1870 by G.W. Beale. [M18; R:99; R1:43-11]

Jones, Thomas Sydnor to Alice Virginia Anthoney. THOMAS SYDNOR JONES, farmer, age 24, single, b. Westmoreland Co., son of Amelia Jones, father unknown, to ALICE VIRGINIA ANTHONEY, age 22, single, b. Westmoreland Co., daughter of Thomas and Nancy Anthoney. License 27 DEC 1876. Married 28 DEC 1876 by R.N. Reamy. [M19; R:121; R1:68-3]

Jones, William to Sarah Frances Weldon. WILLIAM JONES, farmer, age 29, single, b. Westmoreland Co., son of Lucy Jones, father unknown, to SARAH FRANCES WELDON, age 22, single, b. Westmoreland Co., daughter of Sally Weldon, father unknown. License 5 DEC 1878. Married 8 DEC 1878 at Salem Church by F.B. Beale. [M20; R:127; R1:75-11]

Jones, William Henry to Mary Bernice Barrack. WILLIAM HENRY JONES, farmer, age 30, single, b. Westmoreland Co., res. DeKalb Co., Mo., son of William P. and L. Jones, to MARY BERNICE BARRACK, age 30, single, b. Westmoreland Co., son of Charles and Sarah Barrack. License 22 NOV 1880. Married 23 NOV 1880 at *Cherry Hill* by Wm. C. Latane, Presbyter P.E. Church, wit. by Mr. Jones from DeKalb Co., Mo. [M20; R:134; R1:84-4; WP]

K

Kay, Franklin to Ann Maria Dodd. FRANKLIN KAY, farmer, age 36, single, b. Caroline Co., son of Taylor and Elizabeth Kay, to ANN MARIA DODD, age 22, single, b. King George Co., daughter of Margaret Dodd, father unknown. Consent 18 JUN 1866 by bride. License 19 JUN 1866. Married 20 JUN 1866 at St. Peter's rectory by Rev. Thomas E. Locke. [M18; R:83; R1:24-8; WP]

---

[1] DR:23-16, entry for Susan Jones, housekeeper, d. 15 OCT 1871 of consumption, age 30, daughter of Benjamin and Nancy Tate, wife of Patrick Jones.
[2] Jordan Tate and Betsy Thompson, daughter of Bennett Thompson, were married by bond 6 AUG 1838 in Westmoreland Co., with William B. Butler, security.

Kay, Humphrey (d. 1897), to Jane Ferrell (d. 1874 in childbed). HUMPHREY KAY, farmer, age 42, widowed, b. Essex Co., son of Taylor Kay and Elizabeth [Green],[1] to JANE FERRELL, age 33, single, b. Westmoreland Co., daughter of John T. and Eliza[beth] Ferrell [d. testate 1877[2]]. Signed Humphrey [his X mark] Kay, wit. W.S. McKenney. License 12 JAN 1874. Married 15 JAN 1874 at Humphrey Kay's residence by Jno. Payne. [DR:32-16; M19; R:111; R1:56-13; WP]

Kay, James to Julia Kay. JAMES KAY, sailor, age 35, single, b. Essex Co., son of Taylor and Elizabeth Kay, to JULIA KAY, age 23, single, b. Westmoreland Co., daughter of Emily Kay. Signed by James [his X mark] Kay, wit. W.S. McKenney. License 12 JAN 1874. Married 15 JAN 1874 at Humphrey Kay's residence by Jno. Payne. [M19; R:111; R1:56-12; WP]

Kay, Robert to Lucinda Bradshaw. Married 30 JUL 1872 at *Cavalla* by Rev. John Payne. [WP]

Kelly, David to Agness Hodge. DAVID KELLY, farmer, age 23, single, b. Richmond Co., son of Thadeus Kelly and Deannah [Gaskins] (C),[3] to AGNESS HODGE, age 21, b. single, b. Westmoreland Co., daughter of Nancy Hodge, father unknown. Signed David [his X mark] Kelly, wits. J.W. Hutt and J.H. Sisson. License 29 OCT 1868. Married 29 OCT 1868 by D.M. Wharton. [M18; R:92; R1:35-9]

Kelly, George (C) to Sarah Richardson. License 15 JAN 1856. [R:53]

Kelly, James Washington to Sarah Frances Kelly. JAMES WASHINGTON KELLY, farmer, age 24, single, b. Westmoreland Co., son of John and Judy Kelly, to SARAH FRANCES KELLY, age 22, single, b. Westmoreland Co., daughter of Vincent Kelly and [Attaway Astin]. License 25 JAN 1870. Married 3 FEB 1870 by John C. Smith. [M18 license not on film, R:98; R1:41-15]

Kelly, Jesse (C) to Mary Elizabeth Gaskins. JESSE KELLY, blacksmith, age 23, single, b. Westmoreland Co., son of Vincent Kelly and Attaway [Astin], *q.v.*, to MARY ELIZABETH GASKINS, age 22, single, b. Westmoreland Co., daughter of Bartlett Gaskins and Mary [Ann Peck], *q.v.* License 28 DEC 1864. Married 8 JAN 1865 at the house of Bartlett Gaskins by W.W. Walker. [M17a:65-1; R:81; R1:21-13]

Kelly, John Richard to Mary Ann Eskridge. JOHN RICHARD KELLY, laborer, age 23, single, b. Westmoreland Co., son of John and Elizabeth Kelly, to MARY ANN ESKRIDGE, age 29, single, b. Westmoreland Co., daughter of Burrell S. and Fanny Eskridge. Signed Jno. R. [his X mark] Kelly, wit. J.H. Sisson. Consent 2 APR 1860 by bride, wit. Ely Padison Ramy. License 2 APR 1860. Married 2 APR 1860 by H.P.F. King, M.G. [M17:60-19, 19a, 19b; R:74; R1:17-8]

Kenerly, John to Georgianna Payne. Married 16 JAN 1866 at Mrs. Payne's residence, King George Co., by Rev. T.E. Locke. [WP]

---

[1] Taylor Key and Elizabeth Green were married by bond 27 OCT 1834 in Essex Co., security Warner McDowney.
[2] Deeds & Wills No. 41, p. 211, will of Elizabeth Ferrill, proved 24 DEC 1877, names Key grandchildren. WP shows she died 5 SEP 1877, age 72, and was buried at her residence.
[3] Thaddeus Kelly and Dinah Moore Gaskins, both free persons of colour, daughter of David Gaskins, were married by bond 21 OCT 1819 in Richmond Co.

Kennedy, Thomas Allen, Jr. (1830-1907),[1] to Jane Frances English (d. 1886 age 45).[2] THOMAS ALLEN KENNEDY, plasterer, age 29, single, b. Westmoreland Co., son of Thomas A. [Allen] Kennedy and Sarah D. [Davis Pursell],[3] to JANE FRANCES ENGLISH, age 18, single, b. Westmoreland Co., daughter of Benjamin S. English and Mary F. [Smith], *q.v.* License 7 MAR 1860. Married 8 MAR 1860 by G.H. Northam. [M17:60-15 and 15b; R:72; R1:16-11]

Kent, James to Mrs. Emily Jane Stephens, widow of James M. Stephens, *q.v.* JAMES KENT, farmer, age 35, widowed, b. and res. Northumberland Co., son of James Kent and Catharine [A. Dameron],[4] to EMILY JANE STEPHENS, age 30, widow, b. Westmoreland Co., parents unknown [John B. Stephens and Alice Hall]. License 24 JUL 1878. Married 28 JUL 1878 by R.N. Reamy. [M19; R:126; R1:74-6]

Kent, Joseph Benson, served in Co. H, 9th Va. Cav., C.S.A., to Susan Priscilla Rust. JOSEPH BENSON KENT, farmer, age 26, single, b. Anne Arundel Co., Md., son of James and Mary Kent, to SUSAN PRECILLA RUST, age 23, single, b. Delaware, daughter of John and Elizabeth Rust. License 7 SEP 1864. Married 8 SEP 1864 at the residence of John Rust by Thomas E. Locke. [M17a:64-8; R:80; R1:21-1; WP]

Kent, William to Elizabeth Ann Hogan. WILLIAM KENT, waterman, age 35, single, b. Northumberland Co., son of James Kent and Catharine [A. Dameron], *q.v.*, to ELIZABETH ANN HOGINS [sic], age 30, single, b. Westmoreland Co., daughter of Richard J. Hogan and Mary [King], *q.v.* Signed Wm. [his X mark] Kent, wit. J.W. Hutt. License 23 OCT 1867. Married 23 OCT 1867 at Richard Hogins' [sic] by R.J. Sanford. [M18; R:88; R1:29-15]

Kerchimber, John to Emily Crawley. JOHN KERCHIMBER, sailor, age 36, single, b. St. Mary's Co., Md., son of Jacob and Emily Kerchimber, to EMILY CRAWLEY, age 25, single, b. Westmoreland Co., daughter of Harriet Fauntleroy, [father blank]. Signed John [his X mark] Kerchimber. License 15 AUG 1867. Married 16 AUG 1867 at Robt. W. Murphy's by R.J. Sanford. [M18; R:87; R1:29-4]

Key (see Kay)

Keys, William H. (C) to Margaret Jackson. WILLIAM H. KEYS, sailor, age 28, single, b. Caroline Co., son of Robert and Lucy Keys, to MARGARET JACKSON, age 23, single, b. Westmoreland Co., daughter of Henry and [Penelope] Jackson. License 1 DEC 1871. Married 2 DEC 1871 by Emanuel Watts, Pastor of Little Zion Church. [M18; R:103; R1:48-5]

Kilman [also Killman], Martin and Elizabeth Gutridge (b. 1832 in Richmond Co., d. 1916). MARTIN KILMAN, sailor, age 53, widower, b. Dorchester Co., Md., son of Martin and Elizabeth Kilman, to ELIZABETH GUTRIDGE, age 21, single, b. Richmond Co., daughter of Newton Gutridge and Harriet [Scates].[5] License 11 AUG 1857. Married 13 AUG 1857 at the residence of John Robinson by H.P.F. King, minister of the M.E. Church. [DC; M16a:57-27; R:61; R1:10-1]

---

[1] Thomas A. Kennedy, Jr. was buried at Ebenezer United Methodist Church, Oldhams, Va.
[2] Jane Frances Kennedy was buried in the English Family Cemetery, located off of Route 603 near Acorn, Va.
[3] Thomas A. Kennedy and Sarah Pursell were married by bond 6 OCT 1825 in Richmond Co. Thomas Allen Kennedy, b. 22 JUL 1796 at Falmouth, Stafford Co., d. 31 JUL 1871 at Lyells, Richmond Co., m. Sarah Davis Pursell, b. 14 AUG 1802, d. 7 APR 1875, daughter of George and Sarah Pursell of Richmond Co.
[4] James Kent and Catharine A. Dameron were married by bond 10 JAN 1827 in Northumberland Co., with William B. Lewis, security.
[5] Newton Gutridge and Harriet Scates were married by bond 10 JUL 1833 in Richmond Co., with William Balderson, security.

King, Adolphus to Mrs. Sallie Pursley Bowler, bapt. 8 JUL 1855 at St. Peter's Church. ADOLPHUS KING, confectionary man, age 34, single, b. King George Co., son of Sandy and Sarah King, to SALLIE BOWLLER [sic], age 29, widow, b. Westmoreland Co., daughter of A. [Attaway] [d. 1866] and Ellen Pursley. License 14 JUL 1880. Married 18 JUL 1880 at the bride's residence by D.G.C. Butts. [M20; R:134; R1:83-7; SP; WP]

King, Baldwin Compton (d. 1877 of pneumonia), served in Co. A, 15th Va. Cav., C.S.A., to Hannah Jane Jeffries (1837-1913).[1] BALDWIN C. KING, farner, age 23, single, b. Westmoreland Co., son of William and Sarah ["Sallie"] King, to HANNAH J. JEFFRIES, age 22, single, b. Westmoreland Co., daughter of George and Elizabeth Jeffries. Consent 30 AUG 1859 by bride, wit. William B. Robinson. License 31 AUG 1859. Married 1 SEP 1859 by H.P.F. King, M.G. in the Methodist Protestant Church. [DR:40-55; M16a:59-20, 20a and 20b; R:70; R1:15-4]

King, Benjamin Lamkin, served in Co. C, 9th Va. Cav., C.S.A., to Susan Wilkins. BENJAMIN LAMKIN KING, soldier, age 19, single, b. Westmoreland Co., son of John W. King and Ann [Beale],[2] to SUSAN WILKINS, age 21, single, b. Northumberland Co., parents unknown. License 11 MAR 1862. Married 12 MAR 1862 at the residence of Wesley King by James A. Weaver. [M17:62-9; R:78; R1:18-15]

King, Elijah William to Ann Cash. ELIJAH W. KING, farming, age 20, single, b. Westmoreland Co., son of William Sutton and Ann King, to ANN CASH, age 22, single, b. Westmoreland Co., daughter of John and Mary Cash. Wit. Thomas Parker. Signed Elijah W. [his X mark] King. License 9 FEB 1859. Married 9 FEB 1859 at Chilton's X Roads by H.P.F. King, M.G. [M16a:59-7 and 7a; R:68; R1:14-5]

King, George Morland (1846-1914),[3] served in Co. E, 15th Va. Cav., C.S.A., to Lucy Jane Dishman (1843-1908). GEORGE MORLAND KING, farmer, age 20, single, b. Westmoreland Co., son of Henry King and Malissa [Dishman],[4] to LUCIE JANE DISHMAN, age 20, single, b. Westmoreland Co., daughter of James [Andrew] Dishman and Ann [V. Kent]. License 16 NOV 1866. Married 22 NOV 1866 at James Dishman's by John Pullen. [M18; R:84; R1:25-10]

King, Henry Dobyns (1847-1935), to Mary Brown Atwill (1850-1911).[5] HENRY DOBINS KING [sic], farmer, age 22, single, b. Richmond Co., son of [Rev.] Henry P.F. King and Elizabeth [N. Dobyns],[6] to MARY BROWN ATWILL, age 19, single, b. Westmoreland Co., daughter of Samuel B. Atwill and Jane [A. Brown].[7] License 27 NOV 1869. Married 30 NOV 1869 by H.P.F. King. [M18; R:96; R1:40-17]

---

[1] Hannah Jane Jeffries King was buried in the Jeffries Family Cemetery, located 3 miles east of Carmel United Methodist Church on *Level Green Farm.*
[2] John W. King and Ann Beale were married by bond 30 DEC 1841 in Westmoreland Co., with James O. King, security.
[3] George Moreland King was buried in the King Family Cemetery, located at *Kingswood,* located off of Route 637. His wife Lucy Jane Dishman may be buried there as well.
[4] Henry King, son of William Triplett Dishman, and Milly Dishman, sister of Samuel [Marcus] Dishman, were married by bond 2 JUL 1833 in Westmoreland Co., with Samuel Dishman, security.
[5] Henry Dobyns King and his wife Mary Brown were buried in Rock Creek Cemetery, Washington, D.C.
[6] Rev. Henry P.F. King was married second to Elizabeth N. Dobbins [Dobyns] by bond 22 FEB 1841 in Westmoreland Co., with James O. King, security. Also Henry P.F. King, bachelor, and Juliet Ann Dobyns, were married by bond 15 MAY 1839 in Richmond Co.
[7] Samuel B. Atwill and Jane A. Brown were married by bond 20 DEC 1842 in Westmoreland Co., with Thomas Brown, security.

King, Hiram H. [or S.] (d. 1895 age 66), served in Co. A, 15th Va. Cav., C.S.A., to Sarah Elizabeth King (1829-1916),[1] daughter of William and Sally King. License 19 AUG 1851. Married 21 AUG 1851 by W.W. Walker of the Methodist Protestant Church. [DC; DR:102-30; M15:51-17; R:11]

King, James W. (1830-1903), to Mary A. Garner (b. 1838, d. 1915 of bronchitis).[2] JAMES W. KING, occupation: follows the water, age 24, single, res. Alexandria, Va., son of Matthew and Martha King, to MARY A. GARNER, age 23, single, [b. Indiana], res. Westmoreland Co., daughter of [Joshua] Garner [and Elizabeth Roe]. License 4 JAN 1858. Married 5 JAN 1858 at [*Pacram*] by T. Grayson Dashiell. [DC; M16a:58-3; R:63; R1:11-1]

King, John H. to Lucinda L. Dement. JOHN H. KING, wheelwright, age 22, single, b. Northumberland Co., son of Benedict B. King and Elizabeth [Campbell],[3] to LUCINDA L. DEMENT, age 19, single, b. Westmoreland Co., daughter of George Dement and Elizabeth [Harrison]. [4] License 5 APR 1858. Married 7 APR 1858 at Carmel Church by H.P.F. King, minister of the M.E. Church. [M16a:58-11; R:63; R1:11-8]

King, John William (d. 1862 of measles), served in Co. A, 15th Va. Cav., C.S.A., to Sarah Ann Wright. JOHN WILLIAM KING, farmer, age 27, single, b. Westmoreland Co., son of Hiram S. King and Hannah [Harrison],[5] to SARAH ANN WRIGHT, age 20, single, b. Westmoreland Co., daughter of Francis W. and Jane J. Wright. License 15 APR 1861. Married 17 APR 1861 at the residence of Hiram King by H.P.F. King. [M17:61-8[6]; R:77; R1:18-1]

King, Lomax to Jane Purcell. LOMAX KING, fisherman, age 32, single, b. King George Co., son of Sandy and Sarah King, to JANE PURCELL, age 20, single, b. Westmoreland Co., daughter of [Ordivy] and Columbia Purcell. Signed Lomax [his X mark] King, wit. W.S. McKenney. License 27 DEC 1875. Married 29 DEC 1875 at Mr. Bohler's by Wm. C. Latane, minister P.E. Church. [M19; R:116; R1:63-1 has Columbia Purcell; WP]

King, Richard B. to Nancy T. Dawson. RICHARD B. KING, sailor, age 24, single, b. Westmoreland Co., son of James and Nancy King, to NANCY T. DAWSON, age 17, single, b. Northumberland Co., daughter of Benjamin Dawson and Patsy [R. Holliday].[7] License 22 AUG 1855. Married 23 AUG 1855 by H.P.F. King, minister of the Methodist E. Church. [M16:55-17; R:49; R1:4-1]

King, Richard R. (d. 1893 of dropsy), to Frances R. Robinson. RICHARD R. KING, farmer, age 51, widower, b. Westmoreland Co., son of William D. and Ann M. Robinson, to FRANCIS R. ROBINSON [sic], age 33, single, b. Westmoreland Co., daughter of William and Sarah King. License 20 FEB 1871. Married 23 FEB 1871 at Francis Wright's by R.J. Sanford. [DR:94-35; M18; R:101; R1:46-1]

---

[1] DC: Sarah E. King was buried near Kinsale, Va.

[2] James W. King and his wife Mary A. were buried in Bethel Cemetery, Alexandria, Va.

[3] Benedict B. King, son of John King, and Elizabeth Campbell, were married by bond 16 DEC 1830 in Northumberland Co., with William Walker, security.

[4] George Dement and Elizabeth Harrison were married by bond 31 JAN 1827 in Westmoreland Co., with William Gilbert, security.

[5] Hiram S. King, son of Sally R. King, and Hannah Harrison were married by bond 1 JUL 1822 in Richmond Co., with William Brickey, Sr., security.

[6] This is the earliest record found on a new form that includes "Marriage License" at the top, "Certificate to Obtain a Marriage License" in the middle, and "Minister's Return" of Marriage at the bottom.

[7] Benjamin Dawson and Patsy R. Holliday were married by bond 19 DEC 1837 in Northumberland Co., with Joseph B. Lewis, security.

King, Rufus to Martha S. Andrews.[1] RUFUS KING, farming, age about 40, widower, b. Mattox District, Westmoreland Co., son of Thomas King and Mary his wife, to MARTHA S. ANDREWS, age about 23, single, b. Essex Co., daughter of James Andrews [d. testate 1868[2]] and Catherine [B. Sale][3] his wife. License 20 DEC 1855. Married 22 DEC 1855 by John Pullen, M.G. [M16:55-26; R:51; R1:4-8]

King, Thomas Sandy (d. 1899), to Martha Ann Nash (d. 1899). THOMAS SANDY KING, farmer, age 30, single, b. Westmoreland Co., son of John T. King and Juliet [Mothershead],[4] to MARTHA ANN NASH, age 32, single, b. Westmoreland Co., daughter of James R. and Martha Nash. License 8 JAN 1862. Married 8 JAN 1862 at the residence of Mrs. Nash by H.P.F. King. [M17:62-4; NN; R:78; R1:18-11]

Kirk, John (d. 1892), to Alice Ann Kirk (d. 1876)[5]. JOHN KIRK, farmer, age 42, single, b. Westmoreland Co., son of John and Ann Kirk, to ALICE ANN KIRK, age 34, single, b. Westmoreland Co., daughter of William Kirk and Mary [Wheeler].[6] License 6 FEB 1866. Married 8 FEB 1866 by G.H. Northam. [DR:35-35; M18; NN; R:82; R1:23-8]

Kitching, Seymour to Ellen Miranda Bryant. SEYMOUR KITCHING, surgeon, age 38, single, b. Warwickshire, Eng., res. Indian Territory, son of Charles and Frances Kitching, to ELLEN MIRANDA BRYANT, age 25, single, b. Richmond Co., daughter of George and Martha Bryant. License 15 MAY 1877. Married 22 MAY 1877 at Jesse[y] G. Bryant's by R.J. Sanford. [M19; R:122; R1:69-12]

L

Lamkin, James Sydnor (d. 1882 of congestion of the brain), served in Co. C, 47th Va. Inf., C.S.A., to Sarah "Sally" Louisa Craft. JAMES SYDNOR LAMKIN, mechanic, age 27, single, b. Westmoreland Co., son of Matthew and Mary Lamkin, to SARAH LOUISA CRAFT, age 22, single, b. Talbot Co., Md., daughter of Lemuel and Elizabeth Craft. License 23 NOV 1870. Married 24 NOV 1870 by Robert N. Reamy. [DR:56-26; M18; R:100; R1:44-7]

Lamkin, Lewis ap Lewis[7] to Mrs. Mary Ann Clarkson (b. 1814, d. 1887), widow of Carter Croxton, Jr. (b. 1802, d. testate 1858[8]). LEWIS ap Lewis LAMPKIN, farmer, age 46, widowed, b. Northumberland Co., son of Lewis and Griffentello [Claughton] Lamkin,[9] to MARY ANN CROXTON, age 45, widow, b. Essex Co., parents Clarkson [daughter of Richard Clarkson and Susan Lorinda Crittenden]. Signed L.A.L. Lamkin. License 23 MAY 1859. Married 2 JUN 1859 by G.H. Northam. [DR:71-37; M16a:59-15 and 15a; R:68; R1:15-9]

Lampkin, Overton Brook (d. 1888 of pneumonia), to Phebe Gouldman. OVERTON BROOK LAMPKIN, wheelwright, age 17, single, b. Westmoreland Co., son of Matthew W. and Mary M. Lampkin, to PHEBE GOULDMAN, age 17, single, b. Westmoreland Co., daughter of John and

---

[1] CF1860-23, *James P. Woody v. Arena H. Woody &c.* The bride's surname also appears as Andress.
[2] Essex Co. Wills, Bk. 29, p. 3, will of James Andrews, proved 21 SEP 1868.
[3] James Sale and Catharine B. Sale, daughter of William Brooking Sale (d. 1805), were married by bond 20 DEC 1815 in Essex Co.
[4] John T. King and Julyett Mothershead were married by bond 24 DEC 1830 in Westmoreland Co., with Thomas Mothershead, security.
[5] DR:35-35, entry for Alice J. Kirk, d. 9 MAY 1876 of disease of womb, age 43, daughter of William and Mary Kirk, wife of John Kirk.
[6] William G. Kirk and Mary Whealler, sister of Richard Whealler, were married by bond 6 JAN 1824 in Westmoreland Co., with Griffin R. Kirk, security.
[7] Lewis Lamkin was buried in the Croxton Family Cemetery.
[8] Westmoreland Co. Deeds & Wills, Bk. 35, p. 622, will of Carter Croxton.
[9] Lewis Lamkin, Jr. was married by bond 29 OCT 1811 in Northumberland Co., with F. Bates, security.

Martha Gouldman. License 14 DEC 1869. Married 16 DEC 1869 to Robert N. Reamy. [DR:78-154; M18; R:96; R1:40-23]

Lamkin, William Payne (d. 1893 age 65),[1] son of George Lamkin, first to Mrs. Anna M. Cox Bowcock (d. 1866 age 45), daughter of James L. and Lucie Cox, and widow[2] of Henry P. Bowcock (d. 1849). License 2 FEB 1852. Married 4 FEB 1852 by James McDonald. [DR:11-30; M15:52-5, R:15; WP]

Lamkin, William Payne (d. 1893 of cancer), second to Cornelia Northen. WILLIAM PAYNE LAMKIN, merchant, age 37, widower, b. Westmoreland Co., son of George Lamkin and [Ursula] [Payne],[3] to CORNELIA NORTHEN, age 22, single, b. Westmoreland Co., daughter of John H. and Margaret R. Northen. License 14 JUN 1867. Married 18 JUN 1867 at the residence of the bride's mother by Thomas J. Bayton, M.G. [DR:94-9; M18; R:87; R1:28-9]

Landon, John (C) to Sophia Gaskins. JOHN LANDON, farmer, age 23, single, b. Westmoreland Co., son of James and Rose Landon, to SOPHIA GASKINS, age 21, single, b. Westmoreland Co., daughter of Tascar and Sarah Gaskins. Signed John [his X mark] Landon, wit. W.S. McKenney. Married 15 OCT 1874 at Zion Church by Thomas T. Johnson. [M19; R1:59-2]

Landrum, Richard to Henrietta Ashton. RICHARD LANDRUM, laborer, age 25, single, b. Essex Co., son of Reuben Landrum and Lucy [Green],[4] to HENRIETTA ASHTON, age 24, single, b. Westmoreland Co., daughter of George Ashton and Julia [Tate].[5] License 6 DEC 1878. Married 8 DEC 1878 by H.H. Fones. [M20; R:127; R1:75-12]

Latane, William Catesby, Rev. (b. 1847 in Essex Co., d. 1906), Rector of Washington Parish for 30 years, to Susan Wilson (1857-1938),[6] of *Wakefield*. WILLIAM CATESBY LATANE, minister of the Gospel, age 29, single, b. Essex Co., son of James H. [Henry] Latane [b. 1820, d. 1897 at *Mahockney*, Essex Co.] and Janet J. [Juliet Rowzee] [1823-1880], to SUSAN WILSON, age 20, single, b. *Waterfield*, daughter of John E. and Bettie Wilson. License 23 OCT 1876. Married 1 NOV 1876 at St. Peter's Church, Oak Grove, by Beverley D. Tucker. [M19; R:119; R1:66-8; SC; WP]

Lawrence, Albert to Mrs. Betsey Hall Robb. ALBERT LAWRENCE, farmer, age 28, single, b. Westmoreland Co., son of James and [illegible] Lawrence, to BETSEY ROBB, age 26, widow, b. Westmoreland Co., daughter of Henry Hall, mother unknown. Signed Albert [his X mark] Lawrence, wit. J.W. Hutt. License 29 JUN 1869. Married 1 JUL 1869 by John C. Smith. [M18; R:95; R1:38-13]

Laurence, John to Ann Garner. JOHN LAURENCE, no occupation, age 73, single, b. Westmoreland Co., son of Jonathan and Jane Laurence, to ANN GARNER, age 43, single, b. Northumberland Co., daughter of Presl[e]y and Catherine Garner. License 1 MAR 1858. Married 2 MAR 1858 in the Poor House by H.P.F. King, minister of the M.E. Church. [M16a:58-8; R:63; R1:11-5]

---

[1] William P. Lampkin and his wife Anna M. Bowcock were buried near the Garnett Family Cemetery, located off of Route 205.
[2] CF1856-36, *Brent & Bryan v. Admr. of Henry P. Bowcock.*
[3] George Lamkin and Ursley Payne, daughter of Ann Payne, were married by bond 10 JAN 1822 in Westmoreland Co., with William Redman, security. Married 16 JAN 1822 by Rev. John Neale.
[4] See Essex Co. marriage for George Landrum to Georgiana Lewis, 28 DEC 1872.
[5] George Ashton and Julia Tate were married by bond 3 JAN 1844 in Westmoreland Co., with Blain Ashton, security.
[6] Rev. William C. Latane and his wife Susan Wilson were buried at St. Peter's Cemetery, Oak Grove, Va.

Lawrence, Robert (C) to Lucy Johnson. License 26 SEP 1855. [R:49]

Lawrence, Roderick Starling, Col., of *Fort Hill* (d. 1886 at Cole's Point), teacher, served in Co. C, 9th Va. Cav., C.S.A., to Margaret Louisa Bowie, daughter of Walter Bowie and Mary Todd. License 15 JUN 1853. Married 16 JUN 1853 by George Northam, L.M.G. [M15:53-17; NN; R:31]

Laws, Joseph Edmond to Margaret A. Brandican. License 8 DEC 1853. Married 13 DEC 1853 by John Pullen. [M15:53-22; R:35]

Lawson, Henry to Mary Claughton. HENRY LAWSON, miller, age 60, widowed, b. Northumberland Co., son of Charles and Sarah Lawson, to MARY CLAUGHTON, age 27, single, b. Westmoreland Co., daughter of Elizabeth Claughton [no father given]. Signed Henry [his X mark] Lawson, wit. J.W. Hutt. License 17 MAY 1869. Married 23 MAY 1869 at Carmel Church by R.J. Sanford. [M18; R:95; R1:38-7]

Lee, Baldwin to Hannah Fisher. BALDWIN LEE, farmer, age 25, single, b. Westmoreland Co., son of Edward and Maria Lee, to HANNAH FISHER, age 22, single, b. Westmoreland Co., daughter of Isaac and Susan Fisher. Signed Baldwin [his X mark] Lee, wit. W.S. McKenney. License 9 APR 1873. Married 10 APR 1873 at Isaac Fisher's by G.W. Beale, minister. [M19; R:109; R1:54-1]

Lee, Edmund (C) to Mrs. Jane Williams. EDMUND LEE, farmer, age 37, widowed, b. Westmoreland Co., son of Robert and Ann Lee, to JANE WILLIAMS, age 42, widow, b. Westmoreland Co., parents unknown. Signed Edmund [his X mark] Lee. License 17 DEC 1873. Married 30 DEC 1873 at Zion Church by Thomas T. Johnson. [M19; R:110; R1:55-9]

Lee, Edward to Mrs. Sarah A. Saunders. EDWARD LEE, farmer, age 62, widower, b. Westmoreland Co., son of Henry and Annie Lee, to SARAH A. SAUNDERS, age 35, widow, b. Boston, Mass., parents unknown. License 6 JUN 1879. Married 6 JUN 1879 near Beale's Mill by F.B. Beale. [M20; R:129; R1:77-15]

Lee, Eppy (C) to Rose Hackett. EPPY LEE, laborer, age 23, single, b. and res. Northumberland Co., son of Henry and Sophia Lee, to ROSE HACKETT, age 20, single, b. Westmoreland Co., daughter of Jesse and Jane Hackett. Signed Eppy [his X mark] Lee, wit. W.S. McKenney. License 14 AUG 1872. Married 14 AUG 1872 at Salem [Baptist Church] by John C. Smith. [M19; R:106; R1:51-1]

Lee, Henry to Mary Lawrence. HENRY LEE, farmer, age 26, single, b. Westmoreland Co., son of Edward and Maria Lee, to MARY LAWRENCE, age 21, single, b. Westmoreland Co., daughter of Mary Lawrence, father unknown. License 25 JUL 1878. Married 28 JUL 1878 by F.B. Beale. [M19; R:126; R1:74-7]

Lee, Jacob to Frances Landon (d. 1893 in child birth). JACOB LEE, farmer, age 35, widower, b. Westmoreland Co., son of Jacob and Dinah Lee, to FRANCES LANDON [sic], age 23, single, b. Westmoreland Co., daughter of James and Rose Landon. Signed Jacob [his X mark] Lee, wit. Wm. Green. License 30 JAN 1869. Married 4 FEB 1869 by G.W. Beale. [DR:95-22; M18; R:94; R1:37-14]

Lee, John Noah (C) to Henrietta Thompson. JOHN NOAH LEE, farmer, age 25, single, b. Westmoreland Co., son of Moses and Susan Lee, to HENRIETTA THOMPSON, age 25, single, b. Westmoreland Co., daughter of James and Sally Thompson. Signed John Noah [his X mark] Lee, wit. J.H. Sisson. License 22 MAR 1870. Married 24 MAR 1870 at *Pea Hill* by John C. Smith. [M18; R:98; R1:42-12]

Lee, Lazarus (C) to Ella Gibson. LAZARUS LEE, farmer, age 26, single, b. Richmond Co., son of Robert and Edie Lee, to ELLA GIBSON, age 20, single, b. Richmond Co., daughter of Joseph and Betsy Gibson. Signed Lazarus [his X mark] Lee, wit. W.S. McKenney. License 2 DEC 1873. Married 25 DEC 1873 by Jerry Graham. [M19; R:110; R1:55-16]

Lee, Linsey (C) (1865-1943),[1] to Nelly Campbell. LINSEY LEE, farmer, age 22, single, b. Westmoreland Co., son of Edmond and Mary Lee, to NELLY CAMPBELL, age 28, single, b. Westmoreland Co., daughter of Tasker and Maria Campbell. License 28 DEC 1880. Married 30 DEC 1880 at *Springfield* by Charles Rust. [DC; M20; R:134; R1:84-13]

Lee, Meredith Robinson (C) to Fannie Diggs. MEREDITH ROBINSON LEE, farmer, age 23, single, b. Westmoreland Co., son of P. and Mary Lee, to FANNIE DIGGS, age 22, single, b. Westmoreland Co., daughter of John and Sarah Diggs. License 25 MAR 1879. Married 27 MAR 1879 at *Drumbay* by Thomas T. Johnson. [M20; R:128; R1:77-5]

Lee, Moses to Mahala Harris (d. 1885 of pneumonia). MOSES LEE, farmer, age 28, single, b. Westmoreland Co., son of Moses and Sucky Lee, to MAHALA HARRIS, age 22, single, b. Northumberland Co., daughter of Maria Harris, father unknown. Signed Moses [his X mark] Lee, wit. C.C. Baker. License 26 FEB 1868. Married 27 FEB 1868 at *Barnesville* to J.H. Davis. [DR:64-46; M18; R:90; R1:32-10]

Lee, Samuel to Julia Cole. License 14 NOV 1853. Married 17 NOV 1853 by Wm. McGuire, M.G. [M15:53-19; R:35]

Lee, Thomas (C) to Silva Corbin. THOMAS LEE, farmer, age 23, single, b. Westmoreland Co., daughter of Moses and Sucky Lee, to SILVA CORBIN, age 26, single, b. Westmoreland Co., daughter of Thomas and Nancy Corbin. Signed Thomas [his X mark] mark, wit. J.W. Hutt. License 22 DEC 1870. Married 29 DEC 1870 by Thomas T. Johnson, minister of Potomac Colored Baptist Church. [M18; R:100; R1:44-14]

Lee, Washington to Eliza Jane Henderson. WASHINGTON LEE, farmer, age 24, single, b. Westmoreland Co., son of Jerry and Hannah Lee, to ELIZA JANE HENDERSON, age 19, single, b. Westmoreland Co., daughter of Mary Henderson, [no father named]. Signed Washington [his X mark] Lee, wit. C.C. Baker. License 25 MAY 1868. Married 26 MAY 1868 by D.M. Wharton. [M18; R:91 incorrectly has Mary Henderson; R1:33-13]

Lee, William Henry (1834-1902),[2] to Elizabeth Jane Yeatman. WILLIAM H. LEE, age 24, single, b. Westmoreland Co., son of William [Ludwell] Lee and Sarah [McKenney],[3] to ELIZABETH YEATMAN, age 2[4], single, b. Westmoreland Co., daughter of Lucy Yeatman. License 16 DEC

---

[1] DC: Linsey Lee was buried at Zion Church.
[2] William H. Lee was buried at St. John's Episcopal Church, Warsaw, Va.
[3] William L. Lee and Sarah McKenney were married 20 APR 1829 in Westmoreland Co., with James McKenney, security.

1856. Married 17 DEC 1856 by G.H. Northam, minister of the Baptist Church. [M16a:56-35; R:57; R1:7-8 has Wm. T. Lee]

Lefever, John (d. 1872 of consumption), to Harriet R. "Hattie" Crabbe. JOHN LEFEVER, farmer, age 43, widowed, b. Westmoreland Co., son of Nathaniel Lefever and Winny [Short],[1] to HATTIE CRABBE, age 21, single, b. Westmoreland Co., daughter of Benedict P. and Eliza Crabbe. License 15 JAN 1867. Married 17 JAN 1867 by G.H. Northam. [DR:20-22; M18; R:85]

Lefever, William to Mrs. Artimesa Payton Balderson. WILLIAM LEFEVER, farmer, age 42, widowed, b. Westmoreland Co., son of Nathaniel and Winny [Short] Lefever, *q.v.*, to ARTIMESA BALDERSON, age 34, widow, b. Westmoreland Co., daughter of John A. Payton. License 10 SEP 1867. Married 12 SEP 1867 by G.H. Northam. [M18; R:87; R1:29-7]

Leggin, Edmund (C) to Harriet Crawlie. EDMUND LEGGIN, sailor, age 28, widower, b. Powhatan Co., res. Richmond Co., son of Daniel and Jane Leggin, to HARRIET CRAWLIE, age 26, single, b. Westmoreland Co., daughter of Lewis and Sarah Crawlie. License 16 SEP 1876. Married 17 SEP 1876 at Lewis Crawlie's house by Thomas T. Johnson. [M19; R:119; R1:66-4]

Lewis, Aaron (1838-1903),[2] served in Co. D, 15th Va. Cav., C.S.A., second* to Mildred Lindsey Thrift. AARON LEWIS, farmer, age 30, widowed, b. and res. Northumberland Co., son of Hiram [B.] Lewis and Nancy [Winstead],[3] to MILDRED LINDSEY THRIFT, age 23, single, b. Westmoreland Co., daughter of Samuel R. Thrift and Eliza [A. Tinsley].[4] License 17 SEP 1867. Married 19 SEP 1867 at Saml. Thrift's by J.H. Davis. [M18; R:87; R1:29-8]

Lewis, Frank to Maria Smith. FRANK LEWIS, carpenter, age 37, single, b. Westmoreland Co., son of Frank and Catharine Lewis, to MARIA SMITH, age 28, single, b. Essex Co., daughter of Daniel and Judy Smith. License 1 JUL 1869. Planned marriage 8 JUL 1869. [R:95; R1:38-14 no return]

Lewis, George to Mrs. Felicia Smith Beale Barber. GEORGE LEWIS, farmer, age 55, widowed, b. Northumberland Co., son of George and Alice Lewis, to FELICIA SMITH BARBER, age 34, widow, b. Westmoreland Co., daughter of Smith Beale and Ann [Beale].[5] License 22 DEC 1864. Married 22 DEC 1864 at the residence of Mrs. Beale by H.P.F. King. [M17a:64-16; R:81; R1:21-10]

Lewis, George Downing (d. 1868), to Mary Eugenia Wilson. GEORGE DOWNING LEWIS, shoemaker, age 26, single, b. Northumberland Co., son of George and [Mary] "Polly" Lewis, to MARY EUGENIA WILSON, age 18, single, b. Westmoreland Co., daughter of Robert and Lucy Wilson. License 6 MAR 1866. Married 6 MAR 1866 by G.H. Northam. [DR:15-42; R:83; R1:23-14]

Lewis, George Washington (b. 1804 at *Shellfield*, d. testate 1879[6]), judge, member of the Virginia State Senate, served in 47th Va. Inf., C.S.A., of *Claymont*, second to Lucy Anne Robb (1823-1891).[7] GEORGE W. LEWIS, lawyer, age 51, widowed, b. Port Royal, Caroline Co., son of Samuel and

---

[1] Nathaniel Lefever and Winney Short were married by bond 3 MAY 1820 in Westmoreland Co., with William Short, security.
[2] Aaron Lewis is buried with his first wife Frances (1841-1866)* at Henderson United Methodist Church, Hyacinth, Va.
[3] Hiram B. Lewis and Nancy Winstead were married by bond 31 DEC 1831 in Northumberland Co., with Thomas B. Haydon, security.
[4] Samuel R. Thrift and Eliza A. Tinsley, daughter of Cinthia Tinsley, were married by bond 19 DEC 1838 in Westmoreland Co., with Richard H. Donnahaw, security.
[5] Smith Beale and Ann Beale were married by bond 13 MAY 1837 in Westmoreland Co., with Thomas C. Beacham, security.
[6] Deeds & Wills No. 41, p. 378, will of George W. Lewis, proved 26 MAY 1879, names wife L.R. Lewis, small farm *Claymont*, and scrapbook of letters and sword of Gen. George Washington. He was buried in Marmion Cemetery, King George Co.
[7] Lucy A. Robb Lewis was buried at Meade Memorial Episcopal Church, White Post, Clarke Co., Va.

Sarah A. Lewis, to LUCY A. ROBB, age 32, single, place of birth blank, daughter of Patrick [Carrick][1] Robb [1790-1851[2]] and Maria [Pratt] [1795-1871]. License 14 MAY 1856. Married 19 MAY 1856 at St. Peter's Church, Oak Grove by J.W. Chesley, minister of the Prot. Epis. Church. [M16a:56-16; R:55; R1:6-5; SP; WP]

Lewis, James to Mariah Smith. JAMES LEWIS, farmer, age 21, single, b. Northumberland Co., son of John and Matilda Lewis, to MARIAH SMITH, age 23, single, b. Westmoreland Co., daughter of [Meeker] and Easter Smith. Signed James [his X mark] Lewis, wit. J.W. Hutt. License 7 JAN 1868. Married 8 JAN 1868 at the residence of Elizabeth Sexton by Elder James A. Weaver. [M18; R:89; R1:31-9]

Lewis, Jesse to Elizabeth A. Ambrose. JESSE LEWIS, farmer, age 30, single, b. King George Co., son of Charles and Ann Lewis, to ELIZABETH A. AMBROSE, age 30, single, b. Richmond Co., parents unknown. License 12 MAR 1867. Married 14 MAR 1867 at the residence of G. Moss by R.N. Reamy. [M18; R:86; R1:27-11]

Lewis, John to Eliza Waughn (C) (d. 1887 of cancer). JOHN LEWIS, farmer, age 40, single, b. Westmoreland Co., son of Sydnor and Betsy Lewis, to ELIZA WAUGHN, age 40, single, b. Westmoreland Co., daughter of Walter Waughn and Mary [McKay].[3] License 25 SEP 1865. Married 27 SEP 1865 at the house of Eliza Waughn by W.W. Walker. [DR:71-35; M18; R:81; R1:22-3]

Lewis, John Simeon (1850-1893),[4] to Sarah Frances Yardley. JOHN SIMEON LEWIS, farmer, age 27, single, b. Alexandria, Va., son of Thomas and Mary A. Lewis, to SARAH FRANCES YARDLEY, age 19, single, b. Westmoreland Co., daughter of Elizabeth Yardley. Lewis 25 JUN 1877. Married 28 JUN 1877 by H.H. Fones. [M19; R:122; R1:70-3]

Lewis, John W. (d. 1885 of liver disease), son of George and Polly Lewis, to Ellen E. King. License 7 JAN 1851. Married 9 JAN 1851 by E.L. Williams, M.G. [DR:64-44; M15:51-2; R:5]

Lewis, Peter (C) to Sarah Bankhead. PETER LEWIS, farmer, age 22, single, b. Hanover Co., son of Barney and Charity Lewis, to SARAH BANKHEAD, age 22, single, b. Westmoreland Co., daughter of Dunmon and Caroline Bankhead. Signed Peter [his X mark] Lewis, wit. J.W. Hutt. License 23 SEP 1871. Married 23 SEP 1871 by Emanuel Watts, Pastor of Little Zion Church. [M18; R:102; R1:47-10]

Lewis, Samuel to Mrs. Mary Richardson Henry, widow of John Henry, *q.v.* SAMUEL LEWIS, farmer, age 36, single, b. Westmoreland Co., son of Betsy Lewis, father unknown, to MARY HENRY, age 25, widow, b. Westmoreland Co., daughter of Arrenas Richardson, father unknown. License 14 JAN 1865. Married 14 JAN 1865 at the residence of the bride by H.P.F. King. [M17a:65-2; R:81; R1:21-15]

---

[1] Merrow Egerton Sorley, *Lewis of Warner Hall: The History of A Family* ... (1935; reprint ed., Baltimore, Md.: Genealogical Publishing Co., Inc., 1991), p. 157.
[2] SP: Burials, p. 31, and WP. Dr. Patrick G. Robb [sic], aged 60, buried at *Camden* in Caroline Co. on the 28th of July 1851.
[3] Walter Wayghan and Polly McKy, daughter of James and Mary McKy [McKay], were married by bond 22 SEP 1807 in Westmoreland Co., with Samuel Gilbert, security.
[4] John S. Lewis was buried at Grant United Methodist Church, Lerty, Va.

Lewis, Thomas M., Dr., of Westmoreland Co., to Alice A. Tayloe, daughter of the late Charles Tayloe, of King George Co., were married 25 MAY 1859 at *Oaken Brow*, King George Co. [SP; WP]

Locust (see Lucas)

Lomax, Frank (C) to Jane Lee. FRANK LOMAX, farmer, age 48, widowed, b. Westmoreland Co., son of John and Violet Lomax, to JANE LEE, age 46, single, b. Westmoreland Co., daughter of Philip and Mary Lee. Signed Frank [his X mark] Lomax, wit. Wm. S. McKenney. License 16 OCT 1872. Married 17 OCT 1872 at Zion Baptist Church by Thomas T. Johnson. [M19; R:106; R1:51-3]

Lot, Allen (C) to Willie Ann Newman. ALLEN LOT, laborer, age 25, single, b. Coffee Co., Ga., son of Joseph and Mary Lot, to WILLIE ANN NEWMAN, age 20, single, b. Westmoreland Co., daughter of Jacob and Isabella Newman. Signed Allen [his X mark] Lot, wit. Wm. S. McKenney. License 28 DEC 1871. Married 31 DEC 1871 by Emanuel Watts, pastor of Little Zion Church, Oak Grove. [M19; R:104; R1:49-4]

Love, Richard John Worthington (1838-c.1913), teacher, served in Co. D, 40th Va. Inf., C.S.A., to Letty F. Harvey. RICHARD J.W. LOVE, no occupation, age 20, single, b. Baltimore, Md., son of Castro and Sarah Love, to LETTY F. HARVEY, age 19, single, b. Westmoreland Co., daughter of Octavius Harvey and [Susanna] Maria [Muse].[1] License 24 OCT 1856. Married 26 OCT 1856 at the residence of John M. Harvey by H.P.F. King, minister of the Methodist E. Church South. [M16a:56-30; R:57; R1:7-4]

Lowe, John Henry (C) (b. 1835, d. 1924 of entero-colitis), to Ann Whirly. JOHN LOWE, farmer, age [2]5, single, b. Westmoreland Co., son of Jerry and [Rachel] Lowe, to ANN WHIRLY, age 20, single, b. Westmoreland Co., daughter of Harvy and Maria Whirly. Signed John [his X mark] Lowe, wit. J.H. Sisson. License 15 JAN 1870. Married 15 JAN 1870 by John C. Smith. [DC; M18; R:97; R1:41-10]

Lucass, Anderson to Bettie Lee. ANDERSON LUCASS, farmer, age 48, widower, b. Westmoreland Co., son of Duley Lucass, to BETTIE LEE, age 23, single, b. Westmoreland Co., daughter of Humphrie and Lucy Lee. Signed A. [his X mark] Tate [sic], wit. J.W. Hutt. License 9 DEC 1870. Married 10 DEC 1870 by D.M. Wharton, Rector of Montross Parish. [M18; R:100; R1:44-8]

Lucas, Arnold to Willie Ann McGuire. ARNOLD LUCAS, farmer, age 2[5], single, b. Westmoreland Co., son of Polly Lucas, father unknown, to WILLIE ANN McGUIRE, age 23, single, b. Westmoreland Co., daughter of [Racardia] Templeman alias McGuire, father unknown. License 21 AUG 1866. Married 23 AUG 1866 by G.H. Northam. [M18; R:83; R1:24-14]

Lucas, Edward to Mrs. Mary Catharine Washington Lucas. EDWARD LUCAS, farmer, age 29, single, b. Westmoreland Co., son of Newton [d. 1873 of pneumonia near *Longwood*] and Sally Lucas, to MARY CATHARINE LUCAS, age 26, widow, b. Westmoreland Co., daughter of John and Kitty Washington. Signed Edward [his X mark] Lucas, wit. Wm. S. McKenney. License 14 FEB 1876. Married 15 FEB 1876 at Mrs. Lucas' by F.W. Claybrook. [DR:28-28; M19; R:118; R1:64-7]

---

[1] Octavius and Susanna Maria Muse, daughter of Charles Muse, were married by bond 23 DEC 1816 in Westmoreland Co., with Joseph Fox, security.

Lucas, George to Elizabeth Harrison. GEORGE LUCAS, farmer, age 20, single, b. Westmoreland Co., son of Beedy and Jinny Lucas, to ELIZABETH HARRISON, age 24, single, b. Westmoreland Co., daughter of Easter Thompson, father unknown. License 25 APR 1868. Married 30 APR 1868 at *Hickory Hill* by J.H. Davis. [M18; R:90; R1:33-3]

Lucas, Jacob (C) to Vina Tinsley. JACOB LUCAS, farmer, age 26, single, b. King George Co., son of Anthony and Felitia Lucas, to VINA TINSLEY, age 18, single, b. Caroline Co., daughter of Robert and Mary Tinsley. Signed Jacob [his X mark] Lucas, wit. W.S. McKenney. License 25 NOV 1873. Married 27 NOV 1873 at *White Point* by Emanuel Watts, pastor Little Zion Church. [M19; R:109; R1:54-16]

Lucass, James (C) (1854-1930),[1] to Emma L. Tate (C) (d. 1935). JAMES LUCASS, farmer, age 20, single, b. Westmoreland Co., son of Russell and Arena Lucass, *q.v.*, to EMMA TATE, age 21, single, b. Westmoreland Co., daughter of Catharine Tate. License 20 APR 1880. Married 22 APR 1880 at Providence M.E. Church by Paul Bradley. [DC; M20; R:133; R1:82-6]

Locust [or Lucas], John to Mrs. Martha Garner. JOHN LOCUST, farmer, age 38, single, b. Westmoreland Co., son of Ciggie Locust, to MARTHA GARNER, age 36, widow, b. Westmoreland Co., parents unknown. Signed John [his X mark] Locust, wit. J.W. Hutt. License 28 DEC 1867. Married 29 DEC 1867 at Samuel Washington's by R.N. Reamy. [M18; R:89; R1:31-6]

Locust [or Lucas], Lorance to Mary Catharine Grissett. LORANCE LOCUST, sailor, age 24, single, b. Westmoreland Co., son of William and Nancy Locust, to MARY CATHARINE GRISSETT, age 24, single, b. Westmoreland Co., daughter of Polly Grissett, father unknown. Signed Lorance [his X mark] Locust, wit. J.W. Hutt. License 23 DEC 1870. Married 25 DEC 1870 by Robert N. Reamy. [M18; R:100; R1:44-16]

Lucas, Roderick (d. 1882), to Fannie Chambers. LUCAS RODERICK, age 21, single, b. Westmoreland Co., son of Mary Ann Lewis, father unknown, to FANNIE CHAMBERS, age 19, single, b. Westmoreland Co., daughter of Thomas and Patsy Chambers.[2] License 23 NOV 1864. Planned marriage 24 NOV 1864. [DR:55-13; R:81; R1:21-8]

Lucas, Russell (C) to Arrena Tate (C). License 20 DEC 1854. [R:47]

Lucas, William W., served in Co. C. 15th Va. Cav., C.S.A., second[3] to Mrs. Sarah F. Rollins Fox. WILLIAM W. LUCAS, farmer, age 27, widowed, b. Westmoreland Co., son of William H. and Mary Lucas, to SARAH F. FOX, age 23, widow, b. King George Co., daughter of Robert and Peggy Rollins. License 21 DEC 1866. Married 23 DEC 1866 at the rectory, Washington Parish by Thomas E. Locke. [M18; R:85; R1:26-3; WP]

Luttrell, John Davenport (b. 1831 at Village, Va., d. 1914 at Heathsville, Va.),[4] served in Co. D, 15th Va. Cav. and Co. B, 40th Va. Inf., C.S.A., son of John P. Luttrell and Nancy Davenport, first to Mary

---

[1] DC: James Lucas was buried near Zacata, Va.
[2] In R1:21, p. 8, the names of Thomas and Patsy Chambers are inserted as the parents of the groom.
[3] DR11-31, entry for the death of George Anna Lucas, b. King George Co., d. 10 JUN 1866, daughter of Ginnie Brandson, wife of Wm. W. Lucas.
[4] John D. Luttrell was buried with his second wife Sophronia E. Claughton (1842-1902) at Coan Church, Heathsville, Va.

F. Gawen (d. 1863). License 3 OCT 1851. Married 9 OCT 1851 by George Northam, L.M.G. [DC; R:11]

Lyell, Charles Henry, served in Co. C, 47th Va. Inf., C.S.A., to Bettie Jane Dishman. CHARLES HENRY LYELL, farmer, age 38, single, b. Westmoreland Co., son of Joseph L. Lyell [d. 1859 age c.52] and Susan R. [Dishman], *q.v.*, to BETTIE JANE DISHMAN, age 25, single, b. Westmoreland Co., daughter of Charles [Triplett] Dishman and Eliza [T. Smith], *q.v.* License 22 FEB 1871. Married 23 FEB 1871 by R.N. Reamy. [M18; R:101; R1:46-5; WP]

Lyell, Richard M., second[1] to Sarah F. Marmaduke. RICHARD M. LYELL, farmer, age 43, widower, b. Westmoreland Co., son of Dozier Lyell and Frances [Smith],[2] to SARAH F. MARMADUKE, age 24, single, b. Westmoreland Co., daughter of John [M.] Marmaduke and Sarah [Scates].[3] License 5 MAR 1856 [sic]. Married 5 FEB 1856 by H.P.F. King, minister of the M.E. Church. [M16:56-4; R:53; R1:5-7]

Lynham, John Andrew (1840-1885), served in 3rd Richmond Howitzers, C.S.A., to Bettie C. Hardwick (1845-1908).[4] JOHN ANDREW LYNHAM, clerk, age 25, single, b. Henrico Co., res. Norfolk City, Va., son of William and Emeline Lynham, to BETTIE C. HARDWICK, age 21, single, b. Westmoreland Co., daughter of Samuel R. Hardwick and Rebecca [Marmaduke].[5] License 25 DEC 1865. Planned marriage 28 DEC 1865. [R:82; R1:22-12 no return]

M

Mahorney, Gabriel to Malinda Kelly. GABRIEL MAHORNEY, laborer, age 25, single, b. Anne Arundel Co., Md., son of Harry and [Hany] Mahorney, to MALINDA KELLY, age 25, single, b. Westmoreland Co., daughter of John and Judy Kelly. Signed, Gabriel [his X mark] Mahorney, wit. C.C. Baker. License 4 FEB 1868. Married 6 FEB 1868 at *Pec[k]atone* by J.H. Davis. [M18; R:90; R1:32-3]

Mahorney, Thomas to Mary Thompson. THOMAS MAHORNEY, farmer, age 21, single, b. Westmoreland Co., son of James and Mary Mahorney, to MARY THOMPSON, age 21, single, b. Westmoreland Co., daughter of George and Easter Thompson. License 16 DEC 1879. Married 18 DEC 1879 by F.B. Beale. [M20; R:130; R1:79-12]

Maiden, Daniel, Jr. to Olivia Maiden. DANIEL MAIDEN, carpenter, age 26, b. Richmond Co., son of Daniel Maiden, Sr. and Mary [Johnson],[6] to OLIVIA MAIDEN, age 23, b. Richmond Co., daughter of Maria Maiden, father unknown. Consent by bride Olivia [her X mark] Maidden to marry Daniel Maidden, Jr. [sic], wits. Jas. [his X mark] Lewis, J.W. Porter. License 29 DEC 1860. Married 30 DEC 1860. [M17:60-45; R:76]

---

[1] CF1852-11, *Sarah D. Lyell v. Richard M. Lyell &c.* Richard M. Lyell was married first 26 NOV 1846 to Sarah D. Atwill. Also see CF1857-09, *William H. Sanford v. Joseph S. Lyell &c.*
[2] Dozier Lyell and Fanny Smith, daughter of Peggy Smith, were married by bond 22 AUG 1811 in Westmoreland Co., with Vincent Dozier, security.
[3] John M. Marmaduke and Sarah Scates were married by bond 8 MAR 1827 in Westmoreland Co., with William Hutt, security.
[4] John A. Lynham and his wife Bettie C. were buried in Hollywood Cemetery, Richmond, Va.
[5] Samuel B. Hardwick and Rebecca Marmaduke, daughter of James B. Marmaduke, were married by bond 15 JUN 1843 in Richmond Co., with Isaac S. Jeffries, security.
[6] Daniel Maiden and Mary Johnson were married by bond 10 SEP 1828 in Westmoreland Co., with Samuel Faucett, security.

Manning, John (1820-1896), to Mary Elizabeth "Lizzie" Ditty (1841-1896).[1] JOHN MANNING, farmer and planter, age 35, single, b. District of Columbia, res. Prince George's Co., Md., son of Ignatius and Rosetta Manning, to E.M. DITTY, age 19, single, b. Westmoreland Co., names of parents blank [daughter of Dr. Thomas Roger Ditty and Eliza Ann Payne[2]]. License 7 JUN 1858. Married 9 JUN 1858 at *Eltham*, Dr. Ditty's residence by Thomas E. Locke, Rector of St. Peter's Church, Washington Parish. [M16a:58-18; R:64; R1:12-4; SC; SP; WP]

Marders, Howard Montague to Mary Susan Reamy. HOWARD MONTAGUE MARDERS, farmer, age 22, single, b. King George Co., son of Joseph [H.] Marders and Margaret [A. Ramey],[3] to MARY SUSAN REAMY, age 21, single, b. Essex Co., daughter of Henry [J.] and Betsey Reamy. License 3 SEP 1875. Married 5 SEP 1875 at Oak Grove by Howard W. Montague, M.G. [M19; R:115; R1:61-14]

Mardin, Alfred to Mary A. Tate. License 5 NOV 1858. [R:64]

Mariner, James Wilson to Maggie Maria Dishman. JAMES WILSON MARINER, farmer, age 25, single, b. Westmoreland Co., son of Robert [L.] Mariner and Martha [Mitchell][4] [d. 1885 of apoplexy], to MAGGIE MARIA DISHMAN, age 25, single, b. Westmoreland Co., daughter of Charles [Triplett] Dishman [and Eliza T. Smith], *q.v.* License 12 FEB 1880. Married 12 FEB 1880 by R.N. Reamy. [DR:66-146[5]; M20; R:132; R1:81-4]

Marks, Henry to Elizabeth Omohundro. License 18 OCT 1853. Married 20 OCT 1853 by John Pullen. [M15:53-22; R:33]

Marmaduke, Daniel Benjamin (1846-1911), to Eliza Jane Tallent (1848-1905).[6] DANIEL BENJAMIN MARMADUKE, farmer, age 24, single, b. Westmoreland Co., son of William Marmaduke and Elizabeth [Weaver],[7] to ELIZA JANE TALLENT, age 24, single, b. Westmoreland Co., daughter of James Tallent and Elizabeth [Rowe].[8] License 20 JUL 1871. Married 21 JUL 1871 by D.M. Wharton. [M18; R:102; R1:47-3]

Marmaduke, Daniel to Ann W. Eskridge. DANIEL MARMADUKE, sailor, age 35, widowed, b. Westmoreland Co., son of William and Sarah Marmaduke, to ANN W. ESKRIDGE, age 21,* single, b. Westmoreland Co., daughter of Burrell S. Eskridge and Elizabeth [Kilmon].[9] License 11 OCT 1858. Married 11 OCT 1858 by James A. Weaver. [M16a:58-23[10]; R:64; R1:12-8]

---

[1] John Manning and his wife Lizzie were buried at Christ Church, Accokeek, Prince George's Co., Md.
[2] Brooke Payne, *The Paynes of Virginia* (Harrisonburg, Va.: C.J. Carrier Co., 1990). Thomas Roger Ditty (1806-1876) and wife Eliza Anne Payne (1813-1867) were buried in the Payne Family Burying Ground at Horners, Va. The burying location is also known as Red House (*Cedar Hill*).
[3] Joseph H. Marders and Margaret A. Ramey were married 2 APR 1846 in King George Co.
[4] Robert L. Mariner and Martha Mitchell were married by bond 15 JUN 1843 in Westmoreland Co., with Frederick Poor, security.
[5] DR:66-146, entry for Martha Mariner, d. 17 JUL 1885 of apoplexy, age 66, daughter of Mitchell and Rose Carpenter, wife of Robert L. Mariner.
[6] Daniel B. Marmaduke and wife Eliza J. were buried in the Chisford-Stratford Area Community Cemetery, located off of Route 609 on property owned by the Hinson Family.
[7] William Marmaduke and Elizabeth Weaver, daughter of Elizabeth Sanford, were married by bond 9 MAR 1843 in Westmoreland Co., with Jacob V. Doleman, security.
[8] James Tallant and Elizabeth Rowe were married by bond 30 DEC 1845 in Westmoreland Co., with Henry Rowe, security.
[9] Burrel S. Eskridge and Elizabeth Kilmon were married by bond 14 MAY 1829 in Westmoreland Co., with Tarpley Bryant, security.
[10] Another copy at 58-23a, * gives age of bride as 22, and unknown mother of the bride.

Marmaduke, James B. (c.1829-1880), to Mrs. Martha Clark Camm (c.1830-1899).[1] JAMES B. MARMADUKE, shoemaker, age 28, single, b. Westmoreland Co., son of John [M.] Marmaduke and Sarah [B. Scates], *q.v.*, to MARTHA CAMM, age 27, widow, b. Westmoreland Co., daughter of James and Elizabeth Clark. License 4 AUG 1857. Married 5 AUG 1857 at Andrew Chapel by H.P.F. King. [M16a:57-24; R:61; R1:10-2]

Marmaduke, Milton Miles (b. 1847, d. 1919 at the Soldiers Home Hospital),[2] served in Co. G, 43rd Va. Cav., C.S.A., to Mary Emma Bayne. MILTON MILES MARMADUKE, farmer, age 20, single, b. Westmoreland Co., son of Meredith M. Marmaduke and Mary Ann [Porter],[3] to MARY EMMA BAYNE, age 19, single, b. Westmoreland Co., daughter of Richard V. Bayne [d. testate 1892[4]] and Elizabeth [Marmaduke].[5] License 7 DEC 1868. Married 9 DEC 1868 by G.H. Northam. [M18; R:93; R1:36-6]

Marmaduke, Robert Vinton (1838-1906), first to Mrs. Lucretia Fairfax Self Weaver (d. by 1872), widow of Lewis Andrew Weaver, *q.v.* ROBERT VINTON MARMADUKE, farmer, age 24, single, b. Westmoreland Co., son of William and Elizabeth Marmaduke, to LUCRETIA WEAVER, age 27, widow, b. Westmoreland Co., daughter of Moses Self and Sarah [Crask].[6] License 25 NOV 1867. Planned marriage 28 NOV 1867. [R:88; R1:30-2]

Marmaduke, Robert Vinton (1838-1906), second to Olivia Ann Saunders (1838-1921).[7] ROBERT V. MARMADUKE, sailor, age 28, widowed, b. Westmoreland Co., son of William and Elizabeth Marmaduke, to LIVIA A. SAUNDERS [sic], age 27, single, b. Richmond Co., daughter of James H. and Elizabeth Saunders. Signed Ro. V. [his X mark] Marmaduke, wit. Wm. S. McKenney. License 11 MAR 1872. Married 14 MAR 1872 by H.H. Fones. [M19; R:105; R1:49-15]

Marmaduke, Vincent P. (1823-1908),[8] served in Co. C, Motters Inf., C.S.A., to Martha F. Sanford (1829-1893), daughter of Ethelwald Sanford [d. by 1854[9]]. License 24 JUL 1851. Married 24 JUL 1851 by A. Wiles. [M15:51-15; R:9]

Marmaduke, William Carter (1840-1911), served in Co. C, 9th Va. Cav., C.S.A., to Ruth Ella Bayne (1850-1909).[10] WILLIAM CARTER MARMADUKE, merchant, age 33, single, b. Westmoreland Co., son of William B. [Bragg] Marmaduke and Catherine [Quesenbury],[11] to RUTH ELLA BAYNE, age 23, single, b. Westmoreland Co., daughter of Washington [N.] Bayne [d. 1873 at *Baynesville* of

---

[1] James B. Marmaduke and wife Martha Camm were buried in the Marmaduke Family Cemetery, located near the intersection of Routes 214 and 644.
[2] DC: Milton M. Marmaduke, merchant, died in Richmond, Va. and was buried in Hollywood Cemetery.
[3] M.M. Marmaduke and Mary A. Porter were married by bond 20 MAY 1846 in Westmoreland Co., with John P. Norwood, security.
[4] Deeds & Wills, No. 50, p. 444, will of Richard V. Bayne, of *Ruins*, proved 22 FEB 1892, names wife Elizabeth.
[5] Richard V. Bayne and Elizabeth Marmaduke, daughter of Vincent Marmaduke, were married by bond 7 DEC 1846 in Westmoreland Co., with M.M. Marmaduke, security.
[6] Moses Self and Sally Crask were married by bond 22 DEC 1834 in Westmoreland Co., with Jacob V. Doleman, security.
[7] Robert Vinton Marmaduke and his wife Olivia Ann Saunders are thought to have been buried in the Chisford-Stratford Area Community Cemetery, located off of Route 609 on property owned by the Hinson Family.
[8] Vincent P. Marmaduke and his wife Martha were buried in Oakland Cemetery, Moberly, Randolph Co., Mo. The year on his tombstone is 1824, but a newspaper obituary posted on *Findagrave.com* gives birth date 23 SEP 1823.
[9] CF1854-13, *Lucious Sanford v. Ethelwald Sanford &c.*
[10] Ruth Ella Bayne Marmaduke was buried in the Marmaduke Family Cemetery, located at *Kenwood*, off of Route 659. Her husband William Carter Marmaduke is believed to have been buried here as well.
[11] William B. Marmaduke and Catherine Quisenbury, daughter of Jane Quisenbury, were married by bond 27 MAR 1837 in Westmoreland Co., with N. Quisenbury, security.

erysipelas] and Emily [C. Hill].[1] License 22 DEC 1873. Married 23 DEC 1873 at *Baynesville* by G.W. Beale, minister. [D&W 40, p. 334; DR:28-6; M19; R:110; R1:55-12]

Marshall, Robert Augustine (1825-1916), served Co. C, 9th Va. Cav., C.S.A., to Martha Catharine Noel (1832-1907).[2] ROBERT AUGUSTINE MARSHALL, farmer, age 47, single, b. King George Co., son of R.P. [Robert] Marshall and Frances [Spilman],[3] to MARTHA CATHARINE NOEL, age 40, single, b. Essex Co., daughter of Achilles Noel and Mary R. [Parker].[4] License 25 NOV 1872. Married 28 NOV 1872 by W.F. Bain. [M19; R:107; R1:51-14]

Mason, William Henry to Anna Jackson. WILLIAM HENRY MASON, laborer, age 23, single, b. Brunswick Co., son of Heartwell and Melinda Mason, to ANNA JACKSON, age 21, single, b. Westmoreland Co., daughter of William Jackson. License 1 MAR 1873. [R:108; R1:53-12 no return]

Massey, Thomas George Hambden (b. 1831, d. 1901 in Washington, D.C.), served in Co. C, 9th Va. Cav., C.S.A., to Rosalie Maria Taylor Rice (b. 1850, d. 1922 in Cherrydale, Arlington Co.).[5] THOMAS H. MASSEY, farmer, age 38, widowed, b. Kent Co., Md., son of E.T. and E.H. Massey, to ROSALIA T. RICE, age 21, single, b. Westmoreland Co., daughter of John T. [Taylor] Rice [and Mary Carter Robinson]. License 22 NOV 1871. Married 23 NOV 1871 at the residence of John T. Rice by John Payne. [M18; R:103; R1:48-4; WP]

Matthews, James Washington to Eliza Ann Balderson. JAMES WASHINGTON MATTHEWS, farmer, age 24, single, b. Westmoreland Co., son of Philip Matthews and Ellen [Hill],[6] to ELIZA ANN BALDERSON, age 25, single, b. Richmond Co., daughter of Richard and Kenner "Kitty" Balderson. License 13 JAN 1860. Married 16 JAN 1860 at the residence of Jacob Hess by H.P.F. King, M.G. [M17:60-2 and 2a; R:72; R1:16-2]

Mattox, Littleton (C) to Charlotte Ball. LITTLETON MATTOX, sailor, age 27, widowed, b. Delaware, son of Fanny Mattox, to CHARLOTTE BALL, age 28, single, b. Westmoreland Co., daughter of John R. and Hannah Ball. License 6 AUG 1880. Married 10 AUG 1880 at *Frog Hall* by William Gaskins. [M20; R:134; R1:83-10]

Mayhugh, Joseph Lee (1841-1923),[7] C.S.A., second to Marion F. Griggs. JOSEPH MAYHUGH, farmer, age 32, single, b. and res. Prince William Co., son of Thomas and Catharine Mayhugh, to MARION F. GRIGGS, age 20, single, b. Westmoreland Co., daughter of Henry Griggs and Sarah E. [Mothershead].[8] License 30 NOV 1874. Married 1 DEC 1874 by F.B. Beale. [M19; R:113; R1:59-7]

Mayo, John Campbell, Dr. (1832-1871), second to Ellen Jackson Tyler (1848-1928).[9] JOHN CAMPBELL MAYO, physician, age 34, widowed, b. Westmoreland Co., son of [Hon.] Robert Mayo

---

[1] Washington N. Bayne, son of Richard Bayne and Susan Pope, and Emily Catharine Hill were married by bond 16 DEC 1844 in Essex Co.
[2] Robert A. Marshall and his wife Martha were buried at St. Peter's Cemetery, Oak Grove, Va.
[3] Robert P. Marshall and Fanny Spilman were married 23 DEC 1807 in King George Co. by Rev. James Elliott.
[4] Achilles Noel, Jr. and Mrs. Polly R. Parker were married by bond 23 MAY 1825 in Essex Co.
[5] Thomas H. Massey and his wife Rosalie were buried at St. Peter's Cemetery, Oak Grove, Va.
[6] Philip Matthews and Nelly Hill were married by undated bond c.1822 in Westmoreland Co., with James Carpenter, security.
[7] Joseph Lee Mayhugh was buried with his second wife Grace in the Hixson Cemetery, Manassas, Prince William Co., Va.
[8] Henry Griggs and Sarah E. Mothershead were married by bond 1 DEC 1849 in Westmoreland Co., with G.G. Mothershead, security.
[9] Dr. John C. Mayo and his wife Ellen were buried at Yeocomico Episcopal Church, Kinsale, Va.

and Emily A. [Ann Campbell],[1] to ELLEN JACKSON TYLER, age 18, single, b. Westmoreland Co., daughter of Wat H. [Henry] Tyler and Jane [Louisa Blake]. License 29 OCT 1866. Married 30 OCT 1866 at *Wilton* by Wm. N. Ward. [M18; R:84; R1:25-8; SC]

Mayo, Joseph, Jr., of *Edgewater* (1834-1898), Col., served in Co. C, 9th Va. Cav., C.S.A., to Mary Armistead Tyler [1846-1926].[2] JOSEPH MAYO, JR., lawyer, age 34, single, b. *Kirnan*, son of [Hon.] Robert Mayo and Emily Ann [Campbell], *q.v.*, to MARY ARMISTEAD TYLER, age 21, single, b. Warsaw, Va., daughter of [Dr.] Wat Henry Tyler and Jane Louisa [Blake]. License 19 FEB 1868. Married 20 FEB 1868 at *Locust Farm* by Andrew Fisher. [M18; R:90; R1:32-9; WC]

Mayo, Robert Murphy (1836-1898),[3] served 47th Va. Inf., C.S.A., to Lucy Richardson Claybrook. ROBERT MURPHY MAYO, lawyer, age 31, single, b. Westmoreland Co., son of [Hon.] Robert Mayo and Emily A. [Ann Campbell], *q.v.*, to LUCY RICHARDSON CLAYBROOK, age 27, single, b. Westmoreland Co., daughter of Richard A. and Charlotte T. Claybrook. License 29 NOV 1867. Married 3 DEC 1867 at *Afton* by Andrew Fisher. [CP; M18; R:88; R1:30-3]

Mayo, William, of *Cole's Point* (1847-1919), served in Mosby's Bat., C.S.A., to Mary Elizabeth "Lizzie" Brown (1852-1931).[4] WILLIAM MAYO, farmer, age 25, single, b. Westmoreland Co., son of [Hon.] Robert Mayo and Emily A. [Ann Campbell], *q.v.*, to MARY ELIZABETH BROWN, age 21, single, b. Westmoreland Co., daughter of [Col.] Thomas and Sarah Brown [of *Buena Vista*]. License 17 DEC 1872. Married 19 DEC 1872 at the residence of the bride's father by D.M. Wharton. [CP; M19; R:107; R1:52-6; SC]

McCarty, Robert Mitchell (1840-1928),[5] served in Co. B, 40th Va., C.S.A., to[6] Mrs. Anna Frances Omohundro Harwood. ROBERT MITCHELL McCARTY, teacher, age 27, single, b. and res. Richmond Co., son of Madison P. McCarty and Olivia [Ann Mitchell],[7] to ANNA FRANCES HARWOOD, age 27, widow, b. Westmoreland Co., daughter of Richard F. [Fleming] Omohundro and Mary B. [Claughton].[8] License 30 OCT 1868. Married 1 NOV 1868 by G.H. Northam. [M18; R:92; R1:35-10]

McClannahan, Augustine to Maria Mary Garland. AUGUSTINE McCLANNAHAN, farmer, age 29, single, b. and res. King George Co., son of Augustine McClannahan and Lucy [Hudson],[9] to MARIA MARY GARLAND, age 25, single, b. Richmond Co., daughter of [Newton] and Lucy Garland. License 27 APR 1868. Married 28 APR 1868 at the residence of Solomon Branson by J.H. Davis. [M18; R:90; R1:33-5]

McClannahan, William Edward, Jr. to Roberta M. Hill. WILLIAM EDWARD McCLANNAHAN, farmer, age 21, single, b. King George Co., son of William Edward [Sr.] and Lucy McClannahan,

---

[1] Robert Mayo and Emily Ann Campbell, daughter of E.F. Campbell, were married by bond 2 MAY 1831 in Westmoreland Co., with Joseph Jones, security.
[2] Joseph Mayo and his wife Mary A. were buried at Yeocomico Episcopal Church, Kinsale, Va.
[3] Robert M. Mayo was buried at Yeocomico Episcopal Church, Tucker Hill, Va.
[4] William Mayo and his wife Mary E. were buried at Yeocomico Episcopal Church, Kinsale, Va.
[5] Robert M. McCarty was buried at Menokin Baptist Church, Warsaw, Va.
[6] DR:24-15, entry for Richardanna McCarty, d. 13 APR 1871 of unknown cause, age 29, daughter of Richard and Mary B. Omohundro, wife of Robert M. McCarty.
[7] Madison P. McCarty and Olivia Ann Mitchell, daughter of Robert B. Mitchell, were married by bond 10 JAN 1838 in Richmond Co., with Lyne Shackleford, security.
[8] Richard F. Omohundro and Mary B. Claughton were married by bond 29 MAR 1839 in Westmoreland Co., with Edward B. Omohundro, security.
[9] A. McClanahan and Lucy Hudson were married 25 JUL 1828 in King George Co.

to ROBERTA M. HILL, age 22, single, b. Westmoreland Co., daughter of Edwin Hutt. License 10 JUL 1872. Married 11 JUL 1872 at the residence of Edwin Hutt by J.H. Davis. [M19; R:106; R1:50-15]

McClure, Charles to Mary Sanford. License 17 AUG 1850. Married 29 AUG 1850 by John Pullen. [M15:50-20, R:1 not in *Nottingham*]

McCoy (a.k.a. McKoy), Rhody (a.k.a. Rodham) (C) (d. 1894 of Bright's disease), to Sarah Jane Muse. RHODY McCOY, farmer, age 25, single, b. Westmoreland Co., son of Rhody and Agnes [Douglass] McCoy, to SARAH JANE MUSE, age 20, single, b. Westmoreland Co., daughter of John and Ellen Muse. License 14 DEC 1877. Married 20 DEC 1877 at John Muse's by Thomas T. Johnson. [DR:101-98; M19; R:123; R1:71-10]

McCrea, John Davis to Emma Jane Bartholomew. JOHN DAVIS McCREA, farmer, age 21, single, b. Allegheny City, Pa., son of John and Susan McCrea, to EMMA JANE BARTHOLOMEW, age 17, single, b. Allegheny City, Pa., daughter of Joseph and Elizabeth Bartholomew. License 20 JAN 1874. Married 4 FEB 1874 at *Water View* by R.J. Sanford. [M19; R:111; R1:57-1]

McFarland, Robert Thomas to Emily Davis. ROBERT THOMAS McFARLAND, overseer, 35, widowed, b. Essex Co., res. *Peckatone*, son of James MacFarland and Elizabeth [Jones],[1] to EMILY DAVIS, age 20, single, b. Westmoreland Co., res. *Lee Hall*, daughter of Thomas L. Davis and Nancy [Robinson].[2] License 29 JAN 1859. Married 1 FEB 1859 at *Lee Hall* by T. Grayson Dashiell, clergyman. [M16a:59-6 and 6a; R:68; R1:14-4]

McGuire, Edward Brown, Rev. (1818-1881),[3] son of Edward Charles McGuire, first to Mary L. Murphy. License 15 AUG 1851. Married 20 AUG 1851 at *Spring Grove* by Wm. McGuire [brother of the groom]. [M15:51-16; NN; R:9; SP; WP]

McGuire, Edward Brown, Rev., second to Sarah Nicholas Fitzhugh, daughter of Austin W. Fitzhugh. Married 29 JUN 1869 at *Mill Bank*, King George Co., the residence of Austin [W.] Fitzhugh, by Rev. Thomas E. Locke. [WP]

McGuire, James Edward, served in Co. A, 15th Va. Cav., C.S.A., to Emily Jane McGuire. JAMES EDWARD McGUIRE, farmer, age 39, widowed, b. Westmoreland Co., son of Travis McGuire and Rebecca [Sutton],[4] to EMILY JANE McGUIRE, age 21, single, b. Westmoreland Co., daughter of William McGuire and Lucy [Thomas].[5] License 2 JUN 1863. Married 10 JUN 1863 at the residence of Lucy McGuire by H.P.F. King. [M17:63-6; R:79; R1:20-4]

McGuire, John to Lucy Ann Pope. JOHN McGUIRE, farming, age 34, widowed, b. Richmond Co., son of William and Lucy McGuire, to LUCY ANN POPE, age 18, single, b. Westmoreland Co., daughter of Jeremiah and Susan Pope. License 27 OCT 1862. Married 29 OCT 1862 at her mother's residence by Elder James A. Weaver. [M17:62-14; R:78; R1:19-6 incorrectly has Susan Ann Pope]

---

[1] James McFarland and Elizabeth Jones were married by bond 19 DEC 1808 in Essex Co.
[2] Thomas L. Davis and Ann Robinson were married by bond 8 FEB 1832 in Westmoreland Co., with Newman McKenney, security.
[3] Rev. Edward B. McGuire was buried at Emanuel Episcopal Church, Port Conway, King George Co., Va.
[4] Travis McGuire and Beckey Sutton were married by bond 3 FEB 1809 in Westmoreland Co., with Joseph Sutton, security.
[5] William McGuire and Lucy Thomas were married by bond 7 FEB 1827 in Westmoreland Co., with Henry Pritchet, security.

McGuire, Lamkin to Charlotte T. Crask, daughter of James Crask. LAMKIN McGUIRE, sailor, age 23, single, to CHARLOTTE [T.] CRASK, age 22, single. Minister return by H.P.F. King. License 21 FEB 1854. Married 22 FEB 1854 by H.P.F. King at the residence of Jesse McGuire. [Bible; M15:54-17; R:39; R1:1-3]

McGuire, Oliver C. (d. by 1865), to Maria G. Mothershead. OLIVER C. McGUIRE, laborer, age 21, single, b. Richmond Co., son of John and Julia D. McGuire, to MARIA G. MOTHERSHEAD, age 22, single, b. Richmond Co., daughter of George and Mary Mothershead. License 5 JUL 1856. Married 7 JUL 1856 by G.H. Northam, minister of the Baptist Church. [M16a:56-19; R:55; R1:7-2]

McGuire, William Henry (d. 1895 of heart trouble), to Louisa Harriet Franklin (d. 1871 of typhoid fever). WILLIAM HENRY McGUIRE, milling, age 20, single, b. Westmoreland Co., son of William McGuire and Lucy [Thomas], to LOUISA HARRIET FRANKLIN, age 24, single, b. Westmoreland Co., daughter of Thomas and Harriet Franklin. License 23 DEC 1859. Married 27 DEC 1859 by Elder James A. Weaver. [DR:24-16, 102-11; M16a:59-30 and 32; R:70; R1:16-1]

McHarvey, James to Mary Lucas. License 16 OCT 1856. [R:57]

McKay (a.k.a. McKoy), James (C) to Isabella Burrell. JAMES McKAY, farmer, age 22, single, b. Westmoreland Co., son of Rodham McKay and Agness [Douglass],[1] to ISABELLA BURRELL, age 21, single, b. Westmoreland Co., daughter of Nancy Burrell, father unknown. License 1 FEB 1876. Married 3 FEB 1876 at Thomas Burrell's by Thomas T. Johnson. [M19; R:117; R1:64-5]

McKenney, Gerard Robertson [d. testate 1877[2]], to Alice McKenney. GERARD R. McKENNEY, farmer, age 45, widower, b. Westmoreland Co., son of Newman McKenney and Alice [V. McKenney],[3] to ALICE McKENNEY, age 38, single, b. Westmoreland Co., daughter of William McKenney and Catharine [Sanford].[4] License 1 JUL 1857. Marriage 2 JUL 1857 at Lebanon Church by H.P.F. King, minister of the M.E. Church. [M16a:57-20; R:61; R1:9-10]

McKenney, Gerard Robertson (d. 1877 of kidney disease), to Mrs. Mary Muse Bispham Weaver. GERARD ROBERTSON McKENNEY, farmer, age 62, widowed, b. Westmoreland Co., son of Newman McKenney and Alice [V. McKenney], *q.v.*, to MARY MUSE WEAVER, age 46, widow, b. Richmond Co., daughter of William and Mary Bispham.[5] Gerard [his X mark] McKenney. License 26 JAN 1874. Married 28 JAN 1874 by H.H. Fones. [DR:40-62; M19; R:112; R1:57-5]

McKenny, Henry to Martha Ann Brown. HENRY McKENNY [sic], farmer, age 24, single, b. Westmoreland Co., son of Ann McKenny, father unknown, to MARTHA ANN BROWN, age 19, single, b. Westmoreland Co., daughter of Parkerson and Ann Brown. Signed Henry [his X mark] McKenny, wit. W.S. McKenney. License 5 FEB 1873. Married 6 FEB 1873 at Ann Brown's by G.W. Beale, minister. [M19; R:108; R1:53-7]

McKenney, Louis to Jane Graham (C). LOUIS McKENNEY, farmer, age 26, single, b. Westmoreland Co., son of Fanny [McKenney], father unknown, to JANE GRAHAM, age 18, single,

---

[1] Roda McKoy and Agnes Douglass were married by bond 15 DEC 1842 in Westmoreland Co., with Newton Burrell, security.
[2] Deeds & Wills No. 41, p. 212, will of G.R. McKenney, proved 24 DEC 1877.
[3] Newman McKenney and Alice V. McKenney were married by bond 19 SEP 1838 in Westmoreland Co., with Hiram Hutt, security.
[4] William McKenney and Caty Sanford were married by bond 12 JAN 1797 in Westmoreland Co., with Gerard McKenney, security.
[5] William Bispham and Mrs. Mary Asbury were married by bond 19 JUL 1820 in Richmond Co., with Joseph Belfield, security.

b. Westmoreland Co., daughter of Jerry and Harriet Graham. License 26 DEC 1866. Planned marriage 27 DEC 1866. [R:85; R1:26-7 no return]

McKenney, Octavius Lawson, first to Mrs. Eliza Ferguson Davis (b. c.1831, d. 1866 of pneumonia). OCTAVIUS LAWSON McKENNEY, farmer, age 23, single, b. Westmoreland Co., son of Newman and Polly McKenney, to ELIZA DAVIS, age 25, widow, b. Westmoreland Co., daughter of James and Fanny Ferguson. License 23 JAN 1860. Married 26 JAN 1860. Signed O.L. [his X mark] McKenney, wits. H.M. Pursell, C.C. Baker. [DR:11-32; M17:60-6; R:72]

McKenney, Octavius Lawson, second to Mrs. Charlotte Davis Jenkins. OCTAVIUS McKENNEY, farmer, age 37, widowed, b. Westmoreland Co., son of Newman and Mary McKenney, to CHARLOTTE JENKINS, age 25, widow, b. Westmoreland Co., daughter of Thomas and Nancy Davis. License 23 OCT 1866. Married 25 OCT 1866 at the residence of Mr. Peterson by Elder James A. Weaver. [M18; R:84; R1:25-6]

McKenney, Presley to Matilda C. Anton. PRESLY McKENNEY [sic], farmer, age 42, widowed, b. Westmoreland Co., son of Presley McKenney and Nancy [McKenney],[1] to MATILDA C. ANTON, age 29, single, b. Westmoreland Co., daughter of Samuel Anton and Susan [Gregory].[2] License 17 MAY 1858. Married 19 MAY 1858 by James A. Weaver, minister of the Union Baptist Church. [M16a:58-15; R:64; R1:12-1]

McKenney, Samuel Madison to Sarah Elizabeth Collins. SAMUEL MADISON McKENNEY, farmer, age 22, single, b. Westmoreland Co., son of Samuel M. McKenney [d. 1881 of consumption] and Priscilla R. [Sutton][3] [d. 1883], to SARAH ELIZABETH COLLINS, age 20, single, b. Westmoreland Co., daughter of George W. Collins [d. testate 1912] and Ann [Elizabeth Reed], *q.v.* License 10 MAR 1875. Married 10 MAR 1875 at *[Poin]t View* by G.H. Northam. [DR:48-37[4], 58-14; M19; R:115; R1:61-1]

McKenney, Thomas Lawson (1824-1894), first to Ann Tapley Furgerson. THOMAS LAWSON McKENNEY, farmer, b. 19 FEB 1824, single, b. Westmoreland Co., son of Newman and Mary McKenney, to ANN TAPLEY FURGERSON, age 30, single, b. Richmond Co., daughter of James and Frances Furgerson. License 21 JUN 1854. Married 22 JUN 1854 at L.A.L. Lamkin's by W.W. Walker, minister of the Methodist Protestant Church. [M15:54-5; R:43; R1:1-14]

McKenney, Thomas Lawson (1824-1894),[5] served Co. 4, 111th Va. Mil., C.S.A., second to Mrs. Alice Howsen Anton (d. 1871 of dropsy), widow of Benjamin Anton, *q.v.* THOMAS LAWSON McKENNEY, farmer, age 42, widowed, b. Westmoreland Co., son of Newman and Mary McKenney, to ALICE ANTON, age 30, widow, b. Westmoreland Co., daughter of Wesley and Felicia Howsen. License 30 MAY 1866. Married 31 MAY 1866 by Elder James A. Weaver. [DR:23-24; M18; R:83; R1:24-3]

---

[1] Presley McKenney, Jr. and Nancy McKenney were married by bond 31 JUL 1797 in Westmoreland Co., with Gerrard McKenney, security.
[2] Samuel Anton and Susannah Gregory were married by bond 20 JUL 1824 in Westmoreland Co., with Thomas Howell, security.
[3] Samuel McKenney and Priscilla R. Sutton were married by bond 7 JAN 1824 in Westmoreland Co., with James Crask, security.
[4] DR:48-37, entry for Samuel McKenney, farmer, d. 28 JUL 1881 of consumption, age 61, son of Presley and Nancy McKenney, husband of Priscilla McKenney.
[5] Thomas L. McKenney was buried at Carmel United Methodist Church, Kinsale, Va.

McKenney, Thomas Lawson, third to Mary R. Hammonds. THOMAS LAWSON McKENNEY, farmer, age 48, widowed, b. Westmoreland Co., son of Newman and Mary McKenney, to MARY R. HAMMONDS, age 31, single, b. Westmoreland Co., daughter of Alice Hammonds. License 9 MAY 1872. Married 12 MAY 1872 at Carmel [Church] by E.A. Gibbs. [M19; R:105; R1:50-6]

McKenney, Willis to George Anna Morris. WILLIS McKENNEY, farmer, age 23, single, b. Westmoreland Co., son of Ellen McKenney, father unknown, to GEORGE ANNA MORRIS, age 15, single, b. Westmoreland Co., daughter of Joseph and Elizabeth Morris. License 30 JAN 1878. Married 31 JAN 1878 at Mr. Fleet B. Anton's by F.W. Claybrook. [M19; R:125; R1:72-16]

McKoy (see McKay)

McLain [or McLane], John Henry to Mrs. Elmira Green Bartlett. JOHN HENRY McLAIN, farmer, age 50, widower, b. New Jersey, son of [Bassit] and Elizabeth McClain, to ELMIRA BARTLETT, age 35, widow, b. Westmoreland Co., parents unknown [George and Sarah Green, *q.v.*]. License 12 MAY 1870. Married 15 MAY 1870 by Robert N. Reamy. [M18; R:99; R1:43-4]

McNiel, Charles Hugh (b. 1845, d. 1887 of paralysis),[1] to Mary F. Weaver. CHARLES HUGH McNEIL, farmer, age 27, single, b. Westmoreland Co., son of John [d. testate 1884[2]] and Elizabeth McNiel, to MARY WEAVER, age 19, single, b. Westmoreland Co., daughter of John W. and Mary Weaver. License 26 FEB 1873. Married 27 FEB 1873 at the residence of the bride's parents by D.G.C. Butts. [DR:73-109; M19; R:108; R1:53-10]

McNiel, John to Sophronia Hinson. JOHN McNIEL, farmer, age 69, widow, b. Westmoreland Co., son of John McNiel and Lucy [Moxley],[3] to SOPHRONIA HINSON, age 22, single, b. Westmoreland Co., daughter of Andrew and Maria Hinson. License 8 DEC 1879. Married 17 DEC 1879 by H.H. Fones. [M20; R:130; R1:79-6]

Mealy, Charles (C) to Mrs. Alcy Piper. CHARLES MEALY, farmer, age 66, widowed, b. Westmoreland Co., son of Charles and Edie Mealy, to ALCY PIPER, age 46, widow, b. Westmoreland Co., parents unknown. License 5 SEP 1879. Married 7 SEP 1879 at my home by Thomas T. Johnson. [M20; R:129; R1:78-11]

Mercer, Richard (C) (d. 1873 on the Potomac River in the burning *Wawasett*[4]), to Kitty Johnson. RICHARD MERCER, farmer, age 23, widowed, b. Essex Co., son of Killis and [Rachel] Mercer, to KITTY JOHNSON, age 27, single, b. Westmoreland Co., daughter of Hanna Winter. Signed Richard [his X mark] Mercer, wit. Wm. S. McKenney. License 23 DEC 1871. Married 29 DEC 1871 by Emanuel Watts, pastor of Little Zion Church, Oak Grove, Va. [DR:28-31; M19; R:104; R1:48-15]

Middleton, Benjamin J. to Sarah J. Wroe. License 25 AUG 1851. Married 10 SEP 1851 by Wm. N. Ward. [R:11]

---

[1] Charles Hugh McNiel was buried in the McNiel Family Cemetery, located on the Poor House Tract, off Route 648 near Chilton's Crossroads.

[2] Deeds & Wills No. 45, p. 148, will of John McNiel, proved 28 JUL 1884, names wife Jane and two sons Charles H. McNiel and Andrew J. McNiel. See Deeds & Wills No. 51, p. 218 for will of Andrew J. McNiel of *Poor Jack Farm*, proved 22 AUG 1892.

[3] John McNiel and Lucy Moxley, daughter of Robert Moxley, were married by bond c.1807 in Westmoreland Co., with John Davis, security.

[4] The steamboat *Wawasett* caught fire 8 AUG 1873 and sank in the Potomac River, a few miles upriver from Colonial Beach near King George Co. The wreckage was located in June 2010 by Navy divers.

Middleton, Jeremiah L. (1825-1896),[1] served in Co. E, 40th Va. Inf., C.S.A., son of Jerry Middleton and Nancy S. Harrison, to Susan Anton. License 13 MAR 1857. [R:59]

Middleton, William Parker (d. 1897), to Almeda E. Lewis. WILLIAM PARKER MIDDLETON, brickmason, age 50, widowed, b. Westmoreland Co., son of Jeremiah and Nancy [S. Harrison] Middleton, to ALMEDA E. LEWIS, age 21, single, b. Richmond Co., daughter of Thomas [P.] Lewis and Elizabeth [Dameron].[2] License 1 APR 1863. Planned marriage 3 APR 1863. [NN; R:79; R1:19-15 no return]

Miller, Charles L. to Alice P. Young. CHARLES L. MILLER, blacksmith, age 26, single, b. Caroline Co., son of C.P. and Eliza Miller, to ALICE P. YOUNG, age 21, single, b. Caroline Co., daughter of William B. and Melinda Young. License 26 JUL 1856. Married 29 JUL 1856 at St. Peter's Church, Oak Grove by J.W. Chesley, minister of the Prot. Epis. Church. [M16a:56-23; R:55; R1:6-7; SP; WP]

Miller, James Munroe (d. 1893 of pneumonia), to Ann Maria Mothershead. JAMES MUNROE MILLER, farmer, age 25, single, b. Westmoreland Co., son of Richard and Lucinda Miller, to ANN MARIA MOTHERSHEAD, age 23, single, b. Westmoreland Co., daughter of Humphrey and Ellen Mothershead. License 3 FEB 1866. Married 5 FEB 1886 at the residence of Mrs. Mothershead by Robt. N. Reamy. [DR:94-11; M18; R:82; R1:23-6]

Miller, John Francis (1848-1922), to Bettie S. Balderson. JOHN FRANCIS MILLER, farmer, age 26, single, b. Westmoreland Co., son of Lewis F. Miller [d. testate 1884[3] of heart disease] and Mary C. [Young[4]] [d. 1874 of hemorrhage], to BETTIE L. BALDERSON, age 21, single, b. Richmond Co., daughter of Marlborough [B.] Balderson and Susan [D. Olliffe].[5] License 19 MAY 1874. Married 20 MAY 1874 at Marlborough Balderson's by Robert N. Reamy. [DC; DR:32-21[6], 63-158[7]; M19; R:113; R1:58-8]

Miller, William A. to Mary E. Baker. WILLIAM A. MILLER, farmer, age 19y6m, single, b. Westmoreland Co., son of Richard and Lucinda Miller, to MARY E. BAKER, age 18, single, b. King George Co., daughter of James Baker. License 11 MAR 1859. Married 19 MAR 1859[8] at Henry Baker's by John Pullen. [M16a:59-8, 8a and 8b; R:68; R1:14-10]

Miller, William Henry Harrison (d. 1881 of hemorrhage), to Emma Ida Purcell. WILLIAM HENRY HARRISON MILLER, farmer, age 27, single, b. Caroline Co., son of Lewis F. and Mary E. [Eliza] Miller, to EMMA IDA PURCELL, age 19, single, b. Westmoreland Co., daughter of Stephen Purcell and [Julia F. Oliffe], *q.v.* License 3 JAN 1879. Married 5 JAN 1879 at the residence of the bride's father by Wm. C. Latane, Presbyter P.E. Church. [DR:51-27; M20; R:128; R1:76-8; WP]

---

[1] Jeremiah L. Middleton was buried in a Middleton Family Cemetery, located off of Route 600 near Oldhams, Va.
[2] Thomas P. Lewis and Elizabeth Dameron were married by bond 23 OCT 1822 in Westmoreland Co., with Matthew Harrison, security.
[3] Deeds & Wills No. 45, p. 199, will of Lewis F. Miller, proved 22 SEP 1884, names son John F. Miller.
[4] DC: John F. Miller's death certificate gives mother Mary C. Jones.
[5] Marlborough B. Balderson and Susannah D. Olliffe, daughter of William S. Olliffe, were married by bond 11 NOV 1846 in Richmond Co., with Theoderick N. Balderson, security.
[6] DR:32-21, entry for Mary C. Miller, b. Caroline Co., d. 18 MAR 1874 of hemorrhage, age 48, daughter of Wm. K. and Malinda Young, and wife of Lewis Miller.
[7] SE:63-158, entry for Lewis F. Miller, d. 8 SEP 1884 of heart disease, age 60, son of Conrad and Elizabeth Miller, widower, father of John F. Miller.
[8] On the reverse of the license is found a minister return by John Pullen for date of marriage 19 APR 1859.

Minor, John Lewis (1850-1882), to Emma Sophia Peed (1854-1922).[1] JOHN LEWIS MINOR, farmer, age 25, single, b. King William Co., res. Richmond Co., son of Reubin and Melissa J. Minor, to EMMA SOPHIA PEED, age 20, single, b. Westmoreland Co., daughter of John and Catharine K. Peed. License 18 JAN 1875. Married 20 JAN 1875 at Catharine Peed's by Robert N. Reamy. [M19; R:114; R1:60-14]

Minter, William to Jane Jett. WILLIAM MINTER, farmer, age 24, single, b. Caroline Co., son of Joseph and Mary Minter, to JANE JETT, age 23, single, b. Richmond Co., daughter of Mortimer and Delia Jett. Signed William [his X mark] Minter, wit. Wm. S. McKenney. License 27 MAR 1872. Married 27 MAR 1874 by B.R. Battaile. [M19; R:105; R1:50-2]

Mitchell, Isaac Jefferson (1851-1937), to Myra Roslie Hinson (1858-1924).[2] ISAAC JEFFERSON MITCHELL, farmer, age 29, single, b. Westmoreland Co., son of Winifred Mitchell, father unknown, to MIRA ROSLIE HINSON [sic], age 22, single, b. Richmond Co., daughter of Presley Hinson and Ann Hinson.[3] License 1 MAY 1880. Married 2 MAY 1880 by R.N. Reamy. [M20; R:133; R1:82-9]

Mitchell, John to Sally Tricker. Married 5 JUL 1866 at *Campbellton* (the residence of Lawrence Washington) by Rev. Thomas E. Locke. [WP]

Mitchell, William Bladen (b. 1824 at *Grove Mount*, d. at 1895 *Belle Mount*), served in Co. B, 40th Va. Inf., C.S.A. to Julia E. Peake. License 26 JAN 1852. Married 3 FEB 1852 by George Northam, L.M.G. [M15:52-4; R:15]

Monroe, Richard to Jane Munday, colored persons. RICHARD MONROE, farmer, age 38, single, b. Caroline Co., son of Robert and Betsey Monroe, to JANE MUNDAY, age 38, single, b. Westmoreland Co., son of Moses and Lucy St[rats]. License 21 OCT 1865. Married 22 OCT 1865 at the rectory of Washington Parish by Thomas E. Locke. [M17a:65-9; R:81; R1:22-5; WP]

Montague, Porter to Jane Lee. PORTER MONTAGUE, farmer, age 23, single, b. Westmoreland Co., son of Richard and Priscilla Montague, to JANE LEE, age 18, single, b. Westmoreland Co., daughter of Richard and Agnes Lee. Wit. Wm. S. McKenney. License 11 APR 1868. Married 11 APR 1868 by Jer. Grayham [sic]. [M18; R:90; R1:32-15]

Montague, Walter Griffin (C) to Georgianna Montague. WALTER GRIFFIN MONTAGUE, farmer, age 22, single, b. Westmoreland Co., son of Richard and Priscilla Montague, to GEORGIANNA MONTAGUE, age 18, single, b. Westmoreland Co., daughter of Peter and Sophie Montague. License 24 JUL 1873. Married 24 JUL 1873 at her father's by Thomas T. Johnson. [M19; R:109; R1:54-6]

Moon, William Hitherly to Jennie Barnett. WILLIAM HITHERLY MOON, farmer, age 22, single, b. Northumberland Co., son of Joseph and Elizabeth Moon, to JENNIE BENNETT, age 18, single, b. Westmoreland Co., daughter of Levi Barnett and Martha [Pope], *q.v.* Signed Wm. H. [his X mark] Moon, wit. Wm. S. McKenney. License 26 JAN 1876. Married 27 JAN 1876 by F.B. Beale. [M19; R:117; R1:64-3]

---

[1] John L. Minor and his wife Emma were buried in the Peed Family Cemetery, Peeds, Va.
[2] Isaac J. Mitchell and his wife Myra R. were buried in a Mitchell Family Cemetery, located near the intersection of Routes 625 and 677 at Foneswood, Va.
[3] Presley Hinson and Ann Hinson were married by bond 16 JAN 1849 in Westmoreland Co., with Meredith Hinson, security.

Moore, James Henry (C) to Martha Ann Wilson. JAMES HENRY MOORE, farmer, age 21, single, b. Westmoreland Co., son of Daniel [d. 1883] and Amy Moore, to MARTHA ANN WILSON, age 21, single, b. Westmoreland Co., daughter of Mitchel[l] D. and Isabella Wilson. License 22 NOV 1876. Married 23 NOV 1876 by Rev. William Gaskins. [DR:58-62; M19; R:120; R1:67-1]

Moore, Robert to Elizabeth Nelson. ROBERT MOORE, farmer, age 23, b. Nansemond Co., son of James and Dianna Moore, to ELIZABETH NELSON, age 21, single, b. Westmoreland Co., daughter of James and Fanny Nelson. Signed Robert [his X mark] Moore, wit. C.C. Baker. License 7 FEB 1868. Married 15 FEB 1868 at *Hickory Hill* by J.H. Davis. [M18; R:90; R1:32-4]

Morgan, John [Aaron] to Alice Virginia Winkfield. JOHN [AARON] MORGAN, farmer, age 25, single, b. Westmoreland Co., son of Joseph and Alice Morgan [d. 1865], to ALICE VIRGINIA WINKFIELD, age 23, single, b. Westmoreland Co., daughter of Beckwith and Mary Winkfield. License 27 AUG 1880. Married 29 AUG 1880 by R.N. Reamy. [DR:9-38; M20; R:134; R1:83-11]

Morgan, William to Lucy Ann Combs. WILLIAM MORGAN, farmer, age 24, single, b. King George Co., son of Meredith and Mary Jane Morgan, to LUCY ANN COMBS, age 22, single, b. Westmoreland Co., daughter of William and Lucinda Combs. License 23 DEC 1870. Married 2 JAN 1871 at Capt. Robinson's estate by Rev. John Payne. [R:100; R1:44-15 no return; WP]

Morriss, John Daniel to Margaret Frances Figgett. JOHN DANIEL MORRISS, farmer, age 22, single, b. Richmond Co., son of Margaret Sanders, father unknown, to MARGARET FRANCES FIGGETT, age 22, single, b. Westmoreland Co., daughter of Mary Figgett, father unknown. License 10 NOV 1864. Married 10 NOV 1864 at L. Jenkins' by John Pullen. [M17a:64-12; R:80; R1:21-5]

Morris, Joseph to Mary E. Gregory. License 7 MAR 1853. Married 9 MAR 1853 by George Northam, L.M.G. [M15:53-7; R:27]

Morris, Robert C. to Isabella Ann Steel. License 22 JUL 1853. [R:31 no return]

Morris, William to Virginia Short. WILLIAM MORRIS, farmer, 4[0], widowed, b. Westmoreland Co., son of William and Catherine Morris, to VIRGINIA SHORT, age 23, single, b. Westmoreland Co., daughter of George Short and Ellen [Enniss].[1] Signed Wm. [his X mark] Morris. License 30 JUN 1868. Married 1 JUL 1868 at the home of Wm. Morris by J.H. Davis. [M18; R:91; R1:34-8]

Morris, William G. to Elizabeth Anthony. License 2[1] APR 1852. Married 21 APR 1852 by Wm. N. Ward. [M15:52-16; R:19]

Moss, George to Julia Ann Hinson. GEORGE MOSS, farmer, age 40, widowed, b. Richmond Co., son of [Thomas] and Polly Moss, to JULIA ANN HINSON, age 38, single, b. Westmoreland Co., daughter of Vincent Hinson and Fanny [Roe].[2] Signed Geo. [his X mark] Moss, wit. J.W. Hutt. License 12 DEC 1872. Married 12 DEC 1872 at Francis Hinson's by Robert N. Reamy. [M19; R:107; R1:52-2]

---

[1] George Short and Ellen Enniss were married by bond 4 NOV 1830 in Westmoreland Co., with John W. Howsen, security.
[2] Vincent Hinson and Fanny Roe were married by bond 11 FEB 1829 in Westmoreland Co., with Thomas P.W. Neale, security.

Moss, James Henry to Elizabeth Douglass. JAMES HENRY MOSS, farmer, age 23, single, b. Scott Co., son of Helms and Nancy Moss, to ELIZABETH DOUGLASS, age 22, single, b. Westmoreland Co., daughter of Elizabeth Douglass, father unknown. License 17 NOV 1865. Married 17 NOV 1865 at the residence of Mr. Morriss by H.P.F. King. [M17a:65-10; R:81; R1:22-6]

Mothershead, Albert Augustus (d. 1891 by drowning), served in Co. K, 40th Va. Inf., C.S.A., to Julia Ann Cole. ALBERT AUGUSTUS MOTHERSHEAD, carpenter, age 35, single, b. Richmond Co., son of [James] Henry Mothershead and Eliza [Peed], to JULIA ANN COLE, age 19, single, b. Westmoreland Co., daughter of George W. Cole and Mary M. [Sandford].[1] License 21 NOV 1862. Married 25 NOV 1862 at the house of her father by W.W. Walker. [M17:62-15; NN; R:79; R1:19-7]

Mothershead, Charles Andrew (1843-1918), served in Co. G, 15th Va. Cav., C.S.A., to Embrosier Jane Wilkins. CHARLES ANDREW MOTHERSHEAD, farmer, age 25, single, b. and res. Richmond Co., son of James H. [Henry] Mothershead and Eliza [Peed], to EMBROSIER JANE WILKINS, age 21, single, b. Westmoreland Co., daughter of Mathew Wilkins and Lucretia [Atkins].[2] License 7 DEC 1868. Married 9 DEC 1868 by Robert N. Reamy. [DC; M18; R:93; R1:36-5]

Mothershead, George Muse to Eliza Ann Bartlett. GEORGE MUSE MOTHERSHEAD, farmer, age 28, widowed, b. Richmond Co., son of George M. and Mary Mothershead, to ELIZA ANN BARTLETT, age 34, single, b. Westmoreland Co., daughter of Joel Bartlett [d. 1854][3] and Sarah [Wilson].[4] License 1 JAN 1859. Married 2 JAN 1859 by G.H. Northam. [M16a:59-1; R:66; R1:15-11]

Mothershead, Richard Henry to Alice F. Kennedy. RICHARD HENRY MOTHERSHEAD, farmer, age 49, widowed, b. and res. Richmond Co., son of George [M.] and Mary Mothershead, to ALICE F. KENNEDY, age 29, single, b. Westmoreland Co., daughter of Thomas A. [Allen] Kennedy and Sarah [Pursell].[5] License 14 MAY 1872. Married 15 MAY 1872 by G.H. Northam. [M19; R:105; R1:50-7]

Mothershead, Richard Humphrey, served in Co. C, 15th Va. Cav., C.S.A., to Emma Catharine Miller. RICHARD HUMPHREY MOTHERSHEAD, farmer, age 21, single, b. Westmoreland Co., son of Humphrey Mothershead and Jane E. [Rose],[6] to EMMA CATHARINE MILLER, age 28, single, b. Westmoreland Co., daughter of Richard Miller and Lucy [Gutridge].[7] License 18 OCT 1866. Married 21 OCT 1866 by Robert N. Reamy at the residence of Lucy Miller. [M18; R:84; R1:25-5]

Mothershead, Thomas Daniel to Charlotte Temple Sanders (d. 1888 of heart disease). THOMAS DANIEL MOTHERSHEAD, farmer, age 40, single, b. Westmoreland Co., son of Charles C. Mothershead [d. testate 1882[8]] and Elizabeth H. [Dozier] [d. 1884], *q.v.*, to CHARLOTTE TEMPLE SANDERS [sic], age 28, single, b. Westmoreland Co., daughter of John H. [d. testate 1882[9]] and

---

[1] George W. Cole and Mary M. Sandford were married by bond 28 DEC 1842 in Westmoreland Co., with Richard R. King, security.
[2] Mathew Wilkins and Lucretia Atkins, daughter of Jane Atkins, were married by bond 15 JUL 1843 in Westmoreland Co., with Joseph Atkins, security.
[3] CF1860-12, *Ann Eliza McGuire v. Robert H. Bartlett &c.*
[4] Joel Barlett and Sally Wilson were married by bond 24 DEC 1821 in Westmoreland Co., with Lemuel G. Sandy, security.
[5] Thomas A. Kennedy and Sarah Pursell were married by bond 6 OCT 1825 in Richmond Co., with LeRoy Pursell, security.
[6] Humphrey Mothershead and Jane E. Rose were married by bond 29 MAY 1838 in Westmoreland Co., with Matthew Deatley, security.
[7] Richard Miller and Mrs. Lucinda Guttridge were married by bond 9 OCT 1833 in Richmond Co., with Henry H. Hazard, security.
[8] Deeds & Wills No. 43, p. 132, will of Charles C. Mothershead, proved 25 DEC 1882, names wife Elizabeth H. Mothershead.
[9] Deeds & Wills No. 42, p. 367, will of John Saunders, proved 25 SEP 1882, names wife Mary, and children: Sharlotty T. Mothershead, Ruth Ellin Jinkins, Richard T. Saunders, Sarah J. Moxley.

Mary Sanders. License 17 MAY 1880. Married 19 MAY 1880 by R.N. Reamy. [DR:55-14[1], 61-84[2], 76-94; M20; R:133; R1:82-14]

Moxley, Edward Newton, served in Co. C, 15th Va. Cav., C.S.A., to Sarah Jarvis Saunders. EDWARD NEWTON MOXLEY, farmer, age 23, single, b. King George Co., son of Joseph E. and Ellen Moxley, to SARAH JARVIS SAUNDERS, age 24, single, b. Westmoreland Co., daughter of John [d. testate 1882] and Mary Saunders. License 19 NOV 1868. Married 19 NOV 1868 by Robt. N. Reamy. [M18; R:93; R1:35-15]

Moxley, Rodney [Rodham] to Mrs. Rebecca Jones Cash. RODNEY MOXLEY, farmer, age 47, single, b. Westmoreland Co., son of Rhody [Rodham] Moxley and Mary [Weldon],[3] to REBECCA CASH, age 39, widow, b. Richmond Co., daughter of Vincent Jones, mother unknown. License 21 JUL 1864. Married 21 JUL 1864 at Rodney Moxley's by H.P.F. King. [M17a:64-5; R:80; R1:20-14]

Mozingo, James O. to Mary Inscoe, of King George Co. Married 25 JAN 1861 in the rectory of Washington Parish, by Rev. T.E. Locke. [SC; WP]

Mozingo, Richard to Mary Elizabeth Bowen. RICHARD MOZINGO, farmer, age 22, single, b. Westmoreland Co., res. Richmond Co., son of John Mozingo and Ruth [Bragg],[4] to MARY ELIZABETH BOWEN, age 22, single, b. Richmond Co., daughter of Frederick and Mary Bowen. License 13 MAY 1875. Married 14 MAY 1875 by H.H. Fones. [M19; R:115; R1:61-4]

Mozingo, William to Mary Jane McKenney. WILLIAM MOZINGO, farmer, age 31, single, b. Westmoreland Co., son of Thomas [C.] Mozingo and Becky [Jones],[5] to MARY JANE McKENNEY, age 21, single, b. Westmoreland Co., daughter of Matilda McKenney, father unknown. License 5 MAR 1862. Married 6 MAR 1862 at the minister's residence by D.M. Wharton. [M17:62-8; R:78; R1:18-14]

Muir, Joseph Stowell (1848-1919), to Dorothy "Dolly" Jane Rowe (1853-1933).[6] JOSEPH STOWELL MUIRE [sic], farmer, age 24, single, b. Westmoreland Co., son of Stowell and Jane E. Muire, to DOLLY JANE ROWE, age 16, single, b. Westmoreland Co., daughter of William H. and Dorothy Rowe. License 22 MAY 1876. Married 25 MAY 1876 by R.J. Sanford. [M19; R:118; R1:65-6]

Mullins, James to Elizabeth Jane Fones, daughter of Samuel R. Fones and Nancy Wilson, *q.v.* License 9 APR 1851. Married 10 APR 1851 by John Pullen. [M15:51-12; R:9]

Murphy, George Wishart (1829-1905), served in Co. K, 40th Va. Inf., C.S.A., to Olin Lee Turberville Davis (1844-1922).[7] GEORGE WISHART MURPHY, farmer, age 47, single, b. Westmoreland Co.,

---

[1] DR:55-14, entry for Chas. C. Mothershead, d. 17 DEC 1882 of unknown cause, age 72, son of Daniel and Catharine Mothershead, husband of Elizabeth Mothershead, father of Thomas D. Mothershead.
[2] DR:61-84, entry for Elizabeth H. Mothershead, d. 7 DEC 1884 of old age, age 76, daughter of Thomas and Frances Dozier, mother of Thomas Mothershead.
[3] Rodham Moxley, son of John Moxley, Jr., and Mary Weldon were married by bond 8 JUL 1810 in Westmoreland Co., with Henry Lee, security. After the demise of Rodham Moxley, Mary married by bond 7 JUN 1819 to William H. Sanford. Also see D&W No. 14, p. 162.
[4] John Mozingo and Ruth Bragg were married by bond 12 JAN 1841 in Westmoreland Co., with Thomas Mozingo, security.
[5] Thomas C. Mozingo and Rebecca Jones were married by bond 1 FEB 1813 in Richmond Co., with William Thomas, security.
[6] Joseph S. Muir and his wife Dorothy were buried at Carmel United Methodist Church, Kinsale, Va.
[7] George Wishart Murphy and his wife Olin Lee Turverville Davis were probably buried in the Murphy Family Cemetery, located at *Ayrfield*. *Ayrfield* was named by John Ballantine for his native town of Ayr on the southwest coast of Scotland. The house, built about 1806 by John Murphy, was destroyed by fire in January 1994.

son of John B. [Ballantine] Murphy [d. 1867 of bilious fever] and Million B. [Brown Wishart], to OLIN LEE TURBERVILLE DAVIS, age 33, single, b. Richmond Co., daughter of Joseph H. [Hoomes] Davis and Ann T. [Turberville Beale]. License 3 NOV 1877. Married 6 NOV 1877 at Carmel Church by J.H. Davis. [DR:13-37; M19; R:123; R1:70-14]

Murphy, John to Mary Lucy Brown. JOHN MURPHY, lawyer, age 26, single, b. Westmoreland Co., son of Robert Murphy and Eliza B. [Bland Newton],[1] to MARY LUCY BROWN, age 20, single, b. Westmoreland Co., daughter of George F. [Frederick] Brown [d. by 1868[2]] and Martha F. [Fenton] [Taliaferro].[3] Consent 6 OCT 1860 from *Peckatone* by father George F. Brown, wits. Robert Mayo, G.C. Taliaferro. License 8 OCT 1860. Married 9 OCT 1860 [at *Peckatone*] by John M. Rogers [of N.J.]. [M17:60-33, 33a, 33b; R:74; R1:16-14; SC]

Murphy, Murdock Malcomb, served in Co. K, 40th Va. Inf., C.S.A., disabled, to Mrs. Martha Clifford Cheshire. MURDOCK MALCOMB MURPHY, farmer, age 26, single, b. Westmoreland Co., son of James B. Murphy and Susan [B. Lowe],[4] to MARTHA CHESHIRE, age 28, widow, b. Alexandria, Va., daughter of George W. and Mary Ann Clifford. License 25 JUN 1866. Married 4 JUL 1866 by J.H. Davis. [M18; R:83; R1:24-9]

Murphy, Thomas Newton (1827-1902),[5] served Co. K, 40th Va. Inf., C.S.A., to Sarah Elizabeth Bowie (d. 1889 of congestion). THOMAS NEWTON MURPHY, farmer, age 29, b. *Spring Grove*,[6] son of Robert Murphy and Eliza [Bland Newton], to SARAH ELIZABETH BOWIE, age 27, single, b. Essex Co., res. *Kirnan*, daughter of Walter Bowie [d. 1853] and Mary [Todd] Smith [of *Kirnan*]. License 11 DEC 1856. Married 11 DEC 1856 at *Kirnan* by T. Grayson Dashiell, clergyman. [CP; DR:82-163; M16a:56-32; R:57; R1:7-6]

Murray, Thomas (C) to Anna Johnson (C). THOMAS MURRAY, farmer, age 24, single, b. Westmoreland Co., son of Harriet Murray, father unknown, to ANNA JOHNSON, age 17, single, b. Westmoreland Co., daughter of Simeon and Alsey Johnson. License 3 NOV 1876. Married 5 NOV 1876 at Zion Church, Oak Grove, by Emanuel Watts, pastor Zion Church. [M19; R:119; R1:66-13]

Murry, John to Mrs. Elizabeth Marmaduke Doleman. JOHN MURRY, farmer, age 39, single, b. Westmoreland Co., son of William Sanford and Nancy Murry, to ELIZABETH DOLEMAN, age 42, widow, b. Westmoreland Co., daughter of William and Sarah Marmaduke. License 23 JAN 1856. Married 24 JAN 1856 by H.P.F. King, M.G. [M16:56-2; R:53; R1:5-1]

Muse, George Mortimer (1842-1923),[7] served in Co. C, 47th Va. Inf., C.S.A., to Frances Lucy Meriweather Belfield. GEORGE MORTIMER MUSE, farmer, age 25, single, b. Westmoreland Co., son of James H. Muse [d. 1854][8] and Elizabeth B. [Walker],[9] to FRANCES LUCY MERIWEATHER BELFIELD, age 22, single, b. Westmoreland Co., daughter of Thomas M. Belfield and Fannie F.

---

[1] Robert Murphy and Eliza B. Newton were married by bond 18 MAY 1818 in Westmoreland Co., with William L. Rogers, security.
[2] Deeds & Wills No. 37, p. 598, division of lands of George F. Brown, dec.
[3] George F. Brown and Martha F. Taliaferro were married by bond 28 NOV 1838 in Westmoreland Co., with William A. Spence, security.
[4] James B. Murphy and Susan B. Lowe were married by bond 2 SEP 1839 in Westmoreland Co., with James Lowe, security.
[5] Thomas Newton Murphy was buried at Yeocomico Episcopal Church, Tucker Hill, Va.
[6] *Spring Grove*, the home of Robert Murphy, was completed in 1834.
[7] George M. Muse was buried in an unmarked grave at Grant United Methodist Church.
[8] James H. Muse was buried in the Sanford Family Cemetery at *Springfield*, located off of Route 3.
[9] James A. Muse and Elizabeth B. Walker were married by bond 27 JAN 1834 in Westmoreland Co., with James H. Payne, security.

[Sanford] [d. testate 1883[1]].[2] License 23 DEC 1868. Married 24 DEC 1868 at the residence of the bride's father by D.M. Wharton. [M18; R:93; R1:36-15; SC]

Muse, John (C) to Ellen Ashton (C). License 21 FEB 1853. Married 22 FEB 1853 by John Pullen. [M15:53-6; R:27]

Muse, John George to Mary S. Robinson. JOHN GEORGE MUSE, farmer, age 29, single, b. Westmoreland Co., son of William Muse [1817-1879] and Susan [A. Berkley] [1824-1884],[3] to MARY S. ROBINSON, age 25, single, birthplace unknown, daughter of John Robinson. License 20 DEC 1875. Married 21 DEC 1875 by H.H. Fones. [M19; R:116; R1:62-14]

Muse, Richard Brewer (1848-1902), served in 111th Va. Mil. and Home Guards, C.S.A., to Mary Ann Elizabeth Porter (1847-1932).[4] RICHARD BREWER MUSE, farmer, age 29, single, b. Westmoreland Co., son of James H. Muse and Elizabeth B. [Walker], *q.v.*, to MARY E. PORTER, age 27, single, b. Westmoreland Co., daughter of Daniel Porter and Lucy B. [Atwill] [d. testate 1884[5]].[6] License 25 JUN 1877. Married 26 JUN 1877 at the residence of John Omohundro by John W. White. [M19; R:122; R1:70-4]

N

Nash, John Thomas to Charlotte Temple Reamy (1839-1927).[7] JOHN THOMAS NASH, farmer, age 23, single, b. Westmoreland Co., son of Lewis Nash and [Mary] Jane [Gutridge], *q.v.*, to CHARLOTTE TEMPLE REAMY, age 25, single, b. Westmoreland Co., daughter of Alice Reamy. License 28 DEC 1874. Married 29 DEC 1874 at Rich. Peed's by Robert N. Reamy. [M19; R:114; R1:60-5]

Nash, John Wesley to Bettie Ann Davis. JOHN WESLEY NASH, farmer, age 25, single, b. Westmoreland Co., son of William H. and Malinda Nash, to BETTIE ANN DAVIS, age 21, single, b. Westmoreland Co., daughter of John and Sarah Davis. License 14 DEC 1878. Married 17 DEC 1878 by H.H. Fones. [M20; R:127; R1:75-15]

Nash, Lewis (d. testate 1893[8]) to Mary Jane Gutridge. License 26 DEC 1850. Married 26 DEC 1850 by John Pullen. [M15:50-28; R:5 not in *Nottingham*]

Nash, Robert Henry (1840-1901), served Co. E, 15th Va. Cav., C.S.A., to Susan Belinda Poor.[9] ROBERT HENRY NASH, farmer, age 24, single, b. Westmoreland Co., son of Lewis Nash and Malissa [Gutridge], to SUSAN BILAND POOR [sic], age 20, single, b. Westmoreland Co., daughter of Frederick Poor and Elizabeth [Carpenter].[10] License 24 FEB 1864. Married 25 FEB 1864 at the residence of Mrs. Elizabeth Poor by Robert N. Reamy. [M17:64-2; R:80; R1:20-10]

---

[1] Deeds & Wills No. 44, p. 136, will of Fannie F. Belfield, proved 25 JUN 1883.
[2] Thomas M. Bellfield and Frances F. Sandford, daughter of Sebbella Sandford, were married by bond 21 NOV 1821 in Westmoreland Co., with David C. Belfield, security.
[3] William Muse and Susan A. Berkley, daughter of William Berkley, were married by bond 19 JUN 1839 in Westmoreland Co., with George Carter, security. They were both buried in the Muse Family Cemetery, Oak Grove, Va. He served in Co. 8, 111th Va. Mil., C.S.A.
[4] Richard B. Muse and his wife Mary A. were buried at Andrew Chapel United Methodist Church.
[5] Deeds & Wills No. 45, p. 150, will of Lucy B. Porter, proved 28 JUL 1884, resides on *Locust Farm*, names eldest daughter Mary Ann Elizabeth Muse.
[6] David Porter and Lucy B. Atwill were married by bond 13 FEB 1839 in Westmoreland Co., with David Atwill, security.
[7] Charlotte Nash was buried at Ephesus Christian Church, Flat Iron, Va.
[8] Deeds & Wills No. 52, p. 153, will of Lewis Nash, proved 23 OCT 1893, names wife Jane Nash, eldest son Robert Nash.
[9] Robert H. Nash and his wife Susan B. were buried at Popes Creek Baptist Church, Baynesville, Va.
[10] Frederick Poor and Elizabeth Carpenter were married by bond 1 JAN 1839 in Westmoreland Co., with Robert M. Gutridge, security.

Nash, Thomas (C) to Annie Maria Johnson (C) (d. 1881). THOMAS NASH, sailor, age 36, single, b. and res. Prince William Co., son of Thomas and Loucinda Nash, to ANNIE MARIE JOHNSON, age 16, single, b. Richmond Co., daughter of Lieutenant and Mary Susan Johnson. License 2 MAR 1880. Married 4 MAR 1880 at Little Zion Church by Emanuel Watts, pastor. [DR:51-35; M20; R:132; R1:81-10]

Nash, Thomas Lewis to Virginia Jane Bryant (d. 1892). THOMAS LEWIS NASH, farmer, age 29, single, b. Westmoreland Co., son of Thomas Nash and Harriet [Hinson],[1] to VERINA JANE BRYANT [sic], age 30, single, b. Westmoreland Co., daughter of Bazil and Elizabeth Bryant. License 22 MAR 1862. Married 23 MAR 1862 at the residence of Basil Bryant by H.P.F. King. [DR:90-10; M17:62-11; R:78; R1:19-2]

Nash, William to Sydna Green. WILLIAM NASH, farmer, age 27, single, b. Westmoreland Co., son of Lewis Nash and Melissa [Gutridge], to SYDNA GREEN, age 20, single, b. Westmoreland Co., daughter of George and Adelia Green. License 16 NOV 1877. Married 18 NOV 1877 by R.N. Reamy. [M19; R:123; R1:71-1]

Nash, William Henry (C) (b. 1852, d. 1914 of pneumonia), to Tean Newman. WILLIAM HENRY NASH, farmer, age 26, single, b. Westmoreland Co., son of Henry and Susan Nash, to TEAN NEWMAN, age 24, b. Westmoreland Co., daughter of Jacob Newman and Isabella [Sale].[2] License 18 DEC 1877. Married 18 DEC 1877 at Little Zion Church by Emanuel Watts, pastor, Little Zion Church. [DC; M19; R:123; R1:71-13]

Nash, William Henry to Martha Ann Nash (d. 1873 of measles). WILLIAM HENRY NASH, carpenter, age 34, single, b. Westmoreland Co., son of Thomas Nash and Harriet [Hinson], *q.v.*, to MARTHA ANN NASH, age 19, single, b. Westmoreland Co., daughter of Lewis and Jane Nash. License 28 FEB 1871. Married 2 MAR 1871 by G.W. Beale. [DR:27-12; M18; R:101; R1:46-7]

Nash, William Henry to Lucy Virginia Nash. WILLIAM HENRY NASH, farmer, age [3]6, widowed, b. Westmoreland Co., son of Thomas Nash and Harriet [Hinson], *q.v.*, to LUCY VIRGINIA NASH, age 18, single, b. Westmoreland Co., daughter of Lewis and Jane Nash. License 18 FEB 1874. Married 19 FEB 1874 by W.C. Taylor. [M19; R:112; R1:57-14]

Neale, Thomas to Julia Ann Weaver. THOMAS NEALE, farmer, age 22, single, b. Westmoreland Co., res. Washington, D.C., son of John Neale and Margaret [Miller],[3] to JULIA ANN WEAVER, age 22, single, b. Westmoreland Co., daughter of Alexander Weaver and Patsy [Alderson].[4] License 24 DEC 1866. Married 27 DEC 1866 at Patsy Weaver's by John Pullen. [M18; R:85; R1:26-6]

Nelson, George Alfred to Harriet Susan Tymer. GEORGE ALFRED NELSON, farmer, age 24, single, b. Westmoreland Co., son of Joseph and Eliza Nelson, to HARRIET SUSAN TYMER, age 20, single, b. Richmond Co., daughter of Cyrus and Mary E. Tymer. License 9 JAN 1878. Married 14 JAN 1878 by H.H. Fones. [M19; R:124; R1:72-4]

---

[1] Thomas Nash and Harriott Hinson were married by bond 31 DEC 1821 in Westmoreland Co., with Campbell Tate, security.
[2] Jacob Newman and Isabella Sale were married by bond 8 APR 1847 in Westmoreland Co., with Hopeful Tate, security.
[3] John Neale, Jr. and Margaret Miller were married by bond 26 OCT 1831 in Westmoreland Co., with Richard Miller, security.
[4] Alexander Weaver and Marthy Alderson were married by bond 3 JUL 1821 in Westmoreland Co., with James Mariner, security.

Nelson, William Chesterfield to Columbia Ann Berkley (C) (d. 1893 of consumption). WILLIAM CHESTERFIELD NELSON, farmer, age 23, single, b. Westmoreland Co., son of Davy and Louisa Nelson, to COLUMBIA ANN BERKLEY, age 21, single, b. Westmoreland Co., daughter of Charles H. and Caroline Berkley. License 21 JAN 1880. Married 21 JAN 1880 at the house of Charles Berkley by T.G. Thomas. [DR:96-80; M20; R:132; R1:80-15]

Newman, Aaron (C) to Mrs. Amanda Thompson Montague. AARON NEWMAN, farmer, age 31, single, b. Westmoreland Co., son of George and Mary Newman, to AMANDA MONTAGUE, age 35, widow, b. Westmoreland Co., daughter of Joseph and Emily Thompson. License 14 MAR 1877. Married 15 MAR 1877 at Joseph Thomson's by Jerry Graham. [M19; R:122; R1:69-8]

Newman, Cephas (C) (d. 1885), second to Jane Ashton. CEPHAS NEWMAN, farmer, age 56, widower, b. Westmoreland Co., son of [Dennis] and Barbary Newman, to JANE ASHTON, age 30, single, b. Westmoreland Co., daughter of Amelia Ashton, father unknown. License 10 JAN 1871. Married 12 JAN 1871 by Jerry [his X mark] Graham, minister, Baptist Church. [M18; NN; R:101; R1:45-8]

Newman, James to Mrs. Mary Lucas Mahorney. JAMES NEWMAN, laborer, age 19, single, b. Westmoreland Co., son of Emanuel Newman and Caroline [Lucas],[1] to MARY MAHORNEY, age 29, widow, b. Westmoreland Co., daughter of Briddy and Jane Lucas. License 22 DEC 1862. Planned marriage 22 DEC 1862. [R:79; R1:19-9 no return]

Newman, Joseph (C) to Dorcas Johnson. JOSEPH NEWMAN, shoemaker, age 27, single, b. Westmoreland Co., son of Cephas and Fanny Newman, to DORCAS JOHNSON, age 30, single, b. Westmoreland Co., daughter of Thomas and Hannah Johnson. Signed Jos. [his X mark] Newman, wit. W.S. McKenney. License 6 FEB 1871. Married 7 FEB 1871 by Jerry Graham. [M18; R:101; R1:45-14]

Newman, Robert to Gracy Lee, black. ROBERT NEWMAN, farmer, age 21, single, b. Westmoreland Co., son of James [M.] (C) [d. 1881 of brain disease] and Susan Newman, to GRACY LEE, age 17, single, b. Westmoreland Co., daughter of Frances Lee, father unknown. License 20 JAN 1880. Married 22 JAN 1880 at *Ayrfield* by Charles Rust. [DR:48-38[2]; M20; R:131; R1:80-13]

Newman, William H. (C) (d. 1872 of bowel abscess), bricklayer, son of Frederick and Jennie Newman, to Charlotte Tate. License 16 JAN 1856. [DR:20-28; R:53]

Newton, Edward Colston (b. 1848/9 at *Linden*, d. 1913), to Lucy Yates Tyler (1855-1919).[3] EDWARD COLSTON NEWTON, age 26, single, b. Westmoreland Co., son of Willoughby Newton [1802-1874] and Mary S. [Stevenson Brockenbrough] [b. 1811, d. testate 1888[4] of heart disease],[5]

---

[1] Emanuel Newman and Caroline Lucas were married by bond 21 DEC 1836 in Westmoreland Co., with Richard Ashton, security.
[2] DR:48-38, entry for Jas. M. Newman, d. 12 DEC 1881 of disease on brain, age 55, son of Saml. and Betsy Newman, husband of Susan Newman.
[3] Edward C. Newton and his wife Lucy Yates Tyler were buried in the Newton Family Cemetery at *Linden*, located off of Route 202 at Hague, Va.
[4] Deeds & Wills No. 47, p. 428, will of Mary S. Newton of *Linden*, proved 23 APR 1888, names son Edward C. Newton, to inherit residue of *Linden*.
[5] Willoughby Newton III and his wife Mary Stevenson Brockenbrough, daughter of Judge William and Judith Brockenbrough, were married 12 MAY 1829 in Monumental Church of Richmond, Va. They were buried in the Newton Family Cemetery at *Linden*, located off of Route 202 at Hague, Va. This Willoughby Newton is known for serving in the U.S. House of Representatives and the Confederate

q.v., to LUCY YATES TYLER, age 20, single, b. Westmoreland Co., [youngest] daughter of [Dr. Wat Henry] Tyler [and Jane Louisa Blake], *q.v.* License 25 OCT 1875. Married 26 OCT 1875 by John [B.] Newton at *Kelvin Grove*. [CP; DR:71-45; NN; R:115; R1:62-1; SC]

Newton, James (C), to Sarah Waugh (C). JAMES NEWTON, farmer, age 63, single, b. Westmoreland Co., son of Henry and Nancy Newton, to SARAH WAUGH, age 40, single, b. Essex Co., daughter of Peter and Anny [Sale]. Consent 17 MAY 1866 by bride, wit. R.H. Chowning. License 21 MAY 1866. Married 24 MAY 1866 by J.H. Davis. [M18; R:83; R1:24-1]

Newton, Robert Murphy to Annie Emily Arnest. ROBERT MURPHY NEWTON, lawyer, age 26, single, b. Westmoreland Co., son of Willoughby Newton and Mary B. [Stevenson Brockenbrough], *q.v.*, to ANNIE EMILY ARNEST, age 21, single, b. Westmoreland Co., daughter of Thomas M. [d. testate 1887[1]] and Sophia Arnest. License 13 APR 1868. Married 14 APR 1868 at *Nominy Hall* by D.M. Wharton. [CP; M18; NN; R:90; R1:32-16]

Newton, William (C) to Mary Roane. WILLIAM NEWTON, farmer, age 42, widowed, b. Westmoreland Co., son of James and Polly Newton, to MARY ROANE, age 27, single, b. Westmoreland Co., daughter of Thomas and Betsey Roane [or Rone]. License 14 SEP 1876. Married 14 SEP 1876 at King's *Koptsker Farm* by Thomas T. Johnson. [M19; R:119; R1:66-3 gives 14 AUG 1876]

Nicholson, Peter to Lucy Moton. PETER NICHOLSON, farmer, age 42, single, b. Delaware, son of Henry and Mary Nicholson, to LUCY MOTON, age 45, single, b. Westmoreland Co., parents unknown. License signed Peter [his X mark] Nicholson, wit. W.T. Bispham. License 16 JUN 1866. Married 16 JUN 1866 by H.H. Fones. [M18; R:83; R1:24-6]

Nickins, Fielding to Delilah Vessels. FIELDING NICKINS, farmer, age 24, single, b. Westmoreland Co., son of James and Tena Nickins, to DELILAH VESSELS, age 21, single, b. Caroline Co., daughter of Mariah C. Vessels. License 5 SEP 1878. Married 5 SEP 1878 at *Laurel Grove* by Wm. C. Latane, Presbyter P.E. Church. [M19; R:126; R1:74-14; WP]

Nickens, Roy to Rosa Johnson, colored persons. ROY NICKENS, farmer, age 22, single, b. Essex Co., son of Davy and Betty Nickens, to ROSA JOHNSON, age 21, single, b. Westmoreland Co., daughter of [Alex.] and Mary Johnson. Signed Roy [his X mark] Nickins, wit. J.W. Hutt. License 13 DEC 1869. Married 14 DEC 1869 in St. Peter's Church by Thomas E. Locke, Rector, Washington Parish. [M18; R:96; R1:40-21; WP]

Norris, Samuel Farnandis (1841-1901), served in Co. K, 40th Va. Inf., C.S.A., to Mary Frances Murphy (1849-1907).[2] SAMUEL NORRIS, farmer, age 35, single, b. Baltimore City, Md., son of John H. Norris and Jane A. [Attaway Biscoe], to MARY FRANCES MURPHY, age 25, single, b. Westmoreland Co., daughter of Robert Murphy and Mary A. [Jeffries].[3] License 2 DEC 1874. Married 3 DEC 1874 by R.J. Sanford. [M19; R:113; R1:59-9]

Congress. DR:71-45, entry for Mary S. Newton, d. 24 DEC 1887 of heart disease, age 77, daughter of J.W. and Judith Brockenbrough, widow, mother-in-law of E.C. Claybrook.
[1] Deeds & Wills No. 46, p. 465, will of Thomas Arnest, proved 24 JAN 1887, names wife Emily, daughters Emily and Annie E. and others.
[2] Samuel Farnandis Norris and his wife Mary Frances Murphy were buried in the Jeffries Family Cemetery, located 3 miles east of Carmel United Methodist Church, on *Level Green Farm*.
[3] Robert Murphy and Mary Ann Jeffries, daughter of Jeremiah Jeffries, were married by bond 4 JAN 1834 in Westmoreland Co., with Enoch G. Jeffries, security.

Northern, James Braxton to Mary [or Maria] Harvey. JAMES BRAXTON NORTHERN, clerk in country store, age 24, single, b. Richmond Co., son of William S. Northern and Sarah A. [Davis],[1] to MARY HARVEY, age 28, single, b. Westmoreland Co., daughter of Octavius Harvey and [Susanna] Maria [Muse], *q.v.* License 2 JUN 1857. Married 4 JUN 1857 at the residence of G.W. Goldsby by H.P.F. King, minister of the M.E. Church. [M16a:57-17; R:61; R1:9-9]

O

Oliffe (also see Eliff)

Olliffe, Enoch to Robernet Lucas. ENOCH OLLIFFE, age 49 on 1 JUN 1854, widower, b. Westmoreland Co., son of George Olliffe and Mary [Lanthrum] his wife,[2] to ROBERNET LUCAS, age about 24, single, b. Westmoreland Co., daughter of Meredith Lucas and Jane his wife. License 5 JUN 1854. Married 6 JUN 1854 at Rodham P. Olliffe's in Maddox, Va. by John Pullen, M.G. [M15:54-4; R:43; R1:2]

Oliff, John Wesley to Sarah Lorinda Croxton. JOHN WESLEY OLIFF, farmer, age 19, single, b. Richmond Co., son of Wesley B. Oliff and Elizabeth [Kelly],[3] to SARAH LORINDA CROXTON, age 20, single, b. Westmoreland Co., daughter of Carter Croxton and Mary A. [Ann Clarkson], *q.v.* License 25 OCT 1875. Married 27 OCT 1875 at Louis Lampkin's by W.A. Crocker. [M19; R:115; R1:62-2]

Oliffe, Lewis to Mary Ann R. Barker. LEWIS OLIFFE, farming, age about 30, single, b. Westmoreland Co., son of Lofty Oliff and Susan [Jones] his wife,[4] to MARY ANN R. BARKER, age about 18, single, b. Westmoreland Co., daughter of Sandy Barker. License 5 APR 1858. Married 8 APR 1858 at William Deatley's above Leeds Town by John Pullen, M.G. [M16a:58-12; R:63; R1:11-11]

Oliffe, Robert to Loucinda Washington. ROBERT OLIFFE, farmer, age 22, single, b. Westmoreland Co., son of Enoch Oliffe and Robin [Lucas], *q.v.*, to LOUCINDA WASHINGTON, age 25, single, b. Westmoreland Co., daughter of Henry Washington, mother unknown. License 6 JAN 1880. Married 7 JAN 1880 by H.H. Fones. [M20; R:131; R1:80-9]

Oliff, William Bailey to Elizabeth Ann Cole. WILLIAM B. OLIFF, farmer, age 36, widower, b. Culpeper Co., son of James and Susan Oliff, to ELIZABETH ANN COLE, age 18, single, b. Northumberland Co., daughter of William and Eliza Cole. License 25 FEB 1856. Married 29 FEB 1856 by H.P.F. King, minister of the M.E. Church. [M16:56-6; R:53; R1:5-5]

Oliff, William Bailey (1855-1939), to Georgie Allis Moss (1866-1928).[5] WILLIAM BAILEY OLIFF, farmer, age 25, single, b. Westmoreland Co., res. Richmond Co., son of William B. and Mary Oliff, to GEORGIE ALLIS MOSS, age 14, single, b. Westmoreland Co., daughter of George and Emily Jane Moss. License 22 DEC 1880. Married 23 DEC 1880 by R.N. Reamy. [M20; R:134; R1:84-11]

---

[1] William S. Northern and Sarah A. Davis were married by bond 20 DEC 1832 in Richmond Co., with Albert G. Plummer, security.
[2] George Oliffe and Mary Lanthrum were married by bond 14 APR 1789 in Westmoreland Co., with William Quisenbury, security.
[3] Wesley B. Oliff and Elizabeth Kelly were married 16 DEC 1851 in Richmond Co. by Rev. John Pullen.
[4] Lofty Oliffe and Susannah Jones were married by bond 23 AUG 1819 in Westmoreland Co., with William Balderson, security.
[5] William B. Oliff and his wife Georgie were buried at Grant United Methodist Church, Lerty, Va.

Oliff, William Davis (d. 1873 age 45),[1] to Mary Ann Bowen [a.k.a. Bowin]. DAVIS OLIFFE [sic], farmer and timber getting, age 30, single, b. Westmoreland Co., son of John [L.] and Sarah Oliffe, to MARY ANN BOWEN, age 23, single, b. Richmond Co., daughter of Kelly H. and Nancy Bowen. Signed Davis [his X mark] Oliff, wit. J. Henry Sisson. License 13 OCT 1859. Married 16 OCT 1859 by John Pullen at Mrs. Margaret Neale's. [M16a:59-26 and 26b; R:70; R1:15-7]

Oliff, William Samuel (1854-1923), to Camila Bryant. WILLIAM SAMUEL OLIFF, farmer, age 24, single, b. Westmoreland Co., son of Rodham P. [Porter] Oliff and Lucinda [Moore],[2] to CAMILA BRYANT, age 20, single, b. Westmoreland Co., daughter of C. and M.E. Bryant. License 21 MAY 1878. Married 23 MAY 1878 at the residence of J.B. Weaver by Rev. James A. Weaver. [M19; R:125; R1:74-1]

Olive, Nicholas N. (1847-1920), to Mary Jane Carpenter (1856-1930).[3] NICHOLAS N. OLIVE, farmer, age 27, single, b. and res. King George Co., son of George C. and Nancy Olive, to MARY JANE CARPENTER, age 19, single, b. Westmoreland Co., daughter of Robert A. and Mary J. Carpenter. License 28 FEB 1876. Married 29 FEB 1876 at Thomas Carpenter's by Rob. N. Reamy. [M19; R:118; R1:64-10]

Omohundro, John Meredith (1826-1888), served in Co. A, 15th Va. Cav., C.S.A., son of Thomas Omohundro (d. 1869) and first wife Sallie P. Hunter (d. 1852),[4] to Elizabeth F. Porter (1834-1882), daughter of Edward Porter (d. testate 1866[5]) and wife Elizabeth (d. 1849)[6] License 20 MAR 1852. Married 21 MAR 1852 by B.H. Johnson. [M15:52-11; R:17]

Omohundro, Richard Henry (1829-1856), son of Thomas Omohundro (d. 1869), and his first wife Sallie P. Hunter (d. 1852), to Eleanor E. Hutt (b. 1826), daughter of Hiram Hutt and Elizabeth Marmaduke. License 16 DEC 1852. [R:23 no return]

Omohundro, Thomas (1800-1869), second to Mrs. Sarah Ann Frances Reamy[7] Omohundro, widow of Edward B. Omohundro. THOMAS OMOHUNDRO, farmer, age 68, widower, b. Westmoreland Co., res. Richmond Co., son of William Omohundro [1769-1847] and [Nancy] Ann [Marmaduke] [d. 1829],[8] to SARAH ANN FRANCES OMOHUNDRO, age 45, widow, b. Westmoreland Co., parents unknown [see Note]. License 22 JUL 1868. Married 23 JUL 1868 by G.H. Northam. [M18; R:92; R1:34-11]

Omohundro, Thomas Miles (b. 1832 near *Farmers Fork*, d. 1895), served Co. D, 40th Va. Inf. and Co. A, 15th Va. Cav., C.S.A., to Elizabeth "Bettie"[9] Omohundro (b. 1844 on *Edgehill Farm*, d.

---

[1] The death of William Davis Oliff is recorded at the Poor House. DR:27-15, entry Davis Oliff, pauper, d. 15 MAY 1873 of pneumonia, age 45, son of John and Sallie Oliff, husband of Ann Oliff.
[2] R.P. Oliffe and Lucinda Moore were married by bond 26 JUN 1843 in Westmoreland Co., with Robert M. Gutridge, security. Rodham Porter Oliffe served in Co. E, 15th Va. Cav., C.S.A.
[3] Nicholas N. Olive and his wife Mary J. were buried at Round Hill Baptist Church, King George Co.
[4] Thomas Omohundro and Sary P. Hunter were married by bond 23 DEC 1824 in Westmoreland Co., with Charles Mothershead, security.
[5] Deeds & Wills No. 37, p. 317, will of Edward Porter, proved 25 MAR 1867, names daughter Elizabeth Omohundro.
[6] John M. Omohundro and his wife Elizabeth F. Porter, as well as her parents, were buried in the Omohundro Family Cemetery, located near Maple Grove, Va.
[7] *Omohundro*, p. 27, gives her name as Sarah Ann F. Redman Omohudro, widow of Edward Bruce Omohundro, nee Sarah Ann F. Redman (1822-1885), daughter of Solomon Redman and wife Sallie A. Redman.
[8] William Omohundro and Nancy Marmaduke were married by bond 31 JAN 1797 in Westmoreland Co., with Thomas Omohundro, security.
[9] *Omohundro*, p. 27, gives bride as Sarah Omohundro.

1931).[1] THOMAS MILES OMOHUNDRO, merchant, age 29, single, b. Westmoreland Co., son of Thomas Omohundro and [his first wife] Sarah [P. Hunter], *q.v.*, to BETTIE OMOHUNDRO, age 18, single, b. Westmoreland Co., daughter of Edward B. [Bruce] Omohundro and Sarah A.F. [Reamy].[2] License 30 APR 1862. Married 1 MAY 1862 at *Edge Hill* by G.H. Northam. [M17:62-12; R:78; R1:19-3]

Omohundro, William Henry (b. 1840 at *Chantilly*, d. 1915 near Stratford, Va.), served in Co. E, 55th Va. Inf., C.S.A., to Mary Elizabeth Sanford (1851/2-1935). WILLIAM HENRY OMOHUNDRO, merchant, age 29, single, b. Westmoreland Co., son of John Omohundro [1817-1847] and Elizabeth [Crask] [1820-1870],[3] to MARY E. SANFORD, age 18, single, b. Westmoreland Co., daughter of [Capt.] Robert Sanford [1816-1902], mother unknown [Delia Mahala Miller].[4] License 20 DEC 1869. Married 23 DEC 1869 by G.H. Northam. [M18; NN; R:96; R1:40-25]

P

Palmer, John D. to Martha F. Everett. License 16 FEB 1852. Bond 17 FEB 1852 by George Northam, L.M.G. [M15:52-8; R:17]

Palmer, Lewis to Eliza Taylor. LEWIS PALMER, farmer, age 24, single, b. Westmoreland Co., daughter of David and Betsy Palmer, to ELIZA TAYLOR, age 23, single, b. Westmoreland Co., daughter of Sally Taylor, father unknown. Signed Lewis [his X mark] Palmer, wit. Wm. S. McKenney. License 5 FEB 1872. Married 7 FEB 1872 at Gen. R.L.T. Beale's by G.W. Beale. [M19; R:105; R1:49-12]

Palmer, William Washington (d. 1909 in Washington, D.C.), served in Co. C, 9th Va. Cav., C.S.A., first to Rebecca E. Ingram Holliday (d. 1871 in childbirth). WILLIAM WASHINGTON PALMER, farmer, age 28, single, b. Westmoreland Co., son of William W. and Sarah A. Palmer, to REBECCA E. INGRAM HOLLIDAY, age 23, single, b. Westmoreland Co., daughter of William Holliday and Susan [Robinson].[5] License 24 APR 1868. Married 26 APR 1868 at the residence of Capt. Short by H.P.F. King. [DR:23-27; M18; R:90; R1:33-2]

Palmer, William Washington (d. 1909), *q.v.*, second to Columbia Redman Courtney (1857-1932).[6] WILLIAM WASHINGTON PALMER, farmer, age 38, widowed, b. Westmoreland Co., son of William [W.] and Sarah [A.] Palmer, to COLUMBIA REDMAN COURTNEY, age 22, single, b. Westmoreland Co., daughter of James Courtney and Mary [Redman Sutton]. License 17 MAR 1879. Married 19 MAR 1879 at the residence of the bride's father by Rev. John C. Rosser. [M20; R:128; R1:77-3]

Parker, James to Charlotte Smith. JAMES PARKER, farmer, age 21, single, b. Westmoreland Co., son of John and Julia Parker, to CHARLOTT SMITH [sic], age 40, single, b. Richmond Co., parents unknown. Signed James [his X mark] Parker, wit. J.H. Sisson. License 14 APR 1870. Married 14 APR 1870 by H.H. Fones. [M18; R:99; R1:42-15]

---

[1] Thomas M. Omohundro and his wife Elizabeth were buried at Lebanon United Methodist Church, Templeman, Va.

[2] Edward B. Omohundro and Sarah A. Reamy were married by bond 1 JUL 1839 in Westmoreland Co., with Steptoe T. Rice, security. VG:25, p. 26, gives Edward B. Omohundro and Sarah A.F. Redman, married 22 MAR 1839 in Westmoreland Co. by Rev. Charles E. Brown.

[3] John Omohundro, son of William Omohundro, and Elizabeth Crask, daughter of Frances Crask, were married by bond 8 MAY 1837 in Westmoreland Co., with Jacob V. Doleman, security.

[4] Richard Bruce Wright, *The Sanfords and Their Kin, With Additions* (1966).

[5] William Holliday and Susan R. Robinson were married by bond 11 DEC 1837 in Westmoreland Co., with Steptoe T. Rice, security.

[6] William W. Palmer and his wife Columbia were buried at Lebanon United Methodist Church, Templeman, Va.

Parker, Reuben to Amelia Evans. REUBEN PARKER, farmer, age 22, single, b. Westmoreland Co., son of Dennis and Martha Parker, to AMELIA EVANS, age 24, single, b. Essex Co., daughter of Leonard and Lucy Evans. Signed Reuben [his X mark] Parker, wit. W.S. McKenney. License 4 MAR 1871. Planned marriage 5 MAR 1871. [M19 no return; R:101; R1:46-8]

Parker, Richard to Catharine Tate. RICHARD PARKER, farmer, age 26, widowed, b. Westmoreland Co., son of David and Susan Parker, to CATHARINE TATE, age 22, single, b. Westmoreland Co., daughter of Samuel and Eliza Tate. License 24 MAY 1872. [R:105; R1:50-9 no return]

Parker, Robert Foxhall (1836-1908), served Co. C, 47th Va. Inf., C.S.A., to Nannie Lucie Robertson (d. 1928).[1] ROBERT FOXHALL PARKER, merchant, 39, single, b. Westmoreland Co., son of Thomas Parker [d. 1865 of typhoid pneumonia] and Susan R. [Reynolds], to NANNIE LUCIE ROBERTSON, age 29, single, b. Westmoreland Co., daughter of Th. W.N. and Lucy Robertson. License 30 MAY 1876. Married 30 MAY 1876 at the residence of the bride's father in Montross, Va. by D.M. Wharton. [DR:9-35; M19; R:119; R1:65-9]

Parker, Thomas Alexander (1842-1917), served in Co. C, 47th Va. Inf., C.S.A., to Sally Jane Crabb (1842-1919).[2] THOMAS ALEXANDER PARKER, carpenter, age 27, single, b. Westmoreland Co., son of Thomas Parker and Susan R. [Reynolds], *q.v.*, to SALLY JANE CRABB, age 25, single, b. Westmoreland Co., daughter of Benedict [P.] and Elizabeth Crabb. License 11 FEB 1869. Married 11 FEB 1869 by G.W. Beale. [M18; R:94; R1:37-16]

Parks, Washington Lafayette (1839-1906),[3] served in Co. C, 47th Va. Inf., C.S.A., to Elizabeth Haydon. WASHINGTON LAFAYETTE PARKS, carpenter, age 32, single, b. Westmoreland Co., son of Thomas D. Parks and Alice [Lindon Jeffries],[4] to ELIZABETH HAYDON, age 28, single, b. Northumberland Co., daughter of Thomas and Willie Ann Haydon. Married 12 NOV 1872 by R.J. Sanford. [M19; R:106; R1:51-11]

Parks, William Arthur (b. 1838, d. 1886 of cancer on neck), served in Co. A, 15th Va. Cav., C.S.A., to Louise Bailey Reed (b. 1846, d. 1871 of bilious fever).[5] WILLIAM ARTHUR PARKS, ship carpenter, age 28, single, b. Kinsale, Va., son of Thomas D. Parks and Alice L. [Lindon Jeffries] [d. 1889], *q.v.*, to LOUISE BAILEY REED, age 19, single, b. Lebanon, Va., daughter of Joseph Bailey Reed and Elizabeth Reed. License signed by Capt. Edgar B. LeGru, Provost Marshall. Married 16 AUG 1865 at the residence of J.B. Reed[6] by H.P.F. King. [DR:23-29, 65-1, 82-176; M17a:65-6]

Parr, Hedgman (1843-1904),[7] to Lucinda Qualls. HEDGMAN PARR, farmer, age 27, single, b. Fauquier Co., son of Simond [sic] and Mary Parr, to LUCINDA QUALLS, age 22, single, b. Westmoreland Co., daughter of Joshua and Caroline Qualls. License 28 JAN 1870. Married 30 JAN 1870 by Henry Young. [M18; R:98; R1:41-16]

---

[1] Robert Foxhall Parker and his wife Nanny were buried at Andrew Chapel United Methodist Church.
[2] Thomas A. Parker and his wife Sally were buried at Nomini Baptist Church.
[3] Washington L. Parks was buried at Carmel United Methodist Church.
[4] Thomas D. Parks and Alice L. Jeffries were married by bond 27 FEB 1837 in Westmoreland Co., with Robert Murphy, security.
[5] William Arthur Parks and wife Louise B. Reed were buried in the Jeffries Family Cemetery, located 3 miles east of Carmel United Methodist Church, on *Level Green Farm*.
[6] The Certificate gives place of marriage as Lebanon.
[7] Hedgman Parr was buried at National Harmony Memorial Park, Hyattsville, Md.

Patrick, Lawson (C) to Bettie Lumkins. LAWSON PATRICK, farmer, age 21, single, b. Essex Co., daughter of Henry and Mary Patrick, to BETTIE LUMPKINS, age 20, single, b. Essex Co., daughter of Lewis and Millie Lumkins. License 28 DEC 1878. Married 28 DEC 1878 at Little Zion Church by Emanuel Watts, pastor. [M20; R:127; R1:76-5]

Paul, Joseph to Nannie Stowers Rice. JOSEPH PAUL, merchant, age 24, single, b. Winchester, Va., res. Alexandria, Va., son of Isaac and Mary J. Paul, to NANNIE STOWERS RICE, age 25, single, b. Westmoreland Co., daughter of Thomas S. and Lucilia C. Rice. License 16 NOV 1868. Married 17 NOV 1868 by J.H. Davis. [M18; R:93; R1:35-14]

Payne, Richard William (b. 1853), to Lucy Northern, divorced 1902 in King George Co. RICHARD WILLIAM PAYNE, farmer, age 31, single, b. Richmond Co., son of Thomas E. Payne and Louisa J. [James Stiff],[1] to LUCY NORTHERN, age 21, single, b. Westmoreland Co., daughter of Henry Northern and Margaret Ann [Muse]. License 31 JAN 1880. Married 2 FEB 1880 at Mrs. Northern's by Wm. C. Latane, Presbyter P.E. Church. [M20; R:132; R1:81-3; WP]

Payne, Theodoric (C) to Betty Ann Kelsic (1849-1894).[2] THEODORIC PAYNE, farmer, age 26, single, b. Westmoreland Co., son of Theodoric and Sally Payne, to BETTY ANN KELSIC, age 20, single, b. Richmond Co., daughter of Meredith and Lucy Kelsic. Signed Theodoric [his X mark] Payne, wit. W.S. McKenney. License 5 DEC 1872. Married 5 DEC 1872 by Jerry Graham. [M19; R:107; R1:51-15]

Payne, Thomas to Precilla Kief. THOMAS PAYNE, farmer, age 30, single, b. and res. King George Co., son of Letty Payne, to PRECILLA KIEF, age 18, single, b. King George Co., daughter of Lucinda Kief. Signed Thos. [his X mark] Payne, wit. J.W. Hutt. License 3 MAR 1870. Married 5 MAR 1870. [M18; R:98; R1:42-10]

Payne, Walter to Martha Ann Carter (C) (d. 1886 of heart disease). WALTER PAYNE, farmer, age 22, single, b. Westmoreland Co., son of Theodoric and Sally Payne, to MARTHA ANN CARTER, age 21, single, b. Westmoreland Co., daughter of Jane Carter. Signed Walter [his X mark] Payne, wit. J.F. Bispham. License 25 DEC 1867. Married 27 DEC 1867 by R.N. Reamy. [DR:69-75; M18; R:89; R1:30-15]

Pearson, Samuel to Eliza Van Ness. SAMUEL PEARSON, laborer, age 2[1], single, b. Essex Co., son of John and Amy Pearson, to ELIZA VANNESS [sic], age 2[3], single, b. Essex Co., daughter of George [H.] Van Ness and Cath. [L. Powers] [1827-1871].[3] License 19 MAR 1872. [R:105; R1:50-1 no return]

Peed, James C. to Mollie C. Dishman. JAMES C. PEED, farmer, age 21, single, b. Westmoreland Co., son of of John Peed [d. testate 1879[4]] and Catharine [R. Saunders],[5] to MOLLIE C. DISHMAN, age 19, single, b. Westmoreland Co., daughter of Charles [Triplett] Dishman [and Eliza T. Smith],

---

[1] Thomas E. Payne and Louisa James Stiff were married 21 MAY 1846 in Richmond Co. by Rev. [Charles P. Rodefer?].
[2] Betty Payne was buried in the Kelsic Family Cemetery, Zacata, Va.
[3] George H. Van Ness (1815-1869) and Catharine L. Powers, daughter of James Powers (d. testate 1845) and Matilda Brown, were married by bond 20 DEC 1847 in Essex Co., with Edward Powers, security. Catharine was buried at *Plain View*, Essex Co. The original house there burned about 1900, but a later one can now be found adjacent to the small burying ground.
[4] Deeds & Wills No. 41, p. 361, will of John Peed, pproved 24 MAR 1879, names wife Catharine and minor children.
[5] John Peed and Catharine R. Saunders, were married by bond 6 MAR 1848 in Richmond Co., with Richard Saunders, security.

q.v. License 25 DEC 1871. Married 26 DEC 1871 at Charles [Lyell]'s by Robert N. Reamy. [M19; R:104; R1:49-1]

Peed, John Raymond (b. c.1833, d. 1888 in Baltimore, Md.),[1] served in Co. A, 15th Va. Cav., C.S.A., to Elmira Gutridge. JOHN R. PEED, mechanic, age about 23, single, b. Richmond Co., son of John Peed and Rebecca his wife, to ELMIRA GUTRIDGE, age about 17, single, b. Westmoreland Co., daughter of James Gutridge and Susan his wife. License 2 JAN 1857. Married 6 JAN 1857 at James Gutridge's by John Pullen. [M16a:57-1; R:57; R1:8-5]

Peed, Richard Addison (b. 1838, d. 1882 of pneumonia), served in Co. C, 47th Va. Inf., C.S.A., to Sarah Jane Reamy (1837-1925).[2] RICHARD ADISON PEED [sic], farmer, age 19, single, b. Westmoreland Co., son of William S. Peed and Lucy [Nash],[3] to SARAH JANE REAMY, age 21, single, b. Westmoreland Co., daughter of James Reamy and Alice [Saunders]. License 27 DEC 1858. Married 28 DEC 1858 by John Pullen. [DR:51-38; M16a:58-40; R:66; R1:14-9]

Peed, William Herbert (d. 1896 of rheumatism), served in Co. A, 15th Va. Cav., C.S.A., to Louisa [or Louvinia] E. Atkins. WILLIAM HERBERT[4] PEED, house carpenter, age about 22, single, b. upper part of Richmond Co., son of John Peed[e] and Rebecca his wife, to LOUISA E. ATKINS, age about 22, single, b. Westmoreland Co., daughter of Blekey Atkins and Jane his wife. License 14 OCT 1858. Married 14 OCT 1858 at Mrs. Adkins' [sic] by John Pullen, M.G. [DR:106-53; M16a:58-24; R:64; R1:13-8]

Peirce (see Pierce)

Pendleton, John Thomas to Ella Jane Bowie. JOHN THOMAS PENDLETON, lawyer, age 25, single, b. Christian Co., Ky., res. Fulton Co., Ga., son of William and Isabella Pendleton, to ELLEN JANE BOWIE, age 27, single, b. Westmoreland Co., daughter of Walter Bowie and Mary T. [Todd]. License 12 APR 1870. Married 13 APR 1870 by G. Wm. Beale. [M18; R:98; R1:42-14]

Peterson, Mathyas to Sarah T. Davis. MATHYAS PETERSON, farmer, age 25, single, b. Sweden, son of Peter and Ann Peterson, to SARAH T. DAVIS, age 23, single, b. Westmoreland Co., daughter of Thomas L. Davis and Nancy [Robinson], *q.v.* License 7 AUG 1866. Married 9 AUG 1866 at the residence of the bride by Elder James A. Weaver. [M18; R:83; R1:24-12]

Peyton, Philip (C) to Mary Rebecca Maden. PHILIP PEYTON, farmer, age 23, single, b. King George Co., son of Warner and Mary Peyton, to MARY REBECCA MADEN, age 18, single, b. Westmoreland Co., daughter of Julia Maden, father unknown. License 27 DEC 1880. Married 28 DEC 1880 at Little Zion Church by Emanuel Watts, pastor. [M20; R:134; R1:84-12]

Peyton, Washington (C) to Mary Watts. WASHINGTON PEYTON, farmer, age 24, single, b. Westmoreland Co., son of Beverly and Fanny Peyton, to MARY WATTS, age 19, single, b. Westmoreland Co., daughter of Moses and Mary Watts. Washington [his X mark] Peyton, wit. J.W. Hutt. License 28 FEB 1873. Married 1 MAR 1873 by Emanuel Watts, pastor Little Zion Church. [M19; R:108; R1:53-11]

---

[1] John R. Peed was buried at Ephesus Christian Church, Foneswood, Va.
[2] Richard A. Peed and his wife Sarah were buried at Ephesus Christian Church, Foneswood, Va.
[3] William S. Peed and Lucy Nash were married by bond 19 MAY 1837 in Westmoreland Co., with James H. Mothershead, security.
[4] Another copy at 58-24a gives middle name for groom.

Pierce, Andrew (C) (1849-1917), to Susan Ann Thompson. ANDREW PIERCE,[1] farmer, age 27, single, b. Westmoreland Co., son of William Pierce and Hannah [McCoy],[2] to SUSAN ANN THOMPSON, age 27, single, b. Westmoreland Co., daughter of Joseph and Haney Thompson. License 30 JUL 1878. Married 1 AUG 1878 at *Barnesville* by Thomas T. Johnson. [DC; M19; R:126; R1:74-8]

Pierce, Richard to Emily Thompson. RICHARD PIERCE, farmer, age 23, single, b. Westmoreland Co., son of William Pierce and Hannah [McCoy], *q.v.*, to EMILY THOMPSON, age 20, single, b. Westmoreland Co., daughter of George and Easter Thompson. Signed Richard [his X mark] Pierce, wit. W.S. McKenney. License 26 JAN 1871. Married 26 JAN 1871 by G.W. Beale. [M18 parents reversed; R:101; R1:45-12]

Pierce, Thomas H. (C) (d. by 1877), to Sarah Streets. THOMAS H. PIERCE, laborer, age 23, single, b. Westmoreland Co., son of Carter and Ellen Pierce, to SARAH STREETS, age 21, single, b. Westmoreland Co., daughter of Theodoric and Fanny Streets. License 18 DEC 1871. Married 1 JAN 1872 by Emanuel Watts, pastor of Little Zion Church. [M19; R:104; R1:48-10]

Pierce, William to Frances Johnson (C). WILLIAM PIERCE, farmer, age 65, widowed, b. Westmoreland Co., son of Thornton and Betsy Pierce, to FRANCES JOHNSON, age 25, single, b. Westmoreland Co., daughter of Henry and Frances Johnson. License 25 DEC 1865. Married 28 DEC 1865 by Charles P. Rodefer, minister. [CP; M18 license not on film; R:82; R1:22-11]

Pillsbury, Richard Henry to Jane Frances Courtney. RICHARD HENRY PILLSBURY, shoemaker, age 27, single, b. Westmoreland Co., son of Thomas and Maria [Pillsbury], to JANE FRANCES COURTNEY, age 19, single, b. Westmoreland Co., daughter of Jerh. and Ann Courtney. Consent 13 JUN 1860 by Jerh. Courtney for his daughter, wits. Jas. W. English, E.J. Tune. License 14 JUN 1860. Married 19 JUN 1860. [M17:60-26 and 26a; R:74]

Pinn, Leroy Madison (C) to Sarah Payne. LEROY MADISON PINN, farmer, age 22, single, b. Westmoreland Co., son of Jerry and Matilda Pinn, to SARAH PAYNE, age 27, single, b. Westmoreland Co., parents unknown. License 18 MAR 1880. Married 18 MAR 1880 by F.B. Beale. [M20; R:132; R1:81-16]

Piper, George (C) to Sarah Wairer [Ware]. GEORGE PIPER, farmer, age 25, widowed, b. Fredericksburg, Va., son of John and Eliza Piper, to SARAH WAIRER, age 26, single, b. Essex Co., daughter of Judy Wairer, father unknown. License 25 FEB 1879. Married 25 FEB 1879 at Little Zion Church by Emanuel Watts, pastor, Little Zion Church. [M20; R:128; R1:77-2]

Pitts, Carolinas to Victoria Coghill. CAROLINAS PITTS, age 29, single, b. Westmoreland Co., son of Mary Jane Pitts, father unknown, to VICTORIA COGHILL, age 17, single, b. Essex Co., daughter of John Coghill and Jennie [Virginia Parker], *q.v.* License 29 AUG 1878. Married 29 AUG 1878 by B.R. Battaile. [M19; R:126; R1:74-11]

Pitts, Stark to Nancy Adams, both of King George Co. Married [blank] 1855 at St. Peter's Church rectory by Rev. J.W. Chesley. [SP; WP]

---

[1] The surname also appears as Peirce.
[2] William Peirce and Hannah Macoy were married by bond 9 JUL 1828 in Westmoreland Co., with Joseph Thompson, security.

Pitts, William (C) to Agnes Brown. WILLIAM PITTS, laborer, age 25, single, b. Essex Co., son of Thomas and Nellie Pitts, to AGNES BROWN, age 21, single, b. King George Co., daughter of Henry and Priscilla Brown. Signed William [his X mark] Pitts, wit. W.S. McKenney. License 16 MAY 1873. Married 17 MAY 1873 at Oak Grove by Emanuel Watts, pastor Little Zion Church, Oak Grove. [M19; R:109; R1:54-4]

Pomeroy, John to Thirzy Ann Trew [a.k.a. True]. JOHN POMEROY, farmer, age 28, single, b. Westmoreland Co., son of William Pomeroy and Louisa [Lucas],[1] to THIRZY ANN TREW, age 22, single, b. Westmoreland Co., daughter of William J. and Eliza Trew. License 21 FEB 1866. Planned marriage 22 FEB 1866. Married in FEB 1866 at St. Peter's Church by Rev. Thomas E. Locke. [R:82; R1:23-11 no return; WP]

Poor, Richard T. to Elizabeth Neale. License 23 AUG 1853. [R:33 no return]

Poor, Richard Thomas to Lucinda Drake. RICHARD THOMAS POOR, overseer, age 27, widowed, b. Westmoreland Co., son of Frederick and Lucy Poor, to LUCINDA DRAKE, age 27, single, b. Westmoreland Co., daughter of Newton Drake and Margaret [James].[2] Consent 18 DEC 1860 by bride Lucinda [her X mark] Drake, wit. W. Drake. License 18 DEC 1860. Married 20 DEC 1860 by Robert N. Reamy. [M17:60-43, 43a and 43b; R:76; R1:17-5]

Pope, James Socrates to Caroline Gutridge. JAMES SOCRATES POPE, farmer, age 30, single, b. Westmoreland Co., son of Elliot and Elizabeth Pope [d. testate 1894], *q.v.*, to CAROLINE GUTRIDGE, age 23, single, b. Westmoreland Co., daughter of John Gutridge and Elizabeth [Ann Atkins].[3] License 14 APR 1876. Married 14 APR 1876 by H.H. Fones. [M19; R:118; R1:64-13]

Pope, Jeremiah (b. 1838, d. 1892 at *Society Hill*, St. Mary's Co., Md.),[4] to Louisiana Frances Malone. JEREMIAH POPE, sailor, age 24, single, b. Westmoreland Co., son of John Pope and Susan [McCluskey],[5] to LOUISIANA FRANCES MALONE, age 19, single, b. Accomack Co., daughter of Thomas and Nancy Malone. License 28 DEC 1861. Married 1 JAN 1862 at the residence of Mrs. Pope by James A. Weaver. [M17:62-2; R:77; R1:18-7]

Porter, George Henry (1830-1895), second to Harriet Brown Bailey (1839-1912).[6] GEORGE HENRY PORTER, attorney at law, age 43, widowed, b. Talbot Co., Md., res. Baltimore, Md., son of Welman and Sarah Porter, to HARRIET BROWN BAILEY, age 32, single, b. Westmoreland Co., daughter of Stephen G. and Harriet A. Bailey. License 15 DEC 1873. Married 16 DEC 1873 by R.J. Sanford. [M19; R:110; R1:55-6]

Porter, John Wesley (d. 1872 of bilious pneumonia), to Mary Emily King. JOHN WESLEY PORTER, farmer, age 28, single, b. Westmoreland Co., son of Thomas T. Porter and Olivia A. [Harris],[7] to MARY EMILY KING, age 18, single, b. Westmoreland Co., daughter of Griffin T. King and Ann H. [English].[8] Consent 9 MAR 1860 by mother Ann H. King, wit. Saml. Walker. License

---

[1] William Pomeroy and Louisa Lucas, daughter of Meredith Lucas, were married by bond 12 MAY 1837 in Westmoreland Co., with Henry Winkfield, security.
[2] Newton Drake and Margaret James were married by bond 26 JAN 1829 in Westmoreland Co., with George Barrack, security.
[3] John Gutridge and Elizabeth Ann Atkins were married by bond 19 OCT 1844 in Westmoreland Co., with Joseph Atkins, security.
[4] Jeremiah Pope was buried at St. Francis Xavier Church, Compton, Md.
[5] John Pope and Susan McCluskey were married by bond 11 JUN 1834 in Westmoreland Co., with James K. Johnson, security.
[6] George H. Porter and his wives Georgianna (1829-1872) and Harriet were buried in Loudon Park Cemetery, Baltimore, Md.
[7] Thomas T. Porter and Olivia Harris were married by bond 11 DEC 1828 in Westmoreland Co., with John H. Peake, security.
[8] Griffin King and Ann H. English were married by bond 13 APR 1824 in Westmoreland Co., with Vincent Douglass, security.

12 MAR 1860. Married 15 MAR 1860 by G.H. Northam. [DR:21-11; M17:60-16, 16a, 16c; R:72; R1:16-10]

Posey, Washington (C) to Judy Gaskins. WASHINGTON POSEY, farmer, age 25, single, b. Westmoreland Co., son of Lewis and Fannie Posey, to JUDY GASKINS, age 24, single, b. Westmoreland Co., daughter of Edward and Martha Gaskins. Signed Washington [his X mark] Posey, wit. J.W. Hutt. License 13 DEC 1873. Married 18 DEC 1873 by John Roy. [M19; R:110; R1:55-4]

Potter, John Bird, served in Co. C, 40th Va. Inf., C.S.A., to Kate Elizabeth Oliff. JOHN BIRD POTTER, farmer, age 25, single, b. Westmoreland Co., son of William Potter and Ann Maria [McKenney],[1] to KATE ELIZABETH OLIFF, age 23, single, b. Richmond Co., daughter of William B. and Mary Ann Oliff. License 22 DEC 1866. Planned marriage 25 DEC 1866. [R:85; R1:26-4 no return]

Pound, Charles C. (1855-1912), to Margaret "Maggie" Ann Gutridge (1858-1929).[2] CHARLES POUND, farmer, age 23, single, b. Westmoreland Co., son of W.H. [William] Pound and Martha [Green] [1833-1919],[3] to MAGGIE ANN GUTRIDGE, age 22, single, b. Westmoreland Co., daughter of Chas. and Mary Gutridge. License 2 APR 1880. Married 4 APR 1880 by R.N. Reamy. [M20; R:133; R1:82-3]

Powers, David P. (killed 1864 in Louisa Co.), served in Co. A, 15th Va. Cav., C.S.A., to Lucy C. Sanford. DAVID P. POWERS, farmer, age 26, single, b. Westmoreland Co., son of John Powers [d. 1854] and [Eliza Ann Montgomery],[4] to LUCY C. SANDFORD [sic], age 20, single, b. Westmoreland Co., daughter of Ethelwald and Sallie Sanford. License 13 OCT 1857. Married 20 OCT 1857 at Lebanon Church by H.P.F. King, minister of the M.E. Church. [M16a:57-34; R:62; R1:10-14]

Powers, James Andrew (1835-1899), to Mrs. Eleanor Elizabeth Hutt Omohundro (1836-1889),[5] widow of Richard Henry Omohundro, *q.v.* JAMES ANDREW POWERS, merchant, age 25, single, b. Westmoreland Co., son of John Powers and Eliza Ann [Montgomery], *q.v.*, to ELEANOR ELIZABETH OMOHUNDRO, age 25, widow, b. Westmoreland Co., daughter of Hiram Hutt and Ann Payne [Marmaduke].[6] Consent 18 DEC 1860 by bride. License 18 DEC 1860. Married 19 DEC 1860. [M17:60-41; R:76]

Pratt, Archabald "Archie" to Virginia Jane "Jannie" Newman. ARCHABALD PRATT, farmer, age 30, single, b. Westmoreland Co., son of Owen and Jane Pratt, to JANE NEWMAN, age 23, single, b. Westmoreland Co., daughter of Emanuel Newman and Caroline [Lucas], *q.v.* Signed Archabald [his X mark] Pratt, wits. J.W. Hutt, Wm. Green. License 27 MAY 1868. Married 28 MAY 1868 by H.P.F. King. [M18; R:91; R1:33-14]

---

[1] William Potter and Ann M. McKinney were married by bond 16 APR 1829 in Westmoreland Co., with Thomas Cox, security.
[2] Charles C. Pound and his wife Martha were buried at St. Peter's Cemetery, Oak Grove, Va.
[3] William H. Pound and Martha Green, daughter of George Green, were married by bond 17 AUG 1849 in Westmoreland Co., with Samuel Nash, security. Martha was buried at St. Peter's Cemetery, Oak Grove, Va.
[4] John Powers and Eliza Ann Montgomery were married by bond 30 JUL 1828 in Westmoreland Co., with Stephen D. Pitts, security. CF1854-16, *Theophilus Powers v. Eliza Powers &c.*
[5] James A. Powers and his wife Eleanor E. were buried in Augusta Hillside Cemetery, Augusta, Bracken Co., Ky.
[6] Hiram Hutt and Ann P. Marmaduke, daughter of Vincent Marmaduke, were married by bond 25 FEB 1833 in Westmoreland Co., with Dempsey Porter, security.

Pratt, William C. to Eliza H. Turner. Married 8 MAY 1860 by Rev. Thomas E. Locke at *Woodlawn*,[1] the residence of R. [Richard] Turner. [WP]

Prosser, Samuel Coleman, served in Co. D, 40th Va. Inf., C.S.A., to Susan Rebecca Stephens. SAMUEL C. PROSSER, farmer, age 32, widower, b. Northumberland Co., son of Samuel and Lucy Prosser, to SUSAN R. STEPHENS, age 19, single, b. Westmoreland Co., daughter of John B. Stephens and Alice [Hall].[2] License 20 DEC 1859. Married 21 DEC 1859 by H.P.F. King, minister of the M.P. Church. [M16a:59-28 and 28a; R:70; R1:15-8]

Pullen, Thomas Everett (d. c.1896/8), served in Co. G, 15th Va. Cav., C.S.A., to Martha Ann Dishman. THOMAS E. PULLEN, merchant, going on 23 years, single, b. Dist. No. 2 in Richmond Co., son of John Pullen and Henryetta [Bowen] his wife,[3] to MARTHA ANN DISHMAN, age going on 19, single, b. Essex Co., daughter of James [Andrew] Dishman and Ann V. [Kent][4] his [second] wife. License 3 JUN 1856. Married 5 JUN 1856 at *Potomack View* [James Dishman's] by John Pullen, M.G. [M16a:56-17; NN[5]; R:55; R1:6-3]

Purcell, George to Emily Trigger, of King George Co., were married 21 MAY 1853 at St. Peter's Church, Oak Grove, by the Rev. E.B. Tuttle. [SP; WP]

Pursell [or Pursle], Otaway to Sarah C. Eidson. License 22 MAY 1854. [R:43]

Purcell, Robert Henry (1843-1918), served in Co. E, 55th Va. Inf., C.S.A., to Julia Ann English (1853-1934).[6] ROBERT HENRY PURCELL, farmer, age 29, single, b. Westmoreland Co., son of H.M. [Hiram Morgan] Purcell [1816-1877] and H.L. [Hannah Lane Middleton] [1819-1904],[7] to JULIA ANN ENGLISH, age 19, single, b. Westmoreland Co., daughter of B.S. [Benjamin] English and M.F. [Mary F. Smith], *q.v.* License 14 JAN 1873. Married 16 JAN 1873 at the residence of the bride's father by W.A. Crocker. [M19; R:108; R1:53-1]

Purcell, Stephen (1834-1908), served in Co. C, 47th Va. Inf., and Co. D, 40th Va. Inf., C.S.A., to Julia F. Oliffe (d. 1906).[8] STEPHEN PURSELL, farming, age about 22, single, b. Westmoreland Co., son of William Pursell and Ann his wife, to JULIA F. OLLIFFE [sic], age about 22, single, b. Westmoreland Co., daughter of William Oliffe [sic] and Ann his wife. License 22 DEC 1856. Married 25 DEC 1856 at Malbro Balderson's in Richmond Co. by John Pullen. [M16a:56-37; R:57]

Purcell, William to Mrs. Martha Green Pound. WILLIAM PURCELL, farming, age 61, widowed, b. Westmoreland Co., son of John and Sally Purcell, to MARTHA POUND, age 35, widow, b. Westmoreland Co., daughter of George and Sally Green. License 17 OCT 1866. Planned marriage 18 OCT 1866. [R:84; R1:25-4 no return]

---

[1] Located in King George Co., Va.
[2] John B. Stephens and Alice Hall were married by bond 11 SEP 1837 in Westmoreland Co., with Henry Stephens, security.
[3] John Pullen and Hany Bowen, daughter of Thomas and Mary Bowen, were married by bond 9 OCT 1827 in Westmoreland Co., with Smith Jennings, security.
[4] James Dishman and Ann V. Kent were married by bond 31 OCT 1836 in Westmoreland Co., with Thomas Sandy, security.
[5] NN:27 MAY 1898, 3 JUN 1898, 5 AUG 1898 announces the death of Thomas Everett Pullen, and NN:17 MAR 1899 announces the death of Mrs. Thomas Pullen.
[6] Robert H. Purcell and his wife Julia A. were buried at Ebenezer United Methodist Church, Oldhams, Va.
[7] Hiram M. Pursell and Hannah L. Middleton, daughter of Jeremiah Middleton, were married by bond 26 JAN 1841 in Westmoreland Co., with Samuel W. English, security.
[8] Stephen Purcell and his wife Julia F. were buried in a Purcell Family Cemetery at *Chesterfield Farm*, located off of Route 640.

Q

Quesenbury, James Slaughter, second Bettie P. Robinson. License 12 NOV 1850. Married 21 NOV 1850 by John Bayley. [M15:51-23; R:3 not in *Nottingham*]

Quesenbury, Richard Henry (b. c.1830, d. 1863 of dysentery at Point Lookout, Md.), served in Co. K, 9th Va. Cav., C.S.A., to Susan M. Spilman (d. 1873). RICHARD H. QUESENBURY, farmer, age 28, single, b. Westmoreland Co., son of Richard Quesenbury [d. 1844] and Lucy [Mothershead] [d. testate 1868[1]],[2] to SUSAN M. SPILMAN, age 23,[3] single, b. Westmoreland Co., daughter of John Spilman [c.1790-1872] and [Thirza Hoult] [c.1799-1870].[4] License 21 DEC 1858. Married 23 DEC 1858 by H.P.F. King, M.G. [M16a:58-39 and 39a; R:66; R1:13-2]

R

Randall, Beverly to Susan Askins. BEVERLY RANDALL, carpenter, age 60, single, b. Fluvanna Co., son of John and Polly Randall, to SUSAN ASKINS, age 30, single, b. Westmoreland Co., parents unknown. Signed Beverly [his X mark] Randall, wits. J.W. Hutt, Ro. F. Parker. License 5 AUG 1867. Married 28 AUG 1867 at Dr. R.J. Sanford's by R.J. Sanford. [M18; R:87; R1:29-2]

Reamy, Baldwin Monroe (1834-1920), served in Co. A, 15th Va. Cav., C.S.A., to Sarah Emma Moxley (1852-1918).[5] BALDWIN MONROE REAMY, farmer, age 36, single, b. Richmond Co., son of James Reamy [d. 1851] and [his second wife] Alice [Saunders], to SARAH EMMA MOXLEY, age 18, single, b. King George Co., parents unknown [William Moxley and Ellen Jones]. License 26 DEC 1870. Married 6 JAN 1871 by Robert N. Reamy. [DC; M18; R:100; R1:45-3]

Reamy, Benjamin Fairfax to Mary Ella Marders. BENJAMIN FAIRFAX REAMEY [sic], farmer, age 27, single, b. Richmond Co., son of George and Elizabeth Reamey, to MARY ELLA MARDERS, age 28, single, b. King George Co., daughter of Joseph and Margaret [A. Reamy] Marders.[6] Signed B.F. [his X mark] Reamey, wit. Wm. S. McKenney. License 15 DEC 1875. Married 16 DEC 1875 by H.H. Fones. [M19; R:116; R1:62-12]

Reamy, George Sedwick (1856-1927), to Ella Martha Brown. GEORGE SEDWICK REAMEY [sic], farmer, age 2[0], single, b. King George Co., son of Richard R. [Redman] Reamy and Eliza J. [Barrack], to ELLA MARTHA BROWN, age 17, single, b. Westmoreland Co., daughter of Philip [Bush] [Brown] and Alice M. [Collinsworth]. License 26 FEB 1877. Married 1 MAR 1877 by F.B. Beale. [DC; M19; R:121; R1:69-4]

Reamy, Henry Clay (1846-1928), served in Co. A, 55th Va. Inf., C.S.A., first to Mary Peed.[7] HENRY CLAY REAMY, farmer, age 23, single, b. Westmoreland Co., son of John N. Reamy and Jane [Peed],[8] to MARY PEED, age 35, single, b. Westmoreland Co., daughter of James and Catharine Peed. License 3 NOV 1868. Married 4 NOV 1868 by Robt. N. Reamy. [M18; R:92; R1:35-12]

---

[1] Deeds & Wills No. 37, p. 596, will of Lucy Quesenbury, proved 27 JUL 1868, names son Richard H. Quesenbury.

[2] Richard Quesenbury and Lucy Mothershead were married by bond 21 MAY 1835 in Westmoreland Co., with Charles Mothershead, security.

[3] Another copy at 58-39a gives age of groom as 24 and contains signature of groom.

[4] John Spilman and Thirza Hoult were married by bond 3 MAY 1815 in Westmoreland Co., with Abraham White, security.

[5] Baldwin M. Reamy and his wife Sarah E. were buried at Ephesus Christian Church, Foneswood, Va.

[6] Joseph H. Marders and Margaret A. Ramey were married 2 APR 1846 in King George Co.

[7] Henry Clay Reamy and his wife Betty Jones were buried at Ephesus Christian Church, Flat Iron, Va.

[8] John N. Reamy, son of Beriman Reamy, and Jane Peed, daughter of John Peed, were married by bond 16 DEC 1834 in Westmoreland Co., with Samuel T. Reamy, security.

Reamy, Henry Clay (1846-1928), second to Bettie Roane Jones (1948-192_). HENRY CLAY REAMEY [sic], farmer, age 29, widowed, b. Westmoreland Co., son of John N. Reamy and Jane [Peed], *q.v.*, to BETTIE ROANE JONES, age 28, single, b. King & Queen Co., daughter of James I. and Nancey Jones. License 24 JAN 1876. Married 27 JAN 1876 at James Jones' by Robt. N. Reamy. [M19; R:117; R1:64-2]

Reamy, James Broadus to Martha Hinson. JAMES BROADUS REAMY, farmer, age 29, single, b. King George Co., son of Richard R. [Redman] Reamy and Eliza J. [Barrack], to MARTHA HINSON, age 28, single, b. Westmoreland Co., daughter of Rodham and Martha Hinson. License 19 DEC 1876. Married 21 DEC 1876 at Yeocomico Church by John J. Lloyd. [CP; M19; R:120; R1:67-12]

Reamy, John Taliaferro (d. 1923), served in Co. C, 47th Va. Inf., C.S.A., to Agness Dora Peed. JOHN TALIAFERRO REAMEY, farmer, age 30, widowed, b. Richmond Co., son of Robert N. Reamy and Jane [Owens], to AGNESS DORA PEED, age 18, single, b. Westmoreland Co., son of R.A. and Jane Peed. License 6 APR 1878. Married 7 APR 1878 at Richard Peed's by F.W. Claybrook. [M19; R:125; R1:73-12]

Reamy, Presley Garnett (b. 1842, d. 1922 of arterial sclerosis), served in Co. A, 15th Va. Cav., C.S.A., to Angelina Belle Coates (1854-1931).[1] PRESLEY GARNETT REAMEY [sic], farmer, age 31, single, b. Richmond Co., son of James Reamey and Alice [Saunders],[2] to ANGELINA BELLE COATES, age 19, single, b. Westmoreland Co., daughter of William S. Coates and Emily [Gutridge], *q.v.* License 22 DEC 1873. Married 23 DEC 1873 at Sathalial Coats' by Robert N. Reamy. [M19; R:110; R1:55-14]

Reamy, Richard Templeman, served in Co. C, 47th Va. Inf., C.S.A., to Frances Ann Fones (b. 1838 d. 1913 at Foneswood). RITCHARD T. REAMEY [sic], mechanic, age about 22, single, b. Richmond Co., son of Samuel T. Reamy [1812-1891] and Susan [Caroline Fones] [1810-1883] his wife,[3] to FRANCES A. FONES, age about 18, single, b. Westmoreland Co., daughter of [James] B. Fones and Mary [Ann Gutridge][4] his wife. License 5 JAN 1857. Married 8 JAN 1857 at Mrs. Mary Fones' by John Pullen, M.G. [M16a:57-2; R:57; R1:8-7]

Reamy, William Kelley (d. by 1877), to Indiana Jane Armstrong. WILLIAM KELLEY REAMY, farmer, age 22, single, b. and res. Richmond Co., son of James O. Reamy and Mary Jane [Norris],[5] to INDIANA JANE ARMSTRONG, age 20, single, b. Richmond Co., daughter of Henry S. and Jane Armstrong. License 24 APR 1872. Married 25 APR 1872 by Robert N. Reamy. [M19; R:105; R1:50-4]

Reamy, Woody Asberry to Annie Estella Vickers. WOODY ASBERRY REAMY, farmer, age 22, single, b. Westmoreland Co., res. Richmond Co., son of James O. Reamy and Mary J. [Jane Norris], *q.v.*, to ANNIE ESTELLA VICKERS, age 18, single, birthplace unknown, daughter of Thomas Vickers and Elizabeth [Morris].[6] License 22 DEC 1875. Married 23 DEC 1875 by H.H. Fones. [M19; R:116; R1:62-15]

---

[1] Presley G. Reamy and his wife Angelina were buried at Ephesus Christian Church, Foneswood, Va.
[2] James Reamy and Ailsey Saunders were married by bond 9 JAN 1832 in Richmond Co., with James B. Fones, security.
[3] Samuel T. Reamy, son of Beriman Reamy, and Susan C. Fones, were married by bond 25 APR 1832 in Westmoreland Co., with Joshua Reamy, security.
[4] James B. Fones and Mary Ann Gutridge were married by bond 19 DEC 1833 in Westmoreland Co., with Richard C. Gutridge, security.
[5] James O. Reamy and Mary Jane Norris were married by bond 14 SEP 1843 in Richmond Co., with Richard C. Gutridge, security.
[6] Thomas Vickers and Elizabeth Morris were married 30 DEC 1847 in Richmond Co. by Rev. John Pullen.

Redding, Charles C. to Miss [Bettine] Howland (d. 1881).[1] Married 16 DEC 1874 in King George Co. by Rev. John Payne. [WP]

Redman, Jacob Stout (1847-1900), to Lucy Virginia Hardwick (1848-1894).[2] JACOB STOUT REDMAN, merchant, age 22, single, b. Talbot Co., Md., res. Washington, D.C., son of James and Mary Redman, to LUCY VIRGINIA HARDWICK, age 20, single, b. Richmond Co., daughter of S.R. [Samuel] Hardwick and Rebecca [Marmaduke].[3] License 14 JUN 1869. Married 15 JUN 1869 at the residence of the bride's father by J.H. Davis. [M18; R:95; R1:38-11]

Redman, Samuel to Josephine Hacket. SAMUEL REDMAN, farmer, age 25, single, b. Westmoreland Co., son of Lucy Redman, to JOSEPHINE HACKET, age 17, single, b. Westmoreland Co., daughter of Jesse and Jane Hacket. Signed Samuel [his X mark] Redman, wit. W.S. McKenney. License 12 DEC 1872. Married 12 DEC 1872 at James Jordan's by G.W. Beale, M.G. [M19; R:107; R1:52-3]

Reed, Charles to Florence Baker. CHARLES REED, sailor, age 23, single, b. Westmoreland Co., son of George and Charlotte Reed, to FLORENCE BAKER, age 19, single, b. Westmoreland Co., daughter of Henry and Willie Baker. License 20 DEC 1879. Married 23 DEC 1879 by H.H. Fones. [M20; R:131; R1:79-15]

Reed, Edwin Green (d. 1882 of dropsy), to Mrs. Adeline Payne Carter Green (d. 1873 of consumption). EDWIN GREEN REED, farmer, age 59, widowed, b. Richmond, Va., son of [John] and Mary Reed, to ADELINE PAYNE GREEN, age 33, widow, b. Essex Co., daughter of Landon and Cordelia Carter.[4] License 18 JAN 1866. Married 21 JAN 1866 at Prestley Carter's by John Pullen. [DR:27-30, 55-15; M18; R:82; R1:23-3]

Reed, Edwin Green (b. 1810, d. 1882 of dropsy),[5] to Mrs. Mahala Ann Reamy Jenkins, widow of Thomas B. Jenkins. EDWIN GREEN REED, farmer, age 64, widowed, b. Richmond City, Va., son of Joseph and Mary Reed, to MAHALA ANN JENKINS, age 45, widow, b. Richmond Co., daughter of William and Elizabeth Reamy. License 29 DEC 1873. Married 30 DEC 1873 by Walter C. Taylor. [DC; M19; R:111; R1:56-3]

Reed, George (C) (1858-1933), first to Annie Susan Templeman (d. 1887 of pneumonia). GEORGE REED, farmer, age 21, single, b. Westmoreland Co., son of Betsy Reed, to ANNIE SUSAN TEMPLEMAN, age 21, single, b. Westmoreland Co., daughter of James and Jennie Templeman. License 6 JAN 1878. Married 17 JAN 1878 at Templeman's by Thomas T. Johnson. [DC; DR:73-110; M19; R:124; R1:72-11]

Reed, John, Capt. to Matilda W. Noel. License 23 MAY 1853. Married 2 JUN 1853 at the residence of Mr. Noel, Oak Grove, by E.B. Tuttle. [M15:53-16a; R:31; SP; WP]

---

[1] WP shows that Mrs. Charles Redding died 29 SEP 1881 age about 27, buried in King George Co.
[2] Jacob S. Redman and wife Lucy Virginia were buried in Rock Creek Cemetery, Washington, D.C.
[3] Samuel R. Hardwick and Rebecca Marmaduke, daughter of James B. Marmaduke, were married by bond 15 JUN 1843 in Richmond Co., with Isaac S. Jeffries, security.
[4] Landon Carter and Mrs. Delia Carter, widow of Tasker Carter, were married by bond 17 DEC 1831 in Essex Co., with James K. Nash, security.
[5] DC: Edwin Green was buried at Currioman Baptist Church, Chiltons, Va.

Reed, Joseph Edward (b. 1837, d. 1906 in Allamakee Co., Iowa), to Juliet Ann King (1841-1910).[1] JOSEPH EDWARD REED, house carpenter, age 21, single, b. Westmoreland Co., son of Joseph B. and Elizabeth Reed, to JULIET ANN KING, age 17, single, b. Richmond Co., daughter of Henry P.F. King and Elizabeth N. [Dobyns].[2] License 6 NOV 1858. Married 10 NOV 1858 by H.P.F. King, minister of the M.E. Church. [M16a:58-27 and 27a; R:66; R1:12-12]

Reed, Joseph L. to Eliza Jasper. JOSEPH L. REED, carpenter, age about 42, single, b. near Shelton's, Westmoreland Co., son of Joseph Reed and Mary his wife, to ELIZA JASPER, age about 18, single, b. Westmoreland Co., daughter of Philip Countee Jasper and Evelina. License 14 JUL 1856. Married 1[5] JUL 1856 at a stage hear Shelton's X Roads by John Pullen, M.G. [M16a:56-21, R:55; R1:6-10]

Reed, Thompson (C) to Ann Kelley. THOMPSON REED, laborer, age 24, single, b. Westmoreland Co., son of John and Lucy Reed, to ANN KELLEY, age 23, single, b. Westmoreland Co., daughter of Samuel and Taby Kelley. Signed Thompson [his X mark] Reed, wit. Wm. S. McKenney. License 19 MAR 1872. Married 21 MAR 1872 at *Airfield* by Rev. Thomas T. Johnson. [M19; R:105; R1:49-16]

Reed, William Richard (1831-1923), to Julia Ann Johnson (1832-1879).[3] License 23 JUL 185[3]. Married 24 JUL 185[3]. [R:31 no return]

Reynolds, Albert Dangerfield, Rev. (1843-1912), served in Co. D, 9th Va. Cav., C.S.A., first to Sarah Frances Weaver. ALBERT DANGERFIELD REYNOLDS, farmer, age 23, single, b. Westmoreland Co., son of Conway Reynolds and Susan Ann [Weaver],[4] to SARAH FRANCES WEAVER, age 18, single, b. Westmoreland Co., daughter of James A. Weaver and Jane P. [Rose].[5] Signed Albert [his X mark] D. Reynolds, wits. J.W. Hutt, C.C. Baker. License 21 NOV 1866. Married 22 NOV 1866 by G.H. Northam. [M18; R:84; R1:25-11]

Reynolds, Albert Dangerfield, Rev. (1843-1912), second to Lizzie Ann Weaver (1853-1924).[6] ALBERT DANGERFIELD REYNOLDS, farmer, age 24, widowed, b. Westmoreland Co., son of Conway C. Reynolds and Susan A. [Ann Weaver], *q.v.*, to LIZZIE ANN WEAVER, age 16, single, b. Richmond Co., daughter of James A. Weaver and Jane P. [Rose], *q.v.* Signed Albert D. [his X mark] Reynolds, wit. J.W. Harvey. License 4 AUG 1868. Married 6 AUG 1868 by G.H. Northam. [M18; R:92; R1:35-2]

Reynolds, Charles to Susan Sanford. CHARLES REYNOLDS, farmer, age 27, single, b. Richmond Co., son of Edwin [J.] Reynolds and Mary [Mozingo],[7] to SUSAN SANFORD, age 21, single, b. Westmoreland Co., daughter of Lawrence [M.] Sanford and Mary [J. Beale].[8] License 11 JUL 1877. Married 15 JUL 1877 at Lawrence Sanford by R.J. Sanford. [M19; R:122; R1:70-6]

---

[1] Joseph E. Reed and his wife Juliet were buried in New Albin Cemetery, New Albin, Allamakee Co., Iowa.
[2] Henry P. King and Elizabeth N. Dobbins were married by bond 22 FEB 1841 in Westmoreland Co., with James O. King, security.
[3] William R. Reed and his wife Julia A. were buried in Congressional Cemetery, Washington, D.C.
[4] Conway Reynolds and Susan Ann Weaver were married by bond 31 DEC 1842 in Westmoreland Co., with James A. Weaver, security.
[5] James A. Weaver and Jane P. Rose were married by bond 24 NOV 1845 in Westmoreland Co., with Conaway Reynolds, security.
[6] Rev. Albert D. Reynolds and his wife Annie L. were buried at Bethany Baptist Church, Callao, Va.
[7] Edwin J. Reynolds and Mary Mozingo were married 29 DEC 1842 in Richmond Co. by Rev. William N. Ward.
[8] Lawrence M. Sanford and Mary J. Beale, daughter of William L. Beale, were married by bond 14 MAR 1843 in Westmoreland Co., with Willis Garner, security.

Reynolds, Edward to Mary Ann Davis (d. 1893 of heart failure). EDWARD REYNOLDS, sailor, age 23, single, b. Richmond Co., son of Richard and Lina Reynolds, to MARY A. DAVIS, age 22, single, b. Westmoreland Co., daughter of Thomas L. Davis and Ann [Robinson], *q.v.* License 12 AUG 1857. Married 13 AUG 1857 at *Lee Hall* by T. Grayson Dashiell. [DR:95-54; M16a:57-26; R:61; R1:9-13]

Reynolds, James Feriol (1835-1875), to Harriett Susan Mothershead (1843-1912).[1] JAMES FERRYALL REYNOLDS [sic], overseer, age 24, single, b. Westmoreland Co., son of Joseph Reynolds and Martha B. [McKenney], *q.v.*, to HARRIETT S. MOTHERSHEAD, age 16, single, b. Richmond Co., daughter of George and Mary Mothershead. License 8 JUL 1859. Married 10 JUL 1859 at [*Mount Pleasant*] by T. Grayson Dashiell, clergyman. [M16a:59-18 and 18a; R:70; R1:14-13; SC]

Reynolds, Joseph to Anna Ross McGuire. JOSEPH REYNOLDS, farmer, age 24, single, b. Westmoreland Co., res. Northumberland Co., son of Joseph Reynolds and Martha [McKenney], *q.v.*, to ANNA ROSS McGUIRE, age 19, single, b. Westmoreland Co., daughter of Oliver [C.] McGuire and Mariah [Maria G. Mothershead], *q.v.* License 20 DEC 1876. Married 20 DEC 1876 by G.H. Northam. [M19; R:120; R1:67-13]

Reynolds, William Henry to Annie Garner Richardson. WILLIAM HENRY REYNOLDS, farmer, age 22, single, b. Westmoreland Co., son of Joseph Reynolds and Martha [McKenney], *q.v.*, to ANNIE GARNER RICHARDSON, age 25, single, b. Northumberland Co., daughter of Edward [G.] Richardson and Elizabeth [Pursell].[2] Signed Wm. H. [his X mark] Reynolds, wit. C.C. Baker. License 11 MAY 1868. Married 12 MAY 1868 by Elder James A. Weaver. [M18; R:91; R1:33-11]

Rhone (see Roane)

Rice, William H., served in Co. C, 9th Va. Cav., C.S.A., to Maria Ann Barber. WILLIAM H. RICE, farmer, age 27, single, b. Northumberland Co., son of William and Maria Rice, to MARIA ANN BARBER, age 27, single, b. Westmoreland Co., daughter of Thomas Barber and Lucy [Mothershead].[3] License 11 JUL 1856. Married 17 JUL 1856 at the residence of John B. Murphy by H.P.F. King, minister of the Methodist E. Church. [M16a:56-22; R:55; R1:6-4]

Rich, Alexander to Nancy J. Tibbs. ALEXANDER RICH, laborer, age 21, single, b. Westmoreland Co., son of Bladen Tiffey and Fanny Rich now Tate, to NANCY J. TIBBS, age 18, single, b. Westmoreland Co., daughter of Mary Tibbs now Johnson, father unknown. License 25 NOV 1865. Married 25 NOV 1865 at *Woodbury* near Montross, Va. by D.M. Wharton. [M17a:65-11; R:81; R1:22-8]

Rich, Charles (d. testate 1885[4]), to Harriett Cary. License 21 JAN 1851. Married 30 JAN 1851 by John Pullen. [M15:51-8; R:5]

---

[1] J.P. Reynolds and his wife Harriet were buried at Henderson United Methodist Church, Hyacinth, Va.
[2] Edward G. Richardson and Elizabeth Pursell were married by bond 29 JAN 1838 in Northumberland Co., with Peter Self, security.
[3] Thomas Barber and Lucy Mothershead, daughter of Isabella Mothershead, were married by bond 6 NOV 1811 in Westmoreland Co., with James Yeatman, security.
[4] Deeds & Wills No. 45, p. 329, will of Charles Rich, proved 26 JAN 1885, mentions son Hanibal Rich "by my present wife," and children by first wife.

Ritch [or Rich], Charles H. to Ann Carey. License 20 JUL 1853. Married 23 JUL 1853 by George Northam, L.M.G. [M15:53-17; R:31]

Rich, Clabourn to Mrs. Betsy Kelly. CLABOURN RICH, farmer, age 29, widowed, b. Richmond Co., son of Lindsey Rich and Eliza [Tate],[1] to BETSY KELLY, age 25, widow, b. Westmoreland Co., daughter of [H]inson and Attaway Kelly. License 24 JAN 1863. Married 27 JAN 1863 at *Peckatone* by James F. Porter, M.G. [M17:63-1; R:79; R1:19-12]

Rich, Robert to Henrietta Wise Roane. ROBERT RICH, blacksmith, age 50, widowed, b. and res. Richmond Co., son of H. Harford and W. Rich, to HENRIETTA WISE ROANE, age 22, single, b. Westmoreland Co., daughter of John and Lucy Rone [sic]. License 16 DEC 1878. Married 18 DEC 1878 at the residence of the bride by Elder James A. Weaver. [M20; R:127; R1:75-17]

Rich, Tibbs (C) to Elizabeth Ann Newman. TIBBS RICH, farmer, age 21, single, b. Westmoreland Co., son of Charles and Ellen Rich, to ELIZABETH ANN NEWMAN, age 23, single, b. Westmoreland Co., daughter of Francis (C) [d. 1882] and Laurinda Newman. Signed Tibbs [his X mark] Rich, wit. J.W. Hutt. License 1 MAY 1874. Married 3 MAY 1874 by Emanuel Watts, pastor. [DR:56-28[2]; M19; R:113; R1:58-7]

Rich, William (C) to Lucy Taliaferro. WILLIAM RICH, farmer, age 45, widowed, b. Richmond Co., son of Charles and Ellen Rich, to LUCY TALIAFERRO, age 26, single, b. Westmoreland Co., daughter of John Taliaferro. Signed Wm. [his X mark] Rich, wit. Wm. S. McKenney. License 30 DEC 1875. Married 2 JAN 1876 at Little Zion Church by Emanuel Watts, pastor of Little Zion Church. [M19; R:117; R1:63-9]

Richards, Arthur (C) to Mary Frances Fortune (d. 1891). ARTHUR RICHARDS, farmer, age 25, single, b. Essex Co., son of Peter Richards and Sookey [Saunders], to MARY FRANCES FORTUNE, age 21, single, b. Essex Co., daughter of Robert Fortune and Mary [Bird], *q.v.* Signed Arthur [his X mark] Richards, wit. W.S. McKenney. License 12 APR 1871. Married 13 APR 1871 by John Roy, minister. [DR:87-45; M18; R:102; R1:46-14]

Richards, John (C) (d. 1892 of consumption), to Vestilia Byrd. JOHN RICHARDS, farmer, age 29, single, b. Essex Co., son of Peter Richards and Sookey [Saunders],[3] to VESTILIA BYRD, age 35, single, b. Caroline Co., daughter of Martha Byrd. Signed John [his X mark] Richards, wit. W.S. McKenney. License 29 DEC 1873. Married 29 DEC 1873 at Oak Grove, Va. by Emanuel Watts, pastor of Little Zion Church. [DR:92-40; M19; R:111; R1:56-4]

Richards, William (d. by 1868), to Sarah Ann Murphy, daughter of Robert Murphy and Eliza B. [Newton]. License 27 OCT 1852. Married 28 OCT 1852 by E.B. McGuire. [M15:52-25; R:23]

Richardson, Daniel to Letty Johnson. DANIEL RICHARDSON, farmer, age 24, single, b. Westmoreland Co., son of Lucy Richardson, to LETTY JOHNSON, age 22, single, b. Westmoreland Co., daughter of John and Maria Johnson. Signed Daniel [his X mark] Richardson, wits. J.W. Hutt,

---

[1] Linsey Rich and Eliza Tate were married by bond 1 MAY 1823 in Richmond Co., with William R. Jeffries, security.
[2] DR:56-28, entry for Francis Newman (C), laborer, d. 1 JUN 1882 of dropsy, age 60, son of Frederick and Jannie Newman, husband of Laurinda Newman.
[3] Peter Richards and Susan "Sucky" Saunders, daughter of Betty Saunders, were married by bond 19 NOV 1827 in Essex Co.

Frank Sisson. License 26 DEC 1867. Married 26 DEC 1867 by J.H. Davis, Pastor of Westmoreland Circuit, Virginia Conference, M.E. Church. [M18; R:89; R1:31-3]

Roane (a.k.a. Rone), Richard (C) (c.1848-1928),[1] to Lucinda R. Johnson. RICHARD ROAN [sic],[2] farmer, age 22, single, b. Westmoreland Co., son of Thomas Rone and Betsey [Travis] [d. 1874], to LUCINDA R. JOHNSON, age 22, single, b. Westmoreland Co., daughter Armestead and Sarah Johnson. Signed Richard [his X mark] Roan, wit. Ro. F. Parker. License 15 DEC 1869. Married 16 DEC 1869 by Jerry Graham. [DC; DR:30-25[3]; M18; R:96; R1:40-24]

Roane, John Nicholas (C) to Emma Augusta Thompson. JOHN NICHOLAS ROANE, farmer, age 25, single, b. Westmoreland Co., son of John and Lucy Roane, to EMMA AUGUSTA THOMPSON, age 19, single, b. Westmoreland Co., daughter of John and Judy Thompson. Signed John Nicholas [his X mark] Roane, wit. W.S. McKenney. License 21 FEB 1871. Married 23 FEB 1871 by G.W. Beale. [M18; R:101; R1:46-2]

Roane, Thomas (C) (d. 1888[4] of old age), to Frances Pierce. THOMAS RHONE [sic], farmer, age 66, widowed, b. Westmoreland Co., son of Dick and Nelly Rhone [sic], to FRANCES PIERCE, age 35, widow, b. Westmoreland Co., daughter of Henry and Frances Johnson. License 21 DEC 1876. Married 28 DEC 1876 at *Cabin Ford* by F.B. Beale. [DR:76-54; M19; R:121; R1:68-1]

Robb, Spencer (C) to Winnie Vessels. SPENCER ROBB, farmer, age 22, single, b. Essex Co., son of [illegible] and Mittie Robb, to WINNIE VESSELS, age 22, single, b. Essex Co., daughter of James and Delphia Vessels. License 31 MAY 1872. [R:105; R1:50-11]

Robertson, Wilfred (C) to Mrs. Margaret West Taylor. WILFRED ROBERTSON, farmer, age 43, widowed, b. Essex Co., son of Sam. and Milly Robertson, to MARGARET TAYLOR, age 30, widow, b. Westmoreland Co., daughter of Isaac and Emily West. Signed Wilfred [his X mark] Robertson, wit. Wm. S. McKenney. License 31 MAR 1876. Married 2 APR 1876 at Little Zion Church by Emanuel Watts, pastor, Little Zion Church. [M19; R:118; R1:64-12]

Robinson, John to Amanda Jane Drake. JOHN ROBINSON, farmer, age 50, widowed, b. Princess Anne Co., son of William D. and Mary S. Robinson, to AMANDA JANE DRAKE, age 26, single, b. Westmoreland Co., daughter of John and Mary Drake. Married 24 JUL 1867 at the residence of William Weaver by R.N. Reamy. [M18; R1:29-1]

Robinson, Joseph Spence, Dr. (1822-1862), to Mary Susan Rice (1834-1924).[5] JOSEPH S. ROBINSON, physician, age 35, single, b. Westmoreland Co., son of George Robinson and [Sarah Spence] Rice, to MARY SUSAN RICE, age 22, single, b. Westmoreland Co., daughter of John T. Rice and Mary C. Robinson, *q.v.* License 19 SEP 1857. Married 23 SEP 1857 at the residence of John T. Rice by John G. Rowe, M.G. [M16a:57-30; R:61; R1:10-5]

---

[1] Richard Roan was buried at Potomac Baptist Church, Hague, Va.
[2] The surname appears as Rone and Roane.
[3] DR:30-25, entry for Betsy Roane, b. New Kent Co., d. 4 DEC 1874 of tumor on neck, age 50, daughter of Carter Roane and Maria Lewis, wife of Thomas Roane.
[4] Also see Deeds & Wills No. 48, p. 396.
[5] Dr. Joseph S. Robinson and his wife Mary Susan Rice were buried in the Rice Family Cemetery, located on *Laurel Springs Farm* off of Route 202.

Rock, James Andrew to Florence Hugh Ella George. JAMES ANDREW ROCK, farmer, age 30, single, b. Richmond Co., son of James Rock and Sarah [Ann Hardwick], *q.v.*, to FLORENCE HUGH ELLA GEORGE, age 18, single, b. Westmoreland Co., daughter of P.C. [Philander Chinn] George and Ann E. [Atwill], *q.v.* License 23 OCT 1876. Married 24 OCT 1876 at Philander C. George's by John W. White. [M19; R:119; R1:66-9]

Rogers, John to Catharine Trigger. JOHN ROGERS, farmer, age 45, widowed, b. and res. King George Co., son of Major and Elizabeth Rogers, to CATHARINE TRIGER [sic], age 26, single, b. Westmoreland Co., daughter of William and Byram Trig[g]er. License 19 SEP 1878. Married 21 SEP 1878 at Oak Grove Church by F.W. Claybrook. [M19; R:126; R1:75-2]

Rollings, John Francis to Malinda Cook. JOHN FRANCIS ROLLINGS, shoemaker, age 28, widowed, b. Caroline Co., res. King George Co., son of John T.A. and Peggy Rolling, to MALINDA COOK, age 25, single, b. Westmoreland Co., daughter of Austin and Ann Cook. License 10 JUL 1866. Married 15 JUL 1866 at Malinda Cook's by John Pullen. [M18; R:83; R1:24-11]

Roley [or Rolling], Thomas to Virginia S. Allensworth. THOMAS ROLEY, farming, age 24, single, b. King George Co., son of William and Sally Roley [Rolling], to VIRGINIA S. ALLENSWORTH, age 29, single, b. King George Co., daughter of Henry Allensworth and Mildred [Rolling].[1] Signed Thomas [his X mark] Roley, wit. Wm. S. McKenney. License 17 OCT 1871. Married 22 OCT 1871 at the residence of Vinton A. Dickenson by Howard W. Montague, M.G. [M18; R:103; R1:47-16]

Rose, George Julius (1849-1909), to Lucinda "Lucy" Wilkins (1851-1925).[2] GEORGE JULIUS ROSE, engineering, age 26, single, b. King George Co., res. York Co., Pa., son of Horace Rose and Eliza [Ann Crismond],[3] to LUCINDA WILKINS, age 20, single, b. Westmoreland Co., daughter of Mathew Wilkins and Lucretia [Atkins], *q.v.* Signed Geo. J. [his X mark] Rose. License 22 OCT 1873. Married 23 OCT 1873 at Mathew Wilkins' by Robert N. Reamy. [M19; R:109; R1:54-12]

Rose, Hannibal (d. 1883 of malaria) to Mary "Polly" Chambers. HANIBAL ROSE [sic], laborer, age 23, single, b. Westmoreland Co., son of John and Judy Rose, to MARY CHAMBERS, age 16, single, b. Westmoreland Co., daughter of [Thomas] Chambers and Patsy [Astin].[4] License 12 DEC 1872. Married 12 DEC 1872 by H.H. Fones. [DR:58-84; M19; R:107; R1:52-1]

Rose, William Washington, Dr. (d. 1862), served in Cos. C and I, 9th Va. Cav., C.S.A., to Catharine "Kate" Corbin Taliaferro. WILLIAM WASHINGTON ROSE, physician, age 30, single, b. Alexandria, Va., res. King George Co., son of Alexander M. Rose and Anna A. [Smith],[5] to CATHARINE CORBIN TALIAFERRO, age 27, single, b. Westmoreland Co., daughter of William F. and Mary W. Taliaferro [of *Peckatone*]. License 8 OCT 1860. Married 9 OCT 1860 [at *Peckatone*] by Rev. E.B. McGuire. [M17:60-34; R:74; SC]

---

[1] Henry Allensworth and Mildred Rolling were married 18 JUL 1815 in King George Co.
[2] George Rose and his wife Lucy were buried at St. Peter's Cemetery, Oak Grove, Va.
[3] Horace Rose and Eliza Ann Crismond were married 25 MAR 1845 in King George Co. by Rev. John McDaniel.
[4] Thomas Chambers and Patsy Astin were married by bond 8 JAN 1827 in Westmoreland Co., with Rodham Astin, security.
[5] Christine Rose, *Ancestors and Descendants of The Brothers Rev. Robert Rose and Rev. Charles Rose of Colonial Virginia and Wester Alves, Morayshire, Scotland* (San Jose, Calif.: Rose Family Association, 1985), p. 256, Alexander M. Rose and Anna A. Smith were married 28 FEB 1826 in Fairfax Co. by Rev. William H. Wilmer. Anna A. Rose, widow of Alexander M., died 14 SEP 1853 in her 50th year, and was buried at Emanuel Episcopal Church, King George Co.

Rowand, Thomas to Emily Susan McCoy. THOMAS ROWAND, farmer, age 27, single, b. Westmoreland Co., son of Thomas and Mary Rowand, to EMILY SUSAN McCOY, age 18, single, b. Westmoreland Co., daughter of Rody McCoy and Agness [Douglass], *q.v.* License 30 SEP 1867. Married 3 OCT 1867 at Rody McCoy's by J.H. Davis. [M18; R:87; R1:29-10]

Rowe, Andrew Jackson to Martha Susan Bartlett. ANDREW JACKSON ROWE, waterman, age 25, single, b. Westmoreland Co., son of Henry and Jane Rowe, to MARTHA SUSAN BARTLETT, age 20, single, b. Westmoreland Co., daughter of Samuel and Mahaly Bartlett. License 23 DEC 1874. Married 24 DEC 1874 at George Rowe's by Robert N. Reamy. [M19; R:114; R1:60-2]

Rowe, George Washington (1845-1930), served in Co. E, 55th Va. Inf., C.S.A., first to Mary Ann Oliff (d. 1892 age 45).[1] GEORGE WASHINGTON ROWE, sailor, age 24, single, b. Westmoreland Co., son of John Rowe and Lucy Ann [Davis], to MARY ANN OLIFF, age 22, single, b. Richmond Co., daughter of William and Sophia Oliff.* License 22 DEC 1869. Married 23 DEC 1869 by G.H. Northam. [DC; DR:90-13[2]; M18; R:97; R1:40-30]

Rowe, James Augustus to Emmaline Jenkins. JAMES AUGUSTUS ROWE, oysterman, age 23, single, b. Westmoreland Co., son of John Rowe and Lucy [Ann Davis], to EMMALINE JENKINS, age 20, single, b. Westmoreland Co., daughter of Martha Jenkins, father unknown. License 23 FEB 1880. Married 26 MAY 1880 at the groom's brother's by Elder James A. Weaver. [M20; R:132; R1:81-8]

Roy, John to Susan Smith. JOHN ROY, farmer, age 21, single, b. Essex Co., son of John and Eliza Roy, to SUSAN SMITH, age 17, single, b. Essex Co., daughter of Tuns[tall] Smith and Jane [Robb], *q.v.* Signed John [his X mark] Roy, wit. J.H. Sisson. License 24 NOV 1869. Married 2 DEC 1869 by Robert N. Reamy. [M18; R:96; R1:39-15]

Roy, Moses to Harriet Braxton (1865-1924). MOSES ROY, farmer, age 21, single, b. Essex Co., son of William and Mary Roy, to HARRIET BRAXTON, age 19, single, b. Essex Co., daughter of [Bartlett Epps and] Phillis Braxton. Signed Moses [his X mark] Roy, wit. J.W. Hutt, Wm. Green. License 30 MAY 1868. Married 31 MAY 1868 by Robt. N. Reamy. [DC; M18; R:91; R1:34-2]

Roy, Thomas (C) to Fanny Lee. THOMAS LEE, laborer, age 22, single, b. Essex Co., son of John and Eliza Roy, to FANNY LEE, age 22, single, b. Essex Co., daughter of Thomas and Clara Lee. Signed Thomas [his X mark] Roy, wit. W.S. McKenney. License 20 DEC 1873. Married 21 DEC 1873 by John Roy. [M19; R:110; R1:55-10]

Roy, William (C) to Fanny Miles. WILLIAM ROY, farmer, age 23, single, b. Essex Co., son of John and Eliza Roy, to FANNY MILES, age 22, single, b. Essex Co., daughter of Mary Miles, father unknown. Signed William [his X mary] Roy, wit. W.S. McKenney. License 20 DEC 1873. Married 23 DEC 1873 by John Roy. [M19; R:110; R1:55-11]

Roye, William, Jr. (d. 1934) to Martha Ann Lomax (C). WILLIAM ROYE, JR., laborer, age 21, single, b. Essex Co., son of Wm., Sr. [d. 1887 of dysentery] and Jane Roye, to MARTHA ANN LOMAX, age 21, single, b. Westmoreland Co., daughter of Joshua and Sarah Lomax. License 30

[1] George W. Rowe and his wife Mary A. Oliff were buried in the Rowe Family Cemetery, located near the intersection of Routes 606 and 693, now at Currioman Baptist Church, Chiltons, Va.
[2] DR:90-13, entry for Mary A. Rowe, d. 25 JUL 1892, age 45, * daughter of Carter and Mary Oliff, wife of Geo. W. Rowe.

JUN 1880. Married 1 JUL 1880 near Foneswood, by Wm. C. Latane, Presbyter P.E. Church. [DR:74-173; M20; R:134; R1:83-6; WP]

Rust, Charles to Maria Gordon. CHARLES RUST, farmer, age 38, single, b. Westmoreland Co., son of Samuel and Catherine Rust, to MARIA GORDON, age 31, single, b. Westmoreland Co., daughter of [Levi] Gordon. License 29 AUG 1870. Planned marriage 1 SEP 1870. [R:99; R1:43-14 no return]

S

Sanders, Lovell (d. 1899), to Philista Mothershead. License 21 NOV 1851. Married 25 NOV 1851 by John Pullen. [M15:51-24; NN; R:11]

Sanders, Samuel Miskel (b. 1836, d. 1912 at Newland, Va.), served in Co. D, 40th Va. Inf., C.S.A., second to Charlotte Maria Minor (1843-1899).[1] SAMUEL MISKEL SANDERS, farmer, age 29, single [sic], b. and res. Richmond Co., son of James L. and Margaret Sanders, to CHARLOTTE MARIA MINOR, age 20, single, b. Westmoreland Co., daughter of Beverly Minor and Lucy B. [McKenney].[2] License 6 JUN 1866. Married 6 JUN 1866 by Elder James A. Weaver. [M18; R:83; R1:24-5]

Sanders [or Saunders], Thomas to Mrs. Frances Grissett. THOMAS SANDERS, farmer, age 44, single, b. Westmoreland Co., son of William and Polly Sanders, to FRANCES GRISSET [sic], age 32, widow, b. Westmoreland Co., parents unknown. License 7 JAN 1862. Married 9 JAN 1862 at the residence of bridegroom Thomas Sanders by Thomas E. Locke. [M17:62-6; R:78; R1:18-10; WP gives Saunders]

Sanders, Warner (C) to Charlotte Mercer. WARNER SANDERS, laborer, age 21, single, b. Westmoreland Co., son of Agy Rich, father unknown, to CHARLOTTE MERCER, age 27, single, b. Essex Co., daughter of Killis and Rachel Mercer. License 14 MAY 1880. Married 15 MAY 1880 at *Haywood* by Wm. C. Latane, Presbyter P.E. Church. [M20; R:133; R1:82-12; WP]

Sandford (see Sanford)

Sandy, John Edward (d. 1891), served in Co. G, 15th Va. Cav., C.S.A., to Mrs. Mary Catharine Thompson Eliff (d. 1887 of dropsy). JOHN EDWARD SANDY, carpenter, age 34, single, b. and res. Richmond Co., son of Samuel O. Sandy and Elizabeth [Pullen],[3] to MARY CATHARINE ELIFF, age 22, widow, b. King George Co., daughter of William D. Thompson and Ellen [Moxley].[4] License 20 MAR 1873. Married 20 MAR 1873 by G.H. Northam. [DR:72-53; M19; NN; R:108; R1:53-15]

Sandy, John Slicer (d. 1873), served in Co. A, 15th Va. Cav., the 47th and 55th Va., Inf.,C.S.A., to Mrs. Ella Dorsey Fauntleroy Sandford. JOHN SLICER SANDY, farmer, age 34, single, b. Richmond Co., son of John Sandy and Frances R. [Sandford],[5] to ELLA DORSEY SANDFORD,

---

[1] Samuel M. Sanders and his second wife Charlotte M. were buried at Rappahannock Baptist Church, Newland, Va.

[2] Beverly Minor and Lucinda B. McKenney were married by bond 27 APR 1835 in Westmoreland Co., with James McKenney, security.

[3] Samuel Sandy and Elizabeth Pullen were married by bond 8 JAN 1822 in Richmond Co., with Thomas Howe, security.

[4] William D. Thompson and Ellen Moxley were married 14 FEB 1850 in King George Co. by Rev. John McDaniel.

[5] John Sandy and Fanny R. Sandford were married by bond 27 OCT 1819 in Richmond Co., consent by Edward Sandford, with Lemuel G. Sandy, security.

age 31, widow, b. Richmond Co., daughter of Robert and Ann L. Fauntleroy. Signed by both parties. License 22 FEB 1871. Married 23 FEB 1871 by Walter C. Taylor. [M18; R:101; R1:46-4]

Sanford, Adolphus Spence (b. 1842, d. 1931 in D.C.), served Co. K., 40th Va. Inf., C.S.A., to Arnetta Joan Sanford (1842-1915).[1] ADOLPHUS SPENCE SANFORD, farmer, age 23, single, b. Westmoreland Co., son of Richard C. [Corbin] Sanford [d. 1888] and Eliza James Sanford, to ARNETTA SANFORD, age 24, single, b. Westmoreland Co., daughter of Henry Sanford, mother unknown. License 26 DEC 1865. Married 28 DEC 1865 at the home of Hiram S. King by W.W. Walker. [DR:76-56[2]; M18; R:82; R1:22-13]

Sanford, Alfred to Mrs. Susanna Kinzer McClelland. ALFRED SANDFORD [sic], farmer, age 35, single, b. Westmoreland Co., son of Ethelwald Sandford and Sally [M. Robinson],[3] to SUSANNA McCLELLAND, age 26, widow, b. Lancaster Co., Pa., daughter of Henry and Catharine Kinzer. License 10 SEP 1856. Married 11 SEP 1856 at Andrew Chapel by H.P.F. King, minister of the M.E. Church. [M16a:56-26, R:57; R1:6-12]

Sanford, Charles Henry (1846-1920), served in Co. A, 15th Va. Cav., C.S.A., to Sarah Frances Omohundro (1847-1911).[4] CHARLES HENRY SANFORD, farmer, age 22, single, b. Westmoreland Co., son of Thomas Sanford and Adaline [Reamy],[5] to SARAH FRANCIS OMOHUNDRO [sic], age 21, single, b. Westmoreland Co., daughter of John R. [Richard] Omohundro and Elizabeth [Crask], *q.v.* License 5 JAN 1869. Married 5 JAN 1869 at the residence of Mrs. S.T. Hunter by J.H. Davis. [M18; R:94; R1:37-6]

Sanford, Edward Templeman to Sarah Ann Beale. EDWARD TEMPLEMAN SANFORD, laborer, age 51, widowed, b. Westmoreland Co., son of Patrick S. Sanford and Hannah [Butler],[6] to SARAH ANN BEALE, age 21, widowed, b. Richmond Co., daughter of Fanny Gordon, father unknown. Consent 14 MAR 1860 by Sarah Ann [her X mark] Beale, wits. Benjamin S. English and Sarah E. Middleton. License 17 MAR 1860. Married 18 MAR 1860 at the residence of Mrs. Middleton by J.W. Miller, M.G. [M17:60-18, 18a, 18b; R:74; R1:17-11]

Sanford, George Lindsey (d. 1883), served in Co. C, 47th Va. Inf., C.S.A., to Margaret Ann Weaver (b. 1856).[7] GEORGE LINDSEY SANFORD, farmer, age 27, single, b. Westmoreland Co., son of Thomas Sanford [d. 1883 of heart disease] and Adaline [Reamy], *q.v.*, to MARGARET ANN WEAVER, age 16, single, b. Westmoreland Co., daughter of John Weaver [d. testate 1890[8]] and Emily [Maria Bragg], *q.v.* License 11 NOV 1869. Married 11 NOV 1869 by G. Wm. Beale. [DR:58-95 and 96; M18; R:96; R1:39-10]

Sanford, Gerard, served in Co. A, 15th Va. Cav., C.S.A., to Ann Elizabeth Montgomery (1818-1903).[9] GERARD SANFORD, merchant, age 32, single, b. Westmoreland Co., son of Gerard [A.]

---

[1] Adolphus S. Sanford and his wife Aretta were buried at Carmel United Methodist Church, Kinsale, Va.
[2] DR:76-56, entry for Richard C. Sanford, d. 15 JUN 1888 of consumption, age 78, son of Spence and Margaret Sanford, father of A.S. Sanford.
[3] Ethelwald Sandford and Sally M. Robinson were married by bond 29 MAY 1819 in Westmoreland Co., with Thomas S. Muse, security.
[4] Charles H. Sanford and his wife Sarah were buried at Providence United Methodist Church, Chiltons, Va.
[5] Thomas Sanford and Adeline Reamy were married by bond 15 FEB 1834 in Westmoreland Co., with William Johnson, security.
[6] Patrick S. Sanford and Hannah Butler were married by bond 30 OCT 1818 in Westmoreland Co., with Francis Self, security.
[7] George L. Sanford and his wife Margaret Ann were buried in the Weaver-Sanford Family Cemetery, located off of Route 645.
[8] Deeds & Wills No. 49, p. 49, will of John Weaver, proved 24 FEB 1890, names daughter Margaret Ann Sanford.
[9] Ann E. Sanford was buried at Nomini Baptist Church, Montross, Va.

Sanford and Sibe [Sebina B. Jenkins],[1] to A. ELIZABETH MONTGOMERY, age 28, single, b. Westmoreland Co., daughter of Robert T. and E.J. Montgomery [d. 1851].[2] License 20 MAY 1857. Married 21 MAY 1857 at Templeman's X Roads by G.H. Northam, minister of the Baptist persuasion. [M16a:57-14; R:61; R1:9-5]

Sanford, Henry Harrison (a.k.a. William Henry H.) (1840-1920),[3] served in Co. E, 55th Va. Inf., C.S.A., to Sarah Lydia Ann Frances Bryant. HENRY HARRISON SANFORD, farmer, age 29, single, b. Westmoreland Co., son of William J. [James] Sanford and Frances [F. Holbrook],[4] to LIDIA ANN FRANCES BRYANT, age 20, single, b. Westmoreland Co., daughter of Catharine Bryant. Signed Henry H. [his X mark] Sanford, wit. J.W. Hutt. License 12 JAN 1871. Married 12 JAN 1871 by H.H. Fones. [M18; R:101; R1:45-9]

Sanford, John L. (d. 1886 of brain fever), to Annie Belle McGuire. JOHN L. SANFORD, farmer, age 32, single, b. Westmoreland Co., son of William J. [James] Sanford and Frances F. [Holbrook], *q.v.*, to ANNIE BELLE McGUIRE, age 22, single, b. Westmoreland Co., daughter of John McGuire and Julia A. [Ann Mothershead].[5] License 28 MAR 1871. Married 30 MAR 1871 by G.H. Northam. [DR:69-83; M18; R:102; R1:46-13]

Sanford, John Richard to Martha Clarke. JOHN RICHARD SANFORD, farmer, age 27, single, son of [Richard] Corbin Sanford and Eliza [James], to MARTHA CLARKE, age 27, widow, b. England, daughter of John R. and Clara Clarke. License 24 JAN 1879. Married 26 JAN 1879 at Carmel Church by R.J. Sanford. [M20; R:128; R1:76-13]

Sanford, Lemuel (1844-1925), to Rebecca Hall Moxley (1851-1891).[6] LEMUEL SANFORD, age 28, single, b. Westmoreland Co., son of Robert [C.] Sanford and [Delia] Mahala [Miller],[7] to REBECCA HALL MOXLEY, age 21, single, b. Westmoreland Co., daughter of Richard Moxley and Rebecca Ann [Stone].[8] License 13 JAN 1873. Married 15 JAN 1873 at the residence of the bride's father by D.G.C. Butts. [M19; R:108; R1:52-16]

Sanford, Lewis H. to Sarah Luevennia Rowe (1846-1820).[9] LEWIS SANFORD, farmer, age 58, widowed, b. Westmoreland Co., son of Daniel Sanford and Mary [Weaver],[10] to SARAH LIVINIA ROWE, age 25, single, b. Westmoreland Co., daughter of John Rowe and Lucy Ann [Davis]. License 18 DEC 1871. Married 21 DEC 1871 at Mrs. Rowe's by H.H. Fones. [M18; R:104; R1:48-9]

Sanford, Lucius E., first to Willie Ann Sisson (1829-1859). LUCIUS E. SANFORD, coach maker, age 24, single, b. Westmoreland Co., son of Ethelwald Sanford and Sarah M. [Robinson], *q.v.*, to WILLIE ANN SISSON, age 23, single, b. Westmoreland Co., daughter of William R. Sisson and Ann

---

[1] Gerard A. Sanford and Sebina B. Jenkins were married by bond 18 OCT 1820 in Westmoreland Co., with M.M. Marmaduke, security.
[2] SP: Burials, p. 31 and WP. Mrs. Robert Montgomery, aged thirty years, buried at Bluff Point in February 1851.
[3] Henry H. Sanford was buried at Providence United Methodist Church, Chiltons, Va.
[4] William J. Sanford and Fanny Holbrook were married by bond 12 AUG 1830 in Westmoreland Co., with Thomas Belfield, security.
[5] John McGuire and Julia Ann Mothershead were married by bond 10 MAR 1834 in Westmoreland Co., with William McGuire, security.
[6] Lemuel Sanford and his wife Rebecca A.H. Moxley were buried in the Sanford Family Cemetery at Nomini Grove, Va. near a grain elevator.
[7] Robert Sanford and Mahala Miller were married by bond 24 JUL 1837 in Westmoreland Co., with Granville White, security.
[8] Richard Moxley and Ann R. Stone were married by bond 22 NOV 1841 in Westmoreland Co., with James C. Harvey, security.
[9] Luevennia Sanford was buried at Providence United Methodist Church, Chiltons, Va.
[10] Daniel Sanford and Mary Weaver were married by bond 15 SEP 1812 in Westmoreland Co., with James Anthony, security.

[E. Harvey].[1] License 4 MAR 1856. Married 4 MAR 1856 at Andrew Chapel by H.P.F. King, minister of the M.E. Church. [DC; M16:56-7; R:53; R1:5-6]

Sanford, Richard Edward (b. 1800, d. testate 1892[2]), second to Frances Ann Sydnor (1832-1904),[3] daughter of Richard B. Sydnor and Elizabeth Wright.[4] RICHARD SANDFORD [sic], to FRANCES ANN SYDNOR. License 26 JAN 1853. Married 27 JAN 1853 by John Godwin. [M15:53-4; NN; R:27]

Sanford, Robert Andrew, served in Co. C, 9th Va. Cav., C.S.A., to Fenton Rebeca Beale. ROBERT ANDREW SANDFORD [sic], sailor, age 22, single, b. Westmoreland Co., son of Edward T. Sanford and Lydia [Boothe],[5] to FENTON REBECCA BEALE, age 21, single, b. Westmoreland Co., daughter of Thornton and Eliza Beale. License 4 JUN 1868. Married 6 JUN 1868 at *The Narrows* by J.H. Davis. [M18; R:91; R1:34-4]

Sanford, Robert C. (1816-1902),[6] second to Elizabeth Ann Eliff (d. 1869). ROBERT SANFORD, farming, age 39, widower, b. Westmoreland Co., son of Daniel Sanford and Mary [Weaver], *q.v.*, to ELIZABETH ANN ELIFF, age 16, single, b. Westmoreland Co., daughter of Henry Eliff and Frances [Stone], *q.v.* License 14 MAY 1856. Married 15 MAY 1856 by H.P.F. King, minister of the M.E. Church. [M16:56-15; R:55; R1:5-11]

Sanford, Robert C. (1816-1902), third to Lucinda T. Sanford (b. 1847, d. 1881 of consumption). ROBERT SANFORD, merchant, age 54, widowed, b. Westmoreland Co., son of Daniel Sanford and Mary [Weaver], *q.v.*, to LUCINDA T. SANFORD, age 23, single, b. Westmoreland Co., daughter of William [A.] and [Lucinda] Lucy Sanford. License 27 JUL 1870. Married 27 JUL 1870 by G.H. Northam. [DR:50-21; M18; R:99; R1:43-12]

Sanford, Robert James, Rev., M.D. (b. 1822, d. testate 1889[7] of typhoid fever),[8] served in Co. 2, 111th Va. Mil. and Co. B, 40th Va. Inf., C.S.A., *q.v.*, to Ellen Harvey Bailey (d. 1892). ROBERT J. SANFORD, physician, age 31, single, b. Westmoreland Co., son of Robert Sanford and Eliza [B. Harvey], to ELLEN H. BAILEY, age 23, single, b. Westmoreland Co., daughter of Stephen G. and Harriet Bailey. License 13 NOV 1854. Married 16 NOV 1854 at the residence of Stephen G. Bailey by H.P.F. King of the M.E. Church. [DR:82-179, 91-62; M15:54-14; NN; R:45; R1:2]

Sanford, Walter Alexander to Victoria Cleopatra Gawen. WALTER ALEXANDER SANFORD, farmer, age 24, single, b. Westmoreland Co., son of [Richard] Corbin Sanford and Eliza [James], *q.v.*, to VICTORIA CLEOPATRA GAWEN, age 19, single, b. Westmoreland Co., daughter of William [Presley] Gawen and Elizabeth [Ann Murphy], *q.v.* License 10 MAR 1880. Married 11 MAR 1880 at Carmel Church by R.J. Sanford. [M20; R:132; R1:81-14]

---

[1] William R. Sisson and Ann E. Harvey were married by bond 24 MAY 1825 in Westmoreland Co., with Joseph F. Harvey, security.
[2] Deeds & Wills No. 51, p. 198, will of Richard Sandford of Cople District, proved 25 JUL 1892, names wife Frances, sons Ethelwald, George M. and Richard. He was buried at Ebenezer United Methodist Church, Oldhams, Va.
[3] Frances Ann Sydnor Sanford was buried in the Sanford Family Cemetery, located off of Route 600 at Oldhams, Va.
[4] Richard Sydnor and Eliza Wright were married by bond 16 JUL 1821 in Richmond Co., with George M. Wright, security.
[5] Edward T. Sanford and Lydia Boothe were married by bond 17 DEC 1834 in Westmoreland Co., with Presley McKenney, security.
[6] Robert C. "Bob" Sanford and three of his four wives were buried in the Reed-Sanford Family Cemetery, located off of Route 643 near Route 622.
[7] Deeds & Wills No. 49, p. 342, will of Robert J. Sanford, proved 25 AUG 1890, names wife Ellen H. Sanford and five children.
[8] Rev. R.J. Sanford was buried at Carmel United Methodist Church, Kinsale, Va.

Sanford, William Hartwell, Jr. (1849-1933), first to Emma Bland Edwards (b. 1851, d. 1885 of consumption).[1]   WILLIAM HEARTWELL SANFORD [sic], merchant, age 23, single, b. Westmoreland Co., son of [Col.] William H. [Hartwell] Sanford [d. testate 1875[2] of old age] and M.J. [Mary Jane Sandy] [1829-1887], to EMMA BLAND EDWARDS, age 20, single, b. Westmoreland Co., daughter of William Edwards and Josepha [Jones] (now Josepha Crabbe). License 6 NOV 1872. Married 7 NOV 1872 at *Nomini Grove* by G.H. Northam. [DR:34-97[3], 62-1; M19; R:106; R1:51-9]

Saunders, James (C) to Willie Ann White. JAMES SAUNDERS, fisherman, age 23, widowed, b. Westmoreland Co., son of M. and C. Saunders, to WILLIE ANN WHITE, age 23, widow, b. Westmoreland Co., daughter of John and Emma White. License 8 APR 1880. Married 8 APR 1880 at the rectory, Cople Parish, by Pendleton Brooke, P.E. Ch. [M20; R:133; R1:82-4]

Saunders, Richard Templeman (d. 1884 of pneumonia), served in Co. C, 47th Va. Inf., C.S.A., to Mary Ella Vickers. RICHARD TEMPLEMAN SAUNDERS, merchant, age 33, single, b. Westmoreland Co., son of John Saunders [d. 1882 of pneumonia] and Mary [Reamy] [d. 1882 of pneumonia], to MARY ELLA VICKERS, age 22, single, b. Richmond Co., daughter of Thomas and Elizabeth Vickers. License 30 APR 1874. Married 30 APR 1874 at John Saunders' by Robert N. Reamy. [DR:56-37 and 38, 63-173; M19; R:113; R1:58-6]

Saunders, Washington to Margaret Pierce, colored persons. WASHINGTON SAUNDERS, farmer, age 21, single, b. Westmoreland Co., son of Washington and Scilla Saunders, to MARGARET PIERCE, age 21, single, b. Westmoreland Co., daughter of Wallis and Nancy Pierce. Signed Washington [his X mark] Saunders, wit. J.H. Sisson. License 23 DEC 1869. Married 26 DEC 1869 at Quarter on Dr. Ditty's farm by Thomas E. Locke, Rector, Washington Parish. [M18; R:97; R1:41-34; WP]

Scates, James Madison (b. 1836, d. 1884 at Newland, Va.),[4] served in Co. D, 40th Va. Inf., C.S.A., first to Arnetta Virginia Minor. JAMES MADISON SCATES, house carpenter, age 23, single, b. Richmond Co., son of John B. [Bartlett] Scates and Elizabeth [Marks],[5] to ARITER VIRGINIA MINOR [sic], age 24, single, b. Westmoreland Co., daughter of Beverly Minor and Lucy [Lucinda B. McKenney].[6] License 7 JAN 1860. Married 12 JAN 1860 by G.H. Northam. [M17:60-1 and 1a; R:72; R1:16-9]

Scott, Edgar to Frances S. Yeatman. EDGAR SCOTT, farmer, age 22, single, b. Richmond Co., son of John and Emily Scott, to FRANCES S. YEATMAN, age 18, single, b. Westmoreland Co., son of Joseph Yeatman and Mary Ann [Dameron].[7] Signed Edgar [his X mark] Scott, wit. Wm. S. McKenney. License 25 FEB 1876. Married 27 FEB 1876 at *Woodbine* by G.H. Northam. [M19; R:118; R1:64-9]

---

[1] William Hartwell Sanford and his wife Emma Bland Edwards were buried at Nomini Baptist Church, Montross, Va.
[2] Deeds & Wills No. 40, p. 142, will of W.H. Sanford, proved 22 MAR 1875, names wife Mary Jane and son William Hartwell Sanford.
[3] Tombstone at Nomini Baptist Church, Montross, Va., gives her death year 1885.
[4] James M. Scates was buried at Rappahannock Baptist Church, Newland, Va.
[5] John B. Scates and Betsy Marks were married by bond 10 MAR 1830 in Richmond Co., with Newby Berrick, security.
[6] Beverly Minor and Lucinda B. McKenney were married by bond 27 APR 1835 in Westmoreland Co., with James McKenney, security.
[7] Joseph Yeatman and Mary Ann Dameron were married by bond 1 JUN 1849 in Westmoreland Co., with William A. Spence, security.

Scott, James Montague to Mary Ann Moxley. JAMES MONTAGUE SCOTT, farmer, age 27, single, b. Richmond Co., son of James [T.] Scott and Frances [Sandy],[1] to MARY ANN MOXLEY, age 24, single, b. Westmoreland Co., daughter of Richard Moxley and Rebecca [Ann Stone], *q.v.* License 13 JAN 1874. Married 14 JAN 1874 by H.H. Fones. [M19; R:111; R1:56-14]

Scott, Lewis Frederick, served in Co. A, 15th Va. Cav., C.S.A., to Mrs. Emily Franklin Anthony (d. 1888 of tumor), widow of John Anthony, *q.v.* LEWIS FREDERICK SCOTT, farmer, age 30, single, b. Richmond Co., son of Thomas and Mary Scott, to EMILY ANTHONY, age 39, widow, b. Westmoreland Co., daughter of Thomas and Louisa Franklin [sic]. License 20 MAR 1867. Married 21 MAR 1867 by G.H. Northam. [DR:77-105; M18; R:86; R1:27-14]

Scott, Thomas to Malia Mazaro. License 8 DEC 1851. [R:13 no return]

Scott, Tolbert [or Talbert] (1842-1906),[2] served in Co. D, 40th Va. Inf., C.S.A., to Annie Hamilton Wilson. TOLBERT SCOTT, farmer, age 3[3], single, b. Westmoreland Co., res. Richmond Co., son of James [T.] Scott and Frances [Sandy], *q.v.*, to ANNIE HAMILTON WILSON, age 21, single, b. Westmoreland Co., daughter of Robert Wilson and Frances [Bennett].[3] License 21 JAN 1875. Married 21 JAN 1875 by G.H. Northam. [M19; R:114; R1:60-15]

Scrimger, James Washington (1827-1907),[4] second[5] to Frances Lucetta Saunders. JAMES WASHINGTON SCRIMGER, farmer, age 44, widowed, b. Richmond Co., son of James and Sarah Scrimger,[6] to FRANCES LUCETTA SAUNDERS, age 24, single, b. Richmond Co., daughter of Zachariah [Saunders] and Margaret Ann [Oliffe].[7] License 27 SEP 1871. Married 28 SEP 1871 at Zachariah Saunders' by Robert N. Reamy. [M18; R:103; R1:47-12]

Self, Compton Sewell (1846-1923),[8] to Bettie Courtney. COMPSON S. SELF, farmer, age 24, single, b. Westmoreland Co., son of [James Walter] Waddy Self and Lucy [S. Brann],[9] to BETTIE COURTNEY, age 24, single, b. Westmoreland Co., daughter of Malachi Courtney and Mary [Brown].[10] License 4 JAN 1873. Married 5 JAN 1873 by R.J. Sanford. [M19; R:107; R1:52-13]

Self, Moses (d. 1877), to Mrs. Mahala Reamy. MOSES SELF, age 55, b. Westmoreland Co., son of Coley and Debie Self, to MAHALA REAMY, age 50, widow, b. Mathews Co., parents unknown. License 17 AUG 1857. Married 20 AUG 1857 by H.P.F. King, minister of the M.E. Church. [DR:40-90; M16a:57-28; R:61; R1:10-13]

Self, Moses to Mrs. Sarah Yeatman Saunders. MOSES SELF, farmer, age 70, widower, b. Westmoreland Co., son of Coly and Deby Self, to SARAH SAUNDERS, age 40, widow, birthplace unknown, daughter of Jennings Yeatman, [mother] unknown. Signed Moses [his X mark] Self, wit.

---

[1] James T. Scott and Fanny Sandy were married by bond 5 JUL 1820 in Richmond co., with John Davis, security.
[2] Tolbert Scott, U.S. Army, is memorialized at Nomini Baptist Church, Montross, Va.
[3] Robert Wilson and Frances Bennett were married by bond 10 JAN 1850 in Westmoreland Co., with James Johnson, security.
[4] James W. Scrimger was buried at Currioman Baptist Church, Chiltons, Va.
[5] DR:19-9, entry for Adaline Scrimger, d. 15 MAR 1871 of liver constipation, age 45, daughter of Henry and Hannah Miskell, wife of James W. Scrimger.
[6] James Scrimsher and Sarah Fowler, widow, were married by bond 7 JAN 1811 in Richmond Co., with Peter N. Morgan, security.
[7] Zachariah Sanders and Margaret A. Oliffe were married by bond 9 DEC 1844 in Westmoreland Co., with James S. Weaver, security.
[8] Compton S. Self was buried in Bethel Cemetery, Alexandria, Va.
[9] Walter D. Self and Lucy S. Brann were married by bond 15 APR 1845 in Westmoreland Co., with Robert M. Self, security.
[10] Malachi Courtney and Mary Brown were married by bond 15 AUG 1826 in Westmoreland Co., with William Courtney, security.

J.W. Hutt. License 3 NOV 1868. Married 5 NOV 1868 at the residence of Charles Weaver by H.P.F. King. [M18; R:92; R1:35-11]

Self, Samuel Harris to Willie Ann Douglass. SAMUEL HARRIS SELF, farmer, age 33, b. Westmoreland Co., son of Stephen Self and Eliza [Lewis],[1] to WILLIE ANN DOUGLASS, age 31, single, b. Westmoreland Co., daughter of R. and Judy Douglass. License 5 JAN 1867. Planned marriage 12 JAN 1867. [R:85; R1:26-12]

Settle, John Alexander (1845-1908), served in the 9th Va. Cav., C.S.A., first[2] to Laura Priscilla Hall. JOHN ALEXANDER SETTLE, miller, age 23, single, b. and res. Richmond Co., son of Frederick Settle [1819-1902] and [his first wife] Diana<u>h</u> [T. Claughton] [1820-1883], to LAURA PRISCILLA HALL, age 20, single, b. Westmoreland Co., daughter of William B. Hall and Mary B. [Omohundro], *q.v.* License 2 MAY 1868. Planned marriage 3 MAY 1868. [R:91; R1:33-8 no return]

Short, John to Mary Jane Gregory (d. 1888). License 3 MAR 1858. Married [no date] by G.H. Northam. [M16a:58-42; NN; R:63; R1:16-7[3]]

Short, Thomas Daniel (b. c.1844, d. 1908 of apoplexy),[4] served Co. D, 15th Va. Cav., C.S.A., first to Rebecca H. Douglass (d. 1887 of consumption). THOMAS DANIEL SHORT, farmer, age 24, single, b. Westmoreland Co., daughter of George W. Short and Ellen [Enniss], *q.v.*, to REBECCA H. DOUGLASS, age 23, b. single, b. Westmoreland Co., daughter of Vincent H. and Julia A. Douglass. Signed Thomas D. [his X mark] Short, wits. C.C. Baker, J.W. Hutt. License 13 JAN 1868. Married 15 JAN 1868 at Vincent H. Douglass' by J.H. Davis. [DR:73-56; M18; R:89; R1:31-10]

Short, William to Eliza Jane Hudson. WILLIAM SHORT, sailor, age 27, single, b. Westmoreland Co., son of George and [Wincy] Short, to ELIZA JANE HUDSON, age 19, single, b. Westmoreland Co., daughter of William R. Hudson and Catharine [Davis].[5] License 29 MAY 1863. Planned marriage 31 MAY 1863. [R:79; R1:20-3 no return]

Silba, George T. to Mary A. Barker. GEORGE T. SILBA, farming, age about 35, widower, b. upper part of Westmoreland Co., son of Abraham Silba and [Elizabeth] his wife, to MARY A. BARKER, age about 30, single, b. upper part of Westmoreland Co., daughter of Daniel Barker and Leucinda [Davis] his wife.[6] License 10 DEC 1855. Married 11 DEC 1855 at *Foneswood* by John Pullen, M.G. [M16:55-25, R:51; R1:4-7]

Silba [or Silvy], George Taylor to Rosa Ann Covington. GEORGE TAYLOR SILVY, farmer, age 50, widower, b. Westmoreland Co., son of Abraham and Elizabeth Silvy, to ROSA ANN COVINGTON, age 22, single, b. King George Co., daughter of John and Nancy Covington. Signed George T. [his X mark] Silvy, wit. J.W. Hutt. License 27 OCT 1870. Married 31 OCT 1870 by B.R. Battaile. [M18; R:100; R1:44-4]

---

[1] Stephen Self and Eliza Lewis were married by bond 29 DEC 1830 in Westmoreland Co., with Daniel Hardwick, security.
[2] John A. Settle was buried with his second wife Ketura Wilkerson (1855-1896) at Menokin Baptist Church, Warsaw, Va.
[3] License returned is not according to law.
[4] Thomas D. Short was buried at Yeocomico Episcopal Church, Tucker Hill, Va.
[5] William R. Hudson, son of Martha Hudson, and Catharine Davis, daughter of Caty Alderson, were married by bond 18 DEC 1828 in Richmond Co., with George Delano, security.
[6] Daniel Barker and Lucy Smith, daughter of Ann Smith, were married by bond 20 OCT 1803 in Westmoreland Co.

Sisson, Franklin Stuart, served in Co. C, 47th Va. Inf., C.S.A., to Mary Susan Crabb. FRANKLIN STUART SISSON, no occupation, age 21, single, b. Westmoreland Co., son of William Rufus Sisson and Ann [E. Harvey],[1] to MARY SUSAN CRABB, age 21, single, b. Westmoreland Co., daughter of Benedict P. and Eliza Crabb. License 24 NOV 1866. Married 25 NOV 1866 at *Nominy Grove* by G.H. Northam. [M18; R:84; R1:25-13]

Sisson, James Henry, served in Co. A, 15th Va. Cav., C.S.A., to Emily Susan Sanford. JAMES HENRY SISSON, clerk, age 27, single, b. Westmoreland Co., son of William Rufus Sisson and Ann E. [Harvey], *q.v.*, to EMILY SUSAN SANDFORD [sic], age 25, single, b. Westmoreland Co., daughter of Ethelwald Sanford and Sally M. [Robinson], *q.v.* License 8 JAN 1863. Planned marriage 8 JAN 1863. [R:79; R1:19-11 no return]

Sisson, John Taliaferro (1829-1899), to Anna Eliza Clark (1839-1905).[2] JOHN T. SISSON, farmer, age 24, single, b. Richmond Co., son of W.H. [William] Sisson and Susan [W.] Sanford,[3] to ANNA E. CLARK, age 15, single, b. Richmond Co., daughter of Hiempsel Clark and Ann Kent. License 18 AUG 1854. Dated 18 AUG 1854 at Hiempsel Clark's by George Northam, M.G. [M15:54-8; R:43; R1:2]

Sisson, William Henry (b. 1856, d. 1919 near Templeman's Cross Roads), to Willie Ann Collins (1860-1923).[4] WILLIAM HENRY SISSON, farmer, age 22, single, b. and res. Richmond Co., son of William H. Sisson and Elizabeth [Sandy],[5] to WILLIE ANN COLLINS, age 20, single, b. Westmoreland Co., daughter of George W. Collins [d. testate 1912] and Ann Elizabeth [Reed], *q.v.* License 8 DEC 1880. Married 9 DEC 1880 at Nomini Baptist Church by F.B. Beale. [M20; R:134; R1:84-5]

Skinker, Edward H. (1822-1890), served in Co. D, Local Defense Troops, C.S.A., to Roberta Robb Garnett (b. 1838, d. 1927 in Fredericksburg, Va.).[6] EDWARD H. SKINKER, merchant, age 34, single, b. Orange Co., res. Richmond, Va., son of S.T. and M.F. Skinker, to ROBERTA ROBB GARNETT, age 21, single, b. Alabama, daughter of H.T. [Henry] and Eliza S. Garnett. License 15 MAY 1857. Married 9 JUN 1857 at *Ingleside* by Joshua Peterkin, Rector of St. James Church, Richmond, Va. [M16a:57-18; R:59; R1:9-7]

Smith, Alexander to Mary Ella Traverse. ALEXANDER SMITH, farmer, age 26, single, b. Westmoreland Co., son of William and Charlotte Smith, to MARY ELLA TRAVERSE, age 24, single, b. Westmoreland Co., daughter of Abram Traverse and Eliza [Royal]. Signed Alexander [his X mark] Scott, wit. W.S. McKenney. License 26 SEP 1874. Married 1 OCT 1874 by F.B. Beale. [M19; R:113; R1:59-1]

Smith, Charles (C) to Ellen Smith. CHARLES SMITH, farmer, age 27, single, b. Westmoreland Co., son of Marcus and Esther Smith, to ELLEN SMITH, age 30, widow, b. Northumberland Co., daughter of [Alfred] and [Rose] Gaskins. License 28 FEB 1877. Married 7 [MAR] 1877 at Andrew Gaskins' house by Thomas T. Johnson. [M19; R:121; R1:69-5]

---

[1] William R. Sisson and Ann E. Harvey were married by bond 24 MAY 1825 in Westmoreland Co., with Joseph F. Harvey, security.
[2] John T. Sisson and his wife Anna E. were buried at Totuskey Baptist Church, Village, Va.
[3] William H. Sisson and Susanna W. Sandford were married by bond 19 JAN 1824 in Westmoreland Co., with John Sandy, security.
[4] William Henry Sisson and his wife Willie Ann were buried at Nomini Baptist Church, Montross, Va.
[5] William H. Sisson and Elizabeth Sandy were married by bond 21 JUL 1834 in Westmoreland Co., with John B. Sisson, security.
[6] Edward H. Skinker and his wife Roberta Garnett Coontz were buried in Hollywood Cemetery, Richmond, Va.

Smith, Henry to Lizzie Coleman. HENRY SMITH, farmer, age 29, widowed, b. Essex Co., son of Lewis and Sally Smith, to LIZZIE COLEMAN, age 33, single, b. Essex Co., daughter of Daniel and Milly Coleman. License 21 AUG 1876. Married 22 AUG 1876. [R:119; R1:66-1 no return]

Smith, Henry (C) to Ellen Gaskins. HENRY SMITH, farmer, age 22, single, b. Westmoreland Co., son of Henry and Sarah Smith, to ELLEN GASKINS, age 21, single, b. Northumberland Co., daughter of Alfred and Rose Gaskins. Signed Henry [his X mark] Smith, wit. W.S. McKenney. License 23 MAR 1871. Married 23 MAR 1871 by Thomas T. Johnson, minister of Potomac Colored Baptist Church. [M18; R:102; R1:46-12]

Smith, Henry to Cilla Travis. HENRY SMITH, farmer, age 20, single, b. Westmoreland Co., son of William and Charlotte Smith, to CILLA TRAVIS, age 19, single, b. Westmoreland Co., daughter of Abraham and Eliza Travis. License 24 DEC 1879. Married 25 DEC 1879 at *Kenmore* by F.B. Beale. [M20; R:131; R1:80-3]

Smith, Isaac (C) to Mrs. Susan Hoomes Smith. ISAAC SMITH, laborer, age 27, single, b. Essex Co., son of Daniel and Judy Smith, to SUSAN SMITH, age 22, widow, b. Essex Co., daughter of Willis and Ellen Hoomes. License 2 JUL 1875. Married 3 JUL 1875 at Little Zion Church by Emanuel Watts, pastor Little Zion Church. [M19; R:115; R1:61-10]

Smith, Isaac to Margarett Bailor [or Baylor]. ISAAC SMITH, laborer, age 31, single, b. Essex Co., son of Tun[stall] Smith and Jane [Robb],[1] to MARGARETT BAILOR, age 25, single, b. Essex Co., daughter of James and Sedie Bailor. License 5 APR 1879. Married 5 APR 1879 by B.R. Battaile. [M20; R:128; R1:77-7]

Smith, Isaiah to Margaret Jane Bailey. ISAIH SMITH [sic], laborer, age 19, single, b. Northumberland Co., son of William and Charlotte Smith, to MARGARET JANE BAILEY, age 22, single, b. Westmoreland Co., daughter of Milly Bailey. Isaih [his X mark] Smith, wit. W.S. McKenney. License 20 NOV 1872. Married 20 NOV 1872 at *Spring Grove* by G.W. Beale, minister. [M19; R:106; R1:51-12]

Smith, Jacob (C) to Nellie Johnson. JACOB SMITH, laborer, age 21, single, b. Westmoreland Co., son of John and Susan Smith, to NELLIE JOHNSON, age 21, single, b. Westmoreland Co., daughter of Jerry and Bettie A. Johnson. License 22 NOV 1877. Married 29 NOV 1877 at *Reeces* by Rev. William Gaskins. [M19; R:123; R1:71-2]

Smith, Jacob to Lucy Ann Reed. JACOB SMITH, sailor, age 25, single, b. Westmoreland Co., son of Emanuel Smith and Judy [Ashton],[2] to LUCY ANN REED, age 21, single, b. Westmoreland Co., daughter of Betsey Reed. Signed Jacob [his X mark] Smith, wit. W.S. McKenney. License 1 DEC 1873. Married 4 [DEC] 1873 at *Cabin Point* by G.W. Beale. [B19; R:110; R1:55-1]

Smith, James Redman (b. 1824, d. 1894 of cancer), served in Co. 4, 111th Va. Mil. and Co. D, 15th Va. Cav., C.S.A., son of James Stark Smith [1792-1834] and Mary P. Hardwick [1799-1855],[3] to

---

[1] See Essex Co. marriage 8 JUN 1867 for Isaac Robb and Edy Roane. Tunstall Smith and Jane Robb (C) are parents for groom.
[2] Emanuel Smith and Juliet Ashton were married by bond 7 JAN 1830 in Westmoreland Co., with James G. Donoho, security.
[3] James S. Smith and Polly P. Hardwick were married by bond 30 DEC 1816 in Richmond Co., with John Hardwick, security.

Almeida [or Almira] Jane Stephens [1838-1908].[1] License 23 NOV 1857. [DR:99-59; M16a:57-40; R:62; R1:15-12[2]]

Smith, Jerry (C) to Susan Corbin (d. 1868 of dropsy). License 28 APR 1852. Married 29 APR 1852 by E.B. McGuire. [DR:16-54; M15:52-17, R:19]

Smith, Jerry (C) (d. 1888), to Mrs. Margaret Johnson. JERRY SMITH, farmer, age 48, widowed, b. Westmoreland Co., son of Emanuel and Julia Smith, to MARGARET JOHNSON, age 40, widow, b. Westmoreland Co., daughter of John and Susan Johnson. License 5 MAY 1877. Married 10 MAY 1877 at *Allendale*, Cople Mag. Dist. by Chas. [his X mark] Rust, wit. Joseph N. Arnest. [DR:76-59; M19; R:122; R1:69-11]

Smith, John (d. by 1875), to Sarah Lavina Gaskins. JOHN SMITH, farmer, age 23, single, b. Westmoreland Co., son of Emanuel Smith and Julia [Ashton], *q.v.*, to SARAH GASKINS, age 19, single, b. Westmoreland Co., daughter of Patrick Gaskins and Sally [Gaskins], *q.v.* License 11 FEB 1865. Married 16 FEB 1865 by H.P.F. King. [M17a:65-4; R:81; R1:22-1]

Smith, John (M) to Judy Smith. JOHN SMITH, waterman, age 26, single, b. Westmoreland Co., son of Sarah Smith, father unknown, to JUDY SMITH, age 22, single, b. Essex Co., daughter of Daniel and Sarah Smith. License 27 DEC 1872. [R:107; R1:52-12; 1880]

Smith, John (1855-1931), to Fanny Hill. JOHN SMITH, farmer, age 23, single, b. Northumberland Co., son of William and Charlotte Smith, to FANNY HILL, age 20, single, b. Westmoreland Co., daughter of Edward and Julia Hill. License 31 DEC 1877. Married 3 JAN 1878 at *Avries* by F.B. Beale. [DC; M19; R:124; R1:71-17]

Smith, John C. to Maria S. Bailey. JOHN C. SMITH, farmer, age 33, widower, b. Westmoreland Co., son of George W. and Ann Smith, to MARIA S. BAILEY, age 25, single, b. Westmoreland Co., daughter of Stephen G. and Harriet Bailey. License 22 JUN 1855. Married 27 JUN 1855 at Carmel Church by H.P.F. King. [M16:55-13, R:49; R1:3-9]

Smith, Northern to Eliza Gaskins. NORTHERN SMITH, sailor, age 26, single, b. Westmoreland Co., son of Emanuel Smith and Julia [Ashton], *q.v.*, to ELIZA GASKINS, age 21, single, b. Westmoreland Co., daughter of Bartley [Bartlett] Gaskins and Mary [Ann Peck], *q.v.* Signed Northern [his X mark] Smith, wit. J.W. Hutt. License 24 JUN 1869. Married 24 JUN 1869 by G.W. Beale. [M18; R:95; R1:38-12]

Smith, Peter to Virginia Adams Douglas. PETER SMITH, farmer, age about 25, single, b. Westmoreland Co., son of James and Mary P. Smith, to VIRGINIA ADAMS DOUGLAS, age about 20, single, b. Westmoreland Co., daughter of Rhodam and Polly Douglas. License 20 JUN 1857. Married 5 JUL 1857 at B. Walker's by W.W. Walker, M.G. [M16a:57-22; R:61 has Jane A. Douglass; R1:11-2]

---

[1] James Redman Smith and wife Almeda Jane, and his parents, were buried in the Smith Family Cemetery, located off of Route 203 near Oldhams, Va.
[2] R1:11-3 notes that the minister return received 26 DEC 1859 is not according to law.

Smith, Richard Henry (1841-1929), first to Sophronia Ann Conner. RICHARD HENRY SMITH, mechanic, age 30, single, b. and res. Richmond Co., son of James S. Smith and Mary B. [Sisson],[1] to SOPHRONIA ANN CONNER, age 19, single, b. Westmoreland Co., daughter of John H. and [Mildred] A. Conner. License 7 MAR 1877. Married 8 MAR 1877 by F.B. Beale. [M19; R:121; R1:69-6]

Smith, Richard Henry (1841-1929), second to Lucy Ann Elizabeth Scates (1849-1936).[2] RICHARD HENRY SMITH, farmer, age 33, widowed, b. Richmond Co., son of James S. Smith and Mary B. [Sisson], *q.v.*, to LUCY ANN ELIZABETH SCATES, age 20, single, b. Richmond Co., daughter of Alfred Scates and Ophelia J. [Jane Coates].[3] License 15 DEC 1879. Married 17 DEC 1879 at the residence of the bride's father by D.M. Wharton. [M20; R:130; R1:79-11; SC]

Smith, Samuel (C) to Caroline Kelly. SAMUEL SMITH, laborer, age 23, single, b. Westmoreland Co., son of Humphrey and Sarah Smith, to CAROLINE KELLY, age 20, single, b. Westmoreland Co., daughter of John and Judy Kelly. Signed Samuel [his X mark] Smith, wit. J.H. Sisson. License 25 JAN 1870. Married 27 JAN 1870 by John C. Smith. [M18; R:98; R1:41-14]

Smith, Solomon (C) to Rose Blackwell. SOLOMON SMITH, sailor, age 22, single, b. Westmoreland Co., res. Baltimore City, Md., son of Ann Smith, father unknown, to ROSE BLACKWELL, age 21, single, b. Westmoreland Co., daughter of Adam and Sally Blackwell. Signed Solomon [his X mark] Smith, wit. Wm. S. McKenney. License 9 SEP 1875. Married 11 SEP 1875 at Grant's Hill Church by Emanuel Watts, pastor Little Zion Church. [M19; R:115 has groom William Smith; R1:61-15]

Smith, William (C) to Mary Hill. WILLIAM SMITH, farmer, age 32, single, b. King George Co., son of Mathew and Maria Smith, to MARY HILL, age 21, single, b. Va., daughter of Henry Hill, mother unknown. Signed William [his X mark] Smith, wit. W.S. McKenney. License 29 APR 1871. Married 30 APR 1871 at Little Zion Church, Oak Grove by Emanuel Watts, pastor. [M18; R:102; R1:46-15]

Smith, William (C) to Susan Jackson. WILLIAM SMITH, farmer, age 20, single, b. Westmoreland Co., son of Henderson and Matilda Smith, to SUSAN JACKSON, age 18, single, b. Essex Co., daughter of Ellen Jackson. Signed William [his X mark] Smith, wit. Wm. S. McKenney. License 23 DEC 1871. Married 28 DEC 1871 by Emanuel Watts, pastor of Little Zion Church, Oak Grove, Va. [M19; R:104; R1:48-14]

Smith, Willis to Mary Johnson. WILLIS SMITH, laborer, age 23, single, b. Westmoreland Co., son of Henry and Haney Smith, to MARY JOHNSON, age 22, single, b. Westmoreland Co., daughter of James and Betsy Johnson. License 15 DEC 1880. Married 16 DEC 1880 at the residence of the bride's father by D.M. Wharton. [M20; R:134; R1:84-6]

Smoot, George Liston (1848-1928), to Annie Rose Owens (b. 1848, d. 1883 of typhoid fever).[4] GEORGE LISTON SMOOT, farmer, age 21, single, b. Caroline Co., son of Benjamin F. Smoot [b.

---

[1] James S. Smith and Mary B. Sisson were married by bond 27 OCT 1830 in Richmond Co., with William H. Sisson, security.
[2] Richard H. Smith and his second wife Lucy were buried at Nomini Baptist Church, Montross, Va.
[3] Alfred Scates, son of Joseph Scates, and Ophelia Jane Coates, daughter of John A. Coates and Elizabeth Balderson, were married 17 FEB 1859 in Richmond Co. by Rev. John Pullen.
[4] George L. Smoot and his wife Anne Rose Owens were buried in a Smoot Family Cemetery on *Locust Farm* [now *Locust Toft*], located off of Route 638.

1808, d. 1870 of congestive chill][1] and Lucy A. [Ann Mothershead][2] [d. 1872 of pneumonia], to ANNIE ROSE OWENS, age 20, single, b. King George Co., daughter of Edward W. [Wills] Owens, *q.v.*, and A.C. [Smoot].[3] License 16 DEC 1868. Married 17 OCT 1868 by Robert N. Reamy. [DR:16-57, 22-35, 58-98; M18; R:93; R1:36-12]

Smythy, Phillip Henry (C) to Mary Moore. PHILLIP HENRY SMYTHY, laborer, age 24, single, b. Westmoreland Co., son of Rebecca Smythy, father unknown, to MARY MOORE, age 22, single, b. Westmoreland Co., daughter of Daniel and Amy Moore. Signed P. [his X mark] H. Smythy, wit. J.W. Hutt. License 11 JAN 1876. Married 13 JAN 1876 at *Kenmore* near Nominy Ferry by Thomas T. Johnson. [M19; R:117; R1:63-14]

Sorrel, Andrew to Mrs. Nancy Beasely. ANDREW SORREL, farmer, age 21, single, b. Westmoreland Co., son of Spencer and Betty Sorrel, to NANCY BEASELY, age 23, widow, b. Caroline Co., parents unknown. License 19 DEC 1876. Married 21 DEC 1876 in the county by B.R. Battaile. [M19; R:120; R1:67-11]

Sorrell, John Wesley to Mary Jane Sanford (1833-1919).[4] J. WESLEY SORRELL, miller, age 34, widowed, b. Westmoreland Co., son of Enoch and Leanna Sorrell, to MARY JANE SANFORD, age 25, single, b. Westmoreland Co., daughter of Jeremiah Sanford and Harriet [Weaver].[5] Signed J.W. Sorrill. License 10 AUG 1859. Married 11 AUG 1859 by John Pullen at John W. Sorrell's. [M16a:59-19, 19a and 19b; R:70; R1:15-6]

Sorrell, Thomas Edward to Laurah Jane Mozingo. THOMAS EDWARD SORRELL, farmer, age 22, single, b. Westmoreland Co., son of Spencer Sorrell and Letta [Marks],[6] to LAURAH JANE MOZINGO, age 21, single, b. King George Co., daughter of James and Sallie Mozingo. License 24 FEB 1879. Married 25 FEB 1879 by B.R. Battaile. [M20; R:128; R1:77-1]

Sorrell, William Addison to Maria Jane Doleman. WILLIAM ADDISON SORRELL, shoemaker, age 21, single, b. Westmoreland Co., son of Spencer Sorrell and Nancy [Gutridge],[7] to MARIA JANE DOLEMAN, age 25, single, b. Westmoreland Co., daughter of Austin and Elizabeth Doleman. License 8 JAN 1862. Married 8 JAN 1862 at Edwin Balderson's by John Pullen. [M17:62-5; R:78; R1:18-12]

Spence, Thomas B. to Julia A. Scates. License 7 MAY 1853. Married 9 MAY 1853 by Wm. McGuire. [M15:53-14, R:29]

Spilman, Robert Buckner (1838-1917), served in Co. C, 9th Va. Cav., C.S.A., to Mary Telula Bayne (1845-1900).[8] ROBERT BUCKNER SPILMAN, merchant, age 29, single, b. Westmoreland Co., son of John Spilman [d. 1872 of cancer] and Thirza [Hoult], *q.v.*, to MARY T.[9] BAYNE, age 21, single, b. Westmoreland Co., daughter of Washington [N.] Bayne and Emily C. [Hill], *q.v.* License

---

[1] DR: gives death year 1868. Benjamin Franklin Smoot was a son of William Mattox Smoot. He was married 4 MAY 1835 in Richmond Co. to Lucy Ann Mothershead, with Stephen D. Pursell, security.
[2] Benjamin F. Smoot and Lucy Mothershead were married by bond 4 MAY 1835 in Richmond Co., with Stephen D. Pursell, security.
[3] Edward Owens and Alcinda Smoot were married 11 SEP 1845 in King George Co. by Rev. John McDaniel.
[4] Mary J. Sorrell was buried at Providence United Methodist Church, Chiltons, Va.
[5] Jeremiah Sanford and Harriot Weaver were married by bond c.1809 in Westmoreland Co., with John McNeil, security.
[6] Spencer Sorrell and Letta Marks were married by bond 24 DEC 1845 in Westmoreland Co., with William L. Mothershead, security.
[7] Spencer Sorrell and Nancy Guttridge were married by bond 21 JAN 1831 in Westmoreland Co., with Meredith Lucas, security.
[8] Robert B. Spilman and wife Telula Bayne were buried in the Spilman Family Cemetery at *Roxbury*, located off of Route 638.
[9] The license and certificate contain a middle name but it is not legible.

24 JUN 1867. Married 26 JUN 1867 at Washington Bayne's by John Pullen. [DR:22-30; M18; R:87; R1:28-11; WP]

Spilman, William Lansdown (1816-1900), second to Mary Alice Atwill (1839-1881).[1] WILLIAM LANSDOWN SPILMAN, farmer, age 59, widowed, b. and res. King George Co., son of John Spilman and Susan [Greer],[2] to MARY ALICE ATWILL,[3] age 38, single, b. King George Co., daughter of Samuel Atwill and Alice [Jones].[4] License 27 JUN 1878. Married 27 JUN 1878 at B.D. Atwill's residence by D.G.C. Butts. [M19; R:126; R1:74-4]

Stainback, John Moore, Dr. to Izora Louisa Gouldman. JOHN MOORE STAINBACK, physician, age 27, single, b. and res. Brunswick Co., son of Peter and Anna Eliza Stainback, to IZORA LOUISA GOULDMAN, age 2[0], single, b. Caroline Co., daughter of Henry B. Gouldman and Julia Ann [Robinson].[5] License 4 MAY 1869. Married 18 MAY 1869 at *White Point*, the residence of H.B. Gouldman by Thomas E. Locke. [M18; R:95; R1:38-4; SC; WP]

Stallings, Andrew J. to Louisa Van Ness. ANDREW J. STALLINGS, machinist, age 26, single, b. Washington, D.C., son of Benjamin and Mary Stallings, to LOUISA VAN NESS, age 27, single, b. Monroe's Creek, daughter of Benjamin and Delie Van Ness. License 18 MAY 1855. Married 18 MAY 1855 at *Chatham* by J.W. Chesley, minister of the Prot. Episc. Church. [M16:55-11 parties reversed, R:49; R1:3-6; SP; WP]

Stanley, Samuel (C) to Latty Gordon. SAMUEL STANLEY, sailor, age 28, single, b. Massachusetts, son of Monroe and Esther [Stanley], to LATTY GORDON, age 24, single, b. Westmoreland Co., daughter of [Osborn] and Lucy Gordon. License 27 DEC 1870. Married 29 DEC 1870 by Thomas T. Johnson, a minister of Potomac Church. [M18; R:100; R1:45-4]

Stephens, Erastus Sylvanus to Virginia Columbia Straughan. ERASTUS SYLVANUS STEPHENS, farmer, age 22, single, b. Westmoreland Co., son of Henry and Mary C. Stephens, to VIRGINIA COLUMBIA STRAUGHAN, age 23, single, b. Westmoreland Co., daughter of Thomas N. Straughan and Sarah J. [Oldham].[6] License 12 DEC 1877. Married 18 DEC 1877 by G.H. Northam. [M19; R:123; R1:71-8]

Stephens, Henry to Elizabeth C. Oldham. HENRY STEPHENS, farmer, age 22, b. Westmoreland Co., single, son of Jeremiah Stephens and Hannah [J. Cole],[7] to ELIZABETH C. OLDHAM, age 22, b. Westmoreland Co., single, daughter of John T. Oldham and Elizabeth B. [Morris].[8] License 19 OCT 1858. Married 20 OCT 1858 at the residence of James Baily by H.P.F. King, minister of the M.E. Church. [M16a:58-25 and 25a; R:64; R1:12-13]

Stephens, Henry Carter (d. 1882 of bilious fever), to Harriet Ann Hall. HENRY CARTER STEPHENS, farmer, age 56, widower, b. Northumberland Co., son of James [Briscoe] Stephens

---

[1] William Lansdown Spilman was buried with his first wife Maria C. Jones (1817-1857) and second wife Mary A. at Trinity Methodist Church, on Route 3, King George Co.
[2] John Spilman and Susan Greer were married 18 APR 1815 in King George Co.
[3] The license is made out in error to Mary Alice Spilman rather than Mary Alice Atwill.
[4] Samuel Atwell and Alice Jones were married 26 APR 1831 in King George Co.
[5] Henry B. Gouldman and Julia Ann Robinson were married 23 JUN 1843 in Caroline Co.
[6] Thomas N. Straughan and Sarah E. Oldham, daughter of John F. Oldham, were married by bond 18 JAN 1847 in Westmoreland Co., with Joseph A. Booth, security.
[7] Jeremiah Stephens and Hannah J. Cole were married by bond 15 MAR 1826 in Westmoreland Co., with William Cole, security.
[8] John T. Oldham and Elizabeth Morris were married by bond 31 MAY 1825 in Westmoreland Co., with George Delano, security.

and Jane [Hall],[1] to HARRIET ANN HALL, age 35, single, b. Westmoreland Co., daughter of William and Alice Hall. Signed Henry C. [his X mark] Stephens, wit. J.W. Hutt. License 24 DEC 1869. Married 26 DEC 1869 by Robert N. Reamy. [DR:53-71; M18; R:97; R1:41-2]

Stephens, James M. (d. 1876 of pneumonia), to Emily Jane Stephens. JAMES M. STEPHENS, farmer, age 25, single, b. Richmond Co., son of Jefferson Stephens and Ann [M. Askins],[2] to EMILY J. STEVENS [sic], age 23, single, b. Westmoreland Co., daughter of John [B.] and Alice [Hall Stephens], *q.v.* License 21 DEC 1871. Married 21 DEC 1871 at the at the bride's by Elder James A. Weaver. [DR:36-1; M19; R:104; R1:48-13]

Stephens, John (d. by 1868), to Susan Hannah Sanford. JOHN STEPHENS, farmer, age 29, single, b. Westmoreland Co., son of Jeremiah Stephens and Hannah [J. Cole], *q.v.*, to SUSAN HANNAH SANFORD, age 17, single, b. Westmoreland Co., daughter of William S. and Mary B. Sanford. Consent 15 MAY 1866 by bride's mother, wit. Hiram S. King. License 15 MAY 1866. Married 15 MAY 1866 at the residence of Hiram [S.] King by Elder James A. Weaver. [M18; R:83; R1:23-16]

Stephens, John Haley (1848-1933), to Mary Frances Stephens (1841-1907).[3] JOHN STEPHENS, farmer, age 21, single, b. Westmoreland Co., son of [John] Henry Stephens and Mary [E. Wood], to MARY FRANCES STEPHENS, age 22, single, b. Westmoreland Co., daughter of John [B.] Stephens and Alice [Hall], *q.v.* License 24 JUL 1868. Married 26 JUL 1868 at the residence of Geo. W. Beal by R.J. Sanford. [M18; R:92; R1:34-12]

Stephens, Robert W. (1844-1927),[4] to Mrs. Maria G. Mothershead Maguire, widow of Oliver C. McGuire, *q.v.* ROBERT W. STEVENS [sic], farmer, age 21, single, b. Richmond Co., son of Jefferson Stevens and Ann [M. Askins], *q.v.*, to MARIA G. MAGUIRE, age 28, single, b. Richmond Co., daughter of George and Mary Mothershead. License signed by Thos. E. Marshall, Provost Marshall. Married 16 SEP 1865 at G.M. Mothershead's by Elder James A. Weaver. [DC; M17a:65-7]

Stephens, William H. to Sarah A. Boothe. WILLIAM H. STEPHENS, planter, age 24, single, b. Westmoreland Co., son of Jeremiah Stephens and Hannah [J. Cole], *q.v.*, to SARAH A. BOOTHE, age 21, single, b. Westmoreland Co., daughter of Samuel [J.] Boothe and Polly [Mary W. Wright].[5] License 30 JAN 1855. Married 31 JAN 1855 at the residence of Richard Hagans by H.P.F. King, minister of the M.E. Church. [M16:55-5; R:47; R1:3-2]

Stevens (see Stephens)

Stewart, Cornelius (C) to Martha Ann Smith. CORNELIUS STEWART, farmer, age 23, single, b. Westmoreland Co., son of Sam Stewart and Peggy [Watts] [d. 1884 of pneumonia], to MARTHA ANN SMITH, age 19, single, b. Westmoreland Co., daughter of Henderson and Matilda Smith.

[1] James Briscoe Stephens and Jane Hall were married by bond 29 JAN 1799 in Northumberland Co., with Vincent Crutcher, security.
[2] Jefferson Stephens and Ann M. Askins were married 6 APR 1843 in Richmond Co. by Rev. William N. Ward.
[3] John H. Stephens and his wife Mary F. were buried at Gibeon Baptist Church, Village, Va.
[4] Robert W. Stevens was buried at Warsaw Methodist Episcopal Church, Warsaw, Va.
[5] Samuel J. Boothe and Mary W. Wright were married by bond 27 JUN 1817 in Westmoreland Co., with William Brann, security.

License 29 JUN 1875. Married 30 JUN 1875 at Little Zion Church by Emanuel Watts, pastor Little Zion Church. [DR:63-169[1]; M19; R:115; R1:61-9]

Straughan, Henry to Roberta Thompson. HENRY STRAUGHAN, farmer, age 25, single, b. Northumberland Co., son of John and Harriet Straughan, to ROBERTA THOMPSON, age 25, single, b. Westmoreland Co., daughter of Ann Thompson, father unknown. Signed Henry [his X mark] Straughan, wit. J.W. Hutt. License 10 JAN 1867. Married 15 JAN 1867 at the mill by Elder James A. Weaver. [M18; R:85]

Straughan, Sedwick Healey (1847-1921), to Hazeltine Mary Ann Stevens (1853-1931).[2] SEDWICK HEALEY STRAUGHAN, farmer, age 25, single, b. Westmoreland Co., son of Thomas N. Straughan and Sarah J. [Oldham], *q.v.*, to MARY ANN STEVENS, age 20, single, b. Westmoreland Co., daughter of Henry and Mary Stevens. License 17 DEC 1872. Married 18 DEC 1872 at *Chestnut Level* by G.H. Northam. [M19; R:107; R1:52-5]

Streets, Henry (C) to Mrs. Kitty Washington Mercer. HENRY STREETS, farmer, age 27, single, b. Westmoreland Co., son of Spencer and Charlott Street[e] [sic], to KITTY MERCER, age 30, widow, b. Westmoreland Co., daughter of Battle and Hannah Washington. License 30 DEC 1878. Married 31 DEC 1878 at Little Zion Church by Emanuel Watts, pastor, Little Zion Church. [M20; R:127; R1:76-6]

Streets, William Henry (C) to Mary Ellen Brooks. WILLIAM HENRY STREETS, farmer, age 21, single, son of Thornton and [Emily] Streets, to MARY ELLEN BROOKS, age 21, single, b. Westmoreland Co., daughter of Jacob and Hannah Brooks. License 4 JAN 1879. Married 4 JAN 1879 at Little Zion Church by Emanuel Watts, pastor, Little Zion Church. [M20; R:128; R1:76-9]

Suttle, Arthur B. to Fannie J. Green. Married 3 JUN 1877 at the residence of the bride's mother in King George Co. by Rev. William C. Latane. [WP]

Suttle, Robert Vinton, Sr. to Virginia Lovelie Dishman. ROBERT VINTON SUTTLE, farmer, age 23, single, b. and res. King George Co., son of Edwin S. Suttle and Patsey E. [Jones],[3] to VIRGINIA LOVELIE DISHMAN, age 22, single, b. Essex Co., daughter of John T. [Triplett] Dishman and Mary H. [Harlowe McDaniel]. License 12 DEC 1868. Married 17 DEC 1868 by Robert N. Reamy. [M18; R:93; R1:36-9]

Sutton, Frederick T., served in Co. A, 15th Cav., C.S.A., to Susan Sydnor, daughter of Richard B. Sydnor (d. by 1853)[4] and Elizabeth Wright. License 27 SEP 1852. Married 29 SEP 1852 by A. Wiles. [M15:52-23; R:23]

Sutton, James to Dicly J. Harris. JAMES SUTTON, shoemaker, age 47, single, b. Westmoreland Co., to DICLY J. HARRIS, age 28, single, b. Westmoreland Co. Minister return by H.P.F. King. License 22 FEB 1854. Married 28 FEB 1854 at the residence of Stephen Harris. [M15:54-17; R:41; R1:1-4]

---

[1] DR:63-169, entry for Peggy Stewart (C), d. 15 SEP 1884 of pneumonia, age 65, daughter of Sam and Edith Watts, mother of Cornelius Stewart.
[2] Sedwick (a.k.a. Sedrick) H. Straughan and his wife were buried in the Straughan Family Cemetery, Oldhams, Va.
[3] Edwin S. Suttle and Patsey E. Jones were married 27 OCT 1840 in King George Co. by J. Berkley.
[4] CF1857-02, *Samuel M. Lyell v. Exor. of Richard Sydnor &c.*

Sutton, James T. (b. 1822, d. testate 1866[1]), to Elizabeth Reed (1825-1891). JAMES SUTTON, farmer, age 30, single, b. Westmoreland Co., son of Samuel [T.] Sutton [b. 1795, d. 1855] and Elizabeth [Crask] [d. 1854], *q.v.*, to ELIZABETH REED, age 29, single, b. Westmoreland Co., daughter of John Reed and Catherine [Kitty Mariah Kelly].[2] Married 3 JAN 1855 at Chilton's Crossroads by H.P.F. King. [Bible; M16:55-2; R:47; R1:2]

Sutton, John to Mary Ann Bulger. JOHN SUTTON, farmer, age 66, widowed, b. Richmond Co., son of John S. and Rebecca Sutton, to MARY ANN BULGER, age 30, single, b. Westmoreland Co., daughter of Richard Bulger and Mary [Jackson].[3] License 21 JUL 1864. Married 27 JUL 1864 at the residence of John Sutton by H.P.F. King. [M17a:64-6; R:80; R1:20-13]

Sutton, John (d. by 1866), to Mary Young McKenney. JOHN SUTTON, carpenter, age 32, widower, b. Richmond Co., son of John and Martha Sutton, to MARY Y. McKENNY [sic], age 30, single, b. Westmoreland Co., daughter of James McKenney and Sallie [Sutton]. License 16 APR 1856. Married 17 APR 1856 at the residence of the bride's father by W.W. Walker, minister of the Meth. Protestant Church. [M16:56-11; R:55; R1:5-13]

Sutton, Samuel to Elizabeth Sorrell. SAMUEL SUTTON, farmer, age 56, widower, b. Richmond Co., son of Joseph Sutton and Rozee Ann, to ELIZABETH SORRELL, age 22, single, b. Westmoreland Co., daughter of Spencer Sorrell and Nancy [Gutridge], *q.v.* License 1 MAR 1854. Married 1 MAR 1854 at James White's in Richmond Co. by William Balderson. [M15:54-2; R:41; R1:1-6]

Sutton, Thomas Hansford, served in Co. C, 9th Va. Cav., C.S.A., to Hester Ann Hall. THOMAS H. SUTTON, farmer, age 23, single, b. Westmoreland Co., son of Friar and Elizabeth Sutton, to HESTER ANN HALL, age 22, single, b. Westmoreland Co., daughter of William B. Hall and Mary A. [Ann Omohundro], *q.v.* License 23 FEB 1857. Married 25 FEB 1857 at *Plain View* by G.H. Northam, minister of the Baptist Church. [M16a:57-7; R:59; R1:9-1]

Sweeney, William Henry to Mary Ann Newton. WILLIAM HENRY SWEENEY, schoolmaster, age 27, single, b. and res. Washington, D.C., son of Edward and Maria T. Sweeney, to MARY ANN NEWTON, age 27, single, b. Westmoreland Co., daughter of Isaac Newton and Hannah [Mathaney]. License 26 DEC 1867. Married 26 DEC 1867 at the minister's residence by D.M. Wharton, Rector of Montross Parish. [M18; R:89; R1:31-2]

Sydnor, Henry Johnson to Anna Gustas Pope. HENRY JOHNSON SYDNOR, age 31, single, b. Richmond, Va., res. Henrico Co., son of Samuel E. and Mary B. Sydnor, to ANNA GUSTAS POPE, age 24, single, b. Westmoreland Co., daughter of Elliott Pope and Elizabeth M. [Neale] [d. testate 1894[4]].[5] License 24 FEB 1863. Married 5 MAR 1863 at Elizabeth M. Pope's by John Pullen. [M17:63-2; R:79; R1:19-14]

---

[1] Deeds & Wills No. 37, p. 81, will of James Sutton, proved 22 JAN 1866, names wife Elizabeth.
[2] John Reed and Kitty M. Kelly were married by bond 28 NOV 1822 in Westmoreland Co., with Richard Reed, security.
[3] Richard Bulger and Polly Jackson were married by bond 7 JUN 1815 in Westmoreland Co., with Richard Sanford, security.
[4] Deeds & Wills No. 52, p. 367, will of Elizabeth Pope, proved 25 JUN 1894, names daughter Anna G. Sydnor.
[5] Elliott Pope and Mira Neale were married by bond 26 OCT 1826 in Westmoreland Co., with John Bayne, security.

T

Tallent, George William Christopher, served in Co. K, 9th Va. Cav., C.S.A., to Mildred Ann Croxton. GEORGE WILLIAM CHRISTOPHER TALLENT, farmer, age 21, single, b. Richmond Co., son of William Tallent and Amelia A. [Yeatman],[1] to MILDRED ANN CROXTON, age 17, single, b. Richmond Co., daughter of Carter Croxton and Mary Ann [Clarkson], *q.v.* License 12 DEC 1859. Married 14 DEC 1859 by G.H. Northam. [M16a:59-27 and 27b; R:70; R1:16-8; R&I24:38]

Tallent, James Warren (b. 1854, d. 1887 of pneumonia), to Mary Ann Clarke (1860-1907).[2] JAMES WARREN TALLENT, oysterman, age 26, single, b. Westmoreland Co., son of James and [Elizabeth] Betsy Tallent, to MARY ANN CLARKE, age 18, single, b. Westmoreland Co., daughter of Richard and Harriett Clarke. License 26 JAN 1880. Married 28 JAN 1880 by R.N. Reamy. [DR:73-115; M20; R:132; R1:80-16]

Tallent, Thomas Alfred (1848-1923), to Ann Eliza McGuire (d. 1923 of bronchitis). THOMAS ALFRED TALLENT, farmer, age 22, single, b. and res. Richmond Co., son of William Tallent and Amelia [A. Yeatman], *q.v.*, to ANN ELIZA McGUIRE, age 18, single, b. Richmond Co., daughter of John and Sarah McGuire. License 22 NOV 1869. Married 25 NOV 1869 by G.H. Northam. [DC; M18; R:96; R1:39-12]

Taplett, Arthur to Virginia Dunlop. ARTHUR TAPLETT, laborer, age 27, single, b. King George Co., son of William and Mahaley Taplett, to VIRGINIA DUNLOP, age 24, single, b. Westmoreland Co., daughter of John and Jane Dunlop. Signed Arthur [his X mark] Taplett, wit. Wm. S. McKenney. License 5 OCT 1875. Married 5 OCT 1875 by Emanuel Watts, pastor of Little Zion Church. [M19; R:115; R1:61-16]

Tasker, Henry to Mrs. Fanny Hungerford Young, colored persons. HENRY TASKER, farmer, age 50, widower, b. Westmoreland Co., son of Lawrence and Katy Tasker, to FANNY YOUNG, age 45, widow, b. Westmoreland Co., daughter of Anthony and Clara Hungerford. Signed Henry [his X mark] Tasker, wit. H. Chandler. License 13 NOV 1869. Married 17 DEC 1869 at *Laurel Grove* by T.E. Locke, Rector, Washington Parish. [M18; R:96; R1:39-11; WP]

Tate, Benjamin Allen to Harriet Elizabeth Kerry. BENJAMIN ALLEN TATE, farmer, age 41, widow, b. Westmoreland Co., son of Jordan Tate and Betsy [Thompson],[3] to HARRIET ELIZABETH KERRY, age 21, single, b. Westmoreland Co., daughter of Richard and Lucinda Kerry. License 3 DEC 1879. Married 4 DEC 1879 at Richard Carey's by F.W. Claybrook. [M20; R:130; R1:79-3]

Tate, Bennett to Harriet Jones. BENNETT TATE, farmer, age 21, single, b. Westmoreland Co., son of Jordan Tate and Betsy [Thompson], *q.v.*, to HARRIET JONES, age 21, single, b. Westmoreland Co., daughter of Lucy Jones, father unknown. Signed Bennett [his X cross] Tate, wit. Thomas Parker. License 18 JAN 1860. Married 19 JAN 1860. [M17:60-3; R:72]

Tate, Bushrod to Becky Tate, free colored persons. License 14 SEP 1858. Married 17 SEP 1858 at the St. Peter's Church rectory by T.E. Locke. [R:64; SP; WP]

---

[1] William Tallent, Jr. and Amelia S. Yeatman were married by bond 11 JUN 1834 in Westmoreland Co., with John Hunter, security.
[2] James Warren Tallent and his wife Mary Ann Clark were buried in the Chisford-Stratford Area Community Cemetery, located off of Route 609 on property owned by the Hinson Family.
[3] Jordan Tate and Betsy Thompson, daughter of Bennett Thompson, were married by bond 6 OCT 1838 in Westmoreland Co., with William B. Butler, security.

Tate, Campbell to Nancy Tate. License 14 DEC 1857. [R:62 no return]

Tate, Edmond to Clarah Spates, black. EDMOND TATE, farmer, age 21, single, b. Westmoreland Co., son of Frank and Harriet [A.] Tate, *q.v.*, to CLARAH SPATES, age 17, single, b. Westmoreland Co., daughter of James T. Spates [and Cornelia] [Cope] (C) [d. 1885 of pneumonia], mother unknown. License 6 JAN 1880. Married 8 JAN 1880 at the bride's residence by Charles [his X mark] Rust. [DR:65-55[1]; M20; R:131; R1:80-8]

Tate, Frank to Harriet A. Tate. License 18 JAN 1853. Married 20 JAN 1853 by George Northam, L.M.G. [M15:53-3; R:25]

Tate, Garrison (C) to Letty Ann Henry (d. 1921). GARRISON TATE, farmer, age 19, single, b. Westmoreland Co., son of Ephraim and Clara Tate, to LETTY ANN HENRY, age 21, single, b. Westmoreland Co., daughter of Nancy Henry, father unknown [William Henry]. License 14 JUN 1879. Married 15 JUN 1879 at the house of Nancy Henry by W.W. Walker. [DC; M20; R:129; R1:78-3]

Tate, George (C) to Winny Casey. License 7 JAN 1857. [R:59 no return]

Tate, George Henry (C) to Mary Susan Johnson. GEORGE HENRY TATE, laborer, age 22, single, b. and res. Richmond Co., son of Mira Tate, father unknown, to MARY SUSAN JOHNSON, age 20, single, b. Westmoreland Co., daughter of Levi and Kitty Johnson. License 17 MAY 1880. Married 18 MAY 1880 at Montross, Va. by Paul Bradley. [M20; R:133; R1:82-13]

Tate, James Austin to Frances Casey. License 29 OCT 1857. [R:62 no return]

Tate, James Austin to Bettie Newman. JAMES AUSTIN TATE, farmer, age 30, widowed, b. Westmoreland Co., son of Julila Ashton, to BETTIE NEWMAN, age 21, single, b. Westmoreland Co., daughter of Emanuel Newman and Caroline [Lucas], *q.v.* Signed James Austin [his X mark] Tate, wit. W.S. McKenney. License 20 DEC 1871. Married 20 DEC 1871 at Newman's by H.H. Fones. [M18; R:104; R1:48-12]

Tate, James Hampton (C) to Sarah Ann Lawrence (C). Married 26 DEC 1853 by John Pullen. [R:37]

Tate, James Henry to Moriah Jane Thompson. JAMES HENRY TATE, farmer, age 23, single, b. Westmoreland Co., son of Frank and Harriet [A.] Tate, *q.v.*, to MORIAH JANE THOMPSON, age 22, single, b. Westmoreland Co., daughter of Moses Thompson and Haney [Thompson].[2] License 3 JAN 1877. Married 4 JAN 1877 by F.B. Beale. [M19; R:121; R1:68-6]

Tate, John to Catharine Chambers. JOHN TATE, farmer, age 23, single, b. Westmoreland Co., son of Lowry Tate, mother unknown, to CATHARINE CHAMBERS, age 22, single, b. Westmoreland Co., daughter of Polly Chambers, father unknown. Married 1 DEC 1864 at Rodham Ashton's by D.M. Wharton. [M17a:64-15; R:81; R1:21-9]

---

[1] DR:65-55, entry for Cornelia Spates (C), d. 14 JUN 1885 of pneumonia, age 38, daughter of Joseph and Lucinda Cope, wife of James T. Spates.
[2] Moses Thompson and Henrietta Thompson, daughter of Bennett Thompson, were married by bond 7 JAN 1845 in Westmoreland Co., with Solomon Dixon, security.

Tate, John to Eliza Gaskins, colored persons. JOHN TATE, farmer, age 22, single, b. Westmoreland Co., son of George and Julia Tate, to ELIZA GASKINS, age 21, single, b. Westmoreland Co., daughter of Edmond and Milly Gaskins. Signed John [his X mark] Tate, wit. J.W. Hutt. License 8 DEC 1868. Married 24 DEC 1868 at *Laurel Grove Farm* by Thomas E. Locke, Rector, Washington Parish. [M18; R:93; R1:36-8; WP]

Tate, John to Virginia Johnson, black. JOHN TATE, farmer, age 23, single, b. Westmoreland Co., son of William and Fanny Tate, to VIRGINIA JOHNSON, age 18, single, b. Westmoreland Co., daughter of Levy and Kitty Johnson. License 7 JAN 1880. Married 8 JAN 1880 at my residence by D.M. Wharton. [M20; R:131; R1:80-11]

Tate, Joseph to Ellen Rich. JOSEPH TATE, farmer, age 22, single, b. Westmoreland Co., son of Lewis Tate and Hannah [Sale], *q.v.*, to ELLEN RICH, age 24, single, b. Westmoreland Co., daughter of Charles and Fanny Rich. Signed Jos. [his X mark] Tate, wit. Geo. S. Hutt. Consent 10 SEP 1860 at Mattox, Va. by bride Ellen [her X mark] Rich, wit. T.R. Ditty. License 10 SEP 1860. Married 13 SEP 1860. [M17:60-29; R:74]

Tate, Moses (C) (d. 1923),[1] to Judy Chin. MOSES TATE, farmer, age 21, single, b. Westmoreland Co., son of Berryman and Betsy Tate, to JUDY CHIN, age 21, single, b. Westmoreland Co., daughter of Matilda Pin [sic]. Signed by Moses [his X mark] Tate, wit. W.S. McKenney. License 7 JUL 1875. Married 8 JUL 1875 near Warrensville, Va., by F.B. Beale. [DC; M19; R:115; R1:61-11]

Tate, Richard R. (1850-1929), to Amanda Jackson. RICHARD TATE, farmer, age 23, single, b. Westmoreland Co., son of Jordan Tate and Mary [Wilkins], to AMANDA JACKSON, age 20, single, b. Westmoreland Co., daughter of John and Mary Jane Jackson. License 12 JAN 1875. Married 14 JAN 1875 at Mary Tate's by Robert N. Reamy. [DC; M19; R:114; R1:60-12]

Tate, Robert (C) to Willie Ann Johnson. ROBERT TATE, farmer, age 21, single, b. Westmoreland Co., son of John and Sabella Tate, to WILLIE ANN JOHNSON, age 22, single, b. Richmond Co., daughter of Dennis and Mary Johnson. License 12 FEB 1880. Married 12 FEB 1880 at my residence by D.M. Wharton. [M20; R:132; R1:81-5]

Tate, Robert (C) (d. 1914), to Coretta Williams. ROBERT TATE, farmer, age 21, single, b. Westmoreland Co., son of Nancy Tate, father unknown, to CORETTA WILLIAMS, age 21, single, b. Westmoreland Co., daughter of John and Mary Williams. Signed Robt. [his X cross] Tate, wit. J.H. Sisson. License 22 DEC 1869. Married 23 DEC 1869 by D.M. Wharton, Rector of Montross Parish. [DC; M18; R:97; R1:40-32]

Tate, Rufus to Sarah Ann Lucas. RUFUS TATE, farmer, age 25, single, b. Westmoreland Co., son of Jordan Tate and Mary [Wilkins], to SARAH ANN LUCAS, age 21, single, b. Westmoreland Co., daughter of Newton and Nancy Lucas. Signed Rufus [his X mark] Tate, wit. W.S. McKenney. License 4 FEB 1874. Married 4 FEB 1874 by B.R. Battaile. [M19; R:112; R1:57-7]

Tate, Simeon to Alcy Ann Rich. License 18 JAN 1858. [R:63 no return]

---

[1] DC: Moses Tate was buried at Old Quarter Cemetery.

Tate, Sturman to Lucy Tate. STURMAN TATE, farmer, age 25, single, b. Westmoreland Co., son of Hopeful Tate and Maria [Tate],[1] to LUCY TATE, age 24, single, b. Westmoreland Co., daughter of Ewel and Gracie Tate. License signed Sturman [his X mark] Tate, wit. C.C. Baker. License 17 MAY 1866. Married 19 MAY 1866 by D.M. Wharton. [M18; R:83; R1:24-2]

Tate, Thomas Lewis (1840-1918),[2] served in Co. A, 15th Va. Cav., C.S.A., to Roberta Johnson Tate (d. 1907). THOMAS LEWIS TATE, farmer, age 20, single, b. Westmoreland Co., son of William and Ann Tate, to ROBERTA TATE, age 18, single, b. Westmoreland Co., daughter of Henry Tate and Cynthia [Johnson].[3] Signed Thos. [his X mark] L. Tate, wit. J.W. Hutt. License 11 FEB 1860. Married 12 FEB 1860 at the residence of Beckwith Wingfield by H.P.F. King, M.G. [M17:60-10 and 10a; R:72; R1:16-3]

Tate, William (C) to Kitty Tate (C). License 20 DEC 1854. [R:47 no return]

Tate, William to Mary Ashton. WILLIAM TATE, farmer, age 37, widowed, b. Westmoreland Co., son of Jesse and Cordelia Tate, to MARY ASHTON, age 21, single, b. Westmoreland Co., daughter of George Ashton and Julia [Tate].[4] License 28 DEC 1864. Married 29 DEC 1864 at Julia Ashton's by D.M. Wharton. [M17a:64-19; R:81; R1:21-14]

Tate, William to Nancy Tate. License 16 JAN 1850. Married 17 JAN 1850 by John Pullen. [M15:50-17; R:1 not in *Nottingham*]

Tate, William to Fanny Rich. License 21 JAN 1851. Married 30 JAN 1851 by John Pullen. [M15:51-7; R:7]

Tate, William to Eliza Winkfield. WILLIAM TATE, waterman, age about 22, single, b. Westmoreland Co., son of Henry Tate and Zinthy [Cynthia Johnson] his wife, *q.v.*, to ELIZA WINKFIELD, age about 24, single, b. Westmoreland Co., daughter of Henry Winkfield and Zylla [Lucas] his wife.[5] License 15 MAR 1856. Married 19 MAR 1856 at Popes Creek Church by John Pullen, M.G. [M16:56-8; R:53; R1:5-8]

Tate, William James (C) (d. 1889 of paralysis), to Millie Campbell. WILLIAM TATE, farmer, age 62, single, b. Westmoreland Co., son of James and Molly Tate, to MILLIE CAMPBELL, age 62, single, b. Essex Co., parents unknown. Signed Wm. [his X mark] Tate, wit. J.W. Hutt. License 18 DEC 1875. Married 26 DEC 1875 at Little Zion Church by Emanuel Watts, pastor, Little Zion Church. [DR:81-108; M19; R:116; R1:62-16]

Taylor, Daniel to Margaret Watts, colored people. DANIEL TAYLOR, farmer, age 23, single, b. Westmoreland Co., son of Jack and Betsey Taylor, to MARGARET WATTS, age 16, single, b. Westmoreland Co., daughter of Richard and Eliza Watts. Signed Daniel [his X mark] Taylor, wit. J.W. Hutt. License 20 DEC 1867. Married 22 DEC 1867 at the Methodist Church in Oak Grove by Thomas E. Locke, Rector of St. Peter's Church. [M18; R:88; R1:30-10; WP]

---

[1] Hopeful Tate and Maria Tate were married by bond 23 JAN 1832 in Westmoreland Co., with Samuel Tate, security.
[2] Thomas Lewis Tate and his wife Roberta were buried at Grant United Methodist Church, Lerty, Va.
[3] Henry Tate and Sintha Johnson were married by bond 10 JAN 1831 in Westmoreland Co., with Campbell Tate, security.
[4] George Ashton and Julia Tate were married by bond 3 JAN 1844 in Westmoreland Co., with Blain Ashton, security.
[5] Henry Winkfield and Sillar Lucas were married by bond 4 JAN 1826 in Westmoreland Co., with Meredith Lucas, security.

Taylor, John (C) to Judith Betty Richardson. JOHN TAYLOR, farmer, age 24, single, b. Westmoreland Co., son of [James] and Rose Taylor, JUDITH BETTY RICHARDSON, age 18, single, b. Westmoreland Co., daughter of Lucy Richardson, father unknown. Signed John [his X mark] Taylor, wit. J.W. Hutt. License 16 MAY 1868. Married 17 MAY 1868 by Jerry M. Graham. [M18; R:91; R1:33-12]

Taylor, John to Sarah Ann Johnson. JOHN TAYLOR, farmer, age 26, widower, b. Westmoreland Co., son of Rose Ann Taylor, to SARAH ANN JOHNSON, age 23, single, b. Westmoreland Co., daughter of John and Frances Johnson. License 24 SEP 1870. Married 25 SEP 1870 by D.M. Wharton, Rector, Montross Parish. [M18; R:99; R1:43-16]

Taylor, John (C) to Mrs. Lucy Taylor. JOHN TAYLOR, farmer, age 30, single, b. Westmoreland Co., son of Nelson and Polly Taylor, to LUCY TAYLOR, age 27, widow, b. Westmoreland Co., parents unknown. License 2 JUN 1877. Married 7 JUN 1877 at Zion Baptist Church by Chas. [his X mark] Rust, wit. Joseph N. Arnest. [M19; R:122; R1:69-16]

Taylor, John Joseph Aiken Jamesmount[1] to Winny Ann Lee. JOHN JOSEPH A.S. TAYLOR, farmer, age 62, single, b. Northumberland Co., son of Joseph and Silvey Taylor, to WINNY ANN LEE, age 26, single, b. Westmoreland Co., daughter of Moses and Susan Lee. License 1 NOV 1866. Planned marriage 6 NOV 1866. [R:84; R1:25-9 no return]

Taylor, John P. (1832-1913), to Isabella "Belle" Nelson Locke (1842-1909).[2] JOHN TAYLOR, farmer, age 33, single, b. Westmoreland Co., son of Henry Taylor and Julia [D. Leiper], to ISABELLA N. LOCKE, age 2[3], single, b. Lunenburg Co., daughter of [Rev.] Thomas E. [Estep] Locke [1812-1897] and Lucy A. [Armistead Nelson] [1823-1892].[3] License 18 FEB 1867. Married 20 FEB 1867 at the rectory of Washington Parish by Thomas E. Locke. [M18; R:86; R1:27-7; WP]

Taylor, Joseph to Lucinda Newman. License 18 NOV 1857. [R:62 no return]

Taylor, Joseph to Sarah Jenkins. JOSEPH TAYLOR, farmer, age 28, widowed, b. Westmoreland Co., son of Stella Taylor, father unknown, to SARAH JENKINS, age 23, single, b. Westmoreland Co., daughter of Eliza Jenkins, father unknown. Signed Joseph [his X mark] Taylor, wit. J.H. Sisson. Consent by Eliza [her X mark] Jenkins, wit. C. Whitfield McGuire. License 2 SEP 1859. Married 4 SEP 1859. [M16a:59-21 and 21a; R:70 has bride Eliza Jenkins]

Taylor, Joseph (C) (d. 1921), to Letty Elizabeth Reed. JOSEPH TAYLOR, laborer, age 31, single, b. Westmoreland Co., son of [John Rite and] Letty E. Taylor, to LETTY ELIZABETH REED, age 22, single, b. Westmoreland Co., daughter of James and Rose Reed. License 31 DEC 1873. Married 31 DEC 1874 at the house of Rose Reed by D.M. Wharton. [DC; M19; R:111; R1:56-5]

Taylor, Peter (C) to Eliza Grant. PETER TAYLOR, farmer, age 27, single, b. Westmoreland Co., son of Peter and Caty Taylor, to ELIZA GRANT, age 34, single, b. Westmoreland Co., daughter of Orange and [Dorinda] Pitts. License 6 JUL 1867. Married 7 JUL 1867 at T. Tinchcomb's by Jerry Graham. [M18; R:87; R1:28-12]

---

[1] R1:25-9 includes the full name, however, it is partly illegible to this compiler.
[2] John P. Taylor and his wife Isabella were buried in St. Peter's Cemetery, Oak Grove, Va.
[3] Rev. Thomas E. Locke and Lucy Armistead Nelson were married 21 DEC 1841 at *Mount Holly* in Lunenburg Co. by Thomas T. Castleman.

Taylor, Pierson (C) to Nancy Garnett (d. 1935). PIERSON TAYLOR, farmer, age 21, single, b. Caroline Co., son of Caroline Taylor, to NANCY GARNETT, age 19, single, b. Westmoreland Co., daughter of Randal Garnett and Felicia [Reynolds]. Signed Pierson [his X mark] Taylor, wit. J.W. Hutt. License 29 MAY 1868. Married 31 MAY 1868 by Robt. N. Reamy. [DC; M18; R:91; R1:33-15]

Taylor, Robert (C) to Mariah Hogan. ROBERT TAYLOR, farmer, age 22, single, b. Essex Co., son of Caroline Taylor, to MARIAH HOGAN, age 19, single, b. Westmoreland Co., daughter of Payton and Winnie Hogan. License 18 DEC 1879. Married 23 DEC 1879 at Little Zion Church by Emanuel Watts, pastor, Little Zion Church. [M20; R:130; R1:79-13]

Taylor, Solomon to Polly Lawrence. SOLOMON TAYLOR, farmer, age 40, widowed, b. Westmoreland Co., son of Davy and Rachel Gaskins, to POLLY LAWRENCE, age 20, single, b. Westmoreland Co., daughter of Sam and Mary Lawrence. Signed Solomon [his X mark] Taylor, wits. J.W. Hutt, Wm. Green. License 31 JUL 1868. Married 5 AUG 1868 at *Hickory Hill* by J.H. Davis. [M18; R:92; R1:35-1]

Taylor, Solomon (C) to Cressie Gordon. SOLOMON TAYLOR, oysterman, age 50, widowed, b. Westmoreland Co., son of Peter and Rachial Taylor [sic], to CRESSIE GORDON, age 24, single, b. Northumberland Co., daughter of George and Ann Gordon. License 21 JUL 1879. Married 23 JUL 1879 at my residence by Rev. William Gaskings. [M20; R:129; R1:78-6]

Taylor, Thomas Leiper, Dr. (1836-1901), assistant surgeon for the 9th Va. Cav. and 10th Va. Inf., C.S.A., to Rosa Van Doren Locke (1845-1924).[1] THOMAS LEIPER TAYLOR, physician, age 33, single, b. Fredericksburg, Va., son of Henry Taylor and Julia L. [Dunlap], to ROSA VAN DOREN LOCKE, age 23, single, b. Lunenburg Co., daughter of [Rev.] Thomas E. [Estep] Locke and Lucy A. [Nelson], *q.v.* License 19 OCT 1868. Married 27 OCT 1868 at the rectory of Washington Parish by Thomas E. Locke, Rector, Washington Parish. [M18; R:92; R1:35-7; SC; WP]

Taylor, William Penn (b. 1834, d. 1920 at Oak Grove, Va.), served in Co. H, 9th Va. Cav., C.S.A., to Florence Ida Carter (1849-1920).[2] WILLIAM PENN TAYLOR, farmer, age [23], single, b. Westmoreland Co., son of Henry and Julia Taylor, to FLORENCE IDA CARTER, age 23, single, b. Westmoreland Co., daughter of George M. [Monroe] Carter [and Mary T. Rice]. License 18 APR 1873. Married 23 APR 1873 at Oak Grove by John Payne. [DC; M19; R:109; R1:54-2; SC; WP]

Taylor, Wilton (C) to Roberta Jackson, colored people. WILTON TAYLOR, farmer, age 24, single, b. Essex Co., son of Richard and Judy Taylor, to ROBERTA JACKSON, age 22, single, b. Westmoreland Co., daughter of Lawrence and Emily Jackson. Signed Wilton [his X mark] Taylor, wit. C.C. Baker. License 21 DEC 1869. Married 28 DEC 1869 at *Wakefield* by Thomas E. Locke, Rector, Washington Parish. [M18; R:97; R1:40-28; WP]

Templeman, Arthur Richard (C) to Amanda C. Newman (d. 1891 in child birth). ARTHUR RICHARD TEMPLEMAN, farmer, age 31, single, b. Westmoreland Co., son of James [d. 1873 of hemorrhage] and Jane Templeman, to AMANDA NEWMAN, age 22, single, b. Westmoreland Co.,

---

[1] Dr. Thomas L. Taylor and his wife Rosa Van Doren Locke were buried in the Hungerford-Griffith Family Cemetery, located at Leedstown, Va. WP gives his place of burial as *Riverside*.
[2] William Penn Taylor and his wife Florence were buried in St. Peter's Cemetery, Oak Grove, Va.

daughter of Jane Newman, father unknown. License 12 DEC 1877. Married 13 DEC 1877 by H.H. Fones. [DR:27-14[1], 87-42; M19; R:123; R1:71-9]

Templeman, William Taylor (C) to Agness Rebecca McKay. WILLIAM TAYLOR TEMPLEMAN, packer in store, age 28, single, b. Westmoreland Co., res. Baltimore City, Md., son of James and Jane Templeman, to AGNESS REBECCA McKAY, age 21, single, b. Westmoreland Co., daughter of Rodham and Agness [Douglass] McKay, *q.v.* License 21 JUN 1879. Married 23 JUN 1879 by T.T. Johnson. [M20; R:129; R1:78-4]

Thomas, James to Nannie Elizabeth Nelson. JAMES THOMAS, farmer and physician, age 46, widower, b. and res. St. Mary's Co., Md., son of George and Mary Thomas, to NANNIE ELIZABETH NELSON, age 25, single, b. Westmoreland Co., daughter of William D. Nelson and Lettie E. [Chandler].[2] License 14 NOV 1868. Married 2 DEC 1868 by D.M. Wharton. [CP; M18; R:93; R1:35-13]

Thomas, James E. to Josie Virginia Marders. JAMES E. THOMAS, farmer, age 23, single, b. Essex Co., son of Leonard [D.] Thomas [d. testate 1889[3]] and Ann [M. Pitts],[4] to JOSIE VIRGINIA MARDERS, age 16, single, b. King George Co., parents unknown. License 8 FEB 1878. Married 10 FEB 1878 by H.H. Fones. [M19; R:125; R1:73-2]

Thomas, John to Diannah Bundy. JOHN THOMAS, carpenter, age 35, single, b. and res. King George Co., son of Matilda Thomas, father unknown, to DIANNAH BUNDY, age 30, single, b. Westmoreland Co., parents not known. Signed John [his X mark] Thomas. License 19 DEC 1868. Married 20 DEC 1868 by Robert N. Reamy. [M18; R:93; R1:36-14]

Thomas, John Henry, merchant and postmaster at Millville, Va., to Mary Frances Jones. JOHN HENRY THOMAS, merchant, age 24, single, b. King George Co., son of Benjamin F. Thomas and Elizabeth [J. Frank],[5] to MARY FRANCES JONES, age 16, single, b. Westmoreland Co., daughter of Wm. P. [Putnam] and Lucretia Jones. License 30 JAN 1861. Married 3 FEB 1861 at the residence of Putnam Jones by Rev. T.E. Locke. [M17:61-3; R:77; SC; WP]

Thompson, Abraham (1842-1916), to Sarah Ann Johnson. ABRAHAM THOMPSON, farmer, age 24, single, b. Westmoreland Co., son of Benjamin Thompson and Winny [Jenkins], to SARAH ANN JOHNSON, age 22, single, b. Westmoreland Co., daughter of Robert and Polly Johnson. Signed Abram [his X mark] Thompson, wit. C.C. Baker. License 28 JAN 1868. Married 30 JAN 1868 by D.M. Wharton. [DC; M18; R:89; R1:31-15]

Thompson, Daniel (C) to Sarah Newman. DANIEL THOMPSON, farmer, age 21, single, b. Westmoreland Co., daughter of Polly Thompson, father unknown, to SARAH NEWMAN, age 21, single, b. Westmoreland Co., daughter of James and Sallie Newman. License 10 JUN 1879. Married 12 JUN 1879 at my residence by Charles [his X mark] Rust. [M20; R:129; R1:77-16]

---

[1] DR:27-14, entry for James Templeman, farmer, d. 10 OCT 1873 of hemorrhage, age 55, son of Samuel and Betsy Templeman, husband of Jane, father of R.A. Templeman.
[2] William D. Nelson and Lettice E. Chandler, daughter of J. Chandler, were married by bond 24 FEB 1841 in Westmoreland Co., with David H. Tapscott, security.
[3] Deeds & Wills No. 48, p. 463, will of L.D. Thomas, proved 28 OCT 1889, names wife Ann M. Thomas and son James E. Thomas.
[4] Leonard D. Thomas and Ann M. Pitts were married 27 DEC 1853 at the house of Larkin Pitts in Essex Co.
[5] B.F. Thomas and E.J. Frank were married 19 APR 1830 in King George Co.

Thompson, Emanuel to Hannah Ashton. EMANUEL THOMPSON, farmer, age 23, single, b. Richmond Co., son of Benjamin and Agnes A. Thompson, to HANNAH ASHTON, age 25, single, b. Westmoreland Co., daughter of George Ashton and Julia A. [Tate], *q.v.* License 29 DEC 1880. Married 30 DEC 1880 at *Chatham* by D.M. Wharton. [M20; R:134; R1:84-14]

Thompson, George to Mary Ashton. License 8 DEC 1858. [R:66 no return]

Thompson, George Cumberland to Louisa Jane Reed. GEORGE CUMBERLAND THOMPSON, farmer, age 28, single, b. and res. King George Co., son of Hazlewood and Susan [Elkins] Thompson, to LOUISA JANE REED, age 28, single, b. Westmoreland Co., daughter of James and Amelia F. Reed. License 7 JAN 1867. Married 8 JAN 1867 by Joseph A. Billingsley. [M18; R:85; R1:26-13]

Thompson, George Philander to Levicia Hackett. GEORGE PHILANDER THOMPSON, oysterman, age 19, single, b. Westmoreland Co., son of Haney Lee, father unknown, to LEVICIA HACKET [sic], age 16, single, b. Westmoreland Co., daughter of Jesse (C) [d. 1881 of pneumonia] and Jane Hacket[t]. License 29 DEC 1880. Married 30 DEC 1880 at *The Glebe* by F.B. Beale. [DR:48-25[1]; M20; R:134; R1:84-15]

Thompson, Henry B. to Rose Ann Thompson (C) (d. 1882 of pneumonia). HENRY THOMPSON, farmer, age 30, single, b. Westmoreland Co., son of Joseph and Haney Thompson, to ROSE ANN THOMPSON, age 25, single, b. Westmoreland Co., daughter of George Thompson and Easter [Harrison].[2] Signed Henry [his X mark] Thompson, wit. W.S. McKenney. License 25 FEB 1874. Married 26 FEB 1874 at *Bushfield* by G.W. Beale, M.G. [DR:53-77; M19; R:112; R1:58-1]

Thompson, Isaiah to Hannah Cary. ISIAH THOMPSON [sic], farmer, age 21, single, b. Richmond Co., son of Leroy and Harriet Thompson, to HANNAH CARY, age 19, single, b. Westmoreland Co., son of George Cary and Ann [Gaskins].[3] License 28 DEC 1864. Married 29 DEC 1864 at the house of George Cary by W.W. Walker. [M17a:64-18; R:81; R1:21-12]

Thompson, James to Mary Smith. License 22 JAN 1851. Married 30 JAN 1851 by George Northam, L.M.G. [M15:51-3, R:7]

Thompson, James Little to Lucinda Jones (d. by 1867), free Negroes. JAMES L. THOMPSON, farmer, age 26, single, b. Westmoreland Co., son of James and Sally Thompson, to LUCINDA JONES, age 34, single, b. Westmoreland Co., daughter of Betsy Jones, father unknown. Signed James L. [his X mark] Thompson, wits. J.W. Hutt, Benj. P. Atwill. License 25 FEB 1860. Married 1 MAR 1860. [M17:60-13; R:72]

Thompson, James Little (C) to Julia Ann Ball. JAMES LITTLE THOMPSON, farmer, age 36, widowed, b. Westmoreland Co., son of James and Sally Thompson, to JULIA ANN BALL, age 23, single, b. Westmoreland Co., daughter of George Ball. Signed James L. [his X mark] Thompson,

---

[1] DR:48-25, entry for Jesse Hackett, laborer, d. 15 MAR 1881 of pneumonia, age 59, son of John and Ellen Hackett, husband of Jane Hackett.
[2] George Thompson, son of James Thompson, and Easter Harrison, were married by bond 3 JAN 1849 in Westmoreland Co., with Solomon Dixon, security.
[3] George Carey and Ann Gaskins were married by bond 2 SEP 1841 in Westmoreland Co., with William Read, security.

wit. J.W. Hutt. License 10 JUL 1867. Married 11 JUL 1867 at Cabin Point by J.H. Davis. [M18; R:87; R1:28-13]

Thompson, James William to Virginia Frances Thompson. JAMES WILLIAM THOMPSON, farmer, age 19, single, b. Westmoreland Co., son of Benjamin Thompson and Mary [Thompson],[1] to VIRGINIA FRANCES THOMPSON, age 15, single, b. Westmoreland Co., daughter of Bennett and [Barbary] Thompson. Signed by Jas. [his X mark] Thompson, wit. J.W. Hutt. License 10 JAN 1871. Married 12 JAN 1871 by Geo. W. Beale. [M18; R:101; R1:45-7]

Thompson, Jeremiah to Mrs. Jane Pierce Jones. JEREMIAH THOMPSON, farmer, age 23, single, b. Westmoreland Co., son of Garrett and Jincy Thompson, to JANE JONES, age 26, widow, b. Westmoreland Co., daughter of William Pierce and Hannah [McCoy].[2] License 31 OCT 1876. Married 2 NOV 1876 by F.B. Beale. [M19; R:119; R1:66-12]

Thompson, John Richard to Mary Thompson. JOHN RICHARD THOMPSON, farmer, age 23, single, b. Westmoreland Co., son of Lucinda Thompson, to MARY THOMPSON, age 21, single, b. Westmoreland Co., daughter of William and Ann Thompson. Signed John R. [his X mark] Thompson, wit. Wm. S. McKenney. License 20 JAN 1876. Married 20 JAN 1876 by F.B. Beale. [M19; R:117; R1:64-1]

Thompson, John to Judy Johnson. License 18 JUL 1850. Married 19 JUL 1850 by George Northam. [M15:50-19; R:1 not in *Nottingham*]

Thompson, John (C) to Betsy Reed. JOHN THOMPSON, wood cutter, age 27, single, b. Westmoreland, son of James and Sally Thompson, to BETSY REED, age 26, single, b. Westmoreland Co., daughter of James Reed and Catharine Johnson. License 6 SEP 1854. Married 7 SEP 1854 by Wm. N. Ward, M.G. [M15:54-9; R:45]

Thompson, John William to Mary Paggett Thompson (C). JOHN WILLIAM THOMPSON, farmer, age 20, single, b. Westmoreland Co., son of James and Sarah A. Thompson, to MARY PAGGETT THOMPSON, age 19, single, b. Westmoreland Co., daughter of James and Sally Thompson. License 27 DEC 1875. Married 30 DEC 1875 by F.B. Beale. [M19; R:117; R1:63-5]

Thompson, Joseph to Henrietta Johnson. License 8 JAN 1851. Married 9 JAN 1851 by George Northam, L.M.G. [M15:51-1; R:5]

Thompson, Joseph to Eddie Augusta Thompson. JOSEPH THOMPSON, farmer, age 22, single, b. Westmoreland Co., son of Moses and Susan Thompson, to EDDIE AUGUSTA THOMPSON, age 19, single, b. Westmoreland Co., daughter of George Thompson and [Easter] [Harrison], *q.v.* License 17 JAN 1878. Planned marriage 17 JAN 1878. [M19 no return; R:124; R1:72-12]

Thompson, Joseph Nick (C) (1853-1937), to Emily Agusta Wright (1860-1942).[3] JOSEPH NICK THOMPSON, farmer, age 23, single, b. Westmoreland Co., son of Joseph and Haney Thompson, to GUSTA WRIGHT, age 21, single, b. Westmoreland Co., daughter of Solomon and Emily Wright. License 21 JAN 1879. Married 23 JAN 1879 at *The Glebe* by F.B. Beale. [M20; R:128; R1:76-12]

---

[1] Benjamin Thompson and Mary Thompson were married by bond 5 JAN 1847 in Westmoreland Co., with Henry S. Johnson, security.
[2] William Peirce and Hannah Macoy were married by bond 9 JUL 1828 in Westmoreland Co., with Joseph Thompson, security.
[3] Emily A. Thompson was buried at Potomac Baptist Church, Hague, Va.

Thompson, Landon, served in Co. I, 9th Va. Cav., C.S.A., to Lucie Ellen Gouldman. LANDON THOMPSON, farmer, age 24, single, b. and res. King George Co., son of Hazlewood Thompson and Susan [Elkins], to LUCIE ELLEN GOULDMAN, age 2[3], single, b. Westmoreland Co., daughter of Thomas and Pheby Gouldman. License 25 FEB 1867. Married 14 MAR 1867 at Cat Point by Jos. A. Billingsley. [M18; R:86; R1:27-10]

Thompson, Martin to Carrie Ann Harrison (C) (d. 1885 in child birth). MARTIN THOMPSON, sawyer, age 21, single, b. Chatham Co., N.C., son of Lewis and Elizabeth Thompson, to C. ANN HARRISON, age 21, single, b. Westmoreland Co., daughter of Polly Harrison, father unknown. Signed Martin [his X mark] Thompson, wits. John W. Butler, J.W. Hutt. License 10 JUL 1867. Married 11 JUL 1867 by J.H. Davis. [DR:65-63; M18; R:87; R1:28-14]

Thomson, Meredith Davis to Lettice Fauntleroy Brockenbrough. MEREDITH DAVIS THOMSON, farmer, age 26, single, b. Frederick Co., Md., son of William J. and Margaretta Thomson, to LETICE FAUNTLEROY BROCKENBROUGH [sic], age 24, single, b. Westmoreland Co., daughter of John F. [Fauntleroy] Brockenbrough and Frances [Ann Carter], *q.v.* License 1 JUN 1868. Married 3 JUN 1868 at *Chatham* by Andrew Fisher. [M18; R:91; R1:34-3]

Thompson, Moses (d. 1882 of pneumonia), to Lucy Burwell. MOSES THOMPSON, farmer, age 23, single, b. Westmoreland Co., son of Gerard and Ellen Thompson, to LUCY BURELL [sic], age 18, single, b. Westmoreland Co., daughter of Polly Burwell, father unknown. Consent 24 DEC 1860 by Polly [her X mark] Burle, Sen. [sic] for her daughter Lucy Burle to marry, wits. Wm. Thompson, Saml. W. English. License 25 DEC 1860. Married 26 DEC 1860. [DR:53-74; M17:60-44; R:76]

Thompson, Moses (1854-1948),[1] to Ellen Thompson. MOSES THOMPSON, farmer, age 20, single, b. Westmoreland Co., son of George Thompson and [Easter] [Harrison], *q.v.*, to ELLEN THOMPSON, age 17, single, b. Westmoreland Co., daughter of Frances Thompson, father unknown. License 22 JAN 1878. Married 24 JAN 1878 at *Avries* by F.B. Beale. [M19; R:124; R1:72-14]

Thompson, Robert (C) to Mary McKee. ROBERT THOMPSON, farmer, age 24, single, b. Richmond Co., son of Moses and Teny Thompson, to MARY McKEE, age 22, single, b. Westmoreland Co., daughter of Robert and Fanny McKee. Signed Robert [his X mark] Thompson, wit. J.F. Bispham. License 21 MAR 1867. Married 21 MAR 1867 by Jerry Graham. [M18; R:86; R1:27-15]

Thompson, Thomas to Susan Hackett. License 28 SEP 1857. [R:62 no return]

Thompson, William to Ann Hackett. License 21 JAN 1851. Married 28 JAN 1851 by E.B. McGuire. [M15:51-5, R:7]

Thomson (see Thompson)

Thrift, Henry Lindsay (1846-1916), served in Co. C, 9th Va. Cav., C.S.A., to Laura A. Sutton (1854-1908).[2] HENRY LINDSAY THRIFT, wheelwright, age 27, single, b. Westmoreland Co., son of

---

[1] Moses Thompson was buried at Potomac Baptist Church, Hague, Va.
[2] Henry L. Thrift and wife Laura A. were buried at Rehobeth United Methodist Church, Wicomico Church, Va.

Samuel R. Thrift and Eliza A. [Tinsley],[1] to LAURA A. SUTTON, age 19, single, b. Westmoreland Co., daughter of F.T. [Frederick] Sutton and Susan [Sydnor], *q.v.* License 15 OCT 1873. Married 16 OCT 1873 at the home of Richard Sandford by W.A. Crocker. [M19; R:109; R1:54-10]

Thrift, Jeremiah Courtney, of *Tucker Hill* (1823-1909),[2] served in Co. 2, 111th Va. Mil., C.S.A., first to [Mrs.] Eliza Jane Donnahaw Smith (1826-1878), daughter of Richard Henry Donnahaw and Sarah Thrift. License 30 NOV 1853. Married 1 DEC 1853 by W.W. Walker. [M15:53-23; R:35]

Thrift, Jeremiah Courtney (1823-1909), second to Mrs. Anna D. Wright (1834-1909),[3] widow of Thomas Mitchell Dobyns (d. 1873), *q.v.* JEREMIAH COURTNEY THRIFT, farmer, age 57, widowed, b. Westmoreland Co., son of Jeremiah Thrift [d. 1865] and Elizabeth [Self],[4] to ANNA D. DOBYNS, age 44, widow, b. Westmoreland Co., daughter of Mottr[om] [Middleton] Wright [1800-1853][5] and Malinda [Ann Lamkin] [1809-1868].[6] License 29 OCT 1880. Married 2 DEC 1880 at J.N. Wright's residence by W.W. Walker. [DR:9-14; M20; R:134; R1:83-15]

Thrift, Julian Randolph to Bettie English (d. 1921 of uterine cancer). JULIAN RANDOLPH THRIFT, farmer, age 23, single, b. Westmoreland Co., son of Samuel R. Thrift and Eliza Ann [Tinsley],[7] *q.v.*, to BETTIE ENGLISH, age 24, single, b. Westmoreland Co., daughter of John English and Letty Ann [Rice].[8] License 30 JUL 1872. Married 30 JUL 1872 at Mrs. L.A. Beacham's by E.A. Gibbs. [DC; DR:68-31[9]; M19; R:106; R1:50-16]

Tibbs, George (C) (d. 1869 of an accidental fall from a cart), to Octavia Briant. GEORGE TIBBS, farmer, age 40, single, b. Westmoreland Co., son of Harry and Lucy Tibbs, to OCTAVIA BRIANT, age 21, single, b. Richmond Co., daughter of Charlotte Briant, father unknown. License 27 DEC 1865. Married 30 DEC 1865 at *Alwenbury* by W.W. Walker. [DR:17-38; M18; R:82; R1:22-14]

Tiffee, Robert (d. by 1879), to Mary Tate. ROBERT TIFFEE, oyster man, age 22, single, b. Westmoreland Co., son of Blaton and Maria Tiffee, to MARY TATE, age 17, single, b. Westmoreland Co., daughter of Frank Tate and Harriet [A. Tate], *q.v.* License 2 FEB 1876. Married 7 FEB 1878 by F.B. Beale. [M19; R:125; R1:73-1]

Tiffey, Robert Bispham (1830-1881), served in Co. D, 41st Reg. Va. Mil. and Co. A, 15th Va. Cav., C.S.A., to Bettie S. Harvey (1834-1891).[10] ROBERT B. TIFFEY, farming, age 27, single, b. Westmoreland Co., son of John B. Tiffey and Ann [Bispham Harvey],[11] to BETTIE S. HARVEY, age 22, single, b. Westmoreland Co., daughter of Octavius A. Harvey and [Susanna] Maria [Muse], *q.v.* License 8 JAN 1857. Married 8 JAN 1857 in Montross, Va. by H.P.F. King, minister of the M.E. Church. [M16a:57-3; R:59; R1:8-9]

---

[1] Samuel R. Thrift and Eliza A. Tinsley, daughter of Cinthia Tinsley, were married by bond 19 DEC 1838 in Westmoreland Co., with Richard H. Donnahaw, security.
[2] Jeremiah C. Thrift and his wife Eliza Jane were buried in a Thrift Family Cemetery, located off of Route 606.
[3] Anna D. Wright Thrift was buried, with her parents, in the Wright Family Burying Ground, Oldhams, Va.
[4] Jeremiah Thrift and Elizabeth Self were married by bond 25 JAN 1810 in Westmoreland Co., with Francis Self, security.
[5] Deeds & Wills No. 37, p. 602, deed for *Spring View* of which Mottrom M. Wright, father of E.T. Wright died seized.
[6] Mottrom M. Wright and Malinda Lamkin were married by bond 6 APR 1830 in Richmond Co., with Charles L. Bell, security.
[7] Samuel R. Thrift and Eliza A. Tinsley were married by bond 19 DEC 1838 in Westmoreland Co.
[8] John English and Letty A. Rice were married by bond 16 DEC 1833 in Westmoreland Co., with William T. Branson, security.
[9] DR:68-31, entry for Eliza A. Thrift, d. 28 JUL 1886 of bilious fever, age 63, daughter of Anderson and Cynthia Tinsley, mother of W.S. Thrift.
[10] Robert B. Tiffey and his wife Bettie S. were buried at Andrew Chapel United Methodist Church, Montross, Va.
[11] John B. Tiffey and Mrs. Ann (Bispham) Harvey, widow, were married by bond 4 MAY 1829 in Richmond Co., with Joseph S. Lyell, security.

Tinsbloom, John, first to Susan Ann Pitts. JOHN TINSBLOOM, mechanic, age about 22, single, b. King & Queen Co., son of William Bloom [sic] and Mary his wife, to SUSAN ANN PITTS, age about 22, single, b. Westmoreland Co., daughter of William Pitts and Martha. License 24 APR 1856. Married 27 APR 1856 at Mrs. Pitts' by John Pullen, M.G. [M16:56-14; R:55; R1:6-2]

Tinsbloom, John, second to Mrs. Lucinda Peed Dozier, widow of William Churchwell Dozier, *q.v.* JOHN TINSBLOOM, carpenter, age 33, widower, b. King & Queen Co., son of William and Mary Tinsbloom, to LUCINDA DOZIER, age 27, widow, b. Westmoreland Co., daughter of William [S.] Peed and Lucy [Nash].[1] Signed John [his X mark] Tinsbloom. License 11 MAY 1868. Married 12 MAY 1868 by Robt. N. Reamy. [M18; R:91; R1:33-10]

Tinsbloom, John, third to Letty V. Hinson (d. 1881). JOHN TINSBLOOM, farmer, age 44, widowed, b. King & Queen Co., son of William and Polly Tinsbloom, to LETTY V. HINSON, age 20, single, b. Westmoreland Co., daughter of George [W.] Hinson and Jane E. [Poe], *q.v.* License 12 JUN 1879. Married 15 JUN 1879 by B.R. Battaile. [M20; NN; R:129; R1:78-1]

Tinsley, Littleton (C) (d. by 1879), to Sally West. LITTLETON TINSLEY, farmer, age 23, single, b. Caroline Co., son of Robert Tinsley and Mary [Henry] [d. 1881 of heart disease], to SALLY WEST, age 22, single, b. Caroline Co., daughter of Edmond and Ann West. Signed Littleton [his X mark] Tinsley, wit. W.S. McKenney. License 24 DEC 1872. Married 26 DEC 1872 at Little Zion Church, Oak Grove, Va. by Emanuel Watts, pastor. [DR:51-41[2]; M19; R:107; R1:52-9]

Tinsley, Patrick (C) to Eliza Maiden (d. 1941). PATRICK TINSLEY, farmer, age 22, single, b. Caroline Co., son of Robert and Mary Tinsley, to ELIZA MADEN [sic], age 18, single, b. Westmoreland Co., daughter of Mary Maden, father unknown [Charles Lewis]. Signed Patrick [his X mark] Tinsley, wit. W.S. McKenney. License 25 NOV 1873. Married 27 NOV 1873 at *White Point* by Emanuel Watts, pastor of Little Zion Church. [DC; M19; R:109; R1:54-15]

Tobey, Charles Wesley (1841-1886),[3] to Amanda Ebert Augustien. CHARLES WESLEY TOBEY, general contractor, age 33, single, b. Madison Co., N.Y., res. New York City, son of Charles P. Tobey [1815-1891] and Elizabeth [Dunham] [1818-1899], to AMANDA EBERT AUGUSTIEN, age 20, single, b. Fairfax Co., daughter of F.A. [Frederick] and B.B. [Beula] Augustien, *q.v.* License 27 DEC 1875. Married 29 DEC 1875 at Paine's Point by F.W. Claybrook. [M19; R:116; R1:63-2]

Tolson, Alexander (C) to Eliza Eskridge. ALEXANDER TOLSTON [sic], sailor, age 37, single, b. Westmoreland Co., son of Alexander and Sally Tolston, to ELIZA ESKRIDGE, age 37, single, b. Westmoreland Co., daughter of Henry and Chaney Eskridge. Signed Alexander [his X mark] Tolston, wit. J.H. Sisson. License 16 NOV 1870. Married 17 NOV 1870 by Thomas T. Johnson. [M18; R:100; R1:44-6]

Tolson, Joseph to Frances Jenkins (C) (d. 1893 of heart failure). JOSEPH TOLSON, farmer, age 30, widower, b. Westmoreland Co., son of Dennis and Haney Tolson [d. 1889], to FRANCES JENKINS, age 18, single, b. Westmoreland Co., parents unknown. Signed Joseph [his X mark]

---

[1] William S. Peed and Lucy Nash were married by bond 19 MAY 1837 in Westmoreland Co., with James H. Mothershead, security.
[2] DR:51-41, entry for Mary Tinsley, b. Richmond Co., d. 15 MAR 1881 of heart disease, age 40, daughter of Richard and Lavinia Henry, wife of Robert Tinsley.
[3] Charles W. Tobey is buried with his parents in Stockbridge Cemetery, Munnsville, Madison Co., N.Y.

Tolson, wit. W.S. McKenney. License 26 JAN 1871. Married 28 JAN 1871 by D.M. Wharton, Rector of Montross Parish. [DR:80-52, 96-63; M18; R:101; R1:45-13]

Toy, William Maxell to Fenton Jane Laura Sanford. WILLIAM MAXELL TOY, carpenter, age 26, widower, b. Westvell, N.J., son of [Jonathan E.] and Mary B. Toy, to FENTON JANE LAURA SANFORD, age 26, single, b. Westmoreland Co., daughter of [Richard] Corbin and Eliza [James] Sanford, *q.v.* License 24 AUG 1870. Married 25 AUG 1870 at the residence of R.C. Sanford by R.J. Sanford. [M18; R:99; R1:43-13]

Travis, John to Mary J. McCoy. License 27 SEP 1858. [R:64 no return]

Travis, Moses Henry (C) to Mary Frances Montague. MOSES HENRY TRAVIS, farmer, age 26, single, b. Westmoreland Co., son of Carter and Sally Travis, to MARY FRANCES MONTAGUE, age 18, single, b. Westmoreland Co., daughter of Winnie Montague. Signed by Moses Henry [his X mark] Travis, wit. W.S. McKenney. License 3 MAR 1874. Married 5 MAR 1874 at brick house by Rev. Thomas T. Johnson. [M19; R:112; R1:58-2]

Travis, Thomas (C) to Sallie Mitchell. THOMAS TRAVIS, farmer, age 24, single, b. Westmoreland Co., son of [Abram] Travis and Eliza [Royal] [d. 1886], to SALLIE MITCHELL, age 21, single, b. Westmoreland Co., daughter of Richard and Harriett Mitchell. License 5 MAY 1880. Married 6 MAY 1880 at *Cabin Ford* by F.B. Beale. [DR:68-30[1]; M20; R:133; R1:82-10]

Treakle, Henry (1840-1920), to Catharine Elizabeth Mothershead (1845-1918).[2] HENRY TREAKLE, merchant, age 26, single, b. Northumberland Co., son of James Treakle and Elizabeth [Tignor],[3] to CATHARINE ELIZABETH MOTHERSHEAD, age 22, single, b. Westmoreland Co., daughter of Humphry and Ellenor J. Mothershead. License 25 JAN 1868. Married 25 JAN 1868 at Mrs. Mothershead's by Thomas E. Locke. [M18; R:89; R1:31-13; WP]

Treakle, James C. (1830-1886), to Eliza Jane Rose. License 21 JAN 1851. Married 23 JAN 1851 by John Pullen. [M15:51-4; R:7]

True, George Washington to Almira R. True. GEORGE WASHINGTON TRUE, farmer, age 24, single, b. Westmoreland Co., son of James True and Sarah [E. Pitts],[4] to ALMIRA R. TRUE, age 24, single, b. Westmoreland Co., daughter of William True and Eliza [J. Spilman].[5] License 13 FEB 1872. Married 14 FEB 1872 at William True's by Robert N. Reamy. [M19; R:105; R1:49-13]

Tubman, Joseph (C) to Mrs. Julia Wiggins. JOSEPH TUBMAN, sailor, age 24, single, b. Charles Co., Md., son of Peter and Julia Tubman, to JULIA WIGGINS, age 24, widow, b. Westmoreland Co., daughter of Julia Armstrong, father unknown. License 25 SEP 1876. Married 27 SEP 1876 at Mrs. Julia Armstrong's house on Capt. Wm. Allen's farm by Thomas T. Johnson. [M19; R:119; R1:66-6]

---

[1] DR:68-30, entry for Eliza Travers (C), d. 16 JUN 1886 of pneumonia, age 60, daughter of Lipphard and Silla Royal, mother of Aleck Smith.

[2] Henry Treakle and his wife Catharine were buried in the Treakle Family Cemetery, located near the intersection of Routes 630 and 631 at Maple Grove, Va.

[3] James Treakle and Elizabeth Tignor were married by bond 18 FEB 1825 in Northumberland Co., with William Harding, Jr., security.

[4] James True and Sarah E. Pitts, daughter of Patsy Pitts, were married by bond 16 JUN 1845 in Westmoreland Co., with William True, security.

[5] William True and Eliza J. Spilman were married by bond 28 FEB 1838 in Westmoreland Co., with James Mariner, security.

Tucker, George Washington to Mary Ellen Muse. GEORGE WASHINGTON TUCKER, clerk, age 28, single, b. and res. Washington, D.C., son of William and Sarah Tucker, to MARY ELLEN MUSE, age 21, single, b. Westmoreland Co., daughter of William Muse and Susan [A. Berkley].[1] License 22 MAR 1873. Married 25 MAR 1873 at W. Muse's by G.W. Beale, M.G. [M19; R:109; R1:53-16]

Tucker, John William Henry to Eliza Jane Smith. JOHN WILLIAM HENRY TUCKER, laborer, age 22, single, b. Anne Arundel Co., Md., res. Baltimore City, Md., son of John and Sarah Tucker, to ELIZA JANE SMITH, age 20, single, b. Westmoreland Co., daughter of Ann Smith. Signed John [his X mark] W.H. Tucker, wit. Wm. S. McKenney. License 26 SEP 1874. Married 27 SEP 1874 by F.B. Beale. [M19; R:113; R1:58-15]

Tune, Edward Ira to Eliza Virginia Courtney. EDWARD IRA TUNES, farmer, age 28, single, b. Northumberland Co., son of Edward K. Tune and Leannah [Dameron],[2] to ELIZA VIRGINIA COURTNEY, age 17, single, b. Westmoreland Co., daughter of Jeremiah and Ann Courtney. License 27 NOV 1858. Married 1 DEC 1858 by H.P.F. King, minister of the M.E. Church. [M16a:58-32 and 32a; R:66; R1:13-6]

Turner, Charles Blackwell, Jr. (1842-1891),[3] served in Co. C, 9th Va. Cav., C.S.A., to Mary Lee Carey (d. 1880). CHARLES BLACKWELL TURNER, farmer, age 23, single, b. and res. Northumberland Co., son of Charles B. [Blackwell, Sr.] Turner [1798-1892][4] and Judith [Ball Parker],[5] to MARY LEE CAREY, age 23, single, b. Westmoreland Co., daughter of William Carey, mother unknown. License 29 MAY 1867. Married 29 MAY 1867 at the residence of William Cary by Starke Jett. [M18; NN; R:86; R1:28-4]

Turner, Charles P. to Caroline E. Jones. License 5 DEC 1850. Married 5 DEC 1850 by George Northam. [M15:50-25; R:5 not in *Nottingham*]

Turner, Henry to Mrs. Mima Ashton Maiden. HENRY TURNER, farmer, age 81, widowed, b. King George Co., son of Scipio and Rachel Turner, to MIMA MAIDEN, age 50, widow, b. Westmoreland Co., daughter of Meredith and Peggy Ashton. Signed Henry [his X mark] Turner, wit. C.C. Baker. License 17 JUN 1876. Married 19 JUN 1876 at *Cabin Ford* by Frank B. Beale. [M19; R:119 has Maden; R1:65-12]

Turner, Jeremiah to Fenton Thompson (C) (d. 1881 in childbirth). JEREMIAH TURNER, farmer, age 24, single, b. Westmoreland Co., son of James and Milly Turner, to FENTON THOMPSON, age 17, single, b. Westmoreland Co., [illegitimate] daughter of Frances Thompson, father unknown. Signed Jeremiah [his X mark] Turner, wit. Wm. S. McKenney. License 25 JAN 1872. Married 25 JAN 1872 at *Aubie* by G.W. Beale, M.G. [DR:48-47; M19; R:104; R1:49-11]

Turner, John to Mrs. Mary Tate Tiffey, widow of Robert Tiffey, *q.v.* JOHN TURNER, farmer, age 25, single, b. Westmoreland Co., son of James and Minnie Turner, to MARY TIFFEY, age 21,

---

[1] William Muse and Sarah A. Berkley, daughter of William Berkley, were married by bond 19 JUN 1839 in Westmoreland Co., with George Carter, security.
[2] Edward K. Tune and Leannah Dameron were married by bond 6 JAN 1823 in Richmond Co., with Samuel Miskell, security, oath by Peter J. Derieux.
[3] Charles Blackwell Turner, Jr. was buried in the Turner Family Cemetery, Lodge, Va.
[4] Charles Blackwell Turner, Sr. was buried in a Turner Family Cemetery, Harryhogan Rd., Northumberland Co.
[5] Charles B. Turner and Judith B. Parker were married by bond 8 DEC 1838 in Westmoreland Co., with David H. Tapscott, security.

widow, b. Westmoreland Co., daughter of Frank Tate and Harriet [A. Tate], *q.v.* License 9 DEC 1879. Married 11 DEC 1879 at *Sherland* by F.B. Beale. [M20; R:130; R1:79-7]

Turner, Richard to Emma Sophie Baylor. RICHARD TURNER, farmer, age 25, single, b. Westmoreland Co., son of Parish [or Paris] and Fannie Turner, to EMMA SOPHIE BAYLOR, age 21, single, b. Richmond Co., daughter of Lewis and Julia Ann Baylor. License 23 DEC 1878. Married 26 DEC 1878 by H.H. Fones. [M20; R:127; R1:76-3]

U

Uhler, George (b. 1849, d. 1925 in Alexandria, Va.), secretary and treasurer of the Alexandria Water Company, to Nelly Selden Lloyd (1853-1931).[1] GEORGE UHLER, clerk, age 27, single, b. and res. Alexandria, Va., son of Peter G. Uhler [b. 1803 in Philadelphia, Pa., d. 1879 in Alexandria, Va.] and Catharine G. [Griffith Smoot] [1814-1896],[2] to NELLY SELDEN LLOYD, age 23, single, b. Alexandria, Va., daughter of John J. [Janney] Lloyd [1800-1871] and Eliza A. [Armistead Selden] [1820-1870].[3] License 7 AUG 1876. Married 8 AUG 1876 at Yeocomico Church by Beverley D. Tucker. [CP; M19; R:119; R1:65-15]

Unruh, Charles Benner to Julicia A. McKildoe. CHARLES BENNER UNRUH, machinist, age 62, widowed, b. Philadelphia Co., Pa., son of George B. [1797-1884] and Ann Unruh, to JULICIA A. McKILDOE, age 24, single, b. Westmoreland Co., daughter of James S. and Maria McKildoe. License 6 MAR 1876. Married 7 MAR 1876 at Carmel Church by W.A. Crocker. [M19; R:118; R1:64-11]

Unruh, Frank Hughes to Willie Ann Thrift (d. 1877 in childbirth). FRANK HUGHES UNRUH, ordinary keeper, age 25, single, b. Alexandria, Va., res. Kinsale, Va., son of Charles B. [d. 1881 of pneumonia] and Susan Unruh, to WILLIE ANN THRIFT, age 21, single, b. Westmoreland Co., daughter of Jeremiah C. [Courtney] Thrift and wife [E.] Jane. License 11 JAN 1876. Married 13 JAN 1876 at Yeocomico Church by J.H. Davis. [DR:40-96, 49-51[4]; M19; R:117; R1:63-13]

Usual, Robert Arthur (d. 1928), to Lucy Ann Thompson, black. ROBERT USUAL, farmer, age 19, single, b. Westmoreland Co., son of Beverly Usual and Fanny [Buckley], to LUCY ANN THOMPSON, age 19, single, b. Westmoreland Co., daughter of John and Carty Thompson. License 30 DEC 1879. Married 30 DEC 1879 at *Sherland* by F.B. Beale. [DC; M20; R:131; R1:80-7]

V

Van Housen, Christian to Elizabeth Cash. CHRISTIAN VANHOUSEN [sic], farmer, age 48, single, b. Germany, son of Euhon and Christian Vanhousen, to ELIZABETH CASH, age 30, single, b. Richmond Co., daughter of John and Alcey Cash. Groom's signature in German. License 31 MAY 1870. Married 2 JUN 1870 by D.M. Wharton, Rector, Montross Parish. [M18; R:99; R1:43-6]

---

[1] George Uhler and his wife Nellie Selden Lloyd were buried at Ivy Hill Cemetery, Alexandria, Va.
[2] Peter G. Uhler and Catharine Griffith [Smoot] were married by bond 7 NOV 1844 in Alexandria, Va., with Peter G. Uhler, security. *Alexandria Gazette* 13 NOV 1844, p. 3, Catharine is daughter of Rev. Alfred Griffith of the Methodist Church. They were buried in Ivy Hill Cemetery, Alexandria, Va.
[3] John J. Lloyd and Eliza A. Selden were married by bond 15 OCT 1845 in Alexandria, Va., with William C. Yeaton, security. John and Eliza were buried in Ivy Hill Cemetery, Alexandria, Va.
[4] DR:49-51, entry for Chas. B. Unruh, machinist, b. Pa., d. 5 NOV 1881 of pneumonia, age 73, son of Geo. and Anna Unruh, husband of Susan Unruh.

Van Ness, Julius Bishop (1813-1896), to Frances Amanda Porter (1831-1889).[1] JULIUS BISHOP VANNESS [sic], merchant, age 54, widowed, b. Albany, N.H., res. Washington Co., Tex., son of Benjamin and Delia Van Ness, to FRANCES AMANDA PORTER, age 30, single, b. Westmoreland Co., daughter of Sampson Porter and Catharine [Neasom].[2] License 2 JUL 1868. Married 4 JUL 1868 by J.H. Davis. [M18; R:92; R1:34-9]

Van Ness, William Henry (1850-1932), to Sarah Alma Northam (1852-1940).[3] WILLIAM HENRY VANNESS [sic], farmer, age 29, single, b. Richmond Co., res. Bracken Co., Ky., son of W.P. & E.J. Van Ness, to SARAH ALMA NORTHAM, age 28, single, b. Westmoreland Co., daughter of George [H.] Northam and Elizabeth [Walker].[4] License 13 NOV 1879. Married 13 NOV 1879 at Nomini Episcopal Church[5] by F.B. Beale. [M20; R:130; R1:78-15]

Vansant, George to Adalene Augusta Hughlett. GEORGE VANSANT, farmer, age 32, single, b. Pennsylvania, son of L.S. and S.J. Vansant, to ADALENE AUGUSTA HUGHLETT, age 26, single, b. Northumberland Co., daughter of William and S.E. Hughlett. License 25 SEP 1879. Married 29 SEP 1879 at the residence of Mrs. Sarah Jett in Northumberland Co. by Ro. L. Lewis. [M20; R:130; R1:78-13]

Vasselmann, Frederick (d. 1893 of congestion of bowel), to Amanda McKenney. FREDERICK VASSELMAN, farmer, age 41, single, b. Germany, son of John and Catharine Vasselmann, to AMAMDA McKENNEY, age 30, single, b. Westmoreland Co., daughter of G.R. and Mary McKenney. License 4 DEC 1878. Married 5 DEC 1878 near *Prospect Hill* by F.B. Beale. [DR:95-60; M20; R:127; R1:75-10]

Vaughn, Robert to Leonora Griggs. ROBERT VAUGHN, sailor, age 32, single, b. Westmoreland Co., son of Sibby Vaughn, father unknown, to LEONORA GRIGGS, age 21, single, b. Westmoreland Co., daughter of Robert Griggs and Elizabeth [Roane], *q.v.* License 19 MAR 1879. Married 20 MAR 1879 at R. Griggs by T.T. Johnson. [M20; R:128; R1:77-4]

Vessels, David (C) to Lucy Jane Fortune. DAVID VESSELS, farmer, age 29, single, b. Essex Co., son of David and Eliza Vessels, to LUCY JANE FORTUNE, age 18, single, b. Essex Co., daughter of Humphrey and Louisa Fortune. Signed David [his X mark] Vessels, wit. W.S. McKenney. License 1 JUN 1871 [sic]. Married 2[5] MAY 1871 by Jno. Roy, minister. [M18; R:102; R1:46-16]

W

Walker, Addison to Alswitha Casey. ADDISON WALKER, sailor, age 24, single, b. Westmoreland Co., son of John and Caty Walker, to ALSWITHA CASEY, age 25, single, b. Westmoreland Co., daughter of Priscilla Casey, father unknown. Signed A. [his X mark] Walker, wit. W.R. Polk. Consent 16 JAN 1861 by bride Alswitha [her X mark] Carey, wits. Thomas Weldon, John [his X mark] Thompson. License 17 JAN 1861. Married 19 JAN 1861. [M17:61-1 and 1a; R:77]

---

[1] Julius B. Van Ness and his wife Frances were buried in Prairie Lea Cemetery, Brenham, Washington Co., Tex.
[2] Samson Porter [sic] and Catharine Neasom were married by bond 23 MAR 1827 in Richmond Co., with Thomas A. Kennedy, security.
[3] William Henry Van Ness was buried with his wife Sarah at Nomini Baptist Church, Montross, Va.
[4] George H. Northam and Elizabeth Walker were married by bond 20 MAR 1850 in Westmoreland Co., with E.B. Omohundro, security.
[5] Nomini Episcopal Church had been rebuilt by 1848. The initial property was given in 1703 by Youell Watkins for a church to be built over the graves of his grandparents.

Walker, Benedict, Jr. to Emmeline Rice. BENEDICT WALKER, JR., farmer, age 30, single, b. Westmoreland Co., son of Benedict Walker [1783-1861][1] and Hannah [Wright] [1803-1883],[2] to EMMELINE RICE, age 19, single, b. Westmoreland Co., res. *Laurel Spring*, daughter of John T. Rice and Mary [C. Robinson].[3] License 4 NOV 1858. Married 10 NOV 1858 at *Laurel Spring* by T. Grayson Dashiell, clergyman. [M16a:58-28 and 28a; R:64; R1:12-15]

Walker, Benjamin Morgan (1846-1927), to Mary Presley Robinson (1845-1924).[4] BENJAMIN MORGAN WALKER, farmer, age 26, single, b. Northumberland Co., son of Richard W. Walker and Lydia S. [Lewis],[5] to MARY PRESLEY ROBINSON, age 25, single, b. Westmoreland Co., daughter of William [B.] Robinson and Ann [M. Wright].[6] License 3 FEB 1873. Married 4 FEB 1873 at the residence of George D. Jeffries by R.J. Sanford. [M19; R:108; R1:53-6]

Walker, James (1829-1881), to Elizabeth Anna Beale (1840-1921).[7] JAMES WALKER, farmer, age 29, single, b. Westmoreland Co., son of Benedict Walker and Hannah [Wright],[8] to ELISABETH ANNA BEALE, age 18, single, b. Westmoreland Co., daughter of Henry and Susan R. Beale. License 7 APR 1858. Married 13 APR 1858 at the residence of the wife's father by W.W. Walker, M.G. [DR:49-52; M16a:58-13; R:64; R1:11-9]

Walker, William Middleton (1845-1882), served in Co. K, 40th Va. Inf. and 9th Va. Cav., C.S.A., to Hannah Elizabeth Walker (1844-1934).[9] WILLIAM MIDDLETON WALKER, lawyer, age 24, single, b. Westmoreland Co., son of William G. [George] Walker [d. intestate 1847][10] and Elizabeth [Sanford],[11] to HANNAH ELIZABETH WALKER, age 24, single, b. Westmoreland Co., daughter of Benedict and Hannah [Wright] Walker. License 19 FEB 1869. Married 21 FEB 1869 by F.A. Davis. [M18; R:94; R1:38-1]

Wall, Henry, Rev., of Ireland, to Miss Judith W. Hansford, of King George. Married 7 OCT 1856 at *Green Height*, King George Co. [SP; WP]

Wallace, Moses (C) to Mary Nelson. MOSES WALLACE, farmer, age 40, widower, b. Westmoreland Co., son of James and Rose Wallace, to MARY NELSON, age 23, single, b. Westmoreland Co., daughter of John and Sarah Nelson. Signed Moses [his X mark] Wallace, wit. W.S. McKenney. Married 15 OCT 1874 at Zion Church by Thomas T. Johnson. [M19; R1:59-3]

Ware, John Henry (C) to Margaret Jones. JOHN HENRY WARE, farmer, age 34, single, b. Essex Co., son of John and Judy Ware, to MARGARET JONES, age 24, single, b. Essex Co., daughter of William and Peggy Jones (now Lewis). Signed by John Henry [his X mark] Ware, wit. W.S. McKenney. License 2 DEC 1873. Married 4 DEC 1873 by John Roy. [M19; R:110; R1:55-2]

---

[1] CF1863-01, *W.W. Walker v. Hannah Walker &c*, notes that Benedict Walker d. intestate 8 AUG 1861.
[2] Benedict Walker, Sr. and his wife Hannah Wright were buried in the Walker Family Cemetery at *Poplar Plain*, located near the intersection of Routes 600 and 203 at Oldhams, Va. *Poplar Plain* was owned by W.W. Walker. For description of *Poplar Plain*, see *Northern Neck News*, 17 NOV 1891, p. 3.
[3] John T. Rice and Mary C. Robinson were married by bond 29 AUG 1831 in Westmoreland Co., with William M. Dameron, security.
[4] Benjamin Morgan Walker and wife Mary Robinson were buried at Carmel United Methodist Church, Kinsale, Va.
[5] Richard Walker and Lydia S. Lewis, daughter of George Lewis, were married by bond 5 JAN 1839 in Northumberland Co., with George Wilkins, security.
[6] William B. Robinson and Ann M. Wright were married by bond 29 FEB 1836 in Westmoreland Co., with William R. McKenney, security.
[7] James Walker and his wife Anna Elizabeth Beale were buried in the Walker Family Cemetery at *Poplar Plain*.
[8] Benedict Walker and Hannah Wright were married by bond 19 JAN 1825 in Westmoreland Co., with James C. Wright, security.
[9] William M. Walker and his wife Hannah were buried in the Walker Family Cemetery at *Poplar Plain*, located near the intersection of Routes 600 and 203 at Oldhams, Va.
[10] CF1852-13, *Admr. of William G. Walker v. John A. Carter &c*.
[11] William G. Walker and Elizabeth Sanford were married by bond 17 APR 1844 in Westmoreland Co., with Joseph S. Lyell, security.

Ware, Robert (C) to Josephine Fortune. ROBERT WARE, farmer, age 39, widowed, b. Essex Co., son of [John and] Judy Ware, father unknown, to JOSEPHINE FORTUNE, age 28, single, b. Essex Co., daughter of Robert Fortune and Mary [Bird], *q.v.* License 24 APR 1880. Married 29 APR 1880 at John Richards' near Oak Grove by Wm. C. Latane, Presbyter P.E. Church, wit. John Richards. [M20; R:133; R1:82-7; WP]

Warfield, Joseph (C) to Mary McHeart, black. JOSEPH WARFIELD, farmer, age 23, single, b. Baltimore City, Md., son of Joseph and Rose Annah Warfield, to MARY McHEART, age 22, single, b. Westmoreland Co., daughter of Spencer and Mary McHeart. License 6 JAN 1880. Married 8 JAN 1880 at the bride's residence by Charles [his X mark] Rust. [M20; R:131; R1:80-10]

Waring, William Lawson (d. 1900), son of Robert Payne Waring of Essex Co., to Miss Rosalie Virginia Tayloe (1833-1872), daughter of Charles Tayloe and Virginia Anne Turner. Married 4 NOV 1858 at *Oaken Brow*, King George Co. [SP; WP]

Warner, Joseph F. to Laura V. Unruh. JOSEPH F. WARNER, plumber and gas fitter, age 33, single, b. and res. Philadelphia, Pa., son of Adam and Elizabeth Warner, to LAURA V. UNRUH, age 18, single, b. Alexandria, Va., res. Kinsale, Va., daughter of Charles and Susan Unruh. License 24 SEP 1857. Married 30 SEP 1857 at Kinsale, Va. by T. Grayson Dashiell, clergyman. [M16a:57-32; R:62; R1:10-6]

Washington, George to Sophia F. Franklin. GEORGE WASHINGTON, farmer, age 21, single, b. Westmoreland Co., son of Henry Washington [d. 1876 of dropsy] and Jane [Winkfield],[1] to SOPHIA F. FRANKLIN, age 25, single, b. Westmoreland Co., daughter of John and Lucy Franklin. Signed George [his X mark] Washington, wit. Wm. Green. License 12 JAN 1869. Married 14 JAN 186[9[2]] at the residence of William Gutridge by Thomas E. Locke, Rector, Washington Parish. [DR:38-16; M18; R:94; R1:37-10; WP]

Washington, Henry to Catharine Wingfield. HENRY WASHINGTON, age 32, widowed, b. Westmoreland Co., son of John Washington and Lucy [Hinson],[3] to CATHARINE WINGFIELD, age 23, single, b. Westmoreland Co., daughter of Walker Wingfield and Mahala [Locust].[4] License 1 SEP 1858. Married 2 SEP 1858 at the rectory of Washington Parish by Thomas E. Locke, minister of the Prot. Epis. Church. [M16a:58-21[5]; R:64; R1:14-3; SP; WP]

Washington, James Henry to Sally Walker. JAMES HENRY WASHINGTON, farmer, age 21, single, b. and res. King George Co., son of James Washington [c.1826-aft. 1890] and Amelia [McGruder],[6] to SALLY WALKER, age 18, single, b. Westmoreland Co., daughter of Letty Walker, father unknown. James [his X mark] Henry Washington, wit. Wm. S. McKenney. License 20 DEC 1871. Married 23 DEC 1871 at *Bluff Point* by Howard W. Montague, M.G. [M18; R:104; R1:48-11]

Washington, Jesse (C) to Alice Campbell. JESSEY WASHINGTON [sic], farmer, age 23, single, b. Westmoreland Co., son of Stuart and Mary Washington, to ALICE CAMPBELL, age 22, single,

---

[1] Henry Washington and Jane Winkfield were married by bond 6 JAN 1845 in Westmoreland Co., with Walker Winkfield, security.
[2] The date of marriage on the Certificate is 1868; however the year of filing is 1869.
[3] John Washington and Lucy Hinson were married by bond 10 JUN 1816 in Westmoreland Co., with William Nash, security.
[4] Walker Wingfield and Mahala Locust were married by bond 6 JUN 1825 in Westmoreland Co., with James Brown, security.
[5] Another copy at 58-21a gives age of groom 35 and age of bride 21.
[6] James Washington and his wife Amelia were buried at Spy Hill Cemetery, King George Co.

b. Westmoreland Co., daughter of George and Bettie Campbell. License 7 JAN 1878. Married 10 JAN 1878 at the bride's residence by Rev. William Gaskins. [M19; R:124; R1:72-3]

Washington, John (C) to Lilly Garner. JOHN WASHINGTON, farmer, age 22, single, b. Westmoreland Co., son of Stewart and Ditty Washington, to LILLY GARNER, age 21, single, b. Westmoreland Co., daughter of Levi and Mary Garner. License 1 JAN 1877. Married 4 JAN 1877 by Rev. William Gaskins. [M19; R:121; R1:68-5]

Washington, John to Letty Bushard. JOHN WASHINGTON, farmer, age 21, single, b. Essex Co., son of Moses and Jane Washington, to LETTY BUSHARD, age 22, single, b. Westmoreland Co., daughter of West and Easter Bushard. Signed John [his X mark] Washington, wit. J.H. Sisson. License 23 JUN 1870. Married 25 JUN 1870 by H. Young. [M18; R:99; R1:43-10]

Washington, John, first to Lucy G. Franklin (d. 1877 of congestive chill). JOHN WASHINGTON, farmer, age 21, single, b. Westmoreland Co., son of Henry Washington and Jane [Winkfield], *q.v.*, to LUCY G. FRANKLIN, age 25, single, b. Westmoreland Co., daughter of John and Lucy Franklin. Signed John [his X mark] Washington, wit. Wm. S. McKenney. License 24 MAR 1874. Married 26 MAR 1874 by Robert N. Reamy. [DR:41-102; M19; R:112; R1:58-4]

Washington, John, second to Mrs. Amanda Jackson. JOHN WASHINGTON, farmer, age 23, widowed, b. Westmoreland Co., son of Henry Washington and Jane [Winkfield], *q.v.*, to AMANDA JACKSON, age 23, widow, b. Westmoreland Co., daughter of John Jackson and Mary Jane [Head], *q.v.* License 4 DEC 1878. Married 8 DEC 1878 at Oak Grove by F.W. Claybrook. [M19; R:127; R1:75-9]

Washington, Parker (C) to Bettie Turner. PARKER WASHINGTON, farmer, age 27, single, b. Westmoreland Co., son of Stewart and Mary Washington, to BETTIE TURNER, age 18, single, b. Westmoreland Co., daughter of Hetty Turner, father unknown. License 15 NOV 1879. Married 27 NOV 1879 at my residence by Rev. William Gaskings. [M20; R:130; R1:78-16]

Washington, Robert James (b. 1841 at his home *Campbellton*,[1] d. 1910 in Colonial Beach, Va.), served in the 9th Va. Cav., C.S.A., Commonwealth's Attorney, State Senator, to Elizabeth "Bettie" Selena Payne Wirt (1846-1895).[2] ROBERT JAMES WASHINGTON, lawyer, age 26, single, b. Westmoreland Co., son of Lawrence Washington [b. 1791, d. testate 1875[3]] and Sarah T. [Tayloe] Washington [1800-1886],[4] to BETTIE PAYNE WIRT, age 21, single, b. Westmoreland Co., daughter of [Dr.] William Wirt [1815-1899] and [Elizabeth] "Bettie" S. [Selina Payne] [1827-1909].[5] License 18 OCT 1867. Married 30 OCT 1867 at *Wirtland* [the residence of the bride's father] by J.W. Chesley, minister Prot. Epis. Church. [M18; R:88; R1:29-14; SC; WP]

---

[1] Also see NN:18 JAN 1901, p. 2.
[2] Robert J. Washington and his wife Bettie Wirt were buried in a Washington Family Cemetery at *Campbellton*, located near the intersection of Routes 636 and 634.
[3] Deeds & Wills No. 40, p. 234, will of Lawrence Washington, proved 22 NOV 1875, names wife Sarah T. Washington and son Robert. He was buried at *Campbellton*.
[4] Lawrence Washington, of *Oak Grove*, and Sarah Tayloe Washington were married 26 OCT 1819 by Rev. William H. Wilmer, Rector of St. Paul's Episcopal Church in Alexandria, Va. WP shows that Mrs. Sarah Tayloe Washington died 20 DEC 1886 and was buried at *Campbellton*.
[5] William Wirt and his wife Bettie Selena Payne were buried in the Payne Family Cemetery at *Cedar Hill*, located off of Route 640 near Leedstown, Va.

Washington, Walker Hawes, Dr. (1824-1911), to Mary West Washington (1828-1902).[1] WALKER WASHINGTON, age 32, single, b. Caroline Co., son of John Washington and Ann [Hawes], to MARY WASHINGTON, age 26, single, b. Westmoreland Co., daughter of Lawrence Washington and Sallie [Sarah Tayloe Washington], *q.v.* License 18 DEC 1856. Married 29 DEC 1856 at *Blenheim* by J.W. Chesley, minister of the Prot. Epis. Church. [M16a:56-38; R:57; R1:8-2; SC; SP; WP]

Watkins, William to Sarah Ann Johnson. WILLIAM WATKINS, farmer, age 24, widowed, b. Richmond Co., son of George and Lucy Watkins, to SARAH ANN JOHNSON, age 23, single, b. Westmoreland Co., daughter of C. and Ann Johnson. License 13 SEP 1877. Married 13 SEP 1877 by J.H. Davis. [R:122; R1:70-9]

Watson, Rudolph (1852-1928),[2] to Sarah Monroe Northern (d. 1887 of dropsy). RUDOLPH WATSON, farmer, age 24, single, b. Charles Co., Md., son of R.G. [Roderick Green] Watson and Ann [Percy], to SARAH MONROE NORTHERN, age 21, single, b. Westmoreland Co., daughter of John H. [Henry] and Margaret Northern. License 29 JAN 1877. Married 31 JAN 1877 at Mrs. Margaret Northern's by Wm. C. Latane, Presbyter P.E. Church. [DR:74-187; M19; R:121; R1:68-14; WP]

Watts, Emanuel, Rev. (d. 1883 of pneumonia), to Leannah Samuel. EMANUEL WATTS, minister, age 60, widowed, b. Westmoreland Co., son of Sam and Edy Watts, to LEANNAH SAMUEL, age 34, single, b. Essex Co., daughter of Betsy Samuel. License 26 JUL 1877. Married 29 JUL 1877 at Oak Grove Church by Rev. John Dunlop of King George Co. [DR:59-119; M19; R:122; R1:70-7]

Watts, James to Ella West, colored persons. JAMES WATTS, farmer, age 29, widower, b. Westmoreland Co., son of Samuel and Edy Watts, to ELLA WEST, age 18, single, b. Westmoreland Co., daughter of Charles and E. Waters. Signed James [his X mark] Watts, wit. J.W. Hutt. License 27 APR 1868. Married 9 MAY 1868 at the rectory by Thomas E. Locke, Rector Washington Parish. [M18; R:90; R1:33-4; WP]

Watts, James to Mrs. Margaret Watts Taylor (d. 1873 in childbirth at *Monroe Hall*), colored persons. JAMES WATTS, farmer, age 33, widowed, b. Westmoreland Co., son of Emanuel and Hannah Watts, to MARGARET TAYLOR, age 21, widow, b. Westmoreland Co., daughter of Richard and Eliza Watts. James [his X mark] Watts, wit. J.W. Hutt. License 28 DEC 1868. Married 31 DEC 1868 at the Quarter on Dr. Thomas R. Ditty's[3] farm, by Thomas E. Locke, Rector, Washington Parish. [DR:29-52; M18; R:94; R1:37-2; WP]

Watts, James (C) to Mary Carter. JAMES WATTS, farmer, age 39, widowed, b. Westmoreland Co., son of Emanuel and Hannah Watts, to MARY CARTER, age 23, single, b. Westmoreland Co., daughter of Lewis Carter. License 28 NOV 1874. Married 3 DEC 1874 by Emanuel Watts, pastor of Little Zion Church. [M19; R:113; R1:59-6]

Watts, Meredith (C) to Ella Dickerson [or Diggs]. MEREDITH WATTS, farmer, age 21, single, b. Westmoreland Co., son of Robert and Lucy Watts, to ELLA DICKERSON, age 21, single, b. Essex

---

[1] Dr. Walker H. Washington and his wife Mary West Washington were buried in the Washington Family Cemetery at *Campbellton*, located near the intersection of Routes 636 and 634.
[2] Rudolph Watson was buried in St. Peter's Cemetery, Oak Grove, Va.
[3] WP shows that Dr. Thomas R. Ditty died 27 DEC 1876 and was buried at *Cedar Hill*.

Co., daughter of Randell and Polly Dickerson.* License 2 MAR 1880. Married 6 MAR 1880 at Little Zion Church by Emanuel Watts. [DR:74-184[1]; M20; R:132; R1:81-11]

Watts, Moses (C) to Nancy Key. MOSES WATTS, farmer, age 21, single, b. Westmoreland Co., son of Moses and Mary Watts, to NANCY KEY, age 19, single, b. King George Co., daughter of Henry and Winnie Keys. Signed by Moses [his X mark] Watts, wit. P.R. Harvey. License 11 DEC 1874. Married 14 DEC 1874 by Emanuel Watts, pastor of Little Zion Church. [M19; R:113; R1:59-10]

Watts, Samuel to Mrs. Dorcas Barnet Bennett, colored people. SAMUEL WATTS, farmer, age 57, widowed, b. Westmoreland Co., son of Samuel and Edy Watts, to DORCAS BENNETT, age 28, widow, b. Westmoreland Co., daughter of Charles and Hannah Barnet. License 15 NOV 1867. Married 1 DEC 1867 in the Methodist Church at Oak Grove by T.E. Locke, Rector of St. Peter's Church. [M18; R:88; R1:30-1; WP]

Weathers, James to Sally Sutton. License 27 JAN 1851. Married 4 FEB 1851 by Edw. B. McGuire. [M15:51-9; R:7]

Weaver, Bushrod (1846-1912), served in Co. E, 55th Va. Inf., C.S.A., to Virginia Ann Sanders (1848-1889).[2] BUSHROD WEAVER, farmer, age 24, single, b. Westmoreland Co., son of Presley Weaver and Mary A. [Alverson],[3] to VIRGINIA ANN SANDERS, age 21, single, b. Richmond Co., daughter of Zachariah Sanders and Margaret A. [Oliffe].[4] Signed B. [his X mark] Weaver, signed J.W. Hutt. License 6 AUG 1870. Married 7 AUG 1870 by Robert N. Reamy. [M18; R:99; R1:43-12]

Weaver, Charles C. to Mary Ann Self. License 5 FEB 1852. Married 10 FEB 1852 by John Pullen. [M15:52-7, R:17]

Weaver, Charles Lewis to Mary Jane Quesenbury. CHARLES LEWIS WEAVER, farmer, age 40, widowed, b. Westmoreland Co., son of Presley Weaver and Mary [A. Alverson], *q.v.*, to MARY JANE QUESENBERRY [sic], age 23, single, b. Westmoreland Co., daughter of Nicholas and Nancy Quesenberry. License 1 FEB 1866. Married 4 FEB 1886 at Mrs. Quisenberry's by John Pullen. [M18; R:82; R1:23-5]

Weaver, George Amos (d. 1922), to Mary Elizabeth Annadale (d. 1906).[5] GEORGE AMOS WEAVER, farmer, age 28, single, b. Westmoreland Co., son of Henry Weaver and Jane [Nash],[6] to MARY ELIZABETH ANADALE [sic], age 23, single, b. Westmoreland Co., daughter of Robert [P. Annadale] and Mary [M. Tallent], *q.v.* License 20 DEC 1880. Married 21 DEC 1880 by R.N. Reamy. [M20; R:134; R1:84-9]

Weaver, James Henry, served in Co. A, 15th Va. Cav., C.S.A., to Mary Elizabeth Douglass. JAMES HENRY WEAVER, farmer, age 24, single, b. Westmoreland Co., son of Henry and Catharine

---

[1] DR:74-184, entry for Ella Watts (C), d. 1 JUN 1887 of consumption, age 23, daughter of Randall and * Polly Diggs, wife of Meredith Watts.
[2] Bushrod Weaver (a.k.a. Bushard Weaver) and his wife Virginia were buried at Currioman Baptist Church, Chiltons, Va.
[3] Presley Weaver and Mary Alverson were married by bond 21 JAN 1824 in Westmoreland Co., with Joshua Reamy, security. Also found as Allison.
[4] Zachariah Sanders and Margaret A. Oliffe were married by bond 9 DEC 1844 in Westmoreland Co., with James S. Weaver, security.
[5] George A. Weaver and his wife Mary Elizabeth Annadale were buried in the Weaver-Annadale Cemetery, located off of Route 644.
[6] Henry Weaver and Jane Nash were married by bond 1 DEC 1847 in Westmoreland Co., with William Nash, security.

Weaver, to MARY ELIZABETH DOUGLASS, age 23, single, b. Westmoreland Co., daughter of Lemuel Douglass and Sally [Sarah Palmer], *q.v.* License 11 FEB 1868. Married 16 FEB 1868 at Mrs. Sally Douglass' by H.P.F. King. [M18; R:90; R1:32-7]

Weaver, James Samuel (1848-1915), served Co. A, 15th Va. Cav., C.S.A., to Frances "Fannie" Ann Sanford (1839-1929).[1] JAMES SAMUEL WEAVER, farmer, age 28, single, b. Westmoreland Co., son of William Weaver and Nancy A. [Davis],[2] to FANNIE ANN SANFORD, age 27, single, b. Westmoreland Co., daughter of Thomas Sanford and Adaline [Reamy].[3] License 18 JAN 1873. Married 19 JAN 1873 at the residence of the bride's father by D.G.C. Butts. [M19; R:108; R1:53-3]

Weaver, John W. to Mary Ann Drake. License 18 DEC 1850. Married 19 DEC 1850[4] by John Pullen. [M15:50-27; R:5 not in *Nottingham*]

Weaver, John Willis (1840-1921),[5] served in Co. E, 55th Va. Inf., C.S.A., to Mary Ann Weaver. JOHN WILLIS WEAVER, farmer, age 27, single, b. Westmoreland Co., son of William Weaver and Nancy [A. Davis], *q.v.*, to MARY ANN WEAVER, age 25, single, b. Westmoreland Co., daughter of Presley Weaver and Mary [Alverson], *q.v.* License 28 JAN 1868. Married 30 JAN 1868 at Charles Weaver's by H.P.F. King. [M18; R:89; R1:32-2]

Weaver, Joseph to Jane Moss. JOSEPH WEAVER, farmer, age 23, single, b. Westmoreland Co., son of William and Mary Ann Weaver, to JANE MOSS, age 19, single, b. Westmoreland Co., daughter of George and Emily Moss. License 23 DEC 1874. Married 23 DEC 1874 at George Moss' by Robert N. Reamy. [M19; R:114; R1:60-3]

Weaver, Lewis Andrew (d. by 1867), to Lucretia Fairfax Self. LEWIS A. WEAVER, waterman or sailor, age 22, single, b. Westmoreland Co., son of Presley Weaver and Mary [Alverson], *q.v.*, to LUCRETIA F. SELF, age 20, single, b. Westmoreland Co., daughter of Moses Self and Sarah "Sally" [Crask], *q.v.* License 6 NOV 1858. Married 11 NOV 1858 by H.P.F. King, minister of the M.E. Church. [M16a:58-30 and 30a[6]; R:66; R1:12-10]

Weaver, Robert (b. 1835, d. 1903 at Templeman's), served in Co. A, 15th Va. Cav., C.S.A., to Mrs. Mary Ann Haley [or Healy] Hall, (1839-1914),[7] widow of Richard Madison Hall, *q.v.* ROBERT WEAVER, farmer, age 35, single, b. Westmoreland Co., son of Henry [d. 1883] and Nancy Weaver, to MARY ANN HALL, age 32, widow, b. Westmoreland Co., daughter of Nathan and Mary A. Haley. License 15 MAR 1871. Married 16 MAR 1871 by G.H. Northam. [DR:59-17; M18; R:102; R1:46-10]

Weaver, Thomas Collin (d. 1915), to Elizabeth Ann Bryant (d. 1884 of camp colic).[8] THOMAS COLLIN WEAVER, shoemaker, age 26, single, b. Westmoreland Co., son of Henry and Catharine S. Weaver, to ELIZABETH ANN BRYANT, age 25, single, b. Westmoreland Co., daughter of John

---

[1] James S. Weaver and his wife Frances A. were buried at Providence United Methodist Church, Chiltons, Va.
[2] William Weaver and Ann Davis were married by bond 9 JUN 1834 in Westmoreland Co., with Samuel Davis, security.
[3] Thomas Sanford and Adeline Reamy was married by bond 15 FEB 1834 in Westmoreland Co., with William Johnson, security.
[4] The year in the Register of Marriage Licenses with Marriage Certificates, 1850-1920 gives year 1851.
[5] John W. Weaver was buried at Providence United Methodist Church, Chiltons, Va.
[6] Another copy at 58-30a gives middle names for both groom and bride.
[7] Robert Weaver and his wife Mary Ann were buried in the Hall Family Cemetery, located on *Oakville Farm*, located off of Route 202.
[8] Thomas C. Weaver and his wife Elizabeth Bryant (and her parents John B. Bryant (d. 1875) and Elizabeth Eskridge (1810-1867)) were buried in the Eskridge Family Cemetery, located off of Route 214 near the entrance to *Stratford Hall*.

B. Bryant [d. 1875] and Elizabeth A. [Eskridge] [1810-1867].[1] License 12 JAN 1872. Married 14 JAN 1872 at Chilton's X Roads by Robert N. Reamy. [DR:62-111; M19; R:104; R1:49-9]

Weaver, William Alexander, first to Virginia Bryant (d. 1859 of bilious fever). WILLIAM ALEXANDER WEAVER, farmer, age 29, single, b. Westmoreland Co., son of Alexander Weaver and Martha [Alderson],[2] to VIRGINIA BRYANT, age 21, single, b. Westmoreland Co., daughter of John B. Bryant and Elizabeth [A. Eskridge], *q.v.* License 13 NOV 1857. Married 15 NOV 1857 at the residence of Martha Weaver by H.P.F. King, minister of the M.E. Church. [DR:4-36; M16a:57-37; R:62; R1:10-10]

Weaver, William Alexander, second to Frances F. Sanford. WILLIAM ALEXANDER WEAVER, farmer, age 31, widowed, b. Westmoreland Co., son of Alexander Weaver and Martha [Alderson], *q.v.*, to FRANCES F. SANFORD, age 16, single, b. Westmoreland Co., daughter of William and Lucy Sanford. Signed Wm. A. [his X mark] Weaver, wit. E.G. Reed. License 11 OCT 1859. Married 12 OCT 1859 by Elder James A. Weaver. [M16a:59-25 and 32; R:70]

Weaver, William Louis, served in Co. A, 15th Va. Cav., C.S.A., to Lizzie Ann Sanford. WILLIAM LOUIS WEAVER, farmer, age 27, single, b. Westmoreland Co., son of William [H.] and Nancy Weaver, to LIZZIE ANN SANFORD, age 25, single, b. Westmoreland Co., daughter of Thomas Sanford and Adaline [Reamy], *q.v.* License 12 JAN 1866. Married 14 JAN 1866 at the residence of Thos. Sanford by H.P.F. King. [M18; R:82; R1:23-2]

Weldon, David H. (C) to Sarah Ann Thompson. DAVID H. WELDON, farmer, age 24, single, b. Richmond Co., son of Sample Weldon and Sally [Gaskins], *q.v.*, to SARAH ANN THOMPSON, age 21, single, b. Westmoreland Co., daughter of Moses Thompson and Henrietta Thompson, *q.v.* Signed David H. [his X mark] Weldon, wit. Wm. S. McKenney. License 12 DEC 1871. Married 14 DEC 1871 at *Prospect Hill* by G.W. Beale, minister Baptist Church. [M19; R:103; R1:48-8]

Weldon, Thomas (C) to Precilla Montague. THOMAS WELDON, farmer, age 21, single, b. Richmond Co., son of George and Maria Weldon, to PRECILLA MONTAGUE, age 24, single, b. Westmoreland Co., daughter of Novella Montague, father unknown. License 24 JUL 1880. Married 25 JUL 1880 at my residence in Richmond Co. by Edmond Rich. [M20; R:134; R1:83-9]

Weldon, Thomas A. (C) to Caroline Smith. THOMAS A. WELDON, farmer, age 21, single, b. Westmoreland Co., son of Thomas Weldon and Mariah Smither, to CAROLINE SMITH, age 21, single, b. Westmoreland Co., daughter of John Smith. License 13 JAN 1875. Married 14 JAN 1875 near Tucker Hill by Thomas T. Johnson. [M19; R:114; R1:60-13]

Weldon, Thomas (C) to Lucetta Thompson. THOMAS WELDON, farmer, age 26, single, b. Richmond Co., son of Sample Weldon and Sally [Gaskins], *q.v.*, to LUCETTA THOMPSON, age 20, single, b. Westmoreland Co., daughter of Sarah Jenkins, father unknown. Signed Thomas [his X mark] Weldon. License 12 JAN 1872. Married 12 JAN 1872 at the residence of the bride by Elder James A. Weaver. [M19; R:104; R1:49-6]

---

[1] John B. Bryant and Elizabeth Eskridge were married by bond 29 DEC 1831 in Westmoreland Co., with Richard Omohundro, security.
[2] Alexander Weaver and Marthy Alderson were married by bond 3 JUL 1821 in Westmoreland Co., with James Mariner, security.

Wells, Tasker (C) to Mrs. Octavia [Reed] Tibbs. TASKER WELLS, laborer, age 40, widowed, b. Westmoreland Co., son of Arch Campbell and Betsey Wells, to OCTAVIA TIBBS, age 30, widow, b. Westmoreland Co., daughter of Charlotte Reed, father unknown. Signed Tasker [his X mark] Wells. License 30 JUL 1871. Married 3 AUG 1871 at *The Park* by Thomas T. Johnson. [M18; R:102; R1:47-4]

Wharton, Edmund Logwood (1839-1914), served in Co. C, 47th Va. Inf., C.S.A., first to Sophia Eleanor Harvey (1844-1879).[1] EDMUND LOGWOOD WHARTON, farmer, age 26, single, b. Botetourt Co., son of [Rev.] Dabney [Miller] Wharton and Ann [Ophelia Pearce], *q.v.*, to SOPHIA ELEANOR HARVEY, age 21, single, b. Westmoreland Co., daughter of Joseph F. [Fox] Harvey and Ann W. [Washington Hungerford].[2] License 26 JUN 1866. Married 27 JUN 1866 at Montross, Va. by D.M. Wharton, Rector of Montross Parish. [M18; R:83; R1:24-10]

Wharton, Dabney Miller, Rev. (b. 1804, d. 1887 of heart disease),[3] *q.v.*, second to Virginia Ann Hungerford (d. 1879).[4] DABNEY MILLER WHARTON, minister, age 62, widower, b. Bedford Co., son of John and Sally Wharton, to VIRGINIA HUNGERFORD, age 46, single, b. *Twiford*, Westmoreland Co., daughter of John W. [Washington] Hungerford and E.A. [Eleanor Anne Hungerford].[5] License 17 JUN 1868. Married 18 JUN 1868 at *Twiford* (the residence of the bride) by Thomas E. Locke, Rector, Washington Parish. [DR:73-118; M18; R:91; R1:34-6; SC; WP]

Wheeler, John Delozier to Roberta Rowe. JOHN DELOZIER WHEELER, farmer, age 22, single, b. Westmoreland Co., son of William Wheeler and Eliza [Brinon] [d. 1882 of erysipelas], to ROBERTA ROWE, age 21, single, b. Westmoreland Co., daughter of William and Dorothy Rowe. License 11 NOV 1875. Married 14 NOV 1875 by R.J. Sanford. [DR:53-82[6]; M19; R:116 omits Wheeler; R1:62-5]

Wheeler, Richard R. (d. 1881 of consumption), to Mariah Franklin. RICHARD WHEELER, farmer, age 27, single, b. Westmoreland Co., son of William Wheeler and Eliza [Brinon], *q.v.*, to MARIAH FRANKLIN, age 24, single, b. Westmoreland Co., daughter of James and Mary Franklin. License 17 MAR 1879. Married 19 NOV 1879 at Carmel Church by R.J. Sanford. [DR:49-53; M20; R:130; R1:79-1]

White, James H. to Myra Sorrel. License 22 NOV 1852. Married 23 NOV 1852 by John Pullen. [M15:52-27; R:23]

White, John Randolph to Sophia Wood Chandler. JOHN RANDOLPH WHITE, physician, age 34, single, b. St. Mary's Co., Md., son of Nelson B.C. and Sarah C. White, to SOPHIA WOOD CHANDLER, age 24, single, b. Westmoreland Co., daughter of John and Elizabeth Chandler. License 4 DEC 1860. Married 5 DEC 1860 by George F. Bagby. [M17:60-37 and 37a[7]; R:76; R1:17-6]

---

[1] Edmund Logwood Wharton and his wife Sophia were buried at St. James Episcopal Church, Montross, Va.

[2] Joseph F. Harvey and Ann W. Hungerford were married by bond 18 OCT 1843 in Westmoreland Co., with William Hutt, security.

[3] Rev. Dabney M. Wharton was buried in St. James Episcopal Cemetery, Montross, Va.

[4] Virginia Ann Hungerford Wharton was buried in the Hungerford-Griffith Family Cemetery, located near Leedstown, Va.

[5] SP, Baptisms, p. 17, Eleanor Ann Hungerford was baptized at St. Peter's Church, 2 DEC 1855, as an adult.

[6] DR:53-82, entry for Eliza B. Wheeler, d. 8 APR 1882 of erysipelas, age 63, daughter of Benj. and Moss Brinon, widow, mother of John D. Wheeler.

[7] Minister return by George F. Bagby is dated 8 DEC 1860 from *Loch Harbor*.

White, John Willis (b. 1840, d. 1895 of chronic dysentery), served in Co. C, 47th Va. Inf., C.S.A., to Catharine Ann Quesenbury (b. 1843, d. 1884).[1] JOHN WILLIS WHITE, farmer, age 27, single, b. Westmoreland Co., son of Granville White and Leannah [Mothershead],[2] to CATHARINE ANN QUESENBERRY [sic], age 25, single, b. Richmond Co., daughter of Nicholas and Ann [L. Mothershead] Quesenberry.[3] License 10 FEB 1868. Married 12 FEB 1868 at Lucy Quisenberry's. [DR:62-110, gives birth Stafford Co., 101-13 parents Gravette and Laura White; M18; R:90; R1:32-6]

White, William A. (C) (1852-1917),[4] to Bettie Merrick. WILLIAM WHITE, farmer, age 25, single, b. Kent Co., Md., parents unknown, to BETTIE MERRICK, age 20, single, b. Westmoreland Co., daughter of Peggy Johnson, father unknown. License 3 DEC 1879. Married 4 DEC 1879 by H.H. Fones. [M20; R:130; R1:79-2]

Whiting, Alexander (C) to Elizabeth Corbin. ALEXANDER WHITING, farmer, age 60, widowed, b. Westmoreland Co., son of Catesby and Felitia Yates alias Whiting, to ELIZABETH CORBIN, age 25, single, b. Westmoreland Co., daughter of Fleet and Nancy Corbin. License 22 DEC 1873. Married 29 DEC 1873 at *Black Castle* by Thomas T. Johnson. [M19; R:110; R1:55-13]

Wiggins, Fleet, first to Hannah Crabb (C) (d. 1869 in child birth). FLEET WIGGINS, farmer, age 31, single, b. Westmoreland Co., son of John and Patty Wiggins, to HANNAH CRABB, age 22, single, b. Westmoreland Co., daughter of Meredith Crabb and Susan [Morgan]. Signed Fleet [his X mark] Wiggins, wit. J.W. Hutt. License 13 MAY 1869. Married 15 MAY 1869 by John C. Smith. [DR:17-40; M18; R:95; R1:38-5]

Wiggins, Fleet, second to Julia Armstrong. FLEET WIGGINS, farming, age 32, widowed, b. Westmoreland Co., son of John and Patty Wiggins, to JULIA ARMSTRONG, age 21, single, b. Westmoreland Co., daughter of Scipio and Julia Armstrong. Signed Fleet [his X mark] Wiggins, wit. W.S. McKenney. License 20 SEP 1871. Married 21 SEP 1871 at Julia Armstrong's by R.J. Sanford. [M18; R:102; R1:47-9]

Wilburn, Nathaniel J. to Maria A. Deatley (d. 1885). License 28 AUG 1856. [DR:66-113; R:57 no return]

Wilkerson, Thomas Austin (1852-1940), to Sarah "Sallie" Lee Smoot (1857-1920).[5] THOMAS AUSTIN WILKERSON, wheelwright, age 24, single, b. Westmoreland Co., son of Austin P. and Louisa Wilkerson, to SARAH LEE SMOOT, age 19, single, b. Westmoreland Co., daughter of B.F. [Benjamin] and Lucy A. [Mothershead] Smoot, *q.v.* License 21 DEC 1876. Married 24 DEC 1876 at *Locust Farm* by F.W. Claybrook. [M19; R:121; R1:67-16]

Wilkerson, Thomas S. [or J.] to Sydney A. Lamkin. THOMAS S. WILKERSON, no occupation, age 27, single, b. Westmoreland Co., son of Austin Wilkerson and Susan A. [Brennon],[6] to SYDNEY A.

---

[1] John W. White and his wife Catharine Ann were buried in the White Family Cemetery, located near the intersection of Routes 3 and 623.
[2] Granville White and Leannah Mothershead, daughter of Sarah Mothershead, were married by bond 3 MAR 1838 in Westmoreland Co., with James True, security.
[3] Nicholas Quesenberry, widower, and Ann L. Motherhead, spinster, were married by bond 6 JAN 1829 in Richmond Co., with Samuel Morris, security.
[4] William A. White was buried in the White Family Cemetery, located off of Route 640 near Leedstown, Va.
[5] Thomas A. Wilkerson and his wife Sallie L. were buried in Glenwood Cemetery, Washington, D.C.
[6] Austin Wilkerson and Susanna Brennon were married by bond 29 JAN 1823 in Westmoreland Co., with Austin B. Frank, security.

LAMKIN, age 22, single, b. Westmoreland Co., daughter of George Lampkin [sic] and Weston Lamkin. License 23 MAY 1857. Married 31 MAY 1857 by [Y.S.]D. Covington, minister of the M.E. Church South. [M16a:57-15; R:61; R1:9-12]

Wilkins, James Richard (1857-1937),[1] to Aranie Coats. JAMES RICHARD WILKINS, farmer, age 21, single, b. Westmoreland Co., son of Mathew Wilkins and Lucretia [Atkins],[2] to ARANIE COATS, age 21, single, b. Westmoreland Co., daughter of Salathiel and Emily Coats. License 21 DEC 1877. Married 23 DEC 1877 at the residence of the bride's father by F.W. Claybrook. [M19; R:124; R1:71-15]

Wilkins, Thomas Frederick to Virginia Carter. THOMAS FREDERICK WILKINS, farmer, age 24, single, b. Westmoreland Co., son of Mathew Wilkins and Lucretia [Atkins], *q.v.*, to VIRGINIA CARTER, age22, single, b. Westmoreland Co., daughter of John and Nancy Carter. License 14 FEB 1877. Married 15 FEB 1877 by H.H. Fones. [M19; R:121; R1:69-1]

Wilkins, William Augustus (b. 1844, d. 1928 of angina pectoris),[3] to Catharine Gutridge (1855-1928). WILLIAM AUGUSTUS WILKINS, farmer, age 34, single, b. Westmoreland Co., son of Mathew Wilkins and Lucretia [Atkins], *q.v.*, to CATHARINE GUTRIDGE, age 21, single, b. Westmoreland Co., daughter of John Gutridge and Elizabeth [Ann Atkins].[4] License 9 DEC 1879. Married 10 DEC 1879 by H.H. Fones. [DC; M20; R:130; R1:79-8]

Williams, Abraham to Mrs. Frances Smith Johnson (C) (d. 1886 of dropsy). ABRAHAM WILLIAMS, farmer, age 46, single, b. Westmoreland Co., son of Samuel and Patsey Williams, to FRANCES JOHNSON, age 25, widow, b. Westmoreland Co., daughter of Emanuel and Judy Smith. Signed by Abraham [his X mark] Williams., wit. C.C. Baker. License 18 DEC 1866. Married 19 DEC 1866 at *Water View* by J.H. Davis. [DR:68-36; M18; R:84; R1:26-2]

Williams, Dennis (C) to Mrs. Sarah Lavinia Gaskins Smith, widow of John Smith, *q.v.* DENNIS WILLIAMS, farmer, age 30, single, b. Westmoreland Co., son of McKenzie and Jane Williams, to SARAH LAVINIA SMITH, age 27, widow, b. Westmoreland Co., daughter of Patrick Gaskins and Sally [Sarah Gaskins], *q.v.* Signed Dennis [his X mark] Williams, wit. Wm. S. McKenney. License 23 NOV 1875. Married 23 NOV 1875 at Little Zion Church by Thomas T. Johnson. [M19; R:116; R1:62-6]

Williams, Henry (C) to Sarah Blackwell. HENRY WILLIAMS, farmer, age 21, single, b. Westmoreland Co., son of Sarah Williams, father unknown, to SARAH BLACKWELL, age 21, single, b. Westmoreland Co., son of Adam and Sarah Blackwell. Signed Henry [his X mark] Williams, wit. W.S. McKenney. License 24 FEB 1871. Married 26 FEB 1871 by Emanuel Watts, Pastor of Little Zion Church. [M18; R:101; R1:46-6]

Williams, Henry (C) to Winney Burges. HENRY WILLIAMS, farmer, age 26, single, b. Westmoreland Co., son of Jesse and Eliza Williams, to WINNEY BURGES, age 27, single, b.

---

[1] James Richard Wilkins is buried with wife Althea Anne (1856-1937) in St. Peter's Cemetery, Oak Grove, Va.
[2] Mathew Wilkins and Lucretia Atkins, daughter of Jane Atkins, were married by bond 15 JUL 1843 in Westmoreland Co., with Joseph Atkins, security.
[3] DC: William A. Williams was buried at Middlebrough, Va.
[4] John Gutridge and Elizabeth Ann Atkins were married by bond 19 OCT 1844 in Westmoreland Co., with Joseph Atkins, security.

Westmoreland Co., daughter of James and India Burges. Signed Henry [his X mark] Williams. License 27 DEC 1869. Married 10 JAN 1870 by John C. Smith. [M18; R:97; R1:41-3]

Williams, John (C) to Fanny Ashton (C). License 9 DEC 1854. [R:45 no return]

Williams, Phillip (C) to Livina Beale. PHILLIP WILLIAMS, farmer, age 22, single, b. Westmoreland Co., son of Abram and Jane Williams, to LIVINA BEALE, age 22, single, b. Westmoreland Co., daughter of George and Livina Beale. Signed Phillip [his X mark] Williams, wit. Wm. S. McKenney. License 14 OCT 1871. Married 22 OCT 1871 at Potomac Colored Baptist Church by Thomas T. Johnson. [M18; R:103; R1:47-15]

Williams, Samuel to Eliza Gaskins. SAMUEL WILLIAMS, farmer, age 50, single, b. Westmoreland Co., son of Samuel and Patsy Williams, to ELIZA GASKINS, age 32, single, b. Westmoreland Co., daughter of Thomas and Sally Gaskins. Signed Sam [his X mark] Williams, wits. J.F. Bispham, J.W. Hutt. License 4 SEP 1866. Married 5 SEP 1886 at the minister's residence by Elder James A. Weaver. [M18; R:84; R1:24-15]

Williams, Stafford to Sarah Elizabeth Johnson. STAFFORD WILLIAMS, farmer, age 57, single, b. and res. Richmond Co., son of Billy Johnson and Sally Jones, to SARAH ELIZABETH JOHNSON, age 45, single, b. Westmoreland Co., daughter of Peggy Johnson, father unknown. Signed Stafford [his X mark] Williams, wit. C.C. Baker. License 16 AUG 1866. Married 21 AUG 1866 at Sally Elizabeth Johnson's by Wm. N. Ward. [M18; R:83; R1:24-13]

Williams, Sydnor, second[1] to Mrs. Cordelia Parker Nelson (C) (d. 1887 of consumption). SYDNOR WILLIAMS, farmer, age 50, widowed, b. Westmoreland Co., son of [Lazarus] and Mary Williams, to CORDELIA NELSON, age 27, widow, b. Richmond Co., parents unknown [Leroy and Bettie Parker]. Signed Sydnor [his X mark] Williams, wit. J.W. Hutt. License 28 DEC 1869. Married 29 DEC 1869 by D.M. Wharton, Rector of Montross Parish. [DR:73-116; M18; R:97; R1:41-4]

Williams, William Alexander to Sarah Merrick. WILLIAM ALEXANDER WILLIAMS, waiter, age 24, single, b. Westmoreland Co., res. Baltimore, Md., son of Sarah Williams, father unknown, to SARAH MERRICK, age 23, single, b. Westmoreland Co., daughter of Peggy Johnson, father unknown. License 25 SEP 1876. Married 28 SEP 1876 in Richmond Co. by H.H. Fones. [M19; R:119; R1:66-5]

Willing, James Clark, Dr. to Geneveve H. Garnett.[2] License 19 AUG 1850. [R:3 no return, not in *Nottingham*]

Willis, Madison (C) to Lucy Henderson. MADISON WILLIS, farmer, age 24, single, b. Westmoreland Co., son of Richard and Pheby Willis, to LUCY HENDERSON, age 17, single, b. Westmoreland Co., son of Mary Henderson. Signed by Madison [his X mark] Willis, wit. J.W. Hutt. License 29 DEC 1868. Married 31 DEC 1868 by Jerry Graham, parson. [M18; R:94; R1:37-5]

Wilson, George Lewis (C) to Evelina Gaskins. GEORGE LEWIS WILSON, farmer, age 21, single, b. Westmoreland Co., son of Mitchell and Isabella Wilson, to EVELINA GASKINS, age 19, single,

---

[1] DR:16-66, entry for Sophia Williams (C), d. 15 DEC 1868 of bilious, age 50.
[2] Genevieve H. Garnett Willing was buried in the Garnett Family Cemetery, located off of Route 205, just past Mattox Creek Bridge when going toward Colonial Beach from Oak Grove, Va.

b. Westmoreland Co., daughter of B. and Mary Gaskins. Signed Geo. L. [his X mark] Wilson, wit. Wm. S. McKenney. License 4 JAN 1876. Married 7 JAN 1876 at Jesse Kelly's by Thomas T. Johnson. [M19; R:117; R1:63-11]

Wilson, John Ezekiel (1825-1909), served in Co. 8, 111th Va. Mil., C.S.A., owner of *Wakefield*, the birthplace of President George Washington, to Bettie H. Washington (1838-1922).[1] JOHN E. WILSON, farmer, age 31, widowed, b. West River, Anne Arundel Co., Md., son of John F. [Fletcher] and Elizabeth Wilson, to BETTIE WASHINGTON, age 18, single, b. Westmoreland Co., daughter of Lawrence and Sally [T.] [Sarah Tayloe] Washington, *q.v.* License 18 OCT 1856. Married 22 OCT 1856 at *Campbellton* by J.W. Chesley, minister of the Prot. Epis. Church. [M16a:56-29; R:57; R1:7-3; SP; WP]

Wilson, John Thomas (C) to Georgeanna Churchwell. JOHN THOMAS WILSON, farmer, age 24, single, b. Westmoreland Co., son of Mitchell D. and Elizabeth Wilson, to GEORGEANNA CHURCHWELL, age 19, single, b. Westmoreland Co., daughter of Samuel and [Hetty] Churchwell. License 31 OCT 1876. Married 2 NOV 1876 at *Sandy Point* by Thomas T. Johnson. [M19; R:119; R1:66-11]

Wilson, Mitchell, Jr. (C) to Mary Josephine Johnson. MITCHEL WILSON [sic], farmer, age 24, single, b. Westmoreland Co., son of Mitchell [D.] and Elizabeth Wilson, to MARY JOSEPHINE JOHNSON, age 19, single, b. Westmoreland Co., daughter of Joseph Johnson and Arena [Kelly], *q.v.* License 19 NOV 1878. Married 21 NOV 1878 at Horn Point by Thomas T. Johnson. [M19; R:126; R1:75-5]

Wilson, Robert Edward to Mary Louisa Collins. ROBERT EDWARD WILSON, farmer, age 20, single, b. Westmoreland Co., son of Robert Wilson and Fanny [Frances Bennett],[2] to MARY LOUISA COLLINS, age 19, single, b. Westmoreland Co., daughter of George W. Collins [d. testate 1912] and Ann [Elizabeth Reed], *q.v.* License 21 DEC 1876. Married 21 DEC 1876 by G.H. Northam. [M19; R:120; R1:67-15]

Wilson, Robert Henry (C) to Mary Green. ROBERT HENRY WILSON, age 24, single, b. Westmoreland Co., son of Mitchell D. and Isabella Wilson, to MARY GREEN, age 21, single, b. Westmoreland Co., daughter of Henry and Harriet Green. License 13 DEC 1876. Married 14DEC 1876 at *Bankelton* by Thomas T. Johnson. [M19; R:120; R1:67-7]

Wilson, William (C) to Clarissa Ann Gaskins. WILLIAM WILSON, oysterman, age 21, single, b. Westmoreland Co., son of Mitchell [D.] and Elizabeth Wilson, to CLARISSA ANN GASKINS, age 17, single, b. Westmoreland Co., daughter of Bartly [Bartlett] Gaskins and Mary [Ann Peck], *q.v.* Signed William [his X mark] Wilson, wit. J.W. Hutt. License 13 DEC 1870. Married 15 DEC 1870 by Thomas T. Johnson, minister of the colored Baptist Church. [M18; R:100; R1:44-10]

Winkfield [or Wingfield], Beckwith (d. testate 1882[3] of pneumonia), served in Co. A, 15th Va. Cav., C.S.A., to Mary A. Tate. BECKWITH WINKFIELD, farming, age 20, single, b. King George Co., son of [Ezekiel and Polly Winkfield], to MARY TATE, age 18, single, b. Westmoreland Co., parents not

---

[1] John E. Wilson and his wife Bettie were buried in St. Peter's Cemetery, Oak Grove, Va.
[2] Robert Wilson and Frances Bennett were married by bond 10 JAN 1850 in Westmoreland Co., with James Johnson, security.
[3] Deeds & Wills No. 42, p. 351, will of Beckwith Wingfield, proved 28 AUG 1882, mentions wife but not named.

given. License 18 JAN 1854. Married 20 JAN 1854 at Mr. Tate's by Rev. John Pullen. [DR:56-46; M15:54-16b, R:39; R1:1-11]

Winkfield, Richard Henry to Mrs. Lucy Ann Head Barker, widow of Beckwith Barker (d. 1862), *q.v.* RICHARD HENRY WINKFIELD, farming, age 38, widowed, b. and res. King George Co., son of [Ezekiel and] Mary Winkfield, to LUCY ANN BARKER, age 26, widow, b. Westmoreland Co., daughter of Mary Head. Signed Richd. H. [his X mark] Winkfield. License 10 AUG 1867. Married 13 AUG 1867 at the residence of Benj. Yeatman by Thomas E. Locke. [M18; R:87; R1:29-3; WP]

Winkfield, Richard Henry (d. 1884), to Elizabeth Combs. RICHARD WINKFIELD, farmer, age 47, single [sic], b. King George Co., son of Ezekiel and Mary ["Polly"] Winkfield, to ELIZABETH COMBS, age 40, single, b. King George Co., daughter of Edmond and Nancy Combs. License 15 SEP 1877. Married 16 SEP 1877 at Washington Academy by F.W. Claybrook. [DR:63-180; M19; R:123; R1:70-11]

Wirt, Dabney Carr (b. 1817, d. testate 1893[1] of inflamation of the bowel), served in Co. 8, 111th Va. Mil., C.S.A., built *Roxbury*, to Julia Augusta Washington (1830-1888).[2] DABNEY CARR WIRT, lawyer, age 38, single, b. Richmond, Va., son of [Dr.] William Wirt [d. 1899] and Elizabeth [Selina Payne of *Wirtland*], to JULIA AUGUSTA WASHINGTON, age 25, single, b. Princeton, N.J., daughter of William A. [Augustine] and Juliet E. Washington of *Haywood*. License 16 NOV 1855. Married 19 NOV 1855 at St. Peter's Church, Oak Grove, Va. by J.W. Chesley, minister of the Prot. Epis. Church. [DR:90-41; M16:55-22; R:51; R1:4-10; SC; SP; WP]

Withers, William (C) to Sarah Jane Johnson. WILLIAM WITHERS, farmer, age 24, widowed, b. Richmond Co., son of George and Lucy Withers, to SARAH JANE JOHNSON, age 23, single, b. Westmoreland Co., daughter of Charles and Ann Johnson. Married 13 SEP 1877 at Thomas Johnson's home by J.H. Davis. [M19]

World (see Worrell)

Wormley, George (C) to Henrietta Clark. GEORGE WORMLEY, laborer, age 22, single, b. Westmoreland Co., son of James and Sarah Wormley, to HENRIETTA CLARK, age 26, single, b. Westmoreland Co., daughter of Henry and Rebecca Clark. Signed Geo. [his X mark] Wormley, wit. J.W. Hutt. License 16 SEP 1871. Married 16 SEP 1871 at the home of the bride by Jeremiah Graham. [M18; R:102; R1:47-8]

Wormley, Isaac, Jr. (d. 1885 of consumption), to Ann Pierce. ISAAC WORMSLEY [sic], sailor, age 28, single, b. Westmoreland Co., son of Isaac Wormley [Sr.] and Elizabeth [Pierce][3] (C) [d. 1882 of pneumonia], to ANN PIERCE, age 30, single, b. Westmoreland Co., daughter of William Pierce and Hannah [McCoy], *q.v.* License 3 SEP 1878. Married 4 SEP 1878 at *Cabin Ford* by F.B. Beale. [DR:53-79[4], 65-70; M19; R:126; R1:74-12]

---

[1] Deeds & Wills No. 51, p. 452, will of Dabney C. Wirt, proved 22 MAY 1893, names wife Julia Augusta.
[2] Dabney Carr Wirt and his wife Julia Augusta Washington were buried in a Washington Family Cemetery at *Haywood*, now at St. Peter's Episcopal Church, Oak Grove, Va.
[3] Isaac Wormley and Betsy Peirce were married by bond 26 DEC 1842 in Westmoreland Co., with John Wormley, security.
[4] DR:53-79, entry for Elizabeth Wormley (C), housekeeper, d. 12 APR 1882 of pneumonia, age 71, daughter of Thornton and Betsy Pierce, wife of Isaac Wormley.

Worrell, Beckwith to Christiana Adams. BECKWITH WORRELL, wheelwright, age 60, widowed, b. King George Co., son of John and Susan Worrel, to CHRISTIANA ADAMS, age 44, single, b. King George Co., daughter of Thomas and Betsey Worrel [sic]. Signed Beckwith [his X mark] Worrel, wit. C.C. Baker. License 25 OCT 1866. Married 27 OCT 1866 at the residence of William Worrell by Thomas E. Locke. [M18; R:84; R1:25-7; WP]

World [or Worrell], James to Martha S. Winkfield. License 12 MAR 1853. Married 13 MAR 1853 by John Pullen. [M15:53-8; R:29]

Worrell, Putnam to Rachel Worrell (1856-1922), daughter of Beck Worrell and Ruby Purley. Married 12 DEC 1875 at the Parish School House by Rev. William C. Latane, wit. Andrew McGinnis and congregation. [DC; WP]

Worrell, William Henry to Willie Ann Combs (d. 1884 of erysipelas).[1] WILLIAM HENRY WORRELL, farmer, age 37, single, b. King George Co., son of Beckwith Worrell and Leanna [S.] [Pursley],[2] to WILLIE ANN COMBS, age 30, single, b. King George Co., daughter of Edmond and Nancy Combs. Signed Wm. H. [his X mark] Worrell, wit. W.S. McKenney. License 21 JAN 1874. Married 22 JAN 1874 at Wm. Worrell's by Jno. Payne. [DR:63-178; M19; R:112; R1:57-4; WP has Marianne Combs]

Wright, James William (1848-1888), to Naomi Elizabeth Lewis (1853-1888).[3] JAMES WILLIAM WRIGHT, farmer, age 26, single, b. Westmoreland Co., son of Francis [W.] Wright and Jane [Jeffries King], to NAOMI ELIZABETH LEWIS, age 25, single, b. Westmoreland Co., John W. Lewis and Ellen [E. King]. License 11 FEB 1874. Married 12 FEB 1874 at the bride's father's by W.A. Crocker. [M19; R:112; R1:57-11]

Wright, Reuben to Eleanora Mitchell. REUBEN WRIGHT, sailor, age 24, single, b. Alabama, son of Reuben and Charlotte Wright, to ELEANORA MITCHELL, age 20, single, b. Westmoreland Co., daughter of John and Sally Mitchell. License 12 JAN 1876. Married 13 JAN 1876 at Cole's Point by F.B. Beale. [M19; R:117; R1:63-15]

Wroe, John Columbus to Lucinda Jenkins. JOHN COLUMBUS WROE, farmer, age 25, single, b. Westmoreland Co., son of John and Lucy Wroe, to LUCINDA JENKINS, age 21, single, b. Westmoreland Co., daughter of Martha Jenkins, father unknown. License 12 MAR 1878. Married 13 MAR 1878 by H.H. Fones. [M19; R:125; R1:73-8]

Y

Yeatman, Benjamin (d. 1881), to Mrs. Margaret[4] Ann Dameron, widow of Uriah E. Head. BENJAMIN YEATMAN, mail rider, age 52, single, b. Westmoreland Co., son of [Jesse] and Jane Yeatman, to MARGARET HEAD [sic], age 40, widow, b. Westmoreland Co., parents unknown. Signed Benj. [his X mark] Head, wit. Geo. Hutt. Consent 16 JAN 1861 from Oak Grove by bride, wit. William Turner. License 17 JAN 1861. Married 23 JAN 1861 by T.E. Locke. [M17:61-2 and 2a; NN; R:76; SC gives Margaret Head; WP gives date 18 MAY 1861]

---

[1] Mrs. William H. Worrell was buried at Blaggs Cemetery, location unknown. WP shows that Mrs. Wm. H. Worrell died 11 JUN 1884 and was buried at her husband's residence.
[2] Beckwith Worrel and Leanna Pursley were married 13 OCT 1824 in King George Co.
[3] James W. Wright and wife Naomi Elizabeth were buried in a Wright Family Cemetery, located off of Route 602.
[4] Margaret also appears in records as Mahala.

Yeatman, Charles to Emily Augusta Arnest (1845-1888).[1] CHARLES YEATMAN, merchant, age 22, single, b. Richmond Co., son of Alfred J. Yeatman and Emily J. [Jane Hunter],[2] to EMILY ARNEST, age 24, single, b. Westmoreland Co., daughter of Thomas M. [Maund] Arnest and Emily M. [Mildred Beale].[3] License 31 JAN 1870. Married 1 FEB 1870 at the residence of the bride's father by J.H. Davis. [M18; NN; R:98; R1:42-1]

Yeatman, Rodolph to Ann Eliza Crabb. RODOLPH YEATMAN, merchant, age 34, single, b. Fauquier Co., res. Memphis, Tenn., son of George E. Yeatman and C. [Chloe] Ann [Tongue],[4] to ANN ELIZA CRABB, age 25, single, b. Westmoreland Co., daughter of William [P.] Crabb and Eliza [Ann Yeatman].[5] License 21 DEC 1861. Married 22 DEC 1861 at *Nominy Grove* by G.H. Northam. [M17:61-12; R:77; R1:18-5]

Yeatman, Thomas James (d. 1893 of Bright's disease), first to Mary J. Porter (d. 1871 of consumption). THOMAS J. YEATMAN, farmer, age 21, single, b. Westmoreland Co., son of Henry [A.] Yeatman and Ann [W. Reynolds],[6] to MARY J. PORTER, age 21, single, b. Westmoreland Co., daughter of Samson Porter and Catharine [Neasom], *q.v.* License 23 APR 1856. Married 24 APR 1856 at the residence of Samson Porter by H.P.F. King, minister of the M.E. Church. [DR:23-36, 94-45; M16:56-13, R:55; R1:5-12]

Yeatman, Thomas James (d. 1893), second to Medora Dee Beale. THOMAS JAMES YEATMAN, mechanic, age 37, widowed, b. Westmoreland Co., son of Henry A. Yeatman and Ann W. [Reynolds], to MEDORA DEE BEALE, age 22, single, b. Westmoreland Co., daughter of Henry and Susan R. Beale. License 18 OCT 1872. Married 20 OCT 1872 at Ebenezer Church by E.A. Gibbs, minister. [M19; R:106; R1:51-4]

Yeatman, William to Mrs. Mary Ann Bragg Cool (b. *Green Wood*, d. 1864 of pneumonia). WILLIAM YEATMOND, age 46, widower, b. Richmond Co., son of Thomas Yeatman and Elizabeth [McClanahan],[7] to MARY ANN COOL, age 38, widow twice, b. Westmoreland Co., daughter of Thomas [Moore] Bragg and Margaret [Bispham] [d. 1864].[8] License 6 OCT 1854. Married 8 OCT 1854 at John Weaver's by John Pullen. [DR:8-10, 11; M15:54-11; R:45; R1:2]

Young, John F. to Susan A. Miller. JOHN F. YOUNG, farming, age 28 in Feb., single, birthplace blank, son of William Young and Malinda his wife, to SUSAN A. MILLER, age 20 in June, single, birthplace blank, daughter of [Richard] Millar [sic] and Lucy [Gutridge][9] his wife. License 23 JUL 1855. Married 26 JUL 1855 at Richard Millar's, Mattox, Va. by John Pullen. [M16:55-14; R:49; R1:3-11]

Young, Moses (C) to Lizzie Thompson. MOSES YOUNG, farmer, age 23, single, b. Westmoreland Co., son of Thomas and Fanny Young, to LIZZIE THOMPSON, age 21, single, b. Westmoreland

---

[1] Emily Yeatman was buried in an unmarked grave with her parents at Nomini Hall Cemetery, Hague, Va.
[2] Alfred J. Yeatman and Emily Jane Hunter were married by bond 2 DEC 1834 in Westmoreland Co., with William P. Crabb, security.
[3] Thomas M. Arnest and Emily M. Beale were married by bond 5 NOV 1839 in Westmoreland Co., with Richard L.T. Beale, security.
[4] George E. Yeatman and Chloe Ann Tongue were married by bond 11 DEC 1821 in Fauquier Co., with Johnzie Tongue, security. Date of marriage 13 DEC 1821.
[5] William P. Crabb and Eliza Ann Yeatman, daughter of Ann H. Yeatman, were married by bond 7 NOV 1827 in Westmoreland Co., with G.G. Mothershead, security.
[6] Henry A. Yeatman and Nancy W. Reynolds were married by bond 8 JUL 1833 in Richmond Co., with Robert L. Montgomery, security.
[7] Thomas Yeatman and Elizabeth McClanahan were married by bond 21 JAN 1795 in Westmoreland Co., with Edward Porter, security.
[8] Thomas Moore Bragg and Margaret Bispham were married 13 MAY 1813 by Rev. Samuel Templeman in Richmond Co.
[9] Richard Miller and Mrs. Lucinda Gutridge were married by bond 9 OCT 1833 in Richmond Co., with Henry H. Hazard, security.

Co., daughter of Henry and Charlotte Thompson. License 11 JAN 1878. Married 17 JAN 1878 in Washington Township by Emanuel Watts, pastor, Little Zion Church. [M19; R:124; R1:72-5]

No Surname

[ ], Humphrey to Betsy [ ], servants of Col. Henry T. Garnett.[1] Married 8 MAY 1859 in St. Peter's Church. [SP; WP]

[ ], Matthew (a slave belonging to [Mr.] Wheelwright), to Jane [ ] (a slave belonging to D.C. Wirt). Married 19 JAN 1861 at *Roxbury* by Rev. T.E. Locke. [WP]

[ ], Samuel to Stella [ ]. Married 27 JUL 1873 at *Font Hill*, Essex Co. by Rev. John Payne, wit. by the family of R.M.T. Hunter. [WP]

---

[1] WP shows death of Col. Henry Thomas Garnett on 8 AUG 1871, with burial at *Eltham*.

ADDITIONAL MARRIAGES

Below are additional marriages performed in Westmoreland County, where the marriage license is not filed in Westmoreland County.

Richmond County (Note: Refer to Wesley E. Pippenger, *Richmond County, Virginia Marriage Records, 1854-1890: Annotated* (Tappahannock, Va.: Barbour Printing Services, Inc., 2015), in which the references at the end of each entry below are explained):

Ambrose, Joseph to Frances Jenkins. JOSEPH AMBROSE,[1] farmer, age 20y3½m, single, b. Richmond Co., son of Elijah and Caroline [Pratt] Ambrose,[2] to FRANCES JENKINS, age 22, single, b. Richmond Co., daughter of James and Ann [Jenkins] Jenkins.[3] Consent 30 DEC 1873 by bride, wits. John Oliff, Eliza [Ambrose]. B.R. Battaile. 2 JAN 1874 in Westmoreland Co. [C7; R:230; R1:36]

Bartlett, Joseph to Frances Ambrose. JOSEPH BARTLETT, farmer, age 22, single, b. Richmond Co., son of Samuel and Mahala [Carter] Bartlett, to FRANCES AMBROSE, age 18, single, b. Richmond Co., daughter of Elijah and Caroline [Pratt] Ambrose. Consent 14 OCT 1873 by father Elijah Ambrose, no wit. B.R. Battaile. 22 OCT 1873 at *Mulen Hill* in Westmoreland Co. [C6; R:235; R1:34]

Bowen, Frederick to Mrs. Mary F. Yeatman, widow of Levi Yeatman. FREDERICK BOWEN, house carpenter, age 24, single, res. Richmond Co., son of William and Nancy A. [Bowen] Bowen, *q.v.*, to MARY F. YEATMAN, age 26, widow, res. Richmond Co., daughter of Henry and Elizabeth Davis. Consent 23 DEC 1857 from mother Elizabeth [her X mark] Davis, Mary [her X mark] Yeatman, wit. John H. Yeatman. 24 DEC 1857 at res. of Henry P.F. King in Westmoreland Co. Rev. Henry P.F. King, M.E. Church. [C1; R:160; R1:5]

Bowen, William H. to Lizzie H. Jones. WILLIAM H. BOWEN, fisherman, age 28, single, b. Richmond Co., son of James and Ann Bowen, to LIZZIE H. JONES, age 20y10m, single, b. Stafford Co., daughter of Clinton Jones and Catharine [Brown] Jones[4] now Mozingo. Consent 2 NOV 1875 by mother Catherine Mozingo, signed by Lizzie H. Jones, wit. A.L. Saunders. D.M. Wharton. 4 NOV 1875 at the res. of the minister in Westmoreland Co. [C7; R:262; R1:38]

Davis, John A. to Milly Bowen. JOHN A. DAVIS, farmer, age 23, single, b. Richmond Co., son of Henry and Elizabeth [P. English] Davis, to MILLY BOWEN, age 21, single, b. Richmond Co., daughter of John and Maria Bowen. Consent 1 APR 1863 by bride Milly [her X mark] Bowen, wits. Samuel R. Franklin, V. [his X mark] Anthony. G.H. Northam. 5 APR 1863 at *Woodbine* in Westmoreland Co. [C3; R:160; R1:12]

Fones, Charles H. to Mary Susan Moss. CHARLES H. FONES, farming, age 21y4m26d, single, b. Richmond Co., son of Richard [T.] and Susan B. [Ambrose] Fones, *q.v.*, to MARY SUSAN MOSS, age 20y3m, single, b. Richmond Co., daughter of William Moss and Rosey Ann Moss now Nash. Consent 17 APR 1880 by bride's mother Rosey Ann [her X mark] Nash, wit. Wm. [his X

---

[1] Surname is found as Ambers in the Register but is correct at Ambrose.
[2] Elijah Ambrose and Caroline Pratt were married 20 AUG 1849 in Richmond Co. by Rev. William Balderson.
[3] James Jenkins and Ann Jenkins were married 31 MAR 1853 in Richmond Co. by Rev. John Pullen.
[4] Clinton Jones and Catharine Brown were married by bond 19 JUN 1842 in Richmond Co., by consent of her father John Brown.

mark] Cash. D.M. Wharton. 18 APR 1880 at the minister's res. in Westmoreland Co. [C9; R:315; R1:50]

Gutridge, Armistead Carter[1] to Florence B. Reamy. ARMISTEAD C. GUTRIDGE, farmer, age 25, single, b. and res. Westmoreland Co., son of John and Elizabeth [Ann Atkins] Gutridge,[2] to FLORENCE B. REAMY, age 15, single, b. Richmond Co., daughter of James O. and [Mary] Jane [Morris] Reamy. Consent 6 SEP 1878 by A.C. Gutridge, guardian. F.W. Claybrook. 15 SEP 1878 at John Gutridge's in Westmoreland Co. [C8; R:311; R1:45]

Henry, Millard (Col.) to Mary E. "Lizzie" Blue (Col.). MILLARD HENRY, farmer, age 21y4m6d, single, b. Westmoreland Co., son of Frederick and Hannah Henry, to MARY LIZZIE BLUE, age 19, single, b. Westmoreland Co., daughter of George and Fanny Blue. Consent by mother Fanny [her X mark] Blue, wit. T.N. Balderson, Richard [his X mark] Lee. D.M. Wharton. 18 JUL 1878 at res. of the minister in Westmoreland Co. [C8; R:311; R1:45]

Hutchinson, John T. to Lizzie V. Taylor. JOHN T. HUTCHINSON, farmer, age 21, single, b. New Jersey, son of Francis and Mary Hutchinson, to LIZZIE V. TAYLOR, age 22, single, b . Richmond Co., daughter of Daniel and Lydia Taylor. G.H. Northam. 25 MAR 1873 at *Woodbine* in Westmoreland Co. [C6, R:235, R1:34]

Johnson, Sephus to Malinda Burrell. SEPHUS JOHNSON, farmer, age 35, single, b. Westmoreland Co., son of Reuben and Fanny Johnson, to MALINDA BURRELL, age 22, single, b. Richmond Co., daughter of Spencer and Polly Burrell. James A. Weaver. 18 DEC 1860 at James A. Weaver's in Westmoreland Co. [C2, R:154, R1:9]

Jones, Clinton to Dorethea Sanders. CLINTON JONES, farmer, age 21, single, b. Richmond Co., son of Clinton and Catharine [Brown] Jones,[3] to DORETHEA SANDERS, age 21, single, b. Richmond Co., daughter of John and Fanny Sanders. Consent 8 JAN 1872 by bride Dorothea [her X mark] Sanders, wits. Washington [Carter], Henry H. Brown. D.M. Wharton. 10 JAN 1872 at res. of minister in Westmoreland Co. [C6, R:237, R1:31]

Lee, Charles (Col.) to Ellen Johnson (Col.). CHARLES LEE, laborer, age 25, single, b. Westmoreland Co., son of Richard and Lydia Lee, to ELLEN JOHNSON, age 23, single, b. Richmond Co., daughter of Abby Johnson. Consent 2 JUL 1880 by bride Ellen [her X mark] Johnson, wit. Simon Sydnor. D.M. Wharton. 4 JUL 1880 at the res. of the minister in Westmoreland Co. [C9, R:315, R1:51]

Marks, Vincent, Jr. to Mary A. Cash. VINCENT MARKS, JR., farmer, age 22, single, b. Richmond Co., son of Vincent [Sr.] and Mary [France] Marks,[4] to MARY A. CASH, age 22, single, b. Richmond Co., daughter of [William and] Felicia [France] Cash. Consent 27 AUG 1872 by bride, also signed by her mother Felicia Cash, no wit. D.M. Wharton. 29 AUG 1872 at res. of minister in Westmoreland Co. [C6, R:238, R1:32]

---

[1] Armistead Carter Gutridge (b. 10 APR 1853, d. 15 JUN 1921) is bur. at Grant United Methodist Church cemetery, Lerty, Va.
[2] John Gutridge and Elizabeth Ann Atkins were married by bond 19 OCT 1844 in Westmoreland Co.
[3] Clinton Jones and Catharine Brown were married 23 JUN 1847 in Richmond Co. by Rev. John Pullen.
[4] Vincent Marks and Mary France were married by bond 9 MAY 1850 in Richmond Co.

Mozingo, Alexander to Mary Scates. ALEXANDER MOZINGO, farmer, age 20y6m, single, b. Richmond Co., son of Pierce and Sally [Sarah P. Barrett] Mozingo, *q.v.*, to MARY SCATES, age 25, single, b. Richmond Co., daughter of Joseph and Roberta [W. Butler] Scates.[1] Consent 10 NOV 1875 by bride Mary [her X mark] Scates, wits. Richard H. Mozingo, Fauntleroy Mozingo. D.M. Wharton. 11 NOV 1875 at the res. of the minister in Westmoreland Co. [C7, R:262, R1:38]

Mozingo, Fauntleroy to Isabella Weaver. FAUNTLEROY MOZINGO, farmer, age 20y9m, single, b. Richmond Co., son of Pierce and Sally [Sarah P. Barrett] Mozingo (dec'd.), to ISABELLA WEAVER, age 33y10m11d, single, b. Richmond Co., daughter of Henry and Nancy Weaver. Consent 5 JAN 1878 by bride and Nancy Weaver, wit. Pierce Mozingo. D.M. Wharton. 8 JAN 1878 at the res. of the minister in Westmoreland Co. [C8, R:310, R1:44]

Oliff, Thomas to Mahaly Hinson. THOMAS OLIFF, farmer, age 19, single, b. Richmond Co., son of Jesse and [Bethuel] Oliff, to MAHALY HINSON, age 22, single, b. Richmond Co., daughter of George Hinson. Consent 5 DEC 1873 by bride, also Jesse Oliff, wit. W.H. Balderson. B.R. Battaile. 11 DEC 1873 in Westmoreland Co. [C6, R:236, R1:35]

Sargent, Charlie H. to Mary A. Barrott. CHARLIE H. SARGENT, laborer, age 33, widowed, b. Kennebec Co., Me., res. Westmoreland Co., son of Charles and Mariam Sargent, to MARY A. BARROTT, age 34, single, b. Richmond Co., daughter of John and Mary Barrott. D.M. Wharton. 5 DEC 1877 at the res. of the minister in Westmoreland Co. [C8, R:307, R1:43]

Van Ness, Julius B. to Mary M. Porter. JULIUS B. VAN NESS, merchant, age 41, widower, b. Columbia, N.Y., son of Benjamin and Delia Van Ness, to MARY M. PORTER, age 26, single, b. Westmoreland Co., daughter of William and Amanda [C. Baber] Porter.[2] Consent 4 JUN 1855 by bride. B.H. Johnson, Minister of the Methodist Episcopal Church South, 5 JUN 1855 in Westmoreland Co. [C1, R:153, R1:2]

Wilson, Abraham P. to Elizabeth C. Croxton. ABRAHAM P. WILSON, farmer, age 57 on 1 JAN 1870, widowed, b. King and Queen Co., son of Samuel and Fanny Wilson, to ELIZABETH C. CROXTON, age 37, single, b. Richmond Co., daughter of Carter Croxton. Consent 2 DEC 1869 by bride, wit. G.W.C. Tallent. M. Beale, Baptist Church. 19 DEC 1869 at res. of L. Lampkin in Westmoreland Co. [C5, NN:8 OCT 1880, R, R1:27]

---

[1] Joseph Scates and Roberta W. Butler were married by bond 3 MAR 1845 in Richmond Co.
[2] William Porter and Amanda C. Baber were married by bond 11 NOV 1823 in Westmoreland Co.

SELECTED BIBLIOGRAPHY

In addition to original and microfilmed court records, the publications listed below have been consulted.

Anderson, C. Raymond, *Fourteen Generations of A Smoot Family in Virginia and Maryland: Beginning With the Arrival of William Smoot on the Ark in 1634* (Hyattsville, Md.: J.B. Donnellly, 1996)

Chambers, Roger David, *A Southern Legacy: Descendants of John Muse of Virginia* (1994; updated 2012 with corrections)

Davison, Bertha Lawrence Newton, *The Life of Cople Parish, 1664-1964 in Westmoreland County, Virginia* (1990; Westminster, Md.: Heritage Books, Inc., 2008)

Derieux, Susanne P. and Wesley E. Pippenger, *Essex County, Virginia Marriage Records: Transcripts of Consents, Affidavits, Minister Returns, and Marriage Licenses, Volume 1: 1850-1872* (Tappahannock, Va.: Barbour Printing Services, Inc., 2011)

Derieux, Susanne P. and Wesley E. Pippenger, *Essex County, Virginia Marriage Records: Transcripts of Consents, Affidavits, Minister Returns, and Marriage Licenses, Volume 2: 1873-1883* (Tappahannock, Va.: Barbour Printing Services, Inc., 2013)

Derieux, Susanne P. and Wesley E. Pippenger, *Essex County, Virginia Cemeteries: Volume I – County Church Cemeteries* (Tappahannock, Va.: Barbour Printing Services, Inc., 2011)

Dobyns, Kenneth W. and Margaret S. Thorpe, *Daniel Dobyns of Colonial Virginia: His English Ancestry and American Descentants* (Arlington, Va.: By the Author, 1969)

Fisher, Therese, *Marriages of Caroline County, Virginia, 1777-1853* (Bowie, Md.: Heritage Books, Inc., 1998)

Fortier, John, *15th Virginia Cavalry* (Lynchburg, Va.: H.E. Howard, Inc., 1993)

The Genealogical Society of the Northern Neck, *The Shepherd's Fold: Cemetery Records of Northumberland County, Virginia Churches* (Athens, Ga.: New Papyrus Publishing Company, 2012)

Hill, Margaret Lester and Clyde H. Ratcliffe, *In Remembrance: Gravestone Inscriptions and Burials of Lancaster County, Virginia* (White Stone, Va.: By the Compilers, 2002)

Hubard, William Stebbins, *Descendants of William Brockenbrough (1650-1700)* (By the Author, 2000).

King, George Harrison Sanford, *Marriages of Richmond County, Virginia, 1668-1863* (Fredericksburg, Va.: By the Author, 1964)

King George County Historical Society, *Cemeteries of King George County, Virginia, Volume I - Church Cemeteries* (King George, Va.: By the Society, 2000)

King George County Historical Society, *Cemeteries of King George County, Virginia, Volume II - Private Cemeteries* (King George, Va.: By the Society, 2005)

Knorr, Catherine L., *Marriages of Fredericksburg, Virginia, 1782-1850* (Pine Bluff, Ark.: Duplicating Service, The Purdue Co., 1954)

Krick, Robert E.L., *40th Virginia Infantry* (Lynchburg, Va.: H.E. Howard, Inc., 1985)

Krick, Robert K., *9th Virginia Cavalry*, 4th Ed. (Lynchburg, Va.: H.E. Howard, Inc., 1982)

Latane, Lucy Temple, *Parson Latane, 1672-1732* (Charlottesville, Va.: The Michie Co., Printers, 1936)

Lee, Elizabeth Nuckols, *King George County, Virginia Marriages: Volume I, Marriage Bonds Book 1, 1786-1850 [including ministers' returns]* (Athens, Ga.: Iberian Publishing Co., 1995)

Lee, Elizabeth Nuckols, *Westmoreland County, Virginia Loose Chancery Papers, 1804-1864* (Athens, Ga.: New Papyrus Publishing, 2004)

Lee, Ida J., *Lancaster County, Virginia Marriage Bonds, 1862-1850* (Baltimore, Md.: Genealogical Publishing Co., 1972)

Malory, Dalton W., *Westmoreland County, Virginia Cemeteries: Volume One* (Athens, Ga.: New Papyrus Publishing, 2009)

Marsteller, Charles M., *Dishman Index: Tracing the Descendants of Samuel Duchemin/Dishman (c.1640-w1727/Westmoreland Co., VA) ...* (San Francisco, Calif.: By the Author, 2000)

Miller, Thomas Michael, *Alexandria and Alexandria (Arlington) County, Virginia Minister Returns and Marriage Bonds, 1801-1852* (Bowie, Md.: Heritage Books, Inc., 1987)

Musselman, Homer D., *47th Virginia Infantry* (Lynchburg, Va.: H.E. Howard, Inc., 1991)

Norris, Walter Biscoe, Jr., *Westmoreland County, Virginia, 1653-1983* (Montross, Va.: Westmoreland Board of Supervisors, 1983)

Nottingham, Stratton, *The Marriage License Bonds of Lancaster County, Virginia, From 1701 to 1848* (Onancock, Va.: By the Author, 1927; reprint Baltimore, Va.: Clearfield Co., Inc., 1992)

Nottingham, Stratton, *The Marriage License Bonds of Northumberland County, Virginia, From 1783 to 1850* (Onancock, Va.: By the Author, 1929; reprint Baltimore, Md.: Genealogical Publishing Co., Inc., 1976)

Nottingham, Stratton, *The Marriage License Bonds of Westmoreland County, Virginia, From 1786 to 1850* (Onancock, Va.: By the Author, 1928; reprint Baltimore, Md.: Genealogical Publishing Co., Inc., 1975)

Omohundro, Malvern Hill, *The Omohundro Genealogical Record: The Omohundros and Allied Families in America* (Staunton, Va.: McClure Printing Co., 1951)

Payne, Brooke, *The Paynes of Virginia* (Harrisonburg, Va.: C.J. Carrier Co., 1990)

Pippenger, Wesley E., *Alexandria County (Arlington), Virginia Marriage Records, 1853-1895* (Westminster, Md.: Family Line Publications, 1994)

Pippenger, Wesley E., *Death Notices from Richmond, Virginia Newspapers, 1841-1853* (Richmond, Va.: The Virginia Genealogical Society, 2002)

Pippenger, Wesley E., *Essex County, Virginia Marriage Bonds, 1804-1850: Annotated* (Tappahannock, Va.: Barbour Printing Services, Inc., 2015)

Pippenger, Wesley E., *Index to Virginia Estates, 1800-1865, Volume 10* (Richmond, Va.: The Virginia Genealogical Society, 2010)

Pippenger, Wesley E., *John Alexander: A Northern Neck Proprietor, His Family, Friends and Kin* (Baltimore, Md.: Gateway Press, Inc., 1990)

Pippenger, Wesley E., *Richmond County, Virginia Marriage Records, 1854-1890: Annotated* (Tappahannock, Va.: Barbour Printing Services, Inc., 2015)

Reese, William Emmett, *The Settle-Suttle Family* (Carrollton, Ga.: Thomasson Printing Co., 1994)

Rhamy, Bonnelle William, *The Remy Family in America* (Fort Wayne, Ind.: By the Author, 1942)

Ruby, Ann Todd, Florence Isabelle Stacy and Herbert Ridgeway Collins, *Speaking of Families: The Tod(d)s of Caroline County, Virginia and Their Kin* (Columbia, Mo.: Artcraft Press, 1960)

Sorensen, Julian H., *William Moxley: Westmoreland County, Virginia* (Falls Church, Va.: By the Author, 1993)

Tayloe, W. Randolph, *The Tayloes of Virginia and Allied Families* (Berryville, Va.: By the Author, 1963)

Virginia Genealogical Society, *Marriages of Middlesex County, Virginia, 1740-1852* (Richmond, Va.: By the Society, 1965)

Wilkins, Harold E., *The Descendants of Thomas Lamkin of the Northern Neck of Virginia* (Boston, Mass.: Newbury Street Press, 2001)

223

239

243

244

250

283

Heritage Books by Wesley E. Pippenger:

Alexander Family: Migrations from Maryland

Alexandria (Arlington) County, Virginia Death Records, 1853–1896

Alexandria City and Arlington County, Virginia Records Index: Vol. 1

Alexandria City and Arlington County, Virginia Records Index: Vol. 2

Alexandria County, Virginia Marriage Records, 1853–1895

Alexandria, Virginia Marriage Index, January 10, 1893 to August 31, 1905

Alexandria, Virginia Marriages, 1870–1892

Alexandria, Virginia Town Lots, 1749–1801
Together with the Proceedings of the Board of Trustees, 1749–1780

Alexandria, Virginia Wills, Administrations and Guardianships, 1786–1800

Alexandria, Virginia 1808 Census (Wards 1, 2, 3, and 4)

Alexandria, Virginia Death Records, 1863–1896

Alexandria, Virginia Hustings Court Orders, Volume 1, 1780–1787

Connections and Separations: Divorce, Name Change and Other
Genealogical Tidbits from the Acts of the Virginia General Assembly

Daily National Intelligencer *Index to Deaths, 1855–1870*

Daily National Intelligencer, *Washington, District of Columbia*
Marriages and Deaths Notices (January 1, 1851 to December 30, 1854)

Dead People on the Move: Reconstruction of the Georgetown Presbyterian
Burying Ground, Holmead's (Western) Burying Ground, and
Other Removals in the District of Columbia

Death Notices from Richmond, Virginia Newspapers, 1841–1853

District of Columbia Ancestors,
A Guide to Records of the District of Columbia

District of Columbia Death Records: August 1, 1874–July 31, 1879

District of Columbia Foreign Deaths, 1888–1923

District of Columbia Guardianship Index, 1802–1928

District of Columbia Interments (Index to Deaths)
January 1, 1855 to July 31, 1874

District of Columbia Marriage Licenses, Register 1: 1811–1858

District of Columbia Marriage Licenses, Register 2: 1858–1870

District of Columbia Marriage Records Index
June 28, 1877 to October 19, 1885: Marriage Record Books 11 to 20
Wesley E. Pippenger and Dorothy S. Provine

District of Columbia Marriage Records Index
October 20, 1885 to January 20, 1892: Marriage Record Books 21 to 30

District of Columbia Marriage Records Index
January 20, 1892 to August 30, 1896: Marriage Record Books 31 to 40

District of Columbia Marriage Records Index
August 31, 1896 to December 17, 1900: Marriage Record Books 41 to 65

District of Columbia Probate Records, 1801–1852

District of Columbia: Original Land Owners, 1791–1800

Early Church Records of Alexandria City and Fairfax County, Virginia

Essex County, Virginia Deed Abstracts, 1786–1805, Deed Books 33 to 36

Essex County, Virginia, Guardianship and Orphans Records, 1707–1888: A Descriptive Index

Essex County, Virginia, Marriage Bonds, 1804–1850, Annotated

www.ingramcontent.com/pod-product-compliance
Lightning Source LLC
Chambersburg PA
CBHW050239290326
41929CB00048B/3015